KINGDOM
in the
WEST

The Mormons and the American Frontier

Will Bagley, series editor

Volume 10

Utah Expedition Teamster and
Nauvoo Legion Prisoner Charles W. Becker

In October 1857 the Legion captured Charlie Becker east of Fort Bridger and took him to the Salt Lake Valley to work on a farm owned by a son-in-law of Brigham Young. On Christmas Day the Mormons released Becker and two other prisoners and guided them to Fort Bridger. There they provided Colonel Johnston with alarming intelligence about Mormon plans for 1858, including the intent to intercept Captain Marcy's detachment returning with remounts from New Mexico and the establishment of a two-thousand-man standing army to reinforce the existing Nauvoo Legion. Although Becker's claims to have later been a Pony Express rider during 1860–61 are unverifiable, his old-age reminiscences of the Utah War are among the conflict's best captivity narratives. This photo was taken in the early 1920s when Becker was one of the war's last survivors and in his late eighties while still active as a rancher in Malheur County, Oregon. *Courtesy of the Oregon Historical Society, Portland* (#cn 000140).

At Sword's Point, Part 1

A Documentary History of the Utah War to 1858

Edited by
William P. MacKinnon

THE ARTHUR H. CLARK COMPANY
An imprint of the University of Oklahoma Press
Norman, Oklahoma
2008

For Pat MacKinnon
whose loving partnership in this journey
has made all the difference

Second printing, 2008

Library of Congress Catalog Card Number 2007036588
ISBN 978-0-8706-2353-0 (trade edition)
ISBN 978-0-87062-354-7 (collector's edition)
ISBN 978-0-87062-274-8 (entire series)

Library of Congress Cataloging-in-Publication Data
At sword's point / edited by William P. MacKinnon.
v. cm. — (Kingdom in the West: the Mormons and the American frontier ; v. 10)
Includes bibliographical references and index.
Contents: pt. 1. A documentary history of the Utah War to 1858 — pt. 2. A documentary history of the Utah War, 1858
ISBN 978-0-87062-353-0 (v. 1 : hardcover : alk. paper) —
ISBN 978-0-87062-354-7 (v. 1 : collector's ed. : alk. paper) —
ISBN 978-0-87062-274-8
1. Utah Expedition, 1857–1858. 2. Mormons—Utah—History—19th century. I. MacKinnon, William P.

F826.M13 2007
973.6'8—dc22

2007036588

The paper in this book meets the guidelines for permanence and durability of the Committee on Production Guidelines for Book Longevity of the Council on Library Resources. ∞

Contents

Illustrations

Foreword

With the 150th anniversary of the "Utah War" upon us, it is clearly time for a new look at the much-neglected and almost forgotten story of the nation's first "civil war." The telling example of an American president blithely ignoring the advice of his most experienced professional commanders to launch an ill-considered and politically motivated military campaign has eerie echoes in today's headlines. That the traditional, and oft-times inaccurate, tale and much of its attendant mythology has retained a hold on historians all the way into the twenty-first century practically demands a new look.

At Sword's Point offers a new perspective on a complex event and greatly expands our understanding of the dynamics that drove the conflict between Mormon theocracy and the American Republic. Among the surprises in *At Sword's Point,* contained in bright and illuminating documentary gems, are the lengths to which the Mormons went to collect arms and ammunition in 1857 and the fact that rumors surrounding the conflict motivated Tsar Alexander II to first consider selling Alaska. Other surprises include the participation of a U.S. Marine Corps officer in the Utah Expedition, Mormon attempts to develop liquid fire and aerial torpedoes, and the surprising role of a Mormon Texas Ranger in recruiting the support of the hero of San Jacinto, Sam Houston. Perhaps this volume's most important revelation is the picture that it paints of a detail-oriented Brigham Young, who was as involved in concocting the aggressive Mormon strategy in late 1857 as Winston Churchill was in planning the Gallipoli campaign.

This volume is resplendent with new information, previously unheard voices, and original insights that will compel historians to reconsider the causes and conduct of the conflict. The two volumes that make up *At Sword's Point* bring to life dozens of forgotten participants, including women, to tell the war's story and to address the subject in much greater depth than any previous study.

At Sword's Point tells the story of the Utah War's origins, prosecution, and impact, but in the process it also spotlights a crucial crisis in the history of the Mormon people. As 1858 began, the history of the American West reached a balancing point, in which Mormon millennial expectations hung in an equilibrium with the imminence of the Latter Days. Unknowingly, during that heady time the Latter-day Saints in Utah Territory climbed and crossed a watershed in their lives. On the ascending slope to this divide, many frontier Mormons and all their leaders were convinced that the world's end was galloping toward them at breakneck speed. After they crossed the summit of their expectations and began a long descent, they entered a wide desert where the mirage of the Latter Days disappeared over the horizon. Cataclysmic events such as the Civil War or a national panic periodically revived the young religion's millennial hopes, but after federal authority became a dominating force in the territory, the end of time would never again appear so close. "They demoralized the settlement," Jane Richards, an apostle's wife, complained long after the U.S. Army arrived in June 1858. "It has never been the same place since."[1] This book, the product of almost a half-century of diligent work, is the story of how frontier Mormonism crossed that tipping point and how the American Republic handled its first confrontation with theocracy and secession.

It is not hard to comprehend why American historians have generally ignored the U.S. Army's Utah Expedition of 1857 and the subsequent confrontation in the West. The Utah War appeared to be a conflict with no pitched battles or even significant skirmishes, and almost nothing seemed to happen except much boastful blustering, a few colorful guerrilla raids on U.S. Army supply trains, and an appalling atrocity. The Mormons and their leaders creatively resisted what they saw as an unwarranted "invasion" of their beloved mountain Zion, while the army conducted an immensely frustrating mission with admirable restraint and discipline. But if a young lieutenant could complain in 1854 at Great Salt Lake City that "there is no glory in fighting Indians," there was no glory whatsoever in *not* fighting Mormons.[2]

---

[1] Reminis[c]ences of Mrs. F. D. Richards, San Francisco, 1880, from Utah and the Mormons Collection [Bancroft Library], MS 8305, Reel 2, LDS Archives.

[2] LaRhett L. Livingston to James G. Livingston, 16 September 1854, Beinecke Library.

By 1880 the entire nation, Utah included, seemed perfectly happy to simply forget the entire unfortunate episode. Only a handful of old veterans told the story in their memoirs, and it is still odd that an experienced frontiersman like Buffalo Bill Cody would feel compelled to fabricate his adventures as an eleven-year-old boy with the Army of Utah. So perhaps it is not surprising that when members of The Church of Jesus Christ of Latter-day Saints (the people known as Mormons, whose religion is abbreviated throughout this work as "LDS church") recalled the event, they made the story of America's forgotten civil war their own.

Mormon historians have wrestled with how to tell the story of the Utah War ever since Hubert Howe Bancroft arrived in Salt Lake City in January 1880 and asked for their help in writing what became his *History of Utah*. The church's Historian's Office took up the challenge, and Apostle Franklin D. Richards adeptly crafted what became the generally accepted account of the conflict, which basically painted the confrontation as a big misunderstanding largely caused by the American government's reliance on the word of a few disreputable anti-Mormons. Bancroft's collaborators often contradicted Richards's faith-promoting text in their footnotes with counterbalancing comments, such as the observation that Utah's government "was nominally theocratic and practically autocratic." Altogether, however, except for its surprising estimate that the war cost several hundred lives, Bancroft's history helped clothe the story in its modern mythology.[3]

Almost all its early storytellers viewed Utah's past through Mormon spectacles and saw the war as part of an epic conflict between good religion and bad government, a story of persecution and vindication, and the triumphant tale of righteous warriors who marched with orders to "shed no blood." The leading chroniclers of this localized saga—Junius Wells, Richard Young, and Susa Young Gates—were the children and grandchildren of its foremost participants, and they happily promoted the parochial legend of their peoples' glorious defeat of "Johnston's Army," a name that endures in the state's history, perhaps to obscure the fact that it was not a filibustering expedition but the U.S. Army's most complicated campaign between the War with Mexico and the Civil War.

During the twentieth century several fine historians, including LeRoy and Ann Hafen, Norman F. Furniss, Howard R. Lamar, Kenneth M. Stampp,

---

[3] Bancroft, *History of Utah*, 504–38.

Harold Schindler, Richard Poll, and Durwood Ball, have dealt with the Utah War either extensively or at least in passing. None of them, however, pursued the subject with the passion of this volume's editor. I was aware of William P. MacKinnon's reputation as a leading authority on nineteenth-century territorial history long before I made his acquaintance. His interest in Utah, the Mormons, and the most significant conflict between religion and government in American history reaches back to his undergraduate years at Yale University in the late 1950s. With the encouragement of Howard Lamar, who went on to exercise what many consider the greatest influence on the modern interpretation of the American West of any single scholar, MacKinnon spent two years composing an essay for Yale's History Honors Program. Professor Lamar suggested that the Utah War would make an interesting subject, especially since the Yale Collection of Western Americana contained a wealth of material on the Mormon Rebellion.

So began a love affair with the "Mormon Rebellion" that has lasted almost fifty years. MacKinnon's 1963 article for the *Utah Historical Quarterly*, "The Buchanan Spoils System and the Utah Expedition," was the first of his many groundbreaking publications on the subject: the article remains the most valuable resource on the careers of federal mail contractors W. M. F. Magraw and John M. Hockaday and their significant role in the development of the overland mail. During the next two decades, he examined how the Utah War had left "The Gap in the Buchanan Revival," while his "125 Years of Conspiracy Theories: Origins of the Utah Expedition" debunked many beloved historical fables. His 1994 article, "Causes of the Utah War Reconsidered," shared authorship with credit to his late collaborator, Richard Poll. Like all his other works, his recent studies, "Epilogue to the Utah War: Impact and Legacy" and "Lonely Bones: Leadership and Utah Violence" are packed with engaging anecdotes and telling insights. With his bulldog persistence, Bill MacKinnon is the most relentless researcher of my acquaintance.

MacKinnon's achievements as a scholar are especially notable in light of his successful business career. He is a graduate of both Yale University and the Harvard Business School. A veteran of the U.S. Air Force and a former vice president of General Motors, he has been a highly regarded consultant for two decades and has served on the boards of corporations, charitable organizations, educational institutions, and libraries. His considerable personal charm and congeniality make him an excellent mentor for young researchers and a valued colleague for seasoned scholars.

The new light needed to produce an innovative history of the Utah War was scattered in the archives of dozens of libraries, historical societies, and private collections, and MacKinnon has systematically surveyed them all. Perhaps the most revealing new material was hidden in the restricted recesses of the Brigham Young papers at LDS Archives. According to the archivists who moved them out of the old Church Office Building in 1972, many of those records had been boxed up and locked away since they were packed for the "Move South" in the spring of 1858. Historians, including this one, have been denied access to critical parts of the collection, notably the Utah War files. But over the last twenty years, this wonderful resource has become increasingly accessible, and now the collection is open to anyone with the curiosity to explore it.

A separate series volume will be devoted to the Mountain Meadows massacre, which relieves MacKinnon of the burden of addressing the awful tale in detail, but he accurately puts the atrocity in the context of the larger conflict. Due to a combination of circumstances, editorial direction of MacKinnon's volumes fell to the staff of the Arthur H. Clark Company, and their combined effort has produced a work that exceeds the standards we hope readers of KINGDOM IN THE WEST have come to expect.

With their fortuitous appearance during the sesquicentennial of the Utah War, William P. MacKinnon's volumes will provide enough new source material to keep historians busy reinterpreting the conflict for a generation. Bill's wide-ranging interests have contributed substantially to his singular perspective on the Mormon past, and his comprehensive grasp of this controversial subject makes his work pathbreaking, engaging, and balanced. His even-handed judgment of people and events that still provoke passionate responses has won him the respect of historians of all perspectives. His ability to delight and surprise his readers illuminates this study, and the history that this determined scholar has uncovered bears important precedents for Americans who today face similar challenges on a vastly larger scale.

WILL BAGLEY
Salt Lake City, Utah

Acknowledgments

This is the story of the most extensive and expensive American military undertaking during the period between the Mexican and Civil wars. It was a campaign that pitted nearly one-third of the U.S. Army against the country's largest, most experienced militia. The scene was Utah Territory, an area so vast that its counties were more than six hundred miles wide. Here was a military campaign with far-reaching consequences: the near-depletion of the U.S. Treasury; the forced resignation of a secretary of war; the bankruptcy of the nation's largest freighting company; severe damage to the reputation of a president and his nerve for confronting southern secession; the indictment of a church's prophet for treason and murder; the execution of his adopted son for mass murder; the Anglo re-discovery of the Grand Canyon of the Colorado; the organization of England's Pacific Northwest possessions into the province of British Columbia; and Russia's sale of Alaska.

I present this sprawling, complex story as a documentary rather than narrative history, so finding the materials to describe the Utah War has been crucial. Therein has lain much of the fun. Along the way, I have incurred mountainous debts to people helpful in finding this largely unexploited material. So sustained has been the period of their help that three American wars have arisen. In the interim some of these supporters have died, others have experienced name changes, and still others work in institutions that have sustained multiple reorganizations. At the risk of missing some, I want to express my thanks to these benefactors by name while explaining a bit of the underlying research process through which I sought their aid.

Ferreting out these documents has been an odyssey that began in 1958 at Yale. There I encountered nearly simultaneously Howard R. Lamar's frontier history course; Archibald Hanna, Jr.'s, Yale Collection of Western Americana; a young historian named William H. Goetzmann; LeRoy R. and Ann W. Hafen's newly published documentary history of the Utah Expedition; and Richard D. Poll's recent first journal article on the war's political aspects. The combination of these stimuli was catalyst to what became a life-long research and writing effort. I liken this work to prospecting and mining for gold.[1]

Among my most enjoyable research methodologies has been dialogue. Interchanges have been with those few historians who have focused directly on the Utah War and the far larger group probing what I came to realize was the campaign's broader context. Among those people to whom I am most indebted for leads, suggestions, documents, and stimulation are (alphabetically): George Rollie Adams, Polly Aird, Curtis R. Allen, James B. Allen, Lavina Fielding Anderson, Durwood Ball, Darcee Barnes, Steven G. Barnett, John M. Belohlavek, Richard E. Bennett, David L. Bigler, Martha Sonntag Bradley, Robert Briggs, Russell K. Brown, Robert C. Carriker, the late Murray L. Carroll, Lyndia and Robert Carter, William Y. Chalfant, David Chapin, Gregg S. Clemmer, Richard L. Clow, the late Everett L. Cooley (my first editor), Thomas W. Cutrer, Peter H. DeLafosse, Terry A. Del Bene, William Deverell, Gary L. Ecelbarger, Roger R. Ekins, John D. Eldredge, Jessie L. Embry, Max J. Evans, Steven E. Farley, Michael Fellman, Robert Kent Fielding, Jack E. Fletcher, Richard V. Francaviglia, Louis A. Garavaglia, the late Hugh C. Garner, Esq., Edward A. Geary, Jefferson I. Glass, Audrey M. and Kenneth W. Godfrey, William H. Goetzmann, Matthew J. Grow, Kathaleen K. Hamblin, Klaus J. Hansen, B. Carmon Hardy, Helen D. Harris, Ricardo A. Herrera, Harwood Hinton, Val Holley, J. S. Holliday, the late W. Eugene Hollon, Harold Holzer, Michael W. Homer, Esq., Alan F. and Jourdan M. Houston, John T. Hubbell, James S. Hutchins, Marie Irvine, Robert W. Johannsen, Melvin C. Johnson, the late Alvin M. Josephy, Jr., Thomas R. Kailbourn, Violet and the late Stanley B. Kimball, the late Philip S. Klein, Howard R. Lamar, Michael N. Landon, William Lang, Harold D. Langley, Stanford J. Layton, the late Wilford H. LeCheminant, M.D., Glen M. Leonard, Edward E. Leslie, Edward G. Longacre, M. John Lubetkin, Edward Leo Lyman, H.

[1] For the Yale beginnings of this odyssey and its subsequent character, see my "Stranger in a Strange Land: My Forty-Five Years with the Utah War and What I Have Learned" and "Loose in the Stacks: A Half-Century with the Utah War and its Legacy." For other use of the mining metaphor for such research, see Alexander, "Working a 'Gold Mine,'" and Blodgett, "Using Our Faculties: Collecting the Papers of Western Historians at the Huntington Library."

Michael Marquardt, Philip P. Mason, William F. McConnell, David E. Meerse, Leon C. Metz, David H. Miller, William Mulder, Erik L. Myrup, Roger B. Nielson, John C. Oeffinger, Floyd A. O'Neil, Kenneth N. Owens, the late Peter E. Palmquist, Allan Peskin, Charles S. Peterson, Alexander Petrov, Charles Pinnegar, the late Richard D. Poll, Gregory A. Prince, Francis Paul Prucha, S.J., D. Michael Quinn, Bob Rea, W. Paul Reeve, Michael A. Riley, J. Stephen Rizley, Madge Thornall Roberts, Charles P. Roland, Daniel N. Rolph, W. L. (Bud) Rusho, Martha A. Sandweiss, Norman E. Saul, Richard L. Saunders, the late Harold Schindler, William J. Schultz, M.D., Gene A. Sessions, Melvin T. Smith, Kenneth M. Stampp, Clifford L. Stott, Clifford Swanson, Wiley Sword, Jerry Thompson, Robert M. Utley, Michael S. Van Wagenen, James F. Varley, Ronald W. Walker, Peter A. Wallner, Mark R. Wilson, and Eric J. Wittenberg, Esq. I think of my face-to-face chats, telephone conversations, and exchange of letters and e-mail messages with them as invaluable, interactive campfire sessions with generous fellow prospectors.

In addition to these professionals, non-historians located in such diverse places as Lake George, New York, and Roseburg, Oregon, have provided invaluable information, photographs, and documents about their Utah War ancestors. These generous benefactor-descendants include the late George R. Bennett, John Bond, Julie Chitwood, Arvey Drown, Dorothy Henry, Don Hockaday, Inez Jackson, the late LaVonne Cherry Ketchum, Barbara Malin, Joseph P. Malin, Joan Nay, Steven L. Richardson, Arthur Lawrence Taylor, Grace and the late Sidney Hooper (Skip) Young, Jr., and Mrs. Albert L. Zobell, Jr.

Surprising to me at first was the extent to which I also developed leads from antiquarian book sellers. For example, it was from a visit to dealer Rick Grunder of LaFayette, New York, that I first became aware of Brigham Young's revealing 30 June 1857 letter to Horace S. Eldredge, and later of Indian Agent Jacob Forney's papers as well as James C. Van Dyke's 3 January 1858 letter of introduction to John M. Hockaday for Thomas L. Kane. It was from a rare-books catalogue of the Arthur H. Clark Company that I learned of Charles R. Morehead's high-grade account of his Utah War adventures on behalf of Russell, Majors and Waddell—appended to a rare book focused on a quite different subject. Other helpful dealers include: Michael Ginsberg, Bob Heyman, the late Tal Luther, Bill Reese, and Tom Swinford, as well as such Salt Lake City stalwarts as Curt Bench, Ken Sanders, and my earliest such contact, Sam Weller.

Perhaps my most offbeat prospecting has been done among what I call the "tailings"—the research files of deceased historians lodged in the manuscript collections of university libraries and historical societies. Some of these historians died before publishing more than a few tantalizing journal articles based on this material; others, who published more extensively, reserved crucial documents because of religious or cultural inhibitions, publishers' space limitations, or other factors. What they left behind—often prematurely—were dozens of hollinger boxes—some still uncataloged—constituting a virtual El Dorado of documents bearing on the Utah War.[2] Unquestionably the most useful such trove was that of my former colleague and intended collaborator, the late Dick Poll, whose files are now lodged in the University of Utah's Marriott Library. Other collections to which I am indebted are those amassed by Dale L. Morgan at the University of California, Berkeley's Bancroft Library; Charles Kelly at the Utah State Historical Society and University of Utah's Marriott Library; M. Hamlin Cannon and Francis W. Cragin at Colorado College's Tutt Library; Frank Evans and Alfred L. Zobell, Jr., at the LDS Archives; LeRoy R. Hafen, Madeline R. McQuown, and Richard D. Poll at the University of Utah—Marriott; E. Cecil McGavin at Brigham Young University's L. Tom Perry Special Collections, Harold B. Lee Library; and Hamilton Gardner and Stanley S. Ivins at the Utah State Historical Society. To future historians will presumably fall the benefit of the extensive, unexploited research files believed to have been generated by the late Hal Schindler of Salt Lake City but which are as yet unavailable to scholars. Perhaps the lost files of the late Norman F. Furniss of Colorado State University's faculty will also surface; in the interim his published narrative history, footnotes, and bibliography have been invaluable.

Last but not the least rewarding among my research methodologies has been decades of exhaustive pick-and-shovel work among the manuscript collections of institutional repositories as well as those in private hands. This work has flowed from pursuit of an unending series of self-imposed "what-if" questions. My research techniques have ranged from an unstructured receptivity to serendipity to a focused, forensic approach. Evident in all of these methodologies has been a fascinating degree of connectedness suggestive of the prophet Ezekiel's biblical visit to the Valley of the Dry Bones, or at least of the black spiritual's account of the linkages evident there. Since the mid-

[2] Blodgett discusses the value of such research files in his article "Using Our Faculties."

1990s, the availability of optical scanners, e-mail, Internet search engines, fax machines, and courier services have added welcome research power to unearth and exploit these connections. There has been a quantum leap in technology unimaginable when I first started tunneling in the documentary galleries vacated by the Hafens in the late 1950s with such now-quaint hand tools as the fountain pen, index cards, microfilm reader, mechanical typewriter, and telephone.

Through such efforts have surfaced, among other documents: letters of the federal volunteer battalion's Sgt. Maj. William Porter Finlay; reports of U.S. Marine Corps 2d Lt. Robert L. Browning; newspaper dispatches, scrapbook, photographs, and personal papers of Boston's Albert G. Browne, Jr.; the diary, scrapbook, and correspondence of Capt. John W. Phelps of the Fourth U.S. Artillery; letters of 1st Lt. Joseph C. Ives, Corps of Topographical Engineers, re-discoverer of the Grand Canyon, and of Capt. Alfred Cumming, Tenth U.S. Infantry and nephew of Brigham Young's gubernatorial successor; innovative design for an aerial torpedo by Ogden gunsmith Jonathan Browning; letters of Capt. Randolph B. Marcy of the Fifth U.S. Infantry; papers and photographs of David Auguste Burr, who was the son of Utah's first surveyor-general, a daguerreotypist, justice of the peace, and the *New York Times*'s pseudonymous field correspondent "A.B.C."; scrapbook, letters and new sketches of Capt. Albert Tracy, Tenth Infantry; and the extensive papers of the Mormons' key ally, Thomas L. Kane.

In each of these cases, as well as in dozens of others, a form of documentary diaspora constituted a daunting challenge in assembling a coherent story. For example, material generated by or about Sergeant Major Finlay appears in a nineteenth-century newspaper of St. Louis, Missouri; in records in what are now Belfast, Northern Ireland, Calcutta, India, and Melbourne, Australia; in several record groups within Washington's National Archives; in London at the British Library and the British Public Record Office; at Yale's Beinecke Library; and at The Historical Society of Pennsylvania in Philadelphia. Variants of John I. Ginn's Utah War narrative are scattered among at least seven institutional or private manuscript collections.[3] Materials bearing on Kane are located in at least as many repositories, including the private collection of Mrs. Anne Richards Horton of San Marino, California, to whom I am especially indebted. Documents generated by people such as Messrs. Browne,

[3] MacKinnon, "'Unquestionably Authentic and Correct in Every Detail.'"

Burr, merchant William A. Carter, and Captain Phelps also rest in multiple libraries each.

Crucial to locating and accessing these documents has been help from a large group of energetic, accommodating archivists, curators, and librarians to whom I here acknowledge my substantial debt while extending my thanks. The first of this breed to have moved mountains for me while offering high-yield suggestions was Archibald Hanna, Jr., William Robertson Coe Curator of the Yale Collection of Western Americana during the period 1955–81. Archie Hanna steered me to a copy of the rare poem *Mormoniad*, and in his dual role as a reserve marine colonel he told me the enigmatic—and here verified—story of the U.S. Marine Corps's one-man contribution to an otherwise all-army Utah Expedition. It was Archie's successor at Yale, George A. Miles, who surfaced Sgt. Theodore Boos's highly descriptive memoirs of life in the Tenth U.S. Infantry and Capt. Rufus Ingalls's long-lost memorandum on how best to reinforce the Utah Expedition from the Pacific Coast, as well as the records of the Nauvoo Legion's First Brigade, Second Division—the most significant concentration of Legion records outside of Salt Lake City.

Other such archivist-benefactors, most of them accomplished historians, preside over a wide range of welcoming repositories located throughout the United States and internationally. For example, at LDS Archives I am grateful for the help of Elder Marlin K. Jensen, the LDS church's Historian and Recorder, and of Managing Director Richard E. Turley, Jr., and his entire department—especially archivists Ronald O. Barney, Melvin L. Bashore, Jay G. Burrup, W. Randall Dixon, Craig L. Foster, Richard L. Jensen, Jeffery O. Johnson, Michael N. Landon, Chad M. Orton, William W. Slaughter, and Ronald G. Watt. Interestingly, several of these men are descended from Utah War veterans. My thanks also go to their counterpart in Independence, Missouri, the Community of Christ's archivist Ronald E. Romig. In the District of Columbia, my thanks go to Jessica Kratz, David H. Wallace, and others of the National Archives, as well as Edward McCarter at the National Archives and Records Administration II in College Park, Maryland; Bradley Gernand, Jeffrey M. Flannery, and Bonnie B. Coles at the Library of Congress's Manuscript Division; and to Wendy Kail, Archivist of the Tudor Place Foundation, Inc., a little-known Georgetown mansion housing the letters of 1st Lt. Lawrence A. Williams, Col. Albert Sidney Johnston's heretofore unidentified aide-de-camp.

At the special collections libraries of the great research universities other than Yale and at the free-standing research repositories, I received extraordinary help from Alfred L. Bush of Princeton University's Firestone Library, David Kessler of the University of California's Bancroft Library, Brooke M. Black and Peter J. Blodgett at the Huntington Library, Polly Armstrong of the Stanford University Libraries, Daniel N. Rolph and Jack Gumbrecht of the Historical Society of Pennsylvania, John Brady and Matt Rutherford of the Newberry Library, James J. Holmberg of the Filson Historical Society, Elaine Engst and Susette Newberry at Cornell's Carl A. Kroch Library, Daniel Meyer and Debra Levine of the University of Chicago Library, Sidney F. Huttner of the University of Iowa Libraries, Yvonne M. Arnold of the University of Southern Mississippi's McCain Library, Jessy Randall at Colorado [Springs] College's Tutt Library, Chuck Barber at University of Georgia—Hargett, Richard Shrader at the University of North Carolina at Chapel Hill's Southern Historical Collection, Barbara Floyd of the University of Toledo's Ward M. Canaday Center, Linda J. Long of the University of Oregon Library System, John J. O'Shea of Augusta [Georgia] State University's Reese Library, Jim Gerencser of Dickinson College's Waidner-Spahr Library, April A. Ayto of Louisiana State University's Hill Memorial Library, Robert Parks of Manhattan's J. P. Morgan Library, Kim Allen Scott of Montana State University's Burlingame Library, Wilbur E. (Bill) Meneray at Tulane's Howard-Tilton Memorial Library, Sally Cahalan of Lancaster, Pennsylvania's Wheatland Foundation, Susan M. Anderson of the American Antiquarian Society, Roberta Sago of the University of Texas, El Paso, and, at the University of Michigan, John C. Dann, Barbra De Wolfe, and Brian Leigh Dunnigan at its Clements Library, as well as Malgorzata Myc at its Bentley Historical Library. I am especially indebted to Michael Lear of Franklin and Marshall College's Shadek-Fackenthal Library for helping me with the papers of Lt. John F. Reynolds and Asst. Surg. Jonathan M. Foltz, and to Beth Bensman of Thomas Jefferson University's Scott Memorial Library in Philadelphia for introducing me to the power of the Research Library Group/Library of Congress's marvelous RLIN/NUCMC internet search engine. I also extend my thanks to the *New York Times* librarian, Lora Korbut, as well as to Joyce N. Baker at Charleston, South Carolina's Gibbes Museum of Art.

Among the academic curators, none were more helpful than those in Utah's public and private universities, especially David J. Whittaker at Brigham Young

University's Lee Library, Walter R. Jones, Stan Larson, and Gregory C. Thompson at University of Utah—Marriott, Janet Burton Seegmiller of Southern Utah State University's Sherratt Library, and, at Utah State University's Merrill-Cazier Library, Anne Buttars, Noel Carmack, and Stephen C. Sturgeon.

Since this is an account of a military campaign, I have sought technical and archival help by reaching beyond my quite junior air force background to a variety of more senior army sources. Accordingly, I thank Maj. Gen. Bruce G. MacDonald, U.S.A. (Ret'd.), of Birmingham, Michigan; Dr. Richard J. Sommers, Maj. Michael E. Lynch, and Richard L. Baker of the U.S. Army Military History Institute and Army War College at Carlisle Barracks (Pennsylvania); Brig. Gen. Robert S. Voyles, commander of the Utah Self-Defense Force and colonel, Utah Army National Guard, as well as director of the Fort Douglas (Utah) Museum; Maj. Peter J. Rogers of the Maine Army National Guard; Courtney Burns of the New York State Military Museum and Veterans Research Center; and, at the U.S. Military Academy, librarians Susan Lintelmann and Sheila Biles, as well as Col. Patrick Finnegan, West Point's faculty head for Military Law. At Headquarters, U.S. Army, I am indebted to Lt. Col. Sherman L. Fleek, a military aviator and historian from Utah who took time from his contemporaneous work in Baghdad and Washington to share insights about his long-standing interest in the Utah Expedition.

I must also thank the archivist-historians at a very special type of repository—the state-supported historical societies, especially Craig Fuller, Miriam Murphy, Philip F. Notarianni, Allen Kent Powell, and Linda Thatcher (Utah), Riva Dean and Bruce J. Dinges (Arizona), Steve Nielson (Minnesota), William Copeley (New Hampshire), Todd Welch (Oregon), Paul A. Carnahan (Vermont), and Harry L. Miller (Wisconsin). My thanks also to their colleagues at such closely allied governmental institutions as the state archives, including Jeffery O. Johnson, Brandon J. Metcalf, and Arlene Schmuland (Utah), Fred Bassett (New York), Bonnie Linck (Connecticut), Conley L. Edwards (Virginia), Ann Nelson (Wyoming), and Anne Morton, archivist for the Hudson's Bay Company Archives at the Provincial Archives of Manitoba.

At the county level, I also found extraordinary historical-society professionals such as John W. W. Loose (Lancaster County, Pennsylvania), Bernadette M. Rogoff (Monmouth County, New Jersey), Patricia M. Virgil (Buffalo and Erie County, New York), Curt B. Witcher (Allen County, Indiana), and Patricia H. Worthington (El Paso County, Texas). Their helpfulness was matched by the dedicated public librarians in a wide range of towns and cities, especially John D. Stinson (New York), Janice Prater (Denver), John Gibson (Detroit), Catherine Larson (Kalamazoo, Michigan), Rhonda Frevert (Burlington, Iowa), Mary Carpenter (Council Bluffs, Iowa), and Verna Gail Johnson (Independence, Missouri).

Finally, I must acknowledge the extraordinary help of my own local facility, the Bloomfield Township (Michigan) Public Library, led by Karen Kotulis-Carter. Here the professionals of the reference department—especially Linda Sessine, Kelly Williams, Connie Silver, Karrie Yukon, Marcia Preston, and others—labored cheerfully and efficiently to execute a tsunami of my inter-library loan requests. Since 1973 they have provided me with a vital, locally based window to the world of Utah War scholarship, for which I am thankful.

Aside from all of these institutional libraries and archives, I have also benefited from access to wonderful private collections, including not only Mrs. Horton's in San Marino but several others owned by anonymous collectors in Utah and California.

With respect to the downstream task of book-making, my obligations run to Robert A. Clark, publisher of the University of Oklahoma Press's Arthur H. Clark Company, and his KINGDOM IN THE WEST series editor, Will Bagley of Salt Lake City. Bob is the third generation of Clarks engaged in the art of turning ground-breaking manuscripts on Western Americana into beautiful, collectible books bulging with new knowledge. By coincidence—but not without symbolism—he is also descended from Lt. Gen. Daniel Hamner Wells, the Nauvoo Legion's Utah War commander, as well as from LDS church president Heber J. Grant. Bob has been as helpful and skillful a publisher as one could want. His willingness to have me present this story in two volumes directly impacts the completeness and richness of the historical record that we here assemble. Will Bagley, descendant of at least one Nauvoo Legionnaire, has, in turn, been a superb series editor, counselor, and close colleague in what has virtually become a long, two-way tutorial on Western Americana and its written record. Joining Bagley in a reading and critique of my entire manuscript have been Dave Bigler and Rick Turley, historians whose specialized knowledge and quite different perspectives I value along with their friendship. Also of great help as copy editor and book designer has been Ariane C. Smith of Spokane.

As a gifted researcher-historian as well as editor, Will Bagley has also served me in the invaluable but unglamorous role of documents scout extraordinaire. As such, he has responded energetically to countless what-if questions, scouting out manuscript collections (some in private hands) to which I had no prior access, connection, or even awareness. To Will I am indebted for guiding me to such striking finds, among others, as the record book of his own great-uncle, Pvt. John Bagley, the scrapbook of journalist Albert G. Browne, Jr., the journal of newspaper correspondent Lemuel Fillmore, Adjt. Gen. James Ferguson's letters from the Nauvoo Legion's Eastern Expedition, and Maj. Seth M. Blair's correspondence with fellow Texans U.S. senator Sam Houston and Ben McCulloch, a Buchanan peace commissioner. I know of no historian more generous in sharing documentary discoveries than Will Bagley.

Chief among other researchers to whom I am grateful is genealogist–historian–newspaper columnist–friend Ardis E. Parshall of Salt Lake City, distant descendant-cousin of the Legion's James Parshall Terry. Her sensitivity to Mormon heritage, coupled with superb hunting and mining instincts, have guided me into the daylight of wonderful manuscript collections and out of the dark tunnels, blind passages, or potential cultural pitfalls awaiting unwary Wise Men from the East. Ms. Parshall has also played a key role in constantly reminding me that there are at least two sides to every story while transforming my drafts into a form with which Messrs. Bagley and Clark could work their editorial and publishing magic.

Among the typists who have helped with this project in one form or another over five decades are: Dorothy Berry, Helen Denning, Ann Ellis, Kathleen Hadesman, Diana Hunter-Miller, Betty Karras, Rosemarie Setteducate, Mary Steinhilper, and K. Anne Yamamoto. All of these valued former colleagues have moved on to other careers; some occasionally ask how the seemingly unending Utah War turned out. This study is a chance to answer that familiar question while again saying thanks.

Helpful during the latter stages of my work were the inputs of my fellow members on the executive committee of the Utah War Sesquicentennial Committee, a stimulating, eclectic group of historians from Utah and elsewhere committed to shedding light on the experiences of participants on both sides of the conflict.

Foundational to all of these efforts has been the encouragement, emotional support, and love of my family, for which I am profoundly grateful.

My twin, Richard A. MacKinnon, has been both alter ego and steadfast companion throughout this journey of discovery, which for the two of us began in Howard Lamar's early-morning classroom a half-century ago. Although my parents, the late Harold A. and Mary E. MacKinnon, were not westerners, Mormons, or historians, their high standards, inquiring minds, and encouragement of my interests led to my 1956 matriculation at Yale and all that followed from that demanding but magnificent experience. Most influential in my subsequent work on this study have been my wife, Patricia Hanley MacKinnon, and my late wife, Ann Reed MacKinnon. Both ladies contributed more than I can describe or properly acknowledge here. Also important, helpful and encouraging in their own way have been our five delightful children, all of whom have become westerners in spirit and at times through residence in Arizona, California, Oregon, and Texas: Thomas R. MacKinnon, Katherine A. Wen, Lisa A. Hall, Quinn H. Gombert, and William E. Hall.

And so, through an intensive process and the help of this large number of people, I have tried to tell here the story of the Utah War—as colorful, complex, fascinating, and neglected a tale of the American West as I know. My hope is that the documents in *At Sword's Point* will illuminate this struggle in a way that my contemporaries as well as subsequent generations will consider fair, even-handed, complete, and—above all else—revealing. I share historian Dale L. Morgan's 1950 view of one of his own books in progress: "While it is being written with what literary grace I can summon to the task, my main objective is to have a reader say, not 'What a brilliant writer this fellow Morgan is,' but 'So that's the truth of the matter.'"[4] If I succeed, then I will have served well Norman F. Furniss, the Hafens, Dick Poll, and Hamilton Gardner, the historians on whose shoulders I have stood most frequently to survey this scene. So too will I have honored the story itself and the players on both sides for whom the stakes were so high. If errors of fact or judgment appear, they are solely mine, unintended as they are.

WILLIAM P. MACKINNON
Bloomfield Hills, Michigan
July 2007

[4] Morgan to McQuown, 27 February 1950, McQuown Collection.

Editorial Procedures

This collection of Utah War materials goes beyond the traditional definition of "document" to include not only letters; diary entries; newspaper editorials and dispatches; reminiscences, memoirs, and personal narratives; military correspondence, orders, telegrams, and reports; poems; stage dramas; religious discourses; but also commemorative quilts; the lyrics to folk songs and hymns; and images such as photographs, paintings, sketches, and maps. Consequently this compilation presents an eclectic and comprehensive view of the campaign, a perspective that was unavailable to any of the nineteenth-century participants, separated as they were by ideology, self-imposed secrecy, long distances, and communication lags or immersed in the uncertainties of what we now call the fog of war. Most of this primary source material is heretofore unpublished or virtually inaccessible.

One of the hazards in editing this compilation has been the extent to which, anecdotally at least, the trail of Mormon history seems unusually marked with the pitfalls of bogus documents. While documentation for the Utah War is relatively free of such problems, I have nonetheless had to exercise research vigilance as well as skepticism. In about ten cases I have omitted seemingly relevant documents because of the high probability that forgery, deception, or hoaxes were involved. Some of these cases, flowing from the very nature of armed conflict and tactics of disinformation, were contemporaneous to the Utah War. Other problematic documents are relatively modern. Akin to this need for vigilance has been the editorial requirement to determine by what means the correspondence flowed to and from Mormon leaders, especially Brigham Young. If Young used the U.S. mails, what came into play was his high anxiety about postal interception and mail monitoring, an apprehension that directly impacted candor as well as the very construction of his letters. If a trusted courier was used either to hand-deliver a message or to carry it to the protective anonymity of a major midwestern post office for mailing, the confidentiality and directness of such correspondence rose commensurately.[1]

Related to but perhaps even more difficult to navigate editorially has been the long-abandoned practice of some nineteenth-century Mormons to obfuscate when they believed that it would protect their church or themselves. The decades-long, vociferous denial of polygamy by church leaders was perhaps the prime example of such past behavior—one that raises credibility issues for today's historians much as it did for Brigham Young's contemporaries.[2] The credibility of documents relating to the Mountain Meadows massacre is a similar challenge.

Other editorial judgments have run to the more mundane matter of terminology: which descriptive labels to apply to institutions and even events. For example, the formal name of the religious organization on which this study focuses is the Church of Jesus Christ of Latter-day Saints. "Mormon," then, is a long-standing nickname derived from the title of one of the religion's principal scriptures, *The Book of Mormon*. Accordingly, during the 1850s the church's leaders often wrote the term in quotes. While preserving this usage in their documents, for narrative purposes I use the descriptors "Mormon" and "LDS," reflecting the need for brevity as well as the terms used most often today by Latter-day Saints.[3] Conversely I have used the term "non-Mormon" and avoided "Gentile" because of the latter's sometimes pejorative flavor.

A parallel issue arises with respect to the name used for the armed conflict at the heart of this book. Over the centuries, Mormons and Utahns have tended to dub the federal side "Johnston's Army," a label peculiar to these cultures. As I see it, "Johnston's Army" tends to trivialize the campaign, and so I have avoided it except in quotations.[4] The U.S. Army and many mil-

[1] At times Brigham Young would conclude mailed letters with a sarcastic postscript, such as: "P.S. Mr. Postmaster, or his deputy or clerk, or anybody else:—When you have read this letter, please forward it to its destination, for keeping it can do you no good." Brigham Young to Henry W. Bigler and John S. Woodbury, February 1858; see also Young to Bernhisel and Calkin, 5 March and 6 January 1858, LDS Archives. Occasionally in such letters the nub of a sensitive message might be embedded in a single opaque sentence surrounded by other material.

[2] Hardy, "Lying for the Lord: An Essay," *Solemn Covenant*, 362–88.

[3] "Mormons Urge Use of Formal Name," *New York Times*, 5 October 1997, 17/1–3; Gustav Niebuhr, "Adapting 'Mormon' to Emphasize Christianity," *Times*, 19 February 2001, A15/6–8.

[4] For my views and others on this label, see Gene A. Sessions, "The Legend of 'Johnston's Army': Myth and Reality among the Mormons," unpublished paper for Mormon History Association annual conference, Salt Lake City, 26 May 2007.

itary historians prefer "Utah Expedition," a traditional label among such groups for both the campaign and the federal force that prosecuted it, although to me the term seems focused solely on the army side of the conflict. Although there were neither pitched battles nor a congressional declaration of war, this conflict involved two opposing sides, occasional exchanges of gunfire, substantial atrocities, and a massive flow of refugees. Accordingly, I prefer to use "Utah War" in most cases for narrative purposes and footnotes. I reserve "Utah Expedition" for the force commanded by Col. Albert Sidney Johnston, which was also known officially as the "Army of Utah." To avoid confusion, I have tried mightily to bypass "Eastern Expedition," the Nauvoo Legion's occasional designator for that part of its force operating around Echo Canyon and the Green River district during the fall of 1857.

Although a bit counterintuitive for laymen, I have followed for narrative purposes the practice of the U.S. Geological Survey and State of Wyoming in spelling the Green River's tributaries without an apostrophe, as in Hams, Blacks, and Smiths Fork.

I have made maximum effort to present faithfully the text of the war's holograph and printed records in a readable format. With noted exceptions, these transcriptions preserve the grammar, spelling, and style of the originals. Capitalization follows that of the source except that the first letters of sentences and of personal names are capitalized; where the case used in the manuscript is ambiguous, standard capitalization has been followed. I have added periods to the ends of sentences; where a writer employed commas in the place of periods, they are converted to periods. Otherwise I maintained the punctuation (or its absence) of the original document. Transcriptions are as accurate as possible, but this arduous task inevitably has limitations, as in dealing with smeared letterpress copies or damaged materials.

I generally preserved the dating style of the source, including the now-archaic references to month: ultimo (last), instant (current), and proximo (next). The notation *sic* is used sparingly, generally where the item in question is especially significant or could be mistaken for a typo. Brackets enclose added letters, missing words, and conjectural readings. [*Blank*] indicates an empty space, while other bracketed comments, such as [*tear*], note physical defects in the manuscript. Words unreadable for transcriptions are noted as [*illegible*]. Underlined text is italicized, while crossed-out text is rendered as ~~strikethroughs~~. Because the retained (and often only available) copy of Brigham

Young's correspondence was frequently a working draft with indicated deletions, such strikethroughs are displayed as reflections of his thought processes as well as of the efforts by the governor and his secretary-clerks to deal with his often rough language. To a lesser extent, the same is true of Thomas L. Kane's correspondence.

Materials from the extensive sources held at the Archives of the Family and Church History Department of the Church of Jesus Christ of Latter-day Saints in Salt Lake City, Utah, including the Brigham Young Collection, are cited as LDS Archives. Since Utah's principal city was styled Great Salt Lake City until an official name change in 1868, that usage is presented when used in documents, but the name Salt Lake City is used in editorial narratives, footnotes, and introductions.

Except for Chapters 1 and 2, I have organized the material into chapters, sections, and documents. Each document contains an abbreviated heading identifying the source and its location. Full citations for these items are found in the bibliography.

Footnotes cite published sources by author, title, and page number. Where available, newspaper citations are to date and page/column: 2/3. The bibliography contains a complete listing of all the books, articles, newspapers, journals, and manuscripts cited in the footnotes, which consequently are abbreviated. Book titles are italicized, while article, thesis, and dissertation titles are in quotation marks. Manuscript citations appear in plain text without quotation marks. Except when used as adjectives, ages are given as numerals.

Because of the scope of the Utah War's story, it necessarily intersects with multiple aspects of the Mormon frontier saga as presented elsewhere in the KINGDOM IN THE WEST series. Where such is the case, *At Sword's Point* generally cross-references rather than duplicates documents presented in other series volumes. A prime example of this editorial approach runs to the war's atrocities, especially the Mountain Meadows massacre of 11 September 1857 and the attack on the Mormon Salmon River mission, Fort Limhi, on 25 February 1858. Accordingly *At Sword's Point* touches on these events but focuses primarily on other atrocities to provide a broader context for those discussed at book length in two of the series' other volumes. On the other hand, in a few cases, there are documents so important to an understanding of the Utah War story that they appear here as well as in another KINGDOM IN THE WEST volume.

Similarly I have kept the extent to which *At Sword's Point* duplicates those documents appearing in the Hafens' 1958 compilation to a minimum. Consequently in this volume I confine the use of Capt. John W. Phelps's valuable diary to the period after 30 September 1857, the last entry published by the Hafens a half-century ago. By the same token, the published 1858 journal of Capt. Albert Tracy, Phelps's brother officer, is not reprinted here, although his unpublished letters, written during the fall of 1857, appear in this volume for the first time.

Finally, I must note the peculiar editorial challenge and decisions arising from the prolix nature of some of my sources. In the case of newspaper correspondents, they were often paid by the word or line, a compensation system that generated sometimes gargantuan dispatches. In the case of Brigham Young, a similar challenge flowed from a combination of his communications and work style. Because he dictated virtually all of his intertwined personal, church, and governmental correspondence, Young functioned through an office of clerks, confidential secretaries, and bookkeepers. This administrative horsepower—combined with Young's long office hours, loquaciousness, active curiosity, and tendency to micromanage—produced a staggering number of documents, many of rambling, lengthy character, like his extemporaneous hours-long Sunday discourses. Officers of the Utah Expedition were dumbfounded when in October 1857 Captain Marcy received in the wilderness of northeastern Utah a twelve-page argumentative letter from Apostle John Taylor, a total stranger. This paper torrent has forced an editorial ruthlessness in bypassing fascinating but unessential material and in excerpting even crucial documents. These have been vastly different editorial challenges than those prompted by a more cautious, less communicative President Buchanan, who wrote much of his own correspondence while managing the presidential paper flow through a single secretary-clerk. This difference between the two men is alone emblematic of the story that follows.

Introduction

At Sword's Point chronicles the extraordinary armed power struggle between James Buchanan, fifteenth president of the United States, and Brigham Young, second president of the Church of Jesus Christ of Latter-day Saints and first governor of Utah Territory. This study uses key documents drawn from the conflict's enormous paper trail to tell the complex story of what the Utah War was, how it came about, how the two sides prosecuted the war, and its results. Determining which materials best tell this fascinating tale was a daunting challenge.

Notwithstanding its scope, the Utah War has for decades been both obscure and enigmatic—overshadowed by the enormity of the immediately following American Civil War. Compounding this obscurity has been a unique Mormon historiography forged from unequal portions of martial pride, persecution, institutional defensiveness, and twinges of heartburn. For a variety of other reasons, the U.S. Army has also chosen to forget the Utah War. Consequently few major episodes of American military history are so little known. Lost in the process has been an understanding of the nation's most extensive and expensive military undertaking during the period between the Mexican and Civil wars, a campaign that ultimately pitted nearly one-third of the U.S. Army against the Mormon Nauvoo Legion, arguably America's largest, most experienced militia.[1]

Why study a 150-year-old military campaign virtually unknown to non-Mormons and obscure to most Latter-day Saints beyond the ubiquitous descriptor "Johnston's Army"? The answer runs to the matter of cultural context and the importance of the words "understanding," "richness," and "freshness."

[1] For observations about this neglect, see MacKinnon, "The Gap in the Buchanan Revival: The Utah Expedition of 1857–58" and "Loose in the Stacks: A Half-Century with the Utah War and Its Legacy." Buchanan's latest biographer dispatches the Utah War in five badly muddled paragraphs supported by a single citation. Baker, *James Buchanan*, 90–93, 155.

Grasping what took place in Utah, Washington, D.C., and elsewhere on the eve of the American Civil War is not only to understand a vital part of Mormon history, but to appreciate more fully regional western themes. They are events and movements as wildly diverse as army exploration of Arizona's Colorado River and its Grand Canyon; Buchanan's quest for an American protectorate over northern Sonora and Chihuahua; Tsarist Russia's decision to sell Alaska before a feared influx of Utah Mormons simply took it; similar apprehensions by the British Crown about Vancouver's Island and its impact on the defensive creation of British Columbia; violence in bleeding Kansas; bankruptcy of the region's greatest freighting company; establishment of the boundaries of Nevada, Colorado, Nebraska, and Wyoming at Utah's expense; the origins of Utah's boom-bust economic cycles; completion of the transcontinental telegraph and railroad; the phenomenon of today's Sagebrush Rebellion; the Mormon origins of San Francisco, San Bernardino, Las Vegas, and Carson City; and the Mountain Meadows massacre, an atrocity that until 1995 was the greatest episode of organized mass murder of unarmed civilians in American history.[2]

At the same time, the cast of this historical melodrama on both sides includes such wonderfully eclectic frontier bravos as Capt. Orrin Porter Rockwell, Brigham Young's Samson-like bodyguard; Maj. Lot Smith, the Mormons' most audacious horseman; Lt. Bill Hickman, most notorious of the region's confessed killers; Ben McCulloch, Texas Ranger, U.S. marshal, and a Buchanan peace commissioner; William Clarke Quantrill, teamster, card sharp, camp cook, and the Civil War scourge of Lawrence, Kansas; George Washington Shepard, teamster, Quantrill minion, and subsequent rider with the Jesse James–Cole Younger gang; Benjamin Franklin Ficklin, army scout, interim U.S. marshal for Utah, a founder of the Pony Express, and Confederate owner of Jefferson's Monticello; Balduin Möllhausen, Prussian explorer, artist, and protégé of Alexander von Humboldt; Jim Bridger, chief army scout and frontier legend; Christopher (Kit) Carson, Bridger peer and U.S. Indian agent at Taos; Charles R. Morehead, army freight agent and mayor of such tough frontier towns as Leavenworth, Kansas, and El Paso, Texas; Pvt. Charles H. Wilcken, U.S. Army deserter, subsequent bodyguard to two LDS church presidents, and ancestor to George Wilcken Romney and Mitt

[2] The death toll in several nineteenth-century Indian campaigns exceeded the 120 fatalities at Mountain Meadows, but the armed status of many Indian women and some children clouds their status as noncombatants in these actions.

Romney, candidates for president of the United States in 1968 and 2008, respectively; Jonathan Browning, Ogden gunsmith and Mormon pater familias of America's most famous armaments dynasty; 2d Lt. Robert L. Browning, the U.S. Marine Corps's elusive, one-man contribution to an otherwise all-army campaign; and a constellation of military officers and civilians who became Confederate or Union generals less than four years later.[3]

For good reason, then, *At Sword's Point* is not solely a Utah story but rather is an integral part of a broad-gauge series appropriately titled KINGDOM IN THE WEST: THE MORMONS AND THE AMERICAN FRONTIER. What follows is a tale with truly western American and international as well as Utah implications.

In selecting the documents through which to tell this story, I have been guided by two precepts: the need to bring forward new knowledge; and a desire to do so through previously unexploited materials. Over the past eighty years, there has been a tendency to tell this story—if at all—through use of a handful of overused sources such as the letters of Capt. Jesse A. Gove and the journal and sketches of Capt. Albert Tracy, both of the Tenth U.S. Infantry. Valuable as these familiar sources are, there are dozens more voices to be heard on both sides from other regiments, different camps, and varying perspectives. Many of these fresh, untapped accounts of the conflict appear here.

I use these documents to shed light on previously unexplored issues as fairly and evenhandedly as possible. With the volatility and emotionalism surrounding the Utah War's origins, prosecution, consequences, and historiography, it has been my focused intent not to distract readers by either the grinding of editorial axes or the use of narrative hatchets. This was a campaign that began the destruction of James Buchanan's presidential reputation and accelerated the nation's descent into disunion and financial insolvency. At the same time it was an episode that prompted Brigham Young's three federal indictments for treason and homicide, and which eventually brought his religiously adopted son, Nauvoo Legion major John D. Lee, before a firing squad for mass murder at Mountain Meadows. In the sorry spectacle of a probably avoidable war, there is accountability if not culpability for both President Buchanan and President Young, although in quite different ways and in debatable proportions. With a historiography already burdened by extensive scape-

[3] For a narrative discussion of the political, economic, and geographical issues unleashed by the war and the post-1858 experiences of some of its most colorful participants, see MacKinnon, "Epilogue to the Utah War."

goating, vilification, ridicule, and hagiography, neither side deserves anything but the truth. And so on most—but not all—subjects and controversies, this book's documents largely speak for themselves, with verdicts left to the reader's judgment. *At Sword's Point* seeks to present a balanced explanation of the Utah War through its participants' voices, not to win an argument.

One noteworthy, idiosyncratic aspect of the document selection process is the fact that juxtaposed with a plethora of wonderful sources are multiple gaps in the historical record—some at critical junctures of federal as well as Mormon decision making. These voids are more complex and significant than those explained simply by the illiteracy on both sides such as with Porter Rockwell and Jim Bridger. That such should be the case is not surprising given the appalling fact and likely consequences of the Mountain Meadows massacre, the federal criminal indictments that hung over the LDS church's religious and military hierarchy, and the intimate, face-to-face—often paperless—style with which the small Buchanan administration conducted its daily business.

In the case of Mormon leaders, these vexing holes often take the form of missing diary entries or the inexplicable absence of personal correspondence for the period of 1857–58. Examples include the missing personal papers of Lt. Gen. Daniel H. Wells, the Nauvoo Legion's commander, as well as those of Charles Coulson Rich, a Nauvoo Legion brigadier, Mormon apostle, and pioneer leader of Mormondom's most important outpost in California. The apparent absence of any trace of Utah War activity by Ogden's Jonathan Browning, the territory's premier gunsmith, poses a related mystery for a period in which Brigham Young desperately sought firearms. Compounding these voids is the likelihood that since the 1850s the LDS church has surely withheld from public scrutiny some documents bearing on the Utah War, especially its Mountain Meadows massacre, and the certainty that LDS Archives, a private institution, possesses many of the mid-nineteenth century records of the Nauvoo Legion, public documents still unclaimed by today's State of Utah. After decades of reflection on these gaps, one comes to view them as akin to the phenomenon of the dog that did not bark in the Sherlock Holmes case, *Silver Blaze.* This documentary silence speaks volumes, and hopefully will be broken by the forthcoming church-associated monograph tentatively titled *Tragedy at Mountain Meadows.*

With respect to the Buchanan administration, the absence of documents to illuminate important decisions reflects not only intimacy—the seven-man cabinet met at the White House almost daily—but President Buchanan's apparent practice of responding to sensitive correspondence either not at all or only verbally. In this sense the calculating, cautious, lawyerly Buchanan differed substantially in communications style from his more volatile, less schooled adversary in Salt Lake City. The fact that Buchanan or his heirs burned some of his personal papers, while still others disappeared with a putative biographer, further diminished the still-large body of Buchanan papers now lodged at the Historical Society of Pennsylvania, the Library of Congress, and Dickinson College.

Notwithstanding these holes, those interested in the Utah War's record are, on balance, overwhelmingly fortunate rather than deprived. For every missing or expurgated diary of a Mormon leader or Nauvoo Legionnaire, hundreds more—some written and preserved under incredibly adverse circumstances of weather, travel, and legal danger—are still extant, as in the case of the daily pocket journal kept by one of the Legion's most famous, hard-riding officers, Col. Robert Taylor Burton. By the same token, if in its judgment the LDS church and its archivists deny public access to some materials for religious, privacy, or other reasons, they are extraordinarily helpful in making available to researchers far more documents—many highly sensitive—than they sequester.[4] As with other mysteries of life and state secrets, copies of even some of LDS Archives' restricted materials have found their way into a variety of other public and private collections, where they are available for consultation by the enterprising researcher.

Similarly, if President Buchanan chose not to write letters or generate memoranda about sensitive meetings dealing with the Utah War, his cabinet officers and other White House visitors fortuitously did so for their own purposes. I refer to Edward de Stoeckel, the Russian minister to Washington; Dr. John M. Bernhisel, Utah's territorial delegate to Congress; Brevet Lt. Gen. Winfield Scott, the army's general in chief; and James C. Van Dyke, the Buchanan political advisor who was also U.S. attorney in Philadelphia. In this sense, I believe that Professor Kenneth M. Stampp was uncharacteristically mistaken in asserting nearly twenty years ago to Richard D. Poll that there is no "smoking gun," that is to say an unexploited document to explain

[4] Of the editor's voluminous document requests, LDS Archives has rarely denied access to materials, and then only because matters of confidential religious rites or priest-penitent issues were involved. Accordingly the editor considers LDS Archives' current professionals as helpful colleagues.

the Buchanan administration's decision during the spring of 1857 to intervene militarily in Utah Territory. Such a document—indeed several of them—exists; I have collected them.[5]

How, one might ask, does this book differ from LeRoy R. and Ann W. Hafen's classic document compilation of fifty years ago?[6] The distinction runs to the matter of newly discovered sources and their use, a greater emphasis on the sequence and juxtaposition of key events, the cumulative impact of a half-century of additional scholarship and analysis, and an editorial approach that probes a wide range of issues unaddressed by the Hafens. And so *At Sword's Point* builds upon the Hafens' 1958 book as a point of departure rather than rehashing or deconstructing it.

In this first of two volumes, the story of the Utah War's origins and early prosecution carries through to year-end 1857 with Thomas L. Kane's departure from New York for Utah on 5 January 1858. The succeeding volume will contain documents dealing with General Scott's abortive plans to supersede Albert Sidney Johnston and move on Utah from the Pacific Coast, Brigham Young's multi-pronged strategy for dealing with the army, and Kane's important peace-making role. It will also discuss Captain Randolph B. Marcy's arrival in and return from New Mexico, Sen. Sam Houston's response to Mormon pleas for help, the dramatic Mormon mass migration south, and the Buchanan administration's reinforcement of the Utah Expedition from Kansas, concluding with the eventual resolution of the conflict without further bloodshed and the army's non-violent entrance into the Salt Lake Valley after Brigham Young's peaceful replacement as governor and Buchanan's proclamation of a blanket amnesty.

Just as *At Sword's Point* is not solely a Utah story, it should be clear that the conflict neither welled up on a single day with General Scott's issuance of his 28 May 1857 general circular nor ended on 26 June 1858, the day the Utah Expedition marched through Salt Lake City. This was a Mormon-federal conflict nearly a decade in the making that in many respects did not run its course until the early twentieth century. It has taken even longer for the Utah War's story to emerge in reasonably complete fashion.

---

[5] Professor Stampp made this assertion when queried by Poll, a graduate student in his 1947 Civil War seminar, during a 23 October 1990 telephone interview. Memo to file in Richard D. Poll Papers.

[6] Hafen and Hafen, eds., *Mormon Resistance: A Documentary Account of the Utah Expedition, 1857–1858*. This volume, reprinted and retitled by the University of Nebraska Press in 2005, is identical to the Arthur H. Clark Company's study published in 1958 and reprinted in 1982 under the title *The Utah Expedition, 1857–1858: A Documentary Account. . . .*

Chapter 1

"Like a Thousand o' Brick" Tense Prelude to Armed Intervention, 1849–55

Since we came down on the Gentiles lately "like a thousand o' brick," we have nearly scared them all out of the Territory, and we are anticipating a very quiet and peaceable winter.

—First Counselor Heber C. Kimball to James Ferguson, 8 September 1855

The Utah War did not simply spring up on a single day in 1857. It was a conflict nearly ten years in the making, a long period during which already frayed Mormon-federal relations deteriorated steadily, beginning with a minor clash with the army in 1849.

The first U.S. troops to visit the new Mormon settlement at Salt Lake—then an isolated, politically unorganized part of the Mexican Cession—arrived in late August 1849, two years after the Mormons first entered the Great Basin. The troops were detachments detailed by the War Department for quite different purposes. The contingents, traveling only days apart, encountered a suspicious, hypersensitive Mormon community at a time of great political uncertainty. Emblematically, the troops became embroiled in incidents that became part of a long chain of events leading to the Utah War.

The first detachment, 1st Lt. Robert M. Morris's company from the Regiment of U.S. Mounted Riflemen, was escorting Joseph Wilson, superintendent of Indian Affairs for much of the Mexican Cession. Wilson was in transit to California. He and Morris's escort arrived in Salt Lake City on 30 August 1849 and departed two days later. During their brief stay, some of the troops or their civilian packers scuffled with Salt Lake City constables following what was allegedly a rape attempt on the wife of local citizen Rodney Badger. Although a relatively minor and now obscure incident, Apostle George A. Smith recalled it heatedly nine years later during the Utah War.[1]

The day after the Wilson-Morris group departed, 1st Lt. John W. Gunnison entered Salt Lake City from Fort Bridger with the vanguard of Capt. Howard Stansbury's party of topographical engineers. As with the Wilson-Morris group, the War Department had dispatched the Stansbury Expedition without notifying the Mormon community, although Mormon sources had provided Brigham Young with informal intelligence reports of Stansbury's westward movement for weeks. This federal insensitivity and Mormon information-gathering capability were harbingers of future behavior.

Although Captain Stansbury's troops and employees were apparently better disciplined than Lieutenant Morris's party, the melee of a few days earlier must have affected negatively the warmth of their welcome in Salt Lake City. Even more important were severe Mormon apprehensions about the impact on Mormon land claims of Captain Stansbury's mission—charting the Great Salt Lake. Without political organization as either a territory or state, the Salt Lake community was without access to the American system of preemption (homesteading); Mormons were, in effect, squatters on the public domain laboring in a harsh environment to improve land holdings for which they held no title. They pioneered under a church land-allocation system unrecognized by the U.S. government. The unannounced arrival of Stansbury's Expedition, equipped with the paraphernalia of surveyors as well as cartographers, stimulated Mormon apprehensions of land loss while aggravating perceptions of earlier victimization of homesteading Mormons in Missouri during the 1830s. Stansbury and Gunnison had to use all of the diplomacy they could muster before a suspicious, offended Brigham Young would accept and agree to assist their mission.[2]

Although one officer associated with the Stansbury Expedition—2d Lt. George W. Howland—provocatively left the Salt Lake Valley for Oregon Territory with a former plural wife of First Counselor Heber C. Kimball, the main group departed for Washington the next summer on generally good

[1] Morris's diary for this period and his report to the War Department are mute on any such imbroglio, a silence leading Will Bagley to challenge the veracity of Smith's description of the affair. Bagley to MacKinnon, e-mail message, 9 January 2007. George A. Smith's 1858 comments appear in McGavin, *U.S. Soldiers Invade Utah*, 236.

[2] Madsen, *Exploring the Great Salt Lake*, 152–55.

Brigham Young
The former Utah governor and LDS church president is shown in his sixties with postwar beard and in a rare contemplative pose. Projecting vigor as well as careful grooming in photographs throughout his life, a self-educated, controlling Young presented a quite different image from the more elderly, somewhat rumpled President Buchanan of the late 1850s. In 1857 Young held a plethora of overlapping civil and religious titles including those of Utah's governor, superintendent of Indian Affairs, and militia commander while also serving as the LDS church's president, prophet, seer, and revelator. *Courtesy of the LDS Archives.*

terms with the Latter-day Saints.[3] Nonetheless the Compromise of 1850, finalized by Congress as Stansbury rode east, failed to extend the preemption land system to the new Utah Territory. The result was severe Mormon-federal conflicts over land issues that continued into the 1860s, when Congress remedied the situation.

The tensions in Salt Lake City over the first brief presence of federal troops were soon followed by an escalating series of incidents revolving around not only social conduct and survey disputes but a wide range of other matters. The conflicts involved virtually every aspect of federal-Mormon interface: the quality of mail service; the jurisdiction of county, territorial, and federal courts; the evenhandedness of criminal justice; Indian relations and per-

[3] Howland's social behavior is little known but is discussed in Madsen, ibid., 268–70.

ceptions of Mormon tampering with tribal allegiances; Governor Young's handling of congressional appropriations; and the accuracy of the territorial census, an issue important to any Mormon bid for statehood. Reports of Mormon conduct and attitudes from argonauts passing through Salt Lake City to California were mixed, with some travelers positive and grateful about Mormon hospitality while other visitors were sometimes highly critical, citing exploitative, predatory, intimidating, and disloyal behavior.

Aggravating these bitterly contested federal-territorial issues was a series of even more volatile sectarian issues. Chief among these was the obvious but unadmitted practice of plural marriage or polygamy. But at the heart of much of this tension was a collision between Brigham Young's vision of Utah under his leadership as an autocratic theocracy (anticipating the Second Coming of Christ) rather than as a conventional federal territory functioning as a ward of Congress under republican principles of government.[4]

Under territorial status officers were appointed by the president with advice and consent of the Senate. It was by such process, accompanied by intensive lobbying by Thomas L. Kane, a friendly non-Mormon Philadelphia philanthropist, that Pres. Millard Fillmore had designated Brigham Young governor in 1850. Several other Latter-day Saints were also among Utah's first federally appointed officials. In Young's case he held the overlapping roles of governor, U.S. superintendent of Indian Affairs, and militia commander in addition to his church positions. But when such appointees were non-Mormons, Brigham Young and other Mormons challenged them, especially if they were hacks, alcoholics, grafters, libertines or incompetents. When this was done with inflammatory language or occasional violence, such challenges spawned a growing eastern perception of Utah as a disloyal, violent society.

This is not the place for an exhaustive examination of these incidents. But a summary description of the most significant pinch points—some poorly understood today—illustrates an important, foundational concept. The Utah War came about not because of a single critical incident during the spring of 1857. Rather, it was the product of nearly a decade of corrosive incidents, deteriorating relations, and grossly differing philosophies of governance—one secular, conventional, and republican while the other was authoritarian, millennial, and theocratic.

---

[4] Discussion of this long list of pre-1857 conflicts appears in Bigler's two books, *Forgotten Kingdom* and *A Winter with the Mormons,* and in his unpublished paper, "Sources of Conflict: Mormons and Their Neighbors, 1830–90."

Tensions of the Early 1850s

As Congress debated the political organization of the Mexican Cession during 1849–50, it received two petitions bitterly critical of the Mormon Salt Lake community and its loyalty to the U.S. government. These accusations were the dramatic work of a man appearing to be a Mormon insider, William Smith—the erratic, vindictive younger brother of LDS church founder Joseph Smith, Jr. The petitions had a negative impact on Congress's willingness to sanction either a State of Deseret or Brigham Young's early appetite for a vast Mormon political entity stretching from the crest of the Rockies to San Diego Bay. The result was the Compromise of 1850 and Congress's creation of a large but substantially more circumscribed Utah Territory.[5]

During the summer of 1851 Utah's non-Mormon federal appointees arrived in the territory and then abruptly returned to Washington in the fall of 1851 bearing tales of abusive, disloyal behavior on the part of Mormon leaders, especially Gov. Brigham Young. As the departing officials prepared to leave Utah, Brigham Young's quasi-governmental Council of Fifty covertly considered acquiring an exotic weapon developed by elderly, eccentric "Professor" Uriah Brown. At the invitation of Phineas Young, the governor's brother, Brown had traveled to Utah to sell what Young described for the council as "an invention of liquid fire to destroy an army & navy. Many evidences of the power of the invention can be adduced. . . . If pipes were laid in the kanyon he could destroy an army instantly without injuring the operator. If we ever settle on a sea port he could destroy any number of vessels, any navy in an instant."[6] Since Brown's invention was not intended for Indian warfare, the question arises as to the potential application being contemplated by the Mormons. Equally unusual was the request made during the fall of 1851 by Nauvoo Legion general Daniel H. Wells of Samuel Colt, the famous Hartford arms manufacturer. Wells sought information on the price and availability of large quantities of Colt's most powerful, sophisticated, scope-equipped weapons and "any kind of instruments you may be manufacturing, suited to mountain warfare." It was an urgent inquiry of the type that Colt might have expected from the U.S. Army's ordnance bureau rather

[5] MacKinnon, "'Like Splitting a Man Up His Backbone,'" 103.

[6] See entries for 25 August and 13 September 1851, "Council of Fifty Minutes," D. Michael Quinn Papers, transcription in author's possession; entries for 26 August and 13 September 1851, Albert Carrington diary; Brown to Brigham Young, 12 January 1852, LDS Archives. Negotiations with Brown ultimately collapsed.

than from a poorly financed territorial militia concerned about sporadic Indian attacks.[7]

Notwithstanding a national uproar and congressional inquiry into the public aspects of the so-called runaway-officials affair, it largely subsided in 1852 after Young dispatched his second counselor, Jedediah M. Grant, to conduct a campaign of aggressive rebuttal if not attack in eastern metropolitan newspapers with the covert help of Thomas L. Kane.[8] Although these efforts were relatively successful, subsequent widespread rumors of a Mormon independence movement to take the new Utah Territory out of the federal union forced an intense campaign of denial by Mormon leaders in early 1852.[9]

Another national sensation arose in 1852 following the 12 August public disclosure in Salt Lake City that the frequently denied principle of celestial (plural) marriage was and had long been an integral part of Mormon practice as well as theology. The vitriolic uproar over this announcement swelled rather than diminished with time. It nearly cost the church the support of a shocked, disapproving, but ultimately forgiving Kane, a past and future Mormon advocate. Not surprisingly, during 1852 Utah failed in a second attempt to obtain congressional approval for its proposed political transformation from a territory into a State of Deseret. Lost in the process was the Mormons' ability to elect their own officials and to deflect a growing public clamor for federal action over the polygamy issue.[10]

With the departure of a simpatico President Fillmore and the inauguration of an untested Franklin Pierce in March 1853, Brigham Young recognized the political dangers ahead. President Pierce was well aware of the recent runaway-officials predicament, and in 1854 he would need to decide whether to nomi-

[7] Wells to Colt, 27 November 1851, and Brigham Young to Colt, 28 November 1851, LDS Archives; Colt to Wells, 16 February 1852, Utah State Archives.

[8] Many of the charges and counter-charges for the runaway-officials imbroglio are in Bigler, ed., *A Winter with the Mormons*, 194–203. With a loss of confidence in the appointees' credibility, President Fillmore and Sec. of State Daniel Webster ruled in 1852 that they must return to their duties in Utah or forfeit their positions. The most colorful related document, a mammoth 11 June 1852 memo dictated by Brigham Young titled "Beating Against the Air," LDS Archives, has never been published. Aghast at its bulk and aggressive tone, Delegate Bernhisel quietly chose not to transmit this document to President Fillmore on grounds that it would be counterproductive, the tide having already turned in the Mormons' favor.

[9] "Extra," *Deseret News*, 31 January 1852, Beinecke Library. Bernhisel to Young, 10 March 1852, and Young to Bernhisel, 27 May 1852, both LDS Archives.

[10] For Kane's ambivalent reaction to the polygamy announcement, see Kane to Young, 17 October 1852. For an example of Bernhisel's feverish attempts to control the public-relations damage surrounding this issue from the East, see Bernhisel to Young, 11 October and 8 November 1852, LDS Archives.

nate Young for a second four-year term. With a friendly, even chatty tone ("Wishing you a happy, prosperous, and peacefull administration"), Young wrote to Pierce on 30 March in an attempt to influence the president's thinking on appointments at the onset of his administration. Young's letter was essentially an exposition of the need to appoint Mormons to Utah's federal offices on grounds that qualified candidates were locally available and only they understood and could serve effectively for the long term in the territory's isolated, expensive, and culturally unusual environment. In the midst of these arguments, Young included a request "in my own behalf" that he "shall have the honor to be continued in the Office I now hold."[11] This was one of the rare direct communications between Brigham Young and an American president. Four years later his attempts to influence a newly elected James Buchanan would be significantly different—indirect, severe, and only through intermediaries.

On 26 October 1853, along Utah's Sevier River, Capt. John W. Gunnison and seven members of his army topographical engineering party were massacred while surveying one of the routes proposed for a transcontinental railroad. Although the overwhelming likelihood was that the murders were committed by an Indian group (Pahvants), accusations welled up asserting that Mormons were responsible for the atrocity either directly as assassins or indirectly as enablers. Other conspiracy theories associated the massacre with presumed Mormon displeasure over the 1852 appearance of *The Mormons*, a book published by Gunnison following his 1850 return east from a winter in the Salt Lake Valley with the Stansbury Expedition.[12]

During the late summer of 1853 a large Mormon posse expelled frontiersman and national icon Jim Bridger from his trading post on Blacks Fork of the Green River for allegedly violating Brigham Young's ban on trading alcohol and munitions with Indians during the Walker War, a local Mormon-Ute conflict. Responding to lobbying in Washington by Bridger during January 1854, Congress seriously debated but ultimately declined to truncate Utah's eastern frontier while creating boundaries for the new adjacent territories of Kansas and Nebraska.[13]

---

[11] Young to Pierce, 30 March 1853, LDS Archives.

[12] Robert Kent Fielding argues that the Gunnison massacre was part of a chain of events leading directly to the subsequent Utah War and Mountain Meadows massacre. See Fielding, *The Unsolicited Chronicler* and "John Gunnison and the Mormons," 9 December 1993 lecture, Humanists of Utah. A discussion of Captain Gunnison's concerns about the Mormon reaction to his quite simpatico book as he re-entered Utah in 1853 appears in Madsen, "John Gunnison's Letters to His Mormon Friend, Albert Carrington," 264–85.

[13] MacKinnon, "'Like Splitting a Man Up His Backbone,'" 104–107.

Throughout 1854 Pres. Franklin Pierce quietly struggled with the dilemma of whether and how to replace Brigham Young as Utah's governor upon the expiration of his term, a political danger of which Young was well aware through Bernhisel's periodic meetings with Pierce and monthly reports to Salt Lake City. In the midst of this uncertainty U.S. Army brevet lieutenant colonel Edward J. Steptoe arrived in Salt Lake City from Fort Leavenworth on 31 August with a command of about 325 soldiers and civilian packers, as well as nearly 1,000 horses and mules. This was an army presence grossly larger than the detachments of Morris, Stansbury, and Gunnison as well as the early 1854 civilian exploring expedition of John C. Frémont. Steptoe's mission was three-fold: to provide troops and animals for Pacific Coast garrisons; to mark a better road from Salt Lake City to California; and to assist Utah authorities in the capture of those responsible for the prior year's Gunnison massacre. As year-end 1854 approached, relations between Steptoe's troops and civilians in Salt Lake City declined steadily over matters of public drunkenness and what today would be called fraternization with Mormon women. On Christmas Day, following an earlier brawl at the Salt Lake Theater, there was a drunken riot in the city's streets requiring intervention by Steptoe's officers and the Nauvoo Legion.[14] Four days earlier, without Steptoe's awareness, the U.S. Senate confirmed Pierce's nomination of Steptoe as Brigham Young's gubernatorial successor.

By early February 1855 rumors of Steptoe's appointment drifted into Salt Lake City from California and soon became an open secret even though Steptoe kept his own counsel. It was an opportunity about which the colonel agonized throughout the winter and on which he took no action because of his reluctance to leave the army and doubts about his ability to govern Utah. In early spring, three Pahvant Utes were tried in Nephi, Utah, for the Gunnison massacre, resulting in their conviction by a Mormon jury for manslaughter. Perceived as a tepid verdict contrary to the judge's instructions and rendered against perhaps the wrong defendants, it was an outcome that enraged Steptoe's officers—and later many eastern non-Mormons—nearly as much as the convicts' subsequent escape from Utah's porous territorial penitentiary.[15]

[14] The most complete account of the Steptoe Expedition's controversial and enigmatic stay in Utah is in two unpublished studies by Miller, "The Impact of the Gunnison Massacre on Mormon-Federal Relations"; and "Brigham Young, Edward J. Steptoe, and the 1854–55 Gubernatorial Controversy." The Christmas brawl is described in 2d Lt. LaRhett L. Livingston to James G. Livingston, 27 December 1854, Beinecke Library. See also MacKinnon, "Sex, Subalterns, and Steptoe: Army Behavior, Mormon Rage, and Utah War Anxieties," forthcoming in *Utah Hist. Qtly.*

[15] The controversial trial was described at length in a highly critical article in *New York Times*, 18 May 1855, published without attribution but written by Steptoe's Lieutenant Mowry.

In May the Steptoe Expedition left Utah. Its commander had still not decided whether to accept Pierce's appointment. Upon departure the army was accompanied by as many as one hundred married and single Mormon women seeking an exit from the LDS church and the protection of a military escort to California. Here was the 1850 Howland incident writ large. Mormon leaders were livid at the size and character of this female exodus and what they perceived as wholly unacceptable social conduct by Steptoe's command. In the meantime Brigham Young's gubernatorial status remained unaddressed and ambiguous as additional federal appointees—including for the first time a surveyor-general—arrived to fill other territorial positions. Within a remarkably short period of time, the newcomers too were alienated and mutually at odds with Mormon leadership.[16]

1855: A Watershed Year

In the midst of the Steptoe-related tensions, another pinch point in Mormon-federal relations developed in 1855. It arose with Brigham Young's exposition of an old accusation that came to be known as the "ram in the thicket" conspiracy theory. This was a now-bizarre notion asserting that, at the instigation of Sen. Thomas Hart Benton of Missouri, the U.S. government had recruited the Mormon Battalion nine years earlier to place the westering Latter-day Saints somehow in harm's way. The facts were that Pres. James Polk had authorized this recruitment reluctantly and only as an accommodation to Mormon lobbying. The battalion's payroll—paid partially in advance—had been a major source for financing the Mormon exodus from Iowa to the Salt Lake Valley. Nonetheless, beginning in 1855 Jedediah M. Grant and Brigham Young again described the battalion's Mexican War service as illustrative of former and presumably continuing central government persecution.[17]

Of these critical incidents and damaged relationships, the issue surrounding Mormon women and the attentions of outsiders, especially federal troops, is the one least understood and most underestimated by historians. This shortfall is especially important since it has left unexamined an issue that sheds light on Brigham Young's intense reaction two years later to news of the Utah Expe-

[16] Once in California, Steptoe declined Utah's governorship, and an embarrassed Pierce declined to risk the nomination of a new candidate, a chain of events that left Young as de facto governor until Buchanan addressed the issue two years later. For anti-Mormon comments by a recently arrived federal appointee, see Assoc. Justice W. W. Drummond to U.S. Attorney Gen. Caleb Cushing, 1 October 1855.

[17] Bigler and Bagley, eds., *Army of Israel*, 428–29.

dition's approach. By the time Colonel Steptoe's detachment had left the Salt Lake Valley for California in May 1855, Young had vowed to never again allow federal troops into Utah and in proximity to its women, although he expected the federal government to try to garrison Utah soon, perhaps as early as that fall. In September 1855 Young was still so enraged that he told two visiting Europeans that Judge John F. Kinney had "aided the troops of Colonel Steptoe in carrying off women belonging to the Saints. In this forcible abduction the conduct of the American officers, he said, was considered so abominable, that were they to return to the Salt Lake, war would immediately be declared against them; or if fresh troops were to come, the inhabitants would hold no communication with them, either in the way of social intercourse or trade."[18]

That two members of Young's own family—a daughter-in-law and daughter—were involved in the army-Mormon social imbroglios of 1854–55 probably explains in part the months of angry anti-government rhetoric that flowed publicly from Brigham Young and First Counselor Heber C. Kimball. That two of Steptoe's most socially active subordinates—1st Lt. Sylvester Mowry and Capt. Rufus Ingalls—sent severely anti-Mormon reports to Washington after leaving Utah adds to the volatility of that winter's disastrous military-civil encounters.[19]

Recognized or not, the civil affairs damage done by the Steptoe Expedition's conduct in Salt Lake City was a watershed in what by the end of 1855 had become an accelerating, potentially violent deterioration in Mormon-federal relations. Captain Ingalls's subsequent assault and armed confrontation with Apostle Orson Hyde in western Utah, Brigham Young's extraordinary office interrogation of Chief Justice John F. Kinney, the judge's secret but alarming reports to Washington, and the governor's volcanic, provocative Sunday discourses during the late winter, spring and summer of 1855 were straws in the whirlwind to be reaped two years later.[20]

[18] See Young to John Taylor, 25 July 1855, Taylor Family Collection, Marriott Library; Remy, *A Journey to Great-Salt-Lake City*, 1:206–207. Once he returned to New York, Steptoe speculated about an army garrison for Utah in Steptoe to Elias Blackburn, 3 November 1855, LDS Archives.

[19] During the winter of 1853–54, Sgt. John Tobin, a surviving member of the late Captain Gunnison's military escort, bivouacked in Salt Lake City and struck up a problematic and ultimately failed courtship with Alice Young, one of the governor's young daughters; see Parshall, "'Pursue, Retake & Punish,'" 64–86. During the winter of 1854–55 Steptoe's 1st Lt. Sylvester Mowry aggressively pursued, among other women, Mary J. Ayers Young, wife of Brigham Young's son, Joseph A. Young, then absent at the British Mission. Mowry's attentions and plans for elopement drew a death threat from Governor Young. Captain Ingalls, Steptoe's quartermaster, was arrested by Salt Lake City authorities during April 1855 while trying to take thirteen-year-old Rachael Nowell to California. For these imbroglios, see MacKinnon, "Sex, Subalterns, and Steptoe," forthcoming in *Utah Hist. Qtly*.

Reflecting the volatile state of Mormon-federal relations during 1855 was a long discourse delivered by Brigham Young on Sunday, 18 February 1855. He intended this sermon, aptly titled "The Constitution and Government of the United States—Rights and Policy of the Latter-day Saints," to serve multiple purposes as rumors of Steptoe's gubernatorial appointment circulated and as the army continued its disruptive behavior.

First and foremost, this rambling, hours-long sermon was a classic exposition of Mormon love for the U.S. constitution but contempt for the behavior of many of the federal officers charged with its execution. This was a duality expressed in virtually every Mormon commentary on relations with the central government throughout the 1850s. Second, the discourse was a litany of grievances against the government combined with a presentation of the Mormon side of multiple national controversies: the affair of the runaway officials; accusations of a Mormon-independence movement; and the principle of plural marriage. Defiantly, Young covered even the tenor of his own controversial rhetoric, noting, "In my conversation, I shall talk and act as I please. . . . [S]poken words are but wind, and when they are spoken are gone; consequently I take liberties in speaking which I do not allow when I commit my sentiments to writing." Finally, the discourse was a blunt warning to both Colonel Steptoe's men as well as to Mormon women: continued fraternization carried dire, even lethal, consequences.

Although in his discourse Young appeared to express a willingness to cede Utah's governorship to Colonel Steptoe, it is probable that his phrasing was carefully crafted for public consumption. Young spoke at a time when he believed that Steptoe would probably decline President Pierce's nomination—as he eventually did. Brigham Young could afford to be gracious.

The length and intensity of this discourse was stunning—so exhausting that it had to be delivered in two parts. Thomas Bullock, one of Young's senior office clerks, read the first part from a prepared text at the morning tabernacle service, and Young delivered the second segment extemporaneously later that day. It was a sermon and political statement that revealed the intense

[20] For the Ingalls-Hyde confrontation, see Hyde to Young, 19 June 1855, LDS Archives. It is unlikely that the army was aware of this background in evaluating the rabidly anti-Mormon reports later written by Ingalls once he reached California. His 25 August 1855 report to Brevet Maj. Gen. Thomas S. Jesup may be found most conveniently in White, comp., *News of the Plains and Rockies 1803–1865*, 5:288–302. Young's extraordinary interrogation of Judge Kinney is described in Notes of conversation in governor's office, 10 July 1855, recorded by David O. Calder, transcription in possession of David H. Miller, Cameron University; original in LDS Archives.

confrontational style with which Brigham Young met critics and approached challenges at this watershed in his relationship with the federal government.[21]

As the fall of 1855 approached, First Counsel Heber C. Kimball took stock and briefed a protégé, James Ferguson, on what had been happening in Utah since he left for a mission in Ireland. Kimball's description of the fortifications under construction in Salt Lake City were a metaphor for the siege mentality growing in the territory:

> President B. Young has built a strong wall of common cobble stones 11 feet high & 3 feet wide at the base, tapering to one foot at the top, between his orchard and the tithing barn. . . . I am continuing Pres Young's wall northward; so that we shall have a fort within a fort, and a fort within a fort, same as it will be eventually a Kingdom within a Kingdom, and a Kingdom within that, and so on, and so forth, *ad infinitum, ad libitum* nevertheless, notwithstanding, free gratis, and without charge!!! . . .
>
> Since we came down on the Gentiles lately "like a thousand o' brick" we have nearly scared them all out of the Territory, and we are anticipating a very quiet and peaceable winter.[22]

Four days later, with tongue in cheek, the editor of the *Brooklyn Daily Eagle* also assessed the recent past but took a quite different view of what lay ahead:

> The Mormon Imposter Brigham Young, complains very bitterly of the troops who were quartered at Utah last winter. It appears that they created quite a rebellion among the women, and when they left for California, carried off a number with them. Brigham vows vengeance and death to all who shall in future make any such demonstration towards his female flock. The President had better send a regiment out there with instructions to court the women. It would very soon break up that nest. Get the women away and the men would not stay long.[23]

At year-end 1855 Brigham Young turned from vengeful thoughts about Steptoe-like federal intrusions to an apocalyptical view of the American society surrounding Utah. In his role as governor, Young spoke of "sanguinary war" and a "terrible conflagration" ahead not unlike those with which he would himself threaten American cities less than two years later. These were remarkable comments from an American territorial governor.[24]

---

[21] "The Constitution and Government of the United States—Rights and Policy of the Latter-day Saints," *Journal of Discourses*, 2:170–78. Later published in pamphlet form, this two-part discourse is now a collector's item; see copy in Beinecke Library, Yale University.

[22] Kimball to Ferguson, 8 September 1855, Historian's Office Letterpress Copybooks, LDS Archives.

[23] Editorial, *Brooklyn Daily Eagle* (New York), 12 September 1855, 2/1.

[24] Message of Gov. Brigham Young to Utah Legislative Assembly, 11 December 1855, Utah State Archives; text also printed in *Deseret News*, 9 December 1855, 4/1–3.

Chapter 2

"Happy Fighting Led by Inspired Men"

Approaching the Flash Point, 1856

The topic of conversation was war in the future. I remarked that war was not without mitigating circumstances to which Jeddy nodded assent and his countenance shined gloriously. The idea which seemed to be left on my mind was that it would be a happy fighting when led by inspired men.

—Dream of dismissed U.S. Marshal
Joseph L. Heywood, July 1856[1]

If 1855 was a watershed in the accelerating deterioration of Mormon-federal relations—the year during which Brigham Young became intolerant of further colonialism and unacceptable behavior by U.S. troops—1856 took on a different character. It was the year during which Utah's federal appointees and the national establishment bore down on Governor Young's theocracy-in-progress. Meanwhile, the country struggled simultaneously with the slavery issue in the midst of a presidential election, and the potential for conflict between Americans in multiple places, including Utah, neared a flash point.

Mail to Washington continued to flow from federal appointees in Salt Lake City—some of it intercepted, read, destroyed, or even copied and filed with Governor Young's own correspondence. Such letters questioned the sanctity of the mail itself, the peculiar functioning of Utah's courts and criminal justice system,[2] the behavior of Mormon missionaries amongst Indian tribes, and

[1] "Jeddy" in Heywood's dream was Jedediah Morgan Grant, Brigham Young's second counselor in the First Presidency and mayor of Salt Lake City.

[2] Among the multiple controversies was the casual way in which convicted murderers received gubernatorial pardons, in some cases before serving any prison time. Brigham Young pardon of Samuel G. Baker, 3 January 1856, and clerk Daniel Mackintosh to Sheriff of Iron County, 9 January 1856, LDS Archives.

the harassment of federal surveyors.[3] These were new voices sounding familiar alarms in different ways. It was criticism that drove Governor Young to compile a list of twenty-eight suspects whose names he sent east to Apostle George A. Smith and Delegate Bernhisel in Washington "to put us on the track and lead to other testimony and a further development of facts." Within less than a week one of these men, a federal surveyor, was severely beaten in Salt Lake City, and within five weeks another—the federally appointed Mormon territorial secretary—was murdered on the plains near Fort Kearny. Less than two years later a third listee, an apostate-lawyer, would be murdered in southern Utah.[4] Supplementing these criticisms were allegations of violence and unsolved murders in the territory attributed to agents perceived as church assassins.

Arguments also arose as to whether Brigham Young was preaching a violent religious doctrine of blood atonement as part of the frenetic, territorial-wide religious Reformation that began in the fall of 1856 under the leadership of his charismatic second counselor, Jedediah M. Grant.[5] Within the territory—as elsewhere on the frontier—there arose an array of distinctly local euphemisms, for the verb *murder*. In Utah, where this vocabulary was especially rich, such slang was religiously rooted in code terms for excom-

[3] The perception of Mormon tampering with the allegiances of American Indians was an old fear dating back to Missouri but was aggravated in 1855 by the assignment of dozens of LDS missionaries to tribes throughout the West in millennial anticipation of the "final days."

[4] This list is an odd mixture of known church critics as well as Latter-day Saints who appear to have been church members in good standing. It is one of the more curious, revealing documents of the period. Two of the men on Young's list (Babbitt and Williams) were subsequently murdered under controversial circumstances, and one (Troskolawski) was severely beaten in Salt Lake City. The list is contained in Young to George A. Smith, 1–31 July 1856, LDS Archives and listed: [Chief Justice] John F. Kinney; [Associate Justice] W. W. Drummond; [Merchant] Howard Livingston; Surveyor Gen[l] [David H.] Burr; [contract surveyor David A.] Burr; [contract surveyor Frederick H.] Burr; [?] Burr; [?] Burr; Orson Miles; K. L. Briggs; Thomas Bird; Louis Tousig; Henry Standish; Edward Williams; [supreme court clerk] Curtis E. Bolton; [territorial secretary] A. W. Babbitt; [merchant] William Bell; [contract surveyor] Joseph Troskaloskie; E. F. Barr; Richard Thompson; William Camp; [attorney] T. S. Williams; [brewer and soon U.S. Marshal] P. K. Dotson; Samuel Snyder; L. W. Montague; George Kanoy; James Gemmell; George Cronyn.

[5] The thrust of the LDS Reformation was cleansing and purification aimed at returning members to higher standards of personal conduct, hygiene, and religious observance, including rebaptism. Historian Richard E. Turley, Jr., believes that the Reformation may have been prompted in part by reactions to Mormon fraternization with Steptoe's troops. It emphasized excommunication and out-migration of recalcitrant members, often to the accompaniment of raw language and violent Old Testament imagery. The most controversial aspect of the LDS Reformation was the doctrine of blood atonement, the notion that some sins were so heinous that offenders could be redeemed only by having someone shed their blood. Whether, to what extent, and with whose sanction this doctrine led to murders in Utah during 1856–57 has been debated ever since, with church defenders arguing that violent imagery from the pulpit was merely well-intentioned if overzealous rhetoric by leaders attempting to lead their flock to self-improvement. What is clear is that perceptions of homicide, rather than motivational exhortation for back-sliders, spread across the United States. For differing views of the Reformation and its implications, see Peterson, "The Mormon Reformation," 59–87; Alexander, "Wilford Woodruff and the Mormon Reformation of 1855–57," 25–40; Bagley, *Blood of the Prophets*, 50–52.

munication such as *cut-off, hewn-down,* and *cleansing the platter.* Still other, more violent Utah imagery had victims being blood-atoned, pushed over the rim [of the Great Basin], sent home the short-cut, failing to make the connection, and nepoed. When Brigham Young threatened from the tabernacle stand about sending miscreants "to Hell across-lots," his language had a profound impact on non-Mormons, if not Latter-day Saints.[6]

A Highly Political Summer

Outside of Utah, the intensity of anti-Mormon attitudes was such that during 1856 congressional committees received anti-polygamy bills and considered hearings on the wisdom of severing large portions of territory from Utah's eastern and western flanks or even politically obliterating the territory by repealing its organic act. When Apostles George A. Smith and John Taylor traveled to Washington during the summer of 1856 seeking again to establish a State of Deseret, Sen. Stephen A. Douglas of Illinois and Utah territorial delegate John M. Bernhisel both advised against submitting the new statehood petition. They feared unleashing the anti-polygamy forces that were building and stimulating further the territorial dismemberment efforts afoot in Congress.[7] When Apostle Smith traveled to Philadelphia to consult Thomas L. Kane, he found Kane absent for five weeks, the harbinger of an even longer withdrawal a year later with serious consequences.

In anticipation of this third attempt to obtain statehood for Deseret, Young had written to Kane on 14 April to "direct your mind to your old friends in the mountains, and as usual, to again tax the friendship of our valued, and much esteemed friend Col Kane." In addition to seeking Kane's support, Young asked, "May we rely upon your aid and influence in effecting this desirable object? We confidently trust, that we may therefore have taken the liberty of instructing our [constitutional convention] delegates to counsel, and co-operate together with you, and our worthy [congressional] delegate Dr Bernhisel, in regard to this important matter."[8] Here was a consultative and lobbying role for Kane that Brigham Young would press with increasing urgency in 1857 after the November 1856 presidential election.

[6] "Nepo" was "open" spelled backwards, an allusion to the practice of eviscerating a victim and then sinking him in a stream by filling the chest cavity with rocks. Hosea Stout, the Nauvoo Legion's judge advocate, used this obscure code in his diary.

[7] MacKinnon, "'Like Splitting a Man Up His Backbone,'" 107. Smith to Young, 30 June; Taylor, Smith, and Bernhisel to Young, 12 July; Young to Smith, 1–31 July 1856; all in LDS Archives.

[8] Young to Kane, 14 April 1856, LDS Archives.

On 18 June the national convention of the new Republican Party nominated John C. Frémont as its presidential candidate and adopted a platform plank calling for the eradication of polygamy and slavery as the "twin relics of barbarism." The national upset over polygamy rose in intensity, although there was no federal statute prohibiting the practice. Yet as a campaign issue, polygamy did not assume the dramatic character that modern analysts assume and that contemporary Mormon leaders close to Congress feared.[9]

Later that month, exasperated over Utah's controversies, President Pierce summarily dismissed Joseph L. Heywood, Utah's U.S. marshal, after his arrest and indictment in Washington for brawling in the Treasury Department while attempting to bribe a clerk.[10] Utah would not have another Latter-day Saint as U.S. marshal during her long territorial period.

Meanwhile Brigham Young continued with vigorous church exploitation of lead deposits near Las Vegas, New Mexico Territory, with a focus on munitions that evokes his 1851 interest in sophisticated weapons. In addition to this effort to mine ballistic lead outside of Utah, during 1856 General Wells directed Delegate Bernhisel to acquire a variety of military-training manuals from the War Department and multiple private sources. Within Utah, Governor Young pressed on with his longstanding efforts to stimulate a local gunpowder-manufacturing capability, a technically difficult thrust that drove Young to encourage a colorful variety of entrepreneurs and poseurs, including the erratic Swiss chemist-convert Frederick Loba.[11]

Autumn Angst among Utah's Businessmen and Appointees

On 3 October 1856 W. M. F. Magraw, the disgruntled former mail contractor on the Independence, Missouri–Salt Lake City route, wrote a long let-

[9] The 1856 Republican national convention and platform were overwhelmingly about slavery and Kansas affairs rather than Utah and Mormon controversies. The "twin relics" plank was drafted and presented to the convention as the almost-casual work of a single California delegate. See John A. Wills to Historical Society of Southern California, 27 March 1890, published as "The Twin Relics of Barbarism," *Publications of the Historical Society of Southern California*, 40–44. Poll, "The Mormon Question Enters National Politics," 16–44; "Last Chance for Office," Editorial, *The Mormon* (New York), 5 July 1856, 2/1–3.

[10] Heywood had accompanied Apostles George A. Smith and John Taylor to Washington in an attempt to settle his tangled financial accounts as marshal while they lobbied for statehood.

[11] In 1855 Young established an Indian mission at what is now Las Vegas, Nevada. Discovery soon thereafter of substantial lead deposits in the mountains about twenty miles from the mission produced a herculean effort to mine and smelt the ore. Bernhisel to Wells, 14 January; Bernhisel to Young, 17 January; Loba to Young, 20 February 1856; all in LDS Archives.

ter to President Pierce that, rightly or wrongly, has come to be viewed as one of the most damaging anti-Mormon indictments of the pre-war period.[12] Three days later a similar letter to Pierce written by Isaac Hockaday, brother of Magraw's former partner John M. Hockaday, left Independence. Probably motivated by fear of the Mormon seizure of a tannery that the Hockaday brothers operated in Salt Lake, Isaac informed Pierce that they had "suffered repeated wrongs, abuses and outrages" and that "the entire Territory of Utah is under the complete control of a most lawless set of knaves and assassins who disregard and trample under foot the rights of those not belonging to their so called religious community as well as those who are unwilling to sanction and affiliate with them in their most obscene outrages."[13]

Although both Magraw's and Isaac Hockaday's letters were filed in the State Department, which had jurisdiction over territorial affairs, Sec. of State Lewis Cass produced only Magraw's letter fifteen months later in response to a congressional request, describing it as "the only document on record or on file in this department touching the subject of the [congressional] resolution." It is unclear whether Cass's failure to provide Congress with the Hockaday letter was the result of clerical oversight or a deliberate attempt to avoid undercutting the impact of the related Magraw letter. Four years later Brigham Young complained privately that the Hockaday tannery and Magraw mail contract quandaries "are still all that is recognized in Washington concerning Utah."[14]

Election Day, 4 November, dawned in New York emblematically "with a dense black fog; the streets [were] wet and muddy, the falling leaves [were] filling the gutters, and the banners [hung] listlessly, drenched with rain and begrimed with soot."[15] Notwithstanding earlier service in both houses of Congress, as secretary of state, and as ambassador to both Russia and Great Britain, Democrat James Buchanan was largely unknown to the public that elected him president. Among the uninformed was Brigham Young, who knew little about Buchanan and would not learn of his election until more than two months later. But Buchanan was well known to W. M. F. Magraw's family. Magraw's brother Henry, a Democratic Party stalwart, was Pennsylvania's state

[12] MacKinnon, "The Buchanan Spoils System," 127–50. Magraw's letter is printed in this article and elsewhere.

[13] Isaac Hockaday to Pierce, 6 October 1856, Miscellaneous Letters of Dept. of State, National Archives.

[14] Young to W. H. Hooper, 30 January 1860, Hooper Collection.

[15] "United States. The Presidential Election–Success of Mr. Buchanan," *News of the World* (London), 23 November 1856, 2/1–2.

treasurer. Another brother, Robert M. Magraw, was a Baltimore railroad executive who provided the special train that would later transport Buchanan to the White House. There Robert Magraw would become a suitor for the hand of Harriet Lane, the president's niece and official hostess, and Buchanan would appoint him U.S. consul at Liverpool.

Although Frémont and the Republicans had lost the election, Buchanan's victory was a narrow one, signaling his need to deal in some way during 1857 with the "Mormon problem." At the same time Buchanan needed to distance himself from Democratic senator Douglas's favorite political doctrine of "popular sovereignty," a concept that often drew fire from Whigs, Know-Nothings, and Republicans as an enabler for polygamy as well as slavery in the territories.[16]

On election day Brigham Young wrote to Delegate Bernhisel in Washington not about presidential politics but about the continuing mutual angst in his relationship with Utah's federal appointees. Young noted that

> the most [Indian Agent] Dr Hurt complains of is the distinction made between "Mormons and Americans" by the Indians it having as he alleges been taught them by the Mormons. We do not care a groat about all this affair only as we believe that the agent has written to the [Interior] department in relation to it and is disposed in connection with [Surveyor] Genl [David H.] Burr and others to create a disturbance and difficulty between this Territory and the Genl Government if possible. It is to be regretted that the Dr whose course has been so satisfactory heretofore should drink in with such evil disposed spirits as Judge Drummond & Genl Burr. . . . Burr has been watching for evil ever since he has been here. We suspect him to be a regular government spy.[17]

Meanwhile, as Brigham Young was acutely aware, Indian Agent Garland Hurt and Surveyor General Burr undertook to present their own views directly to the Pierce administration, often with their letters or copies of them migrating clandestinely to Young's office courtesy of the Salt Lake City post office. In a letter written to Congressman John M. Elliott during the fall of 1856, Hurt asked rhetorically, "What is to be done with Utah?" and went on to comment about Brigham Young, his supervisor.

---

[16] Douglas's doctrine of popular sovereignty, or local option with respect to "domestic institutions," was the intellectual underpinning for the Kansas-Nebraska Act of 1854. It unleashed political conflict and violence, especially in Kansas Territory, that accelerated the nation's slide toward disunion. See Eyal, "With His Eyes Open," 175–217.

[17] Young to Bernhisel, 4 November 1856; Hurt to Comm. of Indian Affairs George W. Manypenny, 30 August 1856, "The Utah Expedition," House Ex. Doc. 71 (35-1), 1858, Serial 956, 179–81.

HURT TO ELLIOTT, [?] 1856, LDS ARCHIVES.

But it is from the use which he makes of that power [given to him by the Church], that we are to judge of the republican or autocratical despotism of the man himself.

Regardless of his oft protested love for the Constitution of the United States, the whole tenor of his life and actions both public and private, since he advanced into power, has been in violation of the spirit of that sacred instrument.

He has passed laws abolishing the use of the common law in the courts of the Territory.

He has given the Court of Probate concurrent jurisdiction with the United States District Courts, endowing them with the power to convene & instruct grand juries, & dispose of criminal cases.

He has also enacted other laws which are arbitrary and inimical to the spirit of our institutions, and in many respects an insult to the American judiciary. . . .

It seems to be the sole object of His Excellency to rid himself of the influence of the Constitution and laws of the Federal Government. And he has even been heard to say in his private circles, that Mormondom and republicanism were inimical. . . .

Such is the state of affairs in Utah, to which she has been brought by the rein of Brigham Young and his coadjutors while still the anxious enquiry, what is to be done with Utah? remains unanswered. It has been proposed to divide and subdivide the Territory by lines running through the heart of the Mormon settlement, and to attach the fractions to the adjoining Territories. But I am satisfied that such a disposition would not produce any very desirable changes in the present aspect of things

But let Congress repeal her odious statute and establish a wholesome judiciary. Let men be placed in office who will see that the federal laws are respected: and then offer such protection to the oppressed as will guarantee to them those rights to which an American citizen is entitled, whether he be a Mormon, a disaffected Mormon, or no mormon at all, and then, let those who are unwilling to observe the rules and regulations which are necessary for the preservation of those institution which are sacred to the heart of every american citizen take up their household gods and seek a habitation where pries[t]craft and slavery may find a more genial sod.[18]

---

[18] This undated letter appears to be a copy made in the familiar hand of Thomas Ellerbeck, one of Young's office clerks, indicating that the original was intercepted before leaving Utah, perhaps at the Salt Lake City post office, and given to the governor. Presumably the original was returned to the mailbag after copying. The addressee was Rep. John Milton Elliott of Kentucky, to whom Hurt wrote frequently. A member of the House Committee on Public Expenditures, Elliott was an old friend from their college days in Emory, Virginia, and it was to him that Hurt owed his Utah appointment. Bigler, "Garland Hurt: The American Friend of the Utahs," 150.

On the last day of 1856—in a letter that probably never left Salt Lake City—Surveyor General Burr tried to inform his superior in Washington of developments in Utah.

BURR TO THOMAS A. HENDRICKS, 31 DECEMBER 1856, UTAH STATE HISTORICAL SOCIETY.

Night before last the office of the clerk of the U.S. Supreme Court [for Utah], which was also the office of the U.S. District Court, was broken open. Every book of the office and the office Library but the private Library of Judge Stiles. We think the object is to break up the U.S. court if possible and to drive the U.S. Officers out of the Territory. The Mormons are buying up all the arms and ammunition they can find. The merchant [wagon] trains that come annually and all their conductors and employees, and some of the merchants accumulated a considerable quantity [of arms]. All these have been purchased recently. And at [a] select party which Brigham Young gave at his house the other evening, he requested all present to procure arms, for he said they would soon need them. We know not what they mean.[19] Threats are constantly made against the life of Judge Drummond. He is daily expected in this City, and we have great apprehensions for his safety.[20] Threats are also daily made by the Bishops and other leaders of this people against the lives of all the "Gentiles," and they say none shall be permitted to remain in the Territory after the spring opens. Defiance is constantly thrown out against the Federal Government, and the idea of its interference with them is treated with ridicule.

P.S. It has been found that the Library of the U.S. Supreme Court and all the records and other papers were thrown into the vault of a Privy and then the building filled with straw and shingles and then burnt.[21]

[19] For a description of this Christmas party, see *Deseret News*, 31 December 1856, 340/4. These comments attributed to Brigham Young are consistent with the vigorous, ongoing Mormon quest for arms and ammunition.

[20] Drummond never returned to Salt Lake City from his court session in western Utah's Carson Valley but instead left for California near the end of 1856, arriving in New Orleans via Panama at the end of March 1857.

[21] This is the first attempt to report the 29 December 1856 vandalism of Judge George P. Stiles's and lawyer Thomas Williams's office. What was destroyed, by whom, and why became one of the major incidents debated in connection with Mormon affairs before, during, and after the Utah War.

Chapter 3

"See the Red Stuff Run"
Awaiting Buchanan

We are satisfied with the appointment of Buchanan as future President, we believe he will be friend to the good, that Fillmore was our friend, but Buchanan will not be a whit behind.

—Brigham Young to Thomas L. Kane, 31 January 1857

We hear little else worth notice from Washington, besides rumors of the appointment of New Judges—Post Master, Secy. & perhaps Govr*. all of these are surmises, ~~perhaps~~ based upon the public feelings, or rather the feelings of clerks and officials towards Utah. How little they realize that the destinies of men and nations are in the hands of the Great "I Am."*

—Brigham Young to George Q. Cannon, 31 January 1857

With the approach of the new year, Judge George P. Stiles's biggest challenges were reassembling his vandalized office, dealing with his recent excommunication, and determining how best to flee Utah. The latter was a dilemma shared by every non-Mormon federal appointee in the territory. Stiles's problems would soon become a major public-relations nightmare for Brigham Young. But as 1856 closed, the governor had multiple other issues and pressures with which to grapple.

Brigham Young under Pressure

On Utah's periphery there were worries about the viability of the restless Mormon colonies in San Bernardino and Carson Valley, as well as concerns over the launch of an ambitious, expensive Y. X. Carrying Company, the Mormon operation replacing W. M. F. Magraw as mail contractor on the Independence–Salt Lake City route.

Less global but nonetheless punishing were three emotional blows sustained by Young during the fall of 1856: the devastation of the Willie and Martin handcart companies, the uneven execution of the LDS Reformation, and the death of his strongest advisor, Jedediah M. Grant. The enormity of the October–November handcart disaster—the greatest catastrophe of the American overland trails experience—drove Young to lash out in search of managerial scapegoats as some Latter-day Saints quietly questioned his responsibility and leadership. The blow of Grant's unexpected death on 1 December sent Brigham Young into one of his periodic undiagnosed illnesses. In this case it was a debilitating loss of vitality that lingered into the spring of 1857 and kept him from some of the most visible of his church, if not his gubernatorial, responsibilities. Other than what was reported opaquely in the *Deseret News,* there was no disclosure of this condition to Young's federal supervisors in Washington.

In the capital, still other problems beset the governor, including continuing congressional efforts to eradicate polygamy, truncate Utah's borders, repeal her organic act, and split the offices of Utah's governor and superintendent of Indian Affairs. There also remained the dilemma of whether and when to press further the unsubmitted 1856 Deseret statehood petition. Most threatening of all was the outcome of the November election—unknown in Utah until early January. Irrespective of the winner, there was likely to be a backwash of some kind from the "twin relics" agitation, as well as a churning of the federal patronage, including territorial appointments, by the new administration beginning in March. Young knew that because President Pierce had declined to reappoint him for a second term, he was serving only on a continuance, that is, until the new president appointed a successor.

In the face of these forces Brigham Young hoped for the best, but he also prepared for armed conflict. His lead strategy was to use all available influence with the new president to bring about his own retention (if not reappointment) as governor and the appointment of Mormons or at least Mormon-approved men to Utah's federal offices. For this purpose during January 1857 he reached out to Thomas L. Kane of Philadelphia, the church's longest-standing non-Mormon ally. Young asked Kane to lobby covertly for such appointments in Washington.

At the same time, Brigham Young made his case locally for Mormon-friendly federal appointments and against a continuation of what he viewed as colonial treatment for territories by the U.S. government. The forum for this effort was the annual session of Utah's territorial legislative assembly, which convened on 8 December 1856. By all accounts it was a fiery session, wherein Brigham Young presented his views formally and publicly through his gubernatorial annual message. He then worked behind the scenes to have drafted two memorials to Congress and the president that were adopted by the legislative assembly on 6 January 1857. These documents—heretofore unpublished and couched in prolix, provocative rhetoric—had a fateful impact in Washington when read ten weeks later by a presidential cabinet then unknown to Brigham Young.

Simultaneous to these political moves, Young took steps to strengthen his military capabilities. He revitalized the Nauvoo Legion, commanded by Daniel H. Wells, an officer whom he promoted to lieutenant general and also called to be Jedediah Grant's successor as the First Presidency's second counselor. Accompanying this step was a vigorous continuation of the search for both arms and munitions on a scale unique in the activities of territories and their governors. Young also began planning in January 1857 for an arduous long-distance spring trek to inspect Fort Limhi, the new mission at Salmon River, Oregon Territory, as well as the surrounding valleys of what is now southwestern Montana. It was a survey that would have important strategic implications for his conduct in what would soon become the Utah War.

This was a large number of demanding undertakings for any leader, especially an ailing one. Under these pressures, in early February 1857 the full force of Brigham Young's wrath fell secretly upon two petty confidence men—John G. Ambrose and Thomas W. Betts—as they exited the Utah territorial penitentiary and headed haplessly for California on the southern route. What followed was an obscure but nonetheless documented series of murderous attacks that sent shock waves across the country. Within the violent Ambrose-Betts affair lurks an example of gubernatorial leadership gone badly awry just as James Buchanan prepared to take office.

A Rising of the Blood: Brigham Young's Health

Precisely what afflicted Brigham Young briefly during an aborted October 1856 trip to Fort Bridger and less than two months later following the death of Jedediah M. Grant is difficult to determine.[1] At that point in his life, Young's relationship with physicians was as problematic as that involving other professionals, especially lawyers. His dealings with Drs. John M. Bernhisel and Garland Hurt were those of supervisor-subordinate, not patient-doctor. Unlike James Buchanan, whose White House physician left correspondence for posterity, there is no such knowledgeable description of the gubernatorial medical history at this important juncture in federal-Mormon relations.

Throughout January 1857 Young was absent from Sunday services—unable to deliver even brief discourses, let alone his customary long extemporaneous homilies. As the winter of 1856–57 progressed, this weekly responsibility fell to other Mormon leaders. Although there is no sign that Young was totally incapacitated—he often visited his office—it is reasonable to assume that the governor was not at the top of his game during a crucial period. Whether he would have made decisions differently in early 1857 absent such medical problems is an intriguing imponderable.

Without wading deeper into the murky waters of psychohistory, perhaps it is best to let Brigham Young's own comments describe his episodic withdrawals from public view during early 1857. It was a period during which he lashed out at his as-yet unreformed flock, the unloved U.S. government, and occasional criminal miscreants like Messrs. Ambrose and Betts.

Discourse by Young, 1 February 1857, *Deseret News*, 11 February 1857, 386/1.

Let the congregation be as still as possible. I wish to occupy a short time in speaking to you, and I am not able to talk with the ease that I could wish, for my health has for some time obliged me to confine myself pretty closely to my rooms. This is the first time that I have walked so far as to come to this Tabernacle, since the burial of Jedediah M. Grant. My bodily afflictions would not permit me to walk much, and they also still hinder my efforts in speaking or exercising. I have been troubled this winter, as are many in this high altitude, with a rising of the blood to the head; that is what is troubling me this morning, insomuch that I hardly felt able to get here.

Aided by the faith and prayers of the Saints, I will endeavor to speak so that you can hear me, and to edify you according to the best of my ability.[2]

---

[1] For a description of the two-day attack that struck Governor Young while camping in the Wasatch en route to Fort Bridger, see "Return," *Deseret News*, 22 October 1857, 5/2. See also Bush, "Brigham Young in Life and Death: A Medical Overview," 79–103. Judging by the number of silver and rubber catheters personally ordered by the governor through his business agent in St. Louis, it would appear that he (or someone in his family) suffered the discomfort of persistent urological problems during the late 1850s and long thereafter. Young to Horace S. Eldredge, 3 December 1858, LDS Archives.

Snapping and Biting: Governor Young Focuses on Federal Appointments

Although Brigham Young was too ill to attend Sunday services at the tabernacle during much of December and all of January, he did find the energy to involve himself in the crucial business before the territory's legislative assembly during this period. With the exception of his apocalyptical musings about the fate of the "lower world," Young's 8 December 1856 annual message—delivered to the newly convened assembly about a week after Jedediah Grant's funeral—was somewhat bland, providing few overt signals of the storm that would soon rupture Mormon-federal relations. Only with hindsight would an outsider have lingered over the governor's brief exhortation to stockpile arms, ammunition, and camp equipment for an unspecified "emergency." But the assembly's resolutions and Young's correspondence for early January reflected deep anxiety about many of the issues besetting him. Especially revealing was the letter he sent to Washington for Apostles George A. Smith and John Taylor as well as Delegate Bernhisel.

Young to Smith, Taylor, and Bernhisel, 3 January 1857, LDS Archives.

We are not posted in regard to the position of our affairs in Washington. We have however a few suggestions to make which will probably be mostly accomplished or rendered unnecessary in case of our admission into the Union.

We are the more anxious to terminate our Territorial form of Government on account of the appointing power vested in the President, which enables him to fill our offices with men of his own selection . . . it results in some instances most disastrously to both our own and the interests of the General Government.

We find with very few exceptions, that non-resident appointees have always been of that character whose chief delight and business is and has been to stir up strife between us and the General Government by their foul and false statements. They have never manifested any interest in the growth and prosperity of the Territory. . . .

---

[2]Following President Young's return to an active role, Heber C. Kimball commented: "it is a great pleasure to me to see br. Brigham here in this stand once more. I am satisfied that he will be with us a great many years, if this people will do right. . . . How does my heart feel toward br. Brigham? I have felt, time and again, as though I was a good mind to lay my hands upon him and say, br. Brigham, God bless you with health." Kimball, discourse of 1 February 1857, *Deseret News*, 11 February 1857, 388/1, 3. For Brigham Young's later description of his affliction with rheumatism at an unspecified time and his views on health generally, see his unpublished discourse, "The Law of Health," of 22 December 1861 recorded in part in Hiram S. Rumfield to "Frank" (Mrs. Rumfield), 26 December 1861, Rumfield Papers; and Hulbert, ed., *Letters of an Overland Mail Agent in Utah*, 32–41.

We are aware that you are acquainted with all of these matters up to the time you left [last spring]. Since that time Dr Hurt the Indian Agent has been soured in his feelings mostly we think through the influence of Judge Drummonds who accompanied him last season to Carson County. We know that he is now writing and using his influence against us with the Indian department and the Government.

David H. Burr the "General Surveyor" as he calls himself was never anything else than a snarling puppy, snapping and biting at everything that comes in his way. He is unquestionably swindling the Government extensively, all the surveying that has been done by his party is not worth a groat, he has not done any of it himself, and we question his ability to run a line. He has had his given jobs out to Trosky and his own sons, and last fall let one to a Mr Mosheo who it is said killed a man in St Louis and came here as a teamster. We have been informed that this man surveyed 3500 miles in five weeks.[3] They boast of swindling the Government. . . .

If the New administration pursues this course and sends us another batch of such, what shall we call them, Political Demagogues, rest assured they will be sent back as fast as they come, for we are determined not to endure it any longer. It is and has been exceedingly difficult to keep the people from meeting [*sic*] out summary punishment upon them for their misdeeds. . . .

The Legislative Assembly have under consideration a Preamble and set of Resolutions upon this subject which if it is adopted in time we will send by this Mail to you and we wish to have it presented to the new President, and if he will act in accordance with our wishes in regard hereto, and make his appointments from among our citizens, all right. If not, then publish it to the world, as it is our intentions to carry them out, and it will be best for all parties to be timely notified thereof. . . .

We have no intelligence of Judge Drummond but presume he will not return, he did not return to Carson in October as he said he should when he left in July. At that place he decided against the power and jurisdiction of the Probate Courts. We learn that his woman which he had with him here left him so soon as she got where she could get better pay,[4] and he was at Los Angelos waiting for a company to come through with him, but we very much doubt his coming, still he may. Judge Stiles has recently been cut off from the Church [on 22 December] for his corrupt and wicked [adulterous] course of life. . . .

We presume that you will remain until the inauguration and untill the extra

[3] "Trosky" was Joseph Troskowlawski, one of David H. Burr's surveyors. Burr's sons, David A. and Frederick H. Burr, also worked as surveyors. All four men were on Brigham Young's July 1856 list of suspected tale-bearers. "Mosheo" may have been Charles Mogo, another listee who also worked for Surveyor General Burr and fled Utah as did all these men.

[4] This was the soon-to-be notorious Ada Carroll, whom Drummond had brought to Utah and attempted to pass off as his wife. Weary of being demonized over polygamy, Mormons seized on her presence alongside Drummond at court proceedings with a vengeance as the example par excellence of non-Mormon hypocrisy over matters of sexual conduct.

session for making the appointments closes, at least untill those for Utah are decided upon.[5] Unless we gain our admission, which we hardly expect this Congress to grant, we hope and pray for the best, and it will be so let it terminate which ever way it may, and having such dogs and skunks as Drummond, Burr, Hurt and others of a similar stripe sent here by the authority of the Government to rule over men as far above them, as they are above the low and vicious animals they so faithfully represent, that perhaps we are sometimes over anxious about it. . . . We do not expect the present crop to remain any longer than spring and we trust that we may not be favored with another such batch. We know that you will all do the best you can to prevent it. . . .

P.S. I am willing you show this letter to the President if you think best.[6]

The Memorial and Resolutions we want you to show to the new President,[7] If he shall act in accordance with the spirit and meaning thereof, all well, if not it is our particular request and desire that you should publish them in the daily papers in Washington City, [New York] Herald &c for rest assured that we are determined to carry them out. We have been imposed upon long enough by such consummate know nothing scamps as are annually imported to this Territory at the expense of Government. We have seriously resolved to send them back as fast as they come let the consequences be what they may. . . .

We send you a copy of some letters which have been written by Dr Hurt and Genl. Burr to their friends and respective departments. No matter how you came in possession of them. [Just say] You probably obtained them from the departments and can use them as you shall think proper. It is sufficient to know that they are false in every essential particular.[8]

The Yoke of Tyranny: Fateful Petitions

On 6 January 1857 the legislative assembly adopted the two memorials described by Brigham Young for his eastern colleagues, wound up its business, and adjourned. As discussed in a subsequent chapter, these petitions and the cabinet's reaction to them were fateful. Significantly, their text was never published in Washington as Young directed and only appeared in Utah nine months later—during the Utah War—in incomplete fashion.[9] Names of the indi-

[5] This travel advice proved fateful, giving Delegate Bernhisel license to leave Washington in early April 1857 notwithstanding the crisis that had developed there because of the very documents to which Brigham Young here referred.

[6] Here Young appears to mean Franklin Pierce. This letter did not reach Washington until after he left office on 4 March 1857; because of the inflammatory character of the document, Bernhisel did not expose it to Pierce's successor, Buchanan.

[7] Bernhisel did so on 18 March 1857, with disastrous consequences.

[8] These may be the intercepted Burr–Hendricks and Hurt–Elliott letters discussed in the previous chapter.

[9] "Expedition Against Utah," *Deseret News*, 7 October 1857, 244–45/4–5.

viduals nominated in these memorials were not published. Equally strange was the *Deseret News*'s editorial of 28 January 1857 that discussed the subject of appointments at length but without mentioning the two memorials just adopted or the nominees specified in them.[10] This opaque handling in Utah of what should have been significant local news was hardly accidental, although the motives behind it are unclear. It is interesting to find among the names of law-abiding individuals identified as appropriate federal appointees that of the already notorious William Adams Hickman, a backup candidate for U.S. attorney for Utah.

Memorial and Resolutions to the President of the United States, Concerning Certain Officers of the Territory of Utah, 6 January 1857, Utah State Archives.

Whereas the people of Utah Territory desire to live in the quiet enjoyment of those principles which the great charter of our Independence describes as being the inalienable right of all men, "life, liberty, and the pursuit of happiness:"

And Whereas we were driven forth, by our enemies and persecutors to perish on the plains, and were left for upwards of four years, from 1846 until September, 1850, to live or die, not only without the protecting care of the General Government, but on the contrary, having our strength drawn by that Government and sent to the most distant provinces to fight the battles of our country:

And Whereas we complied with this, as we ever have with every requirement of the parent Government, and did raise, and turn out five hundred of our best men, who did actually march, to aid the United States in their war with Mexico, from the Western part of Iowa to Fort Leavenworth and from thence to Santa Fe in New Mexico and from thence to California, under the command of Col. Cooke, who also acted under the direction of Genl. Kearny:

And Whereas those forces did actually perform that journey on foot and essentially aid in bringing into subjection, to the American Government, New Mexico and California and the Territory we now occupy:

And Whereas while these forces were absent upon this tedious and distant march, their families had to be left in a destitute condition, in an Indian country, far from the abodes of civilization, and unsettled, living in tents and wagons, traveling in search of a location where we could be free from our enemies, where we could rest and live in peace:

And Whereas, during this absence of those forces and while our emigrating camps were traveling, halting occasionally to recruit our provisions, which

[10] "United States Appointments and Legislation for Her Territories," *Deseret News*, 28 January 1857, 372/1–4.

we had mostly to rise from the earth as we proceeded, the remaining portion of our people, who through poverty or infirmity were unable to be removed for the time being from Nauvoo, and many of whose fathers and brothers were actually marching in the armies of the United States, as above set forth, to aid the Government in her then existing war with Mexico, were most wantonly and inhumanly attacked with cannon and firearms, without cause or provocation, by mobs who murdered, plundered and indiscriminately drove across the Mississippi river into Iowa, thousands of men, women and children, many of them sick with the fevers incident to the country in that season of the year, causing them to lie on the ground, exposed to the broiling sun by day and damp and chilly air by night, and to rain and tempest, bereft of the shelter of their homes from which they were driven, of food and clothing of which they were robbed; and even of the care and sympathy of friends who were absent in the service of the country, hundreds died and were buried upon the road-side by their companions in affliction, who, on foot, or as best they could by the scanty means left them by the mob, were endeavoring to make their way into the wilderness to overtake the camps who had gone before to find a place and prepare the way, in some far off nook or corner of the earth where we could be free from our oppressors and live in the quiet enjoyment of peace and that liberty which, though denied us, had been handed down by our fathers as a sacred legacy for our joint inheritance:

And Whereas through the blessing and providence of God only, and not of man, we were finally preserved from our adversaries, from the savage tribes and from perishing through hunger and want, which often threatened our destruction, not only upon the desert, the wild and barren plains, but in the repeated destruction of our crops by insects in these parched, unfruitful and inhospitable climes:

And Whereas, after long and repeated solicitation, and after we had gathered strength and limited supplies of provisions, Congress did grant unto us a Territorial form of government, which was thankfully received and under which, until we shall obtain admission into the Union as a free, sovereign and independent State, according to our application and constitution, we expect to live, act and be governed:

And Whereas it is made the duty of the president of the United States, in the Organic Act, passed September 9, 1850, for the organization of this Territory, to appoint, the Senate concurring therein, the following officers in said Territory, namely, our Governor and Superintendent of Indian Affairs, our Secretary, three Judges, our Marshal, our Attorney and, through the Secretary of the Interior and Commissioner of Indian Affairs, two or more Indian Agents:

And Whereas false hearted men, office seekers and corrupt demagogues, from every section of this wide spread Republic, flock to the seat of the federal government, surround the President and influential men thereat, to be appointed to these and similar offices vested in the discretion and patronage of the President and Senate:

And whereas such hangers on and office seekers, who are continually whining around the President for office, are unworthy of the confidence of the Government, and the principle of favoritism is so generally practiced, of throwing a bone to satisfy this hungry hound and a crumb to that yelping cur, cannot be too strongly deprecated by every lover of American liberty, by every person who desires the perpetuity of the free institutions of our country:

And whereas it is our honest conviction that no sensible persons would accept such offices, contrary to the known and expressed wish of the people, only to serve their own selfish purposes, totally regardless of the rights of others:

And whereas the conduct of the large majority of the Appointees has been an insult to humanity, an imposition upon intelligence, and, so far as lay in their power, a serious injury to the interests of this Territory and of this Union:

And whereas thus to appoint Officers and impose them upon a people contrary to their wishes is repugnant to every principle of Republican Government, whose pride and boast is ~~all~~ that all power is inherent in the people and that government should emanate from them:

And whereas the people are continually urging the authorities of this Territory to free them from these abuses and unanimously declare that it is almost unendurable to longer submit to be thus maltreated and trodden under foot by a corrupt and base set of officials, who, without authority of law or right, impose upon us and think to force us into quiet subjection to their base and hellish purposes, simply because they hold offices by the appointment of the Government of the United States:

And whereas we do not understand that such appointments should screen any offender from the just indignation of an insulted, injured and much abused community:

And whereas the practice of appointing to the offices of this Territory strangers and non-residents has frequently thrown into our midst base and corrupt men, whose only business seems to have been to devise mischief, misrepresent us and stir up strife, not only in our midst, but between us and the Indians and also between us and the Federal Government; men who seek to corrupt our community, trample upon our rights, walk under foot our laws, rules and regulations; who neither fear God nor regard man and, whenever checked in their mad career, threaten us with death and destruction by the United States troops, which they seem to consider are ready to march against us at their foul and false instigations:

And whereas our laws, which have been passed by the Legislative Assembly, and not been annulled by Congress, as provided in the Organic Act, have been set at naught and trampled under foot by a portion of said Officers, they having caused, by their rulings and decisions, other laws than those either of our own or the enactment of the Congress of the United States to be enforced, thus subverting the ends of justice and overriding the laws of the Territory, to thwart their operation and insult and oppress the people:

And whereas, in our well founded opinion, there are Citizens of our Territory who are capable and honest, whose interest is identified with the people, who desire the promotion of peace and the prosperity of the Territory and Union:

And whereas we have furnished our worthy Delegate in Congress, the Hon: John M. Bernhisel, a list of the names of certain Citizens of this Territory, with instructions to him to respectfully request the President of the United States to make the appointments for this Territory therefrom, or to select some other citizens of this Republic whose interest is and will be here and somewhat identified in the growth and prosperity of the Territory:

Therefore, be it

Resolved by the Governor and Legislative Assembly of the Territory of Utah, in solemn Assembly convened and having the foregoing acts and suggestion under consideration, that, while we respect the General Government and are at all times willing to observe the laws thereof, so far as they may be applicable to our condition in our Territorial capacity, we will resist any attempt of Government Officials to set at naught our Territorial laws, or to impose upon us those which are inapplicable and of right not in force in this Territory.

Resolved, that, while we will seek to carry out the rules and regulations of the various Departments of the General Government, as we invariably have, we will resist any attempt of any of it[s] Officers to bring us into difficulty, by misrepresentation or otherwise, with either of said Departments of the Government.

Resolved, that we will maintain the Constitution and laws of the United States, so far as they are applicable to our Territory, but we will not tamely submit to being abused by the Government Officials, here in this Territory; they shall not come here to corrupt our community, set at defiance our laws, trample upon the rights of the people, stir up the Indians and use the patronage of the Government to prejudice them against us and endeavour to influence the General Government against us, as a people, by their false statements and misrepresentations, or if they do come and act in this manner, as has been done, we will send them away, asking no odds either of political demagogues or bigots, for we well understand and know that neither the one nor the other is justified by the Constitution and laws in thus trifling with the liberties of the people, or trampling upon their rights.

Resolved, that we are a portion of the great American Republic; that we have rights civil, political and religious, in common with the rest of the States and Territories; that those rights are as sacred to us as they are to any other people, and that it is the duty of the Government to protect us in the peaceable enjoyment thereof, so far as it is in their power, and not to seek to annoy and distress us either with foreign appointments or by fastening upon our necks the yoke of tyranny and oppression, thus depriving us of those rights of freedom pertaining to every Republican Government and held sacred by every State and Territory.

Resolved, that we inherit from our fathers, who declared that Governments "derive their just powers from the consent of the governed," the right to have a voice in the selection of our rulers, and that to deny the right is anti-republican and fraught with evil, not only to us who are unwisely and unjustly held in a Territorial capacity, but to every lover of American freedom.

Resolved, that we desire to live in peace and have ever done so, when let alone by our enemies; that we have sacrificed much to get out of their way, and that, if they follow us up, as in times past, to seek our destruction, we are ready and willing to sacrifice far more, rather than not be rid of them; they shall not live in our midst to plot treason against the Territory and to bring against us the forces of the United States to our destruction.

Resolved, that we eschew as evil and utterly repudiate all social intercourse with those officials who practice under the garb of their official dignity every species of iniquity, also with the murdering thieves and vagabonds with whom such officials associate; and they must and shall leave this Territory, so soon as they manifest themselves to be of the character set forth in these Memorial and Resolutions.

Resolved, that we respectfully solicit the President of the U.S. to make the appointments to the Offices for this Territory from among the Citizens, or else select other good citizens of this great Republic who will endeavour to promote the interest of the Territory and become identified therewith.

Memorial to the President of the United States

We the Undersigned, Members and Officers of the Legislative Assembly of the Territory of Utah, beg leave to present to your honorable notice the following list of names, from which we most respectfully solicit that the appointments to the Offices of this Territory may be made:

For Govr. and Superintendent of Indian Affairs—Brigham Young.
For Secretary—Wm H. Hooper.
For Chief Justice—Elias Smith.
For Associate Justices—Hosea Stout & Wm I. Appleby.
For Marshall—Jesse C. Little.
For U.S. District Attorney—Ja^{s} W. Cummings.
For Surveyor General—Albert Carrington.
For Indian Agents—George D. Grant & Ja^{s} C. Snow.
Agent in Carson County—William Nixon.

These are our first selections, but if there should be any objection to any of them, except that for Governor, we give the following list of names of citizens of this Territory, who, together with those above mentioned, are entitled to the confidence of the Government and are every way capable and worthy to receive any of the above specified appointments:—

For Secretary—William Clayton, Leo Hawkins, Jn° T. Caine, Samuel W. Richards, Hiram B. Clawson.

For Judges—George A. Smith, Isaac Bullock, Aaron Johnson, James Lewis, John D. Parker, Jonathan Wright, Leonard E. Harrington, Chauncey W. West, George Peacock.

For Marshall—Leonard W. Hardy, Alexander M^c^Rae, Robert T. Burton, Wm H. Kimball.

For U.S. District Attorney—Ja^s^ Ferguson, Wm A. Hickman.

For Surveyor General—Jesse W. Fox, Israel Ivins, Thomas W. Ellerbeck.

Indian Agents—Lewis Robison, John Robinson, George W. Armstrong, Levi Stewart.

In recommending Brigham Young to fill the Office of Governor and Superintendent of Indian Affairs, we echo the unanimous wish of the people of this Territory, whose unlimited confidence he has long enjoyed, since he has, during our Territorial existence, administered in that Office not only to our satisfaction, but with credit and honor to himself and the Government.

[Names of fifty-two officers and members of the legislative assembly's council and house of representatives]

Our Constant Friend: Young Reconnects with Kane

As these crucial documents were taking shape, Brigham Young was mindful that soon after New Year's Day, his only winter communications link with the outside world, the monthly U.S. mail, would be leaving Salt Lake City with an anticipated arrival in the East during late February at the earliest. He could delay the carriers briefly, but not for more than a day or so. The timing was perilously close to the 4 March inauguration of the new president. Accordingly, without waiting for the legislative assembly to complete its work, Young mustered the energy to draft a letter to Thomas L. Kane in Philadelphia expressing his concerns and hopes for a positive working relationship with President-elect Buchanan. For reasons unknown Young chose to send this letter via the wintry Salt Lake–Independence route rather than by means of the snow-free California–Panama alternative. The fact that the eastbound contractor was then his own Y. X. Carrying Company may have bolstered his sense of confidence in that choice and its Mormon carriers—men like Bill Hickman and Porter Rockwell.

Young's letter to Kane prompts at least three major conclusions. First, with respect to President-elect Buchanan, it is clear that Young had little insight into his likely behavior, a condition shared with the American people to whom Buchanan was also a cipher. Second, the opening sentence of Young's letter conveys the impression that he and Kane had not communicated for a substantial period of time. On 14 April 1856 the governor had written to Kane seeking political counsel but with no apparent response to that letter or to George A. Smith's unsuccessful follow-up visit to Philadelphia. For that matter, there is no indication that Kane wrote to Young at any time during 1856, although Apostle John Taylor visited Kane at his Philadelphia home on 8 March 1856 and undoubtedly discussed the statehood thrust.[11] Third, in none of his correspondence does Young show awareness that the memorials being adopted by Utah's legislative assembly would be interpreted in Washington as unacceptable territorial behavior.[12]

YOUNG TO KANE, 7 JANUARY 1857, LDS ARCHIVES.

Again do I venture to break the silence of intervening months, and draw upon your time and perhaps patience long enough to read a line or two from your old friend.

Well, we in the mountains are still alive, the loss of crops has not starved us, nor the cold winters frozen us, nor are we disheartened nor discouraged. We have met with a severe loss and affliction in the death of our mutual friend Jedediah M. Grant, who died at his residence in this city on the first day of December last. He had been laboring excessively in a public capacity which brought him upon the bed of sickness, from which he was unable to rise. . . . [13]

In regard to other matters, through the Providence of God and doubtless the influence and favor of *kind friends* I am still Governor of Utah. In this I shall ever appreciate the kindness of Col. Kane and shall hold myself in readiness to reciprocate whenever opportunity shall occur.

A new Administration is about stepping into power and one which if I

[11] Taylor to Young, 16 April 1856, LDS Archives.

[12] Historian Richard E. Turley, Jr., argues that "Young thought Utahns were just doing what was done elsewhere. He forgot the American double standard against minorities . . . majorities could abuse minorities with impunity, but minority wrongs were met with harsh retaliation." Turley, comment on ms. draft.

[13] Young's use of the phrase "public capacity" reflects the interrelation between civil, religious, and military affairs in Utah. Grant was indeed mayor of Salt Lake City, but it was as a result of performing outdoor baptisms to spark the Reformation as part of the LDS First Presidency that he was fatally stricken with pneumonia.

understand aright our *constant friend* will still exercise *at least* his usual amount of influence.[14]

Having the eternal principle of right constantly in view & not fearing the attribution by my friends of any unworthy or selfish motive and not regarding either the opinions or sayings of my enemies, probably emboldens me without apology or misgivings to solicit at this time the interest which you possess or can influence in behalf of my reappointment.

We of Utah consider that we are entitled to some consideration in regard to having behaved so well for several years past, all the interesting features of rebellion, anarchy and confusion have been enacted elsewhere, except indeed what has been enacted in some fast newspapers which can generally hash up a dish of bloody interest to suit the greedy maw of their readers at a moment's notice, who have occasionally located their scenes of tragical romance in this Territory.

What further I wish to suggest is simply this which if we should gain admission into the Union would of course be accomplished. We desire to have a voice in the selection of our officers. We desire that they may be selected from among our citizens. We believe that the interest of the Federal Government as well as of the Territory would be promoted by pursuing this course. Look at the former appointees to this Territory and see what they have done. We allege without fear of successful contradiction that through them alone have we been more in danger of having our peaceful relations interrupted not only with the various departments of government, but with the Indians of the Territory, than from any other cause. . . .

The other case of tampering with the Indians, is using the government patronage by the Agents to predjudice them against the people of the Territory. These appointments will last even if we should be admitted. To the Indians they will say *these* people will take your lands from you, they will give you nothing, the Americans are your friends, they will pay you blankets, guns, powder, lead, tobacco, beads, scarlet cloth &c, for your land & they will be your very good friends. Mormons are kotch wino (no good) and in a thousand other ways seek to make and impress upon their minds a distinction between us and the Americans, and exercise all possible influence to predjudice them against us.[15] The Judges have decided against our laws and endeavored to drag in & enforce common law which had never been adopted as the law of the land by the law-making department. . . . If the non-resident officers were even disposed in our favor, the reverse of which is generally the case, they know

[14] Brigham Young and other Mormon leaders often referred to or addressed Kane cryptically as "our friend," sometimes for confidentiality reasons as well as out of affection.

[15] Here Young appears to be building a backfire with Kane by using against federal agents the argument that they most frequently cited about Mormons: fostering an unhealthy distinction among Indians between Mormons and "Mericats" (Americans).

nothing of our characteristics, are unacquainted with our ways, mode of transacting business, are bound up in strong traditions, forms, and technicalities,—hence unsuited for the times & place, and consequently our peace and quietness constantly endangered.

It is a most foul imposition for men to come here and think act and consider themselves as inheriting a kind of divine right to govern, and rule over a people for whom they entertain no respect, but utterly despise. They cannot think less of us than we do of them.

They come here generally without misses expecting to find the usual accommodations afforded in other parts of the world, and when detected in their endeavors to carry into effect this disgraceful practice they abound in making reports of awful iniquity and treason among the Mormons. How think you must we feel towards men who we know if they had the power would cut our throats? Now we know that we have just such men here by the appointment of the Government, and we also know that they are continually striving to cause a disturbance between us and the Government, in order to have the *aforesaid amiable* object accomplished. For substantiating evidence more forcibly illustrating this view of the case we refer you to facts in the possession of Dr J. M. Bernhisel, Jno Taylor, and Geo A Smith. . . .

Why not kick them out of the Territory say you? That's just it, we intend to, the very first opportunity. We are resolved that their United States' official dignity shall no longer screen them. . . . We can neither vote for President, elect senators, nor representatives, (a delegate cannot vote [in Congress],) our superior officers are all appointed by that President, and Senate, and our laws are liable to be annulled by that Congress. What we ask is this. 1st, Admission into the Union. This failing, that the President select the officers from among the citizens of the Territory including Surveyor General and Indian Agents, that we may have office[r]s who feel an interest in her growth and prosperity, and who will not malign the people, and cause an almost if not quite hostile feeling to spring up between the General Government and the people of the Territory.

We thus recommend ourselves to you honestly believing that we are as willing to serve our country (this part of it) as we are to have anybody else to serve it for us, and being better acquainted with the merits and conditions of the people, better capable of doing it correctly.

Ever retaining a kind remembrance of past favors and wishing you every blessing which you can in righteousness desire, I remain, as ever, Truly your friend,

When early January storms and snow drove the eastbound mail carriers out of the mountains and back to Salt Lake City, Young immediately sent another copy of this letter to Kane by the southern route. For good measure he followed up with an additional, quite different message on 31 January.

Young's second letter to Kane lacked the quasi-statesmanlike tone of his 7 January message. It sank into a gossipy account of the financing practices of Judge Drummond ("excel[s] the Jews of 'Wall St'") and other federal appointees while at the same time taking on the character of a newsletter retailing the shortcomings of Magraw's old mail service, the activities of Mormon missionaries amongst the tribes, the development of the Las Vegas lead mine ("a little for domestic Manufactures"), and his importation of a steam engine from St. Louis. Perhaps the most significant part of Young's 31 January letter to Kane was his closing assertion: "We are satisfied with the appointment of Buchanan as future president, we believe he will be a friend to the good, Prest. Fillmore was our friend, but Buchanan will not be a whit behind."[16]

When Your Finger Crooks, We Move: The Ambrose-Betts Affair

Not long after Brigham Young experienced a dream in which he threatened federal judges W. W. Drummond and George P. Stiles with "oblivion," nightmarish violence indeed broke out in Utah.[17] On the night of 17 February 1857, while en route to California and camped along southern Utah's Santa Clara River, assassins attacked former army sergeant John Tobin, "Colonel" John C. Peltro, and two unknown companions. A fifty-shot fusillade from approximately eight unidentified whites badly wounded the four travelers. In the immediate aftermath of this ambush, the party's horses and saddles were stolen. On the night of 15 March in Springville, Utah, unknown killers simultaneously slashed and shot to death two members of the Parrish family and Gardner ("Duff") Potter. In a familiar pattern many of the Parrishes' valuables also disappeared.

For nearly 150 years the reasons for this violence and even the identities of Tobin and Peltro have been muddled. Contemporary Utahns and subsequent historians mistakenly attributed the Santa Clara ambush to retribution for some combination of an earlier failed romance between Tobin and Brigham Young's daughter, Alice, and an attempt by Tobin to apostatize, notwithstanding the

---

[16] Young to Kane, 31 January 1857, LDS Archives.

[17] For Young's dream about these judges, see Brigham Young "Office Journal," clerk's entry for 9 February 1857, typescript in Leonard J. Arrington Papers. While a mistake to place too much emphasis on Brigham Young's dreams, they are one small indicator of what was on his mind as the Ambrose-Betts affair unfolded. Young thought his dreams important enough to recite their contents periodically to the church historian or his clerk.

fact that he was then married to a daughter of Apostle Charles C. Rich and showed no signs of leaving the church. The Parrishes were believed to have been the victims of an unrelated local act of blood atonement prompted by the belief that they were about to apostatize and decamp for California. In the midst of the nocturnal attack on the Parrishes, Potter, their duplicitous guide, died in a case of mistaken identity—in a hail of what today would be called "friendly fire."

Through recent scholarship by Ardis E. Parshall and Polly Aird—both distant relatives of Nauvoo Legionnaires—we now know otherwise. The casualties in these attacks were the result of a related chain of events launched by circular letters written by Brigham Young on 3 and 6 February 1857 to his bishops in Springville, Nephi, Fillmore, Parowan, and Cedar City.[18] Deeply concerned about a rash of thefts in Reformation Utah, Young's intent was to alert the bishops to the southbound presence of convicts John Ambrose and Thomas Betts and to authorize, if not order, their summary execution.[19]

What followed from this case of gubernatorial leadership gone awry was an example of homicidal vigilantes at work coupled with the law of unintended consequences. Instead of striking Ambrose and Betts, the assassins mistakenly attacked Tobin's party, from whom the ex-convicts had fortuitously separated themselves shortly before their fatal 17 February bivouac on the Santa Clara. Unscathed and perhaps even oblivious to what had happened from the distance of their independent campsite, Ambrose and Betts continued westward via the southern route and disappeared from historical notice in the California goldfields. A few weeks later, either unaware of Brigham Young's real targets or inclined to interpret his letter as an unrestricted license to kill any California-bound apostates of his choice, Springville bishop Aaron Johnson, a Legion brigadier, unleashed plans that resulted in the Parrish-Potter murders. Small wonder that, after reading Brigham Young's letter, Bish-

---

[18] See Parshall, "'Pursue, Retake & Punish,'" 64–86; and Aird, "'You Nasty Apostates, Clear Out,'" 129–207.

[19] At the end of January and in early February 1857 virtually every one of Brigham Young's letters to absent Mormon leaders contained a paragraph like the following to John Taylor: "Some property has been destroyed here this winter, by persons unknown to us, with the intent probably to plunder and rob, this was annoying to me but I think we shall discover the perpetrators." Young to Taylor, 26 January 1857, LDS Archives. The thefts—most often livestock—are described not only in Young's late January letters to absent leaders but in a precursor: Kadz-Ne-Ate, dispatch of 31 January 1856, "From Utah," *New York Times*, 18 April 1856. Historian David L. Bigler notes that "theft" involved cases of apostates fleeing Utah with property they had earlier consecrated to the church through its trustee-in-trust, Brigham Young. Bigler to MacKinnon, e-mail message, 3 January 2007.

op Johnson felt free to predict that "some of us would yet 'see the red stuff run.'"[20]

A thorough analysis of what unfolded along the Santa Clara River and just outside the adobe walls of Springville, Utah, emerges from the ground-breaking articles by Parshall and Aird.[21] What appears below is the first of the two important Brigham Young letters that set the Ambrose-Betts affair in motion, together with context in the form of excerpts from Brigham Young's unpublished 8 April 1853 discourse advocating summary execution of thieves.[22] As discussed in a subsequent chapter, here was advice from the top—couched in language ranging from guardedly cryptic to unmistakably raw—that set a violent tone for the territory. It was a tone that soon resonated with the fate of such early Utah War victims as the Fancher party, Richard E. Yates, Pvt. George W. Clark, Henry Forbes, and the Aiken party.

Young to Bishop Aaron Johnson, 3 February 1857, LDS Archives.

We learn of some noted persons congregating at the Indian farm on Spanish Fork with a view of going out with the mail south or some other time not far distant for California. In this crowd are two persons who have lately served out a short period in the Penitentiary in this Territory. We consider it wisdom to be on our guard in relation to our Stock and the Stock of our settlements generally, especially our horses now on the range near the south end of Utah Lake, lest they attempt to make a break upon them. We have entrusted the care of our stock with bro Andrew Moffatt and Orrice Newell who with the assistance they can obtain from Payson and Summit Creek would be abundantly sufficient unless such circumstances as above alluded to should transpire. What we wish of you is to have a few men on the look out and ready to act in case of emergency. It would be well to have them go out and

[20] Affidavit of Joseph Bartholomew, 29 March 1859, *Valley Tan* (Salt Lake City), 19 April 1859, 1/5, excerpted in Aird, "'You Nasty Apostates, Clear Out,'" 179.

[21] See also MacKinnon, "'Lonely Bones,'" 138–47.

[22] To fathom what drove Governor Young to write and behave as he did, one needs to understand not only his temperament but the Mormon millennial culture of territorial Utah, the impact of leadership burdens and poor health on his judgment, the continuing property destruction and thefts taking place in Reformation Utah, and the governor's likely angry reaction to a confrontational letter written to him by Thomas Betts immediately upon his and Ambrose's release from the penitentiary (Betts to Young, 26 December 1856, LDS Archives). Another important background factor was gubernatorial concern about what Ambrose and Betts as well as their traveling companions—Tobin and Peltro—would say once in California. On 26 January 1857 Young's office clerk recorded: "Then Wm. A. Hickman called and explained the private movements of Peltros, Betts &c. their purpose to go So. to Cala. their fear to stop—their joy in spreading the Report that a new Govr. and new judges are appointed & that with a sufficient Military guard these will be here in the spring to establish order and justice among the Mormons." Brigham Young, "Office Journal," clerk's entry for 26 January 1857, typescript in Leonard J. Arrington Papers.

make a short trip around to see that all things are right. We also write to bro John L. Butler and Geo W. Bradley at Nephi in relation to this subject, with all of whom you will act in concert, and if any such thing as we have suggested should occur we shall regret to hear a favorable report; we do not expect there would be any prosecutions for false imprisonment or tale bearers left for witnesses. We have also received some intimations that the Indians from that vicinity may be induced to make a draw upon our stock by some of our enemies. We wish that you would take a course to ascertain the feelings of the Indians and continue to conciliate them and thereby thwart the purposes of our enemies, who seek to stir them up against us. Be vigilant in these matters and not allow yourself to be taken unawares, or to use an old fashioned phrase, of, not locking the door until after the steed is stolen.

Bro Johnson, you know about these things, have a few men that can be trusted on hand, and make no noise about it and keep this letter safe. We write for your eye alone and to men that can be trusted.

May the Lord bless you forever is the prayer of your brother in the Gospel of Salvation

Three days later Young wrote a similar letter to "Bishops & Presidents South" with nearly identical language describing the traveling felons, the need for secrecy and discretion, and the expectation that "We do not suppose there would be any prosecutions for false imprisonments, or tale bearers for witnesses." Significantly, Young's message of 6 February contained an additional expectation of summary, extra-legal violence that went beyond the language of his earlier letter: "Be on the look out now, & have a few trusty men ready in case of need to pursue, retake & punish."[23]

On 17 February 1857—the day of the Santa Clara ambush of the Tobin-Peltro party—William H. Dame wrote a revealing, action-oriented response to Young's first letter. Dame was president of the Mormon stake in southern Utah and seven months later would be a Nauvoo Legion colonel deeply involved in the 11 September 1857 Mountain Meadows massacre, in which a Nauvoo Legion detachment and Indian auxiliaries killed 120 unarmed men, women, and children emigrating from Arkansas to California. Reporting to Young, he noted, "Tobin, Peltro and those from prison passed with seven or eight more a few days before the mail, our city was under private [guard?] and is now. We could not discover any brand on their poor ponies, but was surprised to see them here." He continued, "I received your letter by mail, &

[23] Young to Bishops & Presidents South, 6 February 1857, LDS Archives.

have prepared a few [men], a word any time is comforting, we try to live so when your finger crooks, we move."[24]

Brigham Young Discourse, 8 April 1853, Journal History.

If you wish to know what you must do hereafter I will tell you in a few words, *keep your powder and lead,* and your guns in good order. . . . *"Be ye also ready for in an hour you think not behold the thief comes,"* and takes away your horse from your stable.

How many complaints have been made to me by men who have had their horses stolen out of their stables; or out of their carals; or of clothes being taken from the line. The reason why people lose their property is because they do not watch it. . . .

If you want to know what to do with a thief that you may find stealing, *I say kill him on the spot,* and never suffer him to commit another iniquity. That is what I expect I shall do, though never, in the days of my life, have I hurt a man with the palm of my hand. I never have hurt any person any other way except with this, unruly member, my tongue. Notwithstanding this, if I caught a man stealing on my premises I should be very apt to send him *straight home,*[25] and that is what I wish everyman to do; to put a stop to that abominable practice in the midst of this people. . . .

If you will cause all those whom you know to be thieves to be placed in a line before the mouth of one of our largest cannon, well loaded with chain shot, I will prove by my works whether I can mete out justice to such persons, or not.[26] I would consider it just as much my duty to do that, as to baptize a man for the remission of his sins. That is a short discourse on thieves, I acknowledge, but I tell you the truth as it is in my heart.

For those inclined to justify or explain Governor Young's advice on the violent disposition of thieves in terms of "frontier justice," it is well to consider the behavior of rancher Theodore Roosevelt in Dakota Territory during early April 1886 upon discovering the theft of a small boat he had moored along the Little Missouri River. With two of his ranch hands Roosevelt immediately jury-rigged a crude boat in the midst of a snowstorm and set out down river in pursuit. After a three-day chase and successful capture, there followed six more days on the icy river with his three captives followed by a forty-five-mile hike across the Badlands to the nearest sheriff's office in Dick-

[24] Dame to Young, 17 February 1857, LDS Archives. For the implications of the well-known Brigham Young hand gesture to which Dame referred, see Parshall, "'Pursue, Retake & Punish,'" 74n24.

[25] One of the euphemisms for murder current in Utah.

[26] In 1857 this would be the method of execution meted out to captured rebels by the British Royal Army during India's sepoy rebellion.

inson, Dakota. During the cross-country part of this trek, Roosevelt limped along—rifle at-the-ready—behind a borrowed wagon carrying his miserable prisoners. When the amazed Dickinson physician who bathed and bandaged T.R.'s feet asked why he had not simply shot the thieves, Roosevelt replied that the thought had never occurred to him. It was a behavior that prompted the doctor to tell his wife "that I had met the most peculiar and at the same time the most wonderful man I had ever come to know."[27]

The two months preceding James Buchanan's inauguration were turbulent ones in Utah in terms of both word and deed. On 8 February 1857—two days after sending his second letter south in the Ambrose-Betts affair—Brigham Young delivered one of the Reformation's most violent sermons in a tabernacle discourse on "blood atonement." In this talk Young asked the congregation rhetorically, "Will you love your brother or sisters likewise, when they have committed a sin that cannot be atoned for without shedding of their blood? Will you love that man or woman well enough to shed their blood? That is what Jesus meant. . . . I could refer you to plenty of instances where men have been righteously slain, in order to atone for their sins. . . . This is loving our neighbor as ourselves; if he needs help, help him; and if he needs salvation and it is necessary to spill his blood on the earth in order that he may be saved, save him." Regardless of whether Young intended his insistence on bloodshed to be taken literally, whether he was engaging in rhetoric only to capture the attention of backsliders, or whether his violent admonitions were ever acted upon, his words provide insight into his frame of mind and the preoccupations of Utah's governor at a critical time in Mormon-federal relations.[28]

[27] McCullough, "Mornings on Horseback," 346–48

[28] Brigham Young, Discourse, 8 February 1857, *Deseret News*, 18 February 1857, 396/4, 397/1–2.

Chapter 4

"Dancing on a Volcano"
The Change in Administrations

Sire, we are dancing on a volcano!
—Comment by Russian minister to Washington at James Buchanan's inaugural ball, 4 March 1857

As the change in administrations took place neither the nation's chief executive nor the adjourning Congress viewed resolution of "the Mormon problem" to be a high priority. In a private valedictory to his cabinet, President Pierce did not even mention Utah. In Buchanan's long public inaugural address later that day, he also was silent on Mormon affairs.[1] Remarkably, by current political standards, this speech was virtually the last public utterance by Buchanan on any subject for the next nine months. With Congress adjourned, a period of official silence descended over the White House during which Mormon-federal relations continued to fester and then explode.

Buchanan immediately turned to four principal tasks: completing his cabinet, distributing federal patronage, appointing a new governor for Kansas, and regaining his health. Within days, the Supreme Court's Dred Scott decision, which stated that those of African descent could not be U.S. citizens and that Congress did not have the authority to prohibit slavery in U.S. territories, created a national furor, especially over violent Kansas.

In assessing how the new president met these challenges, it is important to understand that upon his inauguration Buchanan was in his sixty-sixth year, the nation's oldest chief executive. Since early February 1857 he had been suffering from a severe gastrointestinal illness, a condition aggravated by a

[1] Franklin Pierce to Cabinet, 4 March 1857; James Buchanan, "Inaugural Address," 4 March 1857; Moore, ed., *The Works of James Buchanan*, 10:105–13.

INAUGURATION OF PRESIDENT JAMES BUCHANAN, 4 MARCH 1857
This first photographic image of a presidential inauguration captures Buchanan at the Capitol as it was undergoing extensive renovation, including construction of a massive new dome. Amidst the upheaval of this scene, beset by the "National Hotel" disease, and preoccupied with preserving the Union in the face of a slavery crisis, Buchanan delivered an address that omitted any reference to Mormons or Utah. Photo by John Wood in Montgomery C. Meigs Papers. *Courtesy of the Manuscript Division, Library of Congress.*

punishing influx of visits and mail from office seekers to which Buchanan attended personally. Compounding this workload and extraordinary attention to detail was the near-absence of even clerical support staff for the president.[2] Small wonder that a Princeton College student who attended Buchanan's delivery of his inaugural address reported with disappointment: "I c[ou]ld watch him turn over the leaves [as he read]. You might think he w[ou]ld have had this written on very handsome & costly paper, & then perhaps beautifully ornamented. But it was written on very common blue foolscap, & some parts of it were on little strips only a few inches long."[3]

Based on the foregoing, it is clear that both James Buchanan and Brigham Young were seriously ill in the late winter and spring of 1857. Both men tended to lead their respective organizations with a non-delegatory managerial style that is today called micro-managing. But of the two men Brigham Young, a decade younger than Buchanan, was clearly the more experienced organizer and manager. He had learned to move tens of thousands of people over great distances under adverse conditions, while Buchanan was honing the quite different skills of lawyer, elected legislator, and diplomat. Young's communications style was expansive, earthy, and direct—even occasionally brutal—whereas Buchanan's was crabbed, indirect, and convoluted even with his cabinet. Unwittingly, with this style Buchanan nearly drove Vice President John C. Breckinridge out of Washington and back to Kentucky during the opening weeks of the administration. Recognizing this problem but temperamentally unwilling to confront it himself, Buchanan deputized Sec. of War John B. Floyd, Breckinridge's distant relative, to heal this breach within his official family.[4] Although Floyd was technically successful, "Buck" and "Breck," as their 1856 campaign had styled them, did not meet privately for another three years.

One wonders how the health, stamina, and leadership style of President Buchanan and Governor Young affected the decisions that they made during this critical period as well as the responses of the people they led.

[2] Buchanan's secretary-nephew described the president's orderly but circumscribed office routine in James Buchanan Henry, "Biographical Sketch," Moore, ed., *The Works of James Buchanan*, 12:323–27; a quite different contemporary glimpse of the action in Brigham Young's office appears in Remy, *A Journey to Great-Salt-Lake City*, 1:200–205.

[3] James William Abert Wright to Henry A. Tutwiler, Jr., 2 May 1857, Johnson, ed., "A Southern Student Describes the Inauguration of President James Buchanan," 239.

[4] This incident is described in Stampp, *America in 1857*, 71, and Hatfield, "Strained Relations with Buchanan," 193–99n11. See also Floyd to Breckinridge, 25 March 1857, Jeremiah S. Black Papers.

The Coarsest and Most Brutal Assaults: The Secondary Importance of the Mormon Problem

In its closing pre-inauguration weeks, the thirty-fourth Congress was not focused on "the Mormon problem," although one Republican member of the House of Representatives, Justin S. Morrill of Vermont, took up the issue with an intensity that was to plague the Mormons for decades. From Morrill's zeal would spring the first federal anti-polygamy statute in 1862. In his printed but undelivered remarks dated 23 February 1857, Representative Morrill crafted what was in retrospect a landmark essay—perhaps the most comprehensive attack on Brigham Young and his leadership since that of the discredited runaway officials five years earlier. But at the end of the Pierce administration Morrill's crusade was an individual cause rather than a Congress-wide affair. Morrill laced his remarks with multiple references to the political dilemma that had befuddled Pierce and awaited Buchanan: how to deal with Utah's polygamy without either violating the Democratic Party's doctrine of popular sovereignty for the territories or further aggravating southern fears about the future of slavery, its own peculiar institution. How reflective Morrill's views were of national attitudes about the Mormons is difficult to gauge. Apparently Vermonters noted his views with approval, but it would be an overstatement to argue that Morrill had tapped into one of the country's burning issues given America's overwhelming preoccupation at that time with the slavery issue. The unusual format of Morrill's remarks—a printed but unspoken and therefore largely unreported text—meant that they initially received little attention. But as the winter concluded and alarm over Utah affairs escalated in late March, Morrill's comments surfaced to become an intellectual rallying point for those urging a move on Utah.[5]

Morrill, "Utah Territory and its Laws—Polygamy and its License," 23 February 1857, *Appendix to the Congressional Globe,* U.S. Cong., House (34-2), 284–90.

The House being in the Committee of the Whole on the state of the Union, and having under consideration the bill making appropriations for the Territory of Utah—

[5] For a discussion of Morrill's remarks and his constituents' favorable reactions, see Cross, *Justin Smith Morrill, Father of the Land-Grant Colleges,* 34–36. In the midst of the Buchanan administration's subsequent deliberations on Utah, in a wholly different political climate, editor-publisher Horace Greeley ran the full text of Morrill's remarks and a long related editorial. See *New-York Daily Tribune,* 25 April 1857, 6/4–5, 9/6, 101–106.

Mr. Morrill said:

Mr. Chairman: It was my purpose at an earlier period of the session to have submitted some remarks upon the territorial laws of Utah, and the "patriarchal institution" of polygamy which there prevails. . . . but I felt unwilling to consume the time of the House when it was evident that, from the press of other matters, no legislation could follow. For these reasons, I gave notice of my purpose, and obtained consent to publish what I had to say, with some liberty of expansion. . . .

Hostile to Republicanism.

The Mormons are quite as hostile to the republicanism of government as they are to the usual forms of Christianity. In their official correspondence with Government they are respectful, but at home, publicly and privately, they indulge in the coarsest and most brutal assaults upon the United States Government and its officers. Officially courteous, they are everywhere else malignant backbiters and traducers. . . . They desire a kingly government, in order to make their patriarchal institutions more homogeneous. . . .

Polygamy

There is one topic which has excited some consideration, whenever Utah has been discussed, and seems to acquire greater gravity in each successive year. Stealthily at first, but now openly, the practice of polygamy has become a deep-rooted and notorious institution of the Mormons. Under the Constitution of the United States, they are fostered and protected, and have assigned to them a Territory larger than many of the kingdoms of Europe. Under the guise of religion, this people has established, and seek to maintain and perpetuate, a Mohammedan barbarism revolting to the civilized world. It is polygamy in its most disgusting form, including in its slimy folds sisters, mothers, and daughters; and in order that no element of cruelty and loathsomeness may be wanting, it includes facility of divorce. . . .

And yet we are to be told, because our Constitution declares that "Congress shall make no law respecting an establishment of religion, or prohibiting the free exercise thereof," that we must tamely submit to any burlesque, outrage, or indecency which artful men may seek to hide under the name of religion! But it is impossible to twist the Constitution into the service of polygamy by any fair construction. The fullest latitude of toleration in the exercise of religion could not be understood to license crimes punishable at common law; and, if Congress is prohibited from making an established religion, a Territory must be equally prohibited, for a Territory is the creature of Congress, and Congress cannot authorize a Territory to authorize an incorporated company of priests to do what it may not do itself. The practice under our Constitution has been, and is specially provided for in the organic act of Utah, that territorial laws are annulled and void the moment they are *disap-*

proved of by Congress. We cannot shirk the responsibility by creating a territorial government to do that which the Constitution inhibits to ourselves. If the laws of Utah are in our judgment such as are "not fit to be made," it is our duty to annul them; and if they create an establishment of religion, then it is clearly an open and palpable violation of the Constitution, and not too sacred to go untouched. . . .

What Is to Be Done?

I have no desire to make [political] party capital by making any issues touching Utah. It is a subject requiring the deliberate attention of statesmen. I only aspire to present some facts, in the most authentic form within my reach, calculated to draw attention to the subject. It is quite within the power of [congressional] gentlemen to throw the question into the pool of partisan politics by giving "aid and comfort" to the wildest theories to which any religious imposture ever gave birth. The president and Rulers of the Mormon Church have already sought shelter in the bosom of the Democratic party by their proclamation of the 14th August, A.D. 1856. They find fault with the Republican party for including their "sacred institution" in the phrase of "the twin relics of barbarism." . . .[6]

There is, I hope, room to doubt whether the Democratic party will allow itself to be used for any such purpose. Their political necessities must be great, when they accept of such coadjutors upon the condition indicated.

It may be very properly asked, supposing it should be shown that a state of things exists in Utah which all would admit to be wrong, what are you going to do about it? The subject is not without its difficulties, but they are not altogether insurmountable. . . .

1. We may "disapprove" of all the laws of the Territory that we please, and thereby annul them, and for such reasons as may appear proper.
2. We may circumscribe the boundaries of the Territory, and give the inhabitants much narrower limits.[7]
3. If the second proposition be adopted, we may then abandon them, and leave them to fight out their own independence and salvation, spiritually and temporally, in their own good time.
4. We may cut up the Territory, and annex it to the various adjoining Territories.
5. We may organize a territorial government on the old plan of a Council, consisting of a Governor and judges—not Mormons; and with a military force sufficient to maintain it.

[6] Here Morrill excerpted the text of a bogus handbill asserting before the election of 1856 that Mormons supported the Democratic Party because of its alleged refusal to interfere with territorial institutions. Poll, "The Mormon Question," 128–29 and 130n44; "An Artful Dodge," *The Mormon*, 15 November 1856.

[7] For the history of efforts to pursue this second approach and Morrill's fourth alternative, see MacKinnon, "'Like Splitting a Man Up His Backbone.'"

> I have thus given *in extenso* enough of the statutes of Utah, their doctrines and ordinances, to show their leading characteristics, and that they are dangerous and should be annulled; and I cannot but hope enough of earnest men will ere long be found in Congress ready to devise some action—not of persecution—whereby our common country may be rescued from the great reproach of a barbaric age.

When Franklin Pierce left the presidency a few days after the date of Justin Morrill's remarks, there was much on his mind other than Utah affairs. It seemed as though Pierce had lost interest in dealing with the Brigham Young quandary once Colonel Steptoe declined Utah's governorship. Back in New York, Steptoe later confided to Provo's Bishop Elias H. Blackburn that "The President has conversed very little with me about Utah and has never once asked me to suggest any measures or line of policy."[8] And so when Pierce and Sec. of War Jefferson Davis obtained a four-regiment expansion of the regular army in 1855, it was not, as Young feared, to garrison Utah and drive him out of office.[9] One of President Pierce's last official acts was to sign legislation separating Utah's dual offices of governor and U.S. superintendent of Indian Affairs, both of which Brigham Young held under Utah's organic act. But this law was more a remedy for defective territorial organization than a means of curbing Brigham Young's power and salary since it provided for a similar separation of office in several other territories.[10] Contrary to the fear that Brigham Young had expressed to Thomas L. Kane in January 1857, Pierce did not use his last few months in office to make vindictive, lame-duck appointments for Utah even when he could have named both a new governor and Indian superintendent. This chore and resolution of the associated political problems Pierce gladly left to Buchanan.

His High Functions as Chief Magistrate: Buchanan Forms His Cabinet

Immediately following his 4 November 1856 election, Buchanan had set about forming his cabinet. It was a formidable task driven not only by the president-elect's substantial political obligations but by his quest for sectional balance. With his selections Buchanan sought to set a tone stressing national

---

[8] Steptoe to Blackburn, 3 November 1855, LDS Archives.

[9] Young to Taylor, 25 July 1855, transcription by Raymond W. Taylor in Taylor Family Papers.

[10] The notion of separating these two offices in Utah arose officially as early as 1854 in Comm. of Indian Affairs George W. Manypenny to Sec. of the Interior Robert McClelland, 10 April 1854, House Exec. Doc. 71, Serial 956, 165–66.

unity over regional partisanship. He was determined not to allow sectionalism and the slavery conflict to destroy the union, although some critics perceived a southern tilt to his attitudes and subsequent appointments.

As with the conduct of his 1856 campaign, much of the work of dispensing patronage and cabinet making took place at Wheatland, Buchanan's Lancaster, Pennsylvania, mansion. During a pre-inaugural visit to the capital in January, Buchanan contracted a near-fatal gastrointestinal illness traced to the contaminated water supply at Washington's National Hotel. The president-elect became so ill that conspiracists speculated that an assassination plot was afoot. The affliction killed one of Buchanan's nephews, and another near-fatality was W. M. F. Magraw, who was also staying at the National Hotel, perhaps with his brother Robert, the president-elect's companion, friend, and close political associate.

By the inauguration Buchanan's cabinet selections were still incomplete, a shortfall that required the senate to remain in session a few more days so that it might confirm his nominees. Of the final array of cabinet officers, two were especially important because of their responsibilities for military and territorial affairs: Sec. of War John B. Floyd and Sec. of State Lewis Cass.

Floyd, a second-generation governor of Virginia and attorney-planter, had no military experience beyond his nominal supervision of that state's militia. Although an apparently popular and successful one-term governor, Floyd lacked not only an understanding of military affairs but also significant administrative skills or experience. These background gaps—compounded by Floyd's poor health (back pain), carelessness, and political cronyism—were a problem when one considers that the U.S. Army of the period was the nation's most complex organization, engaged in active operations from Florida to the Pacific Northwest. Floyd's appointment to the War Department was fundamentally a function of his family's prominent social and political standing as well as of his personal connection to Gov. Henry A. Wise, a Virginia kingmaker with presidential aspirations to whom Buchanan felt an intense political obligation.[11] From such limitations, compounded by Buchanan's own lack of management and military background, were to flow the launch of a Utah Expedition seriously flawed in its leadership and instructions as well as critically late in its organization.

---

[11] Floyd's only full-length biography is a somewhat sympathetic one: Pinnegar, *Brand of Infamy*. During the 1930s Robert M. Hughes, a Floyd relative, wrote a series of journal articles defending his conduct as secretary of war. For articles by non-relatives, see Auchampaugh, "John B. Floyd and James Buchanan," 381–88, and Belohlavek, "The Politics of Scandal," 145–60.

Lewis Cass's appointment as secretary of state, the senior cabinet post, was driven not by any personal closeness to Buchanan, who viewed him with contempt, but rather by the overriding need for a midwesterner with a national political following. At age 75, Cass was even older than Buchanan. He had been a general in the War of 1812, a territorial governor, a failed presidential candidate, and most recently an un-reelected U.S. senator from Michigan. Before nominating Cass, Buchanan had exacted from him a humiliating understanding that the substantive work of the department would be done by the president himself, who had been secretary of state in Polk's Mexican War cabinet. Buchanan, in turn, detailed a young protégé, John A. Appleton, to Cass with the rank of assistant secretary. As reinforcement the president maintained an office at the State Department as well as in the White House as he worked closely with Appleton.[12] Through this unusual working arrangement Buchanan was to manage or, more accurately, micro-manage the country's territorial affairs as well as its international relations.

As they took office, neither Buchanan nor his cabinet officers had any substantive experience with the LDS church, its leaders, or the West; none had ever ventured beyond the Mississippi, and the westerly limit of Buchanan's travels in the United States was Pittsburgh. During Martin Van Buren's administration, Buchanan had met with the president and Joseph Smith during Smith's unsuccessful visit to Washington to obtain federal protection for his persecuted people in Illinois. In 1858 Buchanan recalled this encounter for Delegate Bernhisel, who in turn described it to Young: "Spoke in friendly terms of the prophet Joseph, remarked that he had a good deal of conversation with him when in Washington, and liked him. Said Joseph was quite indignant at President Van Buren on account of the manner in which he once treated him when he called on him, and asserted he would not vote for him, and would use his influence to prevent his people from voting for him." Of the cabinet secretaries only Floyd appears to have even met a Mormon leader, in this case a highly unusual 1839 encounter in Virginia with Jedediah M. Grant during which Grant preached so impressively that Floyd took up a collection on the spot to re-clothe the threadbare missionary.[13]

[12] Cass to Lewis Cass, Jr., 27 April 1857, Cass Papers. Appleton had been chief clerk at the State Department when Buchanan was Polk's secretary, and he was later Buchanan's secretary in London before returning to Washington in an editorial role at the *Union*, the Democratic Party newspaper. Stampp, *America in 1857*, 49.

[13] Bernhisel to Young, Account of Conversations with President James Buchanan, 11 June 1859, LDS Archives; Jenson, "Jedediah Morgan Grant," *LDS Biographical Encyclopedia*, 1:57–58.

The Most Remarkable Instance of Indecision: An Ailing Buchanan Fights the Patronage Wars

So ill was Buchanan on inauguration day that he questioned whether he would be able to get through the ceremonies. But he did so in apparent good style with the ministrations of U.S. Navy surgeon Jonathan M. Foltz, a Lancaster physician-friend whom Buchanan soon installed in the White House bedroom next to his own for the period of his affliction.

Compared with the austerity of the Pierce administration, the tone and festivities on inauguration day were glittering, especially with Buchanan's attractive unmarried niece, Harriet Lane, at his side in the role of White House hostess.[14] Nonetheless, at one of the multiple inaugural balls, the Russian minister to Washington, Baron Edward A. de Stoeckl, was filled with foreboding about the prospects for multiple conflicts within the United States. To one dancing partner Stoeckl recalled the comment whispered by Talleyrand to French king Louis Philippe at a ball on the eve of the 1830 revolution: "Sire, we are dancing on a volcano!"[15] Ironically, the elaborately decorated broadside announcing the ball depicted not a volcano but a triumphal arch composed of blocks bearing the names of the thirty-eight states and territories—Utah uppermost among them—just below an image of Buchanan.

Like Stoeckl, the entire country was curious, if not apprehensive, as to what kind of president James Buchanan would become. Even in the isolated mountain valleys and military posts of the trans-Mississippi West, roughhewn citizens paused on inauguration day to consider Buchanan and his new role. At Fort Leavenworth, Kansas Territory, a young cavalry officer contemplated Buchanan's imminent inauguration and a possible summer in the field. He confided to his mother in Woodbury, New Jersey, "But there is no telling what the magnates at Washington may do from one day to another. They are often disposed to listen to illegitimate sources for information."[16] In the wilderness of what is now Montana's Bitterroot Valley, Indian Agent and trader John Owen commented, "I have amused Myself today some little Wondering how the inauguration of Mr. Buchanan Came off and What high times will be carried on the City of Washington to Night."[17] At Fort Laramie,

[14] Klein, "The Inauguration of President James Buchanan," 145–61.

[15] Woldman, *Lincoln and the Russians*, 18.

[16] 2d Lt. George Dashiell Bayard to mother, 3 March 1857, Samuel J. Bayard, *Life of George Dashiell Bayard*, 114.

[17] John Owen, journal entry, 4 March 1857, Dunbar and Phillips, eds., *The Journals and Letters of Major John Owen*, 1:156.

Nebraska Territory, an overworked civilian clerk, Joseph P. Hamelin, Jr., was certain as to what was going on at the capital and lapsed into pathos: "While they are putting Jimmy Buchanan at the head of affairs in Washington, and swilling immense amounts of mean whiskey in honor of the event; I am busily engaged in assisting to invoice the goods of Tutt & D. . . . Industry must be satisfied."[18]

Although in New York the church's newspaper *The Mormon* commented that "President Buchanan enters the White House, the bright star of many hopeful hearts," from Salt Lake City there was no cordial congratulatory note by Brigham Young as there had been for Franklin Pierce four years earlier.[19] Instead the *Deseret News* published its regular issue on 4 March 1857 without a word devoted to either Buchanan or the change in national administrations, but with the full text of an emblematic gubernatorial proclamation announcing the pending election for the Nauvoo Legion's lieutenant general.[20] But all was not quiet in Salt Lake City. From there, "Utah," the *New York Times*'s pseudonymous correspondent, filed a long dispatch questioning Buchanan's interest in confronting "the Mormon problem":

> Yesterday, as we suppose, JAMES BUCHANAN was inaugurated President of the United States, and entered upon the discharge of his high functions as chief magistrate of the Nation. To-day, a trembling band of American citizens, here in this remote quarter of American dominion, vibrates anxiously between hope and distrust as we wonder whether Utah will be deemed by him to be included in the country wherein he has sworn to maintain the Constitution and the laws—whether he will practically regard our peace, prosperity and lives worth an effort for their preservation against lawless violence. Looking back upon the history of the past seven years, and the course of the National Administration during that time, what wonder that we have little confidence in the future.[21]

Buchanan's personal physician, Dr. Foltz, wrote several letters to his wife in Lancaster from his White House quarters. Foltz described the scene as Buchanan took office, struggled with his illness, and tried to cope with the stampede of office seekers who engulfed the new administration as it took shape. These letters, combined with those written by new cabinet officers to

---

[18] Hamelin, "Journal," entry 4 March 1857, Beinecke Library.

[19] "The New President," *The Mormon*, 7 March 1857, 2/2.

[20] "Proclamation," *Deseret News*, 4 March 1857, 413/2. An account of Buchanan's inauguration and the text of his address did not appear for three months until "The Inauguration," *Deseret News*, 10 June 1857, 110/1–4.

[21] "Utah," 5 March 1857, "Highly Interesting from Utah," *New York Daily Times*, 19 May 1857, 1/5.

their own absent wives and press commentary, convey some feel for the patronage pressures and distractions besetting an aging James Buchanan on the eve of the Utah War.[22] The scramble for Buchanan's patronage was such that in New York even Charles A. Scott, destitute and soon driven to enlist as an artillery recruit for the Utah Expedition, entered a hotel to check "the list of the Presidents appointments to make sure that my name was not among them."[23]

Buchanan's illnesses of February–March continued intermittently throughout the spring and early summer, including an attack of what he described to a confidante as a severe bout with "cholera morbus."[24] Even as late as early August Brigham Young speculated, "I should not wonder if we heard he was dead soon," and General Wells added, "this was Buchanan['s] own measure some time ago."[25] Substantially harder to assess is the extent to which Buchanan's health if not judgment were impaired by alcohol during the Utah War period and beyond. Humorous anecdotes about the president's drinking were generated by Buchanan himself and his friends, while less gentle stories flowed from his political enemies. For example, once back on the western plains W. M. F. Magraw frequently stopped eastbound travelers and urged them in an expansive manner to accept a personal letter of introduction to his presidential friend, noting that the best possible such introduction was to appear before Buchanan with the smell of good liquor on the breath.[26] After his falling-out with the president and during a period of presidential recovery, Philadelphia newspaper editor John W. Forney wrote: "Mr. B is delighted at the idea that any member of his Cabinet should get sick, and is in the habit of saying every day, 'I never was in better health in my life; I can take my glass of Old Monongahela [whiskey], dine heartily, indulge in Madeira [wine], and sleep soundly, and yet my Cabinet is always dilapidated.'"

The late Jonas Robitscher, a leading student of presidential health as well as an attorney and forensic psychiatrist, concluded, "Buchanan was never con-

[22] See Charles S. Foltz, *Surgeon of the Seas*, 183–86 and 189–90. For a description of Buchanan's indecision and vacillation in selecting his cabinet, see the March journal entries of former secretary of state William L. Marcy, William L. Marcy Papers, Library of Congress. The crushing patronage burden and Buchanan's health are discussed in the letters of Sec. of the Treasury Howell Cobb to Mary Ann Cobb and John A. Cobb, 8 and 22 March and 8 April 1857, Howell Cobb Papers. See also Sec. of the Navy Isaac Toucey to Catherine Toucey, 13 April 1857, Papers of Isaac Toucey.

[23] Stowers and Ellis, eds., "Charles A. Scott's Diary," 160, entry for 28 March 1857.

[24] Buchanan to Robert Tyler, 11 June 1857, James Buchanan Papers.

[25] Young and Wells quoted in Wilford Woodruff, "Journal," entry for 2 August 1857, 5:71–72.

[26] Jackson, *Wagon Roads West*, 360.

sidered an alcoholic, but steadily drinking over a lifetime—all the Old Monongahela and madeira—takes its toll. Slightly impaired mental performance leads to inflexibility and defensiveness; the pressures of the office require, particularly in older Presidents like Buchanan, that a President keep all his wits about him."[27]

Behold Me, a Lieutenant General: Winfield Scott's Splendid but Conflicted Isolation

One of the few positions atop the national government that did not turn over with the March patronage scramble was that of Brevet Lt. Gen. Winfield Scott, the U.S. Army's general in chief. Given the absence of military experience among both the new president and his secretary of war, General Scott—brave, smart, and vastly experienced—should have been the new administration's lead advisor on military affairs. That he did not become so was a function of three factors: the self-confident, non-consultative administrative style of his civilian superiors; Scott's own prickly hyper-sensitivity; and his unilateral decision in the late 1840s to remove army headquarters from Washington to New York out of pique over the presidential election of his Mexican War rival Gen. Zachary Taylor. Prolonging Scott's self-imposed isolation into the 1850s was his disastrous loss of the 1852 presidential race to Pierce, another Mexican War rival, and the atrocious relationship that developed with Pierce's secretary of war, Jefferson Davis. The conflict between Scott and Davis was so acrimonious that it produced a long exchange of vituperative, mutually insulting letters constituting a near-scandal when published. At the same time Scott conducted an equally rancorous feud over disputed Mexican War issues with Brevet Brig. Gen. William S. Harney, later the Utah Expedition's initial commander.

The result was that throughout the 1850s and until the Civil War, General Scott commanded the U.S. Army's line regiments from the isolation of New York while a succession of cabinet secretaries controlled the army's staff bureaus in Washington. Col. Samuel Cooper, the army's adjutant general, tried to serve as peacemaker by balancing the demands of both the secretary and the general in chief from his awkward post in the capital. Depending upon

---

[27] Robitscher, "Buchanan," 104, unpublished monograph on presidential health. See MacKinnon-Robitscher correspondence 1976–80 in editor's research files.

the season, Scott shuttled the army's small seven-man headquarters between two rented rooms in Manhattan and the more uplifting environment upriver at Scott's beloved West Point. From these changing quarters General Scott pelted the secretary with an endless series of memos delineating his powers and prerogatives, claims for back pay, and suggestions for revising army regulations. When occasionally summoned, he sallied down to Washington for consultation with the president or secretary.[28]

With rumors in late February 1857 that Floyd was to succeed Jefferson Davis at the War Department, General Scott reached out to Floyd in an early attempt to establish an amicable working relationship of the type never achieved with Davis. He offered to return his headquarters to Washington in a fawning, somewhat disingenuous, and premature letter.[29] Here was a key opportunity to rectify a wholly unnecessary communications gap atop the U.S. Army. Three days after the inauguration Scott wrote to Colonel Cooper from New York to notify Floyd that he intended to visit him on 11 March "to make my personal & official respects." Scott added the melodramatic flourish that he intended "to remain in Washington, weeks, months or years to depend on the will of the President &c." Scott closed with the news that "To the suggested expedition against the Cheyenne Indians, I shall invite the early attention of the Secretary of War, & there are some other matters of importance which I shall desire to discuss with him."[30]

Even after Scott's initial courtesy call on Floyd, the matter of his headquarters location remained unresolved. On 24 March, while still in Washington, Scott raised the issue via note and received a response from Floyd the same day, also by letter—a quite different communications style than the face-to-face dialogue more apt to have been used by Brigham Young. "I regret that my numerous and pressing engagements have prevented an earlier attention to the conversation we had upon the subject of the Head Quarters," Secretary Floyd wrote. "In reply to your note of this date, however, I take occasion to say that the subject is one I have been turning in my mind a good deal for the last week, and upon mature reflection, and with a view

[28] Peskin, *Winfield Scott and the Profession of Arms*, 206–28.

[29] Scott to Floyd, 28 February 1857, John B. Floyd Papers.

[30] Scott to Cooper, 7 March 1857, Letters Sent, Headquarters of the Army (Main Series), 1828–1903, National Archives. Noteworthy is the explicit reference to an expedition against the Cheyennes, but not to one involving Utah.

to your own comfort and convenience I have concluded to make no change in the Head Quarters of the Army."[31]

By mid-April 1857 General Scott would be nearly as frustrated with Floyd's inexperience, inattention, and preoccupation with the cabinet's all-consuming patronage deliberations as he had been with Secretary Davis's earlier rancor and overt disrespect. In a candid letter from Washington to one of his aides, Maj. Irvin McDowell, he described his frustrations with Floyd.

SCOTT TO MCDOWELL, 11 APRIL 1857, CLEMENTS LIBRARY.

> I have been here more than 4 weeks & have had official interviews with the new Secretary to the extent, in all, of fifteen minutes. In the meantime I have piled up memorials upon memorials against the new General Regulation; against acts of injustice perpetrated by the same authority upon Majors Leslie & Hunter; protests against taking Lieut. Col. Magruder out of my hands & sending him to Fort Adams [Massachusetts] (the act of the present Secretary) & &c &c. On neither point have I been able to obtain any decision. I also sent in a *projet* for a dividing line between the Secretary's duties & mine. The approval of this *projet* was necessary to give me the control of all the assistant adjutant generals, except those employed in the office of [Adjutant General] Cooper. His approval I have not rec[d]—the Secretary being 9 out of ten working hours in the cabinet, & perfectly green as well as dilatory. . . .
>
> The President rec[d] me kindly & the Secretary with warmth. He touches the acts of his predecessor very hesitatingly.

Although nearly the entire U.S. Army was serving on the frontier, the sense of alienation at its top was so profound that on the day General Scott initiated the Utah Expedition, his headquarters as well as those of the departments of the East and West were located in three New York communities along the Hudson River.

---

[31] Floyd to Scott, 24 March 1857, Sec. of War, Letters Sent Relating to Military Affairs, 1800–89, National Archives.

PRESIDENT JAMES BUCHANAN (1857–61)

This Mathew Brady portrait captures Buchanan as the nation's fifteenth and oldest president. Inaugurated at age 65, he was the country's only bachelor president, a sharp contrast to the then-fifty-five-year-old, much-married Brigham Young. Although an accomplished, well-educated lawyer and vastly experienced politician, legislator, and diplomat, Buchanan lacked important executive and military experience. His shortfalls included directness in communications, ability to delegate, and steadfastness in personal relationships. When he assumed the presidency, Buchanan's highest priority was management of the slavery issue in violent Kansas Territory, not the "Mormon problem" in adjacent Utah. Although he had met Joseph Smith, Jr., in 1839, Buchanan did not know fellow Mason Brigham Young, was not a formal member of any church, and had never traveled west of his native Pennsylvania. *Courtesy of the Brady Collection, National Archives.*

Chapter 5

"It's a Hell of a Place"
The Decision to Intervene

No one has a right to grade a President—not even poor James Buchanan—who has not sat in his chair, examined the mail and information that came across his desk, and learned why he made decisions.

—President John F. Kennedy, February 1962

The [White House] floors pop and crack all night long. Anyone with imagination can see old Jim Buchanan walking up and down worrying about conditions not of his making. . . . [Presidents] who had Boswells and New England historians are too busy trying to control heaven and hell to come back here. So the tortured souls who were and are misrepresented in history are the ones who come back. It's a hell of a place.

—President Harry S. Truman, Diary, 6 January 1947

As winter gave way to spring 1857 the national uproar over the Dred Scott decision grew, but President Buchanan made progress on his other problems: his health improved somewhat; he dispensed much but not all of the federal patronage; and Robert J. Walker, a respected former treasury secretary from Pennsylvania and Mississippi, agreed to serve as Kansas's new governor. What then welled up unexpectedly alongside these top priorities was the need to replace Brigham Young.

Determining how and even when the Buchanan cabinet made decisions is not easy. Unlike the Pierce and Lincoln administrations that bracketed it, Buchanan's cabinet included no insider diarists to record its near-daily meetings.[1] Nonetheless it is possible to assemble an understanding of the deci-

[1] The contrast between this largely unrecorded situation and the cabinet deliberations leading to virtually all other American wars is marked. See, for example, Paige, *The Korean Decision: June 24–30, 1950*.

sion-making process through the documents that flowed to cabinet members and the recorded observations of outsiders who episodically interacted with them. Another useful source is the newspaper coverage of White House affairs, since many Utah-related documents were in the hands of the press virtually as soon as government departments received them.

Almost universally, historians have believed that what brought Utah concerns to the fore was the highly public 30 March 1857 resignation of W. W. Drummond, Utah's venomous, debauched supreme court justice. Not so. The real catalyst for the change in the administration's priorities and its decision making about Utah was not this letter, incendiary as it was. Rather it was the substance and rhetoric in at least three other batches of material received in Washington during the third week of March 1857, weeks before awareness of Drummond's resignation. Notwithstanding an attempt by Thomas L. Kane to convince Buchanan to retain Brigham Young as governor, this material, combined with the cumulative impact of nearly ten years of unremitting tension and the political backwash from the 1856 election campaign, destroyed any vestiges of Young's political viability. It led Buchanan's cabinet to make two related decisions: replace Brigham Young and provide his unidentified successor with some sort of army escort. To assess Buchanan's thought process during this critical period, then, one needs to understand the cumulative private-public effect of all of this material, most of which was never published. Drummond's resignation letter alone represents only part of a far broader tableau.

It Was a Declaration of War: The Utah War's Smoking Gun

In 1990 Professor Kenneth M. Stampp of Stanford University, the leading authority on the political events of 1857, commented that there was no "smoking gun" for the Utah War. By this Stampp meant that he knew of no unexploited nineteenth-century document to explain what had brought on the conflict.[2] Quite to the contrary, at least five such documents had been delivered to Buchanan's cabinet by 20 March 1857. These documents, supported by the 30 March resignation of Judge Drummond and the following press furor, escalated "the Mormon problem" to a burning issue for Buchanan.

[2] Poll notes of a 23 October 1990 telephone conversation with Stampp, research files, Richard D. Poll Papers; Stampp, *America in 1857*, 196–208.

They were transformational: on 9 March Delegate Bernhisel had a "pleasant" interview with Buchanan and noted that "The President appeared free from prejudice himself"; by 19 March the cabinet was offended and interpreted Mormon behavior as "a declaration of war."

Fearful that uncontrolled political consequences might follow public awareness of such volatile material, the Buchanan administration suppressed it. Mormon leaders—who through Bernhisel knew more about the cabinet's thinking than did the general public or even members of Congress—long believed that two of the five documents had been instrumental in the administration's decision making about Utah during the early spring.

The first batch consisted of the Utah legislative assembly's 6 January 1857 memorials and resolutions dealing with federal appointments.[3] Upon adoption, these documents had been sent from Salt Lake City to Bernhisel via the San Bernardino–Panama mail. This material arrived in Washington on 17 March 1857, at which point Bernhisel had already met with President Buchanan—on 9 March—to make the case for Brigham Young's retention. Bernhisel had also filed with multiple government departments old petitions gathered to support this position during 1855–56. What also arrived in Washington on 17 March was an editorial in James Gordon Bennett's *New York Herald* that expressed great confidence in Buchanan's decision making and leadership of the cabinet while advising that "the Kansas question and the Utah Mormon excrescence call for immediate and decisive action. That infamous

[3] Mormon perceptions of the memorials' impact on the administration's Utah decisions were largely derived from Bernhisel's report of Secretary Thompson's face-to-face reactions. This explanation for the Utah War persisted among LDS leaders for several years until the underlying documents themselves were forgotten by both sides of the conflict. For example, on 7 October 1857 Albert Carrington of the *Deseret News* editorialized:

> However, it may be urged that the "expedition AGAINST Utah" is based upon a certain "Memorial and Resolutions to the President of the United States." . . . President Buchanan, do these documents breath[e] aught of a "defiant spirit," aught of a spirit unworthy our Constitution and American citizens? . . . Every American and every intelligent person will at a glance perceive that there [is] naught in the above Memorials and Resolutions but what is strictly and nobly in accordance with the Constitution and Constitutional laws of the United States. . . . And yet we are informed that a grave member of President Buchanan's Cabinet said that those Memorials and Resolutions breathed a "defiant spirit"! "Expedition Against Utah," *Deseret News*, 7 October 1857, 245/1, 3, 4.

In his 15 December 1857 annual message Brigham Young also commented on these documents and noted, "up to this date no official information concerning the action, if any, taken upon that memorial has ever reached us. Time glided by, and travelers and newspapers began to confirm the rumor that the present Executive and a part of his Cabinet had yielded to the rabid clamor raised against Utah." Perhaps the earliest public discussion in Utah of Bernhisel's fateful discussion of the memorials on 19 March was in the editorial "The United States Government and Utah," *Deseret News*, 12 August 1857, 180/4, 181/1–4.

beast, that impudent and blustering impostor, Brigham Young, and his abominable pack of saintly officials, should be kicked out without delay and without ceremony."[4]

Due to the relevance of the new Utah memorials to the appointments process then preoccupying the new administration, Bernhisel immediately returned to visit the president on 18 March. Exhausted by both patronage pressures and illness, Buchanan chose not to examine these documents in Bernhisel's presence. Instead he urged the territorial delegate to deliver them to one of his lead cabinet officers, Sec. of the Interior Jacob Thompson. Bernhisel did so later that day. When he returned to call upon Thompson on 19 March, Bernhisel found that the provocative rhetoric of one of the documents had enraged the secretary and probably the entire cabinet: "it was a declaration of war."[5]

What may well have shaped Secretary Thompson's waspish comments to Bernhisel on 19 March was a letter received that day by the administration from Judge Drummond. This was the second batch of startling reports to reach the cabinet in as many days. Unlike the other Utah materials received that week, portions of this letter immediately appeared in the press—a boon to students of the Utah War, since the original document has disappeared.

"Utah and Its Troubles," 19 March 1857, *New York Herald*, 20 March 1857, 4/5.

A letter was received here to-day from W. W. Drummond, United States Supreme [Court] Judge in Utah Territory, by the Administration. It gives a sad and deplorable picture of matters in that Territory. The following is taken from the letter:

"The leading men of the church are more traitorous than ever. Only a few days since all the papers, records, dockets, and nine hundred volumes of the laws, were taken out of the Supreme Court Clerk's office and burned. And this is not the only instance of the kind. I say to you again, and through you to the President, it is impossible for us to enforce the laws in this Territory. Every man here holds his life at the will of Brigham Young; and here we are without protection. I am firmly of opinion that [Sec. A. W.] Babbitt was murdered by Mormons under directions of Brigham Young, and not by Indians.

---

[4] "Mr. Buchanan's Administration and Our Foreign and Domestic Affairs," *New York Herald*, 17 March 1857, 4/3.

[5] Secretary Thompson's reaction evokes President Franklin Roosevelt's comment to adviser Harry Hopkins on the morning of 6 December 1941 immediately after reading an intercepted cable sent by the Japanese government to its Washington embassy: "This means war." Clausen and Lee, *Pearl Harbor: Final Judgment*, 80.

Murder is a common thing here; and Mormons cannot be punished with a Mormon jury, witnesses, officers, and Governor to pardon. It is too cruel, and must not be endured. A man, not a member of the church, is murdered, robbed, castrated and imprisoned, solely for questioning the authority of the church. Persons are now in the Penitentiary, convicted before the Probate Judge, who are wholly innocent of any crime. Is there any other country where this abuse is or would be endured? Let all, then, take hold and crush out one of the most treasonable organizations in America."

The Administration have had the matter under serious consideration, and will soon appoint a Governor, I understand, who will take sufficient military force into that territory to carry out the laws to the fullest extent.[6]

This letter was probably written by Drummond before leaving California and quite possibly had traveled east aboard the same mail packets that carried the Utah legislative assembly's memorials to Bernhisel. It is not to be confused with Drummond's subsequent 30 March resignation written in New Orleans. Quoting from the Drummond letter received on 19 March, Washington's *National Era* concluded, "Mr. Buchanan has resolved to dispense with the further services of Brigham Young, the present Governor of Utah, and to appoint some Democratic old bachelor, after his own pattern, adverse to the whole theory of polygamy."[7]

Key to understanding the travel, handling, and cabinet reception of these first two batches of documents are three overlapping reports written to Brigham Young by Delegate Bernhisel on 17 and 18 March and 2 April 1857.

Bernhisel to Young, 17 March 1857, LDS Archives.

On Monday last [9 March] which was the fifth day after the inaugeration I had an interview with the President in reference to appointments for our Territory. I stated to him, among other things, that the people of Utah desired exceedingly that Governor Young should be retained in office; that I did not desire your reappointment, though your term of service had expired, but that you be permitted to hold over; also that Colonel Steptoe who was appointed to succeed you, had declined, and united with his brother officers and others in a petition to General Pierce to reappoint you, and that you had hitherto filled the office to the entire public satisfaction.[8] I also requested the

[6] It is likely that Drummond wrote this letter to Attorney General Black, but the letter cannot be found in Black's files. Archivist Fred Romanski (National Archives) to MacKinnon, e-mail message, 1 May 2006.

[7] "Freaks of Popular Sovereignty in Utah—Is the Democracy a Unit," *National Era* (Washington), 2 April 1857, 54.

[8] After signing a petition on 30 December 1854 supporting Young's re-appointment, Steptoe wrote to President Pierce to say that he regretted having done so. Steptoe to Pierce, 25 April 1855; David H. Miller, "Brigham Young, Edward J. Steptoe, and the 1854–55 Gubernatorial Controversy," 11.

appointment of other nominees. His Excellency observed that he had just come into the traces, that he was green yet, but that he thought he was learning fast, that he did not know yet what he should do, but requested me to reduce to writing what I desired, and file the papers in the appropriate Departments. He inquired whether there was no other man who would be as acceptable to the people as Mr Young. I replied that there was no other man living that would be as acceptable, and the [*sic*] you enjoyed the entire confidence of the people. He remarked that if your name were sent to the Senate that it would raise a storm. I answered that I was aware of that, and therefore did not desire your reappointment, but that you be permitted to hold over as you were now doing.[9] He alluded to the prejudice existing against us as a people, but seemed to think it was entirely on account of plurality [polygamy]. I stated that perhaps no other people had ever given a stronger proof of loyalty and patriotism than ours, referring to the battalion that volunteered in the war with the Mexican Republic. He recollected the circumstance very well for he was at that time Secretary of State. I also gave him some account, of the peace, quiet, order, and morality that reigned in our midst. The President appeared free from prejudice himself, and the interview was pleasant, and as satisfactory as could be expected under the circumstances.

Since the interview I have addressed to the President a rather lengthy communication requesting your continuance in office, and filed it in the State Department together with the memorial of the Legislative Assembly of Utah, and a copy of the petition of Colonel Steptoe, his compatriots and others, both of which were addressed to the late incumbent of the Presidency, and preferred a similar request.[10]

I have also deposited in another Department of the Government a letter for his Excellency [Buchanan] relative to other appointments for our Territory.

I deeply regret to inform you that a Mr Nelson, of Indiana has been appointed Superintendent of Indian Affairs for our Territory. The Hon Jacob Thompson, the new Secretary of the Interior, stated to me that the Commissioner of Indian Affairs had reported to him that you had performed the duties of Superintendent very well. . . .[11]

There seems to be a determination in both houses of Congress, and throughout the length and breadth of the land, never to admit Utah into the Union with her "peculiar institution," and I regret to say that within the last few months prejudice against us as a people has greatly increased, not only at

---

[9] Continuance or the holdover approach was the tactic also advocated by Thomas L. Kane but condemned by Representative Morrill in his congressional Utah remarks dated 23 February 1857.

[10] Bernhisel's post–9 March written plea to Buchanan has not been located.

[11] Nelson never took up the appointment, which eventually fell to Jacob Forney. By November 1857 the Department of the Interior's Office of Indian Affairs had changed from this positive assessment of Superintendent Young's stewardship to a highly negative view.

the seat of the Central Government, but throughout this extended Republic. The "peculiar institution" is looked upon with a holy horror.

The Special session of the Senate which convened on the 4th of March . . . , for the purpose of acting on the nominations of the new administration, adjourned on the 14th instant, and I am happy to be able to inform you that [by default] you are still Governor of Utah, but I deeply regret to add that I entertain very serious apprehensions that you may be superceeded. A good deal has recently been said about the people of Utah living in violation of all law, and of establishing a government of laws in our Territory I tell them that our people have violated no law, and that they are a loyal and patriotic people.

There have been no appointments made yet for Utah.

The Salt Lake mail of January 8th via Panama arrived this morning and I was somewhat disappointed that it did no[t] bring me any from you.

I shall return in the mail coach for May, if there be any for that month.

Bernhisel to Young, 18 March 1857, LDS Archives.

[T]wo memorials [dated 6 January 1857] from the Legislative Assembly addressed to the President of the United States, and copies of some papers were received last evening via California, after I had deposited my letter of yesterday to you in the Post office. . . .

This morning I had an interview with the President and presented to him the memorials, and gave him some account of the purport of them, and also some account of the conduct of certain officials, and requested their removal. I again urged upon him your retention as Governor, and told him among other things that it was the universal desire of the people of Utah that you should be retained. His Excellency is constantly surrounded by crowds of office seekers during office hours except when the Cabinet is in session which is daily from 10 to 2. He said you see how it is, that I can do nothing, and desired me to hand the memorials to the Secretary of the Interior and tell him what we wanted, and in due time the Secretary would report to him; that is bring the memorials and whole subject before the Cabinet. I have accordingly had an interview with the Secretary of the Interior, delivered to [him] the memorials, and made a statement of our grievances. The Secretary desired me to call on him to-morrow after he shall have read them, and said he would talk to me freely about them. He seems disposed to do us justice. . . .

I will drop you another note to-morrow after my interview with the Secretary and hope it will be in time for the next steamer.[12] There have been no appointments made yet for our Territory except a Superintendent of Indian Affairs under the new law, and an [*sic*] minor agent for Carson Co.

---

[12] Bernhisel did not write on 19 March as promised, perhaps stunned and demoralized by his meeting with Jacob Thompson that day. His next report to Governor Young was that of 2 April.

Delegate Bernhisel probably wrote the following letter after he withdrew to Pennsylvania. It did not make the April mail to Utah and so traveled in the same coach as Bernhisel, arriving in Salt Lake City on 29 May just after the governor's own return from his five-week Fort Limhi trek and the day following release of General Scott's circular about the Utah Expedition.

Bernhisel to Young, 2 April 1857, LDS Archives.

I remained in Washington after the inaugeration [*sic*] until I had done all I could for Utah, and then took my departure from that metropolis, but I am extremely sorry to say as regards our Territory the clouds are dark and lowering.

In my last [I] informed you that I called again on the President after the receipt of the memorials of the Legislative Assembly with the view of presenting them. . . . [As Buchanan asked] I then sought an interview with the [Interior] Secretary who observed that he would read the memorials, and then speak freely of them, and desired me to call the next day. The next morning I called according to appointment and had a long conversation with him. The Secretary said the memorial containing the nominations was well enough, but that he did not like the tone of the other one, that it was a declaration of war, that it breathed a defiant spirit, that if we got into trouble with the General Government that we would have nobody to blame but ourselves, that the memorial was not respectful, that some respect was due to official station, that it placed him (meaning I suppose the administration) in a position that he did not like to be placed in. The memorial tells us that we must appoint these men, and if we do not, and appoint others, that you will drive them out of the Territory. He said when you tell a man that he *must* do a thing, it excites in him a feeling to resist, and added that the Government had as much power as we had, that we could not agree with any officers. I mentioned Judge [Leonidas] Shaver and Chief Justice ~~Kinney~~ Read [Lazarus Reed] who were very popular, and that the people had endured a great deal from the misconduct of officials for the sake of peace and quiet. He said of [if] an officer misbehaved, his conduct should be properly presented to the appropriate [Washington] Department, and his case would be promptly attended to. He was desirous that if other officers should be sent to our Territory that they should be well received and well treated. I replied that they had always been treated as gentlemen as long as they conducted themselves like gentlemen. He observed that the Government desired to live at peace with us, and inquired whether we did not intend to set up an independent Government. I replied in the negative, and added that we desired to come into the Union as a State. The prejudice or feeling against plurality in both branches of Congress, among the officers of the Government, and throughout the country, is exceedingly

> strong, and is increasing; and the Secretary said that it would be slandering God to say that he approved of polygamy and that the Government intended to put it down, but he did not indicate the mode that they proposed to adopt, but I inferred that it was under the common law.[13] Among other things I entreated him to use his best efforts to prevent any troops being sent to our Territory, stated that the people were loyal and patriotic, and desired to live in peace and harmony with the Government. The Secretary said that if the memorial should get into the newspapers, or if we should be impudent enough to publish it, it would produce great excitement, and we should get ourselves into trouble with the Government.[14] I furnished the Hon Secretary with a printed copy of the [30 December 1854] petitions of Chief Justice Kinney, Colonel Steptoe and others with which he expressed himself pleased. The Secretary of the Interior said too that he knew nothing of our religious principles, but if the[y] lead to such pra[c]tices they must be very bad; also that he did not know how the memorial would strike the President, but that it had made a very unfavorable impression on his mind.

On 20 March 1857, the day after Secretary Thompson informed Delegate Bernhisel of the cabinet's explosive reaction, another shoe dropped. It took the form of two letters from Utah's chief justice, John F. Kinney, to Attorney Gen. Jeremiah S. Black. This was the third batch of Utah-related materials received by the administration in four days.

Kinney had been out of Utah on a leave of absence since 1856. Although moving to Nebraska Territory during March 1857, he was in Washington to assess Buchanan's Utah policy, to lobby for continuation of his paid leave,

---

[13] Presumably for this reason Brigham Young had earlier banned use of both British and American common law as precedents in territorial court cases, a major legal controversy. Young decreed that the only legal arguments permissible in Utah were acts passed by Utah's legislative assembly, thereby dismissing as applicable the resolution of cases decided earlier elsewhere: such cases could have been used to argue against polygamy. See Homer, "The Judiciary and the Common Law in Utah Territory, 1850–61," 97–108.

[14] Apparently taking this warning from Thompson to heart, the only publication of these memorials was a truncated version that appeared in Salt Lake City more than six months later once the Utah War had started, which was reprinted by a New York paper near the end of 1857. See "Expedition Against Utah," *Deseret News*, 7 October 1857, 244–45/1–4 both pages; and "The Mormon War . . . Memorial from the Legislature of Utah to President Buchanan," *New York Herald*, 15 December 1857, 2/3–5. Notwithstanding this suppression, there was some early awareness that the memorials existed as with a report from Washington run by one rural New England newspaper: "We have no doubt that there is positive information in this city that Brigham Young and his crew . . . have demanded the appointment of one of two schedules of federal officers, both headed by Brigham Young for Governor, with the avowal of the purpose of driving any other out of the Territory by force of arms. The truth is, the Mormons are already practically in a state of rebellion." "Most Important from Utah," *The Farmers' Cabinet* (Amherst, N.H.), 26 March 1857, 2. For an example of the type of congressional scrutiny and raucous debate that Buchanan avoided by suppressing the January 1857 materials, see press reports of the subsequent reaction in the U.S. House of Representatives when Utah's January 1858 petitions reached that chamber. "The Mormon Memorial in the House," *New York Herald*, 17 March 1858, 4/5.

and to assert, as he later told the president, that "There was no necessity of returning to Utah until the Government troops started, as testimony and experience both concur in establishing the fact that the [civil] officers are of little or no use in that territory unless sustained by the military arm of the government."[15] In one of his 20 March letters, presumably hand delivered, Kinney reviewed the condition of affairs in Utah. This letter was remarkably like the one Drummond was then formulating aboard ship in the Gulf of Mexico, and it urged Black to share Kinney's views with the president and his cabinet, as he had Drummond's letter, received on 19 March. Kinney did not write spontaneously; Black had asked for his assessment of Utah affairs after reading Drummond's California letter and the 6 January materials delivered by Bernhisel through Thompson. On 20 March Kinney not only recited examples of what he believed to be Brigham Young's perversion of Utah's judicial system, but urged his removal from office and the establishment of a one-regiment U.S. Army garrison in the territory.

From the cabinet's viewpoint, Kinney's inputs must have appeared credible. Prior to his appointment to Utah's bench in 1854, Kinney had been a judge of the supreme court in Iowa. His experience in Utah was relatively long and recent, credentials that Kinney believed qualified him to comment about the territory "advisedly." Both the U.S. Department of State and the Office of the U.S. Attorney General had confidential files amassed during Pierce's administration bulging with Kinney reports criticizing Brigham Young's influence on Utah's judicial and legal systems as well as the indignities suffered by the judge at Young's hands. Probably unknown to the cabinet in March 1857 was Kinney's 1855 indictment in Salt Lake City's probate court on gambling charges, his ownership of a disreputable hotel, and the extent to which he had boldly but unsuccessfully maneuvered for appointment as Utah's governor two years earlier as Colonel Steptoe dithered over President Pierce's offer.

The second letter that Kinney gave to Attorney General Black on 20 March was a document transmitting a letter from Utah surveyor general David H. Burr, the long-time critic of Brigham Young's handling of such disputed federal-territorial issues as disposition of the public lands and Indian affairs. Burr would have been even better known to the cabinet than Kinney. Although Mor-

---

[15] Kinney to Buchanan, 1 August 1857, Office of the Attorney Gen., Correspondence from the President, Letters Received (RG 60), National Archives.

mon leaders would soon begin an intense attack on Burr's character and performance, in March he would have been known in Washington as a nationally famous cartographer who had been employed by both the U.S. House of Representatives and the State of New York. Sandwiched among Burr's litany of alleged Mormon offenses was his shocking assessment that "The great danger to a [new] Governor would be assassination." Notwithstanding his identification of this risk, Burr argued for something other than a large army expedition to execute his recommendations: "To carry out this plan the presence of a small Military force might be necessary. I do not suppose that their services would be needed further than to show the leaders of this people a determination to enforce the laws."[16]

Delivery of the Burr letter by Kinney meant that within two weeks of taking office, James Buchanan and his cabinet had a collection of stunning new inputs on Utah affairs from the territory's truculent legislative assembly, its chief justice, an associate supreme court justice, and the surveyor general. All of these documents were suppressed and never shared with Congress, although the cabinet was surely aware of them. Perhaps this secretive approach reflected Buchanan's belief that Kinney's longstanding request for confidentiality precluded such disclosure. Perhaps there were other reasons for such suppression. The result was that neither the public nor Congress understood fully the documentation available to the administration when it acted on Utah.[17]

Kinney to Black, 20 March 1857, Files of U.S. Attorney General, National Archives.

Confidential & Private

Allow me to call your attention, and through you the attention of the President and Cabinet to the state of things existing in the Territory of Utah. Having resided in Salt Lake City as the Chief Justice of the Supreme Court for about two years, I think I can speak advisedly upon the following points.

[16] The Burr–Black letter is filed with the Kinney–Black letter of 20 March 1857. To date, the only notice of the former document appears in Thomas G. Alexander, "Carpetbaggers, Reprobates, and Liars: Federal Judges and the Utah War," unpublished paper, Mormon History Association annual conference, Salt Lake City, May 2007.

[17] Although he clearly suspected the judge of duplicity as early as 1855, Brigham Young, too, was somewhat in the dark about Kinney's behavior. As a result, after the Utah War President Buchanan reappointed Kinney to be Utah's chief justice, and the Mormons themselves subsequently elected him to be territorial delegate in Congress while appointing one of his sons to West Point under Utah's quota for the military academy.

1st The Mormons are inimical to the Government of the U.S. and to all its officers who are not of their peculiar faith. This was manifested in their attempt last fall to incite the Indians to the murder of Genl. Burr formerly of this [Washington] city, Surveyor General of the Territory, Dr. Garland Hurt Indian Agent, and their party who were on an official visit South; and by the brutal attack made upon Deputy Surveyor Troskolawski last August, by which his life was endangered. It was also repeatedly manifested by their pulpit orators during my residence there in language like the following, to wit: "That they would cut the throats of all the Gentiles, throw their heads into Salt Lake and use their bodies for manure". This remark was made by Bishop Woolley in the presence of Brigham Young to about three thousand people. Similar remarks from Gov. Young and his corrupt associates are common upon the Sabbath. They are particularly hostile to the Gentile Judges as they call them.

In the spring of 1856, Brigham Young attempted to break up my court while in Session by using . . . language. . . . The effect of this was to deprive me of nearly all my jurors, who however on being fined and threatened with imprisonment were induced to return to their duty. The Mormon Legislature attached my District, Salt Lake County where nearly all the business for the Territory is done, to Carson Co[unty], five hundred miles distant, which was presided over by Judge Stiles a Mormon and a willing tool of Brigham Youngs,[18] and created a new district for me in the extreme Northern portion of the Territory inhabited mainly by Indians, where by the terms of the Organic law I would be compelled to reside with my family.

The Governor pardoned one man who was sentenced to the penitentiary, before he reached there and also another man who was sentenced for ten years, after a confinement of thirty days, who was absolutely guilty of murder and ought to have been convicted for that high crime.

2nd The Mormons with Brigham Young at their head, teach continually that he Brigham is the prophet and revelator of God and that when the laws or decisions of the Court are in opposition to his will, the former must yield. In this way were the murderers of the lamented Capt. Gunnison who at the time of his death was an employee of the Government making a reconnoissance and survey, virtually acquitted. The case was tried before me, the testimony of guilt and instructions of the Court were clear and convincing, and yet the foul murderers were only found guilty of manslaughter which subjected them to a imprisonment of only three years.

3rd Innocent and helpless men have been most cruelly murdered for no other reason than that they were gentiles or dissattisfied Mormons.

4th Men are sent out every year for the ostensible purpose of converting the Indians but really to poison their minds against the government and Americans and also to make them their allies in case of any difficulty with the U.S.

---

[18] Kinney was unaware of Stiles's excommunication on 22 December 1856 and the vandalizing of his law office.

5th Universal polygamy exists in Utah and a plurality of wives is inculcated as a religious ~~precept~~ duty.

6th There is little or no security for life, liberty or property among the so-called gentiles and complaining Mormons.

In view of these facts may I not suggest that a reliable man be immediately appointed Governor, in place of Brigham Young whose term of office expired long since.

Also a Secretary in place of Col. A. W. Babbitt killed on the plains last fall. If it were proper I would urge immediate action in the appointment of Judges in places of Stiles a Mormon and Drummond who although an anti-Mormon is in consequence of his immoral conduct, which is unnecessary here to mention, entirely unworthy of a place upon the bench.

In order to sustain the officers of the Govt. in the discharge of their responsible duties I deem it necessary that they should be accompanied by a regiment of the Army, which at the same time would afford protection to the disaffected Mormons.[19]

Mr. Buchanan Is a Timerous, Overworked Man: Thomas L. Kane

In the midst of these inputs to the cabinet during the third week of March, Thomas L. Kane responded to Brigham Young's 7 January plea for help and intervened on his behalf. Kane did so through a 21 March letter to Buchanan pleading that he retain Young in the governorship by taking no action on the position. Later Kane also wrote to Attorney General Black, and perhaps to other influential people. For example, on 1 April William I. Appleby reported to Brigham Young: "I had a long talk with Col. Kane yesterday; he informed me that he received a letter from you a short time since. He has written to the President and also to Judge Black Attorney General of the U.S. in relation to Utah, and the reports, urging your reappointment, how it will terminate [turn out] he says he cannot at present determine, but he will do his best, and use his utmost endeavors and influence for you and the Welfare of Utah. His feelings are good." Two weeks later John Taylor added the news: "Col. Kane has been using all his influence with the administration; he is a true friend. In an

[19] I am indebted to Professor David H. Miller for his transcription of this important letter and to James F. Varley for providing its missing date. The only known published reference to this document is in the bibliography for Varley, *Brigham and the Brigadier*, 309. The "Confidential & Private" notation at the top of the letter differs from the hand in which the body of the letter was written and was presumably entered in Black's office.

interview that I had with him, lately, he informed me that he had received a letter from you & was desirous to carry out your requests as far as possible, he did not think it prudent, however to recommend all [your nominees]; but seemed more desirous to first secure the governorship; enclosed you will find a copy of three letters which he has written, on this subject."[20]

Kane's pro-Mormon lobbying efforts took place during a period of great personal turbulence attributable to continuing grief over the recent death of his older brother Elisha, an internationally famous explorer; the financial and emotional collapse of his father-in-law; his own prolonged illness; and plans for an expedition to the Arctic inspired by Elisha that his family considered and rejected on 27 March. Although he was neither the Democratic Party stalwart nor the Buchanan intimate that his father was, the younger Kane had good reason to assume that the president would give his letter and offer to visit the White House careful thought as the cabinet focused on Utah affairs.

Months later Kane learned from Attorney General Black and the president that both men claimed never to have received his letters. In the meantime, interpreting their silence as a rebuff, annoyed by what he perceived as indiscreet handling of this correspondence, and beset by personal problems, Kane notified Brigham Young of his failure, withdrew from Mormon affairs, and retreated from Philadelphia to Pennsylvania's mountains.

The most polished account of Kane's complex pro-Mormon efforts during March–April 1857 (and subsequently) is a memorandum that he drafted more than a year later, perhaps with the intent to publish it. A more contemporaneous account is Kane's late-March report to Brigham Young. Taken together with his 21 March letter to Buchanan, these documents provide valuable insight into Kane's brief lobbying thrust as well as his poorly understood but fateful disengagement from Mormon affairs during the spring of 1857. Therein also lay the origins of his even more important return to the fray that fall from which sprang his famous 1858 mission to Utah.[21]

[20] Appleby to Young, 1 April 1857, and Taylor to Young, 18 April 1857, LDS Archives. Of the three letters only Kane's 21 March 1857 letter to Buchanan has been located.

[21] Although the late Richard D. Poll did not examine all of the relevant documents, he possessed the most complete and analytical grasp of Kane's intervention with the Buchanan administration to date. See Poll, "Thomas L. Kane and the Utah War," 118–19. Another account of Kane's dealings with the Buchanan administration in 1857 was drafted by his wife after the Civil War, but it is a badly disjointed narrative that seems to conflate the events of the spring and fall of 1857, with Buchanan depicted as hapless and Floyd as insulting. See Elizabeth W. Kane, "The Story of the Mother of the Regiment," unpublished ms., Thomas L. and Elizabeth W. Kane Papers.

KANE, CONCERNING THE MORMONS AND PRESIDENT BUCHANAN, MEMORANDUM, JULY 1858, KANE COLLECTIONS, AMERICAN PHILOSOPHICAL SOCIETY.

By way of introduction there should be noted for you two or three facts:

When I first saw that the present administration were following in the footsteps of Mr. Pierce, I offered to communicate to them what I supposed to be the truth about the state of things in Utah. I was no longer as well posted up as I had been before I wrote my very foolish letters against their polygamy in '52.[22] But I saw enough to satisfy me that Mr. Buchanan was entirely in the dark.

I wrote to Judge Black whom I knew to be an honest man, to this effect, and asked if Mr. Buchanan differed from me, to be allowed to give my own views in detail and offered to come on to Washington for that purpose. I also remember to have written to the President [on 21 March]. No answer came from Washington, but shortly after one of the anti-Mormon correspondents of the New York Times published (perhaps this letter to the President was enclosed in that to Judge Black) a scurrilous half-column which showed me that my letter or letters or the substance of their contents had been communicated to the writer.[23]

I remember particularly that there was some sort of threat about what would be done if I undertook again to lecture the President. (I perhaps ought to say here that both the President and Judge Black, have stated to me since that they had not received these letters and expressed their deep regret).[24] My own apprehension at the time was that those around one or both of these gentlemen were in league with the dishonest persons who were stirring the country up against the Mormons. I felt also that I was the subject of a personal indignity and therefore, [(]I say it with deep regret) made no further effort, to admonish the President of the errors of his course. I must say for myself however that I did not know how grave the consequences might be of my not doing so. This was in the Spring, sometime after I had returned from Havana [with Elisha's body] and was trying to get my affairs in order, and before I was forced by ill health to betake myself to the mountains of Elk County.

---

[22] This may refer to, among other documents, Kane's anguished letter to Brigham Young written after Jedediah M. Grant's visit to break the stunning news of Mormon polygamy. Kane to Young, 17 October 1852, LDS Archives. If Kane intended this piece for publication, he may have been anxious to demonstrate his disapproval of plural marriage.

[23] See "Verastus" to Editor of the *New York Daily Times*, 24 May 1857, in "Col. Thomas L. Kane on Mormonism," *Times*, 26 May 1857, 1/2. "Verastus" was widely believed to be Judge Drummond.

[24] These denials by Buchanan and Black appear problematic. The "Verastus" piece indicates that Kane's correspondence indeed did reach Washington and was shared.

Kane to Buchanan, 21 March 1857, Kane Collection, Harold B. Lee Library, Brigham Young University.

I have been requested[25] to bring to your notice the misconduct of certain individuals holding office under executive appointment in the territory of Utah.

These persons have not lessened their offences in the estimation of the inhabitants of Utah by defaming numerous influential citizens whose evidence against them they might anticipate would secure their punishment. That they are in every respect unfit for the stations which they hold I have no hesitation in believing. I must however in candor admit that you will find difficulty in filling their places by appointments of your own. The Mormons are right in asserting that the experience of two presidential terms has proved that "none but second rate men both as regards talents and integrity" will accept office for their territory.[26] They have a country where an honest livelihood is only obtained by a life of unremitting labor, where there is no hope of advancement for the political adventurer, and quite as little for the speculator who fails altogether to unite a community of a peculiar temper to second his designs. Even the man content with present ease must not expect happiness unless he can unite himself cordially in sympathy with a society the good among whom are in more than one sense cloistered by their attention to religious observances and their habitual calculations upon a future state of existence. The Mormons are used to ask for "a stakeholder"—"one devoted to some useful art of productive industry"—"in circumstances to keep house and rear a family among them"—but who answering this description among us wd. exchange a residence in our own community for theirs?[27]

I wish the Mormons to be contented because I wish them to be efficient citizens of the United States. If they have no other claims to consideration, they are excellent workers in coal and iron, and they have found inexhaustible mines of both. Their other resources wd. enable them on a season's warning to feed and clothe all the RailRoad Laborers we could employ among their midway mountains. Destiny in fact seems to have planted them there for the purpose of rendering the Pacific R.R. a possible achievement for your Administration.[28]

But, however strongly I desire to secure prompt justice for the Mormons, I shd. be wanting to my duty as a citizen and my feeling as your personal supporter, if I were not to recognize the existence of peculiar difficulties that must

[25] A reference to Brigham Young's letter of 7 January 1857.

[26] Brigham Young made this point to President Pierce in his letter of 30 March 1853.

[27] During 1854 Kane had declined Young's invitation to move to Utah so that he might stand for election as territorial delegate in Congress. Young renewed this invitation to relocate in September 1857 as the Utah War unfolded.

[28] Presumably unknown to Kane, Buchanan was as ambivalent about a railroad to the Pacific as Brigham Young was enthusiastic. During the election campaign of 1856 he endorsed this notion only at the last minute in a bid for California's support. Kane's repeated references to Mormon involvement with a transcontinental railroad to pique Buchanan's interest may have been counterproductive.

connect themselves with any executive interference with the status quo of their Territory. The character of the present imbroglio there is vexatious and intricate enough of itself, yet you wd. in vain attempt to settle it by cutting any Gordian knot. Besides, the enemies of the principles of self government [popular sovereignty] are on the watch for every act on the part of a Democratic President which may be presented either as an inconsistency or as a bad precedent.

I have reason to know how much you are engaged at the present time with matters of greater moment. The object of my letter is to ask you to do me the favor to consult with me before taking order upon the affairs of Utah. I shall be most happy to come on to Washington at any time upon notice, and impart to you freely the information and views of which I am in possession. There is at least one point, I think, connected with the construction of the Pacific Rail Road which I am confident will have great weight with you.

Kane to Young, Circa March 1857, Thomas L. Kane Papers, Stanford University Libraries.

I have to day leisure to enclose you a copy of a letter written to the President upon receiving your letter of the [blank]. I could not second your wishes in respect of the subordinate territorial appointments ~~subordinate to the Governorship your own~~ as I wd. desire, because your own is in danger, and it will only be by great address that we succeed in saving it. I heard from the President (at second hand) a week ago, and conclude either that my friends have not ~~pressed~~ brought your matter upon his notice as forcefully as I have requested, or else that there exists where there shd. not be a spirit of determined hostility to your interests. The best thing that can be done at present, as I am advised, is to ~~procure~~ obtain delay—at any price. I have accordingly procured an influential friend to represent to Mr. Buchanan how complicated as well as embarrassing the whole Utah question was to be considered, and ~~advise him not to stir in it [at] all~~ tell him he is half sure to go wrong if he stirs before his mind is less ~~bedevilled~~ harrassed than it is at present. This is about the drift of my own letter: I ~~use~~ press the matter of the inferior appointments ~~only for the purpose of~~ ~~producing~~ for better men no further than will produce the impression that there is something disagreeable to be examined into besides the question of the Governorship. Mr. Buchanan is a timerous man, as well as just now an overworked one.[29]

---

[29] This unsigned, undated document in Kane's hand is undoubtedly a draft used by Kane as his retained copy. The finished (mailed) version cannot be found among the incoming correspondence of the Brigham Young Collection, LDS Archives. Over the years this document has not been associated with the Utah War because of a misleading annotation to it in another hand: "Copy of letter to Gov. Cummings [*sic*] / P.K." I believe that the annotation is that of Robert Patterson (Pat) Kane, written in error by him while assembling and labeling Thomas L. Kane's papers, perhaps after Thomas's death. Stanford's cataloguers have administratively added the descriptive date "1857," which does not appear on the draft. I also believe that this draft was written soon after Kane's 21 March 1857 letter to Buchanan but probably before month-end and the excitement associated with the Drummond resignation.

The sands of executive action were shifting rapidly in Washington, although at this point many observers were at a loss to discern the direction of Buchanan's Utah policy.[30]

I Will Make Open War on This Administration: Judge Drummond as Loose Cannon

After leaving California Judge W. W. Drummond's first American landfall after crossing the Isthmus of Panama was New Orleans. There on 30 March 1857 he wrote a long letter of resignation, sent it to Attorney General Black on 2 April, and gave a copy as well as a long interview to a New Orleans newspaper. In flamboyant language that matched Brigham Young's own, Drummond recited nearly every accusation of Mormon disloyalty and perfidy that had accumulated during the prior ten years. To this litany he added graphic details of new violence and injustices. He called for Governor Young's removal as well as the appointment of a non-Mormon successor with a military escort. Drummond's portrayal of Utah was that of a territory out of control, with its federally sworn governor as the prime offender. Drummond called for appointment of a non-Mormon governor "supported with a *sufficient* military aid."

Like his own earlier letter from California, but unlike Judge Kinney's 20 March letter to Black, Drummond's resignation immediately became public. Its text was telegraphed to newspapers throughout the United States. Unaware of or indifferent to Drummond's seamy character, newspapers reprinted his sensational resignation as news accompanied by editorial calls for a military move on Utah. For the cabinet, unaware of the full background, there were now before it pointed calls for change in Utah by multiple territorial appointees. Soon a clamor for action from the press arose to rival the controversies over the Dred Scott decision and the fate of slavery in Kansas.

There have been few subsequent discussions of the Utah War that do not focus on Drummond's sensational letter of resignation. The text of that document is readily accessible, and so is not included here.[31] What has not been available is the series of supplemental, provocative letters that Drummond

[30] Buchanan's party "organ," the *Washington Union*, did little at this time to shed light on the president's thinking or decision making, although in early 1858 it attempted to do so. The *Union* remained essentially mute on Utah affairs until 10 June 1857, a silence that matched the president's own public uncommunicativeness.

[31] For Drummond to Black, 30 March 1857, see Hafen and Hafen, eds., *Mormon Resistance*, 363–66, and House Ex. Doc. 71, Serial 956, 212–14.

wrote during the spring of 1857. There are unmistakable signs that Drummond's principal motive in this campaign was not only to stoke an anti-Mormon vendetta, but to advance his hope that he might return to Salt Lake City as a militarily backed governor. In a 2 April letter to a friend, Drummond summarized his plans and expectations: "I have stirred the waters of the Saints and shall keep up the war in all time to come. . . . A new Government and Military aid will be sent to Utah now mark it, and Brigham will starve from under the appointments of the Federal Government . . . I may go to Utah as Governor if so look out for a merry time. I will take it with military aid."[32]

Three such Drummond letters to Attorney General Black and Senator Douglas illustrate the extent to which he pushed for action on Utah. In communicating with Douglas, Drummond expressed not only contempt for Black and the entire cabinet but also a threat to both the Buchanan administration and the Democratic Party. Here were early signs of the Democratic Party's self-destructive split into the Douglas and Buchanan wings that facilitated Abraham Lincoln's 1860 election.

DRUMMOND TO BLACK, 18 APRIL 1857, JEREMIAH S. BLACK PAPERS.

If you have any difficulty in obtaining a man to take the office of Gov. of Utah Territory under this (over due) Admin., you may give me the office which I will accept upon the condition that I can have the aid of a Military force sufficient to enable me to enforce obedience to the Laws. And here let me assure you that it is folly and madness for our Govt. to attempt to do anything with or amongst those Mormons by way of administering the Laws of our Common Country without the aid of the Federal Government backed with a Military force. Then I think that the Laws could be enforced but now I know they cannot. Were there a Military force placed in the Territory soon a goodly number of oppressed and dissatisfied Mormons would join the side of the Law which they *dare not do at* this time. A Temporizing Policy on the part of our Govt. with those Mormons will surely lead to unpleasant and I fear most disastrous consequences to the Laws, Officers and Govt. of this Country.

You are aware that I have been among the Mormons as Dist. Judge for the past two and over years and how I have had the means of becoming acquainted with many of the leading men of the Church and quite well do understand the future designs of that Church and people.[33] Unpleasant therefore as the Position would be to anyone, I am willing to take it under the condi-

[32] Drummond to D. J. Thompson, 2 April 1857, Moorman and Sessions, *Camp Floyd and the Mormons*, 12 and 284n23. This letter is described as filed in LDS Archives but cannot now be found.

[33] Utah's three federally appointed judges constituted not only the territory's supreme court but also served as judges of the U.S. district court there.

tions of this letter and I give it as my opinion that one who has had such experience among the Mormons would be more likely to do his duty to both Parties than one wholly unacquainted with their character.

You know that I have just got home and as yet have not gone into any business, and should you conclude to appoint me I will prepare at once for this arduous and most responsible task of Governing the Mormons.

Be pleased to confer with the President and your Bro. Cabinet Officers and inform me of your deliberations during the ensuing week. Address me at Chicago, Ills.

P.S. Confer with Douglas if he is in the City [Washington].

DRUMMOND TO DOUGLAS, 16 AND 22 MAY 1857, SPECIAL COLLECTIONS, UNIVERSITY COLLECTIONS, UNIVERSITY OF CHICAGO LIBRARY.

May 16, 1857

I have had an interview with Atty. Gen. Black today on Utah, and find him as ignorant as a man can be. Cannot for the life of him appreciate the power of the Mormons.[34] He says *they* will enforce the laws in Utah and intimates that 1,000 [military] men will do it.[35] I think I will make open war on this Admin. on this dread question and with the men who have been there since the Organic Act was passed. [I will] make it as hot as Judge Black and the President can well bear it[36] but before I begin I will have a talk with you in regard to the future for I assure you that now it looks as though the present Cabinet were determined to throw away our chances for success in [the election of] 1860 by a foolish procrastination. . . .[37]

May 22, 1857

I have had an interview with the President, Floyd, Cass, Black and Thompson on affairs of Utah and find them ignorant beyond comparison. Mr. Brayman is here & cordially agrees with me. So also does Judge Williams

[34] In view of Kane's subsequent perception that his correspondence had been handled indiscreetly in Washington, an interesting question is whether, during Drummond's May meetings with first Black and then the cabinet, they shared with him Kane's 21 March letter to Buchanan and any Kane–Black correspondence. For an account of Drummond's meeting with Black—supposedly derived from a journalist's subsequent conversation with the attorney general—see *New York Times*, 18 May 1857. The *Times* also speculated that Buchanan would appoint Drummond governor if Ben McCulloch declined.

[35] An expedition of this size would be equivalent to one fully manned regiment, a force comparable to that recommended by Judge Kinney to Black.

[36] In his 30 March resignation letter, Drummond's implied threat to the Democratic Party under Buchanan's leadership was a bit more subtle although unmistakable: "My reason, sir, for making this communication thus public is, that the Democratic party, with which I have always strictly acted, is the party now in power, and, therefore, is the party that *should now* be held responsible for the treasonable and disgraceful state of affairs that now exists in Utah Territory."

[37] The last half of this letter is a discussion of Illinois patronage appointments and Douglas's presidential prospects in the next (1860) national election, and by inference Douglas's 1858 bid for re-election to the Senate. I believe that pressure from Drummond on Utah was instrumental in shaping Douglas's hostility to the Mormons in his 12 June 1857 Springfield speech.

> of Iowa. But still they have the idea that less than one thousand men would be ample, sufficient to enforce the laws and also coerce the Mormons into fear. With me this idea is so ridiculous as to call down my pity instead of bitterness upon the Cabinet. But certain it is that nothing of value will be done. Hence it is to be a damnable question for us to meet for years to come and particularly in the next Presidential campaign. I see a desire to place some responsibilities on you because you are Chairman of Com[mittee] on T[erritorie]s. Such shuffling and dodging will and ought to ruin any man and Party on God's Earth. Notwithstanding the newspaper reports I most positively told the President that I was not an applicant for any office under *his* gift but would most assuredly & publically [*sic*] make the point on his Admin. as to the desperate state of affairs in Utah. I have read many letters rec'd here since my arrival all of which conclusively show that the most treasonable state of society now exists in Utah, and instead of sending men off at once to relieve and protect the men now in Utah they will dally along until it is too late to reach there this season. . . . I shall be at Home in a few days to compare notes.

In response to Drummond's public outbursts, Kane undertook his last effort on behalf of the Mormons during that spring. With the help of Mormon leaders in St. Louis (an itinerant George A. Smith) and New York (John Taylor and William I. Appleby), Kane sparked a bare-knuckle campaign to discredit Drummond patterned after Jedediah M. Grant's and his 1852 attack on Utah's runaway officials. The resulting information about Drummond's libertine behavior in Illinois, Washington, and Utah remains central to this day to the Mormon justification for Brigham Young's anti-federalism and much that flowed from it.

The anti-Drummond strategy—as John Taylor explained it to Brigham Young—was that, at Kane's request, he had "written to George A. Smith now in Saint Louis to write me a letter giving an account of United States officers acts. Br. Snow & Appleby will do the same. I shall then add some remarks & forward them to Col. Kane for the eye of Administration."[38] The result was Kane's 27 April letter to Attorney General Black in which he facilitated the attack on Drummond and again urged a delay in decision making on Utah. Unwittingly, it was an approach that kept the pot of Utah controversy roiling rather than putting "the Mormon problem" to rest.

KANE TO BLACK, 27 APRIL 1857, BLACK PAPERS.

Remarking to what extent the accusations in circulation against the Mormons are based upon Judge Drummond's widely circulated [30 March] letter

[38] Taylor to Young, 18 April 1857, LDS Archives.

> to yourself, I thought I wd. write the enclosed [letter] to Mr. John Taylor, a worthy and conscientious man in whose statements I place great confidence. From various papers sent me in reply I have selected two letters from gentlemen also personally known to me, W. I. Appleby the respectable clerk of the U.S. Courts [in Utah], who seems to have taken a personal interest in the reputation of the Territorial Judiciary, and George A. Smith, the oracle of the Deseret frontier and an admirable whole souled fellow, whom I wd. suspect of any act sooner than telling a lie.
>
> I am sorry that Mr. Bernhisel, the Utah delegate, has left these parts for the Salt Lake, and hope no harm will be done his constituents in his absence. I ask that they shall at least be informed upon what ground action unfavorable to their interests is based. Give them reasonable time to refute statements to their prejudice, and I will engage they will discover their accusers and prove them to be as unworthy of confidence as this man Drummond.[39]

Once Drummond became aware of Kane's intervention with the Buchanan administration, he, in turn, counterattacked publicly through the *New York Times* under the pen name "Verastus." It was a pointed, bruising thrust that referred to the Mormons' friend as "this young man Kane" and closed with a warning: "As soon as he lectures the President on his duties on Mormonism, I may refer to him again, but trust the necessity will not exist."[40] This public attack contributed to Kane's retirement from the field of Mormon-related controversies until the fall of 1857.

Mr. Bernhisel Has Left These Parts: Washington's Mormon Vacuum

During the fall of 1856 a weary, homesick Delegate Bernhisel had booked a seat on the mail coach scheduled to leave Independence, Missouri, for Salt Lake City in early May 1857, by which time he expected Congress would have adjourned. Brigham Young's subsequent letters of January 1857 encouraged

---

[39] Kane transmitted to Black a 25 April 1857 letter to him from John Taylor, which, in turn, transmitted lengthy letters to Taylor from Appleby and George A. Smith about Judge Drummond's conduct and credibility plus materials about the Gunnison massacre.

[40] "Verastus" to Editor, 24 May 1857, printed as "Col. Thomas L. Kane on Mormonism," *New York Daily Times*, 26 May 1857, 1/2. A number of Mormon contemporaries and subsequent historians asserted that "Verastus" was Judge Drummond, a not-unreasonable speculation in view of the contents of these letters as well as the little-noted and perhaps obsessive pattern in which Drummond had given most of his male and female children middle names beginning with the letter V, as with such offspring as America Virginia, Austria Vienna, Alwilda Verla, America Vespucia, Angelica Vandalia, Artemica Viola, and Arabella Victoria.

these travel plans. But during the intervening months a sea change occurred in governmental attitudes about Utah and "the Mormon problem." Shocked on 19 March 1857 over Interior Secretary Thompson's unanticipated reaction to Drummond's *Herald* article and the 6 January petitions from Utah's legislative assembly, Bernhisel made at this juncture what with hindsight appears to have been a strange, fateful decision. Instead of swinging into action to moderate the administration's negative reaction, Bernhisel grew lethargic if not fatalistic. He withdrew from the fray and pursued his original travel plans. Bernhisel left Washington to rest and visit relatives in Pennsylvania, wrote his discouraging 2 April report to Brigham Young, and took his seat on the May westbound mail stage from Independence.

Overlooking his own pending disengagement from Mormon affairs, Kane had observed to Attorney General Black on 27 April that he was "sorry" for Bernhisel's withdrawal from Washington and hoped that "no harm will be done his constituents in his absence." In July 1858 Kane referred retrospectively to Bernhisel's "timidity" and described him as "lying perdu" in Pennsylvania. Perhaps sensing his vulnerability to criticism, Bernhisel later lamented Kane's own simultaneous withdrawal.[41]

In Independence Bernhisel boarded the westbound coach for Utah with Mormon architect Truman O. Angell, then returning from England. At Fort Leavenworth, Apostle George A. Smith joined them on what was for him the last leg of a year-long, ten-thousand-mile journey that had begun with the failed attempt to deliver to Congress the 1856 Deseret statehood petition. He had spent March and April 1857 shuttling between church branches along the Atlantic Coast, as well as throughout the South and Midwest. That Smith had been so engaged, rather than in exerting the influence of a Mormon apostle in Washington, compounded the lobbying vacuum created by the unrelated but coincident withdrawals of Bernhisel and Kane. At this point Brigham Young was also incommunicado on his five-week trek to Oregon Territory.

---

[41] In 1859 James C. Van Dyke informed Kane that Bernhisel "expressed great regret that you had not thought of going out [to Utah] at an earlier date; and said he had no doubt that had you gone there during the latter part of the summer and given them assurances of the prosecution of offenders and of the pardon from the President of such persons as they might desire, his belief was that you could have exerted a powerful influence in persuading his people to return to their allegiance to the U.S." Van Dyke to Kane, 28 March 1859, Kane Collection, Pennsylvania State Archives.

Well Informed on All Subjects: Buchanan Hears from Advisors and Strangers

With first the scramble for patronage and then the notoriety following Drummond's resignation, the administration's mail swelled during March–May with a stream of gratuitous advice about "the Mormon problem." Much of this material advocated a military move on Utah or inquired about anticipated openings in the territory's federally appointed offices, including Brigham Young's. Secretary Floyd received military advice about the Mormon threat from an aging former army officer turned St. Louis lawyer.[42] A committee of citizens in Naperville, Illinois, sent the president their suggestions about the governorship, to which he replied in lawyerly fashion, "The decision in regard to the appointment of a Governor for Utah was delayed mainly *because there is no existing vacancy,* Young still continuing Governor under the terms of the law creating his office. It was postponed *for the present* for further considerations; & not at all because of the opposition of any person to the appointment of M^r^. Eccles."[43] An anonymous citizen from Long Island mailed Buchanan a copy of Judge Drummond's grisly public letter of 27 April to the widow Gunnison describing her husband's 1853 dismemberment in Utah.[44]

Yet for all of the clatter from strangers—rational and otherwise—there were also comments from Buchanan's friends, including those from his home state. Two of Buchanan's closest political advisors in Philadelphia, both of them attorneys, wrote to the president on 27 April: Robert Tyler, son of former president John Tyler; and James C. Van Dyke, grandson-in-law of a former Pennsylvania governor and a man whom Buchanan had installed as U.S. attorney for the eastern district of Pennsylvania. The coincidence of timing and location raises the question of whether these men had coordinated their advice to Buchanan about Utah. The likelihood is that they had not done so, for Tyler and Van Dyke were often rivals for influence with Buchanan. One of the leading historians of Buchanan's controversial Kansas policy described the two advisers thusly: "Mr. J. C. Van Dyke of Philadelphia was

---

[42] John J. Schuler to Floyd, March/April 1857, photostatic copy in M. Hamlin Cannon Papers.

[43] Buchanan to Naperville, Ill., Committee, 14 March 1857, Naperville Heritage Society, photocopy at Utah State Historical Society. This is virtually the only available Buchanan letter touching on Utah affairs. "Eccles" was probably a reference to Delana Eckels of Indiana, who was appointed during the summer of 1857 to be chief justice of Utah's supreme court, replacing the absent Kinney.

[44] A copy of this unsigned letter is in the James Buchanan Papers, Historical Society of Pennsylvania.

also very intimate with both Mr. Tyler and the President. The two former made frequent visits to the White House; and these men doubtless exercised considerable influence upon Buchanan."[45] Buchanan himself argued that Tyler was virtually without peer among those who had worked "to elevate me to my present position and . . . I am personally attached to him very warmly."[46]

In his letter Robert Tyler proposed to Buchanan "an Anti-Mormon Crusade" so that the nation might "forget Kansas." Today such advice seems fantastic in terms of the gravity and irresponsibility of such a notion, but nineteenth-century politics were awash with such schemes or at least speculation about them. Notwithstanding Tyler's longstanding influence with Buchanan, there is no record that the president responded to this suggestion or based his direction concerning Utah on the notion of such a diversion. Nonetheless, absent an understanding of the other material presented to the cabinet, some conspiracist-historians have clung to Robert Tyler's type of advice as a simple means of explaining the Utah Expedition's origins.[47]

What might have prompted Tyler's provocative advice? Conceivably the catalyst was a long editorial that appeared two days earlier in Horace Greeley's influential *New-York Tribune*, which criticized the Democratic Party's handling of the thorny dilemmas in both Kansas and Utah. After rehashing at length Representative Morrill's 23 February remarks about Utah, Greeley closed with a pointed observation reminiscent of the Republican Party's "twin relics" platform plank: "There is a curious analogy in the conduct of the General Government toward the Mormons in Utah and toward the Border Ruffians in Kansas. It would be hard to say to which of the two patriarchal institutions, Polygamy or Slavery, the late President [Pierce] and his Cabinet have most submissively knuckled."[48]

By 1890 conspiracy theories about Buchanan's motives had flourished to

---

[45] Harmon, "President James Buchanan's Betrayal of Governor Robert J. Walker of Kansas," 86.

[46] Buchanan to Joseph B. Baker, 1 July and 9 September 1857, quoted in Stampp, *America in 1857*, 82.

[47] For the role of such a conspiracy theory in the Utah War's historiography, see MacKinnon, "125 Years of Conspiracy Theories," 92–94. In early 1858 President Buchanan's own "organ" promoted a notion that was the direct opposite of Tyler's, that is to say that Brigham Young and the anti-slavery faction in Kansas were in league to keep the army in that territory rather than to send it to Utah. See "The Mormons in Kansas," *Washington Union*, 20 January 1858, 2/3. For contextual analysis, see speculation that President William Jefferson Clinton used military strikes against Osama bin Laden and Iraq to divert public attention from the Monica Lewinski scandal, in Hendrickson, "Clinton's Military Strikes in 1998: Diversionary Uses of Force?" 309–32.

[48] Editorial, *New-York Daily Tribune*, 25 April 1857, 6/5.

an extent that in his study of the Utah War 1st Lt. William R. Hamilton asserted without documentary support that "There is no doubt that the troubles in Utah were made an excuse whereby the administration hoped to turn the eyes of the people from the then greater and more absorbing question of slavery as related to the Kansas-Nebraska dilemma, and at the same time turn to the credit of the administration the obliteration of an eyesore of the nation [Mormonism] of forty years' growth."[49]

TYLER TO BUCHANAN, 27 APRIL 1857,
JAMES BUCHANAN PAPERS, HISTORICAL SOCIETY OF PENNSYLVANIA.

> The public mind is becoming greatly excited on the subject of *Mormonism.* The Popular Idea is rapidly maturing that Mormonism (already felt slightly in our large Northern cities) should be put down and utterly extirpated.
>
> *I believe that we can supercede the Negro-Mania with the almost universal excitements of an Anti-Mormon Crusade.* Certainly it is a subject which concerns *all* the Religious Bodies & reaches every man's fireside with a peculiar interest. Should you, with your accustomed grip, seize this question with a strong fearless & resolute hand, the Country I am sure will rally to you with an earnest enthusiasm & the pipings of Abolitionism will hardly be heard amidst the thunders of the storm we shall raise. Were I President I would put down & cast out this hideous imposture, equally at War with Conscience, Reason & Philosophy, at all hazards. I would take the ground that the case was anomalous & altogether exceptional—without the limits of ordinary Constitutional treatment—& that the principles of the Democratic Party in regard to Territories consequently had no application. The eyes & hearts of the Nation may be made to find so much interest in Utah as to forget Kansas.[50]

Interestingly, a year before Tyler made this suggestion to Buchanan, the British minister to Washington had accused President Pierce's attorney general, Caleb Cushing, and the U.S. attorney in Philadelphia, James C. Van Dyke (a Buchanan protégé), of fomenting Anglophobia, if not war fever, in order to distract the American public from agitation over the slavery issue in Kansas. In Cushing's case, the minister reported to London that he "would if he could push things somewhat further and get the United States into a foreign war;

[49] Hamilton, "History of the Mormon Rebellion of 1856–57" (July 1890), 14.

[50] For the text see also Auchampaugh, *Robert Tyler*, 180–81; and Williams, "President Buchanan Receives a Proposal for an Anti-Mormon Crusade, 1857," 103–105. Auchampaugh comments on Tyler's correspondence thusly: "Men cannot live like salamanders in devouring flame without occasionally spitting fire, which the politicians North and South all did with rare exception. Some of the letters of Robert Tyler appear rather unnecessarily severe in the light of these [1934] quiet days." Williams's judgment was: "The fact that it could be seriously advanced by a son of a former president to the incumbent President in and of itself, makes it a significant document in the political history of Mormonism in America."

this being the great cure for the black disease which is now tearing at the vitals of the Union." James Buchanan would have been acutely aware of British perceptions of such maneuvering by Cushing and Van Dyke for a variety of reasons, not the least of which was his 1856 role as the U.S. ambassador to the Court of St. James. Whether Tyler's 1857 recommendation for a similar diversionary gambit was stimulated by his awareness of the earlier controversy involving his fellow Democrat and Philadelphian, Van Dyke, remains an intriguing but unexamined possibility.[51]

James C. Van Dyke's letter to Buchanan was of a vastly different character than Tyler's. Van Dyke limited his advice to the recommendation that Buchanan grant an interview to John M. Hockaday, Utah's U.S. attorney and Magraw's former mail partner, whom he had just seen. Nearly a month before John Hockaday swung by Philadelphia to consult with Van Dyke, his brother Isaac had visited Washington to complain about the still-festering issue of the Mormon seizure of the Hockadays' Salt Lake City tannery, to which Isaac had presumably alluded in his earlier letter to President Pierce. As William I. Appleby reported it to Governor Young, "Hockaday is at Washington, and he feels quite sore about it."[52]

Van Dyke to Buchanan, 27 April 1857, James Buchanan Papers, Historical Society of Pennsylvania.

> I have just closed an interview of several hours with John M. Hockaday Esqr. and without his knowledge have concluded to write you that in my opinion you should improve the first possible opportunity to listen to the very many interesting statements which he can make in relation to the Territory of Utah and Govr Young. He is well informed on all subjects relating to that curious people, and has a most intimate knowledge of the many conflicting interests which disturb the nation at Salt Lake and which might easily be turned to an advantage to our Government.
>
> Mr H. tells me he will visit Washington tomorrow. I have told him he must not fail to call to see you. I expect he will do so.[53]

---

[51] Belohlavek, *Broken Glass: Caleb Cushing and the Shattering of the Union*, 268–70.

[52] Appleby to Young, 1 April 1857, LDS Archives. Appleby does not indicate to which Hockaday brother he refers, but I infer that the Washington visitor in late March was Isaac because of the travel conditions that would have confronted John in leaving Utah during the winter.

[53] It is highly likely that John M. Hockaday did visit Buchanan. On 6 June 1857 Hockaday dispensed with Van Dyke as an intermediary and wrote directly to the president to urge him to meet with his fellow federal appointees from Utah—then nearing Washington—before replacing U.S. Marshal Peter K. Dotson. Buchanan accepted this advice and retained Dotson in his position. Hockaday to Buchanan, 6 June 1857, Office of the Attorney Gen., Correspondence from the President, Letters Received (RG 60), National Archives.

Orders Having Been Dispatched in Haste: Planning for Military Intervention

Aside from the political issue of replacing Brigham Young, determining precisely when the Buchanan administration decided upon an expeditionary force to escort a new governor and of what size is difficult because of the incomplete record. Among the conflicting advice before the cabinet as Buchanan feverishly sought someone willing to take Utah's governorship was the recommendation of Kinney and Burr for a relatively small force and Drummond's aggressive demand for a far larger expedition. Keying to the rising volume of newspaper coverage of Mormon affairs but without citing firm sources, Norman F. Furniss argued in 1960 that a cabinet meeting on or about 20 May 1857 was decisive.[54] Press speculation about a military move against Utah had begun actively as early as April 1857 with the controversy over Drummond's resignation and the abrupt, unexplained reassignment of Brevet Brig. Gen. William S. Harney from the campaign against Florida's Seminoles to Fort Leavenworth, Kansas Territory.

At that post as early as 15 April, a new lieutenant in Col. E. V. Sumner's First Cavalry reported to his father in New Jersey Harney's transfer together with the garrison's speculation about both a new governor and military expedition for Utah.

2d Lt. George Dashiell Bayard to Samuel J. Bayard, 15 April 1857, *Life of George Dashiell Bayard,* 114–17.

> You will, no doubt before you receive this, have seen in the papers the orders we have just received from headquarters. It has stirred us up here, and all rejoice in the prospect of an active campaign on the Plains for the ensuing summer. I will state the substance of the orders lest you may not have noticed them particularly. . . .
>
> General Harney is to leave Florida and take command at Fort Leavenworth. . . .
>
> Pack-mules not to exceed five hundred, are to be procured for the Quartermaster's Department, and we are to go [to the field] *"fully equipped and prepared for distant service."* That sounds very much like Utah.

[54] Furniss, *The Mormon Conflict,* 63. Furniss appears to have relied heavily on newspaper speculation in focusing on this date. Indicative of the extent to which such speculation was sometimes wrong about confidential decision making is the Washington *National Intelligencer*'s 26 May 1857 assurance that "the reports that have appeared in some of the public journals, purporting to have been telegraphed from Washington, to the effect that a large body of troops—stated at two thousand—have been ordered to Utah, seem to have no foundation in fact."

> This is far better than staying in the [Kansas] Territory all summer, subject to the orders of Governor Walker. I presume we will not return here before late in the fall, if then.
>
> Should we go to Utah, we will not return for a year or more. There is but one consolation we should have in going to Utah; it would cause some resignations in our regiment and make promotion more rapid. . . .
>
> Talking about going to Utah, Col. Sumner and most of the officers here think that we will go; but I will not believe it until I see the order for the march.
>
> That troops will be sent there with the new Governor I have no doubt, but I think they will send infantry and not cavalry. If we were to go there, it would kill all our horses, and we would have to foot it until we got back to a civilized region.
>
> The troops which do go there will have to stay there for two or more years.

Probably out of ignorance Harney himself described the reassignment cryptically as "some important service" and an "important duty," while Capt. Randolph B. Marcy—one of the officers Harney left behind in Florida—confided to a Chicago friend, "General Harney has been ordered to Ft. Laramie, to await instructions from the H.Q. of the Army. The first intimation he had of it was a printed order. He does not know what is to be done, and thinks they have formed various conjunctions as to the object of this move, some thinking that a campaign against the Mormons is on foot and others that it is an expedition against the Indians. Time will tell the story."[55]

In mid-April William I. Appleby, a Mormon leader in New York, also speculated on these matters:

> I wrote you a few days since in relation to the prevailing sentiments, that appears to pervade the people in general, in relation to Utah & the Mormons.[56] And being desirous according to promise to keep you advised of what is going on, take up my pen again. A few days since Gen. Scott issued his orders ~~a few days sin~~ directing Gen. Harney to leave Florida where he is at present and move to Fort Leavenworth, and several other officers, with their companies some to proceed to Fort Kearney, others to Fort Laramie, while others were to move along the Platte River, with mules horses &c their to receive their instructions, the whole amounting to some 2500 men. It is the belief of some,

[55] Harney to Col. Samuel Cooper, 23 April 1857, Records of Adjt. Gen.'s Office, Letters Received (RG 94), National Archives; Marcy to George B. McClellan, 24 April 1857, McClellan Papers, Library of Congress.

[56] From St. Louis Apostle George A. Smith described these "prevailing sentiments" pungently: "All Hell appears to be wide awake against us, the Press is doing its wickedness, Drummond is one of the most popular men of the Nation at present." Smith to Young, 15 April 1857, LDS Archives.

> [Editor James Gordon] Bennett of the Herald in particular that it is the intention of the Government to send them to Utah and appoint a Governor to follow. The report of the burning of the Records & Laws of the United States, belonging to the Supreme Court, appears to have caused the excitement, together with Drummonds letters—some of which I enclose, also a letter from some one, that appeared in yesterday's Herald, who offers to go to Utah in the capacity of a Governor, his name I cannot learn.[57]

The fact is that Harney's reassignment was almost certainly a function not of a move on Utah, but rather on the administration's higher priority need for the regular army to maintain order in Kansas. Robert J. Walker had made it clear in late March that he would not accept Buchanan's proffer of Kansas's governorship unless Harney and his Second Dragoons were assigned to Kansas to support him. The president agreed to Walker's demand.

Notwithstanding speculation by Lieutenant Bayard and *Mormon* assistant editor Appleby, the administration took the official position that no decisions had yet been made on Utah. Buchanan had so informed the Naperville committee on 14 March. On 15 April Secretary of the Interior Thompson replied to a Louisville attorney seeking gubernatorial appointment: "While I shall keep you in mind; yet owing to the great difficulties in Utah, I can give you no idea of what will be done in that Territory."[58]

But coincident with the obvious but unannounced political planning for a gubernatorial succession in Utah, the administration must have given thought as well to whether and what type of military support for a new governor would be required. Judges Kinney and Drummond had explicitly advocated such support privately and publicly on 20 and 30 March, respectively. It is inconceivable that the potential Utah nominees then being approached by Buchanan did not press this military issue, as had Walker vis à vis the Kansas assignment. Consequently General Scott spent the spring shuttling between New York and Washington.

By the last week of May 1857—even with the identity of Brigham Young's successor still undetermined—there had been enough dialogue between Scott and the War Department for thinking to have gelled as to the approximate size of an expeditionary force and which regiments might be involved. Accurate or not, Judge Drummond came away from several meetings with cabi-

---

[57] Appleby to Young, 13 April 1857, LDS Archives.

[58] Thompson to Q. C. Grasty, 15 April 1857, Letter Book of Jacob Thompson, 1857–60, Confederate Records (RG 109), National Archives.

net officers during the third week of May angrily convinced that the administration would commit no more than one thousand troops to Utah.

At this point Scott, too, grew alarmed, probably because he also viewed the size of the contemplated expedition as inadequate and the timing for its launch perilously late. On 26 May—after having consulted his old friend, former general James Shields—Scott wrote a remarkable memorandum in New York to Floyd arguing that a campaign in Utah would be ill fated unless postponed until the spring of 1858. Although by 27 May Scott had traveled to Washington and probably hand delivered this paper to the War Department, Floyd never acknowledged receiving it. In 1864, writing in the third person and with a great deal of conspiracy-oriented hindsight, Scott commented:

> The expedition set on foot by Mr. Secretary Floyd, in 1857, against the Mormons and Indians about Salt Lake was, beyond a doubt, to give occasion for large contracts and expenditures, that is, to open a wide field for frauds and peculation. This purpose was not comprehended nor scarcely suspected in, perhaps, a year; but, observing the desperate characters who frequented the Secretary, some of whom had desks near him, suspicion was at length excited. Scott protested against the expedition on the general ground of inexpediency, and specially because the season was too late for the troops to reach their destination in comfort or even in safety. Particular facts, observed by different officers, if united, would prove the imputation.[59]

Scott's assertion, in turn, prompted Buchanan to make his only published comments about Scott–Floyd communications and the decision to create the Utah Expedition. In his 1868 memoirs Buchanan wrote:

> Nearly eight years after these events had passed into history, Mr. Buchanan was no little surprised to discover that General Scott, in his autobiography, published in 1864, asserts that he had protested against the Utah expedition, and that it was set on foot by Secretary Floyd, "to open a wide field for frauds and peculation." He does not even intimate that the expedition had been ordered by the President. The censure is cast upon Floyd, and upon Floyd alone. The President had, as a matter of course, left the military details of the movement to the Secretary of War and the Commanding General of the Army. From a reference to the instructions from the General to General Harney, the President could not have inferred the existence of any such protest. On the contrary, General Scott explicitly states the fact that they had been "prepared in concert with the War Department, and sanctioned by its authority wherever

[59] Scott, *Memoirs,* 2:604.

> required." . . . And the General, as we have already seen, expresses the belief that the honor and interest of the United States were deeply involved in the result. Most certainly Mr. Buchanan, until he read the autobiography, never learned that General Scott had protested against the Utah expedition.[60]

Buchanan's assertion that he had not seen Scott's important Utah memorandum brings to mind his earlier denial about receipt of Thomas L. Kane's 21 March 1857 letter on the Mormons' behalf.[61]

"Garrison for Salt-Lake-City," Scott to Floyd, 26 May 1857, Headquarters of the Army, Letters Sent (RG 108), National Archives.

> It is proposed to send a military force to that city sufficient to enforce obedience to the civil magistry [*sic*] of the Territory, or to the laws of the United States.
>
> The population of Utah valley is entirely Mormon, or fanatics—that is, religiously hostile to the morals, the authority & laws of the U. States.
>
> As these have been steadily resisted, so will, it is thought, be resisted any inadequate military force that may be sent to coerce obedience.
>
> The population to be coerced may be assumed to be about 40,000 souls.
>
> This estimate would give quite 8,000 males (between 16 & 65) capable of bearing arms. We will, however, take the number at the low figure of 7,000, without including Indian allies.
>
> The military organization & discipline of the Mormons may be set down as indifferent; but we must remember that *religious* fanaticism has *often* proved itself to be an over-match for military discipline.
>
> No divisions of interest or sentiment is known to exist among the Mormons in respect to obedience to their Church or to the laws of the U. States. They are understood to be, *to a man*, on the side of the former & the two are utterly repugnant antagonistic.
>
> The only hope of a schism rests on the women. They may create a party among the *American* men in favour of Christianity, law & order.
>
> But for this hope it would not be safe to propose a garrison for the Mormon Capital, of less than 4,000 troops—; but the President may, it is thought, risk a regiment of Horse, two regiments of Infantry and a company of Artillery, with a field battery—making rather less than 2,500 effective men.

---

[60] Buchanan, *Mr. Buchanan's Administration*, 238–39. It is likely that the hypersensitive comments by both Scott and Buchanan about Utah were related to a public dispute between the two men early in the Civil War on a different subject—Scott's assertion that during the fall of 1860 he had written a memo to warn Buchanan of the vulnerability of federal coastal forts in the event of southern secession.

[61] The only previous publication of this text is in Cannon, "Winfield Scott and the Utah Expedition," 209–11.

This force it would be necessary to keep well massed both in approaching, & after arriving at, the Capital—the occupancy of which would necessarily control the entire Territory.

No detachments from that mass should be risked except when indispensable for gathering in necessaries of life & with a smaller garrison no detachment would be made strong enough to operate at a distance of only a few miles; for the garrison, might, possibly, be obliged to consider itself as besieged for six or twelve months after its arrival.

It is certain that if the occupation be attempted with an inadequate force, &, consequently, be cut off or destroyed, the U. States, after suffering the deep mortification, would be obliged to employ double the force that would, originally, have been necessary. This disgrace ought not to be risked by too great a parsimony in the means first employed.

But can we get together the minimum force (estimated above) & march it to Utah this season?

Remember also, that the little army must arrive out in time to establish itself in an entrenched camp (of huts or tents) before the setting in of the heavy frosts & snows of that region.

Wood for huts & even for fuel, is distant from Salt Lake City & the sun is too feeble to bake *adobes* (sun dried bricks) after the month of October.

As grazing cannot be relied upon after an early day in November, that fact alone fixes the time for arriving out, & as the distance (say) from Fort Leavenworth cannot be less than 1150 miles, we must allow some 90 days for the march. This shows that the movement, from Leavenworth, ought not to be delayed beyond the middle of July.

Can we bring the required force to that point of departure in time this season? It is feared not.

Six companies of the 2d. Dragoons (Gen[l] Harney's regiment) are now in reserve at Fort Leavenworth (under Lieutenant Colonel Cooke) awaiting the call of Governor Walker. The other 4 companies of this regiment are divided between Forts Randall and Kearny and less than half their complement in men & horses. These 4 companies cannot be brought into line with the six, on the route to Utah, & the whole regiment filled up with effective recruits & horses before, probably, the middle of September.

The first Cavalry (Col. Sumner's regiment) is out of position—being (six companies under the Colonel) in march against the Cheyennes & their allies, & the other four with Lieut. Colonel Johnson [Joseph E. Johnston] moving along the southern boundary of Kansas. This regiment, therefore, cannot be disposable for any new service the present season.

The 10th Infantry, now on the Upper Mississippi & the Minnesota, may be replaced in part (at Fort Ridgely) by 4 companies of the 2d. Infantry, & the 10th be brought, after the delay of waiting to be relieved, to Leavenworth, by the middle of July; but cannot march alone, nor with only Captain Phelp's [*sic*] company of artillery (already at that fort) upon the Salt Lake Valley.

There are, however, nine companies of the 2d. Artillery stationed—two at Boston, two at N. York, two on the Upper Lakes, one at Baltimore & three at Fort Monroe—besides about seven companies of the other three artillery regiments not immediately employed against Indians; but all these companies, if full, would not be sufficient with the 10th Infantry & Captain Phelps' company to make up the Salt Lake expedition—besides the extreme injury to the administration & discipline of troops to intermix the companies of different regiments.

It may further be observed that until the late Indian marauders upon the Minnesota border settlements, shall be punished, to give up the pursuit of them would, probably, cause an early repetition of the same outrages. Hence, Gen[l] Shields, a most excellent judge in such cases, urges that a squadron of horse should be placed in pursuit in addition to the present Infantry companies employed in that direction.

For the foregoing reasons—the insufficiency of available troops & the want of time—the conclusion seems to be forced upon us that we cannot make an orderly or safe movement upon the Utah Valley, before the beginning of the summer of 1858.

All which is respectfully submitted to the Secretary of War.

Stunning as the general in chief's memorandum was, even more so was the fact that only two days after he wrote it, Scott did an about-face. Without explaining the reasons behind this reversal except to use the word "haste," Scott issued a circular notifying the bureau chiefs that there was to be a Utah Expedition and tasked them with its support.

It was to be a force of twenty-five hundred troops drawn from the Fifth and Tenth Infantry, Second Dragoons, Phelps's light battery "B" of the Fourth Artillery, and a heavy siege battery from the Ordnance Department. Here was an expedition closer in size to the diversionary anti-Mormon "crusade" advocated by Robert Tyler and Drummond than to the single-regiment force recommended by Judge Kinney or the "small military force" suggested by Surveyor General Burr. Obviously the die was cast, and Scott could do nothing to prevent the decision to move on Utah during 1857. His circular became public immediately.[62] Significantly, there was no companion notification to Brigham Young.

[62] Because this document has been published frequently, it is not reprinted here. It is most readily found in Hafen and Hafen, eds., *Mormon Resistance*, 27–29, and House Ex. Doc. 71, Serial 956, 4–5.

What happened between 26 and 28 May in General Scott's world—a period during which he moved between New York and Washington—remains an intriguing mystery. But the Utah Expedition—at least on paper—had moved from the status of speculation to reality.[63] The communications gaps involved—compounding those discussed in other chapters—were emblematic of conflict, indifference, and ineffectiveness atop the U.S. Army. An inexperienced, ill, but confident Floyd intended to run military affairs during the Buchanan administration unaided. General Scott lacked the interpersonal skills to bridge the polite but yawning chasm dividing him and Floyd. President Buchanan was both temperamentally and experientially ill-equipped to understand the consequences of these shortfalls in competence and communications. These were harbingers of disaster for the way in which the Utah Expedition was to be organized and led.

The Mormon Imbroglio in Its True Light: Decisions Explained Retrospectively

As indicated above, there is no direct insider account of how Buchanan's cabinet decided to intervene politically and militarily in Utah during the late winter and spring of 1857. However there is a description of the administration's thinking written by a source close to Buchanan—the editor of the *Washington Union,* the president's Democratic Party voice in the capital. On 16 February 1858 the *Union* published a unique description of the Utah decision from Buchanan's perspective of less than a year earlier—one that differed somewhat from both the substance and tone of Buchanan's fragmented, formal explanation to Congress on 8 December 1857. If not the narrative of an insider, this unexploited piece was the next best thing. As a *Union* editorial, "Retrospect of the Utah Question" was literally an exposition of what would be called today the "party line," complete with a disingenuously fabricated justification for the Utah Expedition as a means to protect settlers from a fictive Indian menace.

[63] The question arises as to whether Scott argued forcefully or effectively enough for the advice contained in his 26 May Utah memorandum. Four years later, after advising President Lincoln against committing the army to what became the disastrous battle of First Bull Run, Scott attempted to blame Lincoln for the decision by disingenuously telling two Illinois congressmen: "I am the greatest coward in America. I will prove it; I have fought this battle, sir, against my judgment; I think the President of the United States ought to remove me to-day for doing it, I did all in my power to make the Army efficient. I deserve removal because I did not stand up, when my army was not in condition for fighting, and resist it to the last." Donald, *Lincoln,* 308.

"Retrospect of the Utah Question," *Washington Union*, 16 February 1858, 2/5–6.

A very brief retrospect of the Mormon imbroglio will put that somewhat-misunderstood question in its true light. It will be distinctly remembered by the whole population of the United States that about a year ago the judges of the federal courts in Utah were driven out of the Territory by the Mormons, the courts of justice closed, and their records burned; that the federal authorities of the United States, executive and judicial, were banished from the Territory, contemptuously spurned and set at naught.

Immediately upon the inauguration of Mr. Buchanan, he found himself called upon to see that "the laws of the United States were faithfully executed," and to this end his oath compelled him to send civil officers to Salt Lake to take the places of those who had been already expelled by the Mormons. The discontented state of feeling which notoriously pervaded the Indian tribes of that vast region also rendered it imperative upon the administration to send into the military Department of Utah a strong escort. The flagrant insubordination of the Mormons rendered the sending of troops necessary as a *posse* to sustain the authority of the executive and judicial officers of the federal government sent out by Mr. Buchanan, and the discontent of the Indians also required the overawing presence of a strong military force in that military Department. The force which was accordingly sent forward were sent strictly with reference to these two considerations, and not in the character of an invading force against a hostile country.

It had never entered the head of any man outside of the Mormon church that there was even the remote possibility of a collision between the United States troops and the people of this United States Territory. Such an act of madness and treason as should put so large a number of people in open rebellion against the government of their own country was not expected of the Mormons even by those who knew them best. . . .

If the design and intention had been to send forward the army against Utah as an army of invasion against a hostile foreign power, a declaration of war from Congress would have been awaited, and a force despatched of very different proportions and appointments from that which was sent by the administration. As it was, an inconsiderable body of troops were sent out, as to a military department under the jurisdiction of our own government, and in the occupation of our own people. It was sent not for purposes of war, but in obedience to the duty which rested upon the President to see the laws of Congress faithfully executed in our own territory, and the citizens of our country protected from the tomahawk and rifle of the savage.

We Can Place No Reliance upon the President: Kane Turns Fatalistic

Probably unaware of the specific preparations underway at the War Department and distracted by his own months-long move to the mountains of Pennsylvania, Thomas L. Kane sent Brigham Young what amounted to a brief farewell note on the eve of the Utah War. He had done his best. Discouraged by the indifference of an administration with which he anticipated influence and beset by his own burdens, Kane turned inward—at least for awhile.

Kane to Young, 21 May 1857, Thomas L. Kane Papers, Beinecke Library.

I have received another letter from you[64] and ought not to postpone some answer any longer, though I am still without good news to communicate. We can place no reliance upon the President: he succumbs in more respects than one to outside pressure. You can see from the papers how clamorous it is for interference with Utah affairs. Now Mr. Buchanan has not heart enough to save his friends from being thrown over to stop the mouths of a pack of Yankee editors.

For some time past, my efforts have been almost entirely to gain delay. If we can get through the Summer without a Gubernatorial appointment, I shall be in hopes again. But [Ben] McCullo[c]h was really offered the place wch. he has recently refused, and there are a dozen patriots ready to accept of it.

I thank you for writing to me. I am growing old enough to prize the friends whom Time has left me. Jedediah Grant—I had rough talks with him over Deseret matters; and have to think with bitterness that I parted from him without saying in so many words that in my soul I did him justice. Noble fellow; I could give years of my life to have written him before he died one natural and outspoken brother's letter.[65]—Yet this writing, my friend Young;—does it keep down the miles of waste which seem to be growing up between us every year? I wish I had your hand to grasp. I write myself, and it seems but form

Yours faithfully always

---

[64] This would have been Young to Kane, 31 January 1857, LDS Archives.

[65] The late Jedediah M. Grant—as well as the recent death of his own brother Elisha—were much on Kane's mind that spring. On 1 April 1857 W. I. Appleby reported to Brigham Young that in his meeting with Kane, "He spoke feelingly in relation to Br Grants decease, and remarked 'I did not know I loved him so well.'" Appleby to Young, 1 April 1857, LDS Archives. The reference to "rough talks" may be to their summer 1852 meeting about the polygamy announcement.

Why Have You Barked with the Dogs?: Senator Douglas's Betrayal

As General Scott began organizing the Utah Expedition and Kane grappled with personal problems, Sen. Stephen A. Douglas considered his political future—a run for the Senate in 1858 and beyond that the possibility of the White House. In May he returned to Illinois and resolved to turn from a cautious friend of the Mormons to a severe, high-profile critic. The vehicle for this reversal was a 12 June 1857 speech in Springfield that has been interpreted as one of the great acts of villainy in the long history of Mormon persecution. Whether Douglas spoke in response to Judge Drummond's private letters of a few weeks earlier or out of an attempt to rescue his doctrine of popular sovereignty from its dangerous association with the protection of Mormon polygamy, his speech was a landmark. It catapulted him into a position in the Mormon bestiary virtually unrivaled to this day, and did so with one sensational sentence: "When the authentic evidence shall arrive, if it shall establish the facts [about Utah] which are believed to exist, it will become the duty of Congress to apply the knife and cut out this loathsome, disgusting ulcer."[66] The depth of Brigham Young's reaction was such that, even as Douglas lay dying four years later, Young pelted him with a letter asking, "Why have you barked with the dogs, except to prove that you were a dog with them?"[67]

Douglas's Springfield speech is worth noting for at least two reasons. First, his comments reflected the extent to which national concern with "the Mormon problem" had escalated from a secondary to a burning issue during the opening months of the Buchanan administration. Second, Douglas's remarks galvanized into action one member of the audience who aspired to win his Senate seat in the election of 1858—Springfield attorney Abraham Lincoln. Two weeks later Lincoln stimulated an invitation to rebut Douglas and did so with carefully crafted comments in the same chamber. Although not yet

[66] Douglas, "Kansas, Utah, and the Dred Scott Decision," Springfield, Illinois, 12 June 1857, 11–15. Douglas spoke from notes in somewhat impromptu fashion and then took several weeks to organize and edit this material for publication in pamphlet form. For a description of this speech and its reception, see Johannsen, *Stephen A. Douglas*, 566–75. For the enraged Mormon rebuttal to Douglas's speech, see "Comments Upon the Remarks of Hon. Stephen Arnold Douglas," *Deseret News*, 2 September 1857, 204–207.

[67] MacKinnon, "'Like Splitting a Man Up His Backbone,'" 108, 114–15.

recognized as such, these two Utah-related talks were precursor to the nine Lincoln-Douglas debates that began in Illinois twelve months later.[68]

For whatever his reasons, President Buchanan was changing the government in Utah and was intervening there with an unprecedented exercise of force. He did so with Congress absent, unconsulted, and uninvolved. Fifty years later President Theodore Roosevelt would take similar action in Cuba following a governmental collapse in that young republic. When criticized for so acting without consulting Congress, Roosevelt defended himself vigorously, but in the process overlooked Buchanan's Utah decision, by then forgotten. Accordingly Roosevelt focused not on what Buchanan believed he faced with the Mormons in 1857—a year before his birth—but only on his predecessor's 1861 inaction when confronted by Southern secession. Ironically, then, Roosevelt argued in 1906, "I am sure you will agree with me that it would not have been wise to summon Congress to consider the situation in Cuba, which was changing from week to week and almost from day to day. . . . You, my dear Senator, are the last man to advocate my playing a part like President Buchanan or failing to take the responsibility that the President must take if he is fit for his position."[69]

[68] For Abraham Lincoln's rebuttal of Douglas, see Lincoln, Springfield "Remarks," 26 June 1857, Basler, ed., *The Collected Works of Abraham Lincoln,* 2:398–99. One of the few discussions of the linkage between the two speeches is Hubbard, "Abraham Lincoln as Seen by the Mormons," 95–96. On 10 April 1860, while running for president, Lincoln returned to the subject of Mormons and polygamy in a speech delivered in Bloomington, Illinois. The text of these remarks has survived only through incomplete newspaper reports. See Basler, ibid., 4:41–43. For W. W. Drummond's patronizing assessment of Douglas's speech as well as his continuing criticism of Buchanan's timidity over the Mormons, see W. W. Drummond to Hon. Oliver H. Smith, J. A. Wright, A. P. Willard, Dr. Winslow S. Pierce, Ingalsby, Tuttle, Archey, Morrison, Henderson, Wooly and others, of Indianapolis, Ind., 19 June 1857, "The Mormons, Another Letter from Judge Drummond," *New York Daily Times,* 25 June 1857, 2/1–2.

[69] Morris, "Theodore Rex," 459.

Chapter 6

"President Young Says That He Would Build a Fort"

Utah Prepares for the Storm

The President says that he would build a fort 100 feet square of Cob[b]lestone, five feet thick at the bottom, fifteen or sixteen feet high tapering to about a foot at the top . . . I expect to go North with the President starting on the 24th.

—Lieut. Gen. Daniel H. Wells to Nauvoo Legion quartermaster Lewis Robison, 18 April 1857[1]

As James Buchanan struggled with an unexpected Mormon crisis, Brigham Young turned to military measures: the continuing quest for a local source of arms and munitions, a reorganization of the Nauvoo Legion, and a strengthening of the defenses at Jim Bridger's former trading post, which Bridger and his partner sold to the Mormons in 1855.

One of Young's activities along these lines was extraordinary for a territorial governor: the establishment of a revolver factory in Salt Lake City. Perhaps aware that one of Samuel Colt's foundational patents was expiring in 1857, but surely focused on preparations for an uncertain but armed future, Brigham Young launched one of the most ambitious of his multiple local production thrusts—the manufacture of one of Colt's basic pistol designs. This project was managed by two now-obscure Utahns, David Sabin and William Naylor. Starting in March 1857 they operated out of a structure described as

[1] The wall was to be at Fort Bridger; the northern trip was to Fort Limhi. These instructions to Robison, Brigham Young's principal agent in the Bridger area, are a good example of his deep involvement in the details of the Legion's activities.

the public machine shop in Salt Lake City.[2] Here was a vivid example of the entanglement of civil, church, and military affairs in Utah Territory that raised questions warranting investigation beyond the scope of this study.[3]

Irrespective of the technical answers to these questions, the world soon came to view this ambitious but modest local-manufacture thrust as an ominous undertaking by that general bête noire, "the Mormons." The machine shop and its output rapidly assumed highly symbolic, almost mythic, proportions. For example, as early as April 1857 Judge Drummond repeated the assertion by Mormon elder Israel Ivins that "We have the self-loading twenty-four repeating rifle, the Minnié rifle, [Jonathan] Browning's revolving five-shooting rifle, Colt's rifle and pistol, and a revolving cannon or field piece." Drummond then went on to report that "All the above-named fire-arms, powder, ball, &c., are in process of secret manufacture."[4] After Salt Lake City merchant William Bell left Utah in November 1857, he described the revolver works to a New York newspaper.[5] In his first public explanation of the need for a Utah Expedition, President Buchanan complained that Brigham Young "has, therefore, for several years, in order to maintain his independence, been industriously employed in collecting and fabricating arms and munitions of war, and in disciplining the Mormons for military service."[6]

The Moral and Physical Sky Is Clearer: Flight of the Federal Appointees

By the time the latest wave of disgruntled federal appointees left Salt Lake City on 15 April 1857, the die had already been secretly cast within Buchanan's cabinet to replace Brigham Young and to intervene militarily in some way. The

[2] Gibson, "Frontier Arms of the Mormons," 4–26; Schindler, "Settlers in Utah Produced Copycat Colts," *Salt Lake Tribune*, 20 February 1994.

[3] No better example may be found of the extent to which Young's personal, governmental, and church affairs were intertwined than with the shopping list contained in Young to Eldredge, 25 February 1857, M. Hamlin Cannon Papers, typescript copy. The list included not only ordinary household items but multiple types of specialty steel required for the Sabin-Naylor revolver operation. The best glimpse into the modest scale on which such weapons were actually produced in Salt Lake City during 1857 is derived from the year-end report by public machine shop foreman Nathan Davis to the Nauvoo Legion's chief of ordnance, Col. Thomas W. Ellerbeck. Davis to Ellerbeck, 8 January 1858, Nauvoo Legion Papers, Beinecke Library.

[4] "Verastus" [W. W. Drummond] to the Editors of the Washington *National Intelligencer*, "The Military Power and Political Purposes of the Mormons," reprinted in *New York Daily Times*, 21 April 1857, 1/4–5.

[5] "Interesting Correspondence," *New York Herald*, 23 February 1858, reprinted in *Deseret News*, 12 May 1858, 2/1–4.

[6] Buchanan, "First Annual Message," 8 December 1857, Moore, ed., *Works*, 10:153.

spectacle of another federal exodus from Utah was to have a powerful shock effect on the Atlantic Coast. This was a development that intensified the political pressure on the administration while calling into question again the wisdom of President Fillmore's original Utah appointments in 1850 and his 1852 dismissal of the charges lodged by the "runaway officials." In Salt Lake City Postmaster-Judge Elias Smith recorded in his journal a view of the exodus of federal appointees and apostates that smacked of chaos, frenzy, and—surprisingly—surprise.[7] Aware for weeks that such an exodus would take place once the spring thaw began to clear the road and passes, Brigham Young told George Q. Cannon in San Francisco that the departures were an "emetic," but he described the scene somewhat more casually to Horace S. Eldredge:

> Fear hath taken hold of the hypocrites in Zion, they with the gentiles begin to flee, and I think "no man pursueth." T. S. Williams and family, save his eldest daughter who is married to David Kimball, Judge Stiles and family, Genl. Burr, P. K. Dobson [Dotson], Craig and many that had a name among us [flee], even some of the hand cart corp that came in last winter; sad complaints of matters outside of them selves, "no employment"—"lack of bread." The atmosphere breathes more freely and more refreshing this morning, the moral and physical sky is clearer, our streets become duller from the fact that the loafers have deserted them; and the busy crowd that are left, are either occupied in our mechanic shops or quietly tilling the earth and sowing the seeds full of hope of an abundant harvest.[8]

The arrival of this group on the Kansas-Missouri frontier was reported by telegraph during the third week of May. Its tone was far different than Brigham Young's:

> A company of some seventy persons arrived in Leavenworth last Saturday evening, direct from Salt Lake. They left there the 15th of April, and have been about forty-four days on the road. Among the number were Judge Stiles and Surveyor-General W. I. [*sic*] Burr. They were driven out of the Territory by the Mormons. Mrs. Farnum, the keeper of a boarding-house in Salt Lake for "Gentiles," made her escape, and came in the company. Judge Stiles confirms the accounts of Judge Drummond. The Mormons are busily preparing for war with the United States. Brigham Young, instead of being driven out of Utah, has gone up among the [Oregon] Indians to engage their assistance, and to incite them to rob and murder emigrants. Money is very scarce among the Mormons, and they do not hesitate to rob the Gentiles.

[7] Elias Smith, "Journal," entries for 14–17 April 1857.

[8] Young to Eldredge, 17 April 1857, typescript copy in M. Hamlin Cannon Papers, Tutt Library.

> Four Mormons, who were not sufficiently sound on the Mormon "goose," were pursued by Brigham Young—two of them killed—their throats being cut, and the other two escaped and came through with this company.[9]

A Matter of Chemistry: Frederick Loba Flees Utah

Brigham Young did not recruit Frederick A. Loba from Switzerland to manufacture gunpowder, but once he converted and emigrated to Utah during 1854, Loba's skills as an industrial chemist caught the governor's attention.[10] With much gubernatorial encouragement and some backing in the form of materials and financing, Loba set to work to produce gunpowder. Whether he had the talent to accomplish such an assignment is an imponderable, but it is clear that along the way Loba and his partners became distracted by the temptation to focus their skills and equipment on an easier, more profitable, and less risky process—the distillation of alcoholic beverages. Loba's correspondence with Brigham Young reflects a person troubled, anguished, and embarrassed by his distraction and lack of success.[11] Whether it was these dynamics that prompted Loba to flee Utah, or, as he later claimed, it was alarm over the attacks on John Tobin and the Parrishes is unclear. But depart he and his wife did, leaving their eight children behind in hopes that somehow they would follow.

The only contemporaneous account of the Lobas' flight to Kansas during the early spring of 1857 appeared in the midst of a newspaper dispatch from Washington reporting the arrival of Utah's fugitive federal appointees, who had encountered the Lobas in desperate condition in eastern Utah Territory.[12] A far more extensive account appeared in melodramatic fashion in the *New York Times* a year later, thanks to an encounter between Frederick Loba and James W. Simonton, a flamboyant *Times* correspondent then in Kansas

9 "Important from Utah," *Republican* (Lawrence, K.T.), 4 June 1857. This report of two murders was bogus, although the Parrish-Potter murders and Santa Clara ambush had recently occurred.

10 Loba's emigration was primarily the work of T. B. H. Stenhouse, who had in mind Loba's possible usefulness in constructing a paper factory or gas works in Utah. Stenhouse to Lorenzo Snow, 31 January 1853, *Deseret News*, 18 June 1853, 3/3. The years-long attempt by Brigham Young to produce gunpowder in Utah should be viewed not only through the lens of Utah War dynamics but as part of his broader emphasis on economic (if not political) independence through local manufacture of such diverse products and ingredients as paper, sugar cane, cotton, indigo, flax for linen, beer, salt, iron, and lead. Interestingly, when Young commented on efforts to manufacture such products in his December 1857 annual message, he omitted gunpowder and revolvers from the list.

11 Loba to Young, 24 June 1856, LDS Archives.

12 "Affairs in Utah," *New York Times*, 11 June 1857, 1/1.

preparing to travel further west to cover the Utah Expedition.[13] Simonton's dramatic description of the Lobas' flight from Utah and his companion pieces about the chemist prompted fascination in those titillated by the more lurid aspects of Mormon affairs but also drew criticism from pro-Mormon letter-writers skeptical about Loba's motives and credibility, if not Simonton's.[14] For historians, largely oblivious to the Loba story for nearly a century, this sensational material begs the question of whether it was more the editorial work of Simonton than a straightforward narrative dictated by Frederick Loba—a vexing proposition that later dogged the collaboration on other Utah War narratives by Maj. Lot Smith, Lt. Bill Hickman, and Maj. John D. Lee and their editors.[15]

The Earth Seems to Revolve as Formerly: To Oregon and Back with Brigham Young

In the midst of these departures by federal appointees and apostates, Young plunged into preparations for his own long-contemplated, five-week trek to Oregon Territory to visit Fort Limhi, the new Salmon River mission. The journey was to be an unusual one for multiple reasons. Not only was Young undertaking an arduous, cold-weather, high-altitude trip while still recovering from a long illness, it was to be the first time that he had left Utah since 1848. He would never leave Utah again. Furthermore, he was doing so without observing two of the basic protocols of American territorial government: requesting of Sec. of State Lewis Cass a leave of absence from his post, and informing Gov. George Curry of his intent to visit Oregon. The latter omission was especially sensitive since Young took with him at least two chiefs under the jurisdiction of Utah's Indian superintendency, as well as an exten-

---

[13] A summary account of Simonton's complex, sometimes violent Utah War embroilments (as the anonymous correspondent "S") and subsequent career appears in MacKinnon, "Epilogue to the Utah War," 224–25.

[14] "Utah and the Mormons," Statement of Frederick A. Loba, April 1858, *New York Times*, 1 May 1858, 4/5–6, 5/1. For criticisms of the Loba-Simonton collaboration, see letters signed "O.," written from Washington under dates of 28 April 1858, "Supposed New Trick of Brigham Young," *New York Times*, 30 April 1858, 1/4, and 11 May 1858, "Utah and the Mormons," *New York Times*, 15 May 1858, 1/1–2; letter signed "One Who Has Seen the Elephant," written from St. Louis under date of 13 May 1858, "Mr. Frederick Loba and the Mormons," *New York Times*, 19 May 1858, 1/2–3; and "The Loba Hoax," *Millennial Star* (Liverpool), 12 June 1858, 382–83.

[15] Historian Ardis E. Parshall, who has read all of Loba's extant letters written in both English and French, concludes that Loba's long 1858 narrative in the *Times* reflected substantial editing, if not gross rewriting, by Simonton. Parshall to MacKinnon, e-mail message, 18 October 2005.

sive array of presents for northern tribes that were Curry's rather than Young's concern. These were lapses for which Commissioner of Indian Affairs James W. Denver later severely reprimanded him. Historian David L. Bigler has described the entourage that left Salt Lake City on 24 April as involving 142 people, including the entire LDS First Presidency, all but one of the Quorum of Twelve Apostles then residing in Utah, six Nauvoo Legion generals, and two American Indian chiefs, Arapeen of the Northern Wasatch Utahs and Kanosh of the Pahvant Utes.[16]

Given the scope of the journey, the distances involved, and the size as well as character of Young's entourage, here was a trans-territorial jaunt unprecedented for an American governor and perhaps even for a president of the United States. More than a year later Delegate Bernhisel reported to Brigham Young that President Buchanan was still curious about the trip's purpose and meaning: "[Buchanan] inquired where Gov. Young went last Spring. On being informed, asked why it had not been published. I answered that an account of his visit was published at the time. Spoke of the report of our being about to remove to the British possessions."[17] Even with his family and business intimates—with tongue in cheek or for the benefit of prying federal postmasters—Young maintained the fiction that he was trekking to Fort Limhi "to have an out[ting] for the benefit of our health, and see more of the healthy north."[18]

After an absence of thirty-three days, Brigham Young returned to Salt Lake City on 26 May. Weary and still ailing, he was satisfied that he had at last seen and assessed the region to Utah's north and was ready to resume focus on the challenges of what he called the non-Mormon "lower world." Although upon his return Young described what he had seen somewhat negatively in public, Bigler believes that he arrived in Salt Lake City with a quite different private view of the region's attractiveness—as a way station or escape route for a potential Mormon exodus from Utah to Montana's Bitterroot Valley and perhaps beyond to the Pacific Coast.[19]

On 29 May, the day after General Scott announced the Utah Expedition, the mail wagons carrying John M. Bernhisel (and his alarming letter of 2 April), George A. Smith, and temple architect Truman O. Angell rolled into Salt Lake

---

[16] Bigler, *Fort Limhi*, 135–60.

[17] "Account of Conversations with President James Buchanan," untitled, undated memorandum prepared by John M. Bernhisel for Brigham Young, June 1859, LDS Archives.

[18] Young to Horace S. Eldredge, 17 April 1857, M. Hamlin Cannon Papers

[19] Bigler, *Fort Limhi*, 154–55.

City. From Bernhisel and Smith, Brigham Young learned of the intensity of anti-Mormon attitudes in Congress, the reaction of Buchanan's cabinet to the legislative assembly's memorials of 6 January, and the near-certainty that President Buchanan would replace him as governor. From Angell he presumably learned of not only European architectural trends, but of Angell's success in acquiring the best of British revolvers, several of which he carried with him.

Before he could fully absorb the alarming news that arrived that day, Young sent Horace S. Eldredge the charming observations of a man tired but obviously delighted to be back home:

> The earth seems to revolve as formerly, all these affairs notwithstanding, for we found on our return from the North, as we rounded the hill south of the hot springs and east of the lake, our eyes feasting on the City of white houses, peaceful homes and verdant gardens, here still it stands, lovely when seen by the clear beams of silver light now shed nightly upon it from the fair moon, Where is its equal? where do the cooling streams of melted snow water every tree-shaded street as here? Where the same amt of peace, faith—power? Nowhere at present, not even in Washington! and most assuredly neither in St. Louis nor New Orleans!!![20]

Sounding the Alarm: Enter Bill Hickman

Less than a month after the governor's return, on 23 June 1857 Ephraim K. Hanks and Feramorz Little, the governor's nephew, arrived in Salt Lake City bearing the long-awaited June mail from Independence. They had departed from that town in late May unaware that the Post Office Department in Washington was suspending the Mormons' mail contract. A day later gunman Bill Hickman, the third member of the mail party, drifted into town. Decades later Hickman argued that immediately upon arrival he briefed Young on the incendiary nature of anti-Mormon sentiment in Missouri as well as the likelihood of a federal military garrison for Utah. According to Hickman—notwithstanding his status as a trusted Brigham Young agent—he was brushed aside by an inattentive, over-confident governor surrounded by like-minded minions:

> I went to Brigham Young's office and showed my bills of expenditures, and gave a general account of my trip, showing some articles I had published in different papers, rebutting the influences that were going against the people

[20] Young to Eldredge, 29 May 1857, LDS Archives.

> of Utah and the published statement of Judge Drummond, in which I scored him as bad as he had me.[21] I told them that troops would be here; but was laughed at, tantalized, and treated scornfully for making such an assertion. I told them I had been there and ought to know as well as those who sat at home and knew nothing. All hands [in the office] agreed they were not coming, and Brother Brigham said neither should they come so this ended it.[22]

Whether Hickman's account of this meeting and what he saw in Missouri is accurate and credible is problematic because of his notoriety. But it is worth understanding because of the glimpse of Brigham Young that it allegedly provides during the important period between the launch of the Utah Expedition in Washington and first Mormon awareness of the event in Utah.

Mormon historians have traditionally dismissed Hickman's memoirs in toto on grounds that he was a notorious, self-confessed killer excommunicated in 1868; writing his memoirs in 1871, while awaiting trial at Fort Douglas under a murder indictment; and the beneficiary to some unknown extent of a collaboration with the controversial anti-Mormon editor J. H. Beadle. To Hickman's credit, on the day he claimed to be reporting to Brigham Young about the Utah Expedition, Frederick H. Burr recorded in his diary near what is now Montepelier, Idaho, "News of troops coming to Salt Lake."[23] Also, judging by Brigham Young's private correspondence with Hickman and the character of his church assignments, Hickman was clearly a person to whom the governor frequently turned for assistance during the late 1850s. For those anxious to discredit Bill Hickman's 1871 account of his controversial activities during the summer and fall of 1857, it is important to remember that Brigham Young's and the legislative assembly's memorials had insisted that Hickman was worthy of presidential appointment as the territory's senior federal law enforcement officer—U.S. attorney for Utah. Equally telling is the fact that immediately upon arriving in Salt Lake City on 24 June 1857, Brigham Young pressed Hickman into service to attack Judge Drummond in letters to one or more newspaper editors.[24] Eighteen months later Brigham

---

[21] This claim seems credible in view of Hickman's draft letter to the editor of the *Platte Argus* dated 30 June 1857.

[22] Hickman, *Brigham's Destroying Angel*, 116–17. A visit to Brigham Young's office by Hickman during this period is not recorded in Young's multiple diaries and office journals in LDS Archives and the Leonard J. Arrington Papers.

[23] Frederick H. Burr, Journal, entry for 24 June, 1857, Beinecke Library, courtesy of David L. Bigler.

[24] See Hickman to Editor, *Platte Argus* (Weston, Mo.), 30 June 1857, draft letter, retained copy, LDS Archives. That this draft was prepared for Hickman's signature in the hand of Hosea Stout, Brigham Young's principal lawyer, and today may be found in Young's files indicates the extent to which Hickman was then in the gubernatorial good graces.

Young personally renegotiated for Hickman his indebtedness with the non-Mormon mercantile firm of Gilbert and Gerrish, promising that he would pay the principal due if Hickman refused to do so.[25]

Irrespective of when, how, and in what form news of a military move on the Mormons reached Utah, within days after Bill Hickman's arrival it had surely come. The reaction was a mixture of alarm and the blasé. On 30 June Elizabeth Bateman Margetts wrote phonetically to her eastbound husband, Phillip, from Salt Lake City to report her own feelings—surprisingly relaxed ones:

> My dear I do not no that I have eny nuse to tell you at presant. All is pese and prosperity hear at presant tho there is some that are A littel afraid that the solders are A coming here this spring to kill us all of[f] but that is an old story tha [they] have been comin evry sumer for the last sevn years and have not arived yet and I am not eny A fraid that tha will arive in another seven years unles the lord sees fit to let them com for some Wise porpos of [h]is one [own] and if the sa[i]nts will try to do as nere right as the[y] no how soulders not mobers will never be promited [permitted] to harm us agane for Brigam has declard it time and agane and wat he says is so. Wee may rely upon and call it gospel.[26]

The Best Silver Epaulettes: Gubernatorial Outreach

Regardless of whether Brigham Young believed Bill Hickman's report of federal troop movements, during June 1857 the governor oversaw sweeping changes in the organization and readiness of the Nauvoo Legion and made telling preparations for some sort of armed conflict. At the end of the month, with the departure of the July mail imminent, Young advanced these preparations by writing to three of his key links to the outside world: Thomas L. Kane in Philadelphia; Horace S. Eldredge, his Mormon business agent in St. Louis; and Nicholas Groesbeck, an agent on the plains with the Y. X. Carrying Company. The differences in the tone as well as substance of these letters reflects not only the swings in Young's mood as June closed but his ability to tap resources widely varying in character and location.

To Kane, Young addressed an attack on Drummond and eastern editors,

---

[25] Wells to Gilbert and Gerrish, 3 December 1858, LDS Archives.

[26] Margetts to Margetts, 30 June 1857, private collection, typescript of excerpts in editor's possession. Phil Margetts was then on the plains with the first eastbound handcart company destined for the British Mission.

a brief description of his trip to Fort Limhi, and deep appreciation for Kane's help and friendship.

YOUNG TO KANE, 29 JUNE 1857,
THOMAS L. KANE PAPERS, BEINECKE LIBRARY.

Your favor of the 21st May is at hand. I was exceedingly glad to hear from you. . . . I am ever grateful to have a line from you. It gives me great satisfaction to know of your health good feelings and strict integrity, your letter coming when it did with such a vast pile of rubbish was like an oasis in a barren waste. I feel to bless you for it, and for all your kindness to me and to this people in the name of Israel's God whom we serve, and I trust that you and I will yet live to see righteousness prevail and wickedness come to nought yet be permitted to live together to enjoy each others society in peace. I truly regret to learn the loss of your noble hearted brother. . . . O, Colonel will it not be a happy existence when friends can grasp each others hands in a happy immortality beyond the reach of the power of Satan, of wicked and designing men, but we will triumph, God is with us and he is more powerful than all his foes.

I like your policy of staving off [the appointment issue] until a little reason shall have an opportunity to resume its sway. . . . We are fearful that the government is not willing to extend their favorite doctrine of popular sovereignty to Utah, but are desirious [*sic*] of availing themselves of the present furor to operate against us upon the charges of rebellion, insubordination &c all of which, I need not tell you are foul and malignant falsehoods, but I trust in the Lord of hosts to rule and overrule all for the good of his saints.

I wish to have you consider that you and yours have a standing invitation to make us a visit when circumstances shall permit, be assured that you would meet with a warm welcome.

The day after he wrote to Kane, Young sent both a news letter and set of military purchasing instructions to Horace S. Eldredge in St. Louis.

YOUNG TO ELDREDGE, 30 JUNE 1857, LDS ARCHIVES.

I wish you to send by each mail to this place one keg of blasting and two kegs of rifle powder, best quality, take and pack them in an iron bound box, that it may not be known from outside appearances what the box contains.[27]

Bro[s] G. A. Smith, J. M. Bernhisel, and T. O. Angel[l] arrived 29 ult in good health and spirits, from their conversation I do not think that Uncle Sam feels particularly affectionate towards us. . . .

I wish Bro Horace for you to purchase 3 or 4 pairs of the best silver

[27] That Young was so candid was probably a direct reflection of the fact that this letter was carried east—at least far enough to mail it through the anonymity of a large Missouri post office—by Y. X. Carrying Company agent John R. Murdock.

epaulettes, seal them in a tin case, and send them to me by the September mail. I would also like 8 doz of large and 2 doz of small silver military buttons, about 50 yds. of silver cord 1/8 or 3/16 of an inch in thickness, and about 25 yds of the best silver lace 1/2 inch in width.

P.S. I wish you to also send me two red military sashes, not very large, best quality, also two silver sword knobs.

So anxious was the governor about the procurement of these military items that on 30 June and 1 July he wrote two more letters to Eldredge that included reminders and additional instructions: "We very much need . . . powder as you can secure it, and forward every opportunity some coarse, but be careful to get good quality fresh and such as has been taken good care of"; and "Enclosed I send you a Bill of goods for my family & workmen also one for some Military trimmings. I wish you to send these things to me as wisdom and means shall allow without running into debt. In forwarding select those articles most needful for immediate use in the family. The Bill for Military trimmings please fill as near the description as possible. What you cannot obtain in St Louis can be obtained in Philadelphia."[28]

Also on 30 June 1857 Brigham Young wrote to Nicholas Groesbeck, an agent on the Kansas-Missouri frontier with the Y. X. Carrying Company. Although this letter dealt primarily with prosaic matters, it also reflected Young's growing anxiety about anti-Mormon sentiment, especially in Independence ("they are perfectly rabid and are striving to find something against every person that comes here").[29] The next day Groesbeck himself wrote to the governor and reported on the same subject, as well as the disastrous suspension of the Y. X. Carrying Company's important mail contract and Groesbeck's progress in executing an earlier gubernatorial assignment—purchase and shipment of arms and ammunition. Strangely, Groesbeck made no explicit reference to the organization of the Utah Expedition, of which his immediate associates Judson Stoddard and A. O. Smoot were then well aware.

GROESBECK TO YOUNG, 1 JULY 1857, LDS ARCHIVES.

Bro [Judson] Stoddard & myself have just returned from Independence drove all day yesterday and traveled all night to get out of hell whare we could breth without inhalling the atmosphere from the spirits of the damb. It does appear that the spirit of Mobrocracy is a going by telegraph speed through out the lenght and ~~of~~ bredth of this Christinized land whare they think it is and honor

[28] Young to Eldredge, 30 June 1857, M. Hamlin Cannon Papers; 1 July 1857, LDS Archives.

[29] Young to Groesbeck, 30 June 1857, LDS Archives.

to Shoot a latter day saint in Brord daylight in there most promonant streets & then turn to the authorities and bost of their nobel deeds. . . .[30]

I send out some freight 10 kegs powder as you disposed [?] if I could have the money for the powder what it is worth in Salt Lake and amount due in wheat I sent down by express I could purches some four or five thousand in good[s] such as are in demand if it should be gun Powder & lead &c. . . .

I will send out papers to post you up in regard to the feelings of the devels against you and Brs Heber [C. Kimball] & Daniel [H. Wells] they think now is the time to strike & obliterate mormonism from the earth if she is let alone 3 years she will number 1 million of proselites & 100 thousand wariers and then it would be imposable to drive them Salt L. City has ben for the 2 month[s] past been the great Seabastopool[31] of the age. They dred her they fear her and the Name of Brigham Young unnerves them. Fear take hold of them. They want to do sompting to gratify there hellish appetites to oppress the inicent & let the guilty go free. To my Subject again the Powder if you do not want I wish you to see if [Leonard E.] Herington in Deseret store would not take it and advance the money so it can be yoused here againe for the 250 lbs I will take $200,00 Dollors thats 50 Dollors to sell at the yousal price[32] there wont be any goods out before Sep th 15. Enquire of Bro Stoddard and he can Post you up. I have not time to write all particulares. If I should not here from you by an express I shall leave here when the last traine goes out. We aught to send out as large a traine as posable. I shall endeavour to do my best for the general good believe me to be yours in the Kingdom of God.

---

[30] Groesbeck may be referring indirectly to the assassination of Apostle Parley P. Pratt in Van Buren, Arkansas, on 13 May 1857. This murder would have been on Groesbeck's mind for several reasons, not the least of which was that at this time Pratt's distraught widow, Eleanor McLean Pratt, was to accompany Stoddard and Smoot as well as Porter Rockwell on their westbound dash across the plains to the Salt Lake Valley.

[31] Mormons were fascinated by the Russian defensive tactics used during the recently concluded Crimean War, as indicated by this reference to the highly publicized siege of Sebastopol.

[32] Groesbeck's uncertainty as to whether Brigham Young really wanted the gunpowder he had acquired and was shipping is puzzling.

Chapter 7

"To Conquer Both Time and Distance"

Harney Organizes the Expedition

I feel extremely anxious that everything be done to secure the greatest efficiency to your command, and to enable you to achieve success. . . . We have as you are aware to conquer both time and distance.

—Quartermaster Gen. Thomas S. Jesup to Brevet Brig. Gen. William S. Harney, 5 June 1857

Having internally announced an expedition for Utah through General Scott, the Buchanan administration still needed to determine not only who would serve as Utah's next governor but which officer would lead this armed escort. With a cadre of generals and senior colonels who were either seriously ill, superannuated, or both, President Buchanan's and Secretary Floyd's choices were severely limited.[1] Within a slightly different context—an Indian campaign in the Pacific Northwest about fifteen months later—Floyd described to Buchanan the leadership dilemma that they faced in the spring of 1857:

> But one other important consideration remains to be determined, and that is as to the commander of the forces. On this point, I am pretty clear, in my own mind, and cannot doubt but that Genl. Harney is the proper man. I am not sure how Genl. Scott would take this proposition, but Harney is really the only general officer—[A. S.] Johnston alone excepted—who has the physical capacity to conduct such a campaign as this. If therefore, the suggestion meets your approbation, I will give the orders.[2]

---

[1] Most such officers were in their seventies, with some older.

[2] Floyd to Buchanan, 5 August 1858, James Buchanan Papers, The Historical Society of Pennsylvania.

In Due Time: The Tentative Selection of Harney

Coincident with release of his 28 May circular to the army's staff bureaus, Scott notified Brevet Brig. Gen. William S. Harney, the commander at Fort Leavenworth, that in all likelihood he would be designated the Utah Expedition's commander. It was a strange, tentative signal that Scott sent to Harney through Lt. Col. George W. Lay, his aide de camp, especially since much of the country had been speculating on such a command once the War Department had abruptly ordered Harney back to Kansas from Florida in mid-April.

Lay to Harney, 28 May 1857,
Headquarters of the Army, Letters Sent (RG 108),
National Archives.

I am directed by the General in chief to notify you, in anticipation, that you will probably be designated to the command of a force to march to, and winter in, Utah.

That force will consist of the 2d Dragoons, the 5th Infantry (to be replaced in Florida by volunteers), the 10th Infantry, and Phelps' battery of the 4th Artillery.

Meantime, your position and duties in Kansas remain as at present. It is not supposed that the troops destined for Utah can be all assembled at Fort Leavenworth until late in July, if so soon.

Please send an express, if practicable, to Colonel Sumner [on the Cheyenne Expedition], with orders, in the name of the General-in-Chief, that the squadron of dragoons from Fort Kearny are, at such time and in such mode as you can best devise, to be turned over to your command. Horses will be taken to them from Fort Leavenworth, when the Expedition shall march.

You are authorized to announce Captain Pleasonton, or any other officer of the line whom you may select, in orders, as your acting assistant adjutant General. But if you should desire an officer of the [adjutant general's staff] department, one will be assigned to you. The officer so assigned would, however, be senior to Captain Pleasonton.

Copies of orders, and of instructions to the staff departments, relative to the movement for Utah, will be sent you. Your own instructions will be forwarded in due time.

All which is communicated by the order, and the name, of the General-in-Chief.

P.S. The General-in-chief suggests that volunteer missionaries (two or three) accompanying the expedition to Utah might do great good—and should be encouraged and protected. The hope might be held out that, after arrival in the country and the establishment of posts, one or more might possibly be appointed by the post councils of administration, as paid chaplains.[3]

It is unknown whether and with what clarity Buchanan or Floyd had informed General Scott that they had committed to Governor Walker that Harney would remain in Kansas indefinitely. Scott behaved as though Harney indeed was the leader for Utah, and Harney—not officially notified of such an assignment for another month—followed suit immediately while also juggling Walker's demands as disruptive armed bands of civilians and paramilitary forces roamed Kansas. From Washington Brevet Maj. Gen. Thomas S. Jesup, then in his fortieth year as the army's quartermaster general, sent Harney a message that discussed the daunting task ahead while underscoring the tentative nature of his appointment.

Jesup to Harney, 5 June 1857, Records of the Quartermaster Gen., Letters Sent (RG 92), National Archives.

Though I have not yet received the order placing you in command of the Utah Expedition, I have been informed that you are to be assigned to it. I feel extremely anxious that every thing be done to secure the greatest efficiency to your command, and to enable you to achieve success.

Captains [Thomas Lee] Brent and [Stewart] Van Vliet are with you and other officers will be required to join. I beg of you to furnish officers from your regiment of dragoons to aid in promptly obtaining the horses necessary to complete the mounting of the regiment.

All supplies not required for the command on the march can be sent forward by the trains of contractors. The supplies of forage and subsistence for the column in march should be renewed at Fort Kearny, Fort Laramie, and at some point midway between that post and Salt Lake City. To secure the latter, I would suggest that the movement of the troops and trains be so combined that the troops shall overtake the contractors' train about three hundred miles in advance of Fort Laramie. *Subsistence for the troops for the seven months, and corn for at least half rations for the public animals for the same time must be taken forward by the contractors' train.*

I will endeavor to have all the supplies & means necessary for the success of your operations in time for your movement; but you must look into the arrangements yourself, & direct whatsoever you may consider necessary to secure

[3] This was perhaps a subtle attempt on Scott's part at proselytizing among the Mormons. Two months later Floyd deflected a Catholic priest's inquiry about a chaplaincy by informing him that the Utah Expedition had already marched. Floyd to Rev. Z. DeVivaldi, 3 August 1857, Sec. of War, Letters Sent (RG 107), National Archives. In the spring of 1858 Harney successfully lobbied Floyd to commission his personal religious advisor, Rev. P. J. De Smet, S.J., as the Utah Expedition's chaplain.

success. We have as you are aware to conquer both time and distance; and I greatly regret that we have not the advantage of the two months just past to make our arrangements.

On 7 June 1857 Harney took the extraordinary step of sending to Secretary Floyd a private memorandum presenting his unsolicited views of how to conduct the Utah campaign. Harney included the provocative recommendation that he be appointed both civil and military governor of Utah and be empowered to proclaim martial law. Although Harney had little in common with Scott, in many ways his memorandum was strikingly parallel to that written by the general in chief for Secretary Floyd less than two weeks earlier on 26 May. Both military leaders recognized what the inexperienced Buchanan and Floyd apparently did not—the risks inherent in launching a long-distance expedition across the plains and into the Rockies during midsummer that should have been in motion by early May. A week after writing to Floyd, Harney sent a similar memo to Scott, although in this paper he eliminated the recommendation for a governorship and martial law and somewhat reduced the number of regiments he was requesting.

HARNEY TO FLOYD, 7 JUNE 1857, RECORDS OF ADJT. GEN.'S OFFICE, LETTERS RECEIVED (RG 94), NATIONAL ARCHIVES.

I most gladly avail myself of the opportunity you have so kindly offered, thro' Captain Pleasonton, to cultivate an acquaintance which I should have sought on the first occasion of my being near to you. Feeling deeply sensible of the sentiments you so generously entertain towards me, I desire to assure you of the pleasure, as well as agreeable duty, it will always be to me to serve you, not only personally, but also in advancing the interests of the administration in any way, you may deem the most proper to employ my humble efforts.

I have just been notified by the General-in-chief, that it was probable I should be designated to the command of a force to march to, and winter in, Utah; and as a consequence I conceive it is important I should lay before you my views on this subject at the earliest moment.

The proper administration of affairs in Utah, at this time, is one of great delicacy, which will require not only an imposing force, but the establishment of that force in an attitude in the country to impress the minds of the people with the hopelessness of resistance.

The Army must rely entirely upon its own resources, and those resources must be sufficient to furnish one year's supply—Both troops & supplies must pass over a distance of 1200 miles to reach Utah—and assuming the most favorable case, that the troops & supplies arrive at Green river valley by the

1st of December, the Mormons, at that season, could easily prevent the force, which is at present designated, from proceeding further into their country.

There is but one wagon road into the valley of the Salt Lake from this side, and that road, for the last 100 miles, passes thro' a chain of mountains, & is nothing more than a succession of defiles, most difficult to force in the winter season.

I very much question whether it is possible to prepare the command and give it sufficient time to march to Utah before the snow falls.

In a military point of view nothing can be gained by forcing the troops into the valley this winter.

I would most respectfully offer the following suggestion: To establish in the neighborhood of Fort Laramie this winter, a large force fully equipped and supplied, to move early in the Spring upon Utah—Then, in case of resistance, the entire summer can be used in operating.

The moral effect of such a force at Laramie, upon the Mormons, would be more favorable to us, than if placed in a position where they can study our numbers, material &c, besides, the close proximity of our men to the Mormon women that a winter's residence in Utah would necessitate, could only be injurious to discipline and might be productive of disaster.[4]

I was informed yesterday by a person, who, some years since, was a Mormon, and is thoroughly conversant with themselves and their country, that the Mormons are disposed to resist the Government, that they are now collecting their people from California and other places, and that he knows they can bring into the field, well armed & equipped, eight thousand men.

I am not at liberty to give this person's name, but he has been known for some years past to officers of my staff, as a man of character and truth and I have much reliance on his statement.[5]

If the President should think proper to send me to Utah, I hope he will send me as Civil and Military Governor with full powers to declare martial law, if it is necessary. I do not wish this, from any desire of high position, love of power, or any other reason than solely to be enabled to effect the entire wishes of the President; and I feel no doubt as to my success, with a proper force.

I am willing, if the President desires it, to go to Utah with such a force as he may deem sufficient—I have worked hard for the little reputation I have, and I will never lose it, except with my life.

But to effect anything in Utah, I am fully pu[r]suaded that the officer in command of the troops, whoever he may be, should also be the Governor, and have authority to declare martial law.[6]

[4] Whether speaking from personal experience or knowledge of the civil-affairs imbroglio created by the 1854–55 Steptoe Expedition, Harney's observation was perceptive.

[5] The identity of Harney's informant is unknown.

[6] This dual role was not granted to Harney or his successor. The only martial law proclaimed in Utah was to be by Brigham Young on 15 September 1857.

The Mormons will never recognise the authority of any Governor except Brigham Young so long as he lives, unless that other has the power to compel them to do so.

Would it not be well to form Utah into a Military Department? It could give the movement the appearance of an ordinary measure, and remove the apprehensions of those Mormons well disposed.[7]

I enclose a Memorandum which may be useful.

Do me the favor to present my most respectful remembrances to the President, and permit me to subscribe myself, with the warmest feelings of admiration and esteem

Your sincere friend

[enclosure:]

Memorandum concerning the force about to march upon Utah.

I. Besides the troops already designated, viz; 5th & 10th Infantry, 2nd Dragoons, and Phelps' Battery—the 6th Infantry, destined for California, would do good service, by being attached to the Utah Command, with instructions if not needed in Utah, to proceed to California. Also, a battalion of the 2nd Infantry, say six companies.

II. The 1st Cavalry will be necessary to furnish escorts from Fort Laramie to Utah—The main body, 5th, 10th, 6th, & 2nd Infantry & 2nd Dragoons & Phelps' battery, should not be subject to any detail which might separate them, until after the disposition of the Mormons has been made manifest.

III. The Regiments should be filled up to the maximum standard, & all officers who can be spared ordered to join—The Dragoon Companies should be furnished a sufficient number of horses to mount the number of men to the maximum standard—by existing orders, only sixty horses are allowed to each company, which leaves some twenty men in each company on foot.

Phelps's Battery should be increased to six guns with six horses in each piece and caisson.

IV. Orders should be sent immediately to Fort Laramie, to procure a large amount of hay this summer for the use of the Expedition. A cutting machine would be valuable for this purpose & should be sent out at once—

Authority should be granted the Commander of the troops to employ guides, spies & hunters in such numbers as he may deem necessary for the service.

V. It would be well to place Forts Laramie and Kearney [*sic*] under my orders, now, to avoid the inconvenience of referring matters of detail to Washington.[8]

---

[7] The administration adopted this recommendation—also pushed in July by Ben McCulloch, who had declined the governorship of Utah—and used it as a fig leaf to deal with accusations that the expedition was intended to persecute Mormons. It is conceivable that Harney also made this recommendation because command of such an organizational entity might bring him promotion.

[8] The reference to Washington signals Harney's intent to work through Adjutant General Cooper and Secretary Floyd, if not Buchanan, rather than through General Scott in New York.

The companies of the 6th Infantry at Laramie should not be moved, from there, this summer, but should make preparations for wintering the whole command.

VI. Some fifty or sixty miles from Laramie, the troops can easily hut themselves for the winter, but not beyond that point, as the timber becomes scarce.

During the interval between his 7 and 14 June memoranda for Floyd and Scott, respectively, Harney wrote to Adjutant General Cooper in Washington to express alarm over the availability of transportation to supply the expedition while again advancing the notion that the military move on Utah should be delayed. In the process, Harney bypassed General Scott to seek more direct action from "the Government."

HARNEY TO COOPER, 12 JUNE 1857, RECORDS OF ADJT. GEN.'S OFFICE, LETTERS RECEIVED (RG 94), NATIONAL ARCHIVES.

I have just received the enclosed communication from Majors & Russell,[9] the Government contractors for freight to New Mexico, Fort Laramie &c, and I deem the information it contains of such importance as to submit it, at once, for the consideration of the Government, in connection with the contemplated movement of a large force upon Utah.

One of these gentleman, Mr. [Alexander] Majors informed me, in conversation, in very positive terms, that it would be impossible for them to transport all of the necessary supplies for the troops, to Utah, this year—their means of transportation being much too limited. He, also, stated, that should the Government desire it, they could procure any additional amount of transportation, but that the time consumed in so doing, would render the season too far advanced to give any hope of a successful march to the Salt Lake.

The discrepancy between M^r^. Majors verbal statement to me and the written report of the firm of Majors & Russell, has decided me to place them both properly before the Department.

I enclose, also, a copy of a report from the Assistant Quartermaster at this post, showing the means of transportation on hand, as well as the amount which has already been furnished to commands now in the field.

This statement shows, that upwards of 220 six mule wagons have been furnished, to fourteen companies, to be absent in compliance with their orders, during the summer. As the time consumed in marching from this [place] to Utah, will be from three to four months, the above number of wagons may be assumed as a basis for calculation. At this time, by the enclosed report, it will be observed, the entire means of transportation at this depot is confined to 154 mules, 146 wagons & harness, one light wagon and 100 pack saddles—con-

9 See Majors and Russell to Harney, 11 June 1857, Records of Adjt. Gen.'s Office, Letters Received (RG 94), National Archives. The firm was soon to become Russell, Majors and Waddell.

sequently a very large number of mules & horses must be obtained to move the command, alone, from this point. Both mules & horses are very scarce, and the number required cannot be obtained in proper time for the movement. This mule train has no connection with the supply train of Majors & Russell.

It may be important to this department to know, that in the year 1855, when I was in command of the Sioux Expedition, the snow fell on the 3d day of October in the Black Hills, to such a depth, as to cover up the grass completely—the ordure [manure] of the buffalo being the only fuel, the troops suffered very much from the cold—

Between Fort Laramie & Salt Lake, snow generally falls from the middle of October to the 1st of November—Last year a number of Mormon women died, en route, in that part of the country, from cold & starvation—They started from Omaha city about the 1st of August.[10]

In case it is deemed expedient to send troops this season—One Regiment can be, by prompt action, completely organized, equipped & moved in time to obtain safe quarters for the winter in Utah—These troops would offer the necessary protection to the persons of the Governor & the other civil authorities, until the arrival of a larger force in the Spring. Such a course would, also, determine, at once, as to the intentions of the Mormons to resist, as a people, the power of the federal Government.

[(later) endorsement (by Gen. Scott) on reverse:] This communication presents no real difficulties to my mind.

General Harney's doubts about transportation would be cured by an early communication of the orders & instructions prepared by me and waiting to be issued.[11]

The letter of General Harney is dated June 12, at Ft Leavenworth. From St Louis, on the 17th of June, Lt Col Chas Thomas, acting under full powers from the Quartermaster General, reports that ample provision has been made for the public trains & animals and that he has even had to curtail some of the purchases—and that after conference with the government contractor for freight, he has sufficient assurances that the latter will do his part, so far as relied upon.[12]

The proposition [advanced by Harney on 12 June] to risk one regiment alone, in Utah, for the winter, is utterly inadmissible.

Respectfully submitted to the Sec. of War June 22

---

[10] This was the Willie and Martin handcart companies disaster in which hundreds of Mormon children and men as well as women died, the worst trail disaster in the history of America's overland migration.

[11] It would be another week before these orders were released on 29 June. Scott had drafted them on 8 June.

[12] Four days after writing this endorsement, Scott had his aide inform Harney, "The reports and returns from the staff departments, and from the troops, convince him that the problem is now solved satisfactorily and he hopes that your movements may commence at the close of July, or earlier." Lay to Harney, 26 June 1857, Headquarters of the Army, Letters Sent (RG 108), National Archives.

Harney to Scott (via Lt. Col. Lorenzo Thomas), 14 June 1857, Headquarters, Troops Serving in Kansas, Letters Sent (RG 393) National Archives.

I have the honor to acknowledge the receipt of a communication from the Head Qtrs. of the Army dated Washington [May] 28th 1857 . . . notifying me of the probability of my being designated to the command of a force to march to and winter in Utah. . . .

I trust the General-in-chief will excuse the liberty I take in expressing my opinion that the force proposed to be assigned to the service in Utah, viz: 2nd Dragoons, 5th & 10th Infantry, and Phelps' Battery, is scarcely adequate to accomplish the task designed. To effect anything in a moral point of view, its numbers should be largely increased; and, in the event of resistance by the Mormons to such a force, success would be very doubtful when it can be made certain with a larger force.

I propose this increase, viz: 6th Regt. of Infantry if not needed to be sent to California, their destination. 1st Regt. of Cavalry to serve as escorts from Fort Laramie to Utah. A Battalion of 2nd Infantry to garrison Fort Laramie. (6 Cos. at least)

The 2nd Dragoons, 5th, 6th, and 10th Infantry, & Phelps' Battery should not be subject to any details which might separate them from each other until after the disposition of the Mormons has been made known.[13]

This is the very least force that should move upon Utah; with it, by judicious management, the Mormons may be brought to a sense of their duties without blood being shed. A smaller force would invite an attack.

Operating 1200 miles from our depot through a country which for 700 miles has no timber, the only fuel being buffalo dung (and that is becoming very scarce), and having a climate in which the snow falls early in October, where the thermometer stands 38 [degrees] below zero, without depots of any kind on the road; it well behooves the commander of such an expedition to invite the most serious consideration of the government to an understanding, which if not properly met, may be most disastrous not only to the troops but to the country. . . .

Two depots will be absolutely necessary for the troops operating in Utah. One at Fort Laramie, and the other at Green River near Bridgers Fort. This last position is one hundred miles from the Salt Lake, the road from which to the Salt Lake is a succession of defiles through the mountains. It would be unwise to attempt to move the troops and their supplies together through

---

[13] The Fifth Infantry, most of the Tenth Infantry, and Phelps's Battery of the Fourth Artillery moved west from Fort Leavenworth in a body during the last half of July. The Second Dragoons were retained in Kansas until September and did not reach Fort Bridger until the third week of November. The Sixth Infantry was not ordered to Utah until the spring of 1858, and even then was diverted to California without ever passing through Salt Lake City.

> this part of the road. The only other wagon road is round by Fort Hall, and is one hundred fifty miles further. . . .
>
> I respectfully suggest the force for Utah should be instructed to winter near Fort Laramie to move early in the spring to Utah. One Regiment, should it become necessary, could be pushed through to act as an escort and for the protection of any civil officers that may be sent out this year.[14] The remainder would be made very efficient troops by the spring, and could reach Utah in sufficient time for any operations which might be demanded of them. . . .
>
> In the event of the Government being resolved upon sending a force through to Utah this season, a Quartermaster or agent should be sent there immediately to procure as much hay and grain as will supply the animals to be sent. The person sent should be discreet and possess some knowledge of the Mormons. Such a person, I think, can be obtained in this part of the country.[15]

Cold Water upon the Utah Expedition: Controversy over Harney's Enthusiasm

For a variety of complex reasons—including mixed signals sent by Harney himself—rumors arose early in the Utah War that General Harney did not really want to go to Utah. The speculation was so widespread that it caused confusion among Harney's officers as to whether there would indeed be a Utah Expedition in 1857, a hope for delay already fueled by the lateness of the season and the absence of detailed instructions from the War Department. As the rumor went, Harney's personal preference was for duty in Kansas. Even in isolated La Costilla, New Mexico Territory, one observer gossiped that "I don't believe that Harney intended to go out from the start.—He got Governor Walker to make application for him to remain in Kansas and stayed behind to make himself obnoxious to one half of the population of the states."[16]

---

[14] The notion of a one-regiment push into the Salt Lake Valley was not included in Harney's 7 June memorandum for Floyd and may represent Harney's subsequent realization that, for political reasons, an expeditionary force could not be delayed in its entirety until 1858. A week later Scott told Floyd that he viewed such a force as a dangerous half-measure.

[15] Harney may already have had one of his own quartermasters in mind. This memorandum as well as the companion paper for Floyd of 7 June have never been published. Historians Richard D. Poll and Ralph W. Hansen may have alluded to one or both letters in 1961 in arguing that in late June "Harney, fearing the lateness of the season would prevent reaching Salt Lake before winter, unsuccessfully advised against a move at this time." Poll and Hansen, "'Buchanan's Blunder,'" 124.

[16] J. W. Parthoff to W. W. H. Davis, 2 May 1858, W. W. H. Davis Papers. It is unclear who Parthoff was; Davis was a Pennsylvania newspaper editor recently resigned as secretary and acting governor of New Mexico.

In all likelihood Harney's 7, 12, and 14 June memos to Secretary Floyd, Colonel Cooper, and General Scott advising delay for military, professional reasons spawned such rumors about Harney's personal preferences. This advice was technically confidential in the sense of being unpublished, but Harney's written comments had been seen by adjutants at various army headquarters and exposed to both the general in chief and secretary of war. Even though Harney's advice mirrored Scott's own 26 May counsel to Floyd, at the very end of the war's active phase, an exasperated Scott lashed out at Harney in an "unofficial" letter to Floyd. In this message Scott enclosed a confidential note from the Utah Expedition's adjutant "too interesting to be withheld from the Head of the War Department." Paraphrasing a critical Maj. Fitz John Porter, Scott wrote: "General Harney, its first commander, threw cold water upon the Utah Expedition at the outset. Those under him were infected by discouragement, and [enlisted] desertions and tendered resignations [by officers] followed."[17]

Furthermore, it is known that Harney was indiscreet in comments made informally to brother officers at Fort Leavenworth. On 28 June, for example, Capt. Jesse A. Gove of the Tenth Infantry informed his wife, "Now as to Utah. Gen. Harney is opposed to going, strongly so. He has written on that it is impossible to move from here with an army this season with any possible advantage, and it is the general impression here that we will not go. I hope it may prove so."[18] Small wonder that speculation spread throughout the army and beyond as to Harney's enthusiasm.

By the 1890s conjecture about Harney's motives and preferences had blossomed into a full-blown conspiracy theory developed to explain the Utah Expedition's embarrassments while exculpating the army from responsibility for them. Accordingly, when 1st Lt. William R. Hamilton published his history of the campaign, he included a fantastic story of intrigue involving Harney and unidentified political "allies" who allegedly plotted to keep the expedition in Kansas for as long as possible:

> But Harney, who was not adverse to political aspirations, had no desire to leave Kansas and go out to Utah, where he could see ahead of him no glory,

[17] Maj. Fitz John Porter [unsigned] to Maj. Irvin McDowell [September?] 1858, originally included with Scott to Floyd, 30 October 1858, transcription at Utah State Historical Society, 1939 Federal Writers Project Typescripts, Indian Affairs 1855–59 (USHS A458). The Porter to McDowell enclosure is missing, having been returned by Floyd to Scott.

[18] Capt. Gove to Mrs. Gove, 28 June 1857, Hammond, ed., *The Utah Expedition*, 7.

> nothing but hard work, and perhaps defeat. So by the aid of friends his orders were changed. But it took time to do this, so the expedition had to be delayed. Therefore we state that the delay of the troops in Kansas, during the summer, was not justly chargeable to the War Department, but to Harney, who had through his friends influence enough to retard War Department orders. That the expedition started too late there is no doubt.[19]

What were the facts? In early August Harney wrote to Floyd to request "my early release from the service in Kansas" so that he might join the Utah Expedition in the field. Throughout the late summer and fall he also badgered Governor Walker on this subject and even went so far as to lobby Floyd by dispatching his adjutant, Captain Alfred Pleasonton, to Washington so that "his thorough knowledge of the service, as connected with the troops serving in Kansas, may be at the disposal of the department, and that my views, of which he is fully possessed, may be distinctly and clearly submitted."[20] Surely the Mormons, if not the army's skeptics, expected to deal with Harney at close quarters. They took seriously his assignment to Utah, Harney's assertions that he would winter in either the Salt Lake Valley or hell, and his reported threats about personally administering summary justice to church leaders. Harney had never before flinched from difficult or unappealing assignments.[21]

Perhaps the most reliable indicator (other than his own words) of Harney's motivations during the summer of 1857 was the ferocity with which he worked to organize the Utah Expedition. He transferred regiments from Florida and Minnesota Territory, hired the Mormons' old enemy Jim Bridger as his chief guide, assembled a complete staff at Fort Leavenworth, and shuttled recruits west from Governor's Island in New York Harbor.[22] Harney drove his quartermasters relentlessly to acquire horses, mules, draft oxen, pack saddles, wagons, and tents by the thousands while his commissary officers contracted for flour, salt pork, hard bread, dried vegetables, and beef cattle

---

[19] Hamilton, "History of the Mormon Rebellion of 1856–57," 347.

[20] Harney to Floyd, 8 August 1857, Records of Adjt. Gen.'s Office, Letters Received (RG 94), National Archives; Harney to Floyd, 11 October 1857, Adams, ed., *Transactions of the Kansas State Historical Society*, 313.

[21] As recently as 1856 he had accepted command of the campaign against the Seminoles in Florida, the reputational graveyard of multiple senior officers. Before that Harney had interrupted a furlough with his family in Paris to accept command of the Sioux Expedition and a brutal winter bivouac at Fort Pierre, Nebraska Territory.

[22] A complete list of Harney's staff for the Utah campaign appears in a Washington dispatch of 25 July 1857, reprinted in *Sun* (Pittsfield, Mass.), 30 July 1857, 2.

Barracks and Hospital, Fort Leavenworth, Kansas, 1858
This image by C. C. Mills is among the first photographs of the Utah Expedition's main Missouri River staging post. From the Lee-Palfrey Collection. *Courtesy of the Manuscript Division, Library of Congress.*

on a scale unprecedented in the history of American plains warfare.[23] In full pursuit of his Utah mission, Harney was as implacable as he was efficient. Unwilling to brook delay, he was ruthless when confronting obstacles. For example, when Harney set out to secure the services of his favorite field quartermaster, the Second Dragoons' 1st Lt. John Buford, the general perceived Buford's commander at Fort Riley, Brevet Maj. Lewis A. Armistead, to be dilatory in releasing him. Harney retaliated in mid-June by arresting Armistead and ordering him to stand trial before a general court-martial, a vindictiveness that required the intervention of Winfield Scott to ensure not only

[23] "Movement of U.S. Troops" and "The Utah Expedition," *Missouri Republican* (St. Louis), 3 and 4 July 1857, 2/1 both issues.

Buford's orderly transfer to Harney but preservation of both Armistead's effectiveness and reputation.[24]

On balance Harney's temperament and behavior during the summer of 1857 were those of a professional soldier who preferred an active campaign against the despised Mormons—albeit ill-timed and risky—to an indefinite peacekeeping role at the beck and call of Kansas's governor.[25]

This Highly Improper Departure: Re-ignition of the Scott-Harney Feud

All of this activity was undertaken within the context of long-standing enmity between Generals Harney and Scott. It was a conflict aggravated during the summer of 1857 by Scott's geographic and behavioral distance from the War Department and Harney's penchant for circumventing him to deal directly with the president and secretary. When these civilian superiors bypassed Scott, the general either let the matter pass or noted his disapproval with care. But when Harney was the offender, sparks flew.[26]

The catalyst for the worst such interpersonal explosion was the ubiquitous Captain Pleasonton's abrupt 11 July telegram on Harney's behalf to President Buchanan. This wire demanded authority over a regiment and two military posts unsuccessfully requested by Harney in his earlier memos to Floyd and Scott. To Buchanan Pleasonton wired:

> GEN[L] harney desires the troops of sixth infantry now at forts kearney and

[24] The record of the Harney-Armistead clash is fragmentary and elusive. See the charges and specifications preferred against Armistead enclosed with Harney to Thomas, 20 June 1857, Records of the Adjt. Gen.'s Office, Letters Received (RG 94), National Archives; and Special Orders No. 22, 5 July 1857, Headquarters of Troops Serving in Kansas (RG 393), ibid.

[25] Recently evidence has surfaced that during 1857 Harney developed a romantic relationship with Sarah Ashton Stuart, a St. Louis woman, in the long-term absence of his wife in France. One could argue that her consequent pregnancy and the 1858 birth of their daughter, Ada Stuart Harney, could have been as strong a motivator for the general's departure from Fort Leavenworth as for any reluctance on his part to leave Kansas that summer. On 12 September 1872 Harney acknowledged his paternity in an emotional letter to the mother; text attached to e-mail message, John D. Rutledge to MacKinnon, 13 February 2003. Mr. Rutledge is Harney's great-great-grandson through Ada. The earlier birth of another illegitimate Harney daughter, Mary Caroline Harney, to a Winnebago woman in 1829 or 1830 is discussed in Adams, *General William S. Harney*, 36, as well as in an internet posting, "My Relationship to General Harney," http://homepage.mac.com/wieganbr/Harneyrelationship.html (accessed 26 March 2002).

[26] The origins of the Scott-Harney antipathy lay in Harney's Mexican War clash with E. V. Sumner, a Scott protégé; MacKinnon and Ellis, "Edwin Vose Sumner," *The New Encyclopedia of the American West*, 1084–85.

> laramie to be kept there & those positions placed under his orders these measures are indispensible to the success of the movement to utah let instructions be sent by telegraph.[27]

This telegram produced immediate compliance from an anxious president and secretary of war, but when Adjutant General Cooper sent a copy of Floyd's response to army headquarters, the message drew a sharp rebuke from the general in chief. From New York Scott's adjutant informed Harney that:

> [T]he General directs me to express his surprise at this highly improper departure from the plain line of your duty. Nor is this the only case in which you have recently passed by him. . . . The General-in-Chief was specially charged by the War Department with the preparation of the Utah Expedition, and from him you received all your instructions. To him, therefore, more especially should you have addressed yourself in reference to your important command. He further directs me to say that your future communications will be made through the prescribed channel of communication, except in cases where the higher authorities may specially call for direct reports.[28]

An unrepentant, if not belligerent, Harney replied:

> In answer to your first statement, I desire to inform the General-in-chief that I made a direct request of the President, to place Forts Kearney and Laramie under my orders, as I deemed the interests of the service and the success of the movement to Utah depended upon the most prompt and decided action in this matter; which I did not believe would be obtained by the delay necessary to submit it to the General-in-chief. I was the more confirmed in this opinion, from the fact of having made the request of the General-in-chief, fully and distinctly, in my communication to his Head Quarters, of June 14, 1857, to which request no attention was paid.[29]

Scott responded to this rejoinder through yet another adjutant, who informed Harney: "I have submitted your letter to the General-in-Chief, and am instructed, by him, to say he regrets to find it not satisfactory,—but that he will not trouble you further, on the subject, at this time."[30]

---

[27] Pleasonton to Buchanan, 11 July 1857, Records of Adjt. Gen.'s Office, Letters Received (RG 94), National Archives.

[28] Thomas to Harney, 17 July 1857, ibid.

[29] Harney to Thomas, 29 July 1857, Records of the War Department (RG 98), National Archives.

[30] McDowell to Harney, 10 August 1857, Headquarters of the Army, Letters Sent (RG 108), National Archives. At this juncture Scott could afford to step over the confrontation knowing that Harney was being superseded by Johnston.

Squaw Killer and Mad Bear: The Mormons' Adversary

Given these controversies, what kind of man was William S. Harney? In 2001 George Rollie Adams published a first-rate biography, but no contemporaneous description of Harney during 1857 has surfaced of the type generated by his subordinates during the earlier Sioux Expedition of 1855–56.[31] It is helpful, then, to consider descriptions of Harney during the Utah War period that come to us through the obscure old-age reminiscences of two frontier greenhorns: Samuel Adams Drake, a young job-seeking Bostonian who encountered Harney at Fort Leavenworth in the spring of 1858; and Brevet 2d Lt. Samuel Wragg Ferguson of the Second Dragoons, who limned a portrait of Leavenworth City as he saw it during the summer of 1857 immediately after his West Point graduation. Ferguson's narrative especially provides a feel for the raw, wide-open, and frenetic scramble as quartermasters, troop commanders, freighters, and bravos jostled one another at the public trough.

Drake, Recollections of the Old Army in Kansas, Beinecke Library.

General Percifer [*sic*] F. Smith, who was to command the Utah expedition, had just died, and was succeeded by Harney, the old Indian fighter.[32] I was frequently at the general's quarters, where Alfred Pleasonton, his A.A.G. did the honors most acceptably. Pleasonton was then a natty-looking young fellow in a dragoon's jacket. . . .

Harney himself was a man of imposing physique, over six feet, perfectly well made, and though getting along in years, as vigorous and erect as an oak. It was my fancy to picture him as a soldier of the Suwarrow or Blücher type,[33] to whom the prospect of an active campaign was like the sound of the trumpet to an old war horse, after the dull routine of camp and garrison. For those questions requiring delicate handling, constantly arising then and there between the civil and military authorities, no man could have been worse fitted; and for the whole race of politicians he had the professional soldier's undisguised contempt: War was his trade, peace his aversion.

---

[31] Adams, *General William S. Harney*, 159–81; see also MacKinnon, "Review Essay," [Harney] *New Mexico Historical Review*, 431–37. During the Sioux Expedition Harney acquired the nickname "Squaw Killer" because of the number of women and children killed at the battle of Ash Hollow/Blue Water Creek. Appalled at Harney's brutal command style, one officer vowed never again to serve under him, while a Lakota chief with whom Harney later treated at Fort Pierre dubbed him "Mad Bear." Paul, *Blue Water Creek*.

[32] Drake was describing the events surrounding his arrival at Fort Leavenworth in the spring of 1858, not those of a year earlier at the beginning of the Utah War.

[33] Reference to European generals of the Napoleonic Wars.

There were giants in those days. What has become of the men of commanding presence for which the old army was so noted and so notable—the Scotts, Harneys, Sumners, [Pitcairn] Morrisons, [Charles A.] Mays, and many others I could name? . . .

Harney was rather brusque of manner, and abrupt of speech, though I believe not unkind at bottom. I have known a private soldier [to] sense his chance of getting speech of him tell his grievance and get as patient a hearing as if he had worn [officers'] shoulder-straps; but in his moments of wrath I doubt much if ever John Randolph [of Virginia], of famous memory, could have held a candle to Harney in the bigness or originality of his oaths.[34]

Ferguson, "With Albert Sidney Johnston's Expedition to Utah, 1857," Martin, Ed., *Collections of the Kansas State Historical Society*, 12 (1911–12): 304.

We all landed at Fort Leavenworth and were welcomed at the [Missouri River] landing by First Lieutenant [Charles H.] Tyler, of the Second dragoons, and we started under his guidance to pay our respects to the commanding general. On our way there we passed by the quarters of Lieutenant Tyler, who invited us to stop and have a toddy with him (this was before the [temperance] days of Carrie Nation), and we gladly accepted. While thus pleasantly occupied a shot was heard, and shortly an orderly reported that "one citizen had killed another near the guardhouse." Lieutenant Tyler, who was officer of the day, remarked: "Those two men came together to my office, and one asked protection from the other, who he said had threatened to kill him, at the same time stating that they were partners. Whereupon the partner coolly said: 'Yes, I do intend to kill him.' "

Tyler explained to them that it was a case for the civil authorities; that he could not interfere. They went off together. This was an hour before we heard the shot.

The next morning I relieved Lieutenant Tyler as officer of the day. On going together to the commanding officer to report, Tyler, after relating the incident of the murder, said something about having the man buried, when General Harney broke out with: "No! let him lie there. I have reported the case to the civil authorities in Leavenworth city, and in this as in various other matters, they have not taken the slightest notice of my communication."

When I visited the guardhouse in my rounds I found that some kind person had thrown enough dirt over the body to cover it. This was the only notice ever taken of the murder. Such was my welcome to Kansas! On arriving at

[34] This twenty-six-page holograph manuscript was written by Drake in one sitting sometime following the Civil War, in which he served as a lieutenant colonel of Kansas volunteers. Drake's comments about Harney reflect not only his skill as a newspaperman but undoubtedly his awareness of the general's post–Utah War imbroglios.

> Fort Leavenworth I learned that neither the general who was to command it, nor the dragoons that were to form an important part of the expedition, had started, but that both had been detained in Kansas, at the earnest solicitation of Governor Walker, on account of the terrible state of disorder and violence in which the country was. The dragoons were scattered; a company here, another there, assisting the civil authorities—a very disagreeable, thankless duty.[35]

Perhaps one way to view Harney and his character is to consider the fact that by the time of the Utah War, the army had court-martialed him four times and a civil court had tried (but acquitted) him a fifth time for bludgeoning a defenseless female slave to death.

A Suggestion—Not an Order, Nor Even a Recommendation: Orders for General Harney

Notwithstanding General Scott's 28 May alert that he was likely to command the Utah Expedition, Harney did not receive formal orders and detailed instructions for this assignment until early July following their release on 29 June. It was an incredible delay at a time when the expedition was already two months late by the inexorable timetable of the seasons. Through his aide de camp Scott made clear to Harney that the delay was not due to his indecision:

> Orders for the Utah Expedition and instructions for you as its commander were prepared at the desire of the War Department, and forwarded from this office, for approval, on the 8th of this month. More recently they have been discussed between the President, the Secretary of War & the General-in-Chief in person and substantially fixed upon. But the papers, left for formal approval, are not yet received from Washington, though expected daily. They will be immediately issued when received here.[36]

When Scott obtained sanction to release Harney's orders on 29 June, they were sent to Fort Leavenworth by conventional U.S. mail rather than by military courier or telegraph, notwithstanding the urgency involved. Here was another example of the operational differences between the U.S. Army and

---

[35] Ferguson wrote his recollections of service with the antebellum Second Dragoons in the late nineteenth century when he was financially strapped. In addition to this published account, several typescript versions under varying but similar titles are in the Samuel Wragg Ferguson Papers, Hill Memorial Library, Louisiana State University, Baton Rouge. During the Civil War Ferguson received the formal surrender of Fort Sumter in 1861 and raised the first Confederate flag over that post. He rose to be a Confederate brigadier general of cavalry.

[36] Lay to Harney, 26 June 1857, Headquarters of the Army, Letters Sent (RG 108), National Archives.

Nauvoo Legion, to which Brigham Young routinely sent messages by overnight courier, even in the wilderness. Although their text has been published elsewhere, Harney's instructions are presented below because of their importance. This set of material constituted the army's sole official guidance for the Utah Expedition's commander (and his successor) during the entire campaign notwithstanding substantial changes in conditions, circumstances, and challenges over the next two years.

LAY TO HARNEY, 29 JUNE 1857, HOUSE EX. DOC. 71, SERIAL 956, 7–9.

[To the material already sent to you] The general-in-chief desires me to add in his name the following instructions, prepared in concert with the War Department, and sanctioned by its authority, whenever required.

The community and, in part, the civil government of Utah Territory are in a state of substantial rebellion against the laws and authority of the United States.[37] A new civil governor is about to be designated, and to be charged with the establishment and maintenance of law and order. Your able and energetic aid, with that of the troops to be placed under your command, is relied to insure the success of his mission.

The principles by which you should be guided have been already indicated in a somewhat similar case, and are here substantially repeated.[38]

If the governor of the Territory, finding the ordinary course of judicial proceedings of the power vested in the United States' marshals and other proper officers inadequate for the preservation of the public peace and the due execution of the laws, should make requisition upon you for a military force to aid him as a *posse comitatus* in the performance of that official duty, you are hereby directed to employ for that purpose the whole or such apart of your command as may be required; or should the governor, the judges, or marshals of the Territory find it necessary directly to summon a part of your troops, to aid either in the performance of his duties, you will take care that the summons be promptly obeyed.[39] And in no case will you, your officers or men, attack any body of citizens whatever, except on such requisition or summons, or in sheer self-defence.

---

[37] Remarkably, this sentence was the administration's sole declarative statement on the crucial, politically volatile subject of rebellion until the president's conflicting comments in his 8 December 1857 first annual message to Congress.

[38] A reference to the ground rules for use of the army in Kansas.

[39] In 1859 Buchanan and Attorney General Black repudiated their own authorization for the expedition to respond to calls for troops by judges and marshals and vested authority for such levies solely with Utah's governor. Because of this reversal and because the phrasing of Harney's orders here differed from the instructions issued to the new governor by Secretary of State Cass on 30 July 1857, these dynamics created a substantial upset among the federal appointees once the army was actually into Utah. The clearest description of these complex communications and policy disconnects is Furniss, *The Mormon Conflict*, 97–99.

In executing this delicate function of the military power of the United States the civil responsibility will be upon the governor, the judges and marshals of the Territory. While you are not to be, and cannot be subjected to the orders, strictly speaking, of the governor, you will be responsible for a jealous, harmonious and thorough co-operation with him, or frequent and full consultation, and will conform your action to his requests and views in all cases where your military judgment and prudence do not forbid, nor compel you to modify, in execution, the movements he may suggest. No doubt is entertained that your conduct will fully meet the moral and professional responsibilities of your trust, and justify the high confidence already reposed in you by the government.

The lateness of the season, the dispersed condition of the troops, and the smallness of the numbers available, have seemed to present elements of difficulty, if not hazard, in this expedition. But it is believed that these may be compensated by unusual care in its outfit, and great prudence in its conduct. All disposable recruits have been reserved for it.

So well is the nature of this service appreciated, and so deeply are the honor and interests of the United States involved in its success, that I am authorized to say the government will hesitate at no expense requisite to complete the efficiency of your little army, and to insure health and comfort to it, as far as attainable. Hence, in addition to the liberal orders for its supply heretofore given—and it is known that ample measures, with every confidence of success, have been dictated by the chiefs of staff departments here[40]—a large discretion will be made over to you in the general orders for the movement. The employment of spies, guides, interpreters or laborers may be made to any reasonable extent you may think desirable.[41]

The prudence expected of you requires that you should anticipate resistance, general, organized and formidable, at the threshold, and shape your movements as if they were certain, keeping the troops well massed and in hand when approaching expected resistance.[42] Your army will be equipped, for a time, at least, as a self sustaining machine. Detachments will, therefore, not be lightly hazarded, and you are warned not to be betrayed into premature security or over confidence.

A small but sufficient force must, however, move separately from the main column, guarding the beef cattle and such other supplies as you may think

[40] Use of the word "here" betrays either Scott's confusion as to where he was or Buchanan's and Floyd's hand in drafting these instructions—given their issuance from Scott's headquarters in New York and the location of the staff chiefs in Washington.

[41] It was apparently on this authorization that Albert Sidney Johnston recruited a four-company battalion of volunteer infantrymen at Camp Scott in December 1857.

[42] In February 1858 the Buchanan administration's newspaper "organ" maintained that during the summer of 1857 no one in the administration or army anticipated Mormon resistance.

would too much encumber the march of the main body. The cattle may require to be marched more slowly than the troops, so as to arrive in Salt Lake valley in good condition, or they may not survive the inclemency and scanty sustenance of the winter.[43] This detachment, though afterwards to become the rear guard, may, it is hoped, be put in route before the main body, to gain as much time as possible before the latter passes it.

The general-in-chief suggests that feeble animals of draught and cavalry, should be left ten or twelve days behind the main column, at Fort Laramie, to recruit and follow.

It should be a primary object on arriving in the valley, if the condition of things permit, to procure not only fuel, but materials for hutting the troops. Should it be too late for the latter purpose, or should such employment of the troops be unsafe or impracticable, the tents (of Sibley's pattern) furnished will, it is hoped, afford a sufficient shelter.[44]

It is not doubted that a surplus of provisions and forage, beyond the wants of the resident population, will be found in the valley of Utah; and that the inhabitants, if assured by energy and justice, will be ready to sell them to the troops. Hence no instructions are given you for the extreme event of the troops being in absolute need of such supplies and their being withheld by the inhabitants. The necessities of such an occasion would furnish the law for your guidance.[45]

Besides the stated reports required by regulations, special reports will be expected from you, at the headquarters of the army, as opportunity may offer.

The general-in-chief desires to express his best wishes, official and personal, for your complete success and added reputation.

P.S.—The general-in-chief (in my letter of the 26th instant) has already conveyed to you a suggestion—not an order, nor even a recommendation[46]—that it might be well to send forward in advance a part of your horse to Fort Laramie, there to halt and be recruited in strength, by rest and by grain, before the main body comes up.

---

[43] When Indians made off with the army's principal cattle herd in central Kansas and raided a small supply train, Scott severely criticized Harney to Floyd for inattention to this paragraph, which, in turn, led to mutual recriminations.

[44] This new tepee-shaped tent was the patented invention of the Second Dragoons' Brevet Maj. Henry Hopkins Sibley and was being field tested by the Utah Expedition.

[45] Perhaps the most emblematic as well as galling example of this assumption's weakness was the failure to provide the expedition with an adequate supply of salt. This paragraph is remarkably ambiguous and permissive, open to interpretation as an unrestricted license to forage forcibly among Utah's population. In the spring of 1858 Mormon leaders would cite this language in Harney's instructions as proof that the Utah Expedition was attempting to obtain remounts by instigating deadly Indian raids on Mormon horse herds. George A. Smith to T. B. H. Stenhouse, 7 June 1858, Historian's Office, Letterpress books, LDS Archives.

To Bear Our Separation Cheerfully: Home Front Departures

Even before General Scott had released these instructions to Harney, the War Department had assigned him an ordnance officer, Brevet Capt. Jesse L. Reno. By 27 June Reno was hastening west from Philadelphia to Fort Leavenworth, an abrupt, wrenching departure for his wife Mary, then about two months pregnant. Through a quirk of military filing, we have Mrs. Reno's poignant first letter to her newly absent husband—virtually the only such home-front letter to survive from the federal side of the conflict.

Mary C. Reno to Brevet Captain Reno, 28 June 1857, Camp Floyd, U.T., File (RG 92), National Archives.

My darling husband,[47]

You left only last night and here I am seated with a large sheet of paper before me, as though I had a budget of news to write to you. I have no news at all, but more interesting subjects—even for you—myself—yourself—and another little self who came into my room this morning and told me what I already knew to my cost—that—"papa had gone to Utah." Biddy it seems had already taught him the sad truth.[48] He shall not forget you if it is possible for me to keep you in his memory, but I fear indeed that a years absence will efface all but the name with him. Last night after you had left us so sadly and I had watched the last glimpse of that carriage which seemed to carry you off so swiftly, I sat a long time thinking—and it was a great comfort to me to reflect that there has never been anything but truth and kindness and love between us—and I offered up a little prayer to God to keep us so always & to make us both to bear our separation cheerfully. You may imagine my slumbers were often disturbed during the night and I found myself this morning contrary to my resolution, very lazy. I did not wish to go to church this morning—not because I did not feel well—but because every one went from Major Hagner's[49] and I was fearful of intruding upon such a large party. However I read the lesson to myself at home and succeeded in teasing my thoughts away from you. The servants seemed very much distressed at your departure and I heard a good many sobs and groans after you left. I surely believe every

---

[46] This Scott-like phrase is perhaps the murkiest to be found in Utah Expedition orders.

[47] Photocopy and transcription courtesy of Lt. Col. William F. McConnell, U.S.A. (Ret'd.) of Reno, Nev., author of the leading biography of Jesse and Mary Reno, *Remember Reno*. Notwithstanding Mary Reno's hardships, the contrast is marked between her relatively genteel life and the threadbare, hardscrabble existence of the women soon to be left at home by most Nauvoo Legionnaires.

[48] A reference to the Renos' young son Lewis and his nanny, "Biddy."

[49] Brevet Maj. Peter V. Hagner, Reno's former commander at Philadelphia's Frankfurt Arsenal, who had preceded him at West Point by ten years.

> one loves you. There is certainly nothing like occupation to dispel grief and you in your busy wandering life will have an opportunity of testing it. I expect to feel much better tomorrow when I can occupy myself with something else than thinking. I suppose too I shall soon have something which will oblige me to decide upon my plans—and then to work.[50]

Unfeigned Anxiety: Enter Major McCulloch, Exit Captain Van Vliet

Notwithstanding Harney's herculean efforts in Kansas and his earlier success in organizing the Sioux Expedition, Secretary Floyd grew uneasy about the Utah Expedition as June turned into July. Sensing disaster, Floyd turned for help to a fellow southerner and Democrat, Ben McCulloch of Texas, who happened to be in Washington. McCulloch was one of the scrappy Tennesseans who twenty years earlier had rushed to Texas to fight her revolution alongside Sam Houston. A subsequently prominent officer in the Texas Rangers as well as in the Mexican War, McCulloch was U.S. marshal for the eastern district of Texas during the mid-1850s. Either because of or in spite of his reputation for toughness, Buchanan had tendered McCulloch Utah's governorship in May 1857. This offer prompted one editor to write: "Major McCulloch is described as a thin spare man, of great muscle and activity, with a pleasant face, mild and courteous manners, and an air of diffidence. He is a man of cool, determined bravery, and, if he can be prevailed on to accepted, is probably the fittest man in the United States for Governor of Utah."[51] McCulloch declined appointment, reportedly because he believed that his reputation for ferocity would have been a liability among the Mormons.

Although he had refused Buchanan, McCulloch responded to Floyd's 8 July plea that he undertake a mission to Kansas to help Harney with the Utah Expedition's organization and to provide Floyd with an assessment of its prospects for success. There is no indication that Floyd officially consulted General Scott about McCulloch's assignment, although surely Scott became aware of it as soon as army officers and newspapers commented on his presence in Kansas. How and when, if at all, Scott saw McCulloch's 21 July report

---

[50] A probable reference to her pregnancy and need to move from the arsenal during Captain Reno's Utah assignment.

[51] *Daily Republican* (Binghamton, N.Y.), 28 May 1857, 2/2. Although a civilian in 1857, McCulloch held the military rank of major while serving with Texas volunteer troops during the Mexican War.

is also unclear. There are signs that McCulloch may have used a presumed need to consult Governor Walker on Kansas affairs as a ruse to obscure War Department anxieties over prospects for the Utah campaign.[52] This is one of the few U.S. government gambits of the period about which Brigham Young and his agents were unaware.

FLOYD TO MCCULLOCH, 8 JULY 1857, SEC. OF WAR, LETTERS SENT (RG 107), NATIONAL ARCHIVES.

It is a matter of notoriety that an expedition is fitting out under Brigadier General W. S. Harney, U.S. Army, for service in the Territory of Utah. There are many unusual circumstances which make the command of General Harney one of peculiar delicacy and responsibility, and this Department feels unfeigned anxiety that he shall be fully provided with every element of success in its power to place at his disposal. . . .

[Y]ou are accordingly requested and empowered to proceed to Fort Leavenworth to confer with General Harney on matters generally connected with his expedition, for the purpose not only of ascertaining whether the outfit provided for him is in all respects satisfactory, but also *of receiving his views in relation to supplies and aid of any kind which must in future be forwarded to him.*

Some points of enquiry are here suggested, by way of example.

Are the animals furnished for draught &c of a description likely to withstand the fatigues of so long a march at this season?

Can they possibly subsist upon the grass to be found along the route, and has ample provision been made for them in the way of forage?

Are the wagons such as seem, on rigid examination, fit to endure the march?

Are the civil employees, especially the wagon masters and other superintendents, apparently of reliable character?[53]

Are the arms, equipments and other army supplies in good serviceable condition?

What is the reported condition of the route of travel, as to grazing, roads &c?

What is likely to be the reception the troops will meet with in Utah?

Any reliable information concerning the condition of the Mormons, their disposition &c[?]

After returning to Washington less that two weeks later, McCulloch gave Floyd a report summarizing current troop levels in Kansas and making recommendations for dealing with the needs of both that territory and Utah.

---

[52] For an example of eastern newspaper discussion of McCulloch's visit to Kansas, see "The News," *Commercial Advertiser* (Buffalo, N.Y.), 21 July 1857, 2/1.

[53] In retrospect this was an interesting question in view of the fact that among the thousands of teamsters were such subsequent criminals as William C. Quantrill, David Poole, and George Shepard.

With hindsight, it was a document riddled with mistaken assumptions and heavily influenced by Harney's view of the campaign.

McCulloch to Floyd, 21 July 1857, Adjt. Gen.'s Office, Letters Received (RG 94), National Archives.

I beg leave to submit the following report and at the same time assure the Department that it meets the full concurrence of Gen. Harney who commands the Utah Expedition.

The number of troops at Fort Leavenworth, on the morning of July 13 was in the aggregate 1937. . . .

To provide 1st for Kansas—

Retain the 8 Companies of 2nd Dragoons at Fort Leavenworth and order [Capt. Thomas West] Sherman's Battery of the 4th [3d] Artillery from Fort Snelling to Fort Leavenworth *as soon as possible* in order to replace Phelps' Battery under orders for Utah.[54] With this force Gen. Harney can keep Kansas quiet until ordered to Utah. This need not be done before the 1st of October, as he can by making the necessary arrangements overtake the forces for Utah before it reaches Green River, and thus he will be present with the troops at the time they enter those strong mountain defiles through which the road passes to reach Salt Lake City.[55]

Arrangements for Utah

Recall the Cheyenne Expedition and order it to Fort Laramie *at once* and place Forts Kearney [*sic*] and Laramie under Gen. Harney's orders. . . .

This will give for the Utah Expedition 2097[56]

The advantages of this arrangement will be very great. The Cheyenne Expedition if found at Fort Laramie or in that vicinity will be fresh for the march, and will furnish from 80 to 100 Wagons, a great part of which can be used to draw forage from Fort Laramie for a portion of the road almost destitute of grass and when the expedition may suffer materially without some grain at that late season of the year.[57]

---

[54] T. W. ("Tim") Sherman is not to be confused with the later famous W. T. ("Cump") Sherman, who was then a civilian.

[55] The flaw in McCulloch's assessment was that the Nauvoo Legion struck the expedition's vulnerable supply trains on the night of 4–5 October on the high plains east of Green River nearly two months before the commander and the dragoons caught up with the expedition.

[56] McCulloch failed to understand the massive desertions that were taking place at Fort Leavenworth and to anticipate those that would continue on the trail west. He also missed the extent to which the grueling, long-distance campaigning by Sumner's Cheyenne Expedition would make its troops and animals unfit for further service that summer. William Y. Chalfant, *Cheyennes and Horse Soldiers.*

[57] Earlier in the summer, the condition of Sumner's transportation was such that he had largely abandoned his wagons and forged on after the Cheyennes using pack mules for support. After the crucial battle at Solomon's Fork he had to transport his wounded by a form of Indian travois rather than wagons.

The remainder of the Cheyenne Expedition, two Companies of 1st Cavalry and two of the 2nd Dragoons now at Fort Leavenworth, the whole under Col. Sumner's orders as Commander of that Post will afford a sufficient number of mounted men for expresses and escorts as well as for the protection of the Depot at that point.[58]

Fort Kearney to be garrisoned by the 2 companies of 7th Inf. now under orders for Fort Laramie—Should it be necessary, they can be retained in Kansas for a time.

The Company of the 6th Inf. now at Fort Kearney should go to Fort Riley where the Head-Quarters of the Reg^{t} should be retained

Brevet Col. C. F. Smith (Lieut Col. 10th Inf) Senior Col by Brevet of the whole command (including the Cheyenne Expedition) to be placed in his Brevet rank in command of the troops on the march under the orders of Genl Harney. This recommendation is made on the ground of his superior efficiency for the particular duty.[59]

Gen. Harney should send a discreet staff officer by express to Utah in advance of the expedition with a letter to Brigham Young requesting him to facilitate the furnishing of supplies of grain on the road for the use of the troops—[60]

Great efforts are being made to transport sufficient grain to provide the animals of the expedition with a certain allowance each day, until their arrival at Salt Lake. This can be easily accomplished should the Mormons be permitted by Young to send supplies to meet the Army on the road, and by judicious application to Young this may be effected.

At any rate its importance is so great it is at least worth attempting.

Should this fail, the transportation of the Cheyenne expedition will be almost indispensable, as by ~~them~~ it, grain could be transported from Fort Laramie.

It would be unwise to depend wholly upon grass when this can be so easily avoided.

---

[58] Major McCulloch was probably unaware that then hanging over Sumner's head were disciplinary charges, which would be resolved by a November 1857 general court martial of which Harney was the initial presiding officer.

[59] This recommendation was sound, but fatefully it was disregarded, probably for reasons of protocol since Smith's senior (and commander) in the Tenth, Col. Edmund B. Alexander, was also present. Alexander not only provided weak leadership for the regiment but declined to fulfill his role as the expedition's senior officer present until a war council of his own officers virtually shamed him into assuming overall command after the October Lot Smith raid. Without mentioning him here, McCulloch (and Harney) surely understood Colonel Alexander's weaknesses and limitations.

[60] This recommendation reflected wishful thinking as well as a gross, costly miscalculation of Young's willingness to help the army, especially after the 1854–55 peccadilloes of the Steptoe Expedition. Nonetheless, as soon as Floyd read this paragraph he ordered Adjutant General Cooper to telegraph Harney: "You are authorized to send a discreet staff officer to Salt Lake City in advance of the troops, for the purposes suggested by you." Cooper to Harney, 21 July 1857, House Exec Doc. 71, Serial 956, 11.

> With regard to the specific and particular points suggested to me in your letter as worthy of observation I would simply remark that the animals, wagons and their necessary civil employees seem to be such as the Expedition requires and meet the approbation of the Commanding officer. The arms and equipments are in good order and in this connexion I would respectfully suggest the propriety of arming the teamsters or transport an additional quantity of weapons which in case of emergency could be used by them.
>
> The mail service to Utah should also be resumed as soon as practicable.[61]

One of the immediate results of McCulloch's visit to Harney was confirmation of Floyd's belated realization that the army needed to know more about likely Mormon reactions, especially the crucial assumption that they would sell provisions, forage, and lumber for troop quarters once the expedition reached the Salt Lake Valley. That at this late date Floyd felt the need to probe Mormon intentions was an unmistakable albeit hidden sign that the decision to intervene in Utah during 1857 had been based on inadequate forethought and consultation between the cabinet, War Department, and army. A week after the War Department's authorization to do so, Harney ordered one of his assistant quartermasters to Salt Lake City with a small escort to determine the realities of military procurement.

Harney's initial selection for this assignment was Capt. John H. Dickerson, but after a presumably restless night, the general rescinded Dickerson's assignment and ordered Capt. Stewart Van Vliet west in his place. Harney's substitution of Van Vliet for Dickerson was logical, for Van Vliet had a long, positive ten-year relationship with the Mormons. Harney probably calculated that his reception in Salt Lake City stood a better chance of success than that of a complete stranger.[62] What Harney did not anticipate is that Cap-

[61] The U.S. postal service on the Independence–Salt Lake route had been suspended at the beginning of June with abrogation of Hiram Kimball's and the Y. X. Carrying Company's contract; service was not resumed until May 1858. This counterproductive suspension had the unintended consequence of depriving the Utah Expedition as well as the Mormons of mail, a situation that annoyed General Scott and forced him to improvise an army courier service during the winter.

[62] With the emphasis placed by Harney, McCulloch, and Floyd on the need for a "discreet officer" for this detail, it is possible that, notwithstanding his own social peccadilloes, Harney worried about Dickerson's judgment. Later, during the summer of 1858, Dickerson came to the attention of the LDS church's and Legion's most senior leaders when he took up with the wife of Charles Moeller, a Legion lieutenant, whom he allegedly told "he was willing to resign her [back] to Moeller, but he would retain the right to sleep with her occasionally." Journal History, entry for 28 September 1858, LDS Archives. Although neither Dickerson nor Van Vliet have biographers, Professor Mark R. Wilson argues that the two quartermasters were exceptionally able. Wilson, "The Politics of Procurement," 44 and 50. Van Vliet's instructions have been published elsewhere, and so are not included in this compilation. See Hafen and Hafen, eds., *Mormon Resistance*, 36–38.

tain Van Vliet balked at the assignment. Although he went as ordered, Van Vliet wrote to Quartermaster General Jesup from the trail: "I have considered the order for me to repair to Utah as exceedingly hard—as I have already served seven years on these plains—& should have urged to have been relieved from them. . . . I trust that upon my return that I may have the benefit of an equality of service."[63] Here was a grudging reluctance to visit Brigham Young unknown in Van Vliet's subsequently much-publicized mission to Utah.

Not Even the Archangel Michael: Governor Walker Explodes

Even before Governor Walker reached Kansas, a young cavalry officer serving there with Walker's son commented, "The Hon. R. J. Walker, I see, is now appointed Governor, as for some time past, it has been known here he would be. He is an able man, I have no doubt:—but he has no conception of the task he has undertaken to perform. No Governor, not even the archangel Michael, could give satisfaction to all parties here."[64]

It is unclear when Governor Walker fully realized that the Buchanan administration and General Scott indeed intended to send General Harney and his Second Dragoons to Utah, contrary to the president's March commitment that these resources would remain in Kansas. Nor is it clear how President Buchanan and Secretary Floyd expected to reconcile these conflicting needs and commitments.[65] Equally ambiguous is what Scott understood about this dilemma.

At first there was a cordial sparring between Walker and Buchanan. On 8 June Kansas's governor wrote to the president:

> It will never do to send General Harney to Utah until the difficulties in Kansas are settled. He is a terror to the black republicans [here] and just the man for the occasion. When first passing through Lawrence some of these black republicans told me the violent pro-slavery men, if I went for submitting the con-

---

[63] Van Vliet to Jesup, 9 August 1857, transcript courtesy of Professor Wilson, University of N.C. at Charlotte. Perhaps as a sop to Van Vliet, Harney permitted Van Vliet the luxury of traveling aboard an army ambulance rather than by horseback, a perquisite usually reserved for colonels.

[64] 2d Lt. George Dashiell Bayard to Samuel J. Bayard, 3 March 1857, Bayard, *Life of George Dashiell Bayard,* 115.

[65] The contentious relationship between Governor Walker and the administration during the summer of 1857 is convoluted and is presented here only in summary fashion and to the extent that it relates directly to Utah. For specialized analyses of this relationship, see Ponce, "Pledges and Principles," 87–99; Harmon, "President James Buchanan's Betrayal," 51–91.

> stitution to the people, would assassinate me or drive me from Lecompton. I told them I had fixed the exact day for running, namely, when General Harney ran first. They looked serious and did not relish the joke.[66]

In response to this anecdote, the president made a revealing private comment to the governor that the administration guarded for years:

> General Harney has been selected to command the expedition to Utah, but we must continue to leave him with you, at least until you are out of the woods. Kansas is vastly more important at the present moment than Utah. The pressure upon me continues without intermission. I pray that Divine Providence, in which I place my trust, may graciously preserve my life and my health, until the end of my term. But God's holy will be done in any event.[67]

Governor Walker had an earthier way of putting the same thought: "Important as the affairs of Utah may be, they do not threaten the peace of the country, or the stability of the Government. Utah in fact is a wretched excrescence, composed, mainly, of the worst foreign element, which can be readily exscinded at any time, without disturbing in the slightest degree the repose of any one State of this Union. But the difficulties in Kansas menanced [*sic*] the existence of the Government during the Presidential contest, and a successful insurrection here at this time, would be still more alarming."[68]

But as Walker saw armed rebellion unfolding in Lawrence and elsewhere as well as continued plans for Harney to launch and lead the Utah Expedition, he grew frantic and wrote angry letters of protest to Secretary of State Cass on 15 and 20 July.[69] This explosion triggered a chain of events within the administration by which Harney and his dragoons were retained in Kansas while simultaneously stripping the Utah Expedition of its commander and mounted escort. With both absent from the field, this was a decision fateful for the Utah Expedition and the vulnerability of its supply trains. To Harney Adjutant General Cooper telegraphed on 17 July:

[66] Walker to Buchanan, 8 June 1857, "Covode Investigation," House Report. Serial 648, 103–19.

[67] Buchanan to Walker, 12 July 1857, ibid. Buchanan's letter did not become public until April 1860 and only then under the pressure of a congressional investigation, which concluded: "Upon this administration shall hereafter rest the awful responsibility of delaying the removal of the army from Kansas until the winter of 1857, which was the cause of the fearful loss and suffering occasioned by the inability of the army to reach Salt Lake." Ibid., 9.

[68] Walker to Harney, 1 September 1857, Records of Adjt. Gen.'s Office, Letters Received (RG 94), National Archives; transcription courtesy of George Rollie Adams.

[69] An excellent review essay dealing with the historiography of the Kansas unrest is SenGupta, "Bleeding Kansas," 318–41. For the latest assessment of the army's role in this affair, see Mullis, *Peacekeeping on the Plains*. The scale of violence is analyzed in Watts, "How Bloody Was Bleeding Kansas?" 116–29.

THE SECRETARY OF WAR DIRECTS THAT YOU REMAIN IN KANSAS UNTIL FURTHER ORDERS WITH THE COMPANIES OF THE 2D DRAGOONS, AND THE LIGHT ARTILLERY COMPANY ATTACHED TO YOUR COMMAND. LET THE INFANTRY, WITH THE STORES PROCEED ON THE MARCH [TO UTAH], AS ALREADY DIRECTED. ACKNOWLEDGE BY TELEGRAPH.[70]

Ordinary Military Duties: Buchanan Instructs Utah's Governor-Designate

In the midst of these Kansas maneuverings, Buchanan at last found someone willing to accept appointment as Utah's governor. He was Alfred Cumming, the corpulent superintendent of Indian Affairs for the Missouri River's Upper Platte Agency based in St. Louis. Despite his marriage into Boston's patrician Samuel Adams family, Cumming's appointment was a desperate, undistinguished one following embarrassing refusal of the post by multiple more able candidates, including Ben McCulloch. Cumming's only prior executive experience had been as mayor of Augusta, Georgia; his military experience was confined to that of a civilian sutler during the Mexican War. Had Buchanan scrutinized Cumming's more recent record as an Indian Affairs superintendent, what might have surfaced as a cautionary note would have been his severe 1855 conflict with Washington Territory's strong-willed governor, Isaac I. Stevens. This was a warning sign ignored during the summer of 1857 with a price to be paid once Cumming and Albert Sidney Johnston came together at close quarters at Fort Bridger in late November.[71]

Buchanan's 11 July appointment of Cumming was a "recess" one, meaning that with Congress adjourned Cumming's designation as governor took effect immediately without the delay of a Senate confirmation, which ultimately took

[70] Cooper to Harney, 17 July 1857, Records of Adjt. Gen.'s Office, Letters Sent (RG 94), National Archives. Having received this direction, Harney nonetheless allowed Phelps's battery to leave Fort Leavenworth with the Utah Expedition on his own authority because of the extent to which the expedition had been seriously weakened by scores of desertions. The next day Harney received a puzzling, conflicting wire from an out-of-touch Scott—transmitted four days earlier on 14 July—"which will require him to proceed at once to Utah, and Take with him the Second Dragoons as this is intended." Pleasonton to Cooper, 22 July 1857, ibid.

[71] Cumming and Johnston first met at Fort Leavenworth in early September 1857, at which time the governor-designate declined the colonel's offer that he accompany his fast-moving mounted detachment, perhaps out of consideration for his accompanying wife. The result was that Cumming moved west at a slower pace, in effect bringing up the Utah Expedition's rear. Depending upon how Johnston made this offer and the grace with which Cumming deflected it, the tensions between the two officers may have been rooted in this incident.

place in early 1858. Notwithstanding this avoidance of potential bureaucratic delay, the administration determined that Cumming should take the oath of office not in Washington but only after crossing into Utah, a decision that kept Cumming in the powerless status of governor-designate (rather than Utah's chief executive) for an additional four months. As had been the case following Harney's designation to command, a prolonged delay ensued in the State Department's drafting of Cumming's instructions, a process that inevitably involved Buchanan as well as Secretary Cass and Asst. Sec. John Appleton, Buchanan's proxy at the department. The resulting instructions, dated 30 July 1857, were in sharp contrast to the tone of those issued four weeks earlier to Harney by the drafting committee of Buchanan, Floyd, and Scott. Such a disconnect is not unique in American military history. On 26 May 1917 the U.S. Army's acting chief of staff and the secretary of war each issued orders to Maj. Gen. John J. Pershing that differed on such fundamental points as whether his World War I authority extended beyond France and whether his American command was to function separately or be integrated into the Allied forces.[72] Unquestionably Cumming's instructions were influenced by the events rapidly unfolding in Kansas as well as by Ben McCulloch's assessment of the Utah Expedition written nine days before finalization of Cumming's guidance.

Cass to Cumming, 30 July 1857, Gen. Records of the Dept. of State, Territorial Papers, Records of the Territories 1764–1873 (RG 59), National Archives.

> A detachment of the army is under orders to take up a position in that [Utah] country, for the performance of the ordinary military duties of security and protection upon our frontiers, and also, if necessary, to aid in the enforcement of the laws.[73] The commanding officer has been ordered to carry into effect your requisitions for the service of the troops in support of the public peace. A copy of these orders from the War Dept is herewith communicated.[74] . . . With any peculiar opinions of the inhabitants,[75] however

[72] Smythe, *Pershing: General of the Armies*, 11–12.

[73] The phrase "ordinary military duties" reflects Harney's counsel to Floyd of 7 June 1857 and Ben McCulloch's related advice of 21 July to Floyd that the Utah Expedition could be portrayed as the routine establishment and garrisoning of another military organization in the normal course of events—the Department of Utah.

[74] Notwithstanding the administration's care that Cumming be aware of the 29 June instructions issued to Harney, there is no indication that the War Department provided General Harney (or later Colonel Johnston) with these State Department instructions to Governor Cumming. In fact, when Johnston succeeded Harney in the Utah command, he had to retrieve his own orders, the 29 June instructions, from Harney at Fort Leavenworth, rather than receive a copy while meeting with the administration in Washington.

[75] A circumlocution for polygamy.

deplorable in themselves or revolting to the public sentiment of the country, the Executive Gov't. has no legitimate concern, and no design to interfere. Our social and political institutions recognize the utmost freedom of discussion, and men are justly obnoxious to legal penalties for their actions only and not for their opinions. The sentiments so happily expressed by Mr. [Thomas] Jefferson, that, error of opinion may be safely tolerated, where reason is left free to combat it, meets the ready concurrence of the American people. It is your duty to take care that the laws are faithfully executed and to maintain the peace and good order of the Territory, and also to support by your power and authority the civil officers in the performance of their duties. If these officers, when thus engaged, are forcibly opposed or have just reason to expect opposition, they have the right to call such portions of the posse comitatus to their aid, as they may deem necessary. If circumstances should lead you to believe that the ordinary force, at the disposal of such offices, will be insufficient to overcome any resistance that may be reasonably anticipated, then you are authorized to call for such number of troops as the occasion may require, who will act as a *posse comitatus,* and while thus employed they will be under the direction of the proper civil officer, and act in conformity with the instructions you may give, as the Chief Executive Magistrate of the Territory. It is believed that these general suggestions will be found sufficient for such exigencies as may arise. The great object is to assert the supremacy of the law, and to do this in the mode and by the means which the law points out. The President trusts that occasion for resorting to the employment of military force will not arise; but should actual resistance take place, while you meet it with prudence and discretion, it must be met with firmness, and the whole force placed at your disposal must be employed if need be, to put an end to illegal opposition. And should your means not prove sufficient, the President will take care that it be increased, for he is determined to exert all the requisite power of the Executive to preserve the authority of the law in the Territory of Utah.

My Presence Is So Necessary: A Change in Commanders

Having appointed Cumming for Utah and seemingly acceded to Governor Walker's insistence on Harney's retention, the administration nonetheless began to tire of Walker. On 1 August 1857 Secretary Floyd recapitulated for Walker the disposition of regular army units in Kansas. Floyd's accounting was an inflated rather than straightforward or realistic one. He neglected to mention the administration's continuing plans to reinforce the Utah Expedition with both the Second Dragoons and the two-company rear guard of the Tenth Infantry en route from Minnesota. He ignored the exhausted condition of the troops and animals then returning from both the Cheyenne Expedition and the survey of Kansas's southern boundary.[76] Walker immediately perceived this sleight-of-hand, and the administration's duplicity was a factor leading to his stormy November resignation.

Meanwhile, General Harney remained unreconciled to his absence from the Utah Expedition's march west and the loss of its mounted protection. Notwithstanding the debate among the troops over Harney's enthusiasm for a Utah assignment and Scott's earlier fulminations about channels of communication, Harney again took his case for assignment to the Utah campaign directly to Secretary Floyd. In the process Harney revealed not only his willingness to risk Scott's wrath but his qualms about the judgment of the Utah Expedition's subordinate officers, probably Colonel Alexander foremost among them.

HARNEY TO FLOYD, 8 AUGUST 1857, RECORDS OF ADJT. GEN.'S OFFICE, LETTERS RECEIVED (RG 94), NATIONAL ARCHIVES.

. . . my object in thus addressing you, directly, is to inform you at the earliest moment, of the great importance it will be to the success of the movement on Utah, to have an additional mounted force placed at my disposal to guard the road & act as escorts.

Infantry are useless against mounted Indians.

I shall retain the two companies of the 2nd Dragoons at Fort Laramie, and have to request of you that the two companies of the 1st Cavalry under Colonel Sumner, & now under orders for this Post, be directed to take Post at Kearney for the winter—This arrangement, will be of the greatest advantage & I think will sufficiently protect the road until other measures can be adopted. Should this suggestion be approved, will you cause the order to be telegraphed to me—for time is everything at this juncture? . . . [77]

My presence is at this time so necessary to the troops en route—that I am constrained to speak to you upon another subject—my early release from the service in Kansas—everything here is quiet, nor is there any probability that I shall be needed.

---

[76] Floyd to Walker, 1 August 1857, Sec. of War, Letters Sent (RG 107), National Archives.

[77] Floyd did not grant this request, either out of concern over Walker's reaction or awareness of the First Cavalry's exhausted condition upon returning from the Cheyenne Expedition.

The commanders here are discreet & well disposed to co-operate with the Government and they are equal to any emergency that can occur here—but with the troops marching on Utah it is not so—the service is new to the commanders as well as the troops, & my knowledge & experience of that country will do much towards smoothing the way upon their arrival, to a correct & proper understanding with the people, among whom they are to serve—

I can start the 1st week in September & overtake them, having everything in readiness to do so, at a moment's notice from yourself—

I trust you will believe, I am thus free in my explanations, from an earnest desire to serve, faithfully, the cause I am engaged in.

with my most respectful remembrances to the President I remain

Your sincere friend

But as Harney pleaded his case, the die had been cast. The administration and General Scott were already selecting as his successor Col. Albert Sidney Johnston, commander of the newly formed Second U.S. Cavalry in Texas.

Chapter 8

In Pharaoh's Army
Teamsters, Reporters, and Soldiers West

Of course no one in the camp, from the Colonel down to the lowest Corporal, knows what is to be done, or when it is to be done, though be sure every man delivers his own views with great volubility of what ought to be done.
—Capt. Alfred Cumming, Tenth U.S. Infantry, to Mother, 23 September 1857, west of Fort Laramie[1]

Although it was the third week of July before most of the Utah Expedition departed Fort Leavenworth, Russell, Majors and Waddell's supply trains were on the plains by mid-June. In advance of them all were twenty-one-year-old Charles R. Morehead of Lexington, Missouri, and his seasoned boss, James Rupe. As the Utah Expedition's civilian vanguard Morehead left a lively retrospective account of his challenges: Cheyenne raiders; large numbers of young, unruly teamsters; and Mormons of uncertain intent. His reminiscences, as well as those of wagonmaster Percival G. Lowe, provide highly individualized vignettes of this scene. In the process, each man described the Utah Expedition's teamsters, the group of civilian camp followers whose lack of discipline Brigham Young dreaded more than the troops themselves. As Quartermaster Stewart Van Vliet later reported, Young "had no objection to the troops themselves entering the Territory; but if they allowed them to do so, it would be opening the door for the entrance of the rabble from the frontiers, who would, as in former times, persecute and annoy them."[2]

[1] Cumming, a West Pointer and company commander, was the little-known namesake and nephew of Utah's new governor. Their proximity with the Utah Expedition was coincidental, and Captain Cumming spent little time with his uncle.

[2] Van Vliet, Report to Floyd, 20 November 1857, "Report of the Secretary of War," Senate Ex. Doc. 11 (35-1), Serial 920, 38.

For the past eighty years historians have described the experiences of the soldiers and civilians who followed Morehead and Rupe through the papers of just a few of them. Heretofore missing, then, have been soldier voices from the expedition's historically "silent" regiments and insights from a colorful but unknown cadre of civilian participants. For this reason it is revealing to hear now from the Fifth Infantry's Capt. Randolph B. Marcy, the Tenth Infantry's Capt. Alfred Cumming, and Asst. Surgeon A. Roberts Bartholow, medical officer for first the Tenth and then Bee's Battalion of U.S. Volunteers. So too for the extraordinary dispatches written by two newspaper correspondents accompanying the Utah Expedition: Albert G. Browne, Jr., a Boston Brahmin afield for publisher-editor Horace Greeley's *New-York Tribune* with two Harvard degrees, a law license, and a Ph.D. from Heidelberg University; and William Porter Finlay, the ne'er-do-well, homicidal son of Belfast, Ireland's most prominent publisher, a brother of Charles Dickens's boon companion, and a reporter for the *Saint Louis Leader.*

These views from the summer of 1857 are quite different from the more somber, angry, and frustrated accounts of following months. As Generals Scott and Harney had feared, once the troops encountered the autumnal reality of Mormon guerrillas and severe weather near the Continental Divide, the high spirits of a summer campaign faded.

Wide Awake and Out Front: Charlie Morehead

When Charles R. Morehead wrote his reminiscences of the Utah War in 1907 at age 70, he did so at the request of William Elsey Connelley, the energetic secretary of the Kansas Historical Society. Morehead was then the prominent founder-president of El Paso's First National Bank, a leader of that community's public-education thrust, and her former mayor. He had moved to El Paso from Kansas in 1886 as a quintessential frontier "man on the make." Morehead participated full-bore in El Paso's subsequent meteoric transformation from a sleepy border pueblo to a mushrooming, wide-open frontier city in which even the notorious John Wesley Hardin could not escape assassination.

There are signs that Morehead wrote partly to rehabilitate the badly tarnished reputation of William H. Russell, his late uncle and a founding partner in Russell, Majors and Waddell. Morehead also wanted to assure his own place in western history. Connelley, in turn, may have sought out Morehead

Charles R. Morehead, Utah War plains agent for Russell, Majors and Waddell. One of the men who rode far in advance of the Utah Expedition's troops with James Rupe, Morehead was the nephew of the freighting firm's founding partner, William H. Russell. He appears here at the turn of the twentieth century as a powerful bank president and former mayor of wide-open El Paso, Texas. *Courtesy of the El Paso County Historical Society.*

for multiple reasons: his earlier reputation as Leavenworth's mayor as well as one of Kansas's major Santa Fe traders; Morehead's relation to Russell; and his mythic Utah-connected involvement with the creation of the Pony Express.

Morehead, "Recollections," 1907, Appendix C, *Doniphan's Expedition and the Conquest of New Mexico and California*, 600–22.

Early the next spring (1857) the Cheyenne Indians, a numerous and warlike tribe of the plains, went on the war-path, as did the Mormons. . . . [A]nd the contractors for the transportation of army supplies were called upon for almost double the quantity of wagons and teams that had ever been necessary before. . . . So every available wagon, yoke of cattle and teamster was called for and were promptly provided by the transportation company.

Captain James Rupe, the most experienced plainsman then to be had, was appointed general agent of the company, and myself as his assistant and clerk.

. . . [H]is experience in the management of freight trains and Indian warfare was successful up to that time.[3]

We left Fort Leavenworth about the first of May, 1857,[4] in a two-mule spring wagon. Some of the trains and 800 head of loose beef cattle had preceded us. . . .

We expected to overtake the beef cattle and travel with them through the Cheyenne country, or until we reached Fort Laramie, 640 miles out; but at Soldier creek, this side of the Big Blue river, we overtook a train the teamsters of which had mutinied against the wagonmaster. We had to send back for another wagonmaster and settle the mutiny before we could go on, which required several days. We then resumed our journey, passing another train at Big Blue, and pressed on to overtake the beef cattle, when we heard the Cheyennes were infesting the country west of us.

At the point where we first struck the Little Blue our mules began to prick up their ears and act a little strange. Captain Rupe stopped to look around for the cause, when he discerned what appeared to be eight or ten Indians on the opposite side of the river among the trees. He handed me the reins, took up his breech-loading rifle and said:

"You turn around and drive as fast as you can; if they pursue us I will hold them back."

As soon as we made this move the Indians broke for a point up the river to find a crossing, the banks being very steep opposite our position. By the time they got over the river and on the road, we were a considerable distance ahead, and as soon as Rupe saw they were gaining on us and that they were near enough for a shot he opened fire on them. After five or six shots they slackened up, returning the shots. We went on to the train we had left behind us and remained with it that night.

The next evening about dusk we left the train, traveled all night, and reached Fort Kearny about noon the following day. The small band of Indians alluded to were Cheyennes, scouting around to see what was on the road.

At Fort Kearny we met a party of packers, ten in number, from California, who told us they had met our beef cattle between that post and Plum creek; that they had seen Indians popping their heads up from behind the sandhills all the way down the Platte river, and thought the cattle were in danger. So we waited until dark and left to overtake the cattle. By the time we got to the big bend of the Platte, where the road left the river, it began to rain so hard that we had to stop. It was not long before we discerned, by the vivid flashes of

---

[3] Notwithstanding this reputation, Rupe later became embroiled in a controversy in March 1858 in which army officers at Camp Scott accused him of shipping gunpowder to the Mormons clandestinely in his firm's Salt Lake–bound wagons.

[4] The westbound departure of Rupe, Morehead, and several trains was probably not quite this early in the season and would have been primarily because of Col. E. V. Sumner's Cheyenne Expedition—planned during the winter of 1856–57—rather than due to the Utah Expedition.

lightning, a party of men and one mule with a rider coming down the riverbank. We at once concluded that it was our own men, which proved to be the case. They told us the Indians had come down Plum creek into their camp, one at a time, and professed friendship and begged for something to eat, which was given them. After fifteen or twenty had assembled in camp, and while they were eating, a large band of Indians on horseback charged among the cattle and stampeded them. One of the Indians started to get into one of the wagons and a man named Sanborn resisted him, when the Indian stepped back and shot Sanborn dead. The Indians then retreated to a ravine close to the corral, from which they opened fire upon the other herders, numbering thirteen, who had by that time gathered about the wagons. The fight was kept up until the herders retreated to the river-bank. Sanborn was killed outright, and a man named Robb was shot through the thigh and severely wounded. . . .[5]

The following morning we applied to the captain commanding the post for an escort, to try to recover the lost cattle, as we had a right to do under the contract. We were informed that there were but fifty soldiers at the post, all infantry, and that the best he could do was to give us ten men and one six-mule team to carry them. We managed to get ten mules and ponies from the sutler and others about the post, and upon these mounted our men, who were provided with army muskets. We then started for the camp where the cattle were stampeded, under the direction of Captain Rupe. We found the body of poor Sanborn terribly mutilated, and we proceeded to bury it. While doing so [W. M. F.] Magraw's Pacific Wagon Road expedition passed us, and camped at or near Plum creek. Some of his men stopped and viewed the remains and battle-ground, where were found evidences that several Indians had been wounded or killed. The wagons, minus the [covering] sheets, yokes, chains, medicine-chests and Bibles, were all that was left of the equipment.[6]

We then started in the direction in which the cattle had been driven, their trail having been almost entirely obliterated by the previous night's rain-storm. After getting a short distance up in the sandhills we found, scattered about, sixty-five head of the cattle. The mounted men were ahead of the wagon car-

[5] There were two principal attacks by Cheyennes on the Utah Expedition's herds and supply trains during the summer of 1857. The attack described here by Morehead was twenty-eight miles west of Fort Kearny and resulted in the theft of 824 beef cattle on 2 August 1857, a grievous loss that later enraged General Scott because of his belief that General Harney had been cavalier about heeding his 29 June caution to protect the contractor's exposed herds. Intertwined with these emotions was the ongoing Harney-Scott enmity as well as Harney's ill-disguised criticism that Scott's protege and a Harney enemy, Colonel Sumner, was mishandling the then-ongoing Cheyenne Expedition. 1st Lt. E. G. Marshall to Cooper, 2 August 1857, House Ex. Doc. 71, Serial 956, 17–18.

[6] Because of his personal standards, Alexander Majors, the firm's partner responsible for its field operations, issued each teamster a Bible as well as firearms. Majors also administered an oath by which teamsters committed to refrain from profanity; in his memoirs he stated that "Good moral conduct was required of them, and no offense from man to man was allowed, thus keeping them good-natured and working together harmoniously." Majors, *Seventy Years on the Frontier*, 104.

rying the soldiers and our wagon, in which were a young man named Doolittle and myself. When we were on a table-land, skirted by a long cañon, suddenly there appeared, coming down the cañon, a band of mounted Indians, about one hundred and fifty in number, dashing toward us. The sergeant in charge ordered the men to dismount and tie the mules to the wheels, which was instantly done, myself and Doolittle following suit. A gun was fired to attract the attention of our mounted men, who soon came to us. Captain Rupe ordered all of us to repair to a side cañon near by, and as soon as the Indians came within safe range all present (twenty-two in number) were ordered to fire at the line as we stood, our first man aiming at the head of the band, and so on down the line, which was done with good effect. The charge was checked, and by the time we were ready and delivered our second fire they were in flight. They did not locate us until after our first fire, and fired only a few shots in return. They left no dead on the field, but it was believed that eight or ten of them were killed or mortally wounded.

We then gathered the cattle and returned to Fort Kearny. We left the men there to take care of the cattle until some company train should come along, and themselves to be returned to the States,[7] unless they found other employment.

Captain Rupe and myself remained at the post that night and next day until nightfall, when we left for Fort Laramie. . . . [W]e went on to Ash Hollow, and passed through in safety. This was considered one of the most dangerous places on the road, it being mountainous and timbered and forming a gorge putting down between the North and South Platte rivers.

When we reached the valley of the North Platte we drove off from the road and hid ourselves as well as we could, and remained there until dark. We then traveled on up the river to Fort Laramie, passing, a short distance east of that post, the graveyard of Lieutenant Gratton [*sic*] and 28 soldiers, who had been killed by Sioux Indians in 1854.

At Fort Laramie we rested a few days, gathering data about the road beyond, from trappers and traders, for the information of ourselves and the trains to follow. There was no military post beyond Fort Laramie, and there had been no travel except California emigrants and such trains as the merchants in Salt Lake employed to haul their goods. . . .[8]

While at Laramie a party of Indians came into the post with a lot of gold-

[7] "The States" was a widely used term for the established part of the country east of the frontier and territories.

[8] Fort Bridger, west of Laramie, was a civilian trading post. During the winter of 1856–57 the army announced its intent to decommission and abandon Fort Laramie, Nebraska Territory, as a military post, a plan hastily rescinded during the spring of 1857 with the decision to form the Utah Expedition. It was at Fort Laramie that Generals Scott and Harney unsuccessfully advised the concentration of troops in 1857 for an 1858 push into Utah. For the history of the post and its subsequent role in the plains conflicts of the 1860s and 1870s, see Hafen and Young, *Fort Laramie and the Pageant of the West*; Nadeau, *Fort Laramie and the Sioux*; and Hedren, *Fort Laramie in 1876*.

dust and nuggets to trade for such articles as they wanted; and this was not the first time they had come so. They had refused to tell where they got it; but this time it attracted more attention than usual and great inducements were offered them if they would pilot a party to the place. They demanded ponies, sugar, coffee, flour, tobacco, and blankets. A bargain was arrived at finally, and a party was made up and started westward, when the place was found to be Pike's Peak; and in the spring of 1859, after I returned to the States, there was a great rush to Pike's Peak, and thus Colorado has become a great State, and no doubt still greater development of the precious metals will take place in that region.[9]

From Fort Laramie we started out up the North Platte river, with no one ahead of us. The only Indians we met on this branch of the Platte was a band of Arapahoes on a hunt. Captain Rupe could communicate with them enough to give them to understand that we were soldiers and that other soldiers were coming behind us, and as they were not at war they did not molest us, except to try to bulldoze[10] us into trading them our guns, but these we kept close in hand.

We kept on traveling at night until we reached the Sweet Water [River], near the three crossings, when we hid away among the willows along that stream, where we found good grass, water, and plenty of mountain trout, upon which we fed sumptuously.[11]

One morning early I was on a little prominence near our camp, taking my turn on guard watching the road, and saw in the distance a lone man coming on a mule. We supposed it was some trapper, but it proved to be Jesse Jones, who had also been a noted conductor of the mails on the Santa Fé route—a brave and fearless fellow—who had come alone from Fort Leavenworth with a letter from the contractors instructing us to buy all the cattle we could in that country to fill the contract that the cattle captured by the Cheyennes were intended to fill, and to advise us that Captain Stewart Van Vliet, U.S. Quartermaster, was on his way to great Salt Lake Valley to locate a military post, and for us to be governed by his instructions as to the disposition of trains, etc. We also received other letters from friends in the States.

Jones remained with us two days. We compared notes and made out memoranda of the road for the benefit of the trains behind us, and sent him back. . . . Then we hitched up and left for Independence Rock, which stands out

[9] There are multiple accounts in addition to Morehead's of how gold was first discovered along Cherry Creek, Kansas Territory (now Denver) to trigger the Pike's Peak rush. See West, *The Contested Plains*, 145–70. For a summary description of Capt. R. B. Marcy's and the Utah Expedition's tangential 1858 role in the first discoveries, see MacKinnon, "Epilogue to the Utah War," 241.

[10] A good example of a term now associated with construction equipment but derived from an earlier expression from the cattle trade.

[11] The Sweetwater was another famous (and welcome) landmark on the Oregon Trail, the name for which has multiple explanations. The three-crossings stretch took its name from the river's serpentine course relative to the trail.

some distance from the main mountain range. . . . Not far [west] from this was the Devil's Gate, which is a square, vertical cut through the Rocky Mountains, probably fifty feet wide in places, and through which the Sweet Water river flows. The road passed west of it, over the mountain, and then wound down into the valley again.

From the last crossing of the Sweet Water, at the eastern base of Fremont's Peak . . . we turned southwest up through the famous South Pass of the Rocky Mountains, the gateway to the Pacific slope, the dividing-line between the waters of the Atlantic and Pacific. On the Pacific side we came to the famous camping-place known as Pacific Springs, where the Mormons stampeded the mules of the Tenth Infantry sometime later, a splendid description of which is given by Captain Ginn, who was with the regiment at that time. This was the alarm that saved the army from possible starvation that winter, because it hurried Colonel Alexander on to our rescue, which will be more fully set forth hereafter.[12]

We now felt that we were in but little danger from Indians, and we pressed on to the Little Sandy, and then to the Big Sandy, where Simpson's train belonging to the contractors was afterwards burned by the Mormons. Next we came to the beautiful Green river, the valley of which we could not see until we got to the very edge of it, and as we did so and looked down into the valley we could see the trading-post, consisting of a long mud house with dirt roof, in which was a store and other rooms for the family of Baptiste, the trader, consisting of a Shoshone squaw and his children.

For a considerable distance, up and down the river, under the trees, there was a large number of lodges and what appeared to be two or three thousand Shoshone Indians, men, women and children. At first sight we were greatly surprised and alarmed, but there was no turning back, and we went on down to the river, where we were met by a number of Indians on foot and were followed to the house where we met Baptiste. He presented us to Chief Washakie, to whom we made a present of a pair of blankets bought of and as advised by Baptiste, and all was well. . . . [13]

In the meantime Captain Van Vliet arrived, with an escort of fifty soldiers under command of Lieutenant Deshler. The following day Captain Van Vliet

[12] This stampede occurred on the night of 24–25 September 1857. For an account of William I. Ginn's involvement in Utah and with Morehead during this period (and later in El Paso), see MacKinnon, "'Unquestionably Authentic and Correct in Every Detail,'" 322–42. During the period described by Morehead, John I. Ginn was a twenty-one-year-old civilian drover attached to the Tenth Infantry. The title "captain" was honorific, assumed by Ginn at some point during his subsequent western travels. Ginn's colorful but fanciful description of the stampede was contained in a manuscript of his reminiscences that Morehead tried unsuccessfully to help him publish through William E. Connelley in 1907. A description of the stampede by Capt. Alfred Cumming and Nauvoo Legion private John Bagley appears in subsequent chapters.

[13] Baptiste and Shoshone chief Washakie were well known to decades of westbound travelers. Attempting to balance their relations with both the Utah Expedition and the Mormons, these men were uneasy witnesses to, if not shadowy participants in, the Utah War.

moved on to Ham's Fork of Green river, and the next day to Fort Bridger, which was the headquarters of the Mormon army. He was there informed that he would not be allowed to proceed further with his escort, but that he would be sent in under a Mormon escort in his own ambulance to have a conference with Brigham Young. He accepted the proposition, and Lieutenant Deshler was ordered [by Van Vliet] back to Ham's Fork and to camp until Captain Van Vliet returned.[14]

We joined Lieutenant Deshler at Ham's Fork, and awaited the return of Captain Van Vliet.[15]

They Had Mistaken Their Calling: Teamsters and P. G. Lowe

Russell, Majors and Waddell's enormous, rapidly expanding work force was an eclectic mix of experienced hands and greenhorns—people destined to become either solid citizens or villains. The campaign for which the firm hired them was a gigantic national attraction for young men who were restless, destitute, fugitive, larcenous, or simply adventuresome. Before the active phase of the war was over, it would draw not only thousands of upright young men but the likes of William C. Quantrill, Confederate perpetrator of the Civil War's greatest atrocity, as well as George Shepard and David Poole, Quantrill minions. There was also a covey of college drop-outs, incipient Civil War generals, and even future Medal of Honor awardees. Utah's new chief justice, Delana R. Eckels, traveled with the Utah Expedition and described its civilian camp followers to a U.S. senator as "St. Louis wharf rats."

One of the most expert assessments of the Utah Expedition's teamsters came from Percival G. Lowe of Leavenworth, a man who by the summer of 1857 had seen it all. As a youngster Lowe had left his native New Hampshire to seek his destiny in the West. It was to be a path grossly different from that taken by his brother Thaddeus S. C. Lowe, who became a distinguished Harvard professor of science as well as the Union Army's most famous balloonist. By 1857 P. G. Lowe was twenty-nine and a shrewd judge of weather, teamsters, soldiers, Indians, and animals. This astuteness came through a five-year

[14] 1st Lt. James Deshler of Alabama was a West Pointer (1854) serving in the Tenth Infantry. He later became a member of Bee's staff in the Utah Expedition's volunteer battalion formed at Camp Scott. The only biographical sketch of him focuses on his Civil War role as a Confederate brigadier; Sheridan, "Brigadier-General James Deshler, Professional Soldier," 203–16.

[15] For a supplemental description of Morehead's activities and views during this period of waiting, see his anonymous letter to the Lexington, Mo., *Press*, his hometown newspaper, of 13 September 1857.

hitch on the plains as a first sergeant in the tough First U.S. Dragoons and several years as a highly respected civilian wagonmaster for both the army's quartermaster department and its contractors.

Because Lowe was master of transportation for Col. E. V. Sumner's Cheyenne Expedition in the spring of 1857, he missed the opening months of the Mormon campaign. He met the westbound Utah Expedition in mid-Kansas as he returned east to Fort Leavenworth with Sumner's badly jaded troops and animals. Lowe later described the expedition's reinforcements in 1858, limning in the process a sketch of the type of the men who followed Charlie Morehead and Capt. James Rupe to Utah in 1857 as teamsters.

LOWE, "NARRATIVE," 1906, FROM *FIVE YEARS A DRAGOON ('49 TO '54) AND OTHER ADVENTURES ON THE GREAT PLAINS.*

At Two Mile Creek, below the fort [Leavenworth], were located extensive corrals and a "catching-out" crew under experienced "mule tamers," and here all mules were first hitched to wagons and sent to camp some place within a few miles of the post. . . .

I was notified to wind up the feeding business, and bring over mules from Platte the first of April, which I did. Three trains had been organized and camped in Salt Creek Valley. The news that many men would be needed brought them from every direction; some, enterprising young men from the country, ambitious to better their condition or work their way to the Pacific Coast; but there seemed an oversupply of the offscouring of the slums—men leaving their country for their country's good. The variety and makeup of these fellows, many of them fleeing from justice, the arms they carried and their outfits generally, were curious enough.

I was instructed to take charge of the trains. Many complaints had come . . . against a train in the Valley, and he requested me to see to it and do whatever seemed best. I rode out and found a drunken mob—mules scattered, harness in the mud, etc. The wagonmaster was asleep. A mouthy fellow called him "Captain," and he finally crawled out. In a few minutes I saw the utter uselessness of wasting time. He had come with a railroad gang from north Missouri, the most blear-eyed, God-forsaken looking set I ever saw. I told him that he and his men were wanted at the quartermaster's office; that they should take all their belongings with them, because they would not return to this train. Inquiries were numerous, but I quietly cut them off, and in half an hour they were strung out, poor wretches, with the "Captain" in the lead. I promised to meet them at the quartermaster's office, and then rode down the creek a mile to another train, and asked the wagonmaster to give me his assistant, a fine young fellow (Green Dorsey), and loan me half of his men. With them I returned to the drunken train, told Dorsey to take charge as wagonmaster, hire any men that came who suited him, and I would send him more,

> but not to hire one of the old gang, and galloped to the post in time to see them paid off. It was remarked at the office that such an outfit had never before been seen there. I called the "Captain" and his men aside and advised them to seek employment elsewhere; that they had mistaken their calling, and were unfit for the plains, and assured them that not one would ever find employment here. The rain and scarcity of whisky had sobered them some, and they started for the Rialto Ferry and Weston [Missouri].
>
> This incident spread among the trains and camps on the reservation, and I told every wagonmaster not to hire bad men—we did not want to be bothered with them; and it was soon understood that thieves, thugs and worthless characters generally might as well move on. Many of these found employment in ox trains belonging to Government contractors, and were the cause of strikes, mutinies and loss to their employers. Of course, there was no civil law applicable to the management of men on the plains. In a military command the officer in charge was all-powerful, as he must be everywhere within his jurisdiction. Necessity knows no law, and while all well disposed men would perform their duties without friction, the lawless element, sure to crop out from time to time, stood so much in awe of the military power that they did little harm to their fellows or the Government. Where there was no military command the same restraint did not exist, and discontented spirits, schemers and rebellion breeders often caused trouble. The Government trains had more discipline than the contractor's trains transporting Government supplies. The Government train had a sprinkling of discharged soldiers, and the man in charge had himself been amenable to discipline and could not hope to hold a responsible position without maintaining it. He must be a law unto himself or fail. The great contracting firms that transported Government supplies sent numerous ox trains to various military posts, and while they had a good business system, and often accomplished work much better than the Government would have done, yet the immensity of the business left room for many leaks and much defective management. I recall many instances of mutiny—the teamsters in rebellion against their wagonmasters, in some cases possibly with a grievance, and in others through homesickness or the spirit of rebellion that recognizes no authority, always ready to make trouble, delighting in the opportunity to become leaders for more pay, or to show their power when their services were most needed.

Charlie Morehead and P. G. Lowe were authority figures, and naturally they had a substantially different perspective than that of the lowly teamsters they described. Perhaps the best of the teamster narratives was written by a young midwesterner named William Clark, later destined to be mayor of Ames, Iowa, in the 1870s. Because it was published in 1922 and is relatively accessible, Clark's account of his Utah War experiences is not presented here, but it is essential reading for those interested in the adventures of the young, inexperienced, but willing participants in one of the great sagas of the pre–Civil War West.[16] What came with the narratives of Messrs. Lowe and Clark, natives of New Hampshire and probably Illinois, respectively, was a readiness to condemn the behavior and southern attitudes of the campaign's teamsters, many of whom were Missourians. In this sense—if in few others—their views aligned with large numbers of Utah Mormons who awaited them, refugees from brutal persecution during Missouri's Mormon War of 1838–39. Little of this criticism appears in the comments of Morehead, who hailed from the Show Me state.

Marching Is Not Dancing: Field Reports from the Peripatetic, Homicidal Mr. Finlay

Among the least known yet most exotic of the Utah Expedition's civilians was William Porter Finlay. W. M. F. Magraw, who befriended Finlay, described him to President Buchanan as:

> a native of Belfast Ireland; he was educated at the East Indian Company's Military Col[l]ege in England. His father is Francis Dalsele [Dalzell] Finlay, proprietor of The Northern Whig published in Belfast. He arrived in this country in June last [1857], and having previously served in the British Army in Africa and in the East India Co. service in India as Second Lieutenant in the artillery, he naturally had a fondness for the army, and crossed the Plains to Laramie as a guest of the officers of the 10th Regt. having been introduced to them by Genl Harney, to whom he had letters [of introduction]. . . . He is a thorough and accomplished soldier, a man of excellent education. His age is about twenty-five years[17] robust & strong, and should opportunity offer will I doubt not give a good account of himself, as he has done on previous occasions of which he possesses the testimonials, having a letter from Sir Harry Smith mentioning his having been repeatedly brought to notice for gallant conduct during the [South Africa] Caffer [Kaffir] War, and having been promoted in consequence.[18]

[16] William Clark, "A Trip Across the Plains in 1857," 163–223.

[17] Finlay was born 20 April 1831 in Belfast and was named after his maternal grandfather, a Presbyterian minister in County Derry.

[18] Magraw to Buchanan, 2 January 1858, James Buchanan Papers, Historical Society of Pennsylvania. Lt.-Gen. Sir Henry George Waklyn Smith (1787–1860) was one of Britain's most prominent soldiers, especially during the Napoleonic Wars in Europe and England's subsequent colonial campaigns in India and the Cape of Good Hope in southern Africa. President Buchanan would have been well aware of Sir Harry's exploits from his service as minister to the Court of St. James during the mid-1850s. The Kaffir Wars were a series of campaigns between the Royal Army and South Africa's indigenous tribes during the 1840s and 1850s.

Finlay was indeed the oldest son of Belfast's most prominent newspaper publisher, and he had entered Addiscombe, the East India Company's military seminary near London, in 1848 upon the recommendation of a knight and a viscount. Unknown to Magraw, Finlay's "liberal education" as a cadet at Addiscombe had been prematurely terminated by his dismissal in March 1851 following a drinking bout or brawl in a nearby town. This disgrace followed temporary suspension from the academy, a dismal record that brought Finlay's relations with his prominent father to the breaking point.[19]

During the next six years Finlay's travels were global but elusive, although it is known that before the end of 1853 "under circumstances of extenuation [he] was convicted of a Homicide at Calcutta." In 1854 he departed India for a prolonged stay in Australia, where he may have participated in the gold rush then underway north of Melbourne. Precisely how Finlay obtained his release from prison in Calcutta is unclear, but the process involved interventions by a constellation of Francis D. Finlay's influential English and Anglo-Indian allies, including the Duke of Newcastle, Sir James Graham (first lord of the Admirality), Sir Lawrence Peel (chief justice of Calcutta's supreme court and brother of former prime minister Sir Robert Peel), the attorney general of Ireland, and Sir James Hogg (chairman of the East India Company).

In June 1856 Finlay sailed from Australia to Liverpool, and then migrated to the United States.[20] His claims of military service with the East India Company in India and the British Royal Army in South Africa are unverifiable and suspect, although Graham spoke of him as having "fought well" while in South Africa's Cape Colony. After entering the United States in 1857, presumably at New Orleans, he traveled to St. Louis, where he befriended Jedediah Vincent Huntington, the *Saint Louis Leader*'s editor-publisher and/or his partner, Charles L. Hunt. Huntington was scion of a prominent New York family, and it is possible that he had earlier encountered either the Finlay family or mutual friends during the course of his extensive European travels.

Before leaving St. Louis to visit General Harney at Fort Leavenworth, Fin-

[19] The story of Finlay's years at Addiscombe may be found in file L/MIL/9/219/1–13, Oriental and India Office Collections, The British Library, London. Immediately after his son's dismissal, F. D. Finlay wrote to the head of the military department at India House in London, "It has levelled me to the dust! It has broken my heart! . . . My son has not yet written home. He need not turn his feet homeward; for he will not be received here, after all we have endured with him." F. D. Finlay to F. R. Clarke, 5 March 1851, ibid.

[20] For Finlay's international travels, see Helen D. Harris (Melbourne) to MacKinnon, e-mail messages, 3 and 4 March 2006. For the Indian imbroglio, see Graham to Newcastle, 6 December 1853, Public Record Office Victoria, Australia, text courtesy of Ms. Harris.

lay appears to have reached an agreement with Huntington or Hunt to provide the *Leader* with periodic descriptions of his adventures on the plains.[21] Excerpts from the first of these dispatches—all signed "W. P. F."—record Finlay's impressions as he marched west from Fort Leavenworth to Fort Laramie during the period from mid-July to early September 1857. As such they constitute the most extensive daily record yet found of this part of the Utah Expedition's movement.[22] Although Finlay gives the reader the vague impression that he wrote as an American infantryman of ambiguous rank and international background, he traveled as a civilian. As indicated by Magraw, Finlay probably was the guest of the Tenth Infantry's officers, although none of the four captains and lieutenants of the regiment whose letters have survived for this period commented on his presence.

In September 1857 Finlay left the Utah Expedition at Fort Laramie to become an employee in the engineering section of Magraw's disintegrating Pacific Wagon Road crew. Magraw's assistant chief engineer, Henry K. Nichols, was disgusted with the hiring of the "English," unqualified Finlay and recorded in his journal that the men of the Tenth Infantry with whom Finlay had traveled from Fort Leavenworth, "were thoro'ly disgusted with him long before reaching this post."[23]

Finlay, Dispatches of 17 July–2 September 1857, *Saint Louis Leader*, Published 5 October, 4/3–4, 7 October, 4/3–4, 8 October, 4/2–3, and 27 October 1857, 2/2–3. "The Army for Utah."

[From Our Own Correspondent.]
Camp Walbreck [Walbach], near Ft. Leavenworth,
10th Rifle Regiment, July 17th.[24]

At last there appears some prospect of a move in the direction of Utah. All sorts of official messages, and orders and counter orders, returns and req-

[21] While Finlay was filing these dispatches, Huntington sold his interest in the newspaper to Hunt and migrated to France, where he died. For a scathing critique of Huntington's stewardship at the *Leader* and account of his departure from a politically rival (Republican) paper, see "The Wandering Jew Quits Newspapers," *Weekly Tribune* (Liberty, Mo.), 14 August 1857, 2/4.

[22] During this period Belfast's *Northern Whig* ran only one Utah War dispatch from a "young gentleman who is attached to the expedition" in the Second Dragoons, but nothing from Finlay, a sign of his estrangement from his father. "The American Expedition Against the Mormons," *The Northern Whig* (Belfast), 22 March 1858.

[23] Nichols quoted in Leland, ed., *Frederick West Lander*, 91.

[24] Named after Col. John DeBarth Walbach, venerable and respected commander of the Fourth Artillery, who had died 10 June 1857 in his ninety-third year.

uisitions, and the whole of the usual circumlocution office routine,[25] have been going on for some time past, but to-day positive orders have arrived for us to march to-morrow, and neither wagons, clothing, nor even the full complement of arms have been issued. Colonel [Joseph K. F.] Mansfield [the U.S. Army's inspector general] came down and inspected the regiment in heavy marching order, blanket, great coat, complete kit in knapsack, canteen, and with forty rounds of ball cartridge per man in cartouche-box, most minutely, the consequence of which manoeuvre was, that some hundred and fifty men fell out, many of them having fainted in the ranks before the inspection was finished. To a sane and unprejudiced individual, this proceeding, under a burning sun, 110 in the shade, would appear to be at least prejudicial to the good health and condition of the men, and consequently injurious to their efficiency on the long march before them, but even in this country old fogyism flourishes, and they prefer to fatigue men uselessly to varying their usual course. Liberal promises of means of transport had been made to the regiment, but at this last hour orders have arrived diminishing almost one-half what was promised, and giving officers going on a four months march, with the prospect of a residence for an indefinite time in a new country, only 600 pounds, and the men 30 pounds each. . . .

July 18th.—We are positively off at last. The wagons have come down this morning, and according to orders we march to-day. . . . [A]bout half-past five in the evening, the bugle sounded to fall in, the wagons began to move off, the parade was formed, and in five minutes afterwards the 10th Rifles were marching by the river road to Fort Leavenworth, through which lay our path. The band of the 2d Dragoons, and General Harney, with the few officers in garrison, (the 2d Dragoons having previously moved on Lawrence,) bid us good-bye and a safe journey as we traversed the Fort in our flannel shirts, and once outside that we felt that we had at length commenced our arduous march across the plains. Though we had only five miles to go to-day, the men fell out by dozens, and were brought on by the ambulances and wagons in rear of the columns. This state of affairs was to be attributed more to whisky than anything else, as the men who compose our present 10th Rifles are principally recruits, soft and undisciplined, unable to endure the real hardships of a soldier's life at first start. . . .

July 19th.—A long nine miles march to-day. Marching is a very different thing from walking alone, as any one who has tried the two will acknowledge, and we found this quite enough. Four and a quarter miles from our encamping ground on Salt Creek, we found one of the most delicious springs of water it has ever been my lot to taste, though so small that non-commissioned officers were detailed to serve it out to the men and preserve it from being mud-

[25] The "circumlocution office" was a fictive scene of British governmental inefficiency with which Charles Dickens larded several of his novels, including *Little Dorrit.*

died. Talk of cocktails, cobblers, mint juleps, iced champagne, and lager beer, and all the rest of it; but commend me to a spring of pure cold water, on a hot day, after a dusty march, when your eyes, ears, and even the pores of your skin are filled up by a fine penetrating black sand, which nothing can keep out. To enjoy water properly you must first be fatigued and dirty, and hot and thirsty, and exposed to the sun, and then, when you come on a spring of good cold water you will experience a sensation that even joys could not excite. . . .

July 20th.—Short march to-day, and faith the men want it. Marching is not dancing, and requires some preparation. Halted at Stranger creek. . . . Desertion is becoming alarmingly common. Should it continue at this rate, we will not take half our present number to Utah. The men have nothing to complain of, but the prospect of the long and weary march across the plains is too much for some of them, and they go [desert] without taking the trouble to inform any one of their intention. Serves the Government right. What business have they to send a young regiment, undrilled and undisciplined, composed of the rawest possible recruits, on such a long march, with the probability of getting into a shindy at the end of it. The very thing, the chance of a fight, that keeps old soldiers together, and enables them to set at defiance every hardship, is also a great bugbear in the vision of a recruit, and terrifies his undrilled imagination with all sorts of horrors. Recruits are absurdities anyhow, and ought to be abolished so far as the regiment is concerned. They are always in the road except when you want them most, and then are most probably employed in making tracks to the rear as fast as they can. They are a nuisance, and ought certainly to be put down, as Sir Peter Laurie said of suicide.[26] Had the ambulances and spare wagons full again to-day of tired men.

July 21. Reveille, at 4 A.M. Marched at 5-½ o'clock. The men are improving rapidly in their walking, and becoming more used to it. . . . More desertion last night, but a couple of men who had left us without the ceremony of leave taking, were brought in to-day by a citizen and mule driver of another train. The quarter master paid sixty dollars reward for them, and the idea that they would be arrested by the inhabitants if they deserted seemed to have had a good effect among the soldiers. Marched sixteen miles to-day and camped at the first branch of the Grasshopper. Every one pretty tired. . . .

July 23. . . . The sun is most oppressive, and even I, who have marched for months across the sandy plains of South Africa, and been engaged in the jungles of Bengal, where the heat is so intense that life becomes almost a misery to one, find that it is quite as much as any one wants, to be out standing the rays of the sun on the plains for so many hours a day. Marched twenty miles to-y and halted on the Muddy River.

---

[26] Sir Peter Laurie was a former lord mayor of London and English magistrate in Middlesex. Charles Dickens and other writers lampooned him during the 1840s for his attempts to suppress suicide by dispensing severe punishments for those unsuccessful in taking their lives. Gates, *Victorian Suicide*, 51–52.

July 24th. [Mormon Pioneer Day] Having a long march before us, reveille sounded unusually early, at half-past two o'clock, marched at half past four and reached at length the grand rolling prairie of the West. All hail, Columbia! A man has to visit these mighty regions to be enabled to form the least idea of such a wonderful continent; one which will, in that time which must inevitably come round, but which no Englishman ever hopes to see, when the great little island which has fought the world single-handed and is ready to fight it again in the cause of freedom, will sink and become a State like Spain or Prussia, and when the glories of the [Napoleonic War battles of the] Nile and Baltic are among the things that were, then will this country assume the position among the nations of the earth that Great Britain occupies now, and the stars and stripes will float on every sea, and will establish a dominion "on which the sun never sets." . . .

Camp No. 9, July 28th. . . . Met a party of Californians returning to the States, mounted on ponies and carrying their traps on a number of the same animals, to-day. Fine, hardy, athletic looking fellows they were, armed to the teeth, mostly wearing buckskin suits, just the style of men whom killing once would never do for; I should say those fellows would stand half a dozen "wipings out" at least. They have come through Utah and Salt Lake City, and report the Mormons drilling their men and making hostile preparations for our reception, and the same saintly minded but slightly carnally-disposed individuals are endeavoring to stir up the Indians to attack us, and stampede our mules and cattle. Let them try it, that's all. . . .

Camp No. 10, July 29th. Nebraska commences at this point. Farewell for one while to "bleeding Kansas." . . . Met another party of Californians today. Same sort of men and ponies over again, and the same account from Salt Lake. . . .

August 2d. Reveille, at 5 A.M. The men will have an opportunity of washing to-day [in the Little Blue], and will be much refreshed by the operation. No mail has arrived for us yet, and all are anxiously looking out for it. Fort Kearney is only five days' distance from us now, and then I suppose we shall get our letters. Captain Phelps' battery came in at noon, gaining on us a considerable distance during the past week, though some few of his horses are slightly galled by the harness not having been properly fitted to them before starting. A high wind, increasing towards midnight to a regular gale, added to the howling of numerous wolves round the camp, and the flapping of tent flies, gave us a small fore-taste of a windy night on the plains. . . .

August 6th. The bugles blew the reveille this morning at half-past 3 A.M., and we made an early move. From the last camp to the bluffs, through which the road passes and enters the plain of the Platte river, the distance is nine and a quarter miles, and so clear is the atmosphere that you would scarcely think you were more than half of it from them. . . . This valley is a complete plain, level as a bowling-green to all appearance. Marched five miles up the Platte, the banks of which are here well timbered, to the head of Grand Island (this island is one hundred miles in length) an encamped at 12 m, nine miles from Fort Kearney. We have seen a number of Pawnees to-day, friendly Indians they are called, but devil take such friendship as theirs, and dirty, mean looking, truculent scoundrels they seemed. . . .

August 7th. Marched at 5-½ A.M. . . . When we got on the regular track we could see fort Kearney, some nine or ten miles ahead of us, and passed it closely about 10 A.M. A more miserable post I never did see. A few thin wooden houses, admirably calculated to admit both heat and cold, with a small number of poor adobe houses, promiscuously scattered around them, constituted Fort Kearney, and there you have all the description I can afford you of it. It is planted on a bleak open plain, a mile and a half from wood and water, and no one whom I have hitherto asked can give the slightest idea of the reason for this extraordinary arrangement. . . .

Saturday, 8th. Captain Vanderbilt [*sic*], from Fort Leavenworth, arrived today for special duty to Utah, and an escort of one officer [Lieutenant James Deshler] and thirty men is to be furnished him by the Tenth. They are to proceed immediately and travel by mule wagons. All sorts of reports are current as to the course the Mormons will pursue, but the most probable idea is that they will be gld to see us, as we will open a market for all their commodities, and will offer no open opposition to United States authorities. . . .

Sunday, 9th. This day the detachment ordered to proceed as escort left the camp and marched into the fort, whence they will start in the morning. They are to go through in twenty-five days. Visited the Fort and found it as wretched as it appeared at first sight, though some of the officers' quarters are not quite so bad. Men all washing and drying their clothes. Camp presents the appearance of an extensive laundry, with a touch of the old clothes shop.

Monday, 10th.—Our third day's rest. To-morrow we resume our march up the Platte river. . . . The 5th Regiment . . . came up to-day, and halted on the other side of the slough from us. The 5th have had rather a hard time of it lately. They had just returned from Florida, where they were campaigning for several months in the swamps, and are marched straight through, to commence another arduous march, with scarcely any interval of rest. It certainly seems strange to send them, in particular, from the furthest end of Florida, when there are several regiment[s] stationed much nearer the point of departure for Utah, who have done no active service for considerable time. . . .

Camp 25, August 17th. . . . The green-head flies were in perfect swarms today, covering horses and mules with blood, and in some instances, almost obstructing the passage of the train. The infernal torment every living thing, both man and beast, endures from these confounded nuisances no one can imagine till he has tried them. . . .

August 21st to September 2d.—I have become so tired of repeating the same thing over and again every day, that I have concluded to run all these days into one notice. Our progress has been steady, averaging for every day including walk or rest days, within a small fraction of 18 miles. This is first rate work, and the men go it as easily as they used to do half the distance. On one occasion we made 24 miles in 9 hours, or, exclusive of halts, in 8 hours' march, and no one seemed much fatigued. The road followed the general course of the Platte . . . at the point at which we struck the North Fork of the Platte, at a place called Ash Hollow. The appearance of the country changes in a remarkable manner here . . . we come suddenly on the top of the range [between the south and north forks], and below us all is different. A succession of the boldest bluffs intersected by deep ravines running in every possible direction, with some scattered cedar bushes and rocks, present a really pretty and striking scene. One of its greatest charms is the suddenness with which it opens on you, almost like a scene shifting in a theatre. From the summit you can see the battle ground of the Blue water, on the other or North side of the Platte, where General Harney effectually settled all little accounts with the Sioux, leaving a considerable balance in his favor, which they have never attempted to square up. One of the only remarkable objects on the monotonous route is the Chimney Rock, and another the State House [Court House Rock]. . . . The road from this into Laramie is tedious as before, and often difficult for laden wagons to travel, but we managed pretty well, and marched through Fort Laramie about 11 o'clock A.M. on the 2d of September, having marched 637 miles from Fort Leavenworth, and arrived fresher and stronger than when we started. Five and twenty miles is nothing to our men now. We have scarcely an unfit for duty [soldier], and have not lost a man by disease on the route. Our average for every day since leaving Leavenworth is 17¾ miles. I think it would puzzle most regiments to exceed this. Fort Laramie is built on the river Laramie, a fine stream of good water, fordable in the dry season, but deep and rapid in the rainy period and on the melting of the snow. . . . The Fort itself is scarcely more than a few wooden barracks for the men, some wooden houses for officers' quarters, and some adobe huts for the same purpose, with stables for about two troops of dragoons. Having said thus much, you have said nearly all about it. The 10th regiment remain here to rest for three days, and then continue their march across the Rocky Mountains by the South Pass to the Green river, on which it is reported they will halt for the purpose of enabling the troops composing the army for Utah, to concentrate. This distance is estimated to be about 345 miles.[27]

[27] A week after Finlay mailed his dispatch from Fort Laramie, his father died in Belfast at age 64. He left *The Northern Whig* to his younger son, Francis Dalzell Finlay, Jr. (Charles Dickens's friend), an indicator that he may have disinherited William. Neither of his father's two obituaries mentioned him. The newspaper's elegant Georgian stone building still stands, but operates today as an upscale pub of the same name, unconnected to the Finlay family. J. M. R., "Francis Dalzell Finlay," Stephen and Lee, eds., *The Dictionary of National Biography*, 7:29–30. Harris to MacKinnon, e-mail message, 4 March 2006.

SGT.-MAJ. MARTIN MULLINS, Fifth U.S. Infantry. This image shows the regiment's Irish-born senior enlisted man in dress uniform during the late 1850s or early 1860s. Mullins, along with his brother Frank, first sergeant of the Fifth's Company G, held great sway in the regiment in which Captain Marcy was a highly respected company commander. A civilian camp follower described the Sergeants Mullins as "fine looking and handsome men, standing a little over 6 ft. high." Plagued by massive desertions en route from Florida and on the plains, their regiment was the Utah Expedition's smallest and subsequently its most historically "silent." *Courtesy of William J. Schultz, Sugarcreek, Ohio.*

THIS VILE DOG'S LIFE: MARCY'S LAMENTATIONS FROM THE FIFTH

If some of the Utah Expedition's troops looked forward to an adventure, a respite from garrison life, or an opportunity for professional advancement, far more soldiers dreaded the campaign. To them it seemed an arduous, long-term separation from family and even the ordinary pleasures of life. Pessimism was especially rampant in the Fifth Infantry. After a grueling campaign against the Seminoles in Florida, the regiment transferred abruptly to Fort Leavenworth in June 1857. For weeks before and during the transfer the unit had only a murky understanding of its ultimate destination. As General Harney departed Florida for Kansas in April, Capt. Randolph B. Marcy, one of the Fifth's most able company commanders, wrote to a civilian friend from Florida: "Should you see any place for me on your [rail] road that you think would suit me I shall take it as a great favor if you will write me. I am getting tired of being kicked about and separated from my family."[28]

Once it became clear that the Fifth's years of isolated combat in Big Cypress Swamp were to be followed by a twelve-hundred-mile march to remote, desert Utah to campaign against Mormons, desertions and officer resignations escalated. Captain Marcy soldiered on but arranged for his wife Mary and older daughter Mary Ellen ("Nellie") to travel west from the Atlantic coast to meet him at Fort Leavenworth before he departed with the Utah Expedition. Once on the plains Marcy wrote to both ladies at every opportunity. His letters constitute the only narrative account of the Utah War from within the Fifth Infantry; they are now virtually buried amidst the massive volume of papers assembled by George B. McClellan, Marcy's friend and subsequently Mary Ellen's husband as well as one of Lincoln's commanders of the Army of the Potomac.

Captain Marcy to Mary Ellen Marcy, 10 August 1857, McClellan Papers.

> Since I left you at Fort Leavenworth I have been more and more convinced that the life of any officer of the Army is the most disagreeable of all others. You can form an idea of it from what you saw at Fort Leavenworth and that was no specimen. If you had come here [Fort Kearny] you would have seen a fair sample of one of the frontier posts. In [the] midst of a desolate prairie without a stick of timber or anything else to relieve the dread monotony are two or three houses which constitute Fort Kearney. There is one company of the 6th Infantry here, with two officers and an assistant Surgeon. The latter has a wife who is the only lady at the post and I imagine that Mrs. Burns is the first other lady she has seen for many months.[29] What they can do to pass off the time is a mystery to me. It seems to me like being on a rock in the midst of the ocean. I would rather be beggar in the world than to spend my life at such a place and this post is full as good as many others. Dr. Mills, Lieut. Bristol and myself mess together and Simon and wife cook for us.[30]

---

[28] Marcy to George B. McClellan, 24 April 1857, McClellan Papers. McClellan had resigned his army commission 16 January 1857 and was then working in Chicago as chief engineer (soon to be vice president) of the Illinois Central Railroad. By the end of 1857, bored and envious of Marcy's involvement in the campaign, he would be actively scheming to re-enter the army for the Utah War.

[29] Mrs. Burns was the wife of 1st Lt. William W. Burns of the Fifth Infantry. Revealingly, Marcy overlooks here the presence at Fort Kearny of other women—not considered by him as "ladies"—who were usually the laundress-wives of the post's sergeants. Except for the pioneering work of historian Audrey M. Godfrey, the presence of such women with the Utah Expedition has been largely invisible. See Godfrey, "Housewives, Hussies, and Heroines," 157–78.

[30] These officers were Asst. Surg. Madison Mills and newly appointed 2d Lt. Henry B. Bristol of the Fifth Infantry. Simon and his wife Joyce were Marcy's black civilian servants.

> We generally have breakfast at daylight and start immediately afterwards on our march which is about twenty miles per day. As soon as we arrive in camp and get our tents up we have a lunch about 12 o'clock which we all enjoy very much and do ample justice to it. Usually consists of cold ham, bread and butter, but the butter is nearly out. We then lay down and take a nap for a couple of hours and have dinner and tea about sunset. This finishes the day and one day is like all the others. I stopped smoking about ten days since and I am in hopes that I shall improve my hearing, but as yet I cannot discover any change.[31]

The pessimistic tone of Captain Marcy's short family letters is in sharp contrast to the long light-hearted, almost frothy dispatches that he wrote either without attribution or pseudonymously to James Gordon Bennett's *New York Herald.* How Marcy forged this relationship with Bennett, an inactive Nauvoo Legion brigadier,[32] is unknown, although it probably sprang from Marcy's standing as the author of several books about western exploration or from the influence of his late cousin, Sec. of State William L. Marcy. Because Marcy's brother officer, Capt. Jesse A. Gove, also wrote dispatches for the *Herald*—as did civilian Lemuel Fillmore, a relative of former president Millard Fillmore—there has been historiographical confusion as to the authorship of the *Herald*'s multiple Utah War dispatches. Of Marcy's early newspaper dispatches, that of 28 August is perhaps the most useful for its extensive description of the Utah Expedition's illiterate chief guide and Mormon bête noire, Jim Bridger.[33]

Marcy, "The Utah Expedition," 28 August 1857, *New York Herald*, 22 October 1857, 8/1–2.

> This anomalous class of hardy mountaineers—these veritable and unalloyed cosmopolites, whose idiosyncracy enables them to find a home wherever game abounds, their kettles are boiling and their blankets are spread—were in the prosperous days of the fur companies, when beaver skins sold for ten dollars a pound, quite numerous; but since the substitution of silk in the

[31] This text is taken from the late Prof. W. Eugene Hollon's typed transcriptions, which may be found in his research files in the Hollon Collection, Ward Canaday Library, University of Toledo. At the time Marcy wrote to Nellie, she was probably in Amherst, New Hampshire.

[32] Joseph Smith, Jr., had commissioned Bennett during the early 1840s at a time when he sought alliances with newspaper editors and other influential easterners. Bennett never took this arrangement seriously.

[33] The only Utah Expedition letters to the *Herald* subsequently re-published by historians were those written to the newspaper in 1858. Some of these 1858 dispatches may be found in Hammond, ed., *The Utah Expedition,* 205–396, but they are a confusing, undifferentiated mixture of letters written by Gove, Marcy, and Fillmore.

manufacture of hats, and the consequent diminished demand for furs, they have rapidly passed away, and it is seldom now that one of the old stock is seen. We had the good fortune to meet at Fort Laramie that celebrated veteran hunter, trapper, trader, guide, &c., "Jim Bridger," who has passed the greater half of his wild and adventurous life in the mountains, far removed from all intercourse with the civilized world, and surrounded by savage neighbors, who acknowledge no social obligations in common with the pale faces.[34] He is a man of about sixty years of age, with a tall, gaunt figure, somewhat bent by toil and exposure, and possessing a firm, open and generous cast of countenance, indicative of the noble impulses which generally characterize the frontier man and hunter.

His history, teeming as it does with romantic adventure and startling incident, is to me interesting in the highest degree, and, when related by him in the peculiar language of his class, is exceedingly piquant.

A native of the Old Dominion [Virginia], he, thirty-five years ago, while yet a boy, ascended the Missouri river to near its sources, and was employed in that country for several years as a trapper and hunter. His adventures during this period, among the Black Feet, and other hostile tribes, abounded with interest and excitement. From thence he wandered southwest into the "Great Basin" of Utah, visited the present site of Salt Lake city, the Great Salt Lake, and found his way south into Lower California, and was probably the first and only white man who has ever descended the Colorado river of the West.

He was subsequently with Fremont and Stansbury, as guide, and after encountering all the various changes known to that capricious damsel, Fortune, he finally halted upon Black's Fork, of Green river, where he erected an establishment which has since been known as Bridger's Fort. Here he hung up his rifle and hunting implements, laid aside his roving habits, and resolved to spend the remainder of his days in the quiet enjoyment of a home, and for several years did a thriving business both in trading with Indians and California emigrants. But this happy state of things was not destined to continue, as his prosperity excited the cupidity of the Mormons, who demanded a monopoly of the emigrant traffic, and came upon him with a large force, obliging him to escape for his life to the mountains, where he lay secreted for several days, until at length he eluded the search of the "Danites," and made good his retreat to this post, leaving all his improvements, with a large stock of cattle, in the hands of the Mormons, who have held possession of them ever since, but have, as I understand, offered to remunerate him.

From Fort Laramie he returned to the States for the first time in thirty-

[34] Marcy's description of Jim Bridger is one of the earliest and most extensive to have been published. The captain later inserted this description into his famous post-war book *Thirty Years of Army Life*, 400–404. The inclusion of this material in both publications confirms Marcy's authorship of this unattributed dispatch.

one years, and laid his grievances before the authorities at Washington, but up to the present time has not been redressed.[35]

These transactions, as may be supposed, have engendered in his mind a feeling towards the Saints not in strict accordance with that command which requires us to do good to them that persecute us, and it is believed that he will not offer up many petitions in behalf of peace between them and our army. Indeed, those who know him best, think that war would be more in accordance with an answer to his supplications.

Such Miserable, Forlorn Men: Surgeon Bartholow's Patients

Among the most interesting "unknowns" among the Utah Expedition's officers was Dr. A. Roberts Bartholow, a young new assistant surgeon whose first assignment was to the Tenth Infantry. As a regimental physician, Bartholow wrote quarterly "sanitary" reports for the army's surgeon general in Washington to describe his unit's medical condition. These documents are remarkable because of the breadth of his observations and the inquiring, active mind behind them. And so from Dr. Bartholow we have not only a statistical-medical description of the troops in his care but a fascinating account of their habits, behavior, and character, as well as informed observations about the weather, climate, geography, geology, flora, and fauna encountered by the Utah Expedition. What also accompanies these scientific observations are a surprising account of delivering two babies in an army wagon, one of which followed sixty hours of labor. Bartholow has provided somewhat less informed, quasi-anthropological comments about the region's Indian tribes, mountaineers, and even Mormons. The result is a wholly different view of the Utah Expedition than that provided by its line officers, enlistees, and civilian camp followers. In the process Dr. Bartholow's reports also yield a glimpse into both the intellectual power as well as limitations of one of the most talented American military physicians of the mid-nineteenth century.

Dr. Bartholow wrote his report to Surgeon General Thomas Lawson for the quarter ended 30 September 1857 from a bivouac along Hams Fork, a tributary of Blacks Fork and the Green River. He did so shortly before Lot Smith's raid. It was a time when Colonel Edmund B. Alexander, the senior

[35] For an account of Bridger's lobbying in Washington during early 1854, an effort that almost cost Utah the eastern third of her territory, see MacKinnon, "'Like Splitting a Man Up His Backbone,'" 104–107.

Asst. Surg. A. Roberts Bartholow
Newly commissioned medical officer of first the Tenth U.S. Infantry and then Bee's Volunteer Battalion, Dr. Bartholow's quarterly "sanitary" reports provide a unique view of the expedition's troops as well as the kaleidoscope of environmental factors, Indians, mountaineers, and Mormons encountered.
Courtesy of the U.S. Army Center for Military History, Washington, D.C.

officer present, was plagued with uncertainty about how best to move toward Salt Lake City. Here is the work of a highly educated twenty-five-year-old Marylander who had taken both B.A. and M.A. degrees from Maryland's New Windsor College and an M.D. diploma from the University of Maryland in 1854. Dr. Bartholow had entered the military as an assistant surgeon in 1855 with the expansion of the regular army and the creation of the Tenth U.S. Infantry. In 1904 a memorialist, unaware of Dr. Bartholow's Utah War reports for General Lawson, commented:

> While no personal memoranda of this western life are procurable, of one thing we are assured—that the young surgeon had much experience with western fevers, with the bites of venomous reptiles, and in treating gunshot wounds, with plenty of time for thorough study of his cases. At a plastic age, he took a lasting impression from his military duties and surroundings. His naturally positive character accentuated the military manner made necessary in compelling the reckless men of the camp to obey the doctor's order and lead clean and healthy lives.

The same observer described an older Bartholow as "a reserved man who had no intimates outside his own family" and commented on "his independence, his tenacity of opinion, and his nonconformity, which were marked traits of his character, but in him there was little sign of the gay and pleasure-loving temperament."[36]

Dr. Bartholow, Sanitary Report—
Tenth Infantry En Route for Utah, September, 1857, Coolidge, Comp., *Statistical Report on the Sickness and Mortality of the Army of the United States,* 281–88.

On the 8th of July, by order of the general commanding, I reported for duty with the Tenth Infantry. . . .

The regiment arrived at Fort Leavenworth on the 26th of June [from Minnesota], and pitched their camp northwest of the fort, on an alluvial bottom, amid a grove of cottonwood trees, and in the immediate vicinage of the Missouri river. This camp was styled "Camp Walbach."

The total strength of the eight companies upon their arrival was three hundred and forty, less than half their full strength, desertions being the principal cause of this reduction.[37] During the stay at Camp Walbach, three hundred and fifty-seven recruits joined, a majority of whom were enlisted in the Northern States, the remaining in various towns of the West. In subsequent parts of this report, I shall have occasion to remark upon the sanitary condition of many of these recruits, in order to explain the occurrence and results of diseases affecting the command. Here, however, it is necessary to premise that many labored under various forms of chronic disease; many were broken down by habits of dissipation—by intemperance, by syphilis, by the practice of masturbation, &c.; some were too young to endure the fatigues and privations incident to a military life; others too old. Two classes, therefore, the result has shown, are to be considered as a cause of disease constantly operating; young men unaccustomed to new and strange modes of living, and old men worn out by the practice of various vices.

The diseases prevalent at Camp Walbach were such as might be expected from its situation and from the hygienic circumstances to which the men were subjected. . . .

Diarrhoea largely preponderated over all other forms of disease. Several causes [diet and climate] conspired to produce this result. . . .

Changes of temperature, however, had but little influence upon the prudent and temperate men of the command, and especially those old soldiers who had learned in the school of experience the art of taking care of themselves. . . .

---

[36] Holland, "Memoir of Roberts Bartholow," xliii–xlv.

[37] Two of the regiment's ten companies had remained in Minnesota Territory briefly; they joined the Utah Expedition in the fall west of South Pass.

On the 18th July, by order of the general commanding, the Tenth Infantry took up the line of march for Salt Lake City. . . . By way of preparation for the labors and exposure of such a journey, an immense amount of drunkenness was indulged in; and at the outset we had ample demonstration of the fact, that a drunken recruit makes but an indifferent soldier. The afternoon of the 18th July, was excessively warm; the thermometer at Fort Leavenworth hospital indicating 95°. The march was quite short—five miles—and the men carried nothing beside their arms; but quite a number fell from the ranks exhausted, and these were without exception the two classes already mentioned—boys unaccustomed to fatigue, and dissipated men of middle life and more advanced age. To enure the men gradually to the labor of marching, it was found expedient to make short distances at the outset; accordingly for the first three days the regiment traveled but sixteen miles. . . .

The meteorological conditions of the month were not peculiar. In the temperature at noon, not much variation was observed; the thermometer being very uniform at the same hour. Usually at reveille, thick garments were indispensable to comfort, but as the sun rose into the zenith, the heat became oppressive. Rains were unfrequent and inconsiderable. Thunder storms, accompanied with severe wind, passed over us on two nights, but the days were cloudless. No dews were observed. On 31st July, the regiment arrived upon the Little Blue. Distance made, 210 miles; average daily march, including one day's rest, fifteen miles.

The total strength of the eight companies upon arriving at the Little Blue, was 547; having lost by desertion from the time of their departure eighty-two men. No deaths; number treated, 242; ratio of cases per 1,000 mean strength, 442.

As medical officer to the regiment, it became my duty to examine into the condition of those professing themselves unable to walk, and of such as fell ill upon the march. The former class consisted principally of those soldiers who were prostrated by the effects of long-continued inebriation, combined with high temperature; but when whisky and civilization were left behind, the inability to march became the exception, as it had previously been the rule. This class also included those recruits who labored under some physical debility from chronic disease. I was much gratified by witnessing during the march their progressive improvement, especially those in whom a phthisical [consumptive] tendency was marked and imminent. The latter class consisted of such as were overcome by heat, dust, and fatigue. In these cases the symptoms observed were sudden blindness, extreme muscular feebleness, sobbing respiration, a quick small pulse, &c. This state differs in many important particulars from the "coup de soleil," (ictus solis,) especially in its results, for it never was fatal. The treatment required, consisted mainly in rest, brandy, sulphuric ether, and laudanum. Treated upon the march, and having a speedy recovery, they rarely came upon "sick report."

The ambulances provided for the transportation of the sick, were ill suited to such a purpose; so lofty that it was a difficult matter to get a sick man inside, and so rough and jolting that sick men were not improved by the riding. Transportation being limited, I was much embarrassed, during the early part of the march, for the means of carrying those upon sick report excused from marching, and such as were taken sick upon the way.

However, as the causes of disease previously enumerated were removed, the health of the command continued to improve, and my professional labor, happily, became somewhat lightened.

August.—The month of August was occupied in the march from the camp upon the Little Blue, to the vicinity of Fort Laramie, including a detention of three days at Fort Kearny for rest and preparation. . . .

Our first camp in the valley [of the Platte River] was in the vicinity of a large Pawnee encampment. Having received timely information from the commanding officer at Fort Kearny that small-pox was prevailing among these Indians, a rigid non-intercourse policy was at once ordered. Several teamsters in the quartermaster's department, not submitting to strict military rule, were prevailed upon by the charms of filthy squaws, and, as a consequence, suffered from syphilitic inoculation. No soldier, however, was infected.

The march along the Platte valley may be summed up in a few words—marched and encamped. . . .

Diarrhoea, as during the previous month, was the principal disease, but in less proportion and readily amenable to the treatment already indicated.

Diseases of a character somewhat graver began to prevail—[fevers] intermittents and remittents.

During the three days of rest at Fort Kearny the periodical fevers first manifested themselves. This result was to be anticipated. The Platte valley, from the nature of its geological constitution, must be eminently productive of malaria. Beside, the thermometric range for the month was extraordinary, as the following observations exhibit: Highest range, 96°; lowest, 32°; mean, 64°. . . .

The first case of scorbutus [scurvy] occurred in this month. The symptoms were not urgent, and yielded readily under the administration of the iodide of potassium, a diet of "desiccated vegetables," and the use of an alcoholic stimulant.[38] This man is a recruit, an inveterate drunkard, and abstains from the use of whisky only when unable to procure it; and hence, in this man's case, as in many others, a march over the Great Plains is a better temperance sermonizer than Maine ["blue"] law enactments. Regarding this case of scorbutus as an indication of future trouble, I recommended, in a com-

[38] One of the dietary innovations being field tested by the Utah Expedition was a form of dehydrated vegetables—usually potatoes and carrots—that were formed under great pressure into bricks for easy packing and transportation. Once soaked in water, these vegetables expanded substantially and became ingredients for soup.

munication to the colonel commanding, the immediate issue of the desiccated vegetables, and a weekly issue thereafter. . . .

The professional monotony of the march was varied by two cases of labor [childbirth], both in primipara. Both these cases were delivered in a wagon, en route—a novelty in obstetric practice not to be recommended to professors of the art.

The first labor presented no distinctive features, if I may except a rapid recovery under such unwonted conditions. The other labor was remarkable for its duration, a period of sixty hours. The delay I attribute to several circumstances: a somewhat narrowed pelvis, rigidity of the soft parts in consequence of age, and an excessive nervous mobility quite unusual in a camp woman. Distance marched, including six days of rest, 419 miles; average daily march, 13.22 miles; number of cases treated, 158; ratio per 1,000 mean strength, 294.

September.—Beyond Fort Laramie our march lay over a country very different in character from the preceding. . . .

On the 18th of September we leave the Platte river, companion of many miles, and in the space of two days arrive at the Sweet Water, passing over a road continually ascending. The green valley of the Sweet Water, and the clear stream winding through the Rocky Mountains, greatly relieve the barren and desolate scenery. One of the grandest objects upon the road thus far passed over is the Devil's Gate, where the river bursts through the chain of hills. Bare rocks of granite rise up vertically to an immense height. Great boulders of gneiss having fallen in to the bed of the stream, the water boils through with a solemn roar, like the beating of the ocean on a rock-bound shore. For six days we encamped along the Sweet Water, leaving it in the vicinity of the South Pass. On the 24th of September we reached the summit of the Rocky Mountains and marched through the South Pass, attaining the greatest altitude—7,230 feet.

The Pass differs very materially in appearance from what preconceived ideas led us to expect. The ascent is so gradual and extending over so long a distance that it is imperceptible to ordinary observation. Instead of a narrow gorge opening between immense mountains, we find broad table-land insinuating itself among the ranges.[39]

This considerable altitude had a very perceptible effect in increasing the labor of marching. The respiratory acts were rendered more frequent and laborious; fatigue was easily excited, and expistaxis became quite common. A high wind also prevailed, raising clouds of dust and sand. Notwithstanding these adverse circumstances, the necessity of finding a camp compelled a march of twenty-six miles, the longest march in the whole journey. The regiment encamped at the Pacific spring, the head waters of several streams flowing

[39] Bartholow's description of the gentle grade at South Pass is consistent with the surprise of virtually every traveler who recorded it. This, of course, was the pass's great attraction for emigrants.

west; a place memorable from an attempt of the Mormons, in the night, to alarm and stampede the animals. I have to record the death of one of our hopeful recruits on this occasion. The excitement, caused by an alarm at midnight, proved too much for this man's equanimity, and he fell down dead upon the spot, the first victim of the war. Cause, organic disease of the heart.[40]

On the 27th we arrived upon Green river, Utah Territory. Having learned that the Mormons meditated an attack upon government trains lying upon Ham's fork, a night movement was directed, and the regiment marched at 1 o'clock on the morning of the 28th, arriving upon Ham's fork at 9 o'clock, A.M., a distance of twenty-two miles. Upon Ham's fork our march for the month terminated, and my record of it for the quarter closes. Distance marched, 390 miles; average daily march, including eight days of rest, 13 miles; average daily march, excluding eight days of rest, 17.45 miles.

The number of sick continued to decrease until the latter third of the month, when a predisposition to disease was evidently created by several causes.

During the march from the Sweet Water through the South Pass to Ham's fork, very great vicissitudes of temperature were observed. At night, ice formed in my tent, and during the day the thermometer frequently rose to 85°. The atmosphere too was highly rarified, laden with fine particles of sand, and difficult to respire. The unusually lengthy marches, under the operation of these causes, produced a degree of languor and exhaustion highly favorable to the reception of morbific agents. Activity was followed by inaction, except the performance of the ordinary routine duties of camp life. . . .

My report for the month of September, exhibits four cases of scorbutus; these, with the one in August, make five cases during the quarter.[41] These five cases though insufficient to establish a general principle, show clearly that abstinence from vegetable food is not, as some suppose the sole cause of scurvy; nor can its occurrence be ascribed to the use of salted food. These men, in common with the whole command, have eaten per week a certain amount of the "desiccated vegetables," besides apples, peaches, rice, and molasses, and, moreover, the amount of fresh meat consumed greatly preponderated over the salted meat. In my opinion, the previous habits and physical condition act an important part.

A great variety of causes, apparently opposite in character, are, coeteris paribus [all other things being equal], capable of producing scorbutus. The abuse of alcoholic stimulants, and that filthy narcotic, tobacco, a want of cleanliness, indolence, and exhaustion from hard labor, mental despondency, and

[40] For discussion of the death of Pvt. Henry Schulta, Company H, on the night of 24–25 September, see Chapter 13.

[41] At some point during the Utah Expedition, Dr. Bartholow himself fell victim to scurvy. As a result he lost all of his upper teeth, and in 1859 he obtained medical leave so that he might seek dentures in the East. Sohn, *A Saw, Pocket Instruments, and Two Ounces of Whiskey*, 145.

irregular, ill-prepared food, combine in most cases in the production of the scorbutic cachexy. Upon referring to the previous history of these scorbutic men, a sad catalogue of evil habits is presented—most prominent of all, the long continued and excessive use of strong drink; ceaseless tobacco chewing. These men belong to that interesting class, heretofore not unfrequently mentioned, old, broken-down, and inherently worthless recruits.

No more discouraging business can be conducted than the treatment, under present circumstances, of such miserable, forlorn men. . . .

General Summary.—Number treated in the quarter, 499; ratio per 1,000 mean strength, 929; deaths, 3.

In conclusion, it may be interesting to remark the influence of this long march upon the healthy, prudent, and temperate men of the command. They constantly improved in physical vigor and endurance, always performed their arduous duties cheerfully, and, at the termination of the [quarter's] march, had the mens sana in corpore sano.[42]

Notwithstanding the large proportion of sick, I am gratified to be able to state that a considerable number never came upon the sick report; but, unfortunately, these were exceptions to a general rule. Many of those weak, ailing, and unpromising recruits, though frequently sick, have been greatly benefited by the constant, regular, and laborious marching.

I am, therefore, well assured that the eight companies of the Tenth Regiment of Infantry are in a vastly better physical condition this 30th day of September than on the 18th July when they marched out from Fort Leavenworth, en route for Salt Lake City.

Chase after the Infantry Regiments: A. G. Browne's Dispatches

William Porter Finlay sent dispatches to the *Saint Louis Leader* and Captains Marcy and Gove wrote for the *New York Herald* as what today would be called "stringers," informed amateurs who contributed unsolicited but welcome dispatches on a probably unpaid basis. They did so out of personal vanity, a desire to communicate their view of the campaign broadly and at length, and to a certain extent in order to advance their own careers within the delicate conventions of anonymity. Other newspapers also benefited from contributions by stringers among the expedition's officers and even more literate enlistees.

A few papers—New York's *Times* and *Tribune*—had paid correspondents marching among the Utah Expedition's civilian camp followers. Of these writ-

[42] Translation from Latin: "A healthy mind in a healthy body."

WAR CORRESPONDENT
ALBERT GALLATIN BROWNE, JR.
A civilian from Salem and Boston, Browne sent unusually well-informed dispatches from the army to Horace Greeley's *New-York Tribune*. With two Harvard degrees, a law license, a Ph.D. from a German university, and a famous homicide indictment in his background, Browne fascinated illiterate army guide Jim Bridger, who dubbed him "Doc." He is shown here in 1863 at age 31 as a Union Army lieutenant colonel and military secretary to his mentor, Massachusetts governor John A. Andrew. *Courtesy of the Schlesinger Library, Radcliffe Institute, Harvard University.*

ers, none was more talented, better informed, and less known today than Albert G. Browne, Jr., although in November 1857 John M. Bernhisel alerted Governor Young that "The New York Tribune has a special correspondent named Brown with the Utah expedition. The proprietors of that journal pay him an annual compensation of $2000.00 and his expenses."[43] To the extent that historians have connected Browne to the Utah War at all, it has been solely as the anonymous author of a three-part article on the campaign run in 1859 by James Russell Lowell's new *Atlantic Monthly*.[44] This valuable, insightful piece was not the half of Browne's Utah War work.

[43] Bernhisel to Young, 2 November 1857, LDS Archives.

[44] Browne, "The Utah Expedition," 361–75, 474–91, 570–85. Browne was formally identified as the author of this piece in the *Atlantic Monthly*'s first cumulative index during the 1880s, although his authorship was an open secret, at least in Boston, in the late 1850s. He has no biographer, although a brief sketch of his life appears in MacKinnon, "Epilogue to the Utah War," 223, 225–26.

In the summer of 1857 Browne was a twenty-five-year-old native of Salem, Massachusetts, and an alumnus of Harvard College and its law school. He was also a briefly famous participant in the 1854 Boston riot stemming from a failed attempt to free Virginia slave Anthony Burns from federal enforcement of the locally detested Fugitive Slave Act. Because Browne had been indicted with others in connection with the death of a Boston constable during the Burns melee, his prominent family had bundled him off to Germany's Heidelberg University, where Browne became among the first Americans to earn a Ph.D. degree. This academic honor later prompted the Utah Expedition's illiterate chief guide, Jim Bridger, to dub him "doctor" or "doc." Like Marcy's connection with the *Herald*, how Browne struck an arrangement with the *Tribune*'s Horace Greeley is unknown. It is probable that some combination of Browne's family connections, his anti-slavery prominence, and writing skill prompted abolitionist Greeley to engage him as his newspaper's field correspondent with the Utah Expedition. Browne wrote the earliest of his dispatches—all published without attribution—from Fort Kearny.

A. G. BROWNE, JR., "DISPATCHES,"
NEW-YORK DAILY TRIBUNE, 10 SEPTEMBER 1857.
(From Our Special Correspondent)

23 August 1857

Our party arrived here this noon in its chase after the infantry regiments, which we shall probably overtake before they reach Fort Laramie. The 10th Regiment left here on August 11, and the 5th [Infantry] on August 14. The artillery batteries followed a few days after. All of them were considerably thinned by desertions. . . .

A train from California is lying here, which passed through Utah, leaving Salt Lake City on July 29. Its passengers report that the Mormons were much excited by the news of the stoppage of the Utah mail. They learned on July 23 that it had been discontinued. On July 24, they held their annual celebration of the anniversary of their arrival at Salt Lake, and, as on the previous year, not in the city, but at Cottonwood Kanyon, about 25 miles distant. The whole Mormon population trooped out thither, men, women and children; but, contrary to previous practice, Gentiles were carefully excluded. I am therefore unable to obtain any account of their proceedings further than that political speeches were made by Brigham Young, Heber C. Kimball, and others, and two original songs sung, the chorus of one of which ran:

"We'll serve the Lord to-day;
The Prophet we'll obey;

You may find just whom you please,
We'll mind what Brigham says."

Several of these passengers gave accounts of Brigham Young's sermon on July 26, from which it appears to have been the most singular harangue which he had delivered up to that date. It was devoted to discussion of the relations of the Mormons to the General Government. Pointing to the women present, he declared that the Utah expedition was sent to make them all whores, through the interference of the troops. Then, laying his hand upon his coat, he said that he had there "a breast pin eighteen inches long, which he intended to set in the shirt of that Squaw Killer, Gen. Harney, if he should interfere with his (Young's) plans, and send him to hell cross-lots." This "sending to hell cross-lots" appears to be an expression peculiar to Utah—"cross-lots" being equivalent in meaning to "by a short cut." He alluded again to the instrument in his coat as "a pepper-box," [pistol] with which it was his intention "to pepper the General."[45]

The enmity of the Mormons to all persons connected with the office of the Surveyor-General was unabated, and a German named Mogo, who held a contract for executing surveys, joined the train on its passage from the Territory, being apprehensive of an attempt on his life, have been accused of horse stealing and consigned to "hell cross-lots" in a sermon delivered in the Bowery on July 19.[46] They left him at Fort Laramie. . . .

Among the most noted pioneers on the Plains is the old guide [Jim] Bridger, who was dispossessed some years since, by the Mormons, of the little fort which he had erected in a valley about 130 miles from Salt Lake City. The Mormons claim to have bought him out fairly. He claims, I understand, to have been driven away by force. He is now with the 10th Infantry, employed as a guide on the expedition. There is a Mormon settlement in the valley, and when the trains passed about twenty workmen were employed on the fort, around which they had erected a stone wall fifteen feet in h[e]ight, between three and four feet thick at the ground, but tapering to fifteen inches in thickness at its summit. With what intentions they are at work on such a fortification I cannot imagine, for they must be insane to suppose that it can withstand the play [fire] of artillery for ten minutes, especially as it is built of cobblestones loosely cemented with mortar.[47]

---

[45] This is a third-hand rendering of Young's discourse of 26 July 1857, which can be found in *Journal of Discourses*, 5:72–78 and *Deseret News*, 5 August 1857, 172.

[46] Charles Mogo was an employee of Utah's detested Surveyor General David H. Burr. Mogo fled Utah on 29 July, leaving his expectant wife to deliver a son who died a few months later when the infant and his mother arrived in snowy weather in a carriage under Legion escort to Camp Scott.

[47] This was the Fort Bridger cobblestone wall ordered by Brigham Young and D. H. Wells in April 1857 and being constructed under Legion quartermaster Lewis Robison's superintendency. The stones were taken from the bed of Blacks Fork, which flowed through the fort.

Fort Laramie, Nebraska Territory, 1858
For westbound travelers, this post was the last significant settlement and military establishment until the civilian trading post of Fort Bridger. Because of the Buchanan administration's late decision-making and the availability of wood, water, and forage at Laramie, Generals Scott and Harney argued unsuccessfully that the Utah Expedition should winter-over there and push on to the Salt Lake Valley in the spring of 1858. Saved from planned deactivation and abandonment by the substantial requirements of the Utah War, Fort Laramie took on new life as a forward support post and played a key role in the great conflicts with the Plains tribes that followed. *Courtesy of the Lee-Palfrey Collection, Manuscript Division, Library of Congress.*

But whatever they may mean by this building, it is certain that they are receiving constantly large quantities of ammunition. Three trains have passed over the road within a month, which are believed to have been loaded with military stores, and a mule train of forty wagons is six or seven days in advance of us, several of which are suspected to contain powder.[48] All these trains have quitted the road when nearing Fort Kearney, and have passed along the

[48] The mule trains were those being conducted by Mormon mail agent Nicholas Groesbeck of the Y. X. Carrying Company.

north bank of the Platte. They have also avoided encountering Government trains, or those of Government contractors, camping in unusual places and traveling late into the night. They have taken Mormon passengers at the rate of $150 for the trip, supplying all their provisions, but requiring assistance from them in work when needed. . . .

31 August 1857 [Published 15 September 1857]

. . . An express has arrived to-day with the news that Gen. Harney and Gov. Cumming will start from Fort Leavenworth for this post to-morrow. This early departure of the General helps to remove the doubt of the passage of the army beyond Fort Laramie this year.

I Have *Many Many* More Things to Say: Captain Cumming's Voice

From the Tenth Infantry, primarily a northern regiment, may be heard the fresh views of one of its relatively few southern officers, Capt. Alfred Cumming of Georgia. Cumming's involvement with this unit and the Utah Expedition antedated his uncle's appointment by President Buchanan as Utah's governor. The senior Cumming was not a person of military prominence. The more he clashed with Colonel Johnston beginning in late November, the more the family relationship may have been an albatross rather than an advantage for Captain Cumming. Nonetheless, there are signs that young Alfred's appointment to West Point in 1845 was not unrelated to the prominence of his other paternal uncle, William, who had in succession been a distinguished general officer during the army's formative years, a well-known Georgia politician, and a notorious southern duelist.[49] On 23 September, from just east of South Pass and Pacific Springs, Cumming wrote to his mother, Julia Anne Bryan Cumming.

Captain Cumming to Mother, 23 September 1857, Cumming Family Papers.

I avail myself of the first opportunity that has offered since I left Fort Laramie to write home. My short letter to Tom[50] from that Post was not followed up, as I intended it to be, by a longer one. The last Post on the frontier, with no other halting place this side of Salt Lake City, you may suppose that a Commanding officer, even of no greater force than a Company, had

[49] For a biographical sketch of Captain Cumming and much of his family, see Myers, ed., *The Children of Pride*, 1498.

[50] Captain Cumming's younger brother, Thomas William Cumming, who was two years his junior.

considerable to occupy his attention. It was not a matter much to be regretted, however, as all for me to write about, under the circumstances, was to tell you of my health and well-being, which I did in the short note to Tom.

We are now about two hundred and fifty miles from the "City," which, however, I fear is some months off. The opportunity by which I send this is that of the Quarter master [Van Vliet] who was sent in advance some weeks ago to prepare for our reception at Salt Lake. This officer, as was originally intended, is now on his return. From him we hear accounts of the state of feeling in that country which are regarded as pleasant or the reverse according to the nature and circumstances of the hearer. He tells us that the Mormons are preparing for resistance, and that we will not be able to enter the City this winter. Of course there are a great variety of opinions, and a multitude of rumors, about a matter of which we are all equally ignorant. As for myself I am much inclined to the affirmative side of the question. He tells us that ~~the Mormons~~ Brigham Young can at a moment raise 5000 men. He himself represented this number as much greater.[51] Our whole force, if it ever concentrates, will not number over 2500, with a battery of field guns, and a siege train.[52] It is not doubted that if Genl Harney should arrive to take command of us he would immediately march to the city, *were it not* that in case of a fight even should we be successful, we would find ourselves shut up for the winter, without supplies for man or beast. We ourselves, after concentrating, could scarcely reach the City before the heavy snows of this country set in, and should we wait until our subsistence trains, which are to subsist us until a train can arrive in the spring, and which are scattered from [illegible] to Leavenworth, it would be impossible for us to proceed. Going into the Country of an enemy who greatly outnumbers us and from which retreat for ~~the~~ half the year is cut off, these supplies can not be left behind. Such is a kind of rough outline of the position in which we are in at present. Of course no one in the camp, from the Colonel down to the lowest Corporal, knows *what* is to be done, or *when* it is to be done, though be sure every man delivers his own views with great volubility of what *ought* to be done. In the meantime, it is certain that we will in a few days, as was originally intended, go into Camp to await the arrival of the Governor and troops behind us. Our last [news] dates from Leavenworth were up to the 18th ultimo [August]. Uncle Alfred was hourly expected there, and it was thought that he would leave at once, per express. His arrival and that of Genl Harney is much desired, though it is thought the latter will scarcely come out.[53]

---

[51] The consensus estimate by most knowledgeable contemporary sources was that the Legion could field a maximum of about eight thousand troops but never had that many militiamen on duty at any given time.

[52] The size of the Utah Expedition was smaller than the originally specified twenty-five hundred troops, as Captain Van Vliet indiscreetly told Governor Young, because of massive desertions in Kansas.

[53] A reference to rumors of Harney's ambivalence about a Utah assignment.

~~Although be sure eery man believes his own views with great volubility of~~
And now as so for myself. I have only to say that one best thing that persons can say for themselves viz. that I am in excellent health. (I do *not* stand corrected for the first clause of this sentence, for I have come to regard perfect health as better than the existence of all the moral qualities.)[54] this appears to be my present state, and though there is something extremely obnoxious to my feelings in being snowed up for the winter in some cañon of the Rocky Mountains, I am still in good spirits upon the subject. This leads to good feeling spirits upon other subjects, and I am, in my present not enviable position, if not happy, at least content and generally *cheerful*. Notwithstanding my strong expressions of feeling against the Army and Army matters when I was at home, (a feeling I *still* entertain when I give myself time to think,) I could not have borne such a thing as this so philosophically 4 years ago. . . .

I have been writing this whole letter against time, as it were, so please excuse its blemishes. I have *many many* more things to say, and many remembrances to send to each member of the family, but must defer them now.

Give my love to Father.

Most affectionately yours,

P.S. though I shall take every opportunity which may offer to write, do not feel uneasy if you do not get a letter for [from] me for a long time.

---

[54] At about this time, Captain Cumming was struggling with alcoholism as described retrospectively "last fall" in Capt. Gove to Mrs. Gove, 8 July 1858, Hammond, ed., *The Utah Expedition*, 180. Cumming's governor-uncle was also widely perceived to have an alcohol problem.

Chapter 9

"We Will Make a Potter's Field of Every Canyon"

Young and the Legion Respond

We had ridden from Fort Laramie to Salt Lake City in five days and nights, a distance of 520 miles. Truly we were weary and worn out.

—Nauvoo Legion scout Asa S. Hawley on the north plains

. . . the spirit seemed to burn in my bones. . . . I was perfectly running over with it.

—Apostle George A. Smith preaching in southern Utah

When Governor Young first learned that President Buchanan was replacing him and sending an army is complicated and shrouded in Mormon mythology as well as federal fumbling. From Delegate Bernhisel, Young knew as early as February 1855 what he had anticipated as a possibility through 1853–54—that Franklin Pierce would not reappoint him. But legally Young continued as governor until a successor took the oath of office. After Colonel Steptoe declined the honor, finding someone else to accept was no easy task, as first Pierce and then Buchanan discovered. Meanwhile Brigham Young kept his own counsel, saying little except to hint occasionally that he could be replaced or, alternately, to assert aggressively that he would remain in office indefinitely by Divine will.

By early April 1857 Buchanan had privately decided upon a gubernatorial change coupled with military intervention of some sort. Publicly he said nothing about Utah and pressed on with his quest for a new governor. Thus when George A. Smith and John M. Bernhisel arrived in Salt Lake City on 29 May 1857, they bore news not of decisions but rather private indicators of presidential displeasure with Brigham Young, coupled with first-hand glimpses of seething anti-Mormonism along the Kansas-Missouri frontier. But Smith had heard and seen enough in St. Louis and elsewhere that on 19 May when his group stopped at the Y. X. Carrying Company station at Horse Shoe Creek, Nebraska, he openly spoke to the agents about rumors of a two to three-thousand-man expeditionary force for Utah. Surely Smith shared this prospect with Young during their private supper on 29 May.

Additional information arrived in Salt Lake City a month later with mail conductors Ephraim K. Hanks, Feramorz Little, and Bill Hickman on 23–24 June. They brought not only the mail from Independence but press accounts of Apostle Parley P. Pratt's 13 May assassination near Van Buren, Arkansas. These agents also shared their own encounters with escalating hostility in Missouri and news of ominous preparations at Fort Leavenworth. If, as Bill Hickman later claimed, Young discounted these reports, unmistakable confirmation of a military expedition plus shocking news of the cancellation of the Mormon mail contract came a month later with the lathered arrival of the Y. X. Carrying Company's Porter Rockwell, Abraham O. Smoot, and Judson Stoddard, accompanied by the distraught widow Pratt.[1]

It has been debated when and how Brigham Young first heard from this mail trio: on the day they arrived in Salt Lake City (probably 22 July 1857), or on 24 July, when they rode dramatically into the annual Pioneer Day celebration at Big Cottonwood Canyon's Silver Lake.[2] Irrespective of the precise timing, A. O. Smoot's several narratives of their dash across the plains—the only first-hand account—convey the sense of urgency with which the

---

[1] Suspension of mail service was not necessarily the carefully crafted conspiracy suspected by Brigham Young as much as a classic case of independent, uncoordinated action by multiple parts of the federal bureaucracy. The Post Office Department may have acted to terminate Hiram Kimball's (Y. X. Carrying Company) contract without awareness of what was being planned at the War Department. Ultimately, this suspension had the unintended consequence of crippling eastern communications with the Utah Expedition as much as it inconvenienced the Mormons, much to General Scott's rage. Salt Lake City still received an unimpeded (although delayed) flow of U.S. mail via southern California and the occasional westbound private courier who bypassed the army.

[2] As of 7 July Young planned to camp at the mouth of Big Cottonwood Canyon on the evening of 22 July so that he might arrive at Silver Lake early on the morning of the 23rd. On 12 September Young wrote to Thomas L. Kane that he did leave town on 22 July and first heard from the mail trio two days later. On 4 August Young also wrote to George Q. Cannon that the riders had arrived in Salt Lake on 22 July, and Richard E. Turley argues that this was after Young had left town. Postmaster Elias Smith recorded the arrival on a different date—23 July. Everett L. Cooley and Will Bagley have argued that Young heard from the trio soon after they arrived and that their 24 July arrival at Silver Lake was, in effect, staged for dramatic impact. Cooley, ed., *Diary of Brigham Young 1857*, 49–50; Bagley, *Blood of the Prophets*, 80. Young to Aaron Johnson, 7 July 1857, Young to Kane, 12 September 1857, Young to Cannon, 4 August 1857, all in LDS Archives; Thomas, comp., "Elias Smith's Journal," entry for 23 July 1857; Turley to MacKinnon, e-mail message, 29 January 2007.

party carried this news. Rockwell, Smoot, and Stoddard (as well as Buchanan) did not know the name of the rumored new governor, and neither President Buchanan nor Secretary of State Cass ever informed Young that he was being replaced. This was a courtesy that galled Young while providing him the wherewithal to claim into the spring of 1858 that he remained Utah's governor.

A Place Sacred and Devoted to the Service of God: Drama in Big Cottonwood Canyon

In 1856 the annual celebration of the Mormon arrival in Utah—now called Pioneer Day—shifted from Salt Lake City to Silver Lake, an alpine pond on the forested slopes of Big Cottonwood Canyon. Brigham Young was so charmed by the rugged beauty of the place that he immediately determined to return there for the 1857 celebration. In describing the site's sublimity to an absent George A. Smith, Brigham Young provided a private glimpse of his sensitivities—not well understood by his critics—while also conveying some of the peace-war cross-currents that may have been on his mind as he left Salt Lake City a year later for a festive tenth-anniversary "pic-nic."[3]

As time for the 1857 festivities approached, Utah's governor was uneasy. Two weeks before the celebration he wrote to Bishop Aaron Johnson of Springville to urge exploitation of a promising deposit of salt petre, one of the three principal components of gunpowder. A week later, almost in response but from a quite different quarter, Young received a letter from Utah physician-chemist William France seeking gubernatorial support for his development of another critical gunpowder ingredient—sulphuric acid.[4] On 20 July one of Young's plural wives, Augusta Adams Cobb, described quite different preparations: the intriguing fabrication of a new flag. Significantly, this sewing project was under way days before firm confirmation of an army expedition had arrived in Utah: "Brother Brigham has just brought in the flag which you probably purchased, for Sister Eliza Snow and myself to make; she and myself and little daughter live together, at present.[5] The standard is to be raised on the 24 of this month and we expect to proclaim our Independence, I wish I had time to write [you] the addresses and the hymns which

[3] Young to Smith, 28 July 1856, LDS Archives.

[4] Young to Johnson and France to Young, 10 and 16 July 1857, respectively, LDS Archives.

[5] Eliza Roxcy Snow, plural wife of first Joseph Smith and then Brigham Young, was a talented, widely respected figure in the Relief Society's work and the de facto poet laureate of Mormonism.

are to be sung and delivered on that day but I can not for want of time as we are very much hurried in prepareing for the occasion."[6]

While these preparations for the 24 July celebration proceeded, A. O. Smoot, Judson Stoddard, Orrin Porter Rockwell, and Elinor McLean Pratt neared the Salt Lake Valley. Smoot, the late Jedediah M. Grant's successor as Salt Lake City's mayor and subsequently an early leader in Provo, left at least two accounts of their dash across the plains generated twenty-seven years apart. In Smoot's long 26 July 1857 discourse, delivered only three days after his arrival in Salt Lake City, he shared his impressions of the U.S. troops he had seen.

Smoot, "Bowery Remarks," 26 July 1857, *Deseret News*, 5 August 1857, 170/2–4.

Several [Missourians] enquired of me how many men we could raise, able to go into the field and do good service. . . . I told them that I thought we could raise fifty or sixty thousand, more or less, but with me it was only a kind of rough guess. However I spoke candidly and believed all I said, and they also believed it. . . .

But candidly I do not believe that either the officers or soldiers want to come here. A great portion of the soldiers who are ordered to this place will never reach here, for they are deserting every day, and swear that they will not come to fight their own people, the Scotch, the Welsh, the English, etc., they having learned that a great many of this people are foreigners. And the Americans swear that they will not fight the Americans, and thus they are in a fix and do not know how to get out of the snarl they are in. They are deserting nearly all the time, and the officers have to stand with their revolvers and guard the soldiers to keep them from deserting, instead of the soldiers' guarding their officers. . . .

[T]hey are not much more than started now. They are getting a late start, and in a week or ten days the soldiers will begin to have sore feet, and by the time they get to the Platte they will begin to feel so sore that lots of them will take themselves off. . . .

The troops have some 700 very heavy freight wagons destined for Great Salt Lake with two tons and a half in each wagon. Those teams move very

[6] Cobb to "Brother and Sister Badlam" 20 July 1857, Theodore Schroeder Collection, LDS Archives. This flag was probably the one described later in a third-hand account by correspondent A. G. Browne, Jr: "I sent to you from Fort Kearney [*sic*] an account of the Mormon celebration of the 24th of July in Cottonwood cañon, from which all the Gentiles were excluded. Dr. [Garland] Hurt tells me that he has been informed by persons who were present, that on that occasion a resolution was proposed and unanimously adopted, declaring 'Deseret' to be 'a free and independent State,' and that a white flag embroidered with the device of a grizzly bear, was run up on the tallest mountain pine in the cañon, and saluted as the national flag of the Mormon Commonwealth." Browne, dispatch of 25 October 1857 (Camp in the South Pass), "Later from the Mormon War . . . ," *New-York Daily Tribune,* 28 December 1857. With respect to flags, the *Deseret News* reported only that "The stars and stripes were unfurled on two of the highest peaks in sight of the camp and on the tops of two of the tallest trees." "The 24th of July in the Tops of the Mountains," *Deseret News,* 29 July 1857, 165/4.

> slow, and if they reach here before snow falls I shall be a little disappointed, and I think it very probable that they will need some fresh cattle and some yankee [Mormon] drivers to go out and help them in.[7]

Precisely what happened once the mail agents arrived in Big Cottonwood Canyon and reported to Brigham Young is another one of the Utah War episodes from which varying reports and much folklore flowed. The *Deseret News* chose to treat their arrival as almost a non-event: "At about sun set the camp assembled for prayers, when Prest. Wells made a few remarks in relation to the latest tiddings from the States."[8] In his diary Young recorded:

> The bands were playing and every one at peace, when the news came that A. O. Smoot, Judson L. Stoddard, O. Pr Rockwell William Garr & Judge Elias Smith would be in camp in a few minutes.[9] They came, and were welcomed by the band, & 3 deaf[e]ning cheers.
>
> They were ushered into the Lewt. [Lt.] General's (occupied by my family) Marquee. Found that Bros Smoot & Stoddard were from fort Leavenworth 20 days. They informed [me] that a new Govornor and entire set of officers had been appointed, 2500 troops with 15 months provision. Sup[p]osed That General [William S.] Harney would command—to support ~~them~~ officials in their position. I Said if General Harney came here, I Should then know the intention of [the] gover[n]ment; And it was carried unanimously that if Harney crossed the *South Pass* the *buz[z]ards* Should *pick his bones.*[10] The feeling of Mobocracy is rife in the "States" the constant cry is kill the Mormons. *Let them try* it. The Utah mail contract had been taken from us—on the pretext of the unsettled state of things in this Territory. The news helped the people to enjoy themselves. Dancing and mirth continued until a late hour.[11]

Some participants at Silver Lake—apparently oblivious to the arrival of news—recorded only impressions of the scenery, music, dancing, games, and camp routine. Other celebrants left reactions that ranged from the laconic to the highly emotional.[12]

---

[7] A reference to Brigham Young's belief that the Utah Expedition's cattle, munitions, and supplies would end up in Nauvoo Legion hands. Even as Smoot spoke, this notion was being incorporated into a verse of the new Mormon folk song "Du Dah." See also Smoot to Edward W. Tullidge, 14 February 1884, Tullidge, *History of Salt Lake City*, 156–57.

[8] "The 24th of July in the Tops of the Mountains," *Deseret News*, 29 July 1857, 165/4.

[9] Garr was an experienced frontiersman, herder, and early settler of Cache Valley. It is unclear why he was riding with this group.

[10] The significance of South Pass, the Continental Divide, was that it was very near Utah's eastern border, which was defined picturesquely but imprecisely as the crest of the Rockies.

[11] Cooley, ed., *Diary of Brigham Young 1857*, entry for 24 July 1857, 49. For another account of the day's events two months later, see Young to Kane, 12 September 1857, LDS Archives.

[12] A good summary of the range of participant reactions—including unawareness—appears in Cooley, ed., *Diary of Brigham Young 1857*, 51–53n52.

Nauvoo Legion Staff of Lt. Gen. D. H. Wells

U.S. Army officers ridiculed militia grade inflation among the Legion's senior officers shown here, especially Wells's exalted rank. Although the Legion's enlisted men and junior officers were generally without uniforms and sometimes lacked even adequate civilian clothing, Brigham Young took pains on the eve of the Utah War to order "first quality" silver buttons, braid, and sashes for his militia generals, whose uniforms resembled those of the army. *Courtesy of the LDS Archives.*

Still on the plains as Smoot reported was a westbound letter written from a Missouri River steamer by Phil Margetts to his wife, Elizabeth. Like her, he was skeptical about talk on the Kansas-Missouri frontier about a Utah Expedition:

> Now I will tell you a little of the excitement in the states. The first thing we heard on our arrival was the death of our beloved Bro P. P. Pratt . . . the next thing was that their was an army of 2000 going out to Salt Lake to fight the Mormons but I think it is all humbug . . . well *such is life* but I live in hop[e]s of waiting upon them in a few days (& Cry *[h]avock & let slip the dogs of war.*)[13] It is a fact that Mormonism is Creating a great excitement in the States. The news papers is full of the most egrevating & abominable lies you Could possibelly emagine & they say was it not for the law a Mormon Elder would not be safe to travil through those Lieing & evil disigning men.[14]

Our Enemies Are Also Their Enemies: Young Positions Mormons, Leaders, and Indians

Two days later, during services in the Bowery on Sunday, 26 July, a large number of attendees—including a few non-Mormon travelers—heard a fire-and-brimstone discourse delivered by Brigham Young. It was an important talk as Young's first extended public discussion of the Utah Expedition since his brief comments at Silver Lake.[15] Starting with this sermon and continuing on into the fall, the Sunday discourses of Brigham Young, Heber C. Kimball, and John Taylor were filled with volcanic rhetoric, much of which spread nationally and to Europe through *Deseret News* transcriptions. Even when the *News* chose not to reprint some of the most volatile discourses, attending non-Mormon travelers—sometimes dared by Young—described what they heard to California, Kansas, and Missouri newspapers a month later. Although intended primarily as motivational material for local consumption,

---

[13] Phil Margetts was then on the plains heading for the British Mission with the first eastbound handcart company. After the Utah War and his return from England, Margetts would become one of the Salt Lake Theater's most celebrated actors. This passage, an early indication of his interests, is from Shakespeare's *Julius Caesar*, act 3, scene 1.

[14] Margetts to Margetts, 14 June 1857, private collection, typescript of excerpts in editor's possession.

[15] For different versions of what Young said—some expurgated for publication—see Young, "Remarks," 26 July 1857, *Deseret News*, 5 August 1857, 172/1–4 and 173/1; A. G. Browne, Jr., dispatch of 23 August 1857, "The Utah Expedition," *New-York Tribune*, 10 September 1857; *Journal of Discourses*, 5:73–79.

[16] In June 1859 Delegate Bernhisel provided Brigham Young with a memorandum summarizing his multiple meetings with Buchanan. Here Bernhisel recorded that Buchanan "stated that he received the Deseret News and that some of Brigham Young's speeches were terrible." Bernhisel, "Account of Conversations with President James Buchanan," June 1859, LDS Archives.

this language was shocking and offensive elsewhere, especially to non-Mormons including President Buchanan and the Utah Expedition's officers.[16] In this sense Young's choice of words—as with the phrasing of the Utah legislative assembly's 6 January 1857 petition and memorial—was costly to the Mormon cause. Even when editorially scrubbed, his rhetoric reinforced non-Mormon perceptions of Utah as a violent, out-of-control territory led by a disloyal governor. When Young's discourses turned cryptic as well as incendiary—as with several talks in August and September—members of his own church as well as outsiders believed that he was preaching secession through a declaration of independence for Utah. Erroneous or not, this perception was reinforced by descriptions of Augusta Adams Cobb's special Mormon flag first unfurled on 24 July at Silver Lake.

Having thus positioned a substantial portion of his Salt Lake Valley flock on 26 July while providing non-Mormons with the stuff for dramatic, damaging reports of gubernatorial defiance and disloyalty, Brigham Young's thoughts turned to his leaders elsewhere. Beginning on 1 August he or General Wells dictated letters of instruction and positioning to virtually every church and military leader in Utah as well as to those elsewhere in the United States and in Hawaii, Canada, and Europe. Indian chiefs in the territory and on its periphery also received such communications. The rapidity and scope of Young's actions were in sharp contrast to the organizational silences, communications disconnects, political distractions, and bureaucratic fumbling in Washington. The strategy communicated was to prepare the Mormon people psychologically and militarily for another round of persecution. At the same time, Young moved to reach out to allies, determine the Utah Expedition's intent, and accumulate the wherewithal to conduct, if necessary, a medium-term fighting withdrawal to an unspecified destination while preparing to incinerate Utah's infrastructure and property improvements. The model for Young's plan was the Russian defense of Moscow during the Napoleonic Wars and of its southernmost port city during the recently concluded Crimean War—the so-called "Sebastopol strategy."[17]

---

[17] Young had an active interest in the Crimean War as well as in the experiences of British Mormons who had served there with the Royal Army. In March 1857 he asked that notices be placed in Liverpool's *Millennial Star* seeking contact with such veterans, presumably for recruiting purposes; Young to Orson Pratt, 1 March 1857, LDS Archives. Ironically, the Utah Expedition's troops included British veterans of the Crimean War. George A. Smith, then a Nauvoo Legion colonel, had compared notes about Russia's Crimean War preparations during a meeting with Brevet Lt. Col. E. J. Steptoe on 28 December 1854. Church Historian's Office Journal, entry for 28 December 1854, ibid.

Among Brigham Young's most significant early tactical moves were:

- mobilization of Col. Robert Taylor Burton and a small cavalry detachment to patrol the plains as far east as Fort Laramie, Nebraska Territory.[18] Burton's mission was to provide assistance to Mormon emigrants while gathering intelligence on federal troop movements, intentions, and logistics, especially as to whether the Utah Expedition would move west of Laramie during 1857. Burton was also to learn the location of Col. E. V. Sumner's Cheyenne Expedition, a multi-regiment force that had marched west from Fort Leavenworth in May 1857 to punish the Plains tribes. Mormon leaders had come to believe, erroneously but almost obsessively, that Sumner was under orders for a swift, unannounced descent on Salt Lake City to capture and execute them;
- an alert to all Nauvoo Legion units to prepare for imminent activation while repairing firearms and procuring munitions. At the same time Young directed vigorous, covert efforts by Mormon agents to purchase arms and ammunition in California and on the Kansas-Missouri frontier;
- notification to Utah's entire population that grain from 1857's promising harvest was to be conserved—neither fed to animals nor sold to emigrating non-Mormons—in anticipation of a multi-year fighting withdrawal to "the mountains";
- the evacuation of not only the Y. X. Carrying Company stations on the plains but also the outlying Mormon colonies and missions from Carson Valley, San Bernardino, San Francisco, and Hawaii. Young directed their populations to gather in eastern Utah. British emigrants were to be diverted to Canada and away from U.S. Atlantic ports;
- dispatch of Apostle George A. Smith to southern Utah to alert that isolated region to the dangers afoot and plans for dealing with them; and
- communications to Indian tribes urging their alignment with the Mormon side.

Since the first violence of the Utah War took place in southern Utah at Mountain Meadows and involved Indians as well as the Legion, it is important to understand the letters that General Wells sent on 1 and 13 August to William H. Dame of Parowan, stake president and Apostle George A. Smith's successor as colonel commanding the Iron County militia. These and Brigham Young's own 4 August message to Jacob Hamblin, southern Utah's newly appointed Indian "farmer," call into question Young's later position that the

---

[18] Here again, as with his earlier lead-mining venture at Las Vegas, New Mexico; trek to Fort Limhi, Oregon Territory; and establishment of mail stations on the public domain across Nebraska, one finds Brigham Young and his militia operating on an uninhibited, regional (rather than territorial) basis. The act of a territorial governor in sending his militia unilaterally and unannounced into the territory of another was extraordinary, if not unique, in American gubernatorial history.

Mormons urged neutrality on the tribes throughout the war and that it was the army which sought to incite them to violence. Hamblin's instructions and perhaps the first to Dame were carried south by Apostle George A. Smith.

WELLS TO DAME, 1 AUGUST 1857, WILLIAM R. PALMER COLLECTION, SHERRATT LIBRARY, SOUTHERN UTAH UNIVERSITY.

1 August 1857

Reports tolerably well authenticated, have reached this office that an army from the United States is now en route to invade this Territory.

The people of this Territory having lived in strict obedience to the Laws of the parent and home governments, and ever jealous of the supremacy of the Constitution and the rights guaranteed thereby, in such times when anarchy takes place or orderly government and mobocratic tyranny usurp the power to rule; they are left to their inalienable right to defend themselves against aggression against their constitutional privileges. It is enough that for successive years they have witnessed the desolation of their homes; the barbarous wrath of mobs poured upon their unoffending brethren and sisters; their leaders arrested, incarcerated, and slain; and themselves driven to cull life from the hospitality of the desert and the Savage. They are not willing to endure longer these unceasing outrages; but, if an exterminating war is purposed against them, and blows alone can cleanse pollution from the nations bulwarks: to the God of our fathers let the appeal be made. You are instructed to hold your command in readiness to march at the shortest notice to any part of the Territory. See that the law is strictly enforced in regard to arms and ammunition and as far as practicable that each [company of] Ten shall be provided with a good wagon and four horses or mules, as well as the necessary clothing &c for a winter campaign. Particularly let your influence be used for the preservation of grain and report without delay any person from your district that disposes of a kernel of grain to any Gentile merchant or temporary sojourner or suffers to let it go to waste. Avoid all excitement but Be ready.

13 August 1857

You are hereby instructed to keep one or two tens out in the mountains upon the approaches to the settlements as a corps of observation that we may not be taken at any point by surprise.

Get the Indians in your vicinity also to watch & take the most effective measures to be in readiness & to have all the grain secured. Be careful that not a kernel is wasted. Do not have it foolishly and needlessly fed to horses, but let it be preserved, and instruct the people to be economical in using it, use potatoes and vegetables that cannot be preserved and save the grain; have your eye out for good safe places in the mountains where grain can be cached and where women and children can be safe in case we have to take to the mountains. Drop other business and thrash out the grain, and secure it the first thing. This is the first business to attend to. The time may come when we shall have to lay every thing waste & go into the mountains, therefore let us be preparing for such an event; be storing up clothing of a substantial Kind. Fix up and keep in repair our wagons and take care of our property and not let anything go to waste.

Instruct the Indians that our enemies are also their enemies & how they are continually fighting against them somewhere and that it will be come upon them as well as the Sioux & Cheyennes in due time, that they must be our friends and stick to us, for if our enemies kill us off, they will surely be cut off by the same parties.

Find safe retreats in the Mountains for Stock as well as families, and cache some grain to learn how to do it so it will keep. A little "practice you know makes perfect" and it is well to be preparing.

Advise with this Office and keep us posted with every important item of reliable information which you can obtain. Be vigilant and active.

YOUNG TO HAMBLIN, 4 AUGUST 1857, LDS ARCHIVES.

You are hereby appointed . . . as President of the Santa Clara Indian Mission. I wish you to enter upon the duties of your calling immediately.

Continue the conciliatory policy towards the Indians, which I have ever recommended, and seek by works of righteousness to obtain their love and confidence, for they must learn, that they have either got to help us, or the United States will kill us both.[19] Omit promises where you are not sure you can fill them, and seek to unite the hearts of the brethren on that mission, and let all under your direction be knit together in the holy bonds of love and unity.

We have an abundance of "news." The Government have at last appointed an entire set of officials for the Territory. These Gentry are to have a body guard of 2500 of Uncles [Sam's] Regulars. They were to start from Fort Leavenworth July 15th. 400 mule teams brings their personal dunnage, & 700 Ox teams 15 Months provisions, 7000 head of beef cattle are to arrive here to supply them. General Harney it is supposed will command the expedition. There errand is entirely peaceful. The current report is that they somewhat query whether they will hang me with or without a trial. There are about 30 others whom they intend to deal with. They will then proclaim a general jubilee [and] afford means and protection to those who wish to go back to the States. We feel first rate about all this and think every circumstance but proves the hastening of Zion's redemption.[20]

[19] For decades some traditional accounts of the Utah War omitted the last half of this sentence, presumably because of the damage that it did to Brigham Young's reputation, if not legal standing, vis à vis the Indian role at Mountain Meadows.

[20] A reference to Mormon millennial belief that the Utah War reflected the instability in the non-Mormon world and presaged the anticipated Second Coming of Christ.

> All is peace here and the Lord is eminently blessing our labors; Grain is abundant, and our Cities are alive with the busy hum of industry.
>
> Do not permit the brethren to part with their Guns or ammunition, but save them against the hour of need.

On the same day that he wrote to Hamblin in southern Utah, Young wrote to Capt. N. V. Jones on the Nebraska plains: "Have any of the boys learned their [the Cheyennes'] language? If not, lose no time but let some of them go about it immediately that we may have a free communication with them, also the Sioux and other nations in your reach; for they must learn, if they do not know it now, that if they do not help us to whip our enemies they will whip us both if they can."[21]

I Greatly Prefer Fighting to Hanging: Sending George A. South

Apostle George A. Smith was among several leaders dispatched by Young to communicate directly with the settlements some distance from Salt Lake. In early August Smith traveled to isolated southern Utah. For nearly a decade he had been the apostle responsible for shepherding the settlement and well-being of that region. Accordingly, he enjoyed a special relationship with its people—one accompanied by extraordinary regard for his words. What advice George A. Smith dispensed in those hamlets during the third week of August 1857 has also passed into the realm of folklore and controversy over the years, a process complicated almost hopelessly by the region's involvement in the soon-to-follow Mountain Meadows massacre. Some historians have argued that Smith was simply delivering cautionary advice to a people faced with the threatening approach of a large, unanticipated military force reminiscent of earlier Mormon persecution in Ohio, Missouri, and Illinois. Other writers believe that Smith's talks constituted provocative, inflammatory harangues that fanned a spirit of war hysteria in southern Utah, leading directly to the Mountain Meadows massacre less than a month later.

Also open to debate is the matter of whether in early August Smith carried south a gubernatorial proclamation of martial law drafted by Brigham Young, a document that Young did issue on 15 September 1857. A later chapter sets forth the arguments associated with this controversy and concludes that this

[21] Young to Jones, 4 August 1857, LDS Archives.

is not true. For Young to have ordered the preparation and review of such a decree in the midst of the multiple activities already underway during the first week of August—and to do so without leaving a trace of discussion in contemporary accounts of this scene, including Smith's—defies common sense.[22]

Other than Smith's own version, the most extensive account of what he said in this area during August appears in the contemporary notes of James H. Martineau, a young Parowan surveyor who, in the Mormon tradition, had been invited to serve as "historian" for part of Smith's journey. Second Lieutenant Martineau was also the newly appointed adjutant to Col. William H. Dame.

MARTINEAU RECORD, TYPESCRIPT,
WILLIAM R. PALMER COLLECTION, 21–25.

Aug. 9, Sunday. Geo. A. Smith spoke as follows: . . . They intend to hang about 300 of the most obnoxious Mormons; Brigham to be hung any how—no trial necessary for him or the principal leaders; and then go through a form of trial for the rest. They are sending out officers, Governor, judges, jury, and troops. They expect that one half the women will leave their husbands and cut their throats, and that one half of the men will join them. They hope thus to split us in two and have an easy victory over Mormonism and make an end of it. They undertook to get up a Bill for the suppression of polygamy, but the thing failed. . . . As a people we have been long harassed and oppressed, driven, slain and plundered. *I* have got through with it. I am one of the proscribed, but greatly prefer fighting to hanging, being naturally so great a coward. The United States are sending out 2500 infantry, besides Col. Sumner's dragoons, which are to rendezvous in G.S.L. City this winter, and 1000 teamsters, the worst description of men, picked up on the frontiers, which are more to be dreaded than the soldiers. They are making great calculations for "Booty and beauty." This outfit is costing between six and ten million dollars;—it is not a peace establishment, by any means. We must trust in God, for if we trust in any one else, we shall find ourselves the losers. If we trust in God he will give us power over our enemies. . . . If the troops come among us, and we have to flee into the mountains, we will haunt them as long as they live, unless they live longer than we do. Will we sell them grain or forage? I say damn the man who feeds them; I say damn the man who sympathizes with them; I say curse the man who pours oil and water on their heads. Last winter our Legislature sent a memorial to Congress protesting against the appointment of government offi-

[22] Robert Kent Fielding has argued that such a martial law proclamation—nearly identical in text to that issued on 15 September but dated 5 August—was prepared, distributed, and carried south by George A. Smith. Fielding believes that after the Mountain Meadows massacre of 11 September, all copies of the variant proclamation (but not that of 15 September) were returned as incriminating evidence and destroyed. Fielding to Howard R. Lamar, 9 March 2000, copy in editor's files.

cers who would strive to bring us into trouble with the general Government. The memorial was presented to the President, who referred it to Mr. Thompson, Secretary of the Interior, who pronounced it *treason*—a declaration of war, but it was nothing more than a strong protest against the appointment of a set of miserable scoundrels to override the people of this Territory.[23]

Given these events, it is interesting to consider the views of sixteen-year-old Harriet Ann Thatcher, whose Mormon family had just returned to the Salt Lake Valley from California. On 5 August 1857—in the midst of Young's flurry of communications—Harriet wrote to William B. Preston, her twenty-seven-year-old fiancé, then a recent Mormon convert and ex–gold miner farming in California's Yolo County. William and Harriet's biographer, Kenneth W. Godfrey, describes Harriet's unpublished letter as "of more than passing interest because she describes conditions in Utah only four weeks before the Mountain Meadows Massacre, and her account is neither colored nor influenced by the tragic events that occurred there in September."[24]

HARRIET ANN THATCHER TO WILLIAM B. PRESTON,
5 AUGUST 1857, PRESTON PAPERS.

I again take my seat to write you a few lines, to let you know that I am well, and feeling well although I have felt lost since, we parted, for I have missed your company very much, especially on Sundies, but I am feeling first rate now for I expect you home in a few months and consequently I am not going to feel lonely any more. . . .

We arrived on 14th of this [last] month, we stop[p]ed at Centerville about a week, we went to the city to church on the following sunday after we got in, Brigham addressed the audiance his principel subject was *war*, which made his discourse very interesting, not that it was a very desirable subject to talk about, or think of as being actual, and not immaginary, but it filled the peo-

[23] Here Smith is reciting Bernhisel's account of his disastrous 19 March 1857 meeting with Sec. Jacob Thompson and his reaction to the legislative assembly's 6 January 1857 petition and memorial. Smith's use of the word "treason" here goes beyond what Bernhisel had written to Young on 2 April about Thompson's reaction, but may reflect additional information about the Bernhisel-Thompson meeting of 19 March related by Bernhisel during their month-long journey to Salt Lake. As Apostle Smith completed his tour of the southern settlements on 23 August and headed home, Martineau sent an account of the trip to the *Deseret News.* That letter is not presented here because of its extremely bland character. For example, in his published letter Martineau simply noted several times that Smith "preached," whereas in a third document—his personal journal—he recorded, "G. A. Smith and the others preached war sermons to the people." See James H. Martineau to Editor Albert Carrington, 22 August 1857, "Correspondence, Trip to the Santa Clara," *Deseret News,* 23 September 1857, 227/3–4; "James A. Martineau Journal," entries for 5–23 August 1857, LDS Archives. See also Smith's related discourse delivered two weeks after his 1 September return to Salt Lake City; Bowery Discourse of George A. Smith, 13 September 1857, *Deseret News,* 23 September 1857, 226/4 and 227/1–3.

[24] Godfrey, "William Bowker Preston," 93.

ple with fire to think of being driven from their pleasant homes, that they had worked, so hard for, and to think of being driven from them makes them feel like fighting, and that is right way to feel. I suppose you have learned ere this that there ~~were~~ are 2500 troops on their [way] to this place for the purpose of keeping the Mormons at____ted [?], and enforce the laws that are conclid [counseled?] in the constitution, which laws they have always observed, but it is the United States that do not observe, the laws conclid therein, if [they] did they would let the Mormons & Utah alone and mind their own business[25] by doing this, they would be observing the laws of the constitution but as they are doing they are violating and not keeping the laws of theire country. Brigham says, that the troops shall never enter this Vally, if resistance will keep them from it, he says if the United states send enough troops to overpower this people, in war, he will try some other method, and that is to leave this Valley about the time they get here or a little before, and demolish every thing that is in the Vally, he says he will have every house torn down, and all the fences burned, and all the trees and every shrub cut and destroyed, and leave this Vally, or all the improvements, in ashes, he says he will make a Mosco[w][26] of it and flee to the Mountains, for saf[e]ty, he requested all that were willing to demolish their homes and follow him to the mountains, make it manifest by holding up both hands, and every hand that was in the bowery was up in a moment, except it was some gentile merchants, and of course theire hands were not up, but all the saints held up theire hands as a token of theire willingness to follow him. I never saw such unity in all my life as I saw here, all seemed to possess the same spirit that he possessed, this alone is suf[f]icient evidence to prove to me that they are certainly the people of the most high God, for unity is found nowhere else, but among the people of God, consequently this the people of God, at any rate I am willing to be with them in all that they do, for I firmly believe that the heads of this church are guided by his holy spirit, believing this, I am ready to go to the chambers of the mountains or any where else, if we do have this to do, it will be a bitter disappointment, to our enemies, to come and find nothing but a waste of that what was, but it is what they desire, and I [s]hall not pity them a great deal, for this people have [been] oppressed by them long enough, and now God will avenge theire wrongs, the people of this city feel well, and they have reasons to feel well, for they are looking for the redemption of Zion, Yes, beloved Zion it will not be long ere thou art free, then why should we not feel well, we have cause to rejoyce exceedingly—and we do rejoyce!

I shall look for you this fall, for Brigham has sent messengers to call all the elders and saints in, so I will look for you, and my Brothers and I hope I

---

[25] The phrase "mind your own business" used by Miss Thatcher was virtually an informal motto of the LDS church.

[26] These comments were part of Brigham Young's discourse of 26 July 1857.

> shall see you, all in a few months. I expect the Elders will never again be sent out to preach, for Brigham says, the Gospel trump[et] has been sounded to all the nations that he knows of (I heard that he said this) and I do not doubt but what it has been preached to every nation, and I believe peace will be entirely taken from the Earth, I am anxious you should come home this fall, for you can come safer this fall than any other time, that is if this fuss still goes on, and I expect it will. Brigham has called quite a number of men to go out and protect our emigration from the insults of Uncle Sam's troops, and for other purposes, which I am unable to understand.

Let It Be Treason, or Not Treason: The 16 August Discourse and Independence Issue

Of the multiple issues that dogged Mormon-federal relations as well as Utah's national image for years, few were as persistently corrosive as the independence question—the perception that Utah was seeking to exit the American political union by establishing an independent, millennially focused theocratic kingdom. As with arguments over the meaning of blood atonement and the array of code words for murder then used in Utah, the root cause of much of this long-running controversy over independence was Brigham Young's own often-enigmatic choice of words. Aside from the matter of what flags had flown at Silver Lake and for what purpose, Brigham Young's immediately following discourses fueled the belief by many in his audience that Utah Territory was leaving the union. Whether secession—an incendiary issue at the time—was Governor Young's intent is debatable. What is incontestable—as with several other life-and-death issues—is that his choice of words, as a highly visible leader with a large audience and printing press at his disposal, led people to perceive that he had declared Mormon independence.

For example, on Sunday, 16 August 1857 Martha Spence Heywood, plural wife of Utah's dismissed U.S. marshal, wrote in her diary, "Today Brother Brigham declared our independence and for the first time came out with saying that he had the revelation of the Lord that we were His people."[27] On the same day Hannah Tapfield King, a future Brigham Young wife, noted two big events: "At 8 o'clock A.M. news was brought to me of the birth of my grandson, Brigham Young Hampton, being the morning on which Brother Young declared the independence of our people of the United States upon the stand in consequence of the repeated unfilial measures they had taken

[27] Ipson, *Ever Faithful, The Life of Joseph Leland Heywood*, 363.

against us, and in the prospect of a troop of 100 soldiers coming here with sealed orders, etc."[28] Inevitably word of Young's 16 August comments also drifted rapidly into Salt Lake City's small non-Mormon community and from there gained currency throughout the country.[29]

The text of Brigham Young's discourse on 16 August 1857 has never been published—presumably because of its volatility—but church reporter George D. Watt's incomplete notes have survived. Compared to Young's published discourse of 26 July, these later remarks appear to reflect an escalation in Young's level of anger as well as an appetite for conflict. With respect to Young's dramatic comments about the potential for Indian violence, they are open to multiple interpretations. Young's Mormon listeners—steeped in church scriptures—may have interpreted what they heard as a millennially inspired drift into fatalism by a frustrated governor convinced of the scriptural inevitability of retaliatory Indian-on-white assaults irrespective of his past efforts to forestall them.[30] To non-Mormons of the mid-nineteenth century, Brigham Young may have sounded more like a territorial superintendent of Indian Affairs abdicating his responsibility to prevent such destruction and doing so in language easily interpreted as bloody threats.[31]

Young, Discourse, 16 August 1857, Unpublished Discourses, LDS Archives.

> I hope that I may say to the people the things that the Lord would say to them if he were to speak to them with an audible voice . . . what I do say I hope will be in truth and in righteousness dictated by the Holy Ghost. . . .
>
> I have come to this decision, if this people feel like joining me in it, that the last mobb has come to afflict this people that ever has come. . . . [L]et any people whatever rise up against this people to destroy them, and in the name of Isreal's [*sic*] God I say, lift the sword and slay them. (Voices unanimously crying "Amen.") . . .

---

[28] Hannah Tapfield King Journals, entry for 16 August 1857, LDS Archives. The reference to one hundred soldiers and sealed orders may have related to rumors about the intent of Colonel Sumner's Cheyenne Expedition.

[29] "Brigham Young's Declaration of Independence," Liberty (Missouri) *Weekly Tribune*, 1 December 1857, 2/4.

[30] My thanks to Ardis E. Parshall for this possible contemporary Mormon interpretation of Brigham Young's remarks.

[31] The original of Watt's notes are in LDS Archives. The editor thanks Will Bagley for bringing this important unpublished source to his attention. In his diary Young described the discourse as "warning the brethren to prepare for the worst, and bring thier [*sic*] minds to makeing every town a 'moscow' and every mountain pass a 'Potters Field', ere they would permit a mob to desecrate the Land which God has given us." Cooley, ed., *Diary of Brigham Young 1857*, 16 August 1857, 60.

It is a pretty bold statement; it is a pretty bold step for a little handful of men here in the Mountains to think that they can cope with the extensive Government—the powerful Government of the United States. Upon natural principles we cannot, but we can fight them in the name of God Almighty, and with his aid we can keep them off from us.

Let it be treason, or not treason they wilfully turn every thing that we say or do into treason. No "Mormon" can say or do anything but what it is wicked in their eyes, and unlawful. In reality we do and will (as we always have) take the ~~institution of~~ Constitution and the laws of the United States, take the Declaration of Independence and we will walk in the path of our fathers. We have as good a right to declare the Constitution of the United States as any other people, and that guarantees to every man, and to every family and to every community, life and liberty.

Well, as for infringing upon the laws of our Government, as for transgressing or infringing upon the constitution of the United [States], I am at defiance of all Earth and hell to point out the first thing that this people have ever committed wherein in righteousness it could be called an infringement upon our government. I am at the defiance of all ~~hell~~ Governments, but especially ours. ... We are not to blame for their turning good into evil; they alone are responsible for their mad career, but I still say to this people and I have my reasons, and I can show them, let an armed force as is calculating to now [be] ordered out by the Government of the United States [incomplete sentence] ...

The Governor [President] of the United States is sending soldiers here with sealed orders. I know what they are, as well as though I had had the papers and read them. Their sealed orders amount to this, "go there, build your stations, distribute your troops, decoy away every man and woman you can, and bring them to our standard, hatch up any kind of pretext, no matter what, and use up the leaders, break up their organization, disperse the people, and call in our Gentile brethren and break up this kingdom called Latter Day Saints." That is the purport of their sealed orders. ... That is the way they intend to treat us, but I tell you, the Lord Almighty and the Elders of Isreal [*sic*] being our helpers, they shall not come to this territory. I will fight them and I will fight all hell than tamely submit to such outrageous wrong and oppression.

Now sup[p]ose you are brought to that test, let me point it out to you they cannot do anything this fall. We will say we know we are good for them this fall, anyhow, and they may send all they can get here, but in another year, sup[p]ose they send 50,000 troops or 100,000 troops against us, how many is there of the Elders of Isreal and this community that will go with me (here the speaker was inter[r]upted with voices all over the congregation one after another saying, "We are ready".) do as I do and take the road I shall travel? I will tell you what it is, before I ask you to do it or not. If they come here, and if it is necessary I will tell you what I shall do. I shall lay this building in ashes, I shall lay my dwelling house in ashes, I shall lay my mills in ashes, I shall cutt every shrub and tree in the Valley, every pole, every inch of board, and put it all into ashes. I will burn the grass, and the stubble and lay it waste, and make a worse Moscow of every settlement, and then I guess we will make a Potter's field of every Canyon the enemy go into. Dare you all go into the Mountains? (The congregation, at the tops of their voices, shouted, "Yes.") . . . [32]

I will take this people in the midst of these mountains, and I am at defiance of the world. They may come with their fifty thousand men, or a hundred thousand men, or as many as they could raise, and just as sure as they increase their numbers the worse it will be for them.

How do you think they will feel to come here and not find a house, or a barn, or a stick, or a board, nothing under the heavens in the shape of a building of fuel or of lumber? Don't you think the new Governor would feel nice to come here and reign as Governor? (Laughter.) How pretty would a United States Court look here, who will they try? One another, and that will be trying which can be the biggest damned raskel. Excuse me for swearing. . . .

I have no objections to their sending Governors and judges here, but I do object to their injuring this people, and I do not mean they shall do it as they have hitherto. As stated in the last weeks paper the only fault that can be found with this people is that we did not hang up certain poor miserable curses before they got out of this place. I will tell you further, every man and woman that do not callculate to take this shot with me, if we are obliged to, and it is necessary upon natural principles, I want you to pick up and leave now while you can go in peace, for if a man refuses to come to the scratch if the time ever should come that we lay waste to everything, if a man rises up saying "You cannot touch my building," we will hew him down as a cumberer [*sic*] of the ground, and lay waste his heritage. . . .

Can you make the sacrifice? . . . Can you flee to the mountains, men, women and children, and lay wast[e] and desolate every thing before them? (Voices, "Yes.") If you can, show your hands. (All hands were up and not contented with this the whole congregation of thousands of Saints Clap[p]ed their hands. The feeling that prevailed in the meeting cannot be described.)

Now some of you may say, "Why, bro. Brigham, you are unwise to tell this." Not so, and I will tell you why. In the first place, I will commence a little from this. You know that they alledge [*sic*] against me almost every thing they can imagine to my character, proclaiming that I have been the means of doing this mischeif [*sic*] and that and of killing emagrants, and they have laid the death of [Capt. John W.] Gunnison upon me, and the destroying of United States records, every partical [*sic*] of it is a lie. I have treated them kindly. I have done everything I could to make them happy. Don't you see I am clear, I am free? Don't you see I can call upon God to assist me in time of need? Now then, if I warn them, and fore warn them, what fault can they find? None at all.

---

[32] Everett L. Cooley has argued that this portion of the discourse was Young's first public exposition of what in the spring of 1858 would become the Move South. Cooley, ed., *Diary of Brigham Young 1857*, 60–61n61.

If our enemies come here we shall surely lay you waste. Report it, ye gentiles, you hickory Mormons, write to them, publish it abroad, that we callculate to sweep the platter, and to lay this Territory wast[e], and we will take it Indian fashion in the Mountains, and see what you can do with us.[33] Now you need not any of you ask me where you will go, but you just wait until the time comes and it shall be told you. That I shall keep to my self. . . .

I have strove to my uttermost, since I have been in this Territory, to make peace with the Indians, they have all the times been troubling the emagrants, more or less. I have been sending out and expending until the Government of the United States now owes me in my financial capacity some forty or fifty thousand dollars which I have expended for them more than they have paid me. I need not tell you that if they get any property in here, that I mean to put my hand on it to pay myself.[34]

I have preached to the Indians, sent them presents, visited them and prayed for them, that they might become peac[e]able, and let the traveler alone. This Year they are mischieveous [*sic*] on the North rout[e], and our brethren when they came through expected to have a fuss with them. The Indians tried to rob them, but they found them too many of them. Now let me say if the United States send their army here and war commences, the travel must stop; your trains must not cross this continent. To accomplish this I need only say a word to the[m] for the Indians will use them up; unless I continually strive to restrain. I will say no more to the Indians, let them alone, but do as you please.[35] And what is that? It is to use them up; and they will do it. With all my exertions this year, they have killed a good many of the emagrants [*sic*], and it is a matter of regrett.

I warn them and fore warn them if they commence on us, they need not expect me to hold the Indians while they shoot them. What did the first party of Emagrants do this year going to the States, I will show you the foolery of it. Every Indian they saw, they shot at. This raised the ire of the Indians to that degree I cannot keep them peac[e]able.

---

[33] It is not clear what a "hickory" Mormon was. "Sweep (or cleanse) the platter" was a euphemism for bloodshed used in Utah and elsewhere derived from the Bible's Matthew 23:25 and Luke 11:39.

[34] Only weeks later the Nauvoo Legion seized thousands of dollars' worth of government livestock. A discussion of officer-sanctioned looting by the Legion during atrocities at Mountain Meadows and elsewhere appears in Chapter 12. From a leadership-by-example perspective, the question arises as to whether this comment before thousands of people was harmless hyperbole or a license to steal dispensed by a federally sworn governmental leader who also spoke with the force of a territorial governor, superintendent of Indian Affairs, and militia commander.

[35] Young's use of the phrase "do as you please" with respect to potential Indian violence is freighted with importance and destructive ambiguity. The same phrase appears repeatedly in Young's letter to the Nauvoo Legion commander at Mountain Meadows on the eve of the massacre, in his correspondence of the period to absent Mormon leaders, and in his private remarks to Captain Van Vliet two days following the massacre. Young to Haight, 10 September 1857, and Young to Clinton and Orson Pratt, 12 September 1857, LDS Archives; Kenney, ed., *Wilford Woodruff's Journal,* entry for 13 September 1857, 5:96–97.

They lay the ax at the root of the tree to distroy themselves, what can I do? Sit and laugh, and let them. But as for their hanging Brigham, Heber, Daniel, or any of the rest of them, they have to catch them first, for they never can hang us until they have catched us. I am generally pretty wide awake [and] I want you should understand this as I say it. . . .

Write to your friends, if the United States Armies come, but I do not believe they can get here, then say to your friends don't pretend to cross this Contenant [*sic*], for I will tell you honestly, and plainly, and in all good feeling, I will not hold the Indians still while you shoot them, as you have hitherto, but I will say to them, go and do as you please. I tell you that if it was [incomplete sentence]

Had it not been for the "Mormons" in these mountains, this emagration that has past over this contenant this season would have been cut off, 19 out of 20. It would have be[e]n stopped. Had it not been for the settlements here, the overland emigration would have been stopped years ago, and they turn round and condemn me and this people for conniving with the Indians. This people have done the travelers good, they have kept the Indians from injuring them and have done all in our power to save the lives of men, women and children, but this will cease to be, if they commence on us. . . .

I would as leave make my habitation under the bows of these pines, cedars and balsome, gather up the sage brush and make me a wickiup.[36] I would not swap away the good feeling I have, for all the wealth and honer [*sic*] the world can bestow. Another thing I want to say to the brethren.

We are sending our companies to see that our brethren come in safety. There is a good many companies of United States troops in the mountains that have been sent out to hunt the Indians. You have heard of one command's hunting the Shians [Cheyennes] all summer long. [T]hey have been hunting where the Shians [are] not, for fear of meeting them, and the first you know they are in our borders afflicting our emagrants, robbing their property there and reacting the scenes that have been acted before. . . .[37]

"What shall we do? They will take our Cattle." (President Kimball, "they cant do it") I callculate they shall furnish us with Guns, powder, and lead, Beef, Pork, and all that is necessary. (Voices, "Amen") I mean to go to war at their expence and not on ours. . . .

We want to go to work and secure our grain; and those that are not engaged at that prepare to bring in our emagration, and the rest shall be told you in due time.

God bless you: Amen.

---

[36] As events turned out, during the 1858 Move South to Provo President Young and his family were quartered in hotels, private homes, and a specially constructed compound of cabins, while less well-to-do Mormon families sought shelter in friends' homes, wickiups, tents, dugouts, and wagon boxes.

[37] Another reference to anxiety over the mission of Colonel Sumner's Cheyenne Expedition.

Riding Directly into the Lion's Den: Mormon Backtrailing on the Plains

Of the few accounts that survive of the Nauvoo Legion's earliest scouting and intelligence gathering activities, one of the most interesting is the unpublished narrative of Asa S. Hawley, a twenty-two-year-old Canadian convert who wrote his autobiography in 1912 at age 77. In 1857 Hawley was swept up in the Legion's scouting mission because of his work at the Y. X. Carrying Company's important Deer Creek, Nebraska Territory, station under Legion captain (later colonel) Nathaniel V. Jones, a Mormon Battalion veteran.[38] As a result of Brigham Young's and General Wells's orders to Jones, Hawley was assigned to determine whether the Utah Expedition was moving west of Fort Laramie.[39] Because of the lateness of the season and the logic that had motivated Generals Scott's and Harney's recommendations, Brigham Young doubted that the army would do so; but he, Col. Robert Taylor Burton, and Captain Jones needed to know. ("We really do not believe that they will be able to reach farther than Laramie the present season, and then we think that probably some other direction may be given to them;[40] but we have no idea of permitting them to invade our Territory with impunity, and we wish to be prepared for whatever course things may take.") Asa Hawley would find out whether the army was west of Fort Laramie while participating in the greatest adventure of his life. His experiences were those of a low-level, out-of-uniform scout tasked with solving one of the Utah War's early strategic-tactical riddles. Hawley did so while afield amongst a westbound surge of Americans of mixed intent.

Hawley's biggest problem was not hostility from the army's Utah Expedition, but rather his encounter with the civilian Pacific Wagon Road crew so poorly led by "Col." W. M. F. Magraw. It was because of behavior of the

[38] Jones's title during August, before being designated a colonel, is ambiguous. Some letters to Jones by Young and Wells bore no title at all, other than "Brother." During the course of his work with the Y. X. Carrying Company, he was sometimes called "captain," which was perhaps an honorific plains title, although there is at least one Legion order going back to 1851 that describes him as a major.

[39] See Young to Jones, 4 August 1857, and Wells to Jones, 11 August 1857, LDS Archives. Among Young's instructions to Jones were the following urgent questions: "Where is Col. Sumner, and where are the Cheyennes, and what success does he have against them?"

[40] This, of course, was the strategy advocated in May–June 1857 by Generals Scott and Harney. Aside from common sense, Brigham Young's early belief that the Utah Expedition would not move west of Fort Laramie during 1857 was probably grounded in his awareness that the army was two months late in leaving Fort Leavenworth and his painful recollection of the weather-related disaster that had struck the Mormon Willie and Martin handcart companies on the plains during the fall of 1856.

MORMON NEMESIS W. M. F. MAGRAW
A controversial, dissipated, and failed mail contractor hyper-critical of Brigham Young and violent toward some of his followers, Magraw was politically connected to Buchanan. So also were two of his brothers, one of whom courted the president's niece. Rightfully fearful that the Legion was hunting him, Magraw abandoned his troubled Pacific Wagon Road superintendency near South Pass during the fall to seek refuge with the Utah Expedition as a captain in its newly recruited volunteer battalion. *Image from Searight,* The Old Pike: A History of the National Road (*Uniontown, Pennsylvania, 1894*).

type described by Hawley that W. M. F. Magraw soon feared capture, if not assassination, by the Nauvoo Legion.

Magraw has no biographer, but a colorful sketch of his appearance and behavior has survived the nineteenth century. Written thirty years after Magraw's early death at age 46 in 1864, this account focused on his activities not in the West of the 1850s but rather along the old National Road on the Maryland-Pennsylvania border during the years bracketing this period. From this brief description of Magraw's flamboyant, alcohol-fueled, politically oriented style among the mountains of the "Old Pike," one sees a behavior wholly consistent with that displayed in the West. Lurking below the surface of Magraw's convivial persona was the volatile streak of brutality tempered by cowardice encountered by Asa Hawley.[41]

[41] For a description of Magraw's assault on William Hope, editor of the Washington, D.C., *Evening Star,* see "Santa Fe Mail Contractor Fined," *New York Times,* 20 March 1855, 4/1. For his several brawls and avoidance of still others on the plains as well as in Washington involving explorer-engineer Frederick W. Lander, guide Tim Goodale, and others, see MacKinnon, "The Buchanan Spoils System," 140–43.

"W. M. F. Magraw," in Thomas B. Searight, *The Old Pike: A History of the National Road* (Uniontown, Penn: 1894), 327–28.

One of the smartest, best known and most picturesque men of the road forty years ago was William M. F. Magraw. . . . He was a native of Maryland, and belonged to an old influential family of that State. His brother, Harry, practiced law for several years in Pittsburg, and served a term as State Treasurer of Pennsylvania from 1856 to 1859. The Magraws were intimate friend of James Buchanan, and Harry was a leader in the movements that led up to the nomination and election of that old time statesman to the Presidency.[42] W. M. F. Magraw became identified with the National Road as many others did, through a matrimonial alliance. His wife was a daughter of Jacob Sides, who owned the Tomlinson tavern.[43] . . . He was a large, fine looking man, always well dressed, attracting attention wherever he appeared, and making friends by reason of his agreeable manners. He was not fleshy, but broad shouldered, tall and erect, of ruddy complexion, light hair, and habitually wore gold rimmed spectacles on account of some defect of vision. He was generous almost to a fault, and lavish in his personal expenditures. He spent much of his time in Uniontown [Pennsylvania], making his headquarters with his friend Joshua Marsh, [proprietor] of the National House. His habits of living were different from the majority of the old pike boys, especially in the matter of eating, and he enjoyed a good supper at midnight, better than any other hour. He brought in game of all kinds from the mountain and had it served in savory style at the National House. He kept a carriage, and often had it ordered out as early as three and four o'clock in the afternoon, to go to the mountain, but lingered about the town, chatting with friends, until nightfall. He seemed to delight in driving over the mountain in the night. Leaving Uniontown about the dusk of the evening, he would reach the Tomlinson tavern about daybreak the next morning. He called up the old tavern keepers along the road, all of whom knew him, chatted a while with them, took a mint julep, or something stiffer, and pushed on, and this was his habit as long as he remained on the road. . . . During the administration of President Pierce, Magraw had a contract for carrying the mails from the Missouri boundary to western points beyond the plains. He suffered much loss by reason of Indian invasions, and preferred a claim to Congress for a large sum of money to reimburse him. While his bill was undergoing consideration by

---

[42] The Utah Expedition's Captain Phelps referred to Magraw's brother, Henry Slaymaker Magraw, thusly in commenting on W. M. F. Magraw's 1857 appointment to a superintendency with the Pacific Wagon Road project: "It appears that Magraw's brother was a delegate to the [Cincinnati] convention that nominated Buchanan for the Presidency, and hence, in the political logic of the present day *must* be a party chief for a scientific exploring expedition." Phelps diary, entry for 3 September 1857.

[43] Magraw's wife was Elizabeth Sides Magraw. The Tomlinson Tavern was an early nineteenth-century establishment at "Little Meadows," the juncture of the National (Cumberland) and Braddock Roads east of Grantsville, Garrett County, Maryland.

the committee, he appeared before it and emptied upon the floor a number of bags of mules' ears, as evidence of his losses. His bill was passed.[44]

HAWLEY, AUTOBIOGRAPHY, CA. 1912, LDS ARCHIVES.

After circling around to see that all was right we drove inside the corral up in front of the commissary room [at Deer Creek] where much to my surprise out of the house stepped Apostle John Taylor, [Apostle] Erastus Snow and Jim Gammel. . . . [45] We were very diligent in guarding our brethren. This was a very interesting time for me, sitting around the camp-fire hearing the apostles talk and hearing Elder Taylor sing the Mormon Car, a song he had composed while editing a paper in St. Louis.[46] Finally word came from Captain Jones that all was safe and to bring the Apostles down to the station, which we did, and the next morning they started on their way to the [Salt Lake] Valley.

Then came the word that the last train of Handcart company had arrived at or near Fort Laramie. Again I was sent down with some teams to meet them and render them assistance to which I cheerfully complied. We met them in due time finding them full of faith and energy and in good spirits and greatly pleased to think that we had come to their assistance. . . .

It was during my absence that word came that we were released to return home. "Yes," he [Alma H. Bennett] said, "the company starts home in the morning, but you and I have another mission to perform. We are called to go back and find out where the soldiers are, or whether they have passed Fort Laramie or not." . . . [W]e saddled our horses and started on our downward trip, traveling leisurely down the Platte River that day and also the next day until noon, where we met John M. Murdock's freight train loaded with goods for Salt Lake.[47] He told us there was no doubt that the Government was send-

[44] After taking on the mail contract for the Independence–Salt Lake City route in 1854, Magraw incurred heavy operating losses due to inefficiencies and the ravages of Indian attacks, a plague for which he unsuccessfully sought military escorts from Secretary of War Davis. In December 1854 he petitioned Congress for an increase in his annual compensation from $14,000 to $41,800 and was awarded an increase to $36,000. When he subsequently failed to obtain an additional increase, Magraw again petitioned Congress, this time seeking release from the contract. Congress granted this request effective 18 August 1856, and the business was quickly awarded to Hiram Kimball (Brigham Young) and the Y. X. Carrying Company at an annual rate of $23,000.

[45] At about this time Apostle Taylor wrote a long letter from the Platte River to the editor of the *New York Times* describing, among other things, an earlier attempt on Mormon James Gemmell's life by Magraw near Independence. Taylor commented partly in jest, "My private opinion, from the twinkle of his [Gemmell's] eye when speaking on the subject is, that it would not be very good for McGraw's health to meet him on equal grounds." Taylor to Editor, 16 July 1857, *New York Times*, 30 September 1857, 1/1–2.

[46] This song, sung to the upbeat tune of "Jeanette and Jeanot," uses repeated railroad imagery to suggest the past and future of Mormonism. Taylor wrote the words in New York City, not St. Louis. "The Mormon Car," *The Mormon* (New York), 23 February 1856, 1.

[47] Murdock arrived in Salt Lake City on 6 September, bringing first word of Captain Van Vliet's approach and perhaps some of the gunpowder covertly acquired by Nicholas Groesbeck.

ing a large army to Utah and it was his opinion they had already passed Fort Laramie. After remaining with Murdock perhaps for a couple of hours resting our horses and refreshing ourselves with something to eat, we thought it time to ride on. . . .

This was the time and place that tried men's souls, for well did we know that we were riding directly into the lion's den.[48] Gladly would I have turned my face homeward had my mission been fulfilled. . . . [W]e rode on down the river until nearly sundown; then coming to a nice patch of grass on the bank of the river, we conclude to camp for the night. After eating our supper, which consisted of dried buffalo meat straight, we thought we would wander down to the camp of a man named McGraw—he being in charge of a surveying party—and have a chat with him. Here I would state that this McGraw was a very bitter enemy of our people. In fact, one of the main factors in planning and executing the death of Parley P. Pratt. . . .[49]

We had concluded at the same time that we would not linger in McGraw's camp but would pass quietly by. But in this we found ourselves mistaken. When coming opposite his tent he stepped out and hailed us, first inquiring w[h]ere we were from. We told him we were from California. He then wished to know if we came through Salt Lake and what them G–d Mormons was doing there. Stating further that if he caught a Mormon in his camp he would string him higher than Gildiray's [Gilroy's] kite. We then told him we had to ride on as we wished to reach Fort Laramie that night. He then remarked, "You are a couple of fine boys—to come from California alone." Then stepping back into his tent he brought out a bottle of brandy of which he made us a present.[50] We thanked him very much, and bidding him good-morning, we rode on. Here I would state that he told us he expected to go down to Fort Laramie himself that afternoon.

We had gone but a short instance when we met a Government freight wagon train. We had a chat with the wagon-master. He told us the soldiers were but a short ways behind. He also showed us the wagon that was loaded with rope which they intended to hang all the Mormons with, except the women, who they would preserve for their own convenience.[51] Passing on we soon met anoth-

[48] A paraphrase of the famous opening sentence of Thomas Paine's *The American Crisis.*

[49] Magraw was certainly anti-Mormon, but he had nothing to do with Pratt's assassination. The fact that Hawley believed this to be true is significant in terms of Mormon attitudes about him. His assumption resembles those made in southern Utah a few weeks later, in which local residents came to believe that the Fancher party, predominantly from near Harrison, Arkansas, included people involved in Joseph Smith's 1844 murder as well as in the Pratt assassination.

[50] Magraw's drinking habits were described frequently in letters and journals of his disaffected employees and passing travelers. MacKinnon, "The Buchanan Spoils System and the Utah Expedition," 139–40.

[51] Talk of this type by General Harney, his troops, and civilian camp followers—what George A. Smith characterized in southern Utah as loose talk of "booty and beauty"—had a significant impact on Mormon attitudes and stiffened resolve to resist the Utah Expedition's entrance into Salt Lake Valley. Belief in these violent intentions persisted in Utah for decades, especially those related to lynching.

er train, and passed it. A short distance on, from the top of the ridge we beheld the advance guard of the army. Knowing that the goal had been reached and that the army had passed Laramie, for we had seen them with our own eyes, and that there was nothing more to be gained, we could conscientiously turn our faces homeward. . . .

We traveled the rest of that day and that night and the next day until two o'clock. We came down onto the Platte again. Then we stopped. . . . I had laid there but a few minutes when Alma gave a low whistle. I immediately rose to my feet, at the same time picking up my belt and pistols, and buckling them around me. Two men were onto us heavily armed, whom we readily recognized that we had seen in the McGraw camp the morning before. We were not altogether taken by surprise for we had surmised that as soon as McGraw got to Fort Laramie and found we had not been there it would arouse his suspicions, which it evidently did and he sent those two men to follow us and capture us. When they rode up we saluted them by saying, "How are you, gentlemen?" They wanted to know where we were going. We told them we were going to Salt Lake. They asked us if we were Mormons. We told them yes. By this time our tea was steeped and we very graciously invited them to come and partake with us. Our menu consisted of dried buffalo meat, but on this special occasion we had tea.[52] It reminded me very much of General Marion dining with the British officer on sweet potatoes served on pine bark. . . .[53] This was a very peculiar condition, for we knew by intuition that they were only waiting to get the drop on us. You can better imagine than I can describe it. They were desperate looking fellows. Their pistols outside their scabbards sticking loose in their belts, but we were ready for them in any move they might take. I never will forget that meal; talking and laughing and at the same time watching each other like hawks. I finally said to my partner, "Had we not better ride?" He answered, "Yes, we better be moving on." . . .

Thus we worked ourselves out of pistol shot. Riding up over the ridge, we took out our pistols, putting on fresh [percussion] caps, and feeling that we were not done with those fellows yet. We rode on for a while, then upon looking up we saw a great dust. As it drew nearer, we discovered it to be the McGraw men. As they came up I jumped off my horse, turned around, and met them in the road. They asked me if I knew what six men it was coming back there. I replied that I did not, stating that it might be some of our boys, as we had plenty of them strung along. Of course, this was a canard, we well knowing that there were no Mormons anywhere near. The gentlemen passed us and went on. . . .

If anything was lacking to convince us McGraw had sent them to capture or kill us, surely this clinched it. . . .

---

[52] In 1857 Mormon interpretations of the Word of Wisdom's prohibition on alcohol, tobacco, and caffeinated beverages were different than they became at the end of the nineteenth century.

[53] Gen. Francis Marion of South Carolina, the American Revolution's "Swamp Fox."

We were now fully on our way for Salt Lake. At Devil's Gate we met Col. R. T. Burton with a company of fifty men, who had been sent out from Salt Lake to retard the progress of the army as much as possible. Truly, this was a happy meeting. After being in the midst of enemies an those that sought our lives, to be able to grasp the hands of our friends and brethren made us feel that we had made a most miraculous escape and that God had protected us. We had no time to linger. After delivering our message to Col. Burton, also receiving one from him to take to Major McCallister who then was with a battalion on Rocky Ridge [near South Pass], we changed horses and started on. . . .

On arriving at Green River we caught up with our company from Deer Creek. . . . At Hams Fork we passed Capt. Vanvlet's camp, he having gone on to Salt Lake. We arrived at Ft. Bridger about 2 o'clock the next day, where we found Louis Robinson [*sic*] who kindly supplied us with fresh horses. There was no stopping. Now all aboard for Salt Lake, which we reached the next day, just as the sun was coming up over the mountains. We rode immediately to President Young's office and delivered our message. General D. Howells [D. H. Wells] took us then to a restaurant and gave us our breakfast. We were then at liberty to go home. . . . Ours was at Pleasant Grove, some thirty-six miles south, where we arrived about midnight, happy in the thought of once more meeting our wives, our kindred, and our friends.

First Comes the Catching: Anxieties over Colonel Sumner's Mission

Recent historians of the Utah Expedition and those of Col. E. V. Sumner's Cheyenne Expedition have overlooked the substantial apprehension in Utah about Sumner's mission.[54] In part this apprehension was rooted in an understandable Mormon fear of lynching; in part they were the unintended consequence of General Scott's emphasis on secrecy in organizing Sumner's campaign. To appreciate better the implications of Mormon near-obsession with Sumner's whereabouts and intentions, it is instructive to consider the rumors that swept Salt Lake City and as far west as California before washing back into Utah to stoke Mormon anxieties.

On 4 August Brigham Young had queried Capt. N. V. Jones about the whereabouts of Sumner and his troops. A week later Elias Smith wrote, "A rumor

[54] Chalfant's *Cheyennes and Horse Soldiers* is silent on this issue, and neither Juanita Brooks nor Will Bagley discuss concern over Sumner's mission in connection with the war anxiety that arose in southern Utah during August 1857. A lone exception is Roger R. Ekins, *Defending Zion: George Q. Cannon and the California Mormon Newspaper Wars of 1856–1857* (Spokane, Wash: Arthur H. Clark Co., 2002), 358–61.

reached the city from some source that part of the troops of the United States have been looking after the Cheyennes in order to deceive the people of Utah, as we believe it has been their sole intention to get here as slyly as possible, and have had but little intention of fighting Indians, and have made their appearance on the Sweetwater. If so, our expectations as to their intentions have been correct, and I presume their movements will be closely watched hereafter."[55] Later that month George Q. Cannon, editor of the Mormon *Western Standard* in San Francisco, wrote to Brigham Young with tongue-in-cheek:

> It is astonishing how easily they [non-Mormon priests and editors in California] are sold on every thing pertaining to us, as a people; they greedily swallow the most absurd lies, and prefer them, all the time, to plain straightforward, reasonable truth. The latest lie in circulation here, is one concerning your arrest, on a charge of treason, by Col. Sumner, with 86 dragoons, and his departure with you in custody for Washington, "unmolested by the Mormons"! This happened on the 25th of June, and as you did not seem to be aware of it on the 4th of July, the date of your letter, I send you the news. What Gen. Harney, with three thousand men, was scarcely thought able to accomplish, Sumner with eighty-six men, has performed with ease and without the loss of a drop of blood![56]

In isolated southern Utah—alerted by George A. Smith's preaching and his explicit references to Sumner—concern about a possible descent from the east by the Cheyenne Expedition seemed strongest. As a result, during the period 3–11 September 1857 Lt. James H. Martineau again took to the field with three comrades to scout through the high peaks and alpine plateaus above the Sevier River Valley. It was an arduous, cold, and lonely assignment resembling Asa S. Hawley's to the northeast. Although theirs was a scout that proved unsuccessful in terms of turning up signs of approaching troops, it was an expedition that fortuitously for Martineau spared him almost-certain involvement at Mountain Meadows. There his regiment and commander, Col. William H. Dame, played a disastrous part during his absence.[57]

---

[55] Journal of Elias Smith, entry for 11 August 1857.

[56] Cannon to Young, 31 August 1857, LDS Archives.

[57] James H. Martineau, "A Scouting Party," *The Contributor*, August 1890, 395–97. Martineau obviously wrote this reminiscence relying on his 1857 "Journal," a photocopy of which was acquired in 2005 by LDS Archives. The editor thanks managing director Richard E. Turley, Jr., for access to this document.

The Intelligence We Have Thus Far Obtained: Trail Reports for Brigham Young

Not discussed often among the strategies and tactics created by Brigham Young in early August was his 13 August dispatch of Elder Samuel W. Richards from Salt Lake City to Philadelphia and Liverpool to brief Thomas L. Kane and leaders of the British Mission. While crossing the plains, Richards and later John M. Bernhisel made careful observations of troop and supply-train movements, which they reported to Brigham Young. Their reports provide insight into Young's fascination with intelligence gathering and his skill in directing it, as well as his intense curiosity about Sumner's Cheyenne Expedition and W. M. F. Magraw. One of the more colorful aspects about Bernhisel's collection of information is that it took place in the midst of the hospitality and military protection extended to him by his traveling companion-host, U.S. Army captain Stewart Van Vliet.

Richards and Briant Stringham to Young, 18 August 1857, lds Archives.

We take pleasure in availing ourselves of this opportunity to write you a few lines, that you may be posted of our where-abouts, the intelligence we have thus far obtained upon the road &c. &c. . . .

We leave here early in the morning for Horse shoe Creek, and will look after the rear companies of our Emigration and forward them with all possible speed. We shall also endeavour to learn all that we can about the Troops and report as often as expedient.

Bro. N. V. Jones informs us that on the 16th he had conversation with Reshaw[58] who had just arrived from Laramie from whom he learned that word had been passed from Gen. Hearney [*sic*] to the Fort that he had orders to remove our stations from the line, and assured Bro. Jones that he and the bretheren would have to leave & that his information was from a reliable source. Bro. Jones further inquired as to the where abouts of Genl. Hearney, but Reshaw said he could not find out.—that the commander at the Fort knew but would only give him to understand that it was the intention to remove everything from the road and pass over it under a forced march so that no news should go in advance. In the plan of their operations, secretiveness seems to be a very prominent feature. He thought they would not be along here before the first of September.

Col. Sumner's Command have now been gone among the Schyennes sev-

[58] John Baptiste Richard, proprietor of the trading post at Platte Bridge, near what is today Casper, Wyoming. "Reshaw" was a corruption of the French pronunciation of Richards's surname.

eral days longer than they were rationed for, and have not been heard from. It is already believed by the Mountaineers that he and his party have been *"used up"* by the indians. The Cheyennes have already succeeded in stealing some 440 head of Beef Cattle from one of the rear Government trains.

From report we expected to find a company of M^c^Graw's men at Markhams station say about 30 men and very bad at that, but on arriving there we found the full number was only 14 men under Surveyor [Frederick W.] Lander, that they were very civil, and were waiting M^c^Graw's arrival so that they could proceed on through to California and complete the surveying they have to do on the line. Some two or three Routes are being surveyed through south of this by the soldiers which perhaps accounts for the report that soldiers were in Sweet Water &c. Col. Johnson[59] *is said* to be out with a Battalion, and also Col. [Philip St. George] Cooke on different routes.

After Samuel W. Richards left Deer Creek on 20 August, he continued to take notes on military movements as he moved east, but his subsequent report to Brigham Young cannot be located. Richards's observations can be reconstructed from a letter that he wrote to Apostle Orson Pratt immediately after landing in Liverpool on 3 October 1857:

RICHARDS TO PRATT, 4 OCTOBER 1857, *MILLENNIAL STAR*, 17 OCTOBER 1857, 668–71.

Thursday morning, 20th, at daybreak, we crossed the Platte opposite Laramie, and passed down the north side of the river. From this point to Kearney it was a frequent occurrence to see large trains, both in motion and in camp, with enormous herds of cattle, horses and mules. Seventy-eight wagons moving in one train, with about 1000 head of cattle, were as many as we saw together. They generally moved and camped in companies of about twenty-six wagons.

Monday, 24th. The first company of troops that we discovered were in camp 118 miles below Laramie. We camped on the opposite side of the river, in view of some 200 tents or upwards, and five or six distinct trains of Government stores and equipage for the troops. Evidently Government has designed to make the Utah Expedition a magnificent affair.

On the 28th we called at Kearney, where we were informed that most of the troops for Utah had passed that point, and many heavy trains of merchandize [*sic*], in view of a rare chance for speculation, purchasing wheat, grain,

---

[59] This is a reference to Lt. Col. Joseph E. Johnston, First U.S. Cavalry, who was then leading a detachment to survey the southern boundary of Kansas Territory. Because of the similarity of names, ranks, and unit designators, and the presence of both officers in Kansas, Joseph E. was often mistaken in Utah War documents for Albert Sidney.

forage, &c., for the troops in Utah. Poor dear creatures, what a pity they should be disappointed!

At Fort Kearney we learned that many were deserting from the expedition, both troops and teamsters, and the officers had been obliged to hold out inducements, and adopt rigid regulations, withholding pay for one year, &c., to suppress, as far as possible, the spirit of desertion. It was thought this spirit would greatly increase as they advanced towards the mountains, and encountered the severity of the mountain storms, which must necessarily overtake them. Even at Kearney the soldiers were in very high glee at the idea of wintering sumptuously in Utah, where, as the [Irish] Paddy said, "the women are as thick as blackberries," and it was a great wonder to them what Brigham Young would say to see them with his wives parading the streets of Great Salt Lake City. Every dirty, foul-mouthed Dutchman [German] and Irishman, of which many of the troops were composed, fully expected some "Mormon" woman would jump into his arms upon his arrival in Utah, and hail him as a heavenly messenger sent to bring deliverance from "Mormon degradation, wretchedness, and despair." Who don't wait with almost breathless suspense for the issue? Suffice it to say, the information we received at this point was of the most interesting character to such as have families in Utah, and afforded us considerable amusement. With but a short detention at this point, we proceeded on our way, and on Sunday morning, the 30th, we drove into the flourishing little town of Genoa [Nebraska Territory], a settlement of the Saints near the mouth of Loup Fork, where we found Elder Allen in charge.

Berhnhisel to Young, LDS Archives.

Sweetwater River, 21 September 1857

Between nine and ten o'clock this morning near the ice Spring we met Col. Alexander with the 10th Regiment. This evening we expect to meet the 5th Regiment. Neither General [Harney] nor Col Johns[t]on is with the troops, and the officers do not know where they are. M[r] Magraw and his train consisting of thirty two wagons were just behind the troops. Brother [N. V.] Jones will give you all the information in regard to the detachment that we have been enabled to gather. . . .

I am getting on quite comfortably. I have written this scrawl on my knee. On Ham's Fork I was informed by Lieut. Deshler that there were ordered from Fort Laramie to our beloved City, eight more companies of U.S. troops part of whom were dragoons, but that they were now under the command of Col Sumner in the expedition against the Cheyennes, but he thought they would not return to Fort Laramie in season to go to Salt Lake this fall. . . .

Aboard Missouri River Steamboat F. X. Aubry at Leavenworth, 17 October 1857

I addressed a few lines to you from the Sweet Water which I trust have reached you.

September 22nd we met near the Ice Spring the 10th regiment of United States Infantry under the command of Colonel Alexander, and a few miles in the rear of which we passed the 5th regiment commanded by Colonel [Carlos] Wait[e]. The former consisted of about 750 men, and the latter of about 475, having lost about 400, and the first mentioned about 150 by desertion. Mr Magraw and his train followed in the wake. Two of his engineers and some of his men had left him, and he said he did not know what he should do. The two batteries each consisting of six guns, some of which were large, brought up the rear.

Sept. 25th Passed Livingston Kinkead & Cos train a few miles west of Deer Creek. On the same day Mr Morrell the newly appointed postmaster for Salt Lake City accompanied by a Mr Allen, near Faurch Boise; also on the same day the first train (Mr Perry's) of the Sutler to the 10th regiment, and 1½ miles east of LaPrele, and on the following day his second train, about 12 miles west of Horse Shoe creek. The train of Mr Radford who is Sutler to the 5th we met about 5 miles west of Fort Laramie. On the afternoon of the 27th we arrived at Fort Laramie, where we found Lieut Col [Charles F.] Smith with two [Tenth Infantry] companies en route to join the 5th regiment. Here I learned that Colonel Sumner in his rencounter with the Cheyennes killed 13 of them, and had five of his men wounded, who were sent to Fort Kearney, and where they finally arrived in safety. At Fort Laramie were also two companies of dragoons destined for Utah. October 1st Met brother Groesbeck and train some three or four miles below Chimney Rock, traveling at the rate of about 20 miles a day.[60] On the same day met Colonel Johns[t]on Commander in Chief of the Utah Expedition, with a pretty long train of light spring wagons, each drawn by four mules, a mile or two below the Court House Rock. He left Fort Leavenworth on the 17th of September. October 8th on Plum creek 35 [miles] west of Fort Kearney met Lieut Colonel [Philip] St. George Cook[e] with six companies of dragoons, though not all full, and about one hundred baggage wagons, each drawn by six mules, and traveling at the rate of about 22 or 23 miles per day. The Colonel took his departure from Fort Leavenworth on the 19th of September, and was accompanied by Governor Cummings [*sic*], his lady and private Secretary.[61] Mr Eccles [*sic*] the Chief Justice of Utah was at Fort Laramie on his way to the scene of his official labors. It appears that Emery D. Potter, of Ohio, and Mr Charles E. Sinclair are the associate Justices, and Mr John Har[t]nett, of St. Louis, the Secretary.[62] It seems also from the journals that Mr Saunders of Indiana, who was

[60] See a subsequent chapter for Groesbeck's gun-running mission.

[61] The secretary was not an additional person; Mrs. Cumming played this role.

[62] Potter declined the appointment and was succeeded by John Cradlebaugh. Sinclair, a Virginian, chose not to attempt the daunting western trek that fall and did not reach Utah until 1858, as was also the case with Judge Cradlebaugh.

last March appointed Superintendent of Indian Affairs of Utah, resigned; then Mr John C. O. Neill received the appointment, and he also resigned, and then the office was tendered to Mr Meek of Pennsylvania who declined.[63] So you see the office is going a begging. The whole number of horses and mules in the Utah Expedition are over four thousand. On the 10th instant Messrs. Livingston & Hockaday were at Fort Kearney on their return to Utah. On the same day we met the Salt Lake mail of the first of October about nine miles east of Fort Kearney. Mr Miles of St. Joseph, Mo. has the contract at the annual compensation of $32000.[64]

I saw [former Chief] Judge [John F.] Kinney at Leavenworth City; he resides at Nebraska City, . . . General Harney who is in command of Fort Leavenworth, has gone to Washington. . . .[65] I have had quite a pleasant & prosperous journey across the plains. Captain Van Vliet is an agreeable and gentlemanly man. He will leave for Washington to-morrow or next day. His report [to the army] will be favorable.

---

[63] Finally Jacob Forney of Pennsylvania, a political ally of U.S. Attorney General Black, accepted appointment at about the time Bernhisel wrote. Forney traveled west with the Utah Expedition.

[64] This was the interim monthly arrangement that followed cancellation of Hiram Kimball's contract and preceded provision for a weekly mail service awarded to John M. Hockaday in the spring of 1858.

[65] Harney had gone east to lobby for a new [non-Kansas] assignment.

Chapter 10

"Bring Home All the Powder and Lead"
The Quest for Arms and Munitions

Bring me my bow of burning gold!
Bring me my arrows of desire!
Bring me my spear! O clouds unfold!
Bring me my chariot of fire!
I will not cease from mental fight;
Nor shall my sword sleep in my hand
Till we have built Jerusalem
In ev'ry green and pleasant land.

—"Jerusalem," traditional early nineteenth-century English hymn

Due to Utah's isolation, lack of manufacturing capabilities, and freighting costs, Brigham Young's greatest military problem was a shortage of firearms and ammunition. From the beginning of transcontinental Mormon migration in 1847, emigrants to Utah were instructed to arm themselves against Indians. This included British converts and returning missionaries. It is not surprising, then, that even the church's architect returned from Europe to Salt Lake City in May 1857 armed with the finest of English pistols. With the onset of the Utah War, rumors of trans-Atlantic gunrunning fueled by reports from apostates drove the alarmed American ambassador to monitor Mormon-chartered vessels steaming west out of Liverpool. In New York municipal authorities confiscated weapons from British converts at the city's docks.[1]

[1] Bennett and Jewsbury, "The Lion and the Emperor," 56–57. One Mormon historian has posited that terms like "smuggling" and "gunrunning" are less objective than more neutral terms like (*continued next page*)

Earlier chapters have discussed the 1851 Mormon dealings with both Samuel Colt and Uriah Brown, "the liquid fire man," as well as the March 1857 thrust to produce revolvers in Salt Lake City's municipal machine shop. But munitions, rather than weapons, constituted the Nauvoo Legion's critical need. Gunpowder and ballistic lead were the biggest worry.

Daunting problems of quality, cost, labor, logistics, and Indian relations had forced closure of the Mormon Las Vegas, New Mexico Territory, mining and smelting operation by early March 1857. Nonetheless this effort had yielded at least eighty-five hundred pounds of usable lead.[2] And so when nineteen-year-old Joseph F. Smith returned to Salt Lake City after a two-year mission in Hawaii, he galloped off to cavalry service in Echo Canyon only after he "sat up all night molding rifle bullets from a pig of lead I had brought with me from a 'Mormon' smelter at Las Vegas, the ore for which had been carried by teams from the mountains about twenty miles distant."[3]

During the preparatory period between the arrival of the Independence mail on 23 June 1857 and the appearance of Messrs. Stoddard, Smoot, and Rockwell a month later, Brigham Young had returned to his longstanding desire to manufacture gunpowder locally. Eleazar Edwards eventually succeeded in this effort later in the war, but not with timeliness or on a scale that contributed significantly to meeting the Nauvoo Legion's needs. Purchases from California and Missouri would continue to provide the overwhelming bulk of the Legion's powder.[4]

"Big Nose" Threads the Needle: Across the Plains and into the Mountains with Nicholas Groesbeck

In the spring of 1857 Young ordered a large quantity of Missouri powder through Nicholas Groesbeck, a Y. X. Carrying Company agent on the eastern end of

"shipping" or "transporting." While Brigham Young's large-scale quest for arms and munitions was not illegal, his explicit instructions about concealment and the behavior of Mormon agents imply a self-acknowledged impropriety to the whole effort. Parshall to MacKinnon, e-mail message, 28 January 2007.

[2] For a report on the mine's output, see N. V. Jones to Young and Jones to Wells, 9 and 10 January 1857, LDS Archives.

[3] Joseph F. Smith, "My Missions," in "Reminiscences of the First Presidency," *Deseret News*, 21 December 1901, 57. In 1901 Smith, the nephew of Joseph Smith, Jr., became sixth president of the Mormon church, the last of five such connected directly with the Utah War.

[4] Young to Johnson and France to Young, 10 and 16 July 1857, LDS Archives. For a parallel Civil War situation in the South four years later, see Smith, "In Quest of a Supply of Salt Peter and Gunpowder," 96–111.

the Independence–Salt Lake mail route. Groesbeck's effective response was an exhausting, high-risk hounds-and-hare evasion of the Utah Expedition. His was one of the war's more colorful, unknown stories of derring-do.

After Abraham Lincoln became president, Nicholas Groesbeck of Utah often bragged that Lincoln had been his attorney back in Illinois.[5] There were no similar stories about the moniker by which the Indians and mountaineers of the Green River district knew Groesbeck—"Big Nose." In Groesbeck's case his nickname was not a matter of size, as photographs confirm, but rather one of cross-cultural interpretation in the wilderness. Assuming mistakenly that Groesbeck's surname was Gallic rather than Dutch, some frontiersman keyed to what he thought were the two French words "Gros" and "Bec" and translated them into the English descriptor "Big Nose."

Regardless of what people dubbed Nicholas Groesbeck and why, Brigham Young trusted him. In early 1857 he called Groesbeck to operate the eastern (plains) end of the Y. X. Carrying Company. Groesbeck's work led to his inclusion with a select group of Utah's most rugged, dependable frontiersmen—Brigham Young's "boys"—a mixed company of solid citizens like Groesbeck and a few bravos like Porter Rockwell and Bill Hickman, who were perceived as ecclesiastical assassins. Sometime during the late spring of 1857 Young again set Groesbeck apart for a daunting mission—the procurement and covert transportation of large quantities of gunpowder from the Kansas-Missouri frontier.

Groesbeck kept no known record of his adventures, but his episodic correspondence with Brigham Young and the newspaper dispatches of Capt. R. B. Marcy and A. G. Browne shed light on this mission as Groesbeck threaded his way through and around the slower Utah Expedition. From this material it is clear how tightly the governor controlled his agent's activities. Two of the most urgent (although unrelated) questions discussed in Brigham Young's office during the summer of 1857 were the whereabouts of Sumner's Cheyenne Expedition and the westward progress of a heavily laden Brother Groesbeck.

On 30 June—as he was instructing Horace Eldredge on the fine art of buying gunpowder and shipping it covertly from St. Louis—Young worried about Groesbeck's safety as he slipped in and out of an inflamed Indepen-

[5] The case involved a dispute between the Groesbeck family and a Sangamon County, Illinois, farmer whose grain they had accidentally destroyed by fire in 1855. Lincoln obtained the acquittal of Nicholas Groesbeck in a jury trial and negotiated a compromise over monetary damages that freed his son to emigrate to Utah in 1856. "Narrative of Nicholas Harmon Groesbeck," *Treasures of Pioneer History,* 6:55–57. The subject of this chapter's analysis did not use a middle initial or name; Nicholas H. Groesbeck was his son.

MORMON PLAINSMAN NICHOLAS GROESBECK A former law client of Abraham Lincoln as well as an audacious Mormon mail agent with the Y. X. Carrying Company, "Big Nose" was called by Brigham Young to bundle rifles and large quantities of gunpowder across the plains to Salt Lake City while evading the Utah Expedition. Groesbeck's efforts were part of a multi-pronged covert procurement-shipping effort that also involved agents Horace S. Eldredge in St. Louis and Peter W. Conover, Howard Egan, and Jefferson Hunt in California. *Lithograph from Whitney's 1892* History of Utah.

dence. Groesbeck reported to Young on his progress on 1 July 1857 and did so again at the end of that month.[6]

GROESBECK TO YOUNG, 31 JULY 1857, LDS ARCHIVES.

I send by Bro J[ohn]. Murdock and Brother C. Webb five tons freight for Livingston K & Co.[7] which I have contracted agreed to Deliver in Great Salt Lake City at the rates of twenty Dollars pr one Hundred lbs. I also send twenty Kegs Powder in said lot good thinking it might not cause suspision being with there freight I could got freight for to load all our waggons at the same rate. I thought it would be advizable for us to load the ballance of the waggons with such articles as we need. I think we shall be able to do even if Bro Eldredge does not get his drafts cashed

Bro. Smoot & Stoddard, I p[r]esume have arived before this date therefor you are acquainted or informed of our condition in these lower regions. We expect to be able to start the last traine by the 20 of Aug. I hope by that time I shall receive some instructions from you if no word comes through I shall come to the conclusion the course I am taken [*sic*] is sanctioned by you which the particulaers you learnt by bro Stoddard & Smoot. I intend fetching all the Powder I can moung [among] things we need and aught to have.

[6] Young to Groesbeck, 30 June 1857, and Groesbeck to Young, 1 July 1857, both in LDS Archives.

[7] Livingston, Kinkaid and Company, one of the principal non-Mormon mercantile firms doing business in Salt Lake City.

Given the relatively benign state of affairs during the late summer, it is unlikely that Groesbeck's sixteen wagons loaded with explosives were subject to army seizure. Perhaps the army's earliest recorded sighting of Groesbeck's caravan was by the Fifth Infantry's Capt. Randolph B. Marcy. On 28 August he wrote to New York's *Herald* from the plains west of Fort Laramie:

> . . . two trains of wagons, said to be freighted with arms and ammunition, and supposed to be for the Mormons, have passed us in rapid transit for Salt Lake City. Unfortunately, the officers in command of the different detachments of the army have no instructions for stopping or detaining these war munitions, and they, I presume, do not consider themselves authorized to assume the responsibility.[8]

On 5 September a letter writer at Fort Kearny reported inaccurately: "Col. Hoffman had seized five hundred kegs of powder in a Mormon train returning to California, as he was informed the Mormons were making preparations to fight, and did not conceal their hostile movements."[9] On 1 October eastbound Delegate Bernhisel and Captain Van Vliet spotted Groesbeck near Chimney Rock traveling at a brisk speed of about twenty miles per day.[10] Near the end of October correspondent A. G. Browne reported from South Pass on Groesbeck's movements.

A. G. Browne, Jr., Dispatch, "Later from the Mormon War," 22 October 1857, *New-York Daily Tribune*, 28 December 1857.

There is a Mormon train between us and Fort Laramie which is said to belong to the church and to be freighted with private property of Brigham Young Col. Johnston passed it at the beginning of this month, a day or two before he arrived at Laramie. During his stay there it caught up, and its conductor, a man named Groesbeck, called on him to request a passport to enable his train to proceed to Salt Lake City. The Colonel had not at that time heard of the burning of the three supply trains on October 5 (although, from his request, it seems probable that Mr. Groesbeck had received news of the affair), and answered that he knew no reason why he should grant anything of the kind; that if a state of peace existed in Utah the train would of course be able to go on, passport or no passport, but if a state of armed hostility existed, nothing would probably be allowed to reach the Mormons in the nature of supplies. Mr. Groesbeck and his train then proceeded, but he has probably drawn off from the road and laid up for the Winter, or else he is endeavoring to reach

[8] Marcy, dispatch of 28 August 1857, "The Utah Expedition: Our Special Correspondence," *New York Herald*, 22 October 1857, 8/1–2.

[9] *Putnam* [County] *Republican Banner* (Greencastle, Ind.), 7 October 1857, 2/2.

[10] Bernhisel to Young, 17 October 1857, LDS Archives.

> Salt Lake City by some intricate route far from the main road. All trace of him further than seventy or eighty miles beyond Laramie seems to be lost, but it will be impossible for his train, if ever seen again, to escape recognition. It consisted of sixteen wagons all gaudily painted, and each drawn by six mules.

Once the hostility associated with Lot Smith's raid on three government supply trains and heavy snow created unavoidable impediments, Groesbeck cached his wagons and some rifles at John Baptiste ("Reshaw") Richard's Platte Bridge trading post. Free of these encumbrances, he then pressed on through the mountains with a powder-laden string of pack mules. In early November the Nauvoo Legion welcomed Groesbeck to Echo Canyon. On the night of 7 November 1857 he reached Salt Lake City. Unrecorded was the text of Groesbeck's brief tabernacle discourse the next day, which postmaster-judge Elias Smith described without further elaboration as "an interesting account of his journey home."[11]

Albert Sidney Johnston was not oblivious to Groesbeck's activities. Although the smuggler had slipped past the army with the lion's share of his purchases, on 13 November Johnston moved on the Mormon cache at Platte Bridge. His adjutant wrote to the commander of Fort Laramie:

> The Colonel Commanding understands that a quantity of arms, powder, lead and shot, were left at Richard's Trading Station—either on Deer Creek or at Platte Bridge—by Grosbeck the man in charge of the Mormon wagon train, which passed your post about October 6th. He directs you to have a thorough search made for these arms and munitions, and, if found, have them seized in the name of the Government. Should an unusual supply be found at the Mormon Station on Deer Creek or at Platte Bridge, the Colonel wishes you to have it removed, leaving sufficient for ordinary trading purposes—no matter who may claim the ownership.[12]

Perhaps the most graphic reflection of Groesbeck's arduous feat was the prosaic record of what he delivered to Brigham Young's clerk in November 1857. Excluding the rifles cached at Platte Bridge, Groesbeck delivered 2,678.5 pounds of what was described as "merchandise," including 1,617 pounds of

---

[11] Elias Smith Journal, entry for 8 November 1857. This discourse is one of the intriguing "lost" records of the Utah War.

[12] Maj. F. J. Porter to Maj. Isaac Lynde, 13 November 1857, Letters Sent, Dept. of Utah (RG 98), National Archives. That Colonel Johnston moved so decisively to seize a Mormon weapons shipment in the fall of 1857 is in stark contrast with the forbearance and wariness with which the Buchanan administration and its War Department dealt with the flow of rifles to secessionist but non-belligerent states from New York less than four years later. For more on this affair, see Scroggins, "Georgia, New York, and Muskets on the Eve of the Civil War," 318–33. Johnston's seizure of the Platte Bridge cache was no more lawful than Brigham Young's confiscation of Richard Yates's trade goods a month earlier (see Chapter 12).

gunpowder, a half-ton of ballistic lead, and tens of thousands of percussion caps. From other receipts in Brigham Young's financial records, it appears likely that Groesbeck may have delivered as part of his mission an additional 1,216 pounds of powder, 207 pounds of lead, and 10,000 caps.[13] This was munitions smuggling on a scale that Washakie's French-speaking Shoshones would have called "gros."

Those Who Cause Us Trouble Will Freight for Us: Smuggling Ammunition

On 8 August Young instructed Horace S. Eldredge in St. Louis to disregard his earlier 30 June order to acquire and covertly ship gunpowder across the plains in sealed metal boxes because of his expectation of an even better secret conduit—his enemies. This alternative was an audacious but ultimately failed attempt to smuggle substantial quantities of gunpowder through the Utah Expedition's own transportation contractors. As with the original instructions to Eldredge, Young's rescission of them was communicated in a way sometimes used by Mormon leaders worried about interception of their messages—through a single cryptic sentence buried in the midst of a rambling letter dealing with multiple unrelated matters: "Concerning the powder arrangements mentioned in my last, you need take no further care of the matter, as I am of the opinion that, those who cause us trouble will freight for us, an abundant supply of ammunition."[14]

This gambit through the army's freighters was apart from and far more extensive than another federal source—the modest flow of rifles, pistols, bayonets, and cartridges that Young expected to acquire directly from individual army deserters and disaffected teamsters.[15] It was also a different arrangement than Nicholas Groesbeck's parallel all-Mormon gunpowder-smuggling mission.

Exactly how and through whom the arrangement described cryptically to Eldredge was to work is murky, but it is clear that Young expected the government's own freighters to serve as the conduit. Starting with the 24 July Silver Lake celebration, the notion began to bubble up and immediately found its way into the Mormon tune "Du Dah." A week after his 8 August letter to Eldridge, the scheme was prominently on Young's mind, and in a Sunday

[13] Receipts issued to Nicholas Groesbeck, Brigham Young Financial Records.

[14] Young to Eldredge, 8 August 1857, LDS Archives.

[15] John T. Caine to George D. Grant, 27 October 1857, Nauvoo Legion (Utah), Adj. Gen. Record 1851–1870, p. 154, LDS Archives.

discourse he commented, "I calculate they shall furnish us with Guns, powder, and lead, beef, pork, and all that is necessary. (Voices, 'Amen') I mean to go to war at their expense, not on ours."[16]

Covert operations—especially in wartime—are by their nature difficult to document. But the outline of what probably took place during the summer of 1857 emerges from multiple sources. As events unfolded over the next nine months, the prime suspect as Brigham Young's secret agent was to become—rightly or wrongly—James Rupe, Russell, Major and Waddell's chief field agent and a man with ready access to a wide range of the war's players, including Young, Porter Rockwell, and the Utah Expedition's officers. For example, on the day after proclaiming martial law, Young issued a safe-conduct pass to Rupe, who was in Salt Lake City on unknown business after leaving Charlie Morehead at Hams Fork with Lt. James Deshler's detachment. The phrasing of this document was perhaps more permissive than that of any pass Young granted during the war: "The bearer, Mr Roup, Agent for Russell and Wardle may have business to transact in the City or other portions of the Territory. Therefore I wish Mr Roup to have the privilege of passing any where in the Territory where his business may call him unmolested. This pass will also extend to any one of his men whom he may wish to send on business legitimately belonging to his operations."[17]

On the same day Young instructed Legion quartermaster Lewis Robison at Fort Bridger to extend an accommodation to Rupe ("If Mr. Roup wants to get his cattle herded [by us] it will be all right, I have referred him to you for that purpose"), who, in turn, was performing courier service for the Mormons by delivering Young's proclamation to Robison.[18]

It is likely, in communicating the smuggling plan to Eldredge in August, that Young was referring to goods being shipped west via Russell, Majors and Waddell and consigned to "Capt." William H. Hooper's Salt Lake mercantile firm. Such an arrangement would have been bold, for Hooper was a well-known Brigham Young confidante and the man whom the governor had unilaterally appointed to be territorial secretary upon the 1856 murder of Almon W. Babbitt.[19] The freight being hauled for Hooper was sufficiently valuable, if not

[16] Brigham Young, unpublished discourse, 16 August 1857, LDS Archives.

[17] Pass to "Mr. Roup," 16 September 1857, Gubernatorial Letterbook, 654, LDS Archives.

[18] Young to Robison, 16 September 1857, LDS Archives.

[19] Nicholas Groesbeck's use of the non-Mormon firm of Livingston, Kinkaid and Company as a consignee was substantially less risky than any use of Hooper's trading house.

explosive, that as summer turned into fall Brigham Young worried about its safety from his own raiders. With a further demonstration of what today would be called micromanaging, he instructed three apostles in the field to take care:

> Cap. W. H. Hooper informs me that he has 5 wagons loaded with goods in one of Russel and Wardle's trains, *No. 13*, and said to be in charge of Henry Hooper[20] wagon master of that train. The wagon master's name may be reported incorrectly, but the number, *13*, is right, and I wish you to instruct bro. Lott Smith and others to be careful and not destroy those wagons, and if possible, aid their safe progress to this city.[21]

Suspicion of Rupe's 1857 actions surfaced at Camp Scott on 25 February 1858 at a time when tensions ran high at the army's winter quarters. The *New York Times*'s field correspondent described the incident:

> On the 25th of February a most important discovery of a large quantity of powder was made at Fort Bridger. It seems that Messrs. Russell and Waddle, the Government freight contractors, had engaged last Spring to bring out several thousand pounds of freight for Mr. Hooper, a Mormon merchant at Salt Lake City, who was indebted to them, in order to secure the payment of the debt. This freight was sent with the Government trains, but its delivery was of course forbidden by Col. Alexander as soon as he was informed of the fact, when he overtook the trains last Fall; it was accordingly brought here with the other Government freight. The boxes were such as are ordinarily sent to this country with merchandise, and were marked dry goods, hardware, crockery, &c., as usual. Upon examination, however, it was found that every box contained hidden among and surrounded with dry goods and other articles, one or more kegs of powder, the whole amounting to eight thousand pounds. This powder was put up in this manner for the Mormons by some mercantile firm in St. Louis, and it should be ascertained who they are, in order to let the public know the traitors who are aiding in this rebellion.[22]

Albert G. Browne, Jr., later reported Rupe's expulsion from Camp Scott for New York's *Tribune*. His dispatch, together with Burr's for the *Times*, escalated the army's local suspicions into a minor national sensation. It was publicity that burnished Brigham Young's reputation for both ingenuity and perfidy while simultaneously tarnishing that of the Russell firm.

---

[20] This was not "Capt." Hooper, who was then in Utah. Although William H. Hooper's middle name was Henry (as was his father's first name), I have not been able to establish a family relationship between this wagonmaster and Utah's prominent merchant.

[21] Young to Wells, Taylor, and Smith, 12 October 1857, LDS Archives. A week earlier Legion major Smith had destroyed seventy-six wagons in three trains between South Pass and Fort Bridger, and Young undoubtedly knew this.

[22] "A. B. C." (David A. Burr), 5 March 1858, "From the Utah Army," *New York Times*, 19 May 1858, 1/1–2.

A. G. Browne, Jr., Dispatch, "The Utah Expedition," 23 April 1858, *New-York Daily Tribune*, 30 April 1858.

I have been surprised at the silence of your Occasional Correspondent[23] from Camp Scott concerning the discovery of a quantity of Mormon gunpowder in one of the United States supply trains. In the absence of any statement from him on the subject I was inclined to doubt that such was the fact, but I have just finished reading some letters from a gentleman of high official position at the Camp, which establish it beyond question.

The powder was concealed in packages of dry goods, which were consigned to William H. Hooper & Co., merchants at Salt Lake City. It does not appear by what authority these packages found place in wagons intended for the transportation of Government stores; but it seems certain that they could not have been so placed without the knowledge of Mr. James Rupe, the principal agent of Russell & Waddell. Rupe is a man about 37 years of age. He resides in Western Missouri, but has an extensive acquaintance among the Mormon community. It would, perhaps, be unjust to charge that he must have been aware of the contents of those packages, but since he is responsible for the fact that they were in the wagons, it is fair to review briefly his course in connection with the movement of the trains last Autumn. You are aware how much depended then upon the efficiency of Messrs. Russell & Waddell's employees, and I wrote to you what a miserable set they were—those of them, at least, who had charge of the trains which reached the army in November under the escort of [Lt.] Col. [Charles F.] Smith.[24] Mr. Rupe was no exception. He was not drunk—at least I did not see him so—but he was most lamentably inefficient; and circumstances occurred in the course of that month which led some persons to believe that his inefficiency was intentional. He was present when a herd of 800 cattle were run off from the rear of Col. Alexander's command on Ham's Fork, about October 13, and on that occasion exhibited an undue familiarity with Porter Rockwell, who figured among the Mormon robbers. I transmitted to you a copy of his affidavit concerning the affair, which was taken before Judge Eckels, about a fortnight after it occurred. It is significant that both he and William Eads, one of his employees, forfeited recognizances into which they had entered in the sum of $500 each to appear before the Grand Jury of the United States District Court and give their testimony concerning the crime. As there was but one other Gentile present when the cat-

[23] The "occasional correspondent" was David A. Burr, the surveyor general's son, to whom Browne entrusted his role in writing to the *Tribune* during the period 5 January–27 May 1858 when Browne was absent from Camp Scott on his mission to the East. As indicated above, Burr was simultaneously writing dispatches for the *Tribune*'s rival, the *New York Times*, under the pseudonym "A. B. C." Browne wrote this dispatch in St. Louis during his return to Utah based on reports that had drifted eastward across the plains from Camp Scott. Because Browne still had access to telegraph service and the regular mail, his dispatch was published three weeks earlier than Burr's, although Burr had written nearly seven weeks earlier.

[24] Browne had traveled west during the fall of 1857 with the two companies of the Tenth Infantry commanded by Smith.

tle were run off, and he had left for the States at an early day, it was impossible for that Jury to procure testimony to identify the criminals, although it was known that Joseph Taylor, the Mormon Major, then in arrest, was conspicuous on the occasion.[25]

William H. Hooper, to whom the dry goods and gunpowder were consigned, is one of the wealthiest Mormons, and is Secretary of State in Young's Administration. The style of his firm was once "Hooper & Williams;" but Williams became a dissenter, and fled from the Territory, with Surveyor-General Burr and Marshal Dotson, in April, 1857. It was at Hooper's house that Captain Van Vliet was a guest during his stay in Salt Lake City last September.

Two questions suggest themselves in reviewing the affair: 1. If the intentions of the Mormons were peaceable up to the date when the Army of Utah began to move from the Missouri frontier, why did Mr. Hooper procure gunpowder to be smuggled on board the supply trains which started previously to that date?[26] 2. Are proper precautions taken with all the trains which Messrs. Russell & Waddell are starting this Spring to guard against a repetition of the offense?

During April 1858 Russell, Majors and Waddell tried mightily to rescue its reputation and that of Rupe from the condemnation flowing from discovery of the 1857 gunpowder arrangement. The firm argued that it had been duped by Eldredge into believing that only household goods were being shipped to Hooper and that Rupe was wholly unassociated with the Mormons' duplicitous shipping arrangements.[27] Ultimately Quartermaster General Jesup seemed satisfied as to Rupe's role although the indignant junior officers of the Utah Expedition were not.

With All the Gun Powder He Could Carry: Howard Egan Scours Southern California

If Nicholas Groesbeck's westbound mission has remained obscure, Brig. Gen. Peter W. Conover's equally successful and grueling trek for a similar purpose but in the opposite direction during August–September is now somewhat better known. Conover led a party from Salt Lake City west across the deserts, over the Sierra Nevada, and back, buying wagon loads of munitions in San

[25] Maj. Taylor and his adjutant, Lt. William R. R. Stowell, had been captured by Utah Expedition troops on 16 October.

[26] Had Browne known of Young's 30 June instructions to Eldredge, he would have been even more accusatory.

[27] Thomas S. Williams to William H. Russell, 14 April 1858, and William H. Russell to Quartermaster General Thomas S. Jesup, 15 April 1858, Letters Received, Records of the U.S. Army Quartermaster General, National Archives, and M. Hamlin Cannon Papers.

Francisco while simultaneously closing down the Mormon colony in western Utah's Carson Valley. Because Kenneth N. Owens has recently published many of the documents relating to Conover's experiences, there is no need to rehash them here.[28] But there is a need to examine the neglected southern half of Brigham Young's quest for gunpowder in California, through the efforts of rugged frontiersman Howard Egan. It was Egan, a Legion major and one of Brigham Young's most trusted agents, who by the end of 1857 bought perhaps as much as seven hundred pounds of California powder, evaded an army detachment from Fort Tejon, California, and bundled it into Salt Lake City via San Bernardino.

If anything, Howard Egan's gunpowder mission to southern California was more dangerous than those undertaken by Peter Conover and Nicholas Groesbeck. As discussed in a later chapter, Egan had to deal with the cumulative uproar created in California by Conover's slightly earlier activities, the sensational Mormon evacuations of Carson Valley and San Bernardino, and the widespread anti-Mormon animosity created by travelers' accounts of the carnage at Mountain Meadows. Egan also lacked the support in men, wagons, animals, and way-stations that Groesbeck was able to assemble from the decommissioning of the Y. X. Carrying Company and that Conover either brought with him from the Wasatch front or acquired from the Mormon colony in Carson Valley. One senses that the resourceful Howard Egan operated not only clandestinely but largely alone.

One of the early concerns about Mormon smuggling from southern California was reflected in an October 1857 letter to the San Francisco *Alta California* from "Yo Mismo," its pseudonymous correspondent who wrote almost immediately after accounts of the Mountain Meadows massacre drifted into San Bernardino and Los Angeles. In this case the gunrunning described was a precursor to the anxiety over Howard Egan's operation and was attributed to the work of Jefferson Hunt, a legendary Mormon frontiersman and Mormon Battalion officer who was also a senior officer in California's militia and state legislature. In the ruse attributed to Hunt, one sees a similarity to Brigham Young's bold willingness to tap into a government's own gunpowder supply if not state-issued firearms.

> I nearly omitted to tell you that I am informed by a person who saw the document, that Capt. Hunt, of San Bernardino, has written by this steamer to

[28] Owens, *Gold Rush Saints*, 328–41.

> the Governor [of California], for rifles and ammunition to suppress insurrection in that country, and also to fight Indians! This is all pretence. All the files [of arms] and ammunition they receive are instantly forwarded to Salt Lake, where the majority of these people are expected soon to depart.[29]

"Yo Mismo" did not know the half of it. As early as 8 January 1857 Peter Conover had written to Hunt from Provo much as Brigham later instructed Eldredge:

> [The Reformation] makes those who are ill disposed towards us make some pretty big threats about destroying the authorities of this church and the Gentile merchants that are here, have refused to let the Mormons have any ammunition to defend themselves with. So I thought . . . I would just say to you to bring or send as much powder in as you can get hold of, for we shall need it by the time we can get it here. I want you to bring me 1000 lbs for my Brigade. It will bring the money before anything else you can bring here at present, if you could send a Keg by the mail every time they come it would be a good plan by that means we could be supplied at Uncle Sams expense. Now Brother Hunt if you feel like helping us any you can do it in this way more than any other, we are expecting some U.S. troops in here next summer, but we do not anticipate as much trouble from them as we do from the apostates that are here in our midst but from all appearances we will need powder and caps before long and if you cannot sent it before you come be sure to bring it with you.[30]

These, then, were the dangers that surrounded Major Egan in the fall of 1857. On 5 December Apostle Ezra Taft Benson wrote to Brigham Young from Los Angeles's port of San Pedro to report on the anti-Mormonism and troop movements encountered during his return from Liverpool via New York, Panama, and California. In a postscript Apostle Benson added, "We have in company with Bro George Q Cannon & his Brethren who were associated with him informing me that he had a letter from Bro Egan stating that he left Stockton a week ago last Monday [23 November] with all the Gun Powder that he could carry."[31]

A further understanding of the hostility encountered by Egan as he made his way south and east through California to the desert comes with the year-end letter to Brigham Young sent from Provo by returned California missionary David P. Rainey.

---

[29] "Yo Mismo," Letter of October 1857, "Later from the South: The Murders at Mountain Canon confirmed.–More Indian Outrages, &c.," *Alta California* (San Francisco), 27 October 1857, 1/2–5.

[30] Conover to Hunt, 8 January 1857, Amasa Lyman Collection, LDS Archives.

[31] Benson to Young, 5 December 1857, LDS Archives. Cannon was returning to Utah via the southern route after closing up the *Western Standard*. The intriguing Egan–Cannon letter has not been found.

RAINEY TO YOUNG, 29 DECEMBER 1857, LDS ARCHIVES.

The Bretheren in San Bernadino was making ev[e]ry effort to get away from there that they possibly Could Br° [William I.] Cox told me he thought there would be forty Waggons ready to start in Ten days from the time I left there was much Talk of the Mob as they were Called of serching the Bretherens waggons for arms and Amunition &c. But I do not think they will attempt to do so untill about the Last is leaving if they do then there was much anxiety felt by all Parties to know what moves would be made towards the Troops out at Bridger and that has had Its wait and influence in Callifornia if they had been Cut Off the Bretheren would have had trouble to have got away from Callifornia or I will say that was the threats of our Enemies they would have Blocked up the Kanyons and prevented all from comming they could. Tho they ~~they~~ do not want the Mormons there neither do they want them to come away so they do not know what to do with them

The Spirit of opposition in Callifornia is about as high as It Could well be, the Editors say that Callifornia Can turn out Twenty thousand Volunteers to come here to drive out the Mormons if uncle Sam wants them but they will find the Sutheran route a hard Road to travel.[32]

Alerted to Egan's progress toward Salt Lake City and perhaps alarmed by the reports of Apostle Benson, missionary Rainey, and others, Young wrote to Egan with instructions for disposition of his freight:

> We learn that you are on the way to this city with a quantity of Ammunition and that you need assistance. This will be readily afforded you by the Bishops and brethren south upon showing them this letter. They are hereby authorised to furnish you any such assistance as any supplies and horse feed as you may need. We send four of your mules in the charge of John Larson to relieve your team.[33]
>
> In regard to disposing of any of the powder in the southern settlements they are making powder in Iron County and we trust will be able to supply themselves, you had therefore better bring it all through.[34]

No doubt relieved but tired, Howard Egan arrived in Salt Lake City on 8 February 1858, about two weeks ahead of Thomas L. Kane. Quartermaster

[32] As Rainey wrote, this was an option being considered by General Scott and the War Department in the wake of the consternation over Lot Smith's raid.

[33] Larson's first name is listed as Thurston rather than John on Quartermaster Robison's receipt for Egan's munitions. Larson's descendants later spoke of his "secret mission" during the Utah War; he had been Howard Egan's companion during earlier trips to California unrelated to this assignment.

[34] Young was mistakenly optimistic about the status of the powder-manufacturing effort in Iron County. Young to Egan, 6 January 1858, Beinecke Library.

Robison issued him a receipt for 337 pounds of powder, 15,000 percussion caps, and 50 pounds of lead.[35]

The Best and Cheapest that Can Be Made in This Place: Creative Weapons Design

As the Utah War unfolded, Atlantic Coast conjectures about Mormon weaponry—to a certain extent deliberately fed by Brigham Young—grew and morphed into wild fantasies. One newspaper report from Washington by way of Buffalo unwittingly evoked image of Uriah Brown's invention of the early 1850s.

"A Formidable Weapon," *Commercial Advertiser* (Buffalo, N.Y.), 12 November 1857, 2/2–3.

> It has been reported that the Mormons are in possession of a very formidable weapon of war, said to have been used by the Russians in the late [Crimean] War, and composed of an explosive material discharged by electricity. The Washington *States* says that at the close of the war the invention was laid before Congress and drawing[s] were submitted to the Secretary of War. General [John A.] Quitman and other officers gave it their attention, and the whole matter was afterwards placed in the hands of several persons for the purpose of making experiments.[36] It is now alleged by the *States* that these men were all Mormons and that after becoming familiar with the invention, they abandoned the inventor and carried their knowledge to Utah. The *States* says: They had satisfied themselves that old kegs, hollow trees, common boxes, anything in short which could be made to contain a bottle of burning fluid, a little powder, and a considerable amount of missiles, whether of iron scraps balls, or pebbles, and fragments of rock, could be converted into cheap and formidable batteries, whose discharge could be governed at almost any distance to a second of time; and the Mormons may be prepared to try the powers of the new system in the defiles [canyons] of Utah.

Aside from such eastern fantasies, the Nauvoo Legion was the beneficiary of a wave of practical Mormon creativity during the Utah War. Among

---

[35] Receipt issued to Howard Egan by Quartermaster Lewis Robison, 8 February 1858, Brigham Young Financial Records. On the same day Robison issued a virtually identical receipt to Thurston Larson, which raises the question of whether Larson's receipt was simply a duplicate of Egan's or whether the two had split Egan's purchases equally in southern Utah for the final push to Salt Lake City. If the latter was the case, then the Egan mission delivered nearly 700 pounds of powder.

[36] Quitman, a former governor of Mississippi, had been a distinguished major general of volunteers during the Mexican War. He took no part in the Utah War. Like Buchanan, he contracted the National Hotel disease in February 1857, suffered for a prolonged period from its lingering effects, and died in 1858.

the most eclectic suggestions were those offered by Governor Young and two Ogden gunsmiths: John Ash, a long-forgotten craftsman; and Jonathan Browning, premier gunsmith and patriarch of what would become America's most talented family of weapons designers. Brigham Young approached the challenge of new weaponry on a practical, technically uncomplicated basis. His biases as a former woodworker were clearly evident in urging adoption of longbows and crossbows for mountain warfare:

> It has been suggested to my mind, so soon as our fall's work is pretty well got along with, and while [grain] caches are being prepared, &c., to select some 2000 of the right kind of men, have them provided with excellent rifles, and let them furnish themselves with good bows and plenty of arrows, and learn to be as adept in their use as in sharpshooting with the rifle.[37]

Young followed up his suggestion with a note to General Wells on 26 November 1857, commenting that "we want to be picking out our men and fitting up our bows, crossbows, &c. in readiness for another year."[38] Young's advocacy of the bow appears not to have stimulated broad Mormon interest in the weapon, an example of the extent to which in some instances his wishes or suggestions were deflected, albeit carefully.[39] An exception to this indifference was Nauvoo Legion musician Myron Brewer, a perpetual schemer who sought unsuccessfully not only to act upon Young's interest in bows but to organize a detachment of archers to use them.[40]

One of the intriguing mysteries of the Utah War has been the apparent absence of a role by Mormon gunsmith Jonathan Browning, whose innovative weapons designs and craftsmanship in his earlier gun shops in Nauvoo, Illinois, and Kanesville, Iowa, were well known prior to his emigration to Ogden in 1852. With the intensive Mormon quest for military self-sufficiency, one would have expected to have seen Browning in the role assumed by pistol manufacturers Sabin and Naylor. But then Browning's temperament and work style may have been more that of an individual contributor and master craftsman than of the brilliant mass-producer into which his young son John Moses Browning and his brothers developed during the last decades of the nineteenth century.

---

[37] Young to Wells, Taylor, and Smith, 17 October 1857, LDS Archives.

[38] Young to Wells, 26 November 1857, ibid.

[39] In late 2002 or 2003 Saddam Hussein urged the Iraqi army to adopt sling shots and crossbows, saying, "Let's use all the methods we can. These methods can be made at home." Scott Shane, "In Video, Hussein Uses Slingshots and Bows to Rally Iraqis for War," *New York Times*, 24 November 2006, A12/1–5.

[40] Brewer to Brig. Gen. William H. Kimball, 5 February 1858, Donald R. Moorman Collection.

Notwithstanding this low profile, it would be a mistake to assume that Jonathan Browning did not give serious thought to helping the Nauvoo Legion. On 20 December 1857 he wrote to General Wells to describe and make available a creative weapons design. It is possible that Browning was motivated by discussions with John Ash, another member of Ogden's small community of gunsmiths. On 1 November Ash had written to Brigham Young to offer designs for three new weapons, two of which operated without gunpowder as a propellant. Why Young, Wells, and their chief of ordnance—Col. Thomas W. Ellerbeck—chose not to pursue Ash's and Browning's ideas is as intriguing as Young's affinity for the bow was offbeat.

ASH TO YOUNG, 1 NOVEMBER 1857, LDS ARCHIVES.

I have for some time past been studeing on the best kind of weapons sutible for the Brouthern under pressant circumstances I belive the following will be the best and Cheapest that can be made in this place I would be happy to make Samples or Make aney Quantity in the shortest posible Notice

First is a New Steel Spring bow and leever Gun. this Gun is verry powerfull and with Little practice may be discharged with as Much certintity as aney Rifle and where Powder and Lead is scarce and the noise of a Gun is not wanted would be founde verry usefull.[41]

Seccond Is a Compact air Gun that will discharge from 15 to 20 Bullits from once Chargeing with Air is of a simple Construction and can be Made at about 35$.[42]

Thired Is a Britch loding and self priming Gun or Pistol Can be fired as quick as Sharps Rifle and not so Liable to be Choked with the filth of exploded Powder. The advantage of this is the simplicity of its Make and much Cheaper then the present Revolver[.]

BROWNING TO WELLS, 20 DECEMBER 1857,
ELLERBECK PAPERS, BEINECKE LIBRARY, YALE UNIVERSITY.

Bro. D. H. Wells with due respects I will sojest to you a plan that I think might be adopted for Bloing up [gunpowder] Magazines, and the wisdome that you can comand will deside whether it would be advisable to adopt it or not. The plan would be to take a rifle that would carey a ½ oz ball or larger and make a large ball of Iron or perhaps peuter or blacktin would doe, and bore the ball from the fo[r]ward end with a small bit down near the lo[w]erend this bit should be the right size to set a pivit in that a pe[r]cusion cap

[41] This suggestion may have brought Young back to his own earlier interest in bows and prompted his 26 November 1857 reminder to Wells on this subject.

[42] This idea seems to resemble the air gun used by Capt. Meriwether Lewis during the Lewis and Clark Expedition more than fifty years earlier.

would fit and after boring this small hole then take a nose bit some larger and bore it down near the botom of the small hole leaving just enough of the small hole in the bottom to set the pivit in on which to set the cap then cut a screw in the uper end of the large hole to screw in a peace of lead then set in the pivit or standard and place the cap upon it and fill the hole or cavity around the standard with powder and screw the led down nearly to the cap and round it off to a nise rounding point, then the projectile is compleet and supose the magazine to bee in a wageon in boxes kegs or what not this ball could be fiered from a propper gun to the distance of ½ mile in to the magazine and the explosion would comence the instent that the ball strikes any hard substance and the powder in the ball would carey a train for some distance now if thought advisable I would make some experiments on the subject or aney other careful workman could doe the same, and those balls could be caried safe as a comon ball and fierd at will, a good Jaugur [Yauger rifle] would doe tho for a corect long shot it should be a good large bored rifle a smooth bore would not doe as the ball would not be likely to go strate and formost with due respect the foregoing is submited for your consideration.

Reverend Beecher and His "Bibles": A Kansas Context for Mormon Gunrunning

In 1857 Brigham Young was not the only American religious leader focused on evading U.S. Army patrols while running guns into or through Kansas Territory. Throughout New England and the mid-Atlantic states, Protestant clergymen, in addition to business leaders, philanthropists, and ordinary abolitionists, had plunged into channeling anti-slavery settlers into Utah's eastern neighbor while arming them with not only religious tracts but with covertly shipped pistols, rifles, swords, and even artillery pieces. The arms were often of what a demanding Brigham Young would call "first quality," including the new breech-loading, rapid-firing Sharps rifle. Although commonly used by buffalo hunters in the West, this was a weapon as yet unavailable in the army except for those few being field-tested by several companies of the Utah Expedition's dragoons. In nicknaming Sharps rifles "Beecher's Bibles," abolitionists paid tribute not only to their misleading packing labels but to a prime mover behind their shipment to Kansas Territory—the Rev. Henry Ward Beecher, a prominent Brooklyn minister and brother to Harriet Beecher Stowe of *Uncle Tom's Cabin* fame. Here was a flow of Kansas-bound weapons and gunpowder on a national scale that dwarfed the arms trafficking of even Messrs. Young, Eldredge, Conover, Groesbeck, and Egan.[43]

The point in raising this Kansas context for Mormon gunrunning is neither to examine in depth the former nor to justify the latter. Rather it is to emphasize the notion that Brigham Young's strategic and tactical thrusts in the Utah War were often reinforced, if not inspired, by what he saw unfolding in adjoining American territories as well as the recent Crimean War. As a military leader, Brigham Young was unschooled but active, alert, highly situational, and instinctive. In some cases—as with the quest for arms and munition—this ad hoc adaptive approach and the leadership style that spawned it produced results. On 12 September 1857 Brigham Young intensified the call for importations across the plains, writing to William I. Appleby in New York and Jeter Clinton in Philadelphia: "I wish you and all the returning brethren to provide yourselves with good Rifles, and Pistols, and bring with you all the powder and lead which you are able to purchase and freight through. Let those who have means invest it in this way."[44] Here was a total effort that prompted President Buchanan to complain to Congress that Brigham Young "has, therefore, for several years, in order to maintain his independence, been industriously employed in collecting and fabricating arms and munitions of war."[45]

---

[43] See estimated weapons flow to Kansas Territory's Free State faction, 1855–56, Isely, "The Sharps Rifle Episode in Kansas History," 565. In addition to Isley's early analysis, see Rutherford, "The Arabia Incident," 39–47; and Watts, "Plows and Bibles, Rifles and Revolvers," 30–45.

[44] Young to Appleby and Young to Clinton, 12 September 1857, LDS Archives.

[45] Buchanan, 8 December 1857, "First Annual Message," see Chapter 18.

Chapter 11

"If We Are Driven into Extreme Measures"
Brigham Young Beleaguered

As to the present case, therefore, it suffices to say, that the power to suspend the laws, and to substitute the military in the place of the civil authority, is not a power within the legal attributes of a governor of one of the Territories of the United States.

—Opinion of U.S. Attorney General Caleb Cushing, 3 February 1857

Throughout the second week of September—the period of Captain Van Vliet's stay in Salt Lake City—Brigham Young was a leader under great pressure. Among the uncertainties besetting him were the advance of the Utah Expedition; the nature of the violence unfolding at Mountain Meadows; the intentions of the Buchanan administration; the need for alliances with Utah's tribes; the disposition of an oncoming tide of British converts; the political obliteration of Utah; and the optimal use of Thomas L. Kane. To understand how Young dealt with these pressures, it is useful to consider five important letters that he dictated on 12 September.

Based on the schedule for the monthly mail, the second week of a month was not normally when Brigham Young would have tended to his correspondence. But the imminent departure of Delegate Bernhisel provided an opportunity for a secure courier service, and Young seized it. Three of his letters were written to Mormons: Jeter Clinton, president of the LDS branch in Philadelphia; William I. Appleby, John Taylor's deputy on the staff of *The Mormon* in New York; and Apostle Orson Pratt, president of the British Mission in Liverpool. Young sent the other two letters to non-Mormons: Commissioner of Indian Affairs James W. Denver in Washington and confidante Thomas L. Kane in Philadelphia. In mid-September Young's mind was moving rapidly as he worked to cope with these issues. In so doing he communicated with his eastern correspondents in highly individualized fashion.

On 15 September 1857, the day after the eastbound departure of Bernhisel and Captain Van Vliet, Brigham Young took the extraordinary step of imposing martial law. He did so by issuing a gubernatorial proclamation that recited a familiar list of Mormon grievances; branded the approaching Utah Expedition a vengeful mob and forbade its entrance into the territory; and proscribed unauthorized travel within and through Utah. Whether this step was the solution to Young's multiple problems, it was unquestionably a bold stroke. Young's martial-law proclamation was also the first of several actions in September–October that reinforced the perception by many Americans that a Mormon rebellion was indeed underway while stoking Secretary Floyd's belief that Young intended to halt transcontinental travel.[1] Strangely, Young's martial-law proclamation was a subject not discussed in any of the five letters he dictated only three days earlier.

Or the Knife and Tomahawk: Positioning Easterners

Brigham Young's letters to William I. Appleby and Jeter Clinton were very similar, although there were a few differences, for reasons not evident, that are worth noting. For example, the first of the batch—the Young–Appleby letter—contained a far greater emphasis on the concept of an armed "gathering" to Utah than did the message to Clinton. It also revealed a unique glimpse into Young's contingency plan in the event that Congress obliterated Utah as a political entity by rescinding its organic act.

Young to Appleby, 12 September 1857, LDS Archives.

> Should this one expedition fail, yet I feel that we should attend to this warning which has been given to us by the Lord, and accept the incidence in regard to the kind intentions which the Parent government hold towards us, and prepare ourselves to meet their demonstrations in a manner worthy of the Servants of God, by giving them the warmest of receptions.

[1] Other events key to shaping such perceptions were publication of General Wells's 4 October orders to Maj. Joseph Taylor (one of the few Legion documents captured during the Utah War); Maj. Lot Smith's 4–5 October destruction of three federal supply trains; rumors of a Mormon declaration of independence and the arrangement of anti-government Indian alliances; and news of the massacre at Mountain Meadows.

> I therefore in accordance with the dictates of the Spirit within me, wish most emphatically to impress upon your mind the importance of the gathering. Let men, women and children Elders, and all those of this people who abide in the United States take up their bundles and walk—do not wait to procure an outfit, but come, come to Zion, and assist in the upbuilding and defence thereof.
>
> The Mission to the United States I wish entirely to withdraw; and leave those who have driven the Saints, killed the Prophets, and miserably placed themselves in opposition to the Almighty, to the judgments of a justly angry God, and the damning influence of their own base passions.
>
> I shall discontinue the Canada Mission, and have the Elders return to this place, bringing the Saints with them; and I wish you and all the returning Brethren to provide yourselves with good Rifles, and Pistols, and bring with you all the powder and lead which you are able to purchase and freight through. Let those who have means invest it in this way.
>
> If the Organic act creating the Territory of Utah is this winter repealed, Delegates will be convened [here]—A constitution be formed—the Standard of Freedom raised, and woe! woe!! to him who attempts to bring it down.[2] Travel across this Continent will be stopped from the Rio Colorado to the Head Waters of the Missouri; and the forts of Israel, will be baptized in the blood of the Oppressor.

The message dictated to Clinton later the same day contained two important thoughts not included in Appleby's letter: the suggestion that Clinton visit President Buchanan, and his views on a possible Indian intervention in the Utah War. As will be discussed in a later chapter, the phrasing on the Indian issue was so provocative that one historian has argued that Clinton may have used it to blackmail President Young ten years later.[3] The tribes, of course, were a subject that Brigham Young had discussed at length in his important unpublished tabernacle discourse of 16 August. The potential for tribal violence and his role in preventing, allowing, or stimulating it was perhaps the most volatile subject on Young's mind as he dictated to his clerks. Whether or how the prospect of Indian involvement at Mountain Meadows shaped Young's thinking on 12 September is a fascinating imponderable.

YOUNG TO CLINTON, 12 SEPTEMBER 1857, LDS ARCHIVES.

> I have an opportunity of sending directly to you by Doctor Bernhisel who has concluded to go down to Washington this fall.

---

[2] This same contingency plan for dealing with repeal of Utah's organic act was still being endorsed by Brigham Young in the early 1860s. Young to William H. Hooper, 5 January 1860 and 21 February 1866, Hooper Collection; MacKinnon, "'Like Splitting a Man Up His Backbone,'" 110.

[3] Walker, *Wayward Saints*, 101–104.

Captain Van Vliet, one of General Harney's Staff arrived here Tuesday the 8th inst. From what I have seen of him I think him a very fine man, and one who can appreciate honesty of purpose in others. He informs us that, with those who have been detained in Kansas, and the desertion of even one third of those who started, there were but 850 men left of the celebrated Army for Utah, when he passed them 100 miles or more below [east of] Laramie.

I think that we may depend upon the Captain to use his best efforts in staving off the expedition this year. But even should they keep away for the present, we cannot place any confidence in their assurances of amity and peaceful relations; we cannot depend upon them. The fitting out so large an expedition—naming General Harney as Commander—the batteries of cannon—all proclaim that it was no peace establishment. From all former experience, we know that they feel evil, even if the Lord does not permit them [to] act out their hellish designs. My feelings are to be ready for them. . . .

I have written to Brother W. I. Appleby instructing him to withdraw all the Elders from the United States and Canada Missions—to bring home all the powder and lead which he can, and to preach the spirit of Gathering to every saint in the U.S. and outside of Utah: I desire you to assist him in so laudable a work.

I think it would be advisable for you to spend a portion of the winter in Washington. Should you have an opportunity to obtain an interview with President Buchanan talk to him, right [*sic*] out the feelings of this people, and what he may expect if we are driven into extreme measures.[4]

For years I have been holding the Indians, the check rein has broken, and cousin Lemuel[5] is at length at large; in fact he has been already collecting some of his annuities. Day after day I am visited by their Chiefs to know if they may strike while the iron is hot. My answer depends on M[r] Buchanan's policy—if he do not mete out justice to us, the war cry will resound from the Rio Colorado to the head waters of the Missouri—from the Black hills to the Sierra Nevada—travel will be stopped across the continent—the deserts of Utah become a battle ground for freedom. It [is] peace and our rights—or the knife and tomahawk—let Uncle Sam choose. . . .[6]

Brother Clinton, it would be well for us to have access through some reliable source to the ear of the Government, through which we may be able to

[4] Interestingly, Young did not request Appleby to make such a presidential visit though he had occasionally accompanied John Taylor to Washington and reported to Young on political affairs. There is no sign that Clinton ever called on Buchanan.

[5] A reference to Indians derived from *The Book of Mormon* that would have carried great meaning for a Latter-day Saint such as Clinton. In Mormon scripture Laman and Lemuel were ancestors of American Indians, who, in turn, were viewed as a "remnant of Jacob." Brigham Young believed that Indians were destined to play a role in joining their cousins of "latter-day" Israel, the Mormons, in defending God's kingdom against its enemies, including the United States.

[6] The Indian portion of this paragraph is also absent from the companion letter dictated to Appleby, although the notion of a halt to emigration was common to both documents.

> reach their real designs, in order that we may learn them at an early day; if troops are to be sent out to Utah the ensuing season, we wish to be advised in time. Seek, therefore, some person who will be true, and through whom you may operate without attracting notice; we wish you, in connexion with Brother Horace [Eldredge], to take measures to send or bring us reliable information.[7] Pick up some of the Elders and come up to Genoa [Nebraska Territory], and from that point fit out across the plains without any one else, except our people's knowing anything about it. Be wise, energetic, prudent, and vigilant; instruct whoever come to avoid the troops at Laramie, or any other point where they may be located for the winter. We wish all the Elders to come early in the Spring.
>
> Your family are all well, I believe; your business in a flourishing condition; and all of your interests in Zion increasing on Brother Heber's plan.
>
> Captain Van Vliet leaves here, Monday the 14th inst., Doctor Bernhisel by especial invitation accompanying.

Although the letters to Messrs. Appleby and Clinton were dated 12 September, there is a possibility that Brigham Young had dictated them the night before and finalized them the next day. In any event, they clearly were written and sealed before the arrival some time on the morning of 12 September of a courier—perhaps young Asa S. Hawley—who brought the alarming news that the army was moving beyond Fort Laramie. Presumably it was from this source that Brigham Young also first learned that a new commander for the Utah Expedition was being brought up from Texas to supersede General Harney.

The reality that there probably would be a fall move on Salt Lake City had a galvanizing effect on Brigham Young. The tone stiffened in what he dictated later in the day to Apostle Pratt. Young informed Pratt that "We have decided to send Doctor J. M. Bernhisel down this fall," rather than mentioning, as he had to Clinton, that, "Doctor Bernhisel . . . has concluded to go down to Washington this fall." Likewise, Brigham Young's description of his role with Utah's Indians shifted from a somewhat passive, almost fatalistic acquiescence in possible violence to a virtual threat to unleash Indian warfare. In writing to Liverpool, Young's thoughts also turned to the north and Canada perhaps more than they had since his return from Fort Limhi almost four months earlier. The gloves were coming off in Salt Lake City.

[7] The notion of selecting and using such an agent first entered Young's correspondence in an 8 September 1857 letter to Horace S. Eldredge and was repeated in the companion 12 September letter to Appleby. It is not clear whether Young had a specific (but here unidentified) person in mind in urging such an arrangement. In view of events discussed in a later chapter, it would be reasonable to speculate that Young might have been thinking about U.S. senator Sam Houston of Texas for such a role.

Young to Pratt, 12 September 1857, LDS Archives.

Since the [13 August] departure of Brother Samuel W. Richards events of some moment have transpired in relation to the future of Mormonism. My last to you supposed General Harney on his way to this Valley, with a command of 2500 soldiers. More recent advices state that he is detained in Kansas; and one Colonel Johns[t]on of Texas is appointed in his stead.[8] In place of three full regiments, about 1400 men only were collected; of those although they reached Laramie about the 31st ult., near one half had deserted.

By express this morning we learned that 700 men left Laramie on the 3rd inst. for Salt Lake. We cannot learn that any of the civil (?) officers appointed for Utah have ever left the States.

Captain Van Vliet of Harney's Staff arrived here the 8th inst; he left his Escort on Hams Fork and came in with Elders Bryant Stringham and N. V. Jones. He feels the spirit of this people and I think we may count upon his assistance in staving off a collision with the United States this year, and he thinks the Union within that time will have ceased to be.[9] We have decided to send Doctor J. M. Bernhisel down this fall; he leaves here on Monday 14th inst. with Captain Van Vliet and by special invitation will accompany him directly through to Washington.

I have informed the Captain that we shall not permit troops to enter our settlements, collision or not collision. We are now free, and we have determined to remain so.[10]

It may interest you to learn what preparations we are making to defend ourselves, if fight is the word. We have thoroughly reconoitred the mountains, passes and kanyons; found the best places for caching our grain and hiding our women and children. The minds of the people are prepared to set fire to, and destroy every house—barn—and fence—tree—and improvement which we have made. Every old gun, and part of a gun, is being turned to the best account in arming the people. Of powder and lead we have a tolerably [*sic*] supply; our enemies will furnish the rest. Besides all this, cousin Lemuel by thousands only wait the word to use their best endeavors to fulfil the prophecies. Just let Uncle Sam make one movement proclaiming actual hostilities, and the war cry will resound over all the central part of the United States.

---

[8] Apparently Young chose not to believe in this command change, as he continued to refer to Harney as the expedition's leader into October. Alternatively, it may have served Young's motivational purpose to act as though the notorious Harney rather than the unknown Johnston was commander.

[9] If this is an accurate account of Van Vliet's comments, it is an opinion—advanced by a serving officer—as remarkable as his disclosures to Young about troop strength and desertion rates. The captain's disclosures call into question his dispatch west by Harney as a "discreet officer."

[10] As discussed in earlier chapters, Brigham Young's choice of words—especially in describing Utah's future—left him open to multiple interpretations and even legal jeopardy. What did "free" mean?

> All is well with us in the Valley. Your family are in good health. We have an abundance of grain, vegetables and fruit; health, peace, and faithfulness are universal, and at no period of our church history have the Saints had so much occasion for rejoicing as at present. The Temple and other public improvements are progressing finely. In fact the Brethren throughout the Territory continue to build and improve with the same degree of interest that would be manifested was there no prospect of trouble in the future.
>
> I mentioned in my last that you had better turn our emigration to the Canadas. You will bear in mind in so doing that good, able men should attend each ship load of passengers, who can calculate for the people, and who are capable of selecting locations suitable for the Saints to colonize. By referring to the Map, you will perceive that on the north side of Lake Superior, and along the chain of small Lakes dividing the United States and British possessions there is abundance of space for settlements, as that country has none at present. I have been informed by mountaineers, acquainted with that Northern country, that the soil is exceedingly fertile—vegetation rank, and the seasons sufficiently lengthy for raising grain. Those Lakes abound in trout and other fish, game is plentiful; and there is also abundant supplies of useful woods an timber. Should we get a foothold there, I think, the climate will be found sufficiently cold to protect us from the rapacity of those too lazy and villainous to work for a living.[11]
>
> Inasmuch as the United States have given us abundant Testimony of their exceedingly kind intentions toward this Territory, I wish to pursue the same policy mentioned in my last to you—that is, let all the Elders gather home to Zion, and come provided with good arms, and as much powder and lead as their means will permit.

Brigham Young's 12 September letter to James W. Denver, U.S. commissioner of Indian Affairs, is important, but it is more appropriately discussed in a later chapter together with Denver's November response. Suffice to say here that although Young's comments to Denver about potential Indian violence were substantially more muted than in his letters to Clinton and Pratt—as well as in his earlier 16 August discourse—they were still highly provocative for a federal superintendent of Indian Affairs.

The fifth letter of that day, Kane's, is as revealing for what it did not say as what it did communicate. Although Kane lived in the same city as Jeter Clinton, there was for him no discussion of a wholesale armed gathering to Utah, diversion of the British emigration to wilderness Canada, a Clinton

[11] The concept here was that Canada—like Utah—was a place so unattractive that non-Mormons would not settle there.

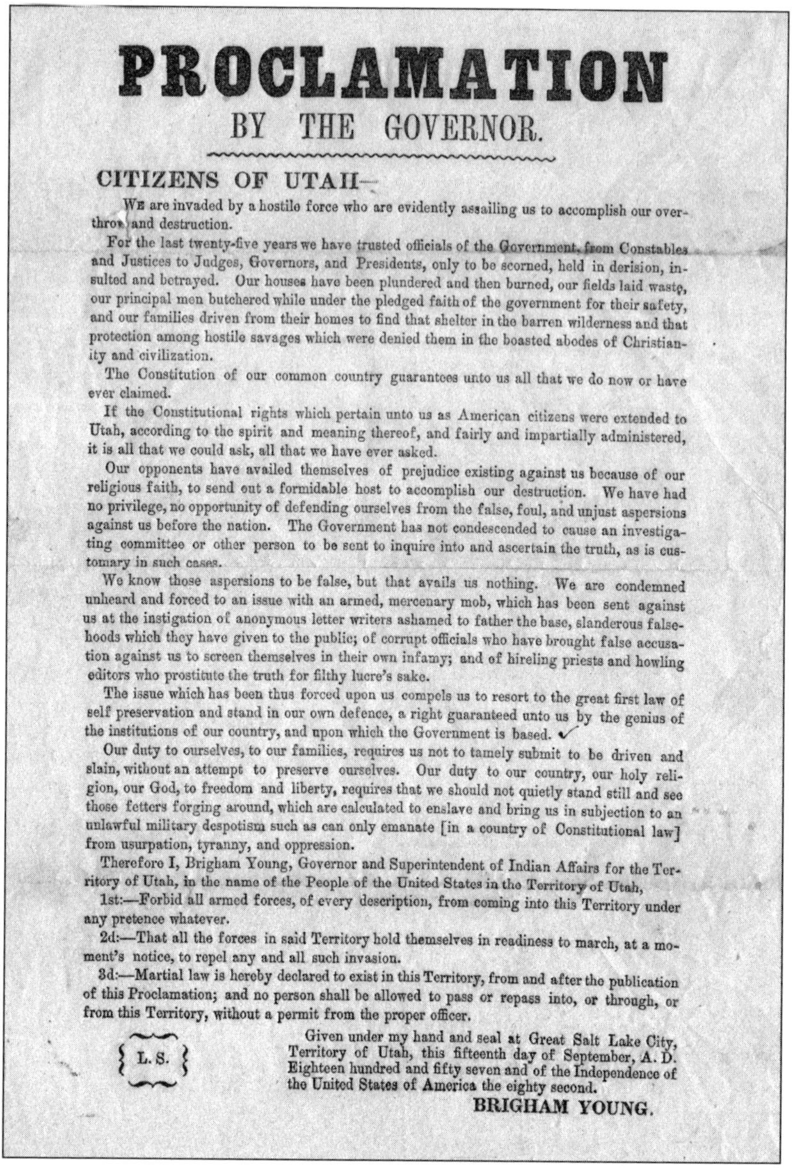

PROCLAMATION

BY THE GOVERNOR.

CITIZENS OF UTAH—

WE are invaded by a hostile force who are evidently assailing us to accomplish our overthrow and destruction.

For the last twenty-five years we have trusted officials of the Government, from Constables and Justices to Judges, Governors, and Presidents, only to be scorned, held in derision, insulted and betrayed. Our houses have been plundered and then burned, our fields laid waste, our principal men butchered while under the pledged faith of the government for their safety, and our families driven from their homes to find that shelter in the barren wilderness and that protection among hostile savages which were denied them in the boasted abodes of Christianity and civilization.

The Constitution of our common country guarantees unto us all that we do now or have ever claimed.

If the Constitutional rights which pertain unto us as American citizens were extended to Utah, according to the spirit and meaning thereof, and fairly and impartially administered, it is all that we could ask, all that we have ever asked.

Our opponents have availed themselves of prejudice existing against us because of our religious faith, to send out a formidable host to accomplish our destruction. We have had no privilege, no opportunity of defending ourselves from the false, foul, and unjust aspersions against us before the nation. The Government has not condescended to cause an investigating committee or other person to be sent to inquire into and ascertain the truth, as is customary in such cases.

We know those aspersions to be false, but that avails us nothing. We are condemned unheard and forced to an issue with an armed, mercenary mob, which has been sent against us at the instigation of anonymous letter writers ashamed to father the base, slanderous falsehoods which they have given to the public; of corrupt officials who have brought false accusation against us to screen themselves in their own infamy; and of hireling priests and howling editors who prostitute the truth for filthy lucre's sake.

The issue which has been thus forced upon us compels us to resort to the great first law of self preservation and stand in our own defence, a right guaranteed unto us by the genius of the institutions of our country, and upon which the Government is based.

Our duty to ourselves, to our families, requires us not to tamely submit to be driven and slain, without an attempt to preserve ourselves. Our duty to our country, our holy religion, our God, to freedom and liberty, requires that we should not quietly stand still and see those fetters forging around, which are calculated to enslave and bring us in subjection to an unlawful military despotism such as can only emanate [in a country of Constitutional law] from usurpation, tyranny, and oppression.

Therefore I, Brigham Young, Governor and Superintendent of Indian Affairs for the Territory of Utah, in the name of the People of the United States in the Territory of Utah,

1st:—Forbid all armed forces, of every description, from coming into this Territory under any pretence whatever.

2d:—That all the forces in said Territory hold themselves in readiness to march, at a moment's notice, to repel any and all such invasion.

3d:—Martial law is hereby declared to exist in this Territory, from and after the publication of this Proclamation; and no person shall be allowed to pass or repass into, or through, or from this Territory, without a permit from the proper officer.

{ L. S. }

Given under my hand and seal at Great Salt Lake City, Territory of Utah, this fifteenth day of September, A. D. Eighteen hundred and fifty seven and of the Independence of the United States of America the eighty second.

BRIGHAM YOUNG.

BRIGHAM YOUNG'S MARTIAL-LAW PROCLAMATION

This sensational 15 September edict sought to bar the army from Utah and halt transcontinental emigration. Although unsuccessful, it shocked non-Mormons, reinforced perceptions of an LDS rebellion, and triggered federal treason indictments (dropped in 1859) for a beleaguered Young and dozens of others. *Courtesy of the LDS Archives.*

visit to the White House, the need for a confidential intelligence source in Washington, or a prospective rampage by "Cousin Lemuel" to halt transcontinental travel. And, of course, there was no discussion of the broadsides then being printed in Salt Lake City preparatory to proclaiming martial law three days later. There were limits to what Brigham Young would share with even a highly valued outside-insider.

What Young did write to Kane was an expression of confidence in Kane's continued help, and a renewal of his 1854 invitation for Kane and his family to move to Utah. He also hinted at still another subject absent from the other four letters: Mormon retaliatory incineration of American cities. It was an extraordinary prospect to which Young had alluded in his 16 August discourse and that he also would mention privately in his last meeting on 13 September with Captain Van Vliet. To Kane Young wrote: "We feel that we can rely upon your aid and influence in averting the fearful storm, but if it breaks upon us it will also break upon the whole country and then friends will be friends in need. Where will you find better warmer or more sincere friends than in the mountains."[12]

Arise Like Men of God: Proclaiming Martial Law

As to the origins of Brigham Young's martial-law proclamation, his office journal indicates that on the morning of 29 August he "instructed President Wells to write out a Proclamation which I intended to pub[l]ish if Harney attempted to enter the Ter[r]itory, declaring Utah under martial Law, and that no one will be permitted to pass into or out of except by permission from the proper officer." By the following evening, at a prayer-circle meeting, several documents including "an official Proclamation were read—the Proclamation I intend making publick in case the troops proceed to enter the Territory. The editorial [about Douglas's speech] & Proclamation were rec[eived]. by acclamation."[13] Whether this subject had been debated even earlier in August is unknown, but the murky, sporadic twentieth-century appearance on the antiquarian manuscripts market of a few copies of a similar proclamation dated six weeks earlier—5 August 1857—has fueled gener-

[12] Young to Kane, 12 September 1857, LDS Archives.

[13] See Brigham Young Office Journal, entry for 29 August, Arrington Papers. The only published, and therefore most available, version of this material is in Cooley, ed., *Diary of Brigham Young 1857*, 68–69.

ations of confusing speculation as to the authenticity and meaning of such a version.[14]

The first recorded discussion of the martial-law proclamation subsequent to these was by postmaster Elias Smith on 14 September: "I attended a council at the Historian's Office in the afternoon by invitation, where the question of the Governor's proclaiming martial law in the Territory was discussed and approved unanimously by those present."[15] On the same day Brigham Young mentioned the imminent release of such a proclamation in letters sent to several religious-military leaders, including Col. William Dame in Parowan.[16]

Aside from the fascinating matter of why, how, and when Brigham Young conceived, drafted, and first issued his martial-law proclamation, there is the more substantive question of the decree's significance and context. Without question Young's release of this document escalated the tensions between the LDS church's leadership and the U.S. government, transforming the conflict from a matter of inflammatory rhetoric to a provocation stunning in its insubordination by a federally sworn governor. The country had seen nothing like it since President Andrew Jackson's confrontation with the State of South Carolina in 1832 over the Nullification Crisis. In several ways and for multiple reasons, Brigham Young's declaration of martial law was his crossing of a Rubicon. From this document would flow, among other consequences, an escalation of the Buchanan administration's armed intervention in Utah as well as Brigham Young's little-known indictment for treason.

Young's Proclamation of Martial Law, 15 September 1857, LDS Archives.

Citizens of Utah,—

We are invaded by a hostile force, who are evidently assailing us to accomplish our overthrow and destruction.

---

[14] Copies of both the 15 September proclamation and very similar 5 August variant may be found in several university libraries. The two versions are printed side by side in Cooley, ed., *Diary of Brigham Young 1857*, 82–83. The definitive analysis of the variant's provenance is a two-part article by Bagley, "Like any other place, Utah history contains share of mysteries" and "If the document is authentic, how can we explain weird dates?" *Salt Lake Tribune*, 3 and 10 August 2003. Here Bagley argues that the 5 August 1857 version was an authentic document but one misdated (for 5 September) and uncirculated. Bagley surmises that, once printed, the variant proclamation was held back because of Captain Van Vliet's imminent (8 September) arrival in Salt Lake City and a subsequent fine tuning of Mormon thinking that necessitated minor phrase changes. Bagley concludes that, in effect, the misdated variant proclamation became a printed (but uncirculated) draft.

[15] Thomas, comp., "Elias Smith's Journal," entry for 14 September 1857.

[16] Young and Wells to Dame, 14 September 1857, LDS Archives.

For the last twenty-five years we have trusted officials of the Government, from Constables and Justices to Judges, Governors, and Presidents, only to be scorned, held in derision, insulted, and betrayed. Our houses have been plundered and then burned, our fields laid waste, our principal men butchered while under the pledged faith of the government for their safety, and our families driven from their homes to find that shelter in the barren wilderness and that protection among hostile savages, which were denied them in the boasted abodes of Christianity and civilization.

The Constitution of our common country guarantees to us all that we do now or have ever after claimed.

If the Constitutional rights which pertain unto us as American citizens were extended to Utah, according to the spirit and meaning thereof, and fairly and impartially administered, it is all that we could ask, all that we have ever asked.

Our opponents have availed themselves of prejudice existing against us, because of our religious faith, to send out a formidable host to accomplish our destruction. We have had no privilege, or opportunity of defending ourselves from the false, foul, and unjust aspersions against us before the nation. The Government has not condescended to cause an investigating committee or other person to be sent to inquire into an[d] ascertain the truth, as is customary in such cases.

We know those aspersions to be false, but that avails us nothing. We are condemned unheard and forced to an issue with an armed, mercenary mob, which has been sent against us at the instigation of anonymous letter writers ashamed to father the base, slanderous falsehoods which they have given to the public; of corrupt officials, who have brought false accusation against us to screen themselves in their own infamy; and of hireling priests and howling editors who prostitute the truth for filthy lucre's sake.

The issue which has thus been forced upon us compels us to resort to the great first law of self preservation and stand in our own defence, a right guaranteed to us by the genius of the institutions of our country, and upon which the Government is based.

Our duty to ourselves, to our families, requires us not to tamely submit to be driven and slain, without an attempt to preserve ourselves. Our duty to our country, our holy religion, our God, to freedom and liberty, requires that we should not quietly stand still and see those fetters forging around, which are calculated to enslave and bring us to subjection to an unlawful military despotism such as can only emanate [in a country of Constitutional law] from usurpation, tyranny, and oppression.

Therefore I, Brigham Young, Governor and Superintendent of Indian Affairs for the territory of Utah, in the name of the People of the United States in the Territory of Utah,

1st:—Forbid all armed forces, of every description, from coming into this Territory under any pretence whatever.

2nd:—That all the forces in said Territory hold themselves in readiness to march, at a moment's notice, to repel any and all such invasion.

3rd:—Martial law is hereby declared to exist in this Territory, from and after the publication of this Proclamation; and no person shall be allowed to pass or repass into, or through, or from this Territory, without a permit from the proper officer.[17]

Given under my hand and seal at Great Salt Lake City, Territory of Utah, this fifteenth day of September, A.D. Eighteen hundred and fifty seven and of the Independence of the United States of America the eighty second.

BRIGHAM YOUNG[18]

General Wells's son, Junius, an editor, later claimed that Brigham Young considered the legal consequences of his proclamation before he acted. Without providing documentary support, Junius Wells argued:

> In preparing this celebrated document the Governor was asked if he realized that the act would be construed by his enemies as treasonable. He replied that he supposed so, but signified that the liberties of a loyal people were worth more than fair fame in the eyes of an administration, so blind and weak as to be goaded on to such acts of folly and wickedness, by the ignorant clamoring of an excited populace. He plainly indicated that defensive action was necessary, not only to preserve the homes and liberties of our people, but to prevent the approaching forces from committing deeds of horrible injustice and cruelty. He expected that a fair investigation and settlement of difficulties would follow the campaign, knowing that it should have preceded it, and proposed that while the excitement of relentless intolerance animated the power raised against us to hold its hand until its head got cool. This was the object and proved to be the effect of Governor Young's proclamation of martial law.[19]

JUSTIFICATION FOR THAT EXTREME MEASURE: CONTEXT FOR YOUNG'S PROCLAMATION

Too often historians have viewed Utah War events in isolation from the rest of American history. They discuss war hysteria and a spirit of vengeance in

[17] This provision of the proclamation did more than deal with an internal Utah restriction. With the territory more than six hundred miles wide and athwart many of the principal emigration trails to the Pacific Coast between New Mexico Territory and the British Possessions, sealing Utah's borders would necessarily have a profound impact on transcontinental travel.

[18] This text is taken from a copy of the original printed proclamation in broadside form; punctuation and capitalization in the document varied when it was published in early 1858 by Congress in House Ex. Doc. 71, Serial 956, 34–35.

[19] "Vaux" [Junius F. Wells], "The Echo Canyon War," 216.

southern Utah without adequate attention to the residual impact of earlier Mormon persecution in Ohio, Missouri, and Illinois. Writers describe the Move South—the Mormon mass exodus from northern Utah to Provo in April 1858—oblivious to the U.S. Army's even more disruptive civilian evacuation of western Missouri during the Civil War.[20] For this reason alone, proper consideration of Governor Young's martial-law decree needs context. To understand better its character and significance, it is useful to compare it to Young's own earlier proclamations as well as to roughly similar edicts issued contemporaneously by governors and mayors in California, Washington Territory, Maryland, and New York. Also relevant are the administrative and legal opinions issued by President Pierce's secretary of state and attorney general on the Washington Territory case only months before Brigham Young declared martial law in Utah.

Young's proclamation of 15 September 1857 was not the first far-reaching military decree that he had issued as governor. For example, in an April 1853 action, the governor issued a decree intended to halt the longstanding Mexican-Ute slave trade involving Indian children. It had the unintended consequence of precipitating a two-year war with Chief Walkara's Utes. In language similar to that four years later Young announced that Utah had been invaded by a "horde of Mexicans;" he ordered out a Legion company to detain suspicious parties and forbade all Mexicans from leaving Utah without permission.[21]

In the region adjoining Utah, there was an even broader context through which to consider Young's 1857 action. In 1856 J. Neely Johnson, California's governor, had proclaimed a form of martial law in San Francisco County to deal with vigilantism and what he termed "insurrection."[22] Earlier in 1856 Washington Territory's Governor Isaac I. Stevens decreed martial law twice for different counties in prosecuting an Indian war.[23] There is evidence that Mormon apostle Wilford Woodruff was aware of at least Stevens's decrees.

Governor Stevens's proclamations also drew notice as well as a challenge in Washington, D.C. President Pierce's secretary of state, William L. Marcy,

[20] See Bohl, "A War on Civilians," 44–51.

[21] Bigler, *Forgotten Kingdom*, 74.

[22] Proclamation of Calif. governor J. Neely Johnson, 3 June 1856, "Correspondence Between the Late Secretary of War and General Wool," 187–88.

[23] The original documents may be found in Miscellaneous Letters, May 1856, General Records of the Department of State (RG 59), National Archives. The text may be found most conveniently in Lokken, "The Martial Law Controversy in Washington Territory, 1856," 99; Cohen, "Martial Law in Washington Territory," 201; and Richards, *Isaac I. Stevens*, 277. The number of such analyses focusing on Stevens's action, its context, and meaning is in sharp contrast to the paucity of attention that historians have given to Brigham Young's more far-reaching proclamation.

sent Stevens a written rebuke. In the 1857 Utah controversy, there is no record that Secretary of State Cass commented officially on Brigham Young's martial-law proclamation, but his predecessor's reaction to such a gubernatorial decree a year earlier is worth understanding.

> MARCY TO STEVENS, 12 SEPTEMBER 1856, STEVENS PAPERS.
>
> I have laid before the President all the documents and papers which you have transmitted to this Department in explanation of your course in declaring Martial law in some parts of the Territory of Washington. After a full consideration of them, he has not been able to find, in the case you have presented, a justification for that extreme measure. Whether in any circumstances whatever, the Governor of a Territory can resort to such a measure, unless under express authority given by legislation, is a question which it is not proposed now to discuss or decide. It is quite certain that nothing but direful necessity, involving the probable overthrow of the civil Government, could be alleged as any sort of excuse for superseding that government temporarily and substituting in its place an arbitrary military rule. The recognition of such an inherent power in any functionary, whatever be his grade or position, would be extremely dangerous to civil and political liberty. While the President does not bring into question the motives by which you were actuated, he is induced, by an imperative sense of duty, to express his distinct disapproval of your conduct, so far as respects the proclamation of Martial law.
>
> Were the President able to adopt the conclusion that Martial law could, in any case, be established without express legislative authority, he could not find such a case in the state of things in Washington Territory as you have presented them. Where rebellion, or a formidable insurrection, had in effect overthrown the civil government, Martial law has been occasionally resorted to as the only means left for its re-establishment. Martial law has also been resorted to in aid of the government when in imminent danger of being overpowered by internal or external foes. In such cases the measure has been regarded as excusable; but it never can be excusable where the object of resorting to Martial law was to act against the existing civil government of the country or to supersede its functionaries in the discharge of their proper duties. The latter seems to have been the principal ground you had for proclaiming Martial law. Your conduct in that respect does not therefore meet with the favorable regard of the President.

Not content to rebuke Governor Stevens himself, Secretary Marcy sought the legal opinion of Attorney General Caleb Cushing on Stevens's actions. A month before Buchanan took office and seven months before Brigham Young proclaimed martial law, Cushing ruled that "the power to suspend the laws, and to substitute the military in the place of the civil authority, is not a power within the legal attributes of a governor of one of the Territories of the United States."[24]

In a different section of the country, Maryland's Gov. T. Watkins Ligon issued a proclamation six weeks after Brigham Young did so in an attempt to cope with ethnic and gang rioting in the streets of Baltimore on the eve of elections. It was a disgraceful scene on which Young later commented critically in emphasizing the orderly election process in Utah. What went with Governor Watkins's proclamation was the mobilization of two divisions of Maryland state militia commanded by a brace of major generals as well as bitter criticism from an embarrassed, outraged mayor of Baltimore.[25] Later in the Utah War period, declaring the citizens of Richmond County to be "in a state of insurrection," New York governor John A. King issued an indignant cease-and-desist proclamation and ordered the state militia to suppress rioting over fears of a yellow-fever epidemic on Staten Island.[26]

Perhaps the most eclectic context in which to consider Brigham Young's action involves a New Mexico incident in August 1850, a month before President Fillmore appointed Young governor of neighboring Utah. In this case acting Secretary of War Winfield Scott instructed the acting governor of the embryonic New Mexico Territory, Brevet Col. John Munroe, on how to handle a boundary dispute with Texas. Anticipating an encroachment ("invasion") by Texas militia units, Scott ordered Munroe to meet them with regular troops and to issue a proclamation to counter one expected to be released by Texas governor Peter H. Bell:

> Accordingly, you are hereby instructed, in the case of any military invasion of New Mexico, from Texas, or by armed men from any other state or states, for the purpose of overturning the order of civil government that may exist in New Mexico at the time, of subjugating New Mexico to Texas, to interpose, as far as practicable, the troops under your command against any such act of violence.
>
> The invaders will probably announce their approach & purposes by proclamation. It may be expedient for you to meet them by a like public declaration in terms at once moderate & firm, intimating the general character of these instructions from the President & your purpose to execute them. You will also profit by all opportunities to remonstrate & use such means of per-

[24] 8 U.S. Op. Atty. Gen. 365 (3 February 1857).

[25] Proclamation of Gov. T. Watkins Ligon, 28 October 1857, Baltimore *Sun,* 29 October 1857, 1/2.

[26] See Proclamation of Governor John A. King, 7 September 1858, *Commercial Advertiser* (Buffalo), 8 September 1858, 1/2.

> suasion as may be in your power with the principal invaders to avoid, if possible, a resort to repulsive violence; but, when necessary & without losing any material advantage, by delay, you will take all preliminary steps for defence, &, in the last resort, resist with vigor.[27]

These state and territorial cases are not raised to justify Brigham Young's declaration of martial law. Rather they serve to illustrate the variety of circumstances in which Young's peers—including several western governors—also used decrees to deal with perceived internal and external threats. What differentiated Young's action from theirs was its anti-federal character, his failure to take intermediate steps before moving to an extreme one, the territory-wide rather than local application of its provisions, and Young's attempt to curb the movement of federal forces as well as civilians.[28]

An Armed Rabble: The Troops React

Brigham Young and his advisors were not the only Utah War players concerned with placing the territory under martial law. On 7 June 1857 General Harney had, of course, twice asked Secretary Floyd for "full powers to declare martial law, if it is necessary."[29] Among the Utah Expedition's junior officers, the barracks lawyers debated the matter of whether the federal side should issue its own proclamation to match Brigham Young's as they approached Utah's eastern border. For his New York readers Albert G. Browne, Jr., reported their debate from a camp on the Big Sandy. Drawing on his Harvard Law School background, Browne essentially took the position expressed by Secretary of State Marcy and Attorney General Cushing in the recent Washington Territory case:

> A. G. Browne, Jr., Dispatch, "Late from the Mormon War," 30 October 1857, *New-York Daily Tribune*, 28 December 1857.
>
> We have been in doubt during the last two days' journey as to whether we have actually entered the Territory of Utah, but to-night we are surely camped within its boundary line. . . .

---

[27] Scott to Munroe, 6 August 1850, Cutrer, "'A Lion in Her Path,'" 79.

[28] For additional sources on martial law—none of which even mention the Utah case—see Rankin, *When Civil Law Fails*; Lieber, "What Is the Justification of Martial Law?" 549–63; Hershey, "Power and Authority of Governor and Militia in Domestic Disturbances," 28–33, and "Constitutional Law—Federal Constitutional Limitation on Military Powers of State Governors"; Ballantine, "Unconstitutional Claims of Military Authority," 189–216; Weida, "A Republic of Emergencies," 1397–438; and Corwin, "Martial Law, Yesterday and Today," 95–104.

[29] See Chapter 7.

It is a matter of regret that Gov. Cumming is not now present to issue his proclamation declaring the Territory to be in a state of rebellion, and calling upon the army to assist him in maintaining the supremacy of the civil power. Although there has been much talk in camp about the necessity of a declaration of martial law by Col. Johnston, doubts are entertained whether such a declaration would be valid, and I do not believe that an officer of his experience and prudence will venture on a step which may, by any possibility, be perverted to palliate the treason of the Mormons. It is a novel and interesting question whether under any circumstance such a suspension of all civil functions as a declaration of martial law effects, would be Constitutional within any portion of the United States. The treason of the Mormons is an offense surely and exclusively within the jurisdiction of the Civil Courts, and I doubt whether it is constitutionally within the power of anybody to remove it, for a trial and punishment, to different tribunals.

How did the troops on both sides of the Utah War react to Brigham Young's proclamation? Governor Cumming's officer-nephew first became aware of Young's proclamation when it reached his bivouac near Hams Fork at the end of September. Aware also of Captain Van Vliet's reception in Salt Lake City as well as his assessment of Mormon resistance, Captain Cumming wrote to his mother, "You can imagine from these things that we are in rather troublous [*sic*] times out here. There is a difference of opinion as to whether we will have any fighting. Certain it is that Governor Young has, in a proclamation, called us 'an armed rabble,' and called upon every good citizen of the Territory to be ready at a moment's notice to repel us by force."[30]

Mormon militiaman John Pulsipher noted at Fort Supply the reading of Brigham Young's proclamation, his supplemental instructions to local leader Isaac Bullock, and the reaction of U.S. troops to the proclamation as reported by Legion scouts.

PULSIPHER, A SHORT SKETCH, LDS ARCHIVES.

September 20 (?) [*sic*]. President Bullock received a letter from Bro. Brigham of the 16th giving us further instructions in regard to carrying into effect the fore going Proclamation. Although the invading army is approaching—but this martial law must be carried out. Be careful of the lives of people. See that there are no more killed than is absolutely necessary to carry out these orders. Mentions in this that it would be well to move the families in from Fort Supply as that is a hard place to live. . . .

Monday, Sept. 28 [1857]. Right from the enemy's camps where he and his company and others have been watching the movements and etc., said they

[30] Capt. Alfred Cumming to mother, 30 September 1857, Cumming Family Papers.

> will not stop by any fair means—are taking any of our boys prisoners that they can catch—When the Government Proclamation was presented to them, they hooted and wanted to know who was Brigham Young—and force-marched harder than before. So our boys commenced giving some hints that they might understand that we meant what we said. These plain hints consisted of taking the herds of beef stock to the Valley where they will winter well—and of burning the heavy freight trains of supplies—these things were done in day time and some of it right in sight of the main army, and when pursued our boys could easily keep out of their way among these ragged rockey mountains.

When General Wells and Apostles Taylor and Smith had forwarded Young's proclamation by courier to Colonel Alexander at the end of September, they were apprehensive. As they reported to Young from their camp at Fort Bridger, "Of course we do not know what will be the result of the documents, but want to be prepared for the worst."[31]

Once Col. Albert Sidney Johnston arrived on the scene, he fulfilled the trio's worst expectations. Treating Brigham Young's proclamation and transmittal letter as though they were plague ridden, Johnston sent the copies that Alexander had been willing to accept back through Legion lines with released Mormon prisoners, although Alexander had already sent one copy east to army headquarters in New York. From Echo Canyon, Legion generals Wells, Rich, and Grant informed Brigham Young of this rejection, adding ruefully that "It would seem as though such documents only meritted silent contempt." Perking up, they then added the observation that "The Proclamation and letter seem to us as an expiring [inspiring] kick, or more likely an *Alexandrian* splurdge."[32]

---

[31] Wells, Taylor, and Smith to Young, 30 September 1857, LDS Archives.

[32] Wells, Rich, and Grant to Young, 28 November 1857, LDS Archives.

Chapter 12

"Lonely Bones"
Violence and Leadership

Yates! He has neither been seen by any of us since the day we purchased his [gun]powder, nor is it probable he will be ever seen by any—in the flesh. . . . In some lone nook, of some lonelier canyon, his bones lie, as do those of many another victim, calling for the vengeance which shall surely come.

—Capt. Albert Tracy, Tenth U.S. Infantry,
journal entry for 10 April 1860

As the army approached Utah's northeastern frontier in late September, it lacked an overall commander. General Harney's absence was obvious; unknown to the expedition was that Colonel Johnston had replaced him and was hastening across Nebraska. The senior officer present in the field, the Tenth Infantry's Col. Edmund B. Alexander, was a timorous officer who chose not to assume leadership of the expedition's disparate regiments and batteries. And so he and they marched west independently—unaware of the War Department's 29 June instructions for the conduct of the campaign as well as the location and even identity of their commander. Oblivious to this federal-leadership vacuum, the Nauvoo Legion scouted, probed, and began to harass its adversary. As it did so, the volatile conditions that can spawn atrocities enveloped this isolated border district as well as that to Utah's far southwest.[1] Unsettling rumors flourished among the Mormons of Salt Lake City and southern Utah of a surprise strike by Colonel Sumner's Cheyenne Expedition. Speculation spread about an anticipated federal invasion of southern Utah from both Texas and the Colorado River. Fear,

[1] This chapter uses the word "atrocity" to mean violence by military forces (or those under their control, such as Indians) against noncombatants or unarmed military prisoners.

tension, hate, covetousness, anger, and uncertainty welled up along Utah's flanks—northern as well as southern—as did ineffective leadership on the Mormon side. Contributing to this shortfall in Mormon leadership were the twin plagues of inflammatory and ambiguous communications as well as a tolerance for, if not encouragement of, undisciplined, opportunistic looting.

And the atrocities came. The loss of life approached the 157 fatalities that contemporaneously earned Utah's eastern neighbor the enduring label "Bleeding Kansas."[2] Here was carnage on a scale that challenges the persistent pernicious myth that, as an LDS church website phrased it until 2007, the Utah War was "a bloodless but costly confrontation . . . and they spilled no blood."[3] Old scores were settled, and simple ageless acts of murder, plundering, and vengeance unfolded in the ambiguity of borderland Utah. Here one's identity as friend or foe often blurred, as two American forces, regular and militia, wearing the same uniform—or none at all—maneuvered in close proximity to tempting targets of prosperous civilians in what later generations would call the fog of war.[4]

The victims fell individually or in small groups. But on 11 September 1857 at Mountain Meadows, an oasis on the rim of the Great Basin more than three hundred miles southwest of Salt Lake City, the group carnage was on an unimaginable scale. The massacre at Mountain Meadows—apparently the war's first such incident—involved the execution at point-blank range of 120 children, women, and disarmed men of the Fancher party of California-bound Arkansas emigrants. The killers, led by field-grade officers, were a Nauvoo Legion detachment and a pick-up tribal group of Paiute auxiliaries. This atrocity was the worst incident of organized mass murder of unarmed civilians in American history until the 1995 Oklahoma City

---

[2] Watts, "How Bloody Was Bleeding Kansas?," 123.

[3] "Struggle for Independence," http://www.lds.org/newsroom/showpackage/0,15367,3899=1-34-2-132,00.html (accessed 18 November 2006). Because of inputs from the editor and others, this phrasing no longer appears on the church's internet "newsroom" and has been replaced by an essay and press release dated 19 June 2007 ("The Mountain Meadows Massacre") in which church historian Richard E. Turley, Jr., asserts to the contrary, "But the atrocity at Mountain Meadows made it [the Utah War] far from bloodless." See http://www.lds.org/ldsnewsroom (accessed 17 July 2007). Today an internet search using Google and the key words "Utah War" and "bloodless" yields more than one hundred sources.

[4] For a recent and apt use of this phrase in connection with a clash in Lebanon between Israeli regulars and Hezbollah militiamen, see Sabrina Tavernise, "Civilians Lose as Fighters Slip into Fog of War, Lebanese Deaths Show Dilemma for Israel," *New York Times*, 3 August 2006, A1/5, A10/1–2. This article comments: "Civilian deaths illustrate the raw dilemma of modern warfare, in which a conventional army fights an elusive militia. . . . In Lebanon, the result has been desperate efforts to flee and military miscalculations in the fog of war."

bombing.[5] The accompanying looting of the victims' cash, livestock, wagons, carriages, household goods, jewelry, and even blood-soaked, bullet-punctured clothing was unprecedented in its callousness and scope. Even in the aftermath of slaughter, the victims' possessions were irresistible for the impoverished Mormons and Indians of hardscrabble southern Utah.

Since the end of the twentieth century—as was the case more than one hundred years earlier—a plethora of novels and nonfiction accounts has appeared to explain and describe the massacre. Since this present work has been the product of prodigious research yielding fresh insights, there is no need here to rehash most aspects of the tragedy.[6] The prime exception to this scrutiny—and therefore the focus of this chapter—is a series of killings that soon followed those at Mountain Meadows and the ineffective leadership that enabled them. This little-examined violence, together with the prewar Ambrose-Betts affair and Parrish-Potter murders, firmly links the Mountain Meadows massacre to a broader context—the military campaign and the territorial culture of violence that spawned it. An understanding of these early atrocities and what prompted them, together with the enormity of the immediately preceding Mountain Meadows massacre, should at long last belie the appalling myth of the Utah War as a bloodless conflict—an expensive but basically harmless affair. With such violence less than one hundred miles from Salt Lake City—and in one case only a few miles from the First Presidency's two counselors—these "other" killings also provide a basis for rethinking another longstanding legend: the notion that wartime murder on the Mormon side was a single event confined to isolated southern Utah's Mountain Meadows and involving panicky locals freelancing more than three hundred miles from senior, disengaged leaders in Salt Lake City.[7]

[5] Some historians are anxious to note that the U.S. Army inflicted even greater casualties on Native Americans during the plains campaigns of the nineteenth century. In these engagements, including Utah's 1863 Bear River massacre, the armed status of Indian women and even children blurred the traditional distinction between combatants and noncombatants.

[6] See Brooks, *The Mountain Meadows Massacre*; and Bagley, *Blood of the Prophets*. Another recent narrative history (Sally Denton, *American Massacre: The Tragedy at Mountain Meadows, September 1857* (New York: Knopf, 2003)) is deeply flawed and far less careful than these other studies. Additional light on this subject will come from two forthcoming studies: Turley, Leonard, and Walker, *Tragedy at Mountain Meadows*; and Bagley and Bigler, *Innocent Blood*. Accompanying this newest material have been several extraordinary acts of reconciliation by the LDS church and descendants on both sides of the atrocity. The most notable such event was the 11 September 1999 rededication of the cairn memorializing the victims at Mountain Meadows, a reconstruction undertaken by the LDS church under the leadership of its president, Gordon B. Hinckley. The ceremony was attended by and involved not only President Hinckley but descendants of both victims and perpetrators.

[7] This chapter is largely adapted from MacKinnon's unpublished paper presented at the Western History Association's 2003 annual conference in Fort Worth and the related journal article, "'Lonely Bones,'" 124–82.

Up the Pocket of the Lord: The Yates Murder

Following the carnage at Mountain Meadows on 11 September 1857, the next Utah War atrocity victimized Richard E. Yates, a mountaineer-trader whom the Nauvoo Legion captured near Fort Bridger around 15 October 1857. Yates's offense was the sale of his substantial stock of gunpowder to the approaching Utah Expedition rather than to the Mormons. Also involved was the Mormon perception of Yates as a federal spy. On 18 October, while Yates was unarmed, manacled, and asleep, Lt. Bill Hickman bludgeoned him to death near the Legion's Echo Canyon headquarters. Hickman admitted the murder publicly in 1871 and reportedly did so informally long before that date. It is on this atrocity that much of this chapter focuses because of its locale and timing, the extensive paper trail, and the availability of comments by one, if not several, of those culpable.

Little is known of Yates's personal background except that he was from Illinois and that he had spent the winter of 1853–54 in the mountains of northeastern Utah, returned east for trade goods, and then, for a year before his 1857 murder, worked as a trader in the region between South Pass and the Salt Lake Valley. The sole contemporary description of Yates is that provided by J. Robert Brown, a young emigrant bound for California, who fell in with Yates and his partner in Missouri during May 1856 as they started across the plains. Brown's journal describes Yates as frequently tipsy, boorish, highly unappealing, and apparently well known to the region's widely scattered Mormon and mountaineer population. Unwittingly, Brown also recorded his impressions of Echo Canyon, and Bill Hickman.[8]

On 16 August 1856, separated from Yates and entering Salt Lake City, Brown wrote, "We passed in front of Gov. Young's house. He was standing in the door of his office, and eyed us closely as we passed."[9] If Brown felt that Brigham Young was personally scrutinizing his passage through town, Richard Yates too had reason to sense Young's interest. Four days later he called on Governor Young seeking Indian trading licenses on behalf of a group of mountaineers. This visit apparently bothered Young. He immediately asked Lewis Robison and others who Yates was representing and on what basis, requesting a reply at "the first opportunity." Robison was Brigham Young's agent for the Fort Bridger area as well as the Nauvoo Legion's quartermaster general.[10]

---

[8] J. Robert Brown, *Journal of a Trip across the Plains of the U.S.*, 34, 66–67, 73–78.

[9] Ibid., 78.

[10] Young to Robison, 20 August 1856, LDS Archives.

Yates's name next appears in correspondence during the early stages of the Utah War among Brigham Young, D. H. Wells, Robison, and Isaac Bullock, Robison's counterpart at the Mormon farming settlement of Fort Supply near Fort Bridger. Since Utah still had no capability to manufacture gunpowder, the Mormon military strategy was to buy privately held supplies before the Utah Expedition seized them. On 18 August 1857 Bullock wrote to Brigham Young:[11]

> There are a good many Mountaineers on Green River & they will be sought for guides for the Army. Should the Army get up clost enough—Yeates a mountaineer has just arrived on Green River with 4 wagons loaded with Indian Goods Powder Lead & [percussion] caps sugar & coffee—he is purposing going to the Utes to traid it, we are getting a long first rate with them. But we can see that the most of the Mountain Men are after money and are not for us but against us and will be on hand to render the soldiers all the aid they can. The Brethren here feel to be & generally are united.

On 7 September 1857, not yet aware of the siege just beginning at Mountain Meadows, Governor Young wrote to Lewis Robison at Fort Bridger:[12]

> We trust that you have secured that Ammunition. . . . Enclosed you will find authority for taking possession of all the property of Yates & Co—We do not wish you to use this authority without you know or can prove that they have been selling or giving liquor to the Indians [illegible] unless they refuse to compromise the terms of which you are at liberty to dictate—perhaps when they find that they are liable to have their property including their wagons cattle horses &c every thing confiscated they will be ~~willing to do~~ willing to compromise fairly. We leave this with you.

A week after Brigham Young authorized Lewis Robison to seize Yates's possessions Charles R. Morehead of Russell, Majors and Waddell encountered Yates near Hams Fork and recorded the trader's apprehensions about looting, and the safety of Jim Bridger and himself.[13] Two weeks later, on 27 September, Capt. Albert Tracy wrote to a friend in Buffalo from the Tenth Infantry's camp on Green River to describe an encounter with a frightened man who was probably Richard Yates's partner: "We saw mounted Mormons today, and an old French trader living here says there are about a hundred some 16 miles above us on the river, and some below us. He told Col. Alexander this

[11] Bullock to Young, 18 August 1857, ibid.

[12] Young to Robison, 7 September 1857, ibid.

[13] Anonymous [Charles R. Morehead] to editor of *Missouri Press* (Lexington, Mo.), 13 September 1857, printed in *Daily Union* (Sacramento, Calif.), 9 December 1857, 1/2.

in my presence, and besides, that there were two Mormons at his house just arrived from Salt Lake. He is a good deal alarmed, and wants us to get between him and the Mormons. We hear that some Mormons wanted to take some powder from him, but that the Snake [Shoshone] Indians would not let them."[14]

At the beginning of October, Apostle George A. Smith was at the Legion's headquarters at Fort Bridger and recorded the next chapter in this tragedy: "[Oct. 3.] At 10 A.M. Mr. Yates and Baptise [?] two Mountaineers or Traders came to the Fort [Bridger], the avowed object of Yates was to purchase flour, propositions were made to him for lead, powder and blankets in his possession, favorable terms were offered but he would not acede to them."[15] Four days after these unsuccessful negotiations, Colonel Alexander ordered a battalion under Capt. Randolph B. Marcy of the Fifth U.S. Infantry to march from Hams Fork to Green River to seize Yates's munitions. Marcy did so, thus outmaneuvering Brigham Young, but it was Richard Yates who paid the price. Mid-October Nauvoo Legion reports or diaries record his arrest and the seizure of his remaining possessions, principally food, clothing, blankets, and livestock.

On 15 October 1857 three senior leaders—General Wells and Apostles Taylor and Smith—sent Brigham Young this field report:[16]

> We have not as yet interrupted their [army] pickets or fired a single gun, but shall continue for the present to carry out your instructions to avoid the shedding of blood. Yates is a prisoner in the hands of Col. [Thomas] Callister at Bridger, having been passing to and from the enemy's camp (and it is believed) as a spy. According to his own statement the [U.S.] troops have got his ammunition. We learn from him that an express is about to start from the troops to the States, by the hands of one Joseph Mageau for which Col. Callister is on the look out. He is a mountaineer, and has sold out to the Government.

Three days later this trio followed up from their new headquarters in Echo Canyon, where Heber C. Kimball, Young's first counselor in the First Presidency, was also present: "We send Yates on the road to the City, a prisoner in charge of Wm. Hickman."[17] On the same day, 18 October, a visitor to the canyon recorded: "At 10 AM W Hickman with Yates a Prisner a Man who has been selling the Troops his Powder Lead Blankets &c &c things he Bought

---

[14] Tracy to Friend, 23–28 September 1857, "From the Utah Expedition," *Commercial Advertiser* (Buffalo, N.Y.), 20 November 1857, 2/2.

[15] Smith, entry for 3 October 1857, Historian's Office Journal, LDS Archives. A confirming description of these negotiations appears in the log kept by the Nauvoo Legion's Brig. Gen. Hiram B. Clawson, entry for 3 October 1857, ibid.

[16] Wells, Taylor, and Smith to Young, 15 October 1857, LDS Archives.

[17] Wells, Taylor, and Smith to Young, 18 October 1857, ibid.

for Indian Trade had refused to sell them to us at 2 pm passed on to the City. Heber Kimball left with his Company for Salt Lake. The night is cold and stormy."[18] That night, Hickman killed Yates and buried him beneath the ashes of their Echo Canyon campfire. As Hickman later described the scene, "About this time all was still, and everybody supposed to be in their beds. No person was to be seen, when Col. [N. V.] Jones and two others, Hosea Stout and another man whose name I do not recollect, came to my campfire and asked if Yates was asleep. I told them he was, upon which his brains were knocked out with an ax."[19]

The enormity of Lieutenant Hickman's atrocity—the slaughter of an unarmed prisoner in his charge—is described most aptly in the comments on soldierly duty by Gen. William Tecumseh Sherman, often viewed as one of the country's most ruthless soldiers. In 1881 Sherman wrote about the behavior of Private Mason of the U.S. Army, who was then under arrest for trying to kill his helpless civilian prisoner Charles Guiteau, the assassin of President James Garfield. Even though Sherman believed that Guiteau had "committed the greatest crime of modern times and deserves to be tortured, torn limb from limb," he argued that Private Mason's attack was "the unsoldierlike conduct of trying to kill a prisoner over whom he was about to be placed on guard. . . . [T]he soldier's duty is to protect him till trial, convicted and executed in the manner prescribed by law. . . . [T]his distinguishes civilization from Barbarism."[20]

Within days, rumors of Richard E. Yates's fate had drifted into both Salt Lake City and the Utah Expedition. A week later, presumably aware of Yates's death, Brigham Young's concern was the disposition of his property rather than a gubernatorial inquiry into his murder: "Yates & partner have sold them [the army] beef oxen, ammunition &c therefore take and keep what you can find belonging to them, keeping an accurate account of the same. Use the blankets and clothing as well as beef and other supplies as needed for the boys, also keeping an accurate account of each issue."[21] At year end corre-

[18] William C. Staines, Diary, 18 October 1857, photocopy, ibid.

[19] Hickman, *Brigham's Destroying Angel*, 125.

[20] Sherman to Mrs. C. Auguster Hooper, 13 October 1881, text in Stuart Lutz Historic Documents, Inc., Catalogue of July 2006, Item # 171.

[21] Young to Grant, Burton, and Robison, 26 October 1857, Nauvoo Legion (Utah). Adjt. Gen. Record 1851–1870, p. 151, LDS Archives. One Mormon historian argues that Young's focus on accounting implied an intent to reimburse, an assumption not necessarily warranted, as with the meticulous records of atrocity victims' property kept by authorities in wartime Germany and Cambodia during the early 1940s and 1970s, respectively. Turley to MacKinnon, e-mail message, 29 January 2007. Turley also argues that it is unknown whether Young was aware of Yates's death on 26 October, an unlikely case in view of the daily flow of messages between Wells and Young, both of whom had demonstrated an active interest in Yates.

spondent Albert G. Browne, Jr., sent a third-hand account of the Yates affair from Camp Scott to New York.

A. G. Browne, Jr., Dispatch, "Later from Utah," 3 January 1858, *New-York Daily Tribune*, 1 March 1858.

He [a returned captive from Salt Lake City, Pvt. Henry Feldman] confirms the suspicion that a most atrocious murder was committed by William A. Hickman, the chief Thug or Danite, on a mountaineer named Yates, in October. To the circumstances attending Yates's disappearance and probable death I have heretofore only distantly alluded, for I was unwilling to lay charges incapable of proof against a man who is already burdened with a greater variety of crimes than any villain mentioned in the *Causes Celébres*.[22]

Yates [illegible] a small post on Green River, [illegible] and lived by raising and trading cattle. When Col. Alexander's command crossed the river last September, Yates disposed to the army of some kegs of gunpowder which he was keeping for sale at his post. He also contracted to supply the [army] commissary with some beef cattle, and a few days afterward drove them up to the camp on Ham's Fork, and received in payment more than $1,000.[23] On his return to Green River a party of Mormons captured him, and conveyed him to Fort Bridger. From there he was taken to Salt Lake City, and after being confined for a few days was allowed to start eastward, accompanied by Hickman.[24] Since the day he started nothing has ever been heard of him except the report which is now brought by Feldmann [*sic*], that he was murdered and robbed by Hickman, as being a man who had forfeited his life to the Mormon god for the sin against the Church of the Latter-Day Saints of having sold gunpowder to the United States Army. It is said that Hickman acknowledges the murder, and has exhibited articles which are known to have been in the dead man's possession.

A year later an ancient Mormon pie vendor, a Welsh woman living in Springville, captivated Captain Tracy with tales of Utah murders, including that of Richard Yates:

I made further inquiry and asked the woman what she knew of her own observation of such things. Glancing around in a nervous manner, she replied . . . "and if I had time, Captain, I could tell you stories of such things that would

[22] *Les Causes célèbres,* an extensive collection of legal decisions in notorious cases compiled by eighteenth-century French lawyer François Gayot de Pitaval, was studied as much for its titillating tales as for its legal precedents.

[23] This amount of cash was essentially the same that Bill Hickman later claimed to have delivered to Brigham Young.

[24] From Charles Morehead it is clear that Yates had been in Salt Lake on business during September, but Browne errs in reporting that he was also there in October as a captive.

> make your hair stand on end in the daytime"—which were her exact words. "Then," said she, "there was Yates, that sold the regulars the powder at Green River, last fall, and afterwards tried to leave. He disappeared—'went up the pocket of the Lord,' we call it—and Bill Hickman—one of the 'Destroyers'—passed through this very town [Springville], wearing the overcoat of Yates and riding his bay pony." Thus the riddle of the man who left the command of [Captain] Marcy, on our return march from the expedition to Green River, was solved. There could be, as there really is, no further doubt as to his fate. Hickman, who was also at one time in our camp by Ham's Fork is noted as one of the most villainous and merciless of all the gang of "Destroying Angels" in their work of freeing themselves of enemies.[25]

And so the Yates murder—one of the Utah War's earliest atrocities—and speculation as to its accountabilities quickly passed into the conflict's folklore.

In 1871 the incident resurfaced with Bill Hickman's public admission of his role. In October a grand jury indicted Hickman, Brigham Young, D. H. Wells, and two other Legion officers—including Hosea Stout, its judge advocate—for murder. The text of this indictment has disappeared, together with much of the court record for the Yates case. Nonetheless, it is possible to piece together much of what happened from other sources. For example, on 31 October 1871, the recently established *Salt Lake Tribune* reported that "The morning [court] session was opened with the case of The People vs. Daniel H. Wells and others, pending an application for a writ of habeas corpus. The indictment is against Brigham Young, Sr., D. H. Wells, Hosea Stout, J. A. Young and William Hickman, and charges that 'on the 15th of November, 1857, in the county of Summit, Territory of Utah, the defendants then and there, with an ax in the hands of said Wm. Hickman, did feloniously and with intent to kill, beat, abuse and wound one Richard Yates, from which wounds he instantly died.' "[26] However, no trials followed from the indictments, for in 1872 the U.S. Supreme Court dismissed hundreds of verdicts and indictments in Utah as procedurally flawed, including those returned by the grand jury in the Yates case.[27]

Who then, if anyone, shares responsibility with Lt. Bill Hickman for Richard Yates's death? Through a book written with anti-Mormon editor

---

[25] Alter and Dwyer, eds., entry for 14 October 1858, "Journal of Captain Albert Tracy, 1858–1860," 45.

[26] "Case of Daniel H. Wells, Charged with Murder," *Salt Lake Tribune*, 31 October 1871, 3/1–2. Why the indictment specified 15 November 1857 as the date of death rather than a month earlier is unknown. Had the case gone to trial, this discrepancy could have been important. Summit County was the organizational successor to Green River County after Congress carved the northeastern "notch" from Utah Territory's borders in 1861.

[27] See *Clinton v. Englebrecht* (U.S. 80:434); Firmage and Mangrum, *Zion in the Courts*, 138, 144–47.

J. H. Beadle and published in 1872, Hickman argued that he had killed Yates on orders from Brigham Young delivered to him in Echo Canyon by his son Joseph A. Young. Hickman stated that after the killing he had personally delivered nearly one thousand dollars of Yates's gold to President Young in his office and had been denied his request for a share in these spoils. Hickman's book, written while in protective custody at Fort Douglas, is well known and readily accessible.[28] But relatively unexploited are two newspaper sources based on a Hickman interview and letters of 1871 and 1877, respectively, which straddled the appearance of *Brigham's Destroying Angel.* This material is worth considering because of its greater spontaneity and freedom from Beadle's editorial influence on Bill Hickman's side of the story. Also relevant are comments of two of Hickman's co-defendants, Joseph A. Young and D. H. Wells, as well as the principal first-hand (but not contemporaneous) challenge to Hickman's account offered by frontiersman and Legionnaire Daniel W. Jones. Taken together, these narratives provide a case study of conflicting accounts of homicide offered by participants of widely varying credibility and mixed motives. As such it is the incomplete stuff from which historical judgments necessarily emerge, including those about Utah's societal tone at the time of the Mountain Meadows massacre.

"Brigham Young's Janissary. Interview with Bill Hickman . . . ," *New York World,* 25 November 1871.

[From Our Own Correspondent.]

Salt Lake City, November 18.—Let the disbelievers in total depravity prepare to renounce that negative faith. Salt Lake is very quiet on the surface, but there is an undercurrent in this social stream equally turbid and fetid. There is, among both Mormons and Gentiles, a half-concealed restlessness that augurs ill. The issue of the approaching trials for murder here is the text for table talk, for street-corner comment, for secret closetings, and the first question asked by new-comers and interested miners.

Bill Hickman

confesses that the blood of ten men is upon his hands, and the "damned spot" will not "out."[29] I have just returned from Camp Douglas and a lengthy interview with this red-handed wretch. He is confined there under indictment for

[28] Hickman (with Beadle), *Brigham's Destroying Angel,* 122–27, 205–206. A substantial amount of material about Bill Hickman and his Utah War activities is available on the Internet at http://www.hickmansfamily.homestead.com. See also his sole biography, Hilton, *"Wild Bill" Hickman and the Mormon Frontier.*

[29] A passage from Shakespeare's *Macbeth* (act 5, scene 1), with Lady Macbeth imagining the murdered king's blood on her hands: "Out, damned spot! out, I say!"

murder, and as the "State's evidence" against Brigham Young, [Salt Lake City] Mayor Wells, [Hosea] Stout, and Kimball,[30] all under indictment for murder—the first two as commanding the murders which Hickman declares that the two latter with himself and others committed. He is writing a book of his life and deeds and what he claims to know of others. It ought to be soup for readers of the most piratical relish. He is 56 years old; a Kentuckian by birth; not tall, but broad, square shouldered and heavy limbed. His head is half covered with a ragged, uncombed crop of hair that seems to have had drought to contend with all its life. His frontal developments are not bad—nature started him in life with an average outfitting for respectability and usefulness, but his face is the clearly written commentary of ancient dissipation revised and enlarged each year down to date. Rum and lechery have there left their tracks. He looks swinish in his habits of person—as foul in body as vile in heart. This walking sprout of poison upas [*sic*] grew up in Missouri, was a clerk, then school teacher, and calls the law his profession. May the law render unto him good for evil and lead him to justice, though he abandoned law! He joined the Mormons in Missouri, followed them to Nauvoo, and came here in 1849.

Correspondent—Were you a member of the band of Mormons called Danites, or Destroying Angels?

Hickman—There never was such a band here with the duty laid on them of cutting off all persons supposed to be unnecessary to the peace and happiness of the Mormon community; but Brigham had his "confidential men," of whom I was one. And whenever any suspicious-looking or acting character appeared in our midst, the president would send for me, or one of the others—Rockwell, Burton, Kimball, and so on—and say, "Hickman, take care of that man;" and he was straightway "cared for," the "job" reported on and approved. These "confidential men" acted separately, and under strict orders to tell no man; so that I have full knowledge of only those crimes in which I took a direct part.[31]

C.—Will you tell me the story of the Yates murder, for which you and the others are indicted?

H.—Yates was a man whom I had known in Missouri, and who brought from St. Louis several thousand dollars worth of arms, ammunition, &c., and halted in the Green River country in 1857 to trade with the Indians. I was at his place frequently, and travelled with him some. Brigham tried to buy his powder, but he refused to sell it, as it would spoil his traffic with the Indians, unless Brigham would buy his whole outfit. This he declined to do. Not

[30] Presumably this was William H. Kimball, who in 1857 was a Legion brigadier, a son of First Counselor Heber C. Kimball, and one of Brigham Young's trusted agents. It is not clear why his name was included.

[31] The descriptor "b'hoys," or "boys" was used more frequently in Utah than "confidential men," which smacks of the newspaper's New York focus.

long afterwards Brigham learned that Yates had sold his powder to the United States troops in that region. I was then commissioned to bring the man into town before Brigham, who was also Governor of the Territory; but on my way in with him I was met by a son of Brigham's, who said his father didn't want that fellow brought to the city, but wished him "taken care of." I then turned back to the mouth of Echo canyon, where one Jones had a camp.[32] There, in the night, while Yates was asleep on the ground, we killed him by knocking out his brains, dug a trench beside him and buried him; we scraped the camp fire on to the fresh dirt to conceal it. We took some $600 and a gold watch from his body. I and one of my men brought the spoils in to Brigham and laid them on his table with the remark that we had had a pretty hard night of it and would like a little of the money to have a little spree with. He replied that the money must go to pay the expenses of the war, and that after such deeds we must keep our heads clear.

C.—Gossip says that you admit the commission of some fifty or sixty murders; is it true?

H.—No; there are not more than eight or ten. I fell out with Brigham some twelve years ago, in consequence of his dislike to General Connor, then in command of Camp Douglas here, and of my refusal to comply with his request to "take care of" the general.[33] I thought him a first-rate man. Since then I have done none of that class of work for Brigham.

C.—Where have you been living?

H.—My home is forty miles south of the city. I have not dared live in the city for the last four years, though my wife is in town now. I have lived in plurality, but only my first wife is living.

C.—Who was Morris?

H.—He was founder of the apostate faction called Morrisites. He claimed to have a revelation for the overthrow of Brigham, and was murdered by one [Robert Taylor] Burton, who is now South [in-transit to St. George] with Brigham.[34]

I have gathered and given this story because Hickman's testimony caused the indictments to be found, and is the main reliance for the trials. It is revolt-

[32] This could be a reference to either of two Legionnaires in the area—Col. N. V. Jones or Pvt. Daniel W. Jones. Hickman knew both men; he probably meant the former.

[33] Notwithstanding the intense Young-Connor enmity, there is no evidence that Brigham Young ever ordered Hickman to assassinate General Connor. It is clear that Hickman's employment with Connor created tensions between him and Young, as did Hickman's escalating alcoholism and violence. See, for example, Young to Hickman, 22 January 1868, and Hickman to Young, 15 September 1868, both LDS Archives.

[34] Burton, acting temporarily as the sheriff of Great Salt Lake County and leader of a large, heavily armed posse, allegedly shot and killed a woman in 1862 in connection with a siege of Joseph Morris's unruly schismatic group. Morris, his wife, and several others also died. This violent chain of events became known in Utah history as the "Morrisite War." Burton was tried and acquitted. See Godfrey, "Did the Bishop Murder the Morrisite Mrs. Bowman?" unpublished paper at May 1999 annual meeting of Mormon History Association, Ogden.

ing in the extreme; and if true would make him a fit consort for the janissaries of Turkey—committing a half score of murders for no gain or interest of his own, but to gratify the spirit of prejudice or revenge in another. I wish to give it no indorsement by relating it. I have set down nothing he did not utter. But I have told you how he looks; and as I have much faith in looks please don't ask me to say I believe this tale of total depravity. He thinks that if Young says fight, the great body of the people are armed and will fight bitterly.

Another side of the Yates affair is that Hickman and a companion were travelling on horseback with Yates when H. said to his companion, "That man Yates was the cause of getting my brother into prison in Missouri, and I wouldn't have him get away." The companion halted for a time, and when he again came up with Hickman Yates was missing.

JOSEPH A. YOUNG, INTERVIEW, "THE WAR ON POLYGAMY," *NEW-YORK TRIBUNE*, 7 OCTOBER 1871, 1/5–6.

With a view of ascertaining the line of defense which the Mormons propose to adopt, your correspondent had brief interviews with several leading men of the Church, and one of special importance with Joseph A. Young, Brigham's oldest son. The following paragraphs contain the results of this conversation, as well as hints from all sources regarding the defense intended by the leaders; but it must not be forgotten in reading them that they present the case only from the Mormon point of view. In the interview with Joseph Young, your correspondent was informed that he (Joseph) together with his father and the other persons whose names I mentioned in my letter of yesterday, were hourly anticipating arrest on a charge of murder, for which, as they had been informed, they had been or were to be indicted. I asked Joseph if he knew anything about the killing of Yates in 1857 by Hickman who had stated that he killed Yates in response to an order from Brigham Young, which order was communicated by Joseph. He replied that his recollection of the affair was that on one occasion in the Fall of 1857, when some Mormon soldiers were guarding the Weber cañon, east of Salt Lake, for the purpose of intercepting Jo. Johnson's [*sic*] army sent by Secretary of War Floyd, he was directed by his father to carry a bundle of dispatches to Gen. D. H. Wells, the commander of the Mormon force;[35] on his way out he met Bill Hickman, who informed him that he had certain deserters from Johnson's army and other prisoners whom he was carrying to Salt Lake, among whom was one Yates, who had been caught as a spy; and that afterward Hickman boasted that he had killed Yates before reaching the city. Joseph expressed it as his opinion that it would be difficult to find any jury of 12 men, however carefully picked, or however unfriendly in character, who would convict any per-

[35] Joseph A. Young's assignment as a courier to Echo Canyon is mentioned in Young to Wells, Taylor, and Smith, 17 October 1857, LDS Archives.

son of the smallest offense on the unsupported testimony of the notorious outlaw Hickman. He further remarked that all the persons who had been mentioned as having been indicted, were holding themselves in readiness for arrest, some of them at no little inconvenience, as they did not propose to be accused of skulking or of seeking to evade the service of any writ, however absurd or illegal. Such, he said, he believed to be the feeling of all whom rumor had connected with the labors of the Grand Jury.

I have taken some pains to find out something about the man Yates, who was killed by Hickman. It appears that he was a mountaineer, who made a living by hunting and by trading with the Indians. The Mormons looked upon him as by no means an unfriendly person, and gave him free admission to their camps when stationed at Weber to intercept the United States forces. On one occasion, as I am informed by Daniel H. Wells, who was the commander of the Mormon militia, one of his officers informed him that Yates was in camp seeking to sell some gunpowder and Indian goods. Wells gave orders that the powder be purchased, but declined to take the Indian trinkets. Yates refused to sell a portion and not the whole of his merchandise, and left the camp in displeasure. It was subsequently learned through a deserter that Yates took the goods to Johnson's army and disposed of them, at the same time giving full information as to the number and position of the Mormon troops.[36] Yates was afterward captured as a spy and forwarded in care of Hickman to Salt Lake, which locality it is believed he never reached.

In view of the fact that the killing of Yates under such circumstances as I have detailed, might be construed as a necessary war measure, rather than as an unprovoked and brutal murder, the question is asked, does not the proclamation of James Buchanan, under date of April 6, 1858, cover the offense, and render it impossible for an indictment to lie against the offenders? Undoubtedly the distinguished attorneys who have been retained for the defense of Brigham Young and his associates, will argue that all crimes growing out of what was known as the "Mormon Rebellion," were pardoned by the President of the United States.

Nearly simultaneous to Bill Hickman's and Joseph A. Young's interviews with the New York *World* and *Tribune*, Daniel H. Wells granted a long interview in October 1871 to George Alfred Townsend—one of the most famous of the young former Civil War correspondents. Townsend was in Salt Lake City on assignment for the Cincinnati *Commercial*. Wells was at the time mayor of Salt Lake City; he was also still commanding general of the Nauvoo Legion and Brigham Young's second counselor in the First Presidency. Notwithstanding these senior roles, he was a worthy to whom the irreverent *Salt Lake Tri-*

[36] This, of course, was precisely the type of intelligence that had been gathered for the Mormon side by Samuel W. Richards, John M. Bernhisel, and others.

bune felt free to refer as "the One-Eyed Pirate of the Wasatch," a liberty indicating that some things had changed in Utah Territory since 1857.[37] Wells was one of the few principals in the Yates case to speak of the affair publicly and out of court.

Other than the perspective that it provides for understanding the Yates case, the prime significance of Wells's session with Townsend is the fact that it constitutes the general's only known public discussion of the Utah War, a near-silence illustrative of certain aspects of the Utah War's challenging historiography. Like Hickman, Wells gave his interview during the emotional, exciting period surrounding his indictment. In evaluating his comments, one should consider that Wells—like Joseph A. Young—realized that Hickman was writing a book, although neither man was yet aware of Hickman's pending interview with the New York *World*. In some respects, then, the Wells and Joseph A. Young interviews took on the form of preemptive strikes against Hickman's credibility and presumably were intended for that purpose. Also relevant is Townsend's ill-defined but close relationship with William Henry Hooper, Utah's then–congressional delegate as well as a fellow native of Maryland's eastern shore.[38]

George A. Townsend, Dispatch, "Interview with the Mayor of Salt Lake," Cincinnati *Commercial*, 25 October 1871.

> . . . this celebrated Mormon warrior, the right-bower of Brigham Young, the Lieutenant General of the great Nauvoo Legion, numbering five thousand men, the commander of the Utah forces in the Sidney Johnston war, and the Fouchet[39] of Salt Lake City, and terror of the criminals there, was ushered into my presence.
>
> I beheld a tall, long-nosed, sharp-browed man, with gray hair, a tuft of gray whiskers on his chin and jaws, a bluish pair of eyes, one of them oblique and not prepossessing, and a bent back, the result of age and unrelieved labor. He would have been several inches over six feet high had he not stooped, but eminent service in the Mormon Church is of almost monastic rigor upon one so distinguished, and this old man had a way of winking which suggested eyes and head worn out in the Secretaryship of that mighty energy, "Uncle

[37] For an example of the newspaper's nickname for Wells, see "Blood-Atoners Testify," *Salt Lake Tribune*, 6 September 1876.

[38] Townsend later published his long dispatches to the *Commercial* from Salt Lake City in book form at Hooper's urging, and Townsend prefaced this collection with a long letter to Hooper that closely resembles a dedication for the book. See Townsend, *The Mormon Trials at Salt Lake City*, 25–26.

[39] Joseph Fouchet (or Fouché) served as Napoleon's minister of police. Fouchet's network of informants was so extensive that he sometimes boasted, "Whenever three men speak together in Paris, two of them are mine."

Brigham," while his clothing was poor and worn, and he talked with gentleness, almost like meekness. The Mormons have admonished me that, although he is a natural fire-eater and a military commander by instinct, he has latterly been a uniform counselor for peace and submission, and has helped to sway Brigham Young to wise advices.

As I never "interview" people off their guard, I took up a quire of paper and a pen, and made notes as the answers came to my questions. . . .

"Who is Bill Hickman?"

"He is a Missouri desperado, who attached himself to our Church many years ago, and was turned out of it several years since. We have had him twice in custody for murder, and once, at least, the United States military authorities have taken him out of our hands. By occupation he is a cattle-stealer. He is the terror of the territory, and children are frightened at the mention of his name. Yet his evidence is admitted to prejudice respectable men in the estimation of their countrymen."

"Who arrested him?"

"One Gibson, one of the numerous deputy Marshals who have been sworn in from the lowest orders of society to overawe us. Gibson has been with Bill Hickman all summer, and there was probably an agreement between them."

"What does Hickman look like?"

"He is a thick-set, burly, sandy man with dyed beard, unable to look you in the eye. We took him up for killing a Mexican who had married his wife. He beat and deserted the woman, and she was divorced from him. He shot the Mexican dead in his doorway, and galloped off. Now, I am told, he is having his life written and embellished for sale. Since his incarceration he has taken to wearing broadcloth."[40]

"Who was Yates, the man he swears he killed at the suggestion of yourself and others?"

"Yates was a trader of some sort whom Hickman brought to my camp in the Mormon war with a shackle on his heel. I ordered him released, and he wanted to go to Salt Lake, which was accorded him. He disappeared with Hichman [*sic*] and was never seen again. Hichman [*sic*] now swears that I said he was a scoundrel, and ought to be dead. Also that Joseph Young said he deserved death. What evidence to indict men of our age and position! I have no recollection whatever of the circumstances. They transpired fourteen years ago. Drown and Arnold were two other men whom Hickman confesses to have killed, and he implicates us there also."[41]

Nearly twenty years after Bill Hickman's published admission appeared, Daniel W. Jones—a Nauvoo Legion infantryman bivouacked near Echo

[40] Wells's implication here is that Beadle and perhaps others were paying Hickman.

[41] The best summary of the circumstances, accusations, and legal proceedings associated with the 1859 murders of Charles M. Drown and Josiah Arnold is Brooks, ed., *On the Mormon Frontier*, 2:702n64.

Canyon during October 1857—provided a quite different perspective on the Yates affair in a memoir titled *Forty Years Among the Indians*. As Jones saw things, Yates was a more sympathetic figure than the loud-mouthed inebriate of 1856 described by J. Robert Brown. According to Jones, Hickman killed Yates solely on his own initiative; Brigham Young was uninvolved, and Hickman acted primarily out of lust for Yates's money.

At the time of the Utah War, Jones was a Mormon convert, Mexican War veteran, and highly experienced frontiersman who had participated in the harrowing 1856 rescue of the Willie and Martin handcart companies. Although a saddler by trade, when called up for Nauvoo Legion service Jones was working as a mail carrier with the Y. X. Carrying Company, a role he shared with Hickman. Writing in 1890, largely from memory, Jones vowed "to speak the truth without malice toward anyone."

Jones, 1890 Rebuttal, Excerpts from *Forty Years Among the Indians*, 129–30.

There is one circumstance connected with my experience while in Echo Canyon [Nauvoo Legion] service which I wish to put on record—the killing of Yates by Bill Hickman. This Mr. Yates was a personal friend of mine, a kind hearted, liberal man of whom I had received many kindnesses, and his being murdered did not agree with my feelings, but I knew of no way to mend the matter, for I knew nothing of the killing till he was buried.

I was camped with a small party about four miles west of the Weber valley and ten or twelve miles from Echo. One very cold morning about sunrise, Hickman and two others came to my camp. They seemed almost frozen, shaking and trembling in an unusual manner. Hickman asked me if I had any whisky. I told him I had not. He then asked if we had coffee. I replied that we had. "Then make us a good strong cup." While the coffee was being made, he took me outside and asked me if I knew Yates. I told him I did. "Well, we have just buried him."

He then told about Yates being taken prisoner for tampering with Indians. And after talking quite excitedly, he said, "We have got [done] away with him. What do you think the Old Boss," (meaning Brigham) "will say?"

Now if Yates had been killed as Hickman related in his book he would not have manifested so much interest in what President Young would say. He tried hard to draw an approval from me of what he had done. I told him I knew nothing about such modes and did not know what Brother Young would say about it.

Hickman killed Yates for his money and horse the same as any other thief and murderer would have done, and then excused himself by telling that he was counseled to do these things. I know positively that Governor Young's

> orders were to avoid bloodshed in every way possible.[42] I was continually acting and around in places and under circumstances that gave me the best of opportunities to know.

The dismissal of Hickman's accusations by Joseph A. Young, Daniel H. Wells, and Daniel W. Jones as the non-credible charges of an excommunicated, self-confessed murderer of no moral standing—a self-aggrandizing freelancer rather than an honorable soldier acting on orders—became the standard reaction of the Mormon side. Over the decades some non-Mormons too were understandably troubled by Bill Hickman's clearly sordid behavior. Perhaps the New York *World*'s Salt Lake City correspondent put it most colorfully in describing Hickman's forthcoming book as "soup for readers of the most piratical relish." In a sense it was a dismissiveness similar to that used later to distance the church's and Legion's hierarchy in Salt Lake City from the actions and even confessions of the troops at Mountain Meadows, especially those of the excommunicated and convicted Maj. John D. Lee. But the 1871 attack on Hickman's credibility about the events of 1857—an interesting somewhat ex post facto argument—is complicated if not clouded by the fact that Hickman was clearly in good standing with Brigham Young as the Utah War began. As indicated in an earlier chapter, it was Brigham Young who during 1857 used Hickman to spy on the Ambrose-Betts and Tobin-Peltro parties, commissioned him as a Legion officer, nominated him to Buchanan and Congress as Utah's U.S. attorney, called him to an active role with the Y. X. Carrying Company, used him to impugn Judge Drummond's character with newspaper editors, and offered to pay Hickman's personal debts. When Bill Hickman killed Richard Yates, if not later, he was one of Young's most trusted, frequently used agents.

Eaten Away by the Crows: The Lynching of Private Clark

Richard Yates's death was not the only Utah War–related murder in northeastern Utah during October 1857. Precisely how many such killings took place will never be known, but there is the verifiable case of Pvt. George W. Clark of the Tenth U.S. Infantry's Company I. On 9 October 1857 Clark took stock of his future, stole an army mule, and disappeared into the mountains

[42] Jones was presumably unaware of the change in Young's orders about lethal force at about the time of the Yates murder, when he feared that the Utah Expedition would move west of Fort Bridger, or in 1890 was serving up the traditional view of the Utah War as "bloodless."

with his rifle, as had dozens of other deserters. It was a crucial time. That evening Captain Marcy's battalion returned to camp with Richard Yates's stock of gunpowder. Colonel Alexander had announced that the next day he would lead the Utah Expedition from Hams Fork to Salt Lake City via Bear River, Soda Springs, and the looping northern route in order to bypass Echo Canyon, which the Nauvoo Legion was defending. Private Clark had had enough and seized his opportunity.

When a federal dragoon patrol found Clark near Smiths Fork of the Green River almost five months later, he was frozen with his eyes and most of his face gone— ravaged by the crows as he hung from a tree limb. Also missing were Clark's army mule and weapon, one of the new .58 caliber rifled models with a special rear sight. First news of this atrocity traveled to the outside world through an unidentified stringer of the *Cincinnati Enquirer,* who stuffed a breathless dispatch into the mail leaving Camp Scott on 1 March 1858, without even knowing the victim's identity. The range and inaccuracy of the correspondent's speculation as to who the victim was (Bill Hickman's brother, Dr. George W. Hickman), who might have conducted this execution (mountaineers), and their motive (vengeance against Bill Hickman) reveals as much about the climate of violence in the Green River district as it does about Hickman's local reputation.[43]

Four days later the *New York Times*'s "A. B. C." submitted a more detailed and accurate account written by David A. Burr, the knowledgeable non-Mormon justice of the peace for Green River County who had empanelled the coroner's jury in the Clark case. After an account of Clark's desertion and a gruesome description of his corpse, Burr reported the jury's findings:

> "He came to his death by hanging by the neck until life was extinct." The Coroner agreed with the verdict of the Jury, adding further that he came to his death by the hands of persons unknown. The probability is, that the deserter (who had stolen a mule on starting) was endeavoring to make his way to Fort Supply (a Mormon village) when he was met by a party of Mormons, who, taking him to be [a] spy, hung him. The spot where he was found is about 30 miles from Ham's Fork and about 16 miles from here.[44]

Who killed Private Clark? Notwithstanding Burr's speculation that the culprits were "a party of Mormons," it is not now possible to determine

[43] Anonymous [probably W. J. McCormick], dispatch of 1 March 1858, "Murder of Dr. G. W. Hickman," *Cincinnati Enquirer,* reprinted in *New-York Daily Tribune,* 16 April 1858, 6; also available at http://www.hickmanfamily.homestead.com/files/murderGWH.htm (accessed 12 April 2001).

[44] "A. B. C." [David A. Burr], dispatch of 5 March 1858, "From the Utah Army," *New York Times,* 19 May 1858, 1/1–2.

responsibility. Because of the Mormon-federal tensions in the region, the fact that the Legion was patrolling Smiths Fork, and common Mormon rhetoric about hangings, it is easy to accuse General Wells's troops. Yet both sides threatened lynchings, and it is significant that no reference to this incident—unlike that involving Yates—appeared in Legion reports. Furthermore Brigham Young was then actively engaged in efforts to encourage rather than frighten military deserters like Private Clark. As with the earlier cases of mistaken identity leading to the Santa Clara attack on the Tobin-Peltro party and Duff Potter's unintended murder in Springville, it is as likely that Private Clark fell victim to vengeful mountaineers as to the Nauvoo Legion. The Cincinnati *Enquirer*'s reporter mistook Clark for Bill Hickman's wandering brother, and mountaineers may also have done so.

We'll Hang Him Yet: Other Threats in the Green River District

That Lt. Bill Hickman relished his role as Richard Yates's executioner—self-appointed or otherwise—is clear from the narrative of another prisoner thrust into his charge at Echo Canyon a month after he murdered Yates there. William Clark, a young discharged teamster, had been captured by the Nauvoo Legion near Fort Bridger in mid-November as he headed for California. Decades after his frightening encounter with Hickman, Clark wrote an account of ominous banter between them. Hickman said of U.S. Indian agent Garland Hurt, who in September 1857 had fled his Spanish Fork post just ahead of the Nauvoo Legion, "I'd like to get in reach of him with my old rifle he wouldn't tell any more tales, and I'll get him yet."[45]

It is not surprising that on 2 November 1857, three days after the Nauvoo Legion ran off mountaineers' cattle at Green River, Wells reported to Young, "Bro Lewis Robison has been to see the mountaineers. They are all scared and very willingly agreed to get out of the way. Some are going in to the Platte and some into the Utah [Ute] Country to winter, with their stock."[46]

On 28 November 1857 Hiram F. Morrell, the federally appointed postmaster of Salt Lake City who had fled Utah the previous April and was returning under the army's protection, wrote to his brother in New Jersey from his refuge

[45] William Clark, "A Trip Across the Plains in 1857," 201.

[46] Wells to Young, 2 November 1857, LDS Archives. Fear of the Legion and its atrocities rapidly spread north and created apprehension even among the tough mountaineers and traders of Montana's isolated valleys.

at Camp Scott. Without providing details, Morrell described what he considered his own close call: "I [recently] received a personal message from Gov. Young's son, through a released prisoner, as follows: 'Tell Morrell, damn him, that we came within one day of catching him and we'll hang him yet;' which was true."[47]

As perhaps the most-hated non-Mormon in Utah, Morrell was hardly an unbiased source on Mormon affairs.[48] But his letter is consistent with the contemporaneous apprehensions of W. M. F. Magraw, Morrell's unsavory Camp Scott mess-mate. Magraw had abandoned his position as a superintendent of the Pacific Wagon Road project in October 1857 after threatening Mormons James Gemmell and Asa S. Hawley (and possibly Porter Rockwell). By the end of 1857, Magraw was an infantry captain in the Utah Expedition's Battalion of U.S. Volunteers, a safe haven which permitted him to escape Yates's fate.[49] Magraw impressed Morrell with his frequent insider references to President Buchanan, and it is known that he described Mormon threats against him to Buchanan directly. From the Nauvoo Legion's records it is clear that it was indeed targeting Magraw and his livestock much as with Richard Yates.[50] During Maj. Lot Smith's early October raid on army supply trains, he told a federal wagonmaster that "they would catch & kill" Magraw and that "there was a special party who had gone out to capture Magraw dead or alive."[51] The Nauvoo Legion's violent plans for Magraw during the fall of 1857 may have arisen as much from a desire to reciprocate Magraw's own threatening behavior as from a proclivity for what Will Bagley has called "plunder."[52]

---

[47] Morrell to brother, 28 November 1857, *Daily Enquirer* (Cincinnati), 22 January 1858, 1/6. See also Whall, The *Salt Lake City Post Office, 1849–1869*, 112. The governor's son was probably Joseph A. Young.

[48] For reactions in early 1857 to Morrell's appointment as Salt Lake City's postmaster, see Thomas, comp., "Elias Smith's Journal," entry for 20 January 1857, and Elias Smith to George A. Smith, 7 February 1857, George A. Smith Papers, LDS Church Archives.

[49] For Magraw's threats and violent actions against Mormons, see MacKinnon, "Unquestionably Authentic and Correct in Every Detail," 333n24; Asa S. Hawley, Autobiography, LDS Archives.

[50] MacKinnon, "The Buchanan Spoils System and the Utah Expedition," 127–50; Magraw to President James Buchanan, 2 January 1858, James Buchanan Papers, Historical Society of Pennsylvania, Philadelphia. Discussion of a plan for Hickman to descend on Magraw's wagon-road party and its animals appears in Hickman, *Brigham's Destroying Angel*, 118.

[51] Lot Smith quoted in David A. Burr to David H. Burr, 7 and 10 October 1857, Burr Papers, Krock Library, Cornell University. Burr also expressed fears for his own safety and that of Morrell, who was then traveling alone near South Pass in an attempt to reach the army.

[52] Bagley devotes an entire chapter ("Plunder") to discussion of the looting—clothes, livestock, wagons, carriages, cash, jewelry, and household goods—that followed the Mountain Meadows massacre. Bagley, *Blood of the Prophets*, 171–87. This behavior—present in all of the atrocities discussed in this chapter (including the pre-war Santa Clara ambush and Parrish-Potter murders)—reflects not only the hardscrabble life of many Utahns but a problematic willingness to relieve non-Mormon emigrants and departing apostates of their property and possessions.

A Fine Looking Party of Men: Assassination of the Aiken Party

The next atrocity case to consider is that of the Aiken party, six well-outfitted, cash-flush civilians from California who entered Utah by the northern route during late October 1857. They mistakenly assumed that the Utah Expedition had already occupied Salt Lake City. Their intent in traveling to Utah is mysterious. Unable to provide a credible explanation for their journey other than tourism, the Mormons immediately concluded that the six were army spies—the view of Richard Yates earlier in October—or that they intended to capitalize on the army's presence in Utah by operating a gambling den of the type that indeed later sprang up adjacent to Fort Bridger and Camp Floyd. The latter assumption may well have been accurate given the very large amount of cash carried by the party. As with Ambrose and Betts a year before them, the Aikens' timing was disastrous in terms of the circumstances awaiting them in Utah. Suspicious Nauvoo Legion officers arrested them near what is now Brigham City and confined the six under house arrest in a Salt Lake City hotel. On about 20 November authorities released the party without trial. Two members remained in Salt Lake City and Lehi to winter over, and the other four men headed back to California by the southern route escorted by Capt. Porter Rockwell and three other men. On the night of 25–26 November these four members of the Aiken party were shot and bludgeoned to death while camped along the Sevier River twenty-five miles south of Nephi. The victims lost not only their lives but cash, weapons, horses, silver-studded saddles, and even their clothes. Later, in 1858, Bill Hickman dispatched a fifth member of the party with a shotgun blast to the head; the sixth man disappeared without leaving a record of his fate.

As with earlier violent incidents, the details of the Aiken party's fate are elusive, but a combination of Utah folklore and trial testimony elicited decades later produced familiar tales of dispatched instructions from Brigham Young, a disregarded plea to the governor from one of the victims, and incompetent but ultimately successful Nauvoo Legion execution squads allegedly led by first Capt. Porter Rockwell and then Lt. Bill Hickman.

With David L. Bigler's recent and comprehensive study, there is no need to probe here the sordid details of the Aiken party killings.[53] However, it is

[53] Bigler, "The Aiken Party Executions," 451–70. See also Schindler, *Orrin Porter Rockwell*, 268–81 and "J. J. G." [John I. Ginn] to Editor Kirk Anderson, 26 March 1859, *Valley Tan* (Salt Lake City), 26 April 1859 reprinted for the first time in MacKinnon, "'Unquestionably Authentic and Correct in Every Detail,'" 334–35. An account of these murders—apparently written by Beadle rather than Hickman—appears in Appendix F to Hickman, *Brigham's Destroying Angel*, 206–11.

important to note the pattern of which they were part. In terms of the chain of events, locale, alleged perpetrators, and the outcomes, the Aiken killings take on a character resembling many aspects of the pre-war Ambrose-Betts affair and Parrish-Potter murders as well as the wartime Yates murder, Clark lynching, and Mountain Meadows massacre. Aside from the violence, perhaps the most striking aspect of the Aiken party atrocities was the familiar looting pattern—a telltale sign of military indiscipline. As with the clothing of Richard E. Yates and the victims at Mountain Meadows, bullet-punctured garments previously worn by members of the Aiken party soon appeared on the backs of citizens near Nephi.

In 1877 a grand jury indicted Porter Rockwell and Sylvanus Collett, presumably a Nauvoo Legion private on detached duty from Fort Limhi, for the murders. Rockwell was awaiting trial when he died in an alcoholic haze in 1878. Collett was later tried and acquitted on the basis of what Bigler considers perjured testimony. Bigler's summary conclusion is that the "circumstantial evidence leaves no doubt in my mind that an authority at Great Salt Lake made a considered decision to allow two of the [Aiken] men to remain at large over the winter and kill the other four. Such an authority could only have been Brigham Young."[54]

The Assassination of Henry Forbes: A Familiar Pattern

In January 1858 Henry Forbes, an armed and well-mounted civilian en route to his home in Illinois, entered Utah from California and, like the Aikens two months earlier, ran afoul of Mormon suspicions and the travel restrictions imposed by martial law. Although not arrested or accused of misconduct, Forbes stopped in Springville and attempted to obtain a pass by which to exit Utah. On 24 January Forbes was assassinated on the road between Springville and Provo after an unsuccessful attempt to flee to Fort Bridger. His distinctive horse and revolvers—originally described as stolen by Indians—were later seen in the possession of James Parshall Terry, a Nauvoo Legion cavalry officer who served with Maj. Lot Smith and the man from whom Forbes had rented a room in Springville. Village speculation attributed the atrocity to two men who were privates in the Legion's Peteetneet Military District commanded by Brig. Gen. Aaron Johnson, bishop of Springville:

[54] Bigler to MacKinnon, e-mail message, 19 June 2006.

Wilber J. Earl, an infantryman who was a member of the bishop's council as well as a city alderman; and cavalryman Sanford Fuller. Notwithstanding these rumors, there was no inquiry into Forbes's murder by the overlapping leadership of the civil community and Nauvoo Legion, and so Earl and Fuller were never charged. Both men were later implicated but not tried in the subsequent investigation of the pre-war Parrish-Potter murders.[55]

Explaining Violence: Gubernatorial Language, Leadership, and Example

How does one explain this Utah War violence in Green River County, near Springville in Utah County, and near Nephi in Juab County? I am not persuaded by the argument that what was at work here was simply a matter of frontier violence common throughout the American West.[56] However, there were at least three other contextual factors worth considering, all peculiar to Utah rather than to the frontier generally:

1. the graphic, unmistakable example of the Ambrose-Betts (Santa Clara) affair and Parrish-Potter murders;
2. the impact of long conflict between the Salt Lake hierarchy and the small group of non-Mormon mountaineers of the sparsely populated Green River district; and
3. the societal tone that Brigham Young as a leader established through his communications with church and military subordinates.

The negative example set by Young's role in the Ambrose-Betts affair and Parrish-Potter murders—leader-stimulated violence that was neither investigated nor punished—has been discussed in an earlier chapter. With respect

[55] Polly Aird to MacKinnon, e-mail message, 2 July 2007; "Discharge of the Grand Jury," *Valley Tan,* 5 April 1859, 2/5.

[56] There is, of course, a plethora of monographs and journal articles about frontier violence in the American West of the nineteenth century. For a creative and relatively recent panel discussion of this subject by a group of non-Mormon and Mormon scholars focusing on its Mormon-Utah aspects, see "Violence on the Mormon Frontier: Fact or Fiction?" comments by Polly Aird, Will Bagley, Edward Leo Lyman, D. Michael Quinn, and William Shepard, 11 August 2001, at 2001 Sunstone Symposium in Salt Lake City, audiotape available through Sunstone Foundation. More recent exploration of this subject as it relates primarily to the Mountain Meadows massacre may be found in the work of two leading Mormon lawyer-historians: Richard E. Turley, Jr., "The Mountain Meadows Massacre and the American Culture of Extralegal Violence," unpublished paper presented 10 October 2003 at Western History Association annual conference in Fort Worth (copy in author's possession); Robert H. Briggs, review of Bagley, *Blood of the Prophets,* downloaded 17 November 2005 from www.leigh.org/familytrees/revedmundleigh/danielleighfamilytree/samuelleigh/reviewofbagleybook.pdf.

to Mormon-mountaineer animosities, as early as 1849 Brigham Young had commented about the region's most famous mountaineer: "I believe that Old [Jim] Bridger is death on us, and if he knew that 400,000 Indians were coming against us, and any man here to let us know, he would cut his throat."[57] This hostility continued throughout the 1850s, and was less a matter of religious conflict than of power and economic rivalry, although the Mormon perception of mountaineers as unprincipled, disheveled freebooters no doubt aggravated differences between the two groups. This is not the place for a detailed description of this conflict's origins. Suffice it to say that at stake was control over the vital, lucrative river ferries west of the Continental Divide operating on federal land to serve the main emigration routes to the Salt Lake Valley and Pacific Coast.[58]

With such longstanding Mormon-mountaineer animosity, it is not surprising that upon learning in January 1857 that Hiram F. Morrell had obtained a federal appointment to replace him as Salt Lake City's postmaster, Judge Elias Smith commented:

> It was rumored early in the morning that . . . a poor lousy fellow named Morelle, a mountaineer that has been roaming through the Indian country between here and Laramie for years had arrived from the East. . . . He has made some preparations to enter upon the duties of the [post] office by getting some *new clothes* in the place of the mountaineer dress of Buckskin Pants and Hunting shirt . . . in the absence of a whore-house, [he] will soon have to turn to his mountain haunts, among the Indians. We have got about sick enough of such impositions to resist them *lawfully*.[59]

As Richard Yates lay in his grave, Private Clark swung from a tree, the Aiken party and Henry Forbes approached their doom, and Messrs. Hurt, William Clark, Ginn, Bridger, Morrell, Magraw, Gemmell, Hawley, and a retreating community of Green River mountaineers contemplated their survival, what orders governed Nauvoo Legion operations in northeastern Utah?

---

[57] Brigham Young, Journal History, entry for 7 May 1849, 1–2, LDS Archives.

[58] For discussion and examples of these Mormon-mountaineer conflicts in the Fort Bridger–Green River district during the 1850s, see Gowans, "The Battle for Green River, 1850–1857," Keynote address at OCTA annual convention, 17 August 2005, summary available at http://www.cavnocta.org/slctalks.html (accessed 19 November 2006); Journal of William Butler, LDS Archives; Gowans and Campbell, *Fort Bridger*, 52–57; Hickman, *Brigham's Destroying Angel*, 93; Cummings to Young, 19 September 1853, LDS Church Archives; MacKinnon, "'Like Splitting a Man Up His Backbone,'" 100–24; Young to Douglas, 29 April 1854, LDS Church Archives and Stephen A. Douglas Papers; and Young to Bernhisel, 29 April 1854, LDS Archives.

[59] Thomas, comp., "Elias Smith's Journal," entry for 20 January 1857, and Elias Smith to George A. Smith, 7 February 1857, George A. Smith Papers, LDS Archives. Emphasis is Smith's.

Even more broadly, what was Brigham Young's command style and through what language did he communicate to the Legion his attitude and authorizations about violence, summary executions, and looting? At the heart of these crucial questions is the third contextual factor—the behavior and effectiveness of Brigham Young as a war leader. Here matters of language and communications were important, especially since Young later argued that the Mountain Meadows massacre was "a wanton, uncalled for affair, one that I never authorized or endorsed. Could we have had a telegraph line in our territory at that time that thing would never have happened."[60] Even more relevant than the imponderable of what Young was unable to communicate is the impact of what he actually said and wrote during 1857.

"If only he could have communicated with his troops!" This voice of what today is called "alternative history" brings to mind another of the persistent Utah War myths—that which speaks ruefully of the impact of broken communications and out-of-touch Legionnaires freelancing at long distance. Not well understood is the fact that unlike Mountain Meadows, the Yates murder took place virtually at Legion headquarters in Echo Canyon, less than one hundred miles east of Salt Lake City. On the day Bill Hickman killed Yates, they were within a few miles of the First Presidency's two counselors, Daniel H. Wells and Heber C. Kimball. The atrocity occurred at a time when written communications between Brigham Young and Mormon commanders flowed on a near-daily basis by courier, often with overnight delivery by his own son.[61] Through this means Governor Young often heaped advice on General Wells about not only strategic issues but in connection with mundane, tactical matters such as the construction of sentries' shelters, the proper use of spyglasses, the positioning of forward observers, and the most effective tone of voice and language to use to entice deserters from federal bivouacs. General Wells, in turn, encouraged such micromanagement by frequently seek-

[60] Josiah Rogerson, "The Guilt of John D. Lee," 18, in Mountain Meadows File, LDS Church Archives, quoted in Bagley, *Blood of the Prophets*, 331. LDS church president Hinckley referred to and reinforced this Brigham Young belief in his remarks dedicating the reconstructed memorial monument at Mountain Meadows on 11 September 1999; see John L. Hart, "Let the Book of the Past Be Closed," *Church News*, 18 September 1999, 3, 8–9. The hypothetical question of whether and how Young would have used a telegraph line in 1857 should be considered in the light of studies indicating that senior army commanders operating in Kansas during 1856 and American diplomats in Paris during the Franco-Prussian War of 1870 had surprising inhibitions about using the telegraph and trans-Atlantic cable, respectively. Mullis, "The Dispersal of the Topeka Legislature," 62–75; Nickles, "Telegraph Diplomats," 1–25.

[61] By contrast, at this time and during the winter of 1857–58, messages between the Utah Expedition and the War Department as well as army headquarters in New York were up to four months in transit.

ing counsel on equally minor issues as well as occasionally on broader, life-and-death matters.[62]

Notwithstanding Young's frequent assertion that commanders in the field knew best and were to be guided by good judgment and local conditions, the practical reality was different. The command philosophy by which the Nauvoo Legion operated was hardly delegatory or characterized by poor communications, even in mountain wilderness.[63] Will Bagley notes this command style, and, in connection with the Mountain Meadows tragedy, concludes with some overstatement as well as aptness that it "poses an untenable paradox—that Brigham Young was aware of 'every sparrow' that fell in Utah Territory but for more than a dozen years knew nothing of the worst crime to take place during his service as territorial governor, Indian superintendent, and commander-in-chief of the militia."[64]

So what did Brigham Young communicate about violence and lethal force during the fall of 1857? Historians have often noted that in the Utah War's most famous military order—General Wells's 4 October 1857 directive to Maj. Joseph Taylor—he admonished Taylor to "take no life." In two even earlier mid-September communications, Young had advised Cols. James W. Cummings and Robert Taylor Burton to attack only the Utah Expedition's animals ("This we think will stop them for this fall and no blood shed, a collision is to be avoided if possible") and, with General Wells, instructed Col. William H. Dame, "Save life always if it is possible—we do not wish to shed one drop of blood if it can be avoided. This course will give us great influence abroad." Restraint was the apparent order of the day.[65]

When Albert G. Browne, Jr., the correspondent-lawyer traveling with the Utah Expedition, became aware of the restrictions in Taylor's orders, he was

---

[62] For a description of Governor Young's intervention in drill procedures, see "Nauvoo Legion," *Deseret News* [Weekly], 1 July 1857, 4/4 and Head Quarters, Nauvoo Legion, General Orders No. 3, 30 June 1857, ibid., 8/3. Other examples of what today would be called micromanaging appear in Young to Wells, 11 and 17 October and 18 November 1857, LDS Archives.

[63] As discussed in the next chapter, a notable exception to his non-delegatory ways was Young's willingness to let General Wells determine in the field just when to burn Fort Bridger and to attack the army's supply trains.

[64] Bagley, *Blood of the Prophets,* 366. A contrary view—that Young did not know everything that happened in Utah and that his counsel was sometimes ignored—appears in Thomas G. Alexander, unpublished "Comments" for panel "The Courts, the War, and the Massacre in Nineteenth-Century Utah," May 2006 annual meeting, Mormon History Association, Casper, Wyoming.

[65] Young to Cummings and Burton, 13 September 1857; Young and Wells to Dame, 14 September 1857, LDS Archives.

not impressed. With blood in his own eye, he asked: "What constitutes the basis for the distinction between their present system of hostilities, and the shedding of blood, I am unable to understand. But whatever it may be, they give us official information that it will cease to exist the moment we attempt to force a passage through the mountains. If it lies in a belief that they do not become traitors till they take human life, they are greater fools than I am willing to believe."[66] Not mentioned in his dispatch was Browne's indictment (and release) in 1854 in the homicide of a Boston constable during a melee over enforcement of a federal statute, the Fugitive Slave Act.

Substantially at cross-currents with the prohibition on bloodshed set forth in these three Mormon communications (possibly phrased to establish what today is called "plausible deniability" in the aftermath of the Mountain Meadows massacre) was the violent tone of Young's unpublished 16 August 1857 discourse and his letters of 12 September 1857 to Messrs. Clinton, Pratt, and Denver. In all of this material Young signaled not only his unwillingness to restrain the territory's tribes, but that he stood ready to unleash than to bring about a bloody halt to transcontinental emigration.

The day after writing these letters, Young told U.S. Army captain Stewart Van Vliet in private, "If the Government Calls for volunteers in California & the people turn out to come to destroy us they will find their own buildings in flames before they get far from home & so throughout the United States. Again if they Commence the war I shall not hold the Indians Still by the fist any longer for white men [emigrants] to shoot at them but I shall let them go ahead & do as they please and I shall Carry the war into their own land and they will want to let out the Job before they get half through."[67] Aware of the impact that such threats would have in Washington, Van Vliet excluded them from his official reports. Nonetheless word of Mormon intent to burn major cities leaked out when the Legion's medical director later repeated this threat to travelers passing through Utah.[68]

Also obscure is that fact that in mid-October and November—as the two military forces closed and tensions rose exponentially—Brigham Young altered his instructions to the Legion about bloodshed. Young may have had in mind such a drastic change on 4 October when overnight he denied Colonel Jones's

[66] Albert G. Browne, Jr., Dispatch, November 1, 1858, "Later from the Mormon War," *New-York Daily Tribune*, 28 December 1857.

[67] Kenney, ed., *Wilford Woodruff's Journal, 1833–1898*, entry for 13 September 1857, 5:96–97.

[68] "A Mormon Threat," *Vermont Watchman and State Journal* (Montpelier), 8 January 1858, 4.

plea for gunpowder to construct Echo Canyon's defense by explaining, "I do not think it advisable to use our powder for blasting purposes at present as we shall probably need it for more effective operations. I consider therefore it is unecessary to forward the tools and powder."[69] He then authorized lethal force against the Utah Expedition and introduced allusions to summary execution into his messages to Utah Expedition officers. For example, on 16 October Young wrote to Col. E. B. Alexander of the Tenth U.S. Infantry, "And if George Washington was now living, and at the helm of our government, he would hang the administration as high as he did [British major John] Andre."[70] On 17 October, the day *before* Bill Hickman murdered Richard Yates, Young instructed Apostles Wells, Taylor, and Smith, "If they [U.S. troops] undertake to swing round into Cache Valley or the Malad, let sleep depart from their eyes and slumber from their eyelids, both by night and by day, until they take their final sleep; pick off their guards and sentries & fire into their camps by night, and pick off officers and as many men as possible by day."[71] These were the instructions, among others, that Joseph A. Young carried to Echo Canyon as he encountered Bill Hickman and Richard Yates. On 8 November President Young told Wells and two of his brigadiers that, if the Utah Expedition should move west of Fort Bridger toward Salt Lake City, "policy dictated that the Officers and mountaineers with them be as rapidly disposed of as possible." As Young wrote these orders, the same trio was sending him a message stating, "We shall watch them close however, and when they demonstrate their intentions by passing Bridger we propose pitching into them in every possible way.... Hence our conclusion not to shoot them till they pass Bridger to come this way, more specially as there is not a good chance to do so beyond Bridger."[72]

As a result of Brigham Young's directives, throughout October and November communications flowed between the Nauvoo Legion's senior field commanders ordering or permitting lethal force. With this change the Legion secretly abandoned the prohibition on killing—widely touted then as well as now, but a fiction after September. Although the world outside of the Nauvoo Legion has been oblivious to this day of the shift in authorizations, General Wells's adjutant general was acutely aware of its potential for bloodshed. On

[69] Jones to Young, 3 October 1857, and Young to Jones, 4 October 1857, LDS Archives.

[70] Young to Alexander, 16 October 1857, House Ex. Doc. 71, Serial 956, 57.

[71] Young to Wells, Taylor, and Smith, 17 October 1857, LDS Archives

[72] Young to Wells, Rich, and Grant, 8 November 1857; Wells, Rich, and Grant to Young, 7 November 1857, ibid.

13 October, from a camp four miles west of Bear River, Brig. Gen. James Ferguson wrote to his plural wives, "We intend none of them shall enter the [Salt Lake] City, though to prevent it, we have to slay them. . . . Pray for me that I may do my duty as a man of God."[73] The next March Young authorized the "destruction" without trial of a party of army deserters, apostates, and emigrants exiting Utah on the northern route to California if they stole from Mormon settlements.[74]

These authorizations targeted U.S. troops, civilian mountaineers, and other noncombatants. That none of these communications can be linked to a specific killing—and they have not been—does not mean they had no effect. They were issued by a leader claiming to be the federally sworn and paid governor of an American territory, and they were issued against other arms of the same government. On 30 December 1857 a federal grand jury sitting near Fort Bridger indicted Brigham Young for treason; fourteen years later another grand jury heard evidence about his 1857 behavior and returned an indictment for murder.[75]

Yet legends to the contrary soon sprang up and persist today. For example, even as Thomas L. Kane returned east by train from Brigham Young's

[73] Ferguson to My dear Jane, Lucy & Phillis, 13 October 1857, quoted in Bagley, ed., "'A Bright, Rising Star,'" 19. It is clear that during the fall General Wells was loathe to shed blood and hoped that an army halt at Fort Bridger would preclude the need to do so. Nonetheless, Wells was unquestionably prepared to use lethal force if the army advanced beyond Bridger and authorized such action at Brigham Young's urging. For other examples of such authorizations, often with shifting descriptions as to where the crucial line of demarcation was, see Young to Wells, Taylor, and Smith, 16 October 1857; Wells to Callister, 10, 17, and 19 October 1857; Wells to Warren S. Snow, 2 and 4 November 1857; Wells to Robison and Burton, 10 and 23 November 1857, all in LDS Archives. Emblematic of an earlier ambiguity (and poor leadership) in the guidance about lethal force dispensed by senior Mormon leaders was the behavior of Apostle George A. Smith, a former Nauvoo Legion colonel, during his mid-August visit to Pinto, the southern Utah hamlet closest to Mountain Meadows. There Smith encountered the local legion commander (probably Maj. John Higbee) who was excited about rumors of a pending descent on the region by Colonel Sumner's Cheyenne Expedition: "The Major seemed very sanguine about the matter. I asked him, if this rumour should prove true, if he was not going to wait for instructions. He replied, There was no time for any instructions; and he was going to take his battalion and use them up before they could get down through the kanyons; for, said he, if they are coming here, they are coming for no good." Instead of using this opportunity to discuss rules of engagement—a not unimportant subject in view of that major's bloody involvement at Mountain Meadows less than a month later—Smith merely said wryly, "I admired his grit, but I thought he would not have the privilege of using them up, for want of an opportunity." Smith, Discourse, 13 September 1857, *Deseret News,* 23 September 1857, 226/4 and 227/1–3.

[74] Young to Col. Chauncey W. West, 12 March 1858, LDS Archives; also discussed in Parshall, "'Pursue, Retake & Punish,'" 85n47. This authorization—never acted upon—was consistent with Young's advice in his 8 April 1853 discourse.

[75] Although neither indictment resulted in a trial, it could be argued, flawed as they were, that they cast a negative pall over this period of Brigham Young's gubernatorial leadership.

1877 funeral, he passed through Echo Canyon and was moved to record a fascinating but jumbled description of the Utah War. Here Kane depicted Young as reserving for himself the right both to order shedding of first blood and to prohibit such violence:

> Coming back on [railroad in] Weber & Echo [Canyons]—The truth upon the Echo fortifications &c—[Brigham Young] had assumed the responsibility of ordering the first blood shed himself. The man who sheds blood before he has my order his blood be on his own head. And he (?) was quite the man at some last moment to have, himself, ~~tossed~~ loosened a mass of rock prepared ~~as if~~ for his lever as if upon the heads of an advancing foe, disregarding his last warning. It was expected by numbers that he would do this from some commanding height where his prophetic figure would be seen cutting against the sky. But this would have been merely as a signal. The best proof of his determination to put off shedding blood is found in his forbidding cavalry attacks. He had a fine body of well-fed horse to bring upon our poor crowbaits, and it was the expectation of an attack from them which first sent the word of alarm that reached Floyd. But he said, "No. Do nothing but assail their transportation" (November 1857) After that when it was plain they would not and could not take up towards Fort Hall—they could not move anywhere he said, "Use no unnecessary violence whatever." About the same time, he said, "They seem bent on starving themselves to death."[76]

Notwithstanding Kane's mythic assertions of twenty years after the war, the 1857 sources indicate that on the Mormon side—as illustrated by the multiple examples discussed above—there was an unhealthy, wholly undisciplined, longstanding use of language by and in the presence of the governor and the Legion's most senior commanders about lynching, other forms of summary execution, and theft.[77] The governor had himself delivered a public discourse on 8 April 1853 advocating the summary execution of thieves. It was strange behavior from a religious community whose own founder-prophet had been lynched.

[76] "Thomas L. Kane's Account of his Journey to Salt Lake City, 30 August 1877–17 September 1877," Thomas L. Kane Collection, Brigham Young University Library.

[77] In instructing Bill Hickman and his fellow carriers with the Y. X. Carrying Company before their first eastbound departure from Salt Lake City, Heber C. Kimball admonished them in Brigham Young's office to "Never touch anything that is not yours unless you have orders from headquarters." Entry for 7 February 1857, Brigham Young Office Journal, Arrington Papers. Kimball's was a strange conditional admonition that brings to mind the title of Sharpe, *Thou Shalt Not Kill Unless Otherwise Instructed.* Small wonder that in 1853 a Legion officer engaged in looting Fort Bridger following Jim Bridger's flight, felt free to recommend to Governor Young that with respect to the district's mountaineers "we send them home the Short cut" while assuring him that "The Boys that are with me are faithful and true and as good as I would wish, they both watch and prey." Cummings to Young, 19 September 1853, LDS Archives.

Should such talk be dismissed as the rough-and-tumble way of the frontier, the effort of rough-hewn leaders attempting to command the attention of their even less-educated followers? Perhaps, but when militia officers—and even their wives—wore victims' clothes astride stolen horses, as happened after the Mountain Meadows massacre, the Yates murder, assassination of the Aiken party, and Henry Forbes's murder, it is appropriate to scrutinize command accountability and the effectiveness of senior leaders. That over the years the governor and senior Nauvoo Legion officers felt free to indulge in such talk as well as to sanction, if not participate in, repeated acts of looting and pillaging set the stage for an unstudied decline in Nauvoo Legion discipline that became a self-fulfilling prescription for disaster.

For example, in his 16 August 1857 discourse Young complained bitterly that the U.S. government owed him forty to fifty thousand dollars in unreimbursed Indian Department expenses. To this disclosure he added the forecast, "I need not tell you that if they get any property in here, that I mean to put my hand on it to pay myself." When a territorial governor and militia commander sends such a message, the restraints on subordinates' behavior loosen commensurately and immediately, as with the Mormon theft of hundreds of government- and contractor-owned cattle a few weeks later. Thus was set a tone to society in territorial Utah of the late 1850s—one that has prompted D. Michael Quinn to argue that it was a time and place "filled with violent incidents breaking out along religious lines of division. LDS leadership did not discourage this, but actually created a culture of violence with sermons, congregational hymns, newspaper editorials, and patriarchal blessings invoking the memories of past persecutions, while urging vengeance against Mormonism's enemies and 'blood atonement' against the wicked."[78]

Complicating this atmosphere was the fact that even some of Brigham Young's closest associates had difficulty determining his wishes long distance. For example, in February 1857, concerning a handcart rather than military matter, Apostle John Taylor had to write bluntly from New York: "When Brs. Grant & Kimball first came, I felt & said that I would give $500 for five minutes conversation with you. You must here excuse me Br. Young, I may be obtuse and so may those who were with me; but however plain your words

[78] Quinn, "LDS 'Headquarters Culture,'" 149. If Quinn implies here that the doctrine of blood atonement was aimed at non-Mormons, he is technically mistaken; to the extent that it was ever acted upon, this practice involved only Mormons whose sins were so grievous that their redemption required shedding of their own blood. For more on territorial Utah's violent tone, see Quinn, *The Mormon Hierarchy*, 242–99.

might be to yourself on this matter, neither I nor my associates could understand them."[79]

Language is far from a military commander's only qualification, but in matters of life and death, its clarity is crucial as well as revelatory about the leader's skill and effectiveness.[80] Brigham Young was a territorial governor and church leader with no formal military experience or education. The phrasing of his discourses, letters, and military orders was at times not only unmistakably violent but also filled with code words as well as indirection. At times his utterances were deliberately phrased to avoid non-Mormon comprehension and perhaps even legal jeopardy if intercepted, as Young expected they would be.

And so the debate continues over the phrasing in Brigham Young's fateful 10 September 1857 letter carried south by James Haslam and delivered too late to stay the hand of his conflicted Legion commanders at Mountain Meadows. What Young wrote then to Legion major Isaac C. Haight was: "In regard to the emigration trains passing through our settlements, we must not interfere with them, until they are first notified to keep away. You must not meddle with them." Yet in the next sentence Young added the enigmatic thought, "The Indians we expect will do as they please but you should try and preserve good feelings with them." What did this mean? Juanita Brooks commented that this letter was "so characteristic" and that the qualifying sentence "sounds as though he [Young] might not condemn an Indian massacre."[81]

The phrase "the Indians we expect will do as they please" in Young's letter to Haight is a strange, unclear one to be used by a wartime territorial superintendent of Indian Affairs. Yet these words were clearly important to Young, for he used them almost mantra-like during the Utah War's opening months: twice in his 16 August discourse; in his crucial 10 September instructions to Haight; in several of his 12 September letters; and during his threat-filled 13 September conversation with Captain Van Vliet. What was Young's message with these important, deliberate, but enigmatic words? Here was a communi-

---

[79] Taylor to Young, 24 February 1857, LDS Archives. For another but slightly earlier example, see the exchange between Apostles Taylor and Smith over a matter of "interpreting" Brigham Young; Taylor to George A. Smith, 17 December 1856, George A. Smith Papers, LDS Archives.

[80] For discussion of the importance of such clarity and its significance in U. S. Grant's Civil War effectiveness, see McPherson, "The Unheroic Hero," 16–19. An example of how a commander's vexingly ambiguous and confusing language provoked the 1789 mutiny aboard the Royal Navy's armed sloop H.M.S. *Bounty*, see Denning, *Mr. Bligh's Bad Language*.

[81] Brooks, *The Mountain Meadows Massacre*, 63–65. For a description of the similarly opaque message passed between local Legion commanders at the beginning of the massacre, see Turley, Leonard, and Walker, *Tragedy at Mountain Meadows* (forthcoming).

cations style that makes it legitimate if not essential to ask whether a few weeks later the operative instructions for the Legion's forces in Echo Canyon and the Green River district were to take no life or to kill the Utah Expedition's officers and mountaineers first. With the answer to this question rested the fate of a large number of people and the continuing historical reputation of a few.

And so the atrocities came. They came once accomplished—but seriously ill and militarily inexperienced—leaders such as James Buchanan and Brigham Young faced their first major military crisis during the spring of 1857. Their ineffective response was to place large numbers of armed men in motion—troops led by commanders with powerful motivation but guided by instructions that ranged from the ambiguous, enigmatic, and sometimes conflicting to those that were unmistakably direct and brutal. In Brigham Young's case even body language—his crooked finger for example—needed to be interpreted by subordinates when violence was under discussion. The unfortunate result, as Captain Tracy's Mormon pie vendor described it, was that unarmed noncombatants went "up the pocket of the Lord," with their killers unprosecuted for decades, if at all.

With ineffective leadership and serious communications problems also present on the federal side, the stage was set for still more atrocities in 1858—this time involving the Utah Expedition rather than Mormon side as provocateur. Still to come was the murderous, federally provoked 25 February assault on the Salmon River Mission (Fort Limhi) by Bannocks and Northern Shoshones. Also lurking in the conflict's future was Albert Sidney Johnston's virtually unknown January attempt to enlist tribal help from the Uintahs and his spring 1858 decision to hire Washakie's Shoshone warriors as mercenary operator-defenders of the Green River ferries.[82]

During the Utah War neither side had clean hands with respect to violence and atrocities. In quite different ways and on a substantially different scale both Brigham Young and James Buchanan were accountable, if not culpable, for what took place as well as for what they authorized and communicated. Intentions together with executions were part of the rough road being traveled by two supreme leaders of uneven effectiveness and problematic communications skills.

[82] These incidents will be discussed in this study's second volume. See MacKinnon, "'Lonely Bones,'" 157–62.

Chapter 13

"Like Stubble before a Wirlwind" The Legion Strikes

I think I tell the feeling of every man when I tell my own, and that is, no desire to return to our beloved homes, our dear associations, and to the Prophet of our God until we have scattered like stubble before a wirlwind the enemies of our God, our religion, our liberties, and our rights.

—Nauvoo Legion private George D. Watt to wife Alice, near Fort Bridger, 1 October 1857

By their nature, the Utah War's atrocities were not isolated incidents. They were acts intertwined with the Nauvoo Legion's most active guerrilla-like operations. With the startling news on 12 September that the army had moved west of Fort Laramie, the issues changed from those of August when the Legion operated through small mounted scouting detachments in Nebraska Territory. Paramount now was determining whether the army would enter Utah, reach Fort Bridger, and push beyond it in 1857. At stake was the safety of the Salt Lake Valley, its women, and the LDS church's leaders. Also of unstated but serious concern was what the army would surely find at Mountain Meadows.

Beleaguered by these issues, Brigham Young had proclaimed martial law, as discussed in an earlier chapter. The Legion then went on the offensive in northeastern Utah. General Wells left Salt Lake City on 27 September to lead a new Nauvoo Legion organization: the Eastern Expedition.[1] He began to implement the early phases of Young's threatened scorched-earth policy by deploying mounted units to harass and raid the Utah Expedition's supply trains, cattle herds, and infantry regiments. Once it was clear that the Utah Expedi-

[1] The term "Eastern Expedition" is used minimally here in order to avoid confusion with the U.S. Army's Utah Expedition.

tion was within striking distance of Fort Bridger, General Wells burned that post as well as nearby Fort Supply while shifting his headquarters from Fort Bridger to Echo Canyon via a brief bivouac on Muddy Creek. These actions were coordinated with Maj. Lot Smith's fiery destruction of seventy-six supply wagons in three contractor trains that were camped at Green River and the Big Sandy to the rear of the army's vanguard. With these acts the Mormons signaled unmistakably their military capabilities (and the army's vulnerabilities) as well as their willingness to incinerate Utah's infrastructure, if not that of the non-Mormon world. For the British and Russian ministers to Washington, these developments brought the unwelcome specter of an armed Mormon exodus to their under-defended possessions on the Pacific Coast.

What followed throughout October were grass fires on a vast scale, intended to destroy forage essential for the army's animals. Simultaneously the Legion stampeded a large proportion of the Utah Expedition's cattle herds, an irreplaceable loss of what was to have been fresh beef for winter rations. For animals as well as troops, October 1857 was stressful.

Within less than a month this destruction—together with the Mountain Meadows massacre, the martial-law proclamation, and the publication of General Wells's captured operational orders to Maj. Joseph Taylor—reinforced the nation's conviction that Utah was indeed a rebellious territory.

Historian and trails expert John D. Eldredge has argued that, in effect, the Utah War was "fought" during the fall of 1857 in the region between the Sweetwater Valley and Fort Bridger.[2] To understand better the nature of this contest as well as the escalation in the Legion's operations, one needs to understand the correspondence between Brigham Young, General Wells, and the remarkable apostolic delegation of John Taylor and George A. Smith, who were sent to assist Wells with what Young called their "united judgment."[3] Also essential is an appreciation of the diary entries and personal correspondence generated during the fall by Legionnaires of all ranks. Thanks to that aspect of Mormon culture stressing the importance of journals and the creation of personal histories, there is a vast body of such sources. It is a trove in sharp contrast to the historiographical "silence" still shrouding such federal units as the Fifth U.S. Infantry, Bee's Battalion of U.S. Volunteers, and Reno's siege battery.

[2] Eldredge discussion with MacKinnon, 7 July 2006.

[3] Wells, like Taylor and Smith, was an apostle, but organizationally he was a member of the First Presidency rather than the Quorum of the Twelve Apostles. Accordingly, he was addressed as "president" rather than "apostle," as well as, of course, "general."

Nauvoo Legion Lt. General Daniel Hamner Wells
Commander of Utah's territorial militia and LDS second counselor to President Young, Wells campaigned in northeastern Utah from field bivouacs and headquarters at Fort Bridger, Muddy Creek, and Echo Canyon before returning to Salt Lake in early December. Federal grand juries indicted him for the October 1857 murder of ammunition trader Richard E. Yates and for treason; both indictments were later dropped for procedural reasons. *Lithograph from Whitney's 1892* History of Utah.

From such Mormon material come fleeting impressions of religiously motivated militiamen episodically engaged in an overlapping series of scouts, patrols, construction details, raids, and bivouacs to defend their adopted homeland. Such activities tend not to be the stuff of an orderly campaign history appropriate to a conventional military conflict of set battles. As with so many other aspects of Brigham Young's thinking and the Nauvoo Legion's operations, these complex, often confusing activities were not confined to a small area or, for that matter, to Utah. They ranged across plains, deserts, canyons, mountains, and river valleys—a sprawling regional "front" over intersecting portions of what were then the territories of Nebraska, Utah, and Oregon, with forays into the state of California and New Mexico Territory as well.

To Waste Away Our Enemies and Lose None: Recalibrating Tactics

As noted, the news from Capt. N. V. Jones's scouts that the army had marched past Fort Laramie shocked Brigham Young. He immediately focused on more drastic action. Any reservations about proclaiming martial law now vanished.

"Brigham Young Mustering His Forces to Fight the United States Troops" This caption for a 28 November 1857 political cartoon in the newly launched *Harper's Weekly* was inspired by First Counselor Heber C. Kimball's August boast that his wives alone could whip the Utah Expedition. With Mormon polygamy and Buchanan's bachelor status as fodder for satire and lampoonery, the war also spawned a wide range of earthy poems, folk songs, novels, sheet music, and stage dramas as well as loftier LDS hymns. *Courtesy of* HarpWeek.

An explanation of the new as well as longer-term tactics appears in Young's 13–14 September instructions to his joint commanders on the plains and to the principal military leader in southern Utah. As discussed in the previous chapter, the prohibition on bloodshed found in these orders immediately followed the awareness in Salt Lake City that something had probably gone violently awry at Mountain Meadows. Although at mid-month it was not clear to Brigham Young what had happened there, what was obvious from the unexpected appearance of courier James Haslam in Salt Lake City was that Mountain Meadows meant, among other things, Mormon legal, if not religious, jeopardy. The phrasing of these orders reflected such a worry, creating in the process what today could be called damage control if not the basis for plausible deniability.[4] Both of these letters also reflected Young's expectation that Captain Van Vliet would be able to halt the army east of Bridger once he reported what he had seen of Mormon resolve.

YOUNG TO COLS. CUMMINGS AND BURTON (ON THE PLAINS), 13 SEPTEMBER 1857, LDS ARCHIVES.

Capt. Van Vliet and Dr. Jno M. Bernhisel leave for Washington early in the morning [tomorrow]. You will know by the time they meet you more in relation to the troops. They will carry the word to them that they will be opposed in attempting to come to this place, they must not be permitted to come here. Bro [N. V.] Jones had better not go down [east] any great distance and return as soon as possible for we want him to be back so that you can operate up on their animals. Take the [army's] baggage train animals first as this you know will stop the troops. Keep your men concentrated as much as possible. If the forces show a determination to come in after the Capt has passed them, pitch in to the animals whenever and wherever you can safely do so and not be seen by them, go the night work on them. This we think will stop them for this fall and no blood shed, a collision is to be avoided if possible that is if they can be kept back by taking their animals

Be wise and discreet and take good care of the men.

May the god of Heaven bless you and give you wisdom in all your movements and enable you to check this movement untill another year.

You have our faith and prayers and if necessary will have assistance.

The freight trains are not to come in this direction any farther than Forts Bridger or Supply. If they should undertake it, their trains and animals *must* also be taken and brought into the city.[5]

YOUNG AND WELLS TO DAME, 14 SEPTEMBER 1857, LDS ARCHIVES.

Herewith you will receive the Governor's Proclamation, declaring Martial law. You will probably not be called out this fall, but are required to continue to make ready for a big fight another year. The plan of operations is supposed to be about these. In case the U.S. Government should send out an overpowering force, we intend to desolate the Territory and conceal our families,

[4] See Chapter 18 for James Buchanan's own employment of the concept of plausible deniability in his year-end dealings with Thomas L. Kane.

[5] The two colonels commanded jointly until Cummings became ill. These instructions were being carried to them by Col. N. V. Jones as he accompanied Delegate Bernhisel and Captain Van Vliet to their rendezvous with Van Vliet's army escort at Hams Fork. Adjt. Gen. James Ferguson, Year-End Report to Brigham Young, 7 January 1858, Nauvoo Legion (Utah), Adj. Gen. Record 1851–1870, pp. 230–43, LDS Archives.

> Stock, and all of our effects in the fastnesses of the mountains, where they will be safe while the men waylay our enemies, attack them from ambush, stampede their animals take the supply trains cut off detachments, and parties sent to Kanyons for wood, or on other service. To lay waste every thing that will burn, houses, fences, trees, fields grass, that they cannot find a particle of any thing that will be of use to them, not even sticks to make a fire for to cook their suppers. To waste away our enemies and lose none, that will be our mode of warfare. Thus you see the necessity of preparing, first secure places in the mountains where they cannot find us, or if they do where they cannot approach in any force; and then prepare for our families building some cabins cacheing flour and grain. Flour should be ground in the latter part of the winter or early in the spring in order to keep. Sow grain in your fields early as possible this is so that the harvest of another year may come off before they have time to get here. Conciliate the Indians and make them our fast friends.
>
> In regard to letting people pass or repass or travel through the Territory, this applies to all strangers and suspected persons. Your self and Bro [Maj.] Isaac C. Haight in your district are authorized to give such permits. Examine all such persons strictly before giving them permits to pass. Keep things perfectly quiet and let all things be done peacefully but with firmness and let there be no excitement. Let the people be united in their feelings and faith as well as works and keep alive the spirit of the Reformation, and what we said in regard to saving the grain and provisions, we say again let there be no waste, save life always when it is possible, we do not wish to shed a drop of blood if it can be avoided. This course will give us great influence abroad.

And so in the last half of September the Legion focused on the Utah Expedition's animals rather than on the destruction of its men and supply trains. Stampede mules, horses, cattle, and work oxen—so went the plan, immobilizing both the army and Russell, Majors and Waddell. In the process, the Utah Expedition would lose its beef-on-the-hoof.

The earliest and boldest such raid in response to Brigham Young's 13 September orders was a descent by a detachment of mounted Legionnaires on the mule herd of the Tenth Infantry on the night of 24–25 September. The regiment—the Utah Expedition's vanguard—was then bivouacked just west of South Pass at Pacific Springs. An understanding of who participated in the raid and with what impact has been clouded by the Utah War's mythology along with several other episodes discussed later in this chapter. In 2003 Steven E. Farley published a highly colorful account of the Pacific Springs raid written by John I. Ginn, a twenty-one-year-old Georgian employed by the Tenth as a civilian livestock drover. Ginn's typescript account, snippets of which have circulated among historians for decades, described Capt. Orrin

Porter Rockwell as the detachment's leader and the raid itself as a farce. According to Ginn, the Legion initially stampeded thousands of animals only to lose them along with the raiders' own mounts. Lost with uncritical acceptance of Ginn's inaccurate narrative is an understanding that he wrote as an aging, impoverished journalist in turn-of-the-century El Paso with an apparent need to associate himself with Rockwell, who was really operating considerably west of Pacific Springs along the Weber River.[6]

The two most verifiable and consistent accounts of what took place at Pacific Springs are encompassed in the heretofore unpublished "record" of Legion private John Bagley and the after-action report written to Brigham Young by Bagley's superiors, Colonels Cummings and Burton. Bagley, a Canadian convert who had emigrated to Utah from New Brunswick in 1854, was the same age as Ginn. Both men wrote later in life, although Bagley did so a decade earlier than Ginn, and each probably worked from contemporary notes no longer extant. Bagley, who died in Idaho in 1923 at age 92, was among the last of the Utah War's surviving veterans. His record provides first identification of the six raiders who attacked the Tenth Infantry's camp. He also provides a glimpse of the extent to which Legionnaires on extremely short rations struggled with the temptation to pilfer army food even in the face of Brigham Young's 16 August signal that such foraging was an acceptable provisioning strategy. Here one also finds a recitation of the pervasive post-war myth that Young ordered an avoidance of bloodshed throughout the Utah War.

John Bagley Record Book, Written in 1894.
Transcription by Will Bagley from
Hawley Bagley Typescript in Family Collection.

I will now say a few words in regard to 1857 and 58. Commencing August 14th 1857, I was working in the head of Big Cottonwood canyon on the 13th of August when I received word from General D. H. Wells to be in Salt Lake City the next day, ready to start in the Army. Obedience was my great aim, so I started in the morning. When I got to the city all hands was ready but myself, forty nine men mounted on horseback and myself afoot, made the

[6] For a review of the flaws in Ginn's manuscript and Farley's uncritical acceptance of it in *The Mormon Mountain Meadows Massacre*, see MacKinnon, "'Unquestionably Authentic and Correct in Every Detail,'" 322–42. The editor is indebted to historians John D. Eldredge and Will Bagley for their justifiable skepticism about Rockwell's involvement in the Pacific Springs raid and to Bagley for a transcription of his great-uncle's account of his own participation. The most prominent acceptance of Ginn's account is Schindler, *Orrin Porter Rockwell*, 255–57. For the editor's own misguided acceptance as recently as 2006 of the seductively appealing but largely inaccurate Ginn account, see Davidson, "America's Forgotten War," *Deseret Morning News*, 9 July 2006, A10/1.

fifty. I had a saddle and gun and larette, so I piled in the bagig wagon and went to Fort Bridger. There I got a horse off Lewis Robinson [*sic*] on trust, gave verbal security, which was at that time far better than hard shelled notes is at the present time. We traveled without any hardships till we got to Devils Gate on Sweetwater, where we camped for some time. Part of the company went to plat [Platte] bridge for the [westbound] YX [Carrying Company] train, which was ahead of [the] troops. The train come and passed on, we lay there till our supplies gave out, all but flour. We had a hard time, game was plenty but we could not kill anything. We tried many times with the whole company for two days and only killed one rabbit for fifty of us. We finally started back, travelling slow, waiting for the trupes [*sic*] to come to Pacific Springs where we calculated to stampede their animals. They had some freight on ahead which we expected to burn later on. I thought it was very foolish to burn and destroy grub when we were almost starving for it, so I tried my hand at confiscating a little bacon one night, which I was successful in obtaining about fifty pounds and a fine shotgun which I had to carry nine miles through the sagebrush and darkness of the night. I had my yogger [Yauger, or Mississippi rifle] and dragoon pistol and 100 rounds of ammunition besides. I dare not let my officers know what I was going to do till I had dun it, so I had to go afoot all the way there and back, nine miles each way, and carry my precious load. I got back to camp just at the break of day, when two of our boys just come to camp had not eaten for two days and nights. They was nearly wild for food. I heard them complaining. I went to them as soon as I could in the dark, and led them over to my pile of bacon. I struck a match and they looked at me and then at the meat. They was both Scotchmen so I had to take a scotch blessing, and then we cooked meat for the first time for over three weeks.[7] We only had flour to live on. What a happy morning to behold, one pound of bacon to each man in camp. This was an act long to be remembered by the boys. Though very small, only one pound of meat to the man.[8]

In a few days we had the trupes camped at Pacific Springs where we thought to get all their animals and leave them there afoot. We made a bold and dar-

[7] A "Scotch blessing" is a severe scolding. Historian Ardis Parshall's interpretation of this passage and Bagley's furtiveness is that although the starving men decided to eat Bagley's bacon, they were upset over the theft. She notes that when Maj. Lot Smith's detachment destroyed seventy-six wagons of government stores and provisions in early October, his troops took almost nothing for themselves before burning the trains. Parshall to MacKinnon, e-mail message, 12 July 2007.

[8] Whether the scanty provisioning of Legion detachments in the field was a matter of unavoidable necessity in hardscrabble Utah or officer neglect is debatable. In an unusually severe assessment of the rigors experienced by his great-uncle and his comrades, historian Will Bagley concludes that "the Legion commanders were as concerned about the well-being of the troops as the Mormon emigration agents who routinely dispatched parties across the plains without enough supplies to get to Fort Laramie." Bagley to MacKinnon, e-mail message, 10 July 2007. For a description of the Spartan rations and game available to 2d Lt. James H. Martineau's scouting detachment in the mountains east of Parowan during early September 1857, see Martineau, "A Scouting Party."

ing strike for all they had and got none of them. Alma Williams, Frank Nolton, Ned Fuller, Jarvis Baker, William Woodland and John Bagley: we left the company about half a mile off and went in afoot and see how they was situated, returned and got our horses and instructions how to do.[9] We rode past three guards and right up to the herd, they was herded just on the outside of camp. No guard halted us and we rode right to the herd and fired two pistles at them and then the fun commenced, dum bull, horse fiddle, bare [bear] skin, and the mare hoop, we run through the band three times.[10] They was chained and hobbled so it was impossible for them to run. A few of them got loose and run the whole length of camp right through the tents and guy ropes. Frank Nolton and I went after them, but they scattered so we lost track of all of them. We run clear through camp and came to our meeting place and counted five [men]. We looked for the other and seen him ride three times around a guard fire after a mule and then give it up and come to us. It was Ned Fuller. I can't tell the condition of the trupes any more than they was in a terrible uproar as long as we was in hearing of them.[11] Our Captain was soon with us, H. C. Kimble Jun, and ordered a force[d] march out of danger. We got to Green River next day for breakfast, where we eat hearty of water whelps as we called them, flour and water mixed and baken in a pan.[12] We had a little meat that morning. We continued our march up to Fort Supply, where we rested for awhile. Our animals being poor, we kept out of the way and gave

---

[9] Of the other five members of Bagley's raiding party relatively little is known. The two youngest, Alma Alanson Williams and Benjamin Franklin Knowlton, ages 18 and 19, were already experienced frontiersmen and herdsmen; they had been among the first Mormons to visit the Flathead country of Montana's Bitterroot Valley as livestock traders. Williams was the brother of Judge Stiles's controversial law partner, Thomas S. Williams, and Knowlton was the brother-in-law of Thomas S. Williams's mercantile partner, William H. Hooper, as well as a son-in-law of the late Willard Richards, Brigham Young's deceased second counselor. At age 27, Edmund Burk (Ned) Fuller of Weber County and Jarvis Young Baker, newly arrived from the former Mormon colony in Carson Valley, were the detachment's elders. The sixth raider was William West Woodland, age 25, who like Private Baker had helped to settle Carson Valley before returning to what is now the Brigham City area in 1856, a year before that community's roll-up in the face of the Utah War. Bigler, *Fort Limhi*, 122n13.

[10] It is not clear what some of these implements were. Colonels Burton and Cummings described the use of "bear skins 'Rattles' 'Dum Bells' &c prepared for the purpose." Cummings and Burton to Young, 27 September 1857, LDS Archives.

[11] The best account of the chaos in the Tenth Infantry's camp appears in Capt. Jesse A. Gove to Mrs. Gove, 25 September 1857, *The Utah Expedition*, 64–65. Gove described the death of one unidentified soldier in Captain Tracy's Company H from a heart attack as did Surgeon Bartholow in his "Sanitary Report" for the quarter ended 30 September. From this unit's regimental return for September 1857 and the "Register of Enlistments," both in the National Archives, Curtis R. Allen of Centerville, Utah, has identified the deceased soldier as Pvt. Henry Schulta, age 31, who had emigrated from Prussia and enlisted in Buffalo only three months earlier. The army also spelled his surname as Shulter and Schulte; it buried him at Pacific Springs but later placed a marker bearing his name in the post cemetery at Camp Floyd, Utah, thereby contributing to the mythic illusion that a number of Utah Expedition soldiers are buried there who actually are interred in places as distant from Utah as Baltimore, Maryland. Allen to MacKinnon, e-mail message, 11 July 2007.

[12] Water whelps were pieces of dough (variously described as a paste, pancake, or dumpling) that were usually boiled rather than baked. This basic fare was common among travelers and miners.

> room for new recruits, who went forth burning wagons, driving off stock and burning grass, ever obeying our great General Brigham Young's command—never take human life but use every possible means to stop the march of the trupes.[13] We soon had them spellbound, or snowbound. We might say the protecting hand of our Heavenly Father raised up between us and our enemies, to give them time to consider what they was sent to do.

While Private Bagley and his five comrades rode through the Tenth Infantry's camp, Colonels Cummings and Burton and nearly forty other men sat their horses "formed in a line paral[l]el with the creek near the camp. We made all the noise we possibly could." Two days later these officers reported the results to Brigham Young in a defensive tone: "we are sorry to say [that the stampede] failed but the failure was not in consequence of any inaction of nonexecution on our part for we went 6 men direct through their camp into the midst of their animals." One of the six, Pvt. Frank Knowlton, was considerably more direct and stated in his post-war reminiscences, "I was one of the five who rode through Col. Alexander's corral and tried to stampede his mules. We failed in the attempt." Burton's and Cummings's sensitivity may have reflected not only embarrassment but their awareness of rumors in Salt Lake City about disaffection and insubordination among their troops. As discussed later in this chapter, in October General Wells alluded to his disappointment in the performance of these officers, and at about this time Colonel Cummings returned home with an eyesight problem. During the following January Adjutant General Ferguson confided to Brigham Young frankly that this and other raids had been ineffective in stopping the army's advance.[14]

In the immediate aftermath of the failed Pacific Springs raid, its commanders warned Brigham Young ominously that "Those that entertain the idea that our Enemies will be prevented from coming into Salt Lake City without a Severe contest we fear will be Saddly disappointed."[15]

---

[13] See Chapter 12.

[14] Cummings and Burton to Young, 27 September 1857, LDS Archives; Cummings and Burton to Wells, 27 September 1857, LDS Archives; Wells to Carrington, 7 October 1857, Carrington Collection, Marriott Library; and Adjt. Gen. James Ferguson, Year-End Report to Brigham Young, 7 January 1858, Nauvoo Legion (Utah), Adj. Gen. Record 1851–1870, pp. 230–43, LDS Archives. Knowlton, *The Utah Knowltons*, 69. Failure that it was, the Pacific Springs raid may have produced a war trophy that delighted Brigham Young—possession of Colonel Alexander's pet white mule.

[15] Cummings and Burton to Young, 27 September 1857, LDS Archives. For the mood of Utah Expedition officers after the Pacific Springs raid, see "From the Utah Expedition," Capt. Albert Tracy (Between South Pass and Big Sandy) to Friend, 23–28 September 1857, *Commercial Advertiser* (Buffalo, N.Y.), 20 November 1857, 2/2; Capt. Marcy to Samuel Colt, 4 October 1857, Colt Papers.

A Cold Seat around the Ashes of Forts Bridger and Supply: Trial by Fire

At the end of September Colonel Alexander was attempting to consolidate as much of the Utah Expedition as he could at Hams Fork above its juncture with Blacks Fork, a good source of grass and water for thousands of army animals. Alexander did so as the "senior officer present" rather than as the expedition's commander. His pause at Hams Fork was in response to Captain Van Vliet's eastbound advice against further forward movement as well as his own hope that his superior officer would soon emerge from the frozen fog of the Continental Divide. Reflecting the fact that he had never seen Winfield Scott's 29 June instructions to Harney, Alexander made the shocking confession that "No information of the position or intentions of the commanding officer has reached me, and I am in utter ignorance of the objects of the government in sending troops here, or the instructions given for their conduct after reaching here."[16]

For the Nauvoo Legion this pause at Hams Fork also presented a dilemma: would the expedition resume its march, reach Fort Bridger, and attempt to enter Salt Lake City? If so, by which route? Would it use the main east–west emigrant road through defended Echo Canyon, or would it loop to the north through Sublette's Cutoff, the Bear River, and Soda Springs to descend on Salt Lake along the undefended Oregon–Fort Hall road? And who was the commander: an absent General Harney, a rumored Colonel Johnston, or some other officer?[17]

On 2 October the Legion's quartermaster general, Lewis Robison, sent a Mexican messenger into Alexander's camp bearing the martial-law proclamation and a letter from Brigham Young addressed to an unnamed commanding officer. In this defiant document Young asserted, "I am still the governor and superintendent of Indian affairs for this Territory, no successor having been appointed and qualified, as provided by law; nor have I been removed by the President of the United States." Young's message went on to "direct that you retire forthwith from the Territory, by the same route you entered. Should you deem this impracticable, and prefer to remain until spring, you can do so in peace and unmolested, on conditions that you deposit your arms

[16] Alexander to the Officers of the United States Army Commanding forces en route to Utah, 8 October 1857, House Ex. Doc. No. 71, Serial 956, 39.

[17] Confusing the identity issue for the Mormons was the fact that an officer of similar name, Lt. Col. Joseph E. Johnston, was afield with a battalion of the First Cavalry in Kansas for a different purpose.

and ammunition with Lewis Robison, quartermaster general of the Territory, and leave in the spring." Legion adjutant general James Ferguson confided to his three wives that "Their answer will decide whether we have to fight them or not. It will be just as God wills." Alexander's response—hardly a stirring rejoinder—was that, "I will submit your letter to the general commanding as soon as he arrives here. . . . [F]uture movements and operations will depend entirely upon orders issued by competent military authority."[18]

With this response, the Legion moved immediately to fire Fort Supply and Fort Bridger, and in two attacks Mormon raiders also burned seventy-six wagons in three undefended trains belonging to Russell, Majors and Waddell. How and by whom the decision was made for these coordinated actions is an important but largely unprobed question. It is easy to attribute the decision to Brigham Young, whose command style was often non-delegatory and patently interventionist.[19] Yet an examination of the sources yields a more complex picture of Mormon decision making at this juncture. If today Brigham Young seems a micromanager, he also understood the value of counsel and the importance of local knowledge when they were essential.

The broad plan for the campaign was, of course, set forth in Brigham Young's martial-law proclamation and the letters to key leaders immediately surrounding it. Ardis E. Parshall, perhaps the leading authority on Brigham Young's correspondence, believes that by the time General Wells and the Eastern Expedition left Salt Lake on 27 September, he and Young had reached an understanding: destroy Fort Bridger and Fort Supply if the army continued to advance, with the timing and circumstances left to Wells's judgment in the field.[20] At month-end, the decisive factor in the general's mind was whether or not the army's commander marched in force from the large bivouac on Hams Fork after receiving the cautionary materials to be delivered by Lewis Robison.

On the evening of 30 September, Wells summarized for Young his preparations. He noted, "Of course we do not know what will be the result of the documents, but want to be prepared for the worst. We shall therefore make every preparation to burn this place [Bridger], and Fort Supply, and

---

[18] Young to The Officer Commanding the forces now invading Utah Territory, 29 September 1857, and Alexander to Young, 2 October 1857, House Ex Doc. No. 71, Serial 956, 33–35. Ferguson to Jane, Lucy, and Phillis Ferguson, 30 September 1857, private collection, photocopy in editor's possession courtesy of Will Bagley.

[19] See other chapters for discussion of Young's degree of involvement with military decisions. For an additional example, see Young's almost comical instructions to his business agent on how to go about buying fifty Sharps rifles; Young to Eldredge, 2 September 1853, LDS Archives.

[20] Parshall to MacKinnon, e-mail message, 22 August 2006.

make a speedy retreat [to Echo Canyon], in case the answer should be unfavorable, and be ready to start as soon as the express by Bro. Robison shall return. We think that they will remain where they are a few days, which would give us a little chance to operate and get things cleaned up, but shall not trust to their doing so."[21]

According to an operational log kept at Wells's headquarters by Brig. Gen. Hiram B. Clawson, Brigham Young's son-in-law and business advisor, Robison and a small escort left Fort Bridger for Hams Fork at 3:00 A.M. on 1 October. Later that day, George D. Watt—Brigham Young's talented scribe and church reporter—wrote to his wife, Alice, in Salt Lake City. He did so in his new role as Legion private. Although bivouacked only two miles south of Fort Bridger, Watt was unaware of the major decisions in process, yet he sensed keenly the importance of what he and his comrades were doing. A man of great intellect, George Watt was Mormonism's first convert in the British Isles, a horticulturist, and co-inventor (with Brigham Young) of the new, eclectic Mormon alphabet. Nonetheless, on 1 October he focused on the typical Legionnaire's concerns about family, health, faith, food, and lost mittens. In so doing, it was also typical of Watt that he wryly described the disintegration of his boots as a matter of "parting soul from the body."

PVT. GEORGE D. WATT TO ALICE WATT,
1 OCTOBER 1857, WATT PAPERS.

> I am in excelent health and spirits. We are now campt about 2 miles South of Fort Briger. The enemies camp is situated on Hams Fork about 35 miles from us. It is reported to us by a detatchment of our boys that the Cavalry has come up and joined the main body of the Soldiery.[22] The enemy is on the alert, their animals are well secured, hobbled and chained, making it imposable to stampede them. A company of our boys rode right into their correl, and even struck the gaurds with their leathers, slaping their animals, and yelling like Indians but all to no purpose.[23] General Harney is expected in in 3 days, then there may be some active work but at present the enemy is lying still, and so are we. I know not what the future will reveal but it is certain that all will go well for Isreal there is no cause for fear in the least. The Lord will give us the victory over our enemies and strike Terror to the hearts of those who thirst for the blood of the p[r]ophets of God. A camp life in the capacity of soldiers is a hard life, and on the other hand there are scenes highly interesting and amusing the one somewhat ballances the other. We have plenty of

[21] Wells, Taylor, and Smith to Young, 30 September 1857, LDS Archives.

[22] This report was inaccurate.

[23] This was the Pacific Springs raid.

beef and flour, but no salt, nor cooking utensils, it would amuse you to see the different inventions in the line of cooking. The meat is roasted over a large camp fire each man holding his stake on the pointed end of a green willo[w] stick, the cooked portion of the meat is then cut off the remainder is cooked again in the same way and so on until it is all cooked and eaten. The flour is mixed up with water alone, then rolled into lengths of a yard long, and rolled round a stick, and then held before the fire until cooked, for plates we use [wood] chips when we can find them. I think I tell the feeling of every man when I tell my own, and that is, no disire to return to our beloved homes, our dear associations, and to the prophet of our God until we have scattered like stubble before a wirlwind the enemies of our God, our religion, our liberties, and our rights. The Lord will show his power at his own time and in his own way, I am satisfied that all depends upon our obedience to our leaders, faith in our God and union among ourselves. We have no mean [small] enemy to cope with and every man will be brought to the test whether he will risk his life for his God his religion and his rights. The saviours words are very aplicable to our case. "He that shall seek to save his life shall lose it, etc.["][24] May God help me to be brave and valient in the defence of every thing that is dear to me and to you, and to every saint of God. *Give us your prayer.* I am in great need of boots the ones I have on are parting soul from the body. Please see Bro. Godsal, and if you can by any means send them to me do.[25] The gloves I got from mother I exchanged for a pair of mittens. I lost one mitten and gave the other away, so I am minus anything for my hands. If you can trade peaches or flour for wood do so, it may be winter before I get home. If you can hire any person to gather my garden, do so. Our present circumstances throws a little more weight upon you than otherwise would have been, but my Dear have a mans heart in you for a little while, and you can do much to help me while I am fighting for your safety and for the good of Israel. My love to my Mother and family to Father and Mother Longstroth to Sarah Nancy Rhodaten and all the little boys and girls.[26] God bless and preserve us both in life until we again shall meet amen.[27]

By the afternoon of 3 October it was clear to General Wells, if not to Private Watt, that the army's response was unfavorable, and that a continuation

[24] Matthew 10:39.

[25] John Godsall, a shoemaker from Birmingham, England, had arrived in Utah the previous December. Other Legionnaires in Echo Canyon had a footwear problem quite different than Watts's. On nearly the same day that he wrote to Alice, Col. N. V. Jones informed Brigham Young from the canyon that "the men are in good health and spirits, although the footmen having started with new Boots or Shoes, their feet have become sore, but they do not complain." Jones to Young, 3 October 1857, LDS Archives.

[26] Father and Mother Longstroth were Alice Watt's parents. It is unknown who the others mentioned were.

[27] The editor thanks Ronald G. Watt of LDS Church Archives for access to his ancestor's letters. For more on Watt, see Watt, "Sailing 'The Old Ship Zion,'" 48–65, and "The Beginnings of 'The Journal of Discourses,'" 134–48; Walker, *Wayward Saints*, 265–67.

NAUVOO LEGION PRIVATE GEORGE D. WATT
Although age 45 and a sedentary member of Brigham Young's office staff, Watt campaigned actively with the Legion near Fort Bridger and in Echo Canyon. His letters to plural wife Alice are among the most interesting to survive the war on either side, reflecting a deep commitment to Mormonism and its armed defense. Shown here at age 36 in an 1848 lithograph made by a London Latter-day Saint, Watt claimed to have been Mormonism's first English convert. *Courtesy of descendant Ronald G. Watt, Salt Lake City.*

of its march from Hams Fork was imminent.[28] Coincidentally, it was a day on which Charles W. Penrose, a Mormon missionary in Liverpool, turned his thoughts prophetically to the scene unfolding at Fort Bridger:

> The troops must by this time be close there I wish I was in the mountains with the b'hoys. My blood boils furiously at the repeated indignities put upon the Saints & my heart beats high with desire to fight with my brethren in the sacred cause of truth & liberty Arise O God and let thine enemies be scattered clothe thy servants with power nerve their arms with strength and let the wisdom of the Holy One be made manifest in all their movements like a mighty torrent may they flow down from the mountains and lick up their enemies like small dust may the armies of the Gentiles be before thy servants like withered leaves before the blast and as dry twigs in the flame of a furnace.[29]

Brig. Hiram Clawson recorded the events of 3 October as a combination of the momentous and the mundane. Clearly the most important event was General Wells's 3:00 P.M. council meeting. With Colonel Burton present at this meeting, there was no apparent discussion of the pressure to execute flowing

[28] As it turned out, Alexander did not fully break camp until 12 October after a slightly earlier false start.

[29] Penrose Journals, entry for 3 October 1857, LDS Archives. In the late nineteenth century Penrose became the leading Mormon apologist with respect to attacks on the church over Mountain Meadows, as well as an apostle and writer of hymns.

Fort Supply

Established in 1853 thirteen miles from Fort Bridger, Fort Supply was intended to be a civilian agricultural settlement to re-provision westbound Mormon emigrants for the final push to the Salt Lake Valley as well as a mission to influence the region's nomadic tribal bands. Notwithstanding herculean efforts, the settlement was only partially successful due to its high altitude, austere climate, and short growing season. *Image from Gowans and Campbell,* Fort Bridger, Island in the Wilderness, *courtesy of the LDS Archives.*

from his failure to immobilize the Tenth Infantry at Pacific Spring eight days earlier. It was a session that sheds light on the Mormon decision-making process: prayerful deliberation by the senior authority guided by direction from above as well as by advice and support from his immediate counselors.

Clawson, Eastern Expedition Log, October–November 1857, LDS Archives.

Oct 3 1857. O. P. Rockwell started with an Express to McAllister he will remain to assist him

10 oclock A.M. Mr Yates & Battise came to the Post. Propositions was made to Yates him [*sic*] for the Powder & Lead, & Blankets he had on hand—to purchase them. 500 & Powder 700 & Lead . . .[30]

[30] As discussed in the previous chapter, Yates refused this offer, thereby setting in motion a chain of events leading to his murder by Lt. Bill Hickman on 18 October. See Chapter 12.

3 o clock P.M. Met in Council Present Gen D H Wells, John Taylor Geo. A Smith, Genl Ferguson Genl Lewis Robinson, O. P. Rockwell, Bryant Stringham, Col Burton & Genl H B Clawson & Judson Stoddard also B Young Jr decided that O. P. Rockwell Express to Maj McAllister and stay to assist him.

Instructions that Maj McAllister use great caution in attacking their trains in stampeding their Cattle, should they be pursued let the cattle go and take care of yourselves.

Question by Genl. Wells shall we destroy their trains & Burn the Grass &c[?] *Decided,* that Col Burton Burn Fort Supply as soon as he can get ready to leave and do that as soon as possible, let the [wheat] field stand for the present also the Mill cash [cache] all you can also that O P Rockwell & Maj McAllister Burn all the grass on the roads & routes to the valley, starting on the [northerly] road to Soda springs. in regard to the trains Capt Lot Smith will do as ~~circumstances shall~~ he has been directed[31]

Should the troops ~~take the~~ move by any route toward the City Col Burton is instructed in cooperation with Maj McAllister to escort the troop on their way and annoy them all in his power without exposing his men

20 minutes after five P.M.

Express from McAllister for D. W. Perkins & Absolum Smith, saying, that the troops are all on the march for by the upper route probably by Bear river & Kinneys cut off[32]

Col Burton will move immediately to this place and find [?] a start ~~without~~ by [any a gld?] delay on the Oregan road to head them

O.P. Rockwell will take 3 men of McAllisters company & and move immediately after the troops and burn & destroy their trains burn the grass &c on both sides & before them . . .

6 o clock P.M

Fort Bridger set ~~a~~ on fire by Lewis Robinson & O P Rockwell left for Maj McAllister he will ~~take~~ move all his men ~~in with him~~ in the same direction

1/2 past 6 P M

Gen Wells started for Muddy [Creek] accompanied by Genl Ferguson Bro Taylor & Smith Gen Clawson, B Stringham Judson Stoddard & Capt B Young Jr . . .

11 o clock.

Prayers by John Taylor returned to rest. Moon shown bright cold night.

From his bivouac on Muddy Creek, General Wells soon moved his headquarters to Echo Canyon, where they remained. In that twenty-mile-long defile Cols. N. V. Jones and W. B. Pace and Maj. Adam Sharp supervised the con-

[31] In the early 1880s, Lot Smith recalled that "General Wells, looking at me as straight as possible, asked if I could take a few men and turn back the trains that were on the road or *burn* them. I replied that I thought I could do just what he told me to. The answer appeared to please him, and he accepted it." "Narrative of Lot Smith," Hafen and Hafen, eds., *Mormon Resistance,* 220.

[32] Kinneys Cutoff was a popular variant of the earlier Sublette Cutoff.

struction of the canyon's defenses with 498 men organized in eight detachments. Jones, the former Las Vegas lead miner, reported to Brigham Young, "We have been busily employed in making fortifications on both sides the kanyon, where men with rocks and firearms can make great destruction to our enemies without being in the least danger themselves, unless the enemi [*sic*] should succeed in flanking which we are making preparations to prevent effectually. The only fear is the enemy will not move through this kanyon."[33]

One of the few first-hand accounts of Fort Supply's destruction appeared in Legionnaire Jesse W. Crosby's journal, which was polished from the original in the early twentieth century and published in 1939.

CROSBY, JOURNAL, *ANNALS OF WYOMING* (JULY 1939), 212–13.

> I went to Fort Supply with a small company of men to help take care of the crops, and to make ready to burn everything if found necessary. After finishing the third day's labor and posting our guards we retired to rest, but were soon disturbed by the arrival of an Express from Bridger, ordering everything destroyed. We took out our wagons, horses, etc., and at 12 o'clock set fire to the buildings at once, consisting of 100 or more good hewed-log houses, one sawmill, one grist mill and thrashing machine; and after going out of the Fort, we did set fire to the Stockade work, straw and grain stacks, etc. After looking a few minutes at the bonfire we had made, thence on by the light thereof.
>
> I will mention that owners of property in several cases begged the privilege of setting fire to their own, which they freely did, thus destroying at once what they had labored for years to build, and that without a word. Thence on the way a few miles we stopped and set fire to the City Supply—a new place just commenced—10 or 16 buildings perhaps, and warmed ourselves by the flames.[34] Thus was laid waste in a few hours all the labor of a settlement for three or four years, with some 500 or 600 acres of land fenced and improved.
>
> Our work of destruction was now finished and we moved silently onward and reached Bridger a little after daylight and found it in ashes, having been fired the night before. We now joined our companions in arms who, with us, after some deliberation evacuated the place and moved back in the brush to await orders on the approach of the enemy. After waiting some myself and a small division of men with disabled horses we left for the main camp in Echo, and again joined Col. Burton's command.

Two months later, David A. Burr, writing as the *New York Times*'s pseudonymous correspondent "A. B. C.," described the ruins of Fort Supply: "On arriving at the spot I realized for the first time in my life what I had imag-

[33] Jones to Young, 3 October 1857, LDS Archives.

[34] "City Supply" was apparently a small settlement ancillary to Fort Supply.

ined of the appearance of a sacked, burned and abandoned village. The place was marked by the blackened and charred timbers sticking up in every direction, and by the tumbling adobe walls and mud chimneys. There was a sense of desolation about those ruins of a recently beautiful settlement which was, to say the least, unpleasant."[35]

Lot Smith's own account of his activities is available in published form. Less well known but nonetheless valuable is the account of James Parshall Terry, one of the Legionnaires who rode with Smith. Terry's autobiographical account of his experiences with Lot Smith was like many pioneer reminiscences, probably based on rougher, contemporaneous notes no longer available. To a modern reader there are signs that Terry's narrative may have been influenced in some ways by Lot Smith's earlier published account. On the other hand, Terry includes comments, vignettes, and information wholly undiscussed in Smith's narrative while excluding any reference to speculation about his possible involvement in the assassination of Henry Forbes in January 1858.[36] This material also includes a unique partial roster of the forty-four men who set out from Fort Bridger on the afternoon of 3 October 1857. Of his leader, Terry commented, "I want to say in honor to Lot Smith that I never travelled or would wish to travel with a better officer than he was. He was a boy with the Boys. Always shared what he had with them and fared just as they did. Was one to do more than his part in standing guard or anything else that needed to be done."

TERRY, AUTOBIOGRAPHY, BRIGHAM YOUNG UNIVERSITY LIBRARY.

Fri [Oct.] 2 [1857] A Company of 44 men was organised with Lot Smith as Captain to scout around the enemy, burn the grass, and otherwise annoy them by stampeding their stock, burning their wagons or any way to cripple them. Generals D. H. Wells and Geo. A. Smith called the boys together preparitory to our starting and gave some instructions. Among other things they said, "Boys, don't let them pen you." Also told us that if the soldiers fired on us we were not to return the fire. We started at 4 P.M. travelling 31 miles and camped for the night on the south side of and near Blacks Fork below the Soldiers' camp.

Sat [Oct.] 3. While getting breakfast we saw a dust on the main road and supposed it to be a company of the enemy. We got up our horses when Capt. Smith with a part of his men went to see what it was. Found to be a small

---

[35] Burr ("A. B. C.") dispatch, 1 December 1857, "The Utah Army," *New York Times*, 21 January 1858, 1. The stumps of the burned pallisades or "pickets" may still be seen in what is now a Wyoming rancher's privately owned pasture.

[36] See Chapter 12.

freight train which he turned towards Green River.[37] We then . . . the balance of our company and rode on to Green River. Found a large [military] company of the enemy there with a light battery. We went in below them on a big island and camped. It is worthy of note that our mules was perfectly quiet all night while the mules of the soldiers camp kept up an incessant braying.

Sun [Oct.] 4. The enemy rolled out of camp very early this morning for Hams Fork. Our company divided this morning. A scouting party went back to Blacks Fork. I remained with Lot. We rode on to the Big Sandy, sent out 3 men as scouts. They returned with the news that one freight train of 26 wagons was on Green River when we held a council whether it would be wisdom to go back to Green River and burn the wagons when it was decided to try it. We arrived at the wagons about 12 o clock midnight and upon examining them, we found instead of 26 wagons, there was 51 of them in 2 corals only a little distance apart. The most of the teamsters had gone to bed, but the wagonmaster [John M. Dawson] with those that was still up was just coming out from the trading post near by as we rode up when we took them prisoners although there was about 66 of the teamsters while there was only 26 of us. We placed guards around the wagons and got the men all up of which I (never) saw a scareder lot in my life until they found that they was not going to be hurt. Then they laughed and said they was glad the wagons was going to be burnt as they would not have to bull whack any more, as they called it. The teamsters was permitted to take their private clothing and guns out of the wagons and then they were burnt. Capt. Smith was very (happy) to see that there was no ammunition or anything to explode to cause axidents. There was one wagon loaded with tar rope ostensibly, as it was said to hang Brigham Young and his danites.[38] But suffice it to say the tar rope made a grand light. The country was lit up for miles around and we returned to Big Sandy and camped till morning. We got word about this time that Fort Bridger and Supply was burnt by our Boys. I will here insert the names of the boys or men that was together at this time. Lot Smith Captain. [Lt.] Horton D. Haight, Henry [C.] Jackson,[39] Thomas Alihat [Lt. Thomas Abbott], Jacob Truman, Lenard Rice, Mark Bigler, Samuel Bateman, Ten I don't know the right name, [Lt.] John Vance, Oren Lee, Edward Westover, Isaiah Cox, [Joseph] Woodmanse, James P. Terry, George Sonekin, Philo Dibble [Jr.], Mahonri M. Cahoon, Orson P. Arnold, Henry Boice, ______ Reeves [Robert W. Reeve, Jr.], Peter Saby, ______ Lenard, M. Halnbrook, Henry Day, Harry Perkins. There is two or three of these names I cannot . . . to be correct.

1857 October Monday 5th. We rode up Big Sandy a little ways and got breakfast and then rode on a little further and on to the main road when we came across another train of 24 wagons stopped for noon. The wagon master [Lewis

---

[37] This was "Captain" Rankin's six-wagon train loaded with corn for the army's animals.

[38] See Asa S. Hawley's comment in an earlier chapter about this intent back on the plains in August 1857.

[39] See below for Jackson's letters to his wife.

Simpson] and some of the teamsters was gone out to bring their cattle and the men that was in camp, we instructed them to take their clothing, guns, and anything that might explode out of the wagons preparitory to burning them. When the wagon master came in, Lot told him he had orders to burn the wagons when he said, "Well you have got the advantage of me. I guess you will have to burn them." Lot answered him, "Oh I guess not if you think so. There is your guns. They were stacked at the head of the corral, you can take them an we will try for it." But the wagon boss declined the proposition and said he would rather let the wagons be burnt. And now began the pleading, he wished to retain a wagon to carry their baggage and some provisions on to Green River but it was some time before Ca[p]t. Smith would consent, but finally he yielded. Then the wagon master wanted another and it took some hard pleading before he got it, but finally Lot consented and they pulled out the two wagons and the other 22 wagons was burnt. Here I want to show an overruling providence in our behalf in letting the teamsters retain the two wagons. A few days after (this) incident we was entirely without anything to eat so we went in to Green River when we found the wagon master with his two wagons which he had been allowed to retain wasn't burnt. And Lot told him our situation when he said, "you acted the gentleman with me and now you can have all you want of anything we have." So you see how the Lord can over rule things for good.[40]

In the immediate aftermath of this destruction, General Wells drafted instructions for one of his mid-level and most active field officers, Maj. Joseph Taylor. These instructions, written from Echo Canyon's Cache Cave, were to be the template for Wells's guidance to his other officers. When captured with Taylor and his adjutant on 16 October, Wells's letter soon became a cause célèbre—one of the two most famous documents of the Utah War.[41] It also became crucial evidence leading to the subsequent treason indictment returned against Taylor, William R. R. Stowell, his adjutant, Brigham Young, and D. H. Wells, among others.

WELLS TO JOSEPH TAYLOR, 4 OCTOBER 1857, LDS ARCHIVES.

You will proce[e]d with all possible dispatch without injureing your Animals to the Or[e]gon Road near the bend of Bear River North by East of this place. Take Close and correct observations of the Country on your route. When you approach the road send Scouts ahead to ascertain if the invading troops have passed that way. Should they have passed take a Concealed route and get ahead of them. Express to Col Burton who is now on that road and in the

[40] A slightly expanded, more polished version of this autobiography, signed pseudonymously by Terry as "Unohoo," appeared in *The Juvenile Instructor* 28, nos. 9–10 (1 and 15 May 1893): 278–80, 310–12.

[41] The other document was Brigham Young's martial-law proclamation. After he became aware that the army had his instructions to Taylor, Wells directed his field commanders to destroy his future messages after reading them.

> vicinity of the troops, and effect a junction with him so as to operate in concert. On ascertaining the Locality or route of the troops proceed at once to annoy them in every possible way. Use Every Exertion to Stampede their animals and set fire to their trains. Burn the whole country before them and on their flanks. Keep them from sleeping by night ~~and by night~~ surprises. Blockade the road by felling trees or destroying river fords when you can. Watch for Opportunities to Set fire to the Grass on their windward so as if possible to envelope their trains. Leave no grass before them that Can be burned. Keep your men concealed as much as possible and guard against surprise. Keep scouts out at all times and communication open with Col. Burton Major McAllister and O. P. Rockwell who are operating in the same way. Keep me advised daily of your movements and every step the troops take and in which direction
>
> God bless you and give you success, Your bro in Christ
>
> P.S. If the troops have not passed or have turned in this direction follow in their rear and continue to annoy them burning any train they may leave. Take no life but destroy their trains and stampede or drive away the animals at every opportunity.[42]

Meanwhile, Brigham Young was stirring in Salt Lake City. On 4 October, unaware of the decisions made by Wells's council of war during the prior afternoon, he provided his own advice through a message that seems almost relaxed if not serene:

> By your letter of Oct. 2nd I can in no wise perceive but what the Spirit of our God guides and blesses you in your views and plans, so far as they can be developed while the advance [U.S. Army] troops are awaiting the orders of the General Commanding, and am in no way concerned but that you will ever be thus guided and blessed. . . .
>
> To enable you to more easily carry out these suggestions, it will probably be best to vacate and lay waste Forts Bridger and Supply at the earliest date that your judgment may dictate.[43]

General Wells received this message by courier late on the night of 4 October, at which time Fort Bridger and Fort Supply—virtually the only communities between Fort Laramie and Salt Lake City—were in ashes, as would be soon three contractor supply trains. Two years later to the day, Apostle George A. Smith recorded: "Prest. [Young] remarked that his natural feelings were not to destroy property, and he thought that if he had been in the

[42] The text of these instructions may also be found in House Ex. Doc. No. 71, Serial 956, 56–57, and Hafen and Hafen, eds., *Mormon Resistance*, 161–62. The former source contains minor editorial changes and mistakes such as in Wells's middle initial, while the Hafens' version unaccountably omits the important postscript containing the "take no life" instruction.

[43] Young to Wells, Taylor, and Smith, 4 October 1857, LDS Archives.

mountains, he would not have given his consent to the burning of the Government Wagons, but still he believed that it was the best thing that could have been done, and it was all right that he did not know any thing about it until it was over, we might have got along without doing it, but perhaps the yarn would not have been dyed thoroughly, and would wash out."[44]

General Wells and his apostolic advisors reported the action as they knew it to Young on 5 October after receiving his letter of the previous day. Among other news, they reported, "We sent Wm Hickman & two or three men to Green R. to endeavour to get a chance to burn the trains that might have made their way there. We directed Col. Burton to burn Fort Supply and move down near Fort Bridger. We then put the torch to the Fort and moved to our Camp near the Muddy."[45] Two days later the same group transmitted a report of 5 October from Maj. Thomas Callister summarizing the early results of Lot Smith's operations, including news "that he destroyed 51 wagons [in two trains] loaded with Government stores on Green River last night about 12 o'clock. . . . Our men at this point are actively engaged in burning the grass on Smith & Black's Fork—Fort Supply is burnt to ashes."[46] On 8 October General Wells and his advisors wrote to Brigham Young to provide additional information on Lot Smith's activities—the destruction of twenty-five more wagons on Big Sandy—as well as about Porter Rockwell's grass-burning efforts, hopes for the theft of six hundred army cattle on Green River, as well as plans to stampede additional herds of horses and mules.[47]

In the midst of this activity General Wells wrote a long, candid letter to his friend Albert Carrington, editor of the *Deseret News*. This private message had a substantially different tone than Wells's official reports, many of which were written in collaboration with Apostles Taylor and Smith. Here one sees more of the general's fatigue, some of the confusion related to the evacuation and destruction of the forts, and even signals of Wells's disappointment with a few of his subordinates.

---

[44] Historian's Office Journal, entry for 4 October 1859, LDS Archives. In mid-November 1857 a Buffalo, New York, newspaper ran a telegraphic dispatch from St. Louis reporting, "Brigham Young disclaims any knowledge of or participation in the destruction of the U.S. supply trains." *Commercial Advertiser* (Buffalo), 17 November 1857, 2/4.

[45] Wells, Taylor, and Smith to Young, 5 October 1857, LDS Archives.

[46] Thomas Callister to Daniel H. Wells, 5 October 1857, LDS Archives. Apparently the destruction was not complete, for a month later another report informed Young, "We left behind . . . about 60 men with Br^s^ Lewis Robison & R. T. Burton to watch the movements of the enemy and burn the hay & grain stacks still left at Supply. The old huts that were still standing at Bridger were burned last night." Wells, Rich, and Grant to Young, 7 November 1857, ibid.

[47] D. H. Wells, George A. Smith, and John Taylor to Brigham Young, 8 October 1857, LDS Archives.

Wells to Carrington, 7 October 1857, Carrington Collection.

Having a little leisure today while waiting the result of the movements of the detachments, I thought that perhaps I could not be better engaged than in writing a few lines to you. We have selected this place as being the most convenient to direct the movements from in any direction that may be necessary and not be liable to be marched upon at any moment as we were at Fort Bridger. When we arrived at that place we found things in a very bad condition for a hasty move[.] Bro. [J. W.] Cummings & Robert [Burton] had not recovered from their hasty retreat from the [South] pass after attempting the stampede of the animals of the Army, and [we] were not fully apprised of their doings and movements. We had therefore to strengthen our guards in that direction and take such other measures as should keep us better advised of their movements ~~and the country~~. We also found ourselves deficient in regard to the lay of the country and found that others were almost as ignorant in regard to this matter as ourselves. A portion of the Men were try[ing] to work a little at Fort Supply to secure the grain without tools and were doing it to very little effect. The stock at Fort Bridger still remained on the range and a considerable lot of Property consisting of wagons, blacksmith tools, about a thousand horse shoes &c &c scattered about. One days forced march such as the Army made coming to Green River would bring them there. We therefore lost no time upon our arrival at that point in sending the message proclamation &c of the Governor and making preparations to suddenly evacuate & burn that place as well as Fort Supply. It was two days after we sent those documents before we got any reply. In the meantime we had been very busy in making our details and preparing for active service. You must also remember that during this time the horse teams which had been sent out with flour were near their camp so if we had been disposed we could not safely move until they were out of reach. The army did not rest but still seemed on the move. They received our communication in the morning just as they were ready to start and answered it after they camped that night having marched some said 5 some 10 Miles that day. Their direction (if you will observe the map) up Ham's Fork brought them nearer Bridger than before and we felt they might by making a night march [to] surprise us at any moment. We therefore considered it best to lay waste [to] that place and Fort Supply so that they could not avail themselves of any benefit at either of those places. We took every thing that we had teams and wagons to carry and cached the balance that could be secured except at Fort Supply some grain would necessarily fall into their hands. as some of the grain was not cut. Other was in the shock in the field five miles from the machine and so long as we continued to bother with it, it seemed as though we could do nothing else. I took the best teams to do the hauling. There was no tools to work with and to tell the truth not much disposition on the part of the boys to work. They felt tired. It disadvantaged our baggage wagons & baggage to have the wagons so far away and you will also observe that it is in the wrong direction. There was nothing but potatoes & turnips there that we could use except feed for animals. No beef nor flour. We therefore secured what we could and burned the rest retaining only such as we could use at a moment's notice for feed for animals. The potatoes and turnips being dug of course remain as they were. Having made our details as you have probably seen in the despatches to the Governor we left for Muddy [Creek] where the sick the poor and worn-out animals and surplus wagons had been forwarded. We sent back sufficient rations to do the boys about fifteen days (with what they had) and the next morning started this camp out of the way. The sick and surplus wagons have been sent into the city and the remainder with supplies remain at the express station near this place. We thought we would rather send back a load or two of supplies from this place if needed than run any risk of having them taken by the enemy. I am aware that this [place] is some distance to operate from and if it were either prudent or wisdom [I would] much rather be with Robert [Burton]. But we all feel that this is the most judicious move we could make.

A word in regard to the instructions to the boys. We felt as though we could not before try the enemy only watching their movements and retreat before them and do nothing towards hedging up their way and we did not know any other way to do this than to stampede their animals or drive them off burn the grass and their wagons & supplies &c if possible. We consider that if we can burn up their wagons they will have to stop as they dare not leave their supplies. As to taking their trains keep a sharp lookout on their horses & mules and their cattle could scarcely travel out of the way of even footmen if they should choose to pursue. We therefore directed the boys to drive off their cattle if they could but if they found themselves pursued to abandon them and try it again some other time and keep doing so it will hinder their progress at least and tend to annoy them of course and will get them if possible as also the horses & mules but to rob a man you must get pretty close to him and run some risk of getting shot. We have therefore to act very cautious and it appeared as though we might do more towards impeding their progress by using up their trains of wagons than any other way. It is not probable that their supplies would all burn but you see they would have to stay by it. This ~~course~~ calculation has already proven true as Major Lott Smith could not secure the cattle belonging to the Fifth [Infantry] and wagons at Green River which he destroyed and now that dragoons have come up it may still be still more difficult to get any more cattle but if we can destroy their wagons they are licked. I am only afraid that we shall not be able to do sufficient of this upon our enemies at this present. We considered the chances very strong of the troops taking the Fort Hall route and considered it best to throw an additional force ahead of them if possible. With this view we detached from the force here fifty men under the command of Major [Joseph] Taylor and sent them across to the Oregon road from the head of this Kanyon to operate with Col. Burton with instructions to express to him when they should arrive in his vicinity but we have since learned that the troops only moved a short distance and that others have come up. It is supposed that General Harney is with them of this we expect to learn tonight. His forces will act perhaps as efficiently in connection with Col. Burton as though they had remained here even if the Army comes that way. Yesterday with Bro Taylor, Judson Stoddard, James Ferguson & Hiram [Clawson] I visited the camp below operating with Col. N. V. Jones. I consider it the best point in the Kanyon to defend and pointed it out to him as we passed up every place is entirely secure from any of the enemy shot except their cannon and there is not a point that the cannon can be brought to bear upon until they arrive with[in] gun shot of our men. They cannot therefore have the advantage of long shot but will be liable to be cut off the very moment they come in sight otherwise they might do some damage with their cannon. I shall take a look at these works so soon as we learn of them coming this way and perhaps before if things are so that I can. Flanking is well guarded against at that point by deep ravines. I directed that the road should be broken up in three places not far apart.[48] All this is immediately under the range of our guns and the shortest yagers [rifles] can reach them. Indeed at many places the common revolvers can be used with perfect impunity. Each place is not only secure from the small arms of the enemy but has a safe retreat if they find they cannot silence their cannon.

Well I have hastily thrown together this office chat the same as tho' we were talking and could say much more but Bro [Lewis] Robinson [*sic*] is now ready to go and I must close. I thought his things were so scattered it was best for him to go in and if he could get round in time come back. Bro George A. [Smith] and all the rest stand this trip so far first rate and feel well. Our trust is in God and we have no fear but that it will all come out right let things turn as they will. We have instructed our men not to kill any body until they get into this Kanyon or until further orders. If we can only defeat them without firing a gun or killing a single one I feel that I should be perfectly satisfied.

If General Wells conveyed to Albert Carrington a scene of uncertainty and some confusion, he was not alone. Colonel Alexander's officers—enraged by Lot Smith's destruction to their rear while Alexander remained passive—virtually forced the colonel to assume command of the expedition and to make a decision on its forward direction. From this 6 October war council came Alexander's decision to move on Salt Lake City via the longer northern route to bypass the defended canyons, a march that began belatedly in fits and starts over the next week.

---

[48] Here Wells is describing a series of ditches dug transversely across the road which, through sluice gates, could be flooded from the stream coursing through Echo Canyon. He believed that these water barriers would stop the Utah Expedition.

Nauvoo Legion Major Lot Smith
The war's most famous Legionnaire and perhaps its best horseman, Smith was the source of the conflict's most enduring utterance ("for His sake"). He led the mounted raiding party that destroyed three Russell, Majors and Waddell wagon trains behind army lines on the night of 4–5 October 1857, thereby vividly demonstrating Mormon military capabilities in guerrilla tactics at the cost of a (subsequently quashed) federal treason indictment. Smith's raid alarmed not only Americans on both coasts but also European diplomats. *Courtesy LDS Archives.*

It Was for His Sake: Of Lot Smith, Myths, and Realities

If Lot Smith's early October raid dealt a severe blow to the aura of army invincibility, the attack unwittingly spawned a new myth to take its place, albeit one that took generations to gain currency. In this sense, the Utah War was like all other American military conflicts—freighted with folklore, tall tales, and legends, some of which assumed mythic proportions. Did the Nauvoo Legion use silver bullets? Was the Utah War indeed bloodless? Did Colonel Cooke doff his hat as the Second Dragoons marched past Brigham Young's Lion House? Did an eighteenth child survive the Mountain Meadows massacre and remain hidden in Utah? Was Thomas L. Kane a secretly baptized Mormon? Were Buchanan's cabinet officers plotting secession as proto-Confederates as early as 1857? Did Jim Bridger, Bill Cody, and Kit Carson spend the winter of 1857–58 together on Blacks Fork?

Over the centuries all of these legends have developed a following, some with good reason and others as the result of pernicious, willful manipulation of the truth. The principal myth associated with Lot Smith's raid ran to what he said while putting the torch to wagonmaster John M. Dawson's train at Green River on the night of 4–5 October. Based on Smith's account, Dawson reacted to his intent "to put a little fire" into his wagons with the excited comment, "For God's sake, don't burn the trains." According to Smith, "I said it was for His sake that I was going to burn them."[49]

Twenty-five years after the raid, Smith worked with Junius F. Wells, talented son of General Wells, to produce a fascinating account of this action, including Smith's recollection of his repartee with Captain Dawson. It was a piece that Wells ran serially in his Salt Lake City magazine, *The Contributor,* during 1882–83.[50] How much of this narrative was the work of which man is an imponderable not unlike attempting to fathom the editorial collaboration between Smith's less savory comrade-in-arms Bill Hickman and J. H. Beadle, or that of John D. Lee and his attorney-editor William Bishop. It is probably safe to conclude that Lot Smith's essay was substantially more polished and fluent than had Junius Wells not been involved. Smith himself commented, "All has been written from memory and the editor has done well to get it in as good shape as it is."

Whether Smith's "for His sake" response to Dawson was included in the material Smith provided in 1882 or was an editorial embellishment by Wells cannot be determined. Nevertheless, the phrase captured the imagination of first Mormons and then others at the height of the late nineteenth-century federal polygamy prosecutions. This was a period during which a polygamous Smith was evading federal marshals in the slickrock canyons of northern Arizona. His words as published by Wells became emblematic of an embattled Legionnaire's cool determination and religiosity in the wilderness of 1857. Through a process still poorly understood, these few words took on a mythic quality, with Lot Smith himself assuming an heroic image that in today's terms could be described as a blend of the Lone Ranger, Robin Hood, and Nathan Hale. As the decades and centuries passed, Smith's "for His sake" comment has become the best-known phrase of a western confrontation that is itself poorly understood. It is an utterance with far more verve and appeal than its nearest rival, President Buchanan's assertion to Congress two months

---

[49] "Narrative of Lot Smith," Hafen and Hafen, eds., *Mormon Resistance,* 222.

[50] Smith's narrative was not a standalone piece but rather was material incorporated into a serial that Wells wrote under the pen name "Vaux" and was titled "The Echo Cañon War." The Lot Smith segments of the story appeared in *The Contributor* 3 (1882):271–74; 4 (1883):27–29, 47–50, 167–69, and 224–26. See also "Narrative of Lot Smith," Hafen and Hafen, eds., *Mormon Resistance,* 220–46.

later that "This is the first rebellion which has existed in our Territories; and humanity itself requires that we should put it down in such a manner that it shall be the last."[51]

Did Lot Smith say it? With all of the contemporaneous affidavits taken from witnesses on the federal side—including John Dawson—and with available reminiscences left by several men who rode with Smith such as James Parshall Terry and Robert W. Reeve, Jr., there is no record to support this now-famous comment. On the other hand, there are at least two reasons to take Smith's "for His sake" comment seriously, if not to accept it at face value: the overall defensibility of Lot Smith's narrative and his personal reputation.

Notwithstanding the fact that Smith worked entirely from memory, his narrative as published holds up in exemplary fashion alongside contemporaneous documents. This applies not only to Smith's recollection of names, dates, places, and the sequence of events but also with respect to his extraordinary grasp of repartee exchanged twenty-five years earlier.[52] With Smith's unusually accurate memory of banter, it is not unreasonable to take seriously his 1882 recollection of the "for His sake" phrase. The fact that this comment appeared casually in the midst of a sentence about a wholly mundane, unrelated subject, and subsequently was never stressed by either Smith or his editor, adds to its credibility.

Finally, there is the matter of Lot Smith's character. Most people who have read and thought about Charles S. Peterson's wonderful biographical sketch of Smith would have difficulty imagining him as a purveyor of hyperbole or tall tales. Smith had a reputation as a wag, but not as a self-promoting liar.[53]

Lot Smith may have been rough, hot-headed, hard on people, and at times even brutal and profane, but in terms of truthfulness his reputation was impeccable.[54] In this sense, he was not a Jim Bridger. Neither was Smith a Buffalo Bill Cody, who in the 1880s began to merchandise shamelessly the tale that he had witnessed Lot Smith's raid as Lew Simpson's eleven-year-old protégé, and that he had spent the subsequent winter at Fort Bridger under the pro-

[51] This sentence was embedded in Buchanan's 8 December 1857 first annual message to Congress.

[52] For several examples of the accuracy of Smith's recollections, see his account of his 5 October 1857 encounter with "Captain" Rankin's six-wagon corn train, his 6 October encounter with wagonmaster Lewis Simpson, and his description of his and Porter Rockwell's 12 October confrontation with James Rupe. "Narrative of Lot Smith," Hafen and Hafen, eds., *Mormon Resistance*, 221 and 237; Hiram B. Clawson, Eastern Expedition Log, October–November 1857, entry for 5 October 1857, LDS Archives.

[53] Peterson, "A Portrait of Lot Smith," 393–414.

[54] Surely W. M. F. Magraw would have viewed Smith as brutal had he heard him say during his famous raid, as wagonmaster Lew Simpson did, that "they would catch & kill" Magraw, and that "there was a special party who had gone out to capture Magraw dead or alive." See Chapter 12.

tection of James Butler (Wild Bill) Hickok. These were both Utah War myths of the worst stripe stoked by an image-building Cody and then accepted by reporters, novelists, and historians in need of colorful anecdotes.[55]

After the Utah War Lot Smith continued to lead a colorful life. Ironically, with the rank of captain in the U.S. Army, Smith commanded the company constituting Utah Territory's contribution to the Civil War. Even after this patriotic service, one Fort Douglas merchant reported to his superior at Fort Bridger in November 1865 that Smith "is not in the habit of visiting any Government office when he can avoid it."[56] In 1892, living in self-imposed exile in the isolated canyons of northern Arizona and somewhat estranged from Mormonism, Smith died of gunshot wounds sustained in a grazing dispute with a Navajo shepherd. In 1902 Smith's body was exhumed and reburied at Farmington, Utah, his former home. Virtually the entire senior leadership of the LDS church attended Smith's recommittal service. For years thereafter Lot Smith's Legion comrades met for annual reunions at his grave. Even today uniformed reenactments of these gatherings continue periodically in Farmington, a gesture of respect for Lot Smith and pride in Mormon military service.[57] Lot Smith (if not Junius Wells) lives!

Left to Your Discretion and Judgement: Young Strategizes and Micromanages

Notwithstanding the havoc created by Lot Smith's raids, the continued advance of the Utah Expedition in an uncertain direction and with unclear intent prompted Brigham Young to rethink his plans. His 17 October letter to General Wells and Apostles Taylor and Smith was a stunning message that ranged through a wide mix of strategic initiatives and operational minutia. In the process Young demonstrated an unmistakable propensity to micromanage while thinking broadly. As indicated in the previous chapter, one finds here abandonment of Young's earlier no-bloodshed admonitions together with clear signals that he fully intended to seize the possessions of private mer-

[55] Neither Cody nor Hickok took part in the Utah War as Cody claimed they did. See Gray, "Fact Versus Fiction," 2–20, and MacKinnon, "Epilogue to the Utah War," 221. The most recent acceptance in toto of Cody's story about his Utah War involvement is Miller, "Bill Cody Gets Buffaloed," 195–200.

[56] Samuel Dean to William A. Carter, 16 November 1865, Judge William A. Carter Papers, Auerbach Collection.

[57] See "After Lapse of Ten Years, Remains of Captain Smith Interred at Farmington. A Most Notable Occasion," *Deseret News*, 9 April 1902, 5. The editor visited Smith's grave on 24 May 2007 with a Mormon History Association tour.

chants as well as government contractors—looting on a grand scale. Mixed with semi-comical instructions about how best to entice federal deserters and an offbeat advocacy of Mormon archery was a little-known vetting of one of Young's major manpower thrusts for 1858—the creation of a one-thousand- to two-thousand-man regular or "Standing Army" to parallel the Legion's militia organization and availability.

YOUNG TO WELLS, TAYLOR, AND SMITH,
17 OCTOBER 1857, LDS ARCHIVES.

The hurry attendant upon dispatching my express to you yesterday let [left out] a few items which may prove beneficial, and I now forward them by my son Joseph A. who expects to leave early tomorrow morning.

The alteration of positions in affairs necessarily induces at times a change of policy, and wisdom now seems to dictate a cessation of the destruction of trains, both individual and Government, for if the troops undertake to come in we shall fall heir to the property in their possession, and the private trains are destined for this market and are too far off to be hauled to any other, and we may need the [blot] they contain. In ceasing to destroy wagons and their loading it does not follow that they are to be altogether let alone, but at every opportunity let such as can be conveniently got hold of be forwarded on towards this city. That at present appears to be the best course to pursue with the trains.

Inasmuch as there are rumors of more or less disaffection in the enemy's camp, if possible to be accomplished it may be productive of good to have br. Lott Smith, or some other clear spoken and loud voiced person who is also a good rider, be furnished with a good horse and instructed at once to proceed to the enemy's camp and upon the first opportunity, at about dusk of a still evening, approach within hailing distance, on the windward side, and on a point or rise of ground if any, and shout something as follows:— "Attention the camp", (to be repeated, perhaps, once or twice, till attention is attracted) "all who wish to fight the Mormons had better stay where they are; and all who do not wish to fight are advised to make for Salt Lake City at every opportunity, where they will be well treated, furnished with employment and permitted to proceed to California when they please". Those words, or others of like purport, should be deliberately spoken with a loud, clear voice, so as to be definitely understood, and in case of an attempt to catch the speaker, his track for escape should be well understood by him beforehand. It may be that their picket guards and sentries are stationed too far out for the practicability of the above plan, of that you will be the better able to judge. But should that plan not be available, it is possible that you may be able to get word to [captive] Dr. [George W.] Hickman, by some of your messengers to the officers, to endeavor to get the above named ideas into the minds of those soldiers who wish to leave; or if that would be unsafe or impossible for Hickman to attempt, you may be able to contrive some plan that will succeed, as you are more familiar with the position and feelings of our enemies. It certainly is but fair that those who wish to leave and come in peaceably, as citizens, should be informed that they have that privilege, so far as we are concerned, and not be compelled to fight when they do not wish to and those whom they do not wish to. With the above suggestions, the most practicable mode of conveying the information is left to your discretion and judgement. But after all, perhaps the word already [seen by] the flight [?] the teamsters is sufficient for the purpose.

As you are already advised, so long as the troops keep on or east of the Fort Hall road, it is still best not to attempt to harm their persons, but to be always ready and on the alert to commence active operations the moment they may leave that road with a view to come into any of our settlements. If they take the road east, let them entirely alone; and if they continue down Bear River and take the Fort Hall road, let them go; but if they undertake to swing round into Cache valley or the Malad, let sleep depart from their eyes and slumber from their eyelids, both by night and by day, until they take their final sleep; pick off their guards and sentries and fire into their camps by night, and pick off officers and as many men as possible by day; but be sure to charge your men to watch against surprise and for some retreats, for the main skill consists in wasting our enemies, with no loss of our own men.

The cattle sent in under charge of br. Woodmansee all arrived safely, except a few weak ones left on good feed a short distance back; they can be driven in at any time.

We thought we would answer Col. Alexander's letter here, as we have office conveniences, &c., and I hope it will be as satisfactory to you and the brethren now out as it is to the brethren to whom it has been read.

If it is necessary to meet the enemy north, the brethren had probably better come down Weber cañon, if they can in safety with their wagons, as it will save some 20 or 30 miles travel. This I presume you have all before you, but it came into my mind and I thought I would mention it.

It has been suggested to my mind, so soon as our fall's work is pretty well along with, and while caches are being prepared &c, to select some 2000 of the right kind of men, have them provided with excellent rifles, and let them be furnished themselves with good bows and plenty of arrows, and learn to be as adept in their use as in sharpshooting with the Rifle, and organize them into a standing army to be most—or all—the time on duty in the field, and so appointed on the different feasable [*sic*] approaches to our Territory as circumstances may from time to time require, and each Ward supporting so many families, so that our solders can be perfectly free. About 100 on the Southern route to California, about 200 on the Mary's River route, 100 north to watch for Oregonians, and the remainder to watch the different eastern routes, the latter so placing their stores and rendezvous that they can operate together or apart. This we have written to you so that you can have something to talk about, when you have nothing more profitable to occupy your attention, though we really do think that 2000 men of the right stripe can prevent all the armies of the world from coming here.[58]

You will perceive that I made no mention, in my letter to Col. Alexander, about Dr. Hickman's being a prisoner, as that course would probably be most chagrining to his feelings, for he had [grannyisd?] upon that subject through over a page of his letter, and we are all perfectly aware that they dare not injure him, and will probably soon make an excuse to send him as a bearer of dispatches, if they have not already done so.[59]

As ever, praying for the success and welfare of Zion and for the confusion and overthrow of her enemies, I remain Your Brother in the Gospel,

I Am on the Lord's Business: Campaigning with Legionnaires

In mid-October Private Watt wrote again to his wife, Alice, describing an active two weeks of campaigning. Watt's letter is best appreciated with those of two other Legionnaires: Henry Clark Jackson and James Ferguson. These men were of widely varying background and accomplishment, yet there are interesting commonalities in what they wrote. Emblematic of early Utah society (as well as of the Utah Expedition), the birthplaces of the three Legionnaires were England, the United States, and Ireland, respectively.

Pvt. George D. Watt to Alice Watt, 14 October 1857, Watt Papers.

After nearly three weeks of constant travel of heats and cold—of wet and dry—of frost and snow—of aches and pains—After traveling over fortie [?] bottoms and saleratus plains, climing mountains and threading canyons, passing through hair breadth escapes—once being upset when in the baggage waggon down a deep declevity, the waggon and its load, with 4 loaded guns all around me being turned upon me, smashing the wagon bows to a thousand pieces. Once narrowly escaping being blow up by gunpowder. A young man by the name of Geo. Spencer one of our mess had his powder flask in his pocket with a 100 rounds of powder in it, also some matches which ignited and exploded the powder blowing the flask into a thousand pieces, envelop-

[58] The standard treatment of the Standing Army thrust is Bigler, *Forgotten Kingdom*, 183–84.

[59] Dr. George Washington Hickman was indeed soon released by the Utah Expedition to carry messages to Salt Lake City. In describing Alexander as a "granny," Young unwittingly echoed the nickname given to the colonel by his own officers: "the old woman."

ing every person near him in smoke and flame, I say after all this and more I am now situated about one days ride from the beloved City and the dear association in it, having escaped every danger without scratch or hurt, how great are the mercies of our God!, how uncearchable are his ways!!, how inscrutable his providences!!! Our tracts [tracks] may be seen for hundreds of miles around our enemies camp, fire from our branch has laid waste the country around in black desolation, 76 waggons loaded with provisions cloathing and armes for the soldier have been distroyed, and the cattle that hauled them driven away. A deserter came into our camp a few days ago he says they are upon half rations in the soldiers camp, and that many are watching their oppertunity to desert, he says they know not what course to take, but they are waiting for their commander to come up whose name is Johnson, Harney is not on the way at all, Johnson is expected up with 800 cavalry when he comes they may make a move either to press their way in or retreat. The defences in Echo Canyon cannot be discribed on paper, suffice it to say that all that can be done by nature, aparently has been done, and what seemed deficient has been, and is being added by the labor of our boys. They have grade rock defences with port holes on every point commanding a good rifle range of the road for a distance of over a mile, then they have dugg ditches clear across the canyon, and have it so fixed that they can stop the water and make a dam large enough to drown both horse and rider. The position is such with its defences as to defy any army that may ever seek to break through it; 500 men or less are all that is necessary to defend this pass. It cannot now be expected that the soldiers will take the northren course so late in the season, they are pretty well used up now, and unfit to travel 200 miles and fight their way against frosts and snows, and the contending forces of the hosts of Isreal, who are so well able to block up their way, and gaul them in every possable way, and all hope of their ever passing this point is totally extinguished. So there is nothing now left for them but to lay down their armes, and search for winter quarters, retreat eastward, or remain where they are, to perish in the snows of winter, how infalable are the words of God through his prophet Brigham "For I the lord will fight your battles." How long we may stay at this point I cannot say, neither does it concern me, I am on the lord's business, I am just as ready to return again close on the enemies borders, as to return home, tho I presume my home is as dear to me, and your sweet society, as home and a wifes society can possably be to any mortal, it is to defend such endearments that I am here, ready if necessary to pour out my blood like water for them, for our holy religion, and for nationl liberty. Such feelings has inflamed my bosome since I have been out on this campain to such an extent as to creat a longing disire to meet the enemy, face to face and with deadly weapons try the contest. I am perfectly ignorant as to the state of your health and the health of your friends. Letters have come to almost every man from their families, and I have stood with cracking ears expecting every next name would be G. D.

Watt but as yet I have not had the satisfaction of receiving a single line from my freinds. The last packet of letters that came and there were none for me, I must say that I felt for a forsaken and freindless. I had just come in from a long and tedious days journey, was hungery—weary—and worn—and dirty, and on the top of this no letter for me, I felt for a moment as tho nobody cared for *me*; but I knew better at the same time. I know that my absense necessarily throws a great deal more care upon you, but if you can steal a moment to drop me a line, you cannot tell the satisfaction it would yeild me. I have written you two notes before this. If bro. Godsal has not made my boots by this time, please tell him he need not make them at all my feet is on the ground and has been, but I can get along now. I think until the end of the campain.[60] Give my kind love to every body that cares for me, and those who dont care for me, care not for my love.

Among Private Watt's comrades in Echo Canyon was a less articulate Pvt. Henry Clark Jackson of Salt Lake City. One of Jackson's letters to his wife is available, together with her response. Remarkably, their letters represent virtually the only two-way husband-and-wife correspondence known to have survived the war from either the Nauvoo Legion or Utah Expedition. In almost all other cases, with the notable exception of Marcy C. Reno's one-sided correspondence with her U.S. Army officer-husband, the letters of the soldier were preserved and those of the wife lost.[61] The exchange of letters between the Jacksons echoes Private Watt's emphasis on warm clothing while providing even more graphic insight into the burden of additional responsibilities thrown on a wife during the Eastern Expedition's campaign. One senses that for Private Jackson his Legion service was something of a lark more than serious church business, yet for Ann Oades Jackson living in Salt Lake City, it was an almost nightmarish period. Incredibly, in his letter of 14 October, Henry Jackson failed to mention that he had just taken part with Lot Smith and James Parshall Terry in what would become the most famous action in Mormon military history.

Pvt. Henry Clark Jackson to Ann Oades Jackson,
14 October 1857, Ward Jay Roylance Collection.

After a Silance of 2 Wheeks I improve this opertunity to Write a few lines to you to Lett you know of my wheare abouts. My health is Very good Considering my Travales Since I Wrote to you Last. Since that time I have Rode on Horse Back about 350 Miles and and [*sic*] have never had tent or Waggon

[60] Watt's descendant-biographer believes that he had returned home by 18 October 1857 and was back at work recording tabernacle discourses a week later. Watt to MacKinnon, e-mail message, 7 November 2006.

[61] See also the long-distance correspondence between a civilian Mormon couple caught up in the Utah War—Elizabeth Margetts and Phillip Margetts—in Chapters 6 and 9.

to sleep in before last Night that I arrived at this place. I Tooke a Little Cold 6 Days since and have been a Little Horse [hoarse] But this morning I Can Speak a little Better But my health is good and my sperits is good as they was the day I Left home. If you Can get me [a] pair of Mittins to send me I think it whould Be a great favour. I have not needed them yet But I think I Shall do if I Remain out much Longer. I have Enjoied my self first rate, Remember me to my Children. Kiss them for me. Rec[e]ive my Love your self. Pleas rite to me [and] let me know how you are geting on in health and Every other respect. Rem[em]ber me to Sister Macintosh. I do not think much fighting will have to be done this season but I guess next year thear will be a Little. Do not neglect to write forth with. Charle[s] Wilken is returning home.[62]

Ann Oades Jackson to Henry Clark Jackson, 18 October 1857, LDS Archives.

Acceding to your request I take up my pen to ad[d]ress a few Lines to you you may think me neglectful by not writing to you sooner but when I tell you how I have fared you will at once no doubt forgive me for the children have all been sick it is three weeks to Morrow since Alma was taken with pukeing and purgeing when he got a little better then Henry William was taken sick a few days after Elizabeth Sarah was taken sick and then Alma again they are getting better know [*sic*] all but Alma he has not been so sick this two days he looks very sick and is very fretful but I hope he will take a turn for the better [very soon?] I have been up night and day all most for they was worse in the night you would have though[t] they could not breathe to help them I [?] put them in warm baths I was taken with the same complaint on wednesday last and have not been able to write since I got your letter before to day for my head [h]as been so bad that I could not look steady at any thing long so you see the way I live and my hands full since you left me and I have had no one to do the first thing for me I am alone day and night well I think I have given you plenty of bad news now well I am glad to hear that you look so well and that you have injoyed your self sine you have been out but I would be more glad if you had got through there and got home I hope you will not be much longer I am [k]nit[t]ing you a pare of gloves for I did not know how to get any mittins I will send them the first oportunity I would like to know how you do for washing for I think you cannot wash much I have heard of some sending in there dirty clothes I think it would be better if you could send yours home Send me word if you have plenty to eat and if you want any thing send word if [?] I must get it I will try and make you a Cap to put on at night as I think your Hat is to[o] cold well I shall have to conclude for it is Morning please write tome as often as you can and tell me how you are getting on I hope you are

[62] While unlikely, it is possible that Wilken was Pvt. Charles H. Wilcken, a German national (and ancestor of Gov. George Wilcken Romney) who deserted from Phelps's battery and was escorted into Echo Canyon on 10 October.

better of your cold by this time take all the care you can of yourself I wish I had something good to send you but I have not but I pray that the Lord God of Israel will bless you and give his Angels charge over you by night and by day that no evil come nigh you the Children often talk about Father [?]illingly [?] when are [?] you coming home Brother Walker is get[t]ing the Potatos up and Jones [?] got [h]is plough left three bushel [?] of wheat and 18 pounds of Mutton there is no wood come yet excuse all blunders

Adjt. Gen. James Ferguson's letters to Jane Robinson Ferguson, one of his three wives, were written from or near Echo Canyon while she was in Salt Lake City. Ferguson, a convert born in Belfast, Ireland, was a man of enormous talents and personal appeal. He had been sergeant major of the Mormon Battalion during the Mexican War and subsequently, as a lawyer, participated in some of Utah's most bruising legal disputes of the late 1850s. After the war, he co-founded a newspaper, *The Mountaineer,* in Salt Lake City with two other lawyers who were veterans of the Utah War. Their newspaper was meant to counteract the 1858 appearance of the anti-Mormon *Valley Tan.* Both newspapers folded in 1860. Tragically, Ferguson died of alcoholism in 1863 at age 35.[63]

Because of Ferguson's senior rank and close proximity to General Wells, his letters discuss some of the Legion's most momentous decisions and greatest risks. But Ferguson's messages also shared many of the less-global concerns found in the letters of Privates Watt and Jackson. An exception is a letter that he gave to Capt. Stewart Van Vliet as he was leaving Salt Lake City. Here one finds a whimsical tone not present in the personal letters, as Ferguson wrote to ask Van Vliet to obtain from the War Department a series of U.S. Army manuals "and such others as you may judge useful to us."[64] His letter to Jane Ferguson of 31 October signals the continuing struggle with alcohol that would kill him six years later. The letter of 17 November is an excellent example of a clear-minded Ferguson's substantial powers of reasoning and expression on behalf of Mormonism.

FERGUSON TO JANE R. FERGUSON, PRIVATE COLLECTION.

Camp Little 3 miles from Weber
Oct. 31, 1857, 8 A.M.

I feel sorry to have left you as I did, and trust you will forgive me. My folly however will result in good, for after I got over my tightness I was seized with

---

[63] Bagley, ed., *"A Bright, Rising Star": A Brief Life of James Ferguson.*

[64] Ferguson to Van Vliet, 14 September 1857, Nauvoo Legion Adjt. Gen.'s Record (1851–1870), p. 104, LDS Archives. The War Department in Washington took no note of Ferguson's cheeky request, although four months earlier—in the midst of planning for the Utah Expedition—Floyd had sent Young copies of the General Regulations for the Army for distribution to the Utah militia. Floyd to Young, 11 May 1857, ibid.

NAUVOO LEGION ADJUTANT GENERAL JAMES FERGUSON
Former sergeant-major of the Mexican War's Mormon Battalion, this talented writer-lawyer was General Wells's chief administrative officer. Like almost half of the Mormon and federal troops, Ferguson had been born abroad in Belfast. His ornate brigadier's uniform is trimmed with silver accessories probably ordered by Young on 30 June 1857; the presentation sword was received during Ferguson's 1855 mission to Ireland.
Courtesy of the late John Sharp Ferguson and of Will Bagley.

vomitting in the night and threw up an immense amount of bile. I vomitted all day yesterday and was very sick but kept travelling. This I believe will save me from bilious sickness on the Campaign which must have been the case if I had not got rid of the bile. Make my apologies to Lucy, Phillis & Mother, and bid them God bless them from me. Also kiss my dear children for me. I remember kissing little Pat, and your kind attentions to me in the wagon. God bless you a thousand times my dear girl. Apologize to Br. Barlow and family for me, and all whom I may have offended.[65] I have heard no additional news from the troops. My faith is still good that we will have no fighting this fall: but God knows best and will order things according to His own good pleasure. My kind love to everybody. Good bye. God bless you.

Camp 15 miles up Echo [Canyon]
Nov[r] 17, 1857

Although I wrote you a few lines in answer to your letter yesterday I thought I would make use of the passing leisure moment to write again inasmuch as I know that the many rumors afloat in the city trouble and perplex you. You want I should tell you the truth about matters and things out here. I can only tell you my own thoughts and reflections. These have ever been that we won't

[65] Much of this letter appears to deal with some alcohol-related embarrassment and illness during Ferguson's recent furlough.

have no war with the enemy this winter. And although by our last report they were within 7 miles of Bridger Ruins, my Faith is still ste[a]dfast that the storm will scatter, and that we shall enjoy our winter in peace.[66] While this is my firm belief, I am resigned to the Will of God, and with His help will abide firmly the result. It is our intention. Our scouts have orders to fire upon them if they come this side Bridger and in that case the war has commenced. But as I before said my firm conviction is that the commencement will be in another year than this. Be not uneasy nor troubled about me. We will both be grey before we part for the last time in this probation. That our pilgrimage will be varied and full of trouble I have no doubt. But our trials and separations will only make future happiness the more rich, and meetings the more joyful. Have we not been separated often, and been preserved by the Hand of the Almighty while the weapons of subtle foes have been exerted to keep us asunder and have we not met safe and unharmed again. For all your anxiety to see me, I know you would not ask me to be idle at home while my brethren were out for the defense of all we hold dear on earth. Are not wife [?] and children and home and friends [?] as dear, and as much the gifts of God to me, as they are to others, and are not they worth the expenditure of my time and ability for their defense? Are not the holy religion and God of my family and myself as dear to me, and do they not call as loudly for the testimony of my actions to prove that I love them, as any one else? Be encouraged then my dear girl, and let your cares be over the house at home, and your prayers ~~only~~ for me only that I may learn to serve my God better, and shrink from no duty whithersoever the path thereto might lead. My love to Lucy, Mother, Eliza, & a kiss each for my little ones. God bless you my dear Jane, and help us to love each other with a pure and holy love, as we have ever done, only more so.[67]

In Regard to Pretended Civil Officers: Dealing with Potential Captives

During the last week in October Brigham Young paused to focus on an offbeat but practical problem for the Legion now unknown to historians: what to do if its troops should encounter any of the Utah-bound federal appointees. On 7 October Young had written about such a possibility somewhat whimsically in terms of the disposition of a hypothetically captive army commander: "It is hoped that Lott [Smith] will genteelly escort Gen'l Harney, if found on the road."[68] But as time passed and the army moved deep-

[66] As Ferguson wrote, the Utah Expedition arrived at Bridger.

[67] The editor expresses his appreciation to Will Bagley through whose thoughtfulness and generosity these letters were made available.

[68] Young to Wells, Taylor, and Smith, 7 October 1857, LDS Archives. Young's tone here was quite different than that of his 24 July 1857 comments about Harney's intended fate if caught west of South Pass.

er into northeastern Utah, contingency planning grew more serious. Near month-end General Wells instructed Gen. George D. Grant, "If any officer such as a Governor, Judges, or other officials should throw themselves in sight with Merchants or any others take them into custody and keep them safely under guard. They cannot in any case be permitted to exercise any official authority in the Territory. You will retain such persons treating them respectfully and careing for their wants and safety."[69] A week later, on 4 November, Brigham Young returned to the subject:

> In regard to pretended civil officers on their way to this Territory, you are of course well aware that there cannot be any civil officers in Utah, except the ones now here, until others shall have presented themselves and are qualified by some person now legally acting here, hence you see the propriety and necessity of knowing no outside pretended civil officers, and of taking the necessary measures in regard to all persons undertaking to crowd themselves into our borders. Also, to our enemies forming a civil government in their camp, who ever heard of any law or precedent for such a nonsensical ideal as unqualified persons undertaking to act in a legal official capacity, more especially when there are no persons over whom to exercise such mock jurisdiction and that solely too in company with troops on their march?[70]

Two days later, with the arrival of the first severe snow storms, Young added: "since rough weather has commenced, and if the enemy are actually going into winter quarters. . . . Should the civil officers that may be with the army go into quarters with them in the region of Green river, let them go and enact such farces of official fantastic tricks as they may please."[71]

When the army *did* go into winter quarters two weeks later, it was dangerously closer to the Salt Lake Valley—at Fort Bridger rather than Green River. On 21 November, the day that Alfred Cumming took the oath of office to succeed him, Brigham Young instructed General Wells anew: "Should the *civil* officers come into your camp, you will take them and hold them as prisoners, not forwarding them to this place as you do other prisoners, but retaining them with you for such exchange or orders as future contingencies may require."[72]

From the distance of the twenty-first century, these instructions resemble what is today called a catch-22 situation. The federal appointees, including Utah's new governor, were not to be recognized since they had not taken

---

[69] Wells to Grant, 28 October 1857, Nauvoo Legion (Utah), Adj. Gen. Record 1851–1870, p. 166, LDS Archives.
[70] Young to Wells, Taylor and Smith, 4 November 1857, LDS Archives.
[71] Young to Wells, Taylor and Smith, 6 November 1857, ibid.
[72] Young to Wells, 21 November 1857, ibid.

the oath of office in the Salt Lake Valley, a requirement rendered impractical by the armed actions of the very leader most skeptical of their legitimacy. In 1857 these were instructions from which treason indictments could flow.

Order and Harmony Were Restored: Life in the Nauvoo Legion

As the Nauvoo Legion operated during the fall of 1857, it was blessed with an extraordinary absence of internal disciplinary problems. As discussed in the previous chapter, some Legion officers and troops did commit atrocities, and there were cases of looting and pillaging. But the victims were non-Mormon outsiders, not one's brother Legionnaire and fellow priest. Within the Legion there was a religiously inspired harmony and cohesiveness, as reflected in the letters of Privates Watt and Jackson and Generals Ferguson and Wells. These were attitudes quite different than the tone of the U.S. Army and its Utah Expedition. There, the rule of the lash prevailed, with 25–30 percent of the troops deserting annually as their officers presided over adjudication of an endless round of court-martial offenses: murder, theft, insubordination, gambling, drunkenness, and desertion.

The tone of the Utah Expedition, of course, flowed from the contentious example set by the army's senior leadership. General Scott had been court martialed and suspended for a year early in his career. During the 1850s, from his self-imposed exile in New York, Scott was in conflict with a succession of secretaries of war as well as with General Harney. That officer, in turn, was engaged in a decades-long vendetta with Colonel Sumner as well as with his army superiors, who had court-martialed Harney four times over a twenty-year period. Sumner, Harney's adversary, spent much of the Utah War defending himself—first before a November 1857 court martial at Fort Leavenworth and then in May 1858 at a trial held at Carlisle Barracks, Pennsylvania, just as the army was court-martialing its second most senior officer, Brevet Maj. Gen. David E. Twiggs, for insulting Secretary Floyd. As discussed in a subsequent chapter, Colonel Cooke was to clash repeatedly with Colonel Johnston, who in turn became embroiled in a feud with Governor Cumming even as Cooke pursued successive attempts to court martial the Second Dragoons' alcoholic Brevet Maj. Henry H. Sibley. It is emblematic of Cooke's combativeness that during October 1857—as he and the Second Dragoons passed through Fort Laramie under extreme pressure—that he found time to pelt Floyd with an argumentative petition demanding reform in officer promotions, a cause in which Harney joined him. The Utah War tensions between Colonel Alexander and his officers in the Tenth Infantry have been discussed.

By their own efforts and religiously guided behavior the Nauvoo Legion and its apostolic leadership spared themselves virtually all of this turmoil, notwithstanding jockeying by such action-oriented rivals as Capt. Porter Rockwell, Lt. Bill Hickman, and Maj. Lot Smith.[73] Yet on infrequent occasions the Nauvoo Legion, like all human institutions, experienced some disciplinary challenges and unharmonious behavior. Understanding these relatively rare cases highlights the atmospheric extremes between which the Legion and its conflicted federal adversary operated. At the same time this material yields deeper insight into the nature of life in the Nauvoo Legion.

One of the early cases of disharmony confronting the Legion took place oddly enough in the field of a prosperous farmer, John Pack, near Salt Lake City. There, in August 1857, six Mormon troopers attempted heavy-handedly to requisition horses for the first detachments heading for the Nebraska plains. Farmer Pack's protest to Brigham Young sets forth his side of the confrontation.

PACK TO YOUNG, 22 AUGUST 1857, LDS ARCHIVES.

I was in my field yesterday morning stacking wheat and six men armed with guns came to me and demanded of me a horse to go back on the Planes. I asked them by what authority they came to me armed and demanded a horse they said by the authorety of Bishop [John] Stoker [of Bountiful.]

I told them that Bishops did not send an armed force to execute their orders and I had no horse to spare. the Captain of the six men whose name is John Allsop then said well then we shall take one, he then commanded the five men to aboutface forward march and went to get a horse that was just turned out to feed but did not get him then went to my horses that was harnised to a load of wheet and the [farm] Boys drove on[.] The six men then cocked their guns and the Captain commanded the boys to standstill and said if you stir one step we will shoot you down in your tracks. They then leveld their guns on the boys and the smallest boy only twelve years of age attempted to move and one of the Company said Boy if you stir another foot I will blow you through. The captain then went to the teeme and on hiched one horse and road him off with the harnis on him and the rest of the men followed him.

I went to Bishop Stoker and asked him if he had sent an armed force to

[73] Lot Smith defined his relationship with Porter Rockwell during the Utah War thusly: "Rockwell and I were good friends, on the following basis: I did as I pleased and he, regularly, damnd me for it." "Narrative of Lot Smith," Hafen and Hafen, eds., *Mormon Resistance*, 236.

> take a horse from me, he said I did. I asked him by what authorety he don so, he gave me no satisfaction but said I am prepared to back it off.
>
> I Remain your affectionate friend and Brother
>
> P.S. . . . Bishop Stoker did not ask me for a horse before he sent the armed force

A month later, Colonels Cummings and Burton—fresh from arduous duty on the plains and still smarting over the failure of their 24–25 September raid on the Tenth Infantry at Pacific Springs—dealt with another form of disharmony—rumor mongering:

> By the last express from your city we learn of a report that was in circulation that the men under our command on this campaign were disobedient "unruly" and paid no respect to our orders We here feel it a duty we owe to our selves "to the men under our charge" and to those associated with us in the one common cause of which we are all engaged to state to you that such a report is false and groundless. We feel it a pleasure to state that our men have ever been ready at every call and emergency which was on hand and paid us that respect that is due to those placed over them[74]

As the war wore on and the Legion's campaign shifted to the Wasatch range, other behaviors and disciplinary challenges arose. With the growing concentration of troops in Echo Canyon, what went along with the camp chores, boredom, and onerous pick-and-shovel work were frayed nerves. In 1884, after he had become Brigham Young's successor, President John Taylor related a story about command style in Echo Canyon involving Col. Nathaniel V. Jones.[75] The anecdote tells us as much about President Taylor as it does about Colonel Jones and his "boys."

In the fall of 1857 Jones had recently been promoted from captain (or major)

[74] Cummings and Burton to Wells, 28 September 1857, LDS Archives.

[75] For another vignette about uneven officership in the Legion mentioning Jones, see the reminiscences of chronic complainer (and later apostate) Pvt. David Davis Bowen. Bowen claimed that in Echo Canyon, "An order was esued by the comanding officerr for evry man to bring all their crackers to the comasary store for inspection. That was complyed with. All most to a man. And after the dilevry of the crackers to the comassary, we never sa[w] any of them any more. Our good crackers was eating [b]y the officers and the poor men had to cook some flower the best way they could, without any fat or meat whatever. This was one of the greater oppretion and tyrany that ever was known in any country. Evry man had to find himself with gun & amunitions, with bed cloths and clothing and provissions. And after all their good crackers was taking away from them and eating by the officers, and the men was feed on dray flower alone. Daniel H. Wells was the Comander General and Nathaniel V. Jones the comassary General. All the officers from the highest to the lowest was as proud as Lucifer and considering the men or (Private) as low as dogs or things to low for them to assosiate with. Such brotherly feeling as that m[a]y go to the divel for my [p]art. That is a poor example of Mormon authority." Bowen, Reminiscence and Journal 1845–1863, LDS Archives, entry for 17 November 1857.

to colonel, a rise in rank that took place in the late summer immediately after his hard and effective service on the plains as Asa S. Hawley's leader. To this officer as well as to Col. William Pace, Maj. John Sharp, and his brother Adam fell much of the responsibility for constructing and manning Echo Canyon's defenses. John Taylor—a veteran at close quarters of Brigham Young's non-delegatory ways—explained in a Sunday discourse how he dealt with Colonel Jones's similar command style.

TAYLOR, DISCOURSE OF 20 FEBRUARY 1884, *JOURNAL OF DISCOURSES* 26:355–56.

I will relate a little circumstance of that kind; for we have all kinds of things among us Mormons. We had a war here a while ago. Brother Wells here was appointed a Lieut. General, and then myself and George A. Smith were appointed his counselors—(laughter). . . . Well, we went out and did the best we could, and I must say that General Wells displayed a good deal of knowledge, tact, vim, life and fidelity, and we tried to step up to him as near as we could—being his counselors. (laughter.) There was a little difficulty arose about Brother Nathaniel Jones—or Colonel Jones—a very excellent, good man, and a thorough disciplinarian . . . he had been in the Nauvoo legion and an officer in the Mormon Battalion,[76] and there he had got a smattering of military tactics, military ideas, military rule and authority, and when he saw all kinds of curious doings among the boys—as they called themselves—who were not strictly under military rule, etc., he wanted to straighten them out. But they, like the associates of Sister Ferguson, felt that "Jack was as good as his master." They didn't want too much military rule; they wanted a great amount of latitude, that they might be able to carry out their ideas and enjoy themselves and kick up their heels and feel like a lot of wild colts. Well, General Wells wanted me to go down, as his counselor, and see if the difficulty could not be put right. I was not even a corporal; I don't know what office I did hold; but he wanted me to go down and adjust matters.[77] So I went. I examined into things generally; talked with the officers, and mixed up with the men, and found out how things were exactly. There were Captains, and Colonels, and Generals, and all kinds of big men there, and they each had men in command; but Colonel Jones, whenever he saw anything wrong anywhere, wanted to go to work himself and put it right. I soon found out the feeling that was against him. The men considered him too straight-laced, and as they expressed it, "had too many epaulets

[76] In the Mormon Battalion, Jones had been first sergeant of Company D but was reduced to private on 18 March 1847 after some of his troops refused to drill. Bigler and Bagley, *Army of Israel*, 124, 202n20, 226–52.

[77] John Taylor held no military rank, but he carried with him the moral authority of his apostolic status as well as by multiple wounds received while trying to shield Joseph Smith from the lynch mob at Carthage Jail in 1844.

on his shoulders," because they saw in him a disposition to exercise authority, and the officers of the several companies did not object to that because it relieved them from responsibility. "Now, Brother Jones" (said I) I called him brother; I had not got the length of calling him colonel, I called him plain Brother Jones—"let me tell you how to fix these matters. Such and such a man is a captain, is he not?" "Yes." "Another, there, is a lieutenant?" "Yes." "And another is major?" "Yes." "And you are in command here?" "Yes." "Well, now, instead of going to work to regulate all these matters yourself, why do you not detail lieutenant so and so, captain so and so, and major so and so, to look after the men who are acting improperly?" He thought the advice was good, and followed it, and order and harmony were restored.

On 26 November 1857, a leadership trio consisting of an apostle, a brigadier general, and a colonel briefed Lieutenant General Wells on several more serious cases, including one that posed a unique disciplinary challenge, bizarre even by Utah Expedition standards.

TAYLOR, RICHARDS, AND JONES TO WELLS,
26 NOVEMBER 1857, LDS ARCHIVES.

Since penning our note to you of last Evening Bro. [George W.] Hill has arrived and informs us that his horsethief prisoner is on his way to this Camp in charge of a guard from Col. [Chauncey W.] West's command.

The thief whose name is Almond Colvin confessed his theft and also that he was & had been an accomplice of some seven or eight others—Government Teamsters &c in stealing horses and getting off for California. It appears that when they were ready to start they stole Colvin's outfit and left him in the lurch. When Colvin arrives we shall get as many of the names of this group as possible.

Some cases of petty thieving in Camp have been brought before us, generally confirmed cases known to be such by the Officers from whom they are reported. As we scarcely hope to reclaim the thieves from their confirmed habits by any discipline which we would like to prescribe we thought best to enquire of you what penalties if any shall be inflicted upon the criminals above alluded to.

A more revolting case requires us to ask what shall we do with a man convicted of sexual ~~intercourse~~ connection with a mare?

Since the case of Davis communicated to you by Bros Taylor & Richards—one Perkins of Major [George W.] Kelsey's Battalion in Col. [Thomas] Callister's Regiment—was convicted of positively refusing to obey his Captain's (Truman's) orders & thereof [?] striking & kicking him. Perkins is dismissed by Order—his arms retained and he held subject to the decision of a Court

> Martial. We state this that you may be aware of the course of discipline that we are pursuing and desire your approval or correction in these matters.
>
> We especially request your counsel how to dispose of the case of bestiality & the cases of thieving.
>
> Your Brethren in the Church & Kingdom of God,

In the "more revolting case," Pvt. James Drake, an eighteen-year-old from North Willow Creek, was the accused. At General Wells's direction he stood trial in Echo Canyon on 30 November 1857. No transcript for Drake's general court martial has survived, but a member of his court, Maj. J. D. T. McAllister, recorded both the outcome and the typically Mormon way of confirming the verdict the next day.

> Tuesday December 1st Some Snow falling Cold Public Meeting at 10 A.M. Assembled in proper order at the time appointed Ogden Brass Band played some lively airs. Gen[l] Wells offered up Prayer, then Spoke concerning the position of our Enimies gave some good Council to the *Armies of Israel* & regretted that any thing had Transpired to mar our peace, he then referred to the case of James Drake, who was tried before the Court Martial yesterday for Beastiality. and Sentenced to be *publicly Shot.* Gen[l] Wells called him into the Square, and then called upon all present that if they felt to sanction the decision of the court Martial to do so by the raise of of [*sic*] the right hand. it was a una[ni]mous vote he made some remarks concerning him, als[o] Bro John Taylor made a few remarks, and Gen[l] G. D. Grant, Gen[l] Wells said the time and place would be appointed for the shooting of Drake hereafter. Received Orders to Break up Camp and start for home. at 2 P.M. moved from Echo and got into comfortable Quarters on the Weber. Gen[l] Wells and Staff Camped with us.[78]

Legionnaire Lorenzo Brown described the formation at which Private Drake's sentence was read and confirmed what occurred in substantially more emotional terms than had Major McAllister:

> He was called out & the congregation were called upon to approve or disapprove the sentence of the court & all therein favor o[f] the sentence were requested to uncover their heads & raise their right hand to High Heaven in token of their assent. Every head was made bare & every hand raised. This was one of the severest trials I have encountered in my checkered path way of life & d[o] not wish to meet another & nothing I think can make a person feel their own littleness more than to raise his hand consenting to the death of even

[78] McAllister Journal, entry for 1 December 1857, 221–22, LDS Archives. For a biographical sketch, see Hinton, "John D. T. McAllister," 106–36.

> the vilest criminal but my hand raised despite my nature feeling that justice should have its perfect way. But had I known the business of the meeting I should I presume I should have absented myself altogether.[79]

Even as this unnerving ceremony unfolded, Brigham Young was considering Private Drake's fate. He quickly arrived at a decision resembling in tone, spirit, and language Abraham Lincoln's later disposition of some of the clemency pleas lodged on behalf of young Union Army soldiers under death sentences: "It will be best to release one [?] Drake and give him a severe reprimand, and let that suffice for his past condt, and inform him that it may [be] permitted to sleep in silence, unless future like acts should require further proceedings."[80]

What happened next was recorded dramatically by Legionnaire Warren Gould Child. At dawn on 3 December, while the troops evacuating Echo Canyon were camped on the Weber River in Round Valley, "Pvt Drake he was marched out of camp into an elevated piece of ground by the guard and there in the presence of the Command who had been formed in [the shape of] an open hollow Squair a hanker chief was plased over his eyes his hands tied behind him and a plattoon detached to execute him when a messenger rode into camp with a reprieve from governor Young which was red in his presents and he was set at liberty a wiser if not a better man on the grounds that owing to his ignorance and unixperienced in the church and not understanding the penalty for sutch a crime."

With that, most of the Eastern Expedition and presumably the wretched Private Drake went home for the winter.

---

[79] Lorenzo Brown Journal, entry for 1 December 1857, LDS Archives

[80] Young to Wells, 1 December 1857, ibid. Earlier, in a letter dated 27 November, Wells had described Drake's offense to Young in the middle of a message filled with more mundane issues. The paragraph devoted to Drake has been blacked out, presumably out of Victorian sensitivity to the subject or out of consideration for the accused soldier's family. Perhaps for the same reason, another member of Drake's court—Colonel Burton—recorded in his field diary that he participated in the trial but made no notation of the unusual offense or the accused's name.

"Never a Complaint": The Epic March of Second U.S. Dragoons

This 1987 painting depicts the Utah Expedition's rear guard and Governor Cumming's escort just west of the Continental Divide at South Pass while passing the Wind River Mountains in early November. With the superb leadership of Lieutenant Colonel Cooke, former commander of the Mormon Battalion, the dragoons executed the longest cold-weather trek in American military history to redress the conflict's balance in cavalry capability. *Courtesy of artist Don Stivers, Waterford, Virginia.*

Chapter 14

"Staggering Along Like So Many Drunken Men" The Army's Ordeal

The King of France marched up the hill,
And then marched down again.
—Pvt. Charles A. Scott, Phelps's Battery,
diary entry for 20 October 1857

If Lot Smith's raid became the best known (and most relished) episode of the Utah War for Mormons, the army's subsequent six-week ordeal for U.S. troops and teamsters was the Utah Expedition's most vivid experience. For the army, it was a nightmarish period of frustration and loss as it marched up Hams Fork and back during the last three weeks of October under Colonel Alexander, and then pushed desperately from Hams Fork to Fort Bridger on Blacks Fork during the first half of November under Colonel Johnston. Several of the troops compared what they endured to Napoleon's retreat from Moscow. From such a humiliating experience at the hands of bad weather and a territorial militia came the institutional army's subsequent amnesia about the campaign.

Albert Sidney Johnston arrived at Fort Leavenworth on 11 September from Texas by way of Washington and his home in Louisville. In Kansas he picked up the orders originally issued to Harney on 29 June; saw to the refitting of the Second Dragoons; met Governor Cumming; greeted his new adjutant, Maj. Fitz John Porter; and headed west on 17 September at top speed with a forty-dragoon escort. Lacking either a sense of urgency or a willingness to subject his wife to Johnston's forced march, Cumming declined the colonel's invitation to accompany him. Instead Cumming's party traveled with Colonel

Cooke's six companies of dragoons and the other civilian appointees as the Utah Expedition's rear guard. It was a decision that may have soured Cumming's relationship with Johnston from the beginning.

Johnston's subsequent letter from Fort Kearny to his West Point classmate, Capt. Amos Beebe Eaton, was full of optimism over the prospects for wintering in Salt Lake City, a destination that he expected to reach by 20 October. Less sanguine about what lay ahead for Johnston were two letters written by his Second Cavalry executive officer in San Antonio, Lt. Col. Robert E. Lee.

What soon followed in the wake of Lot Smith's raid—federal indecision, embarrassment, and near-disaster in extreme weather—has been described frequently. In many respects, it is the most familiar part of the Utah Expedition's story. Yet, as with accounts of the army's march to the Continental Divide during the summer and early fall of 1857, all of these subsequent experiences have come to us through a small number of familiar sources. What follows is a brief retelling of the army's ordeal during October–November through fresh, unexploited material: the post-September diary of the highly intelligent but eccentric Captain Phelps; Colonel Johnston's private correspondence; the letters of his new adjutant, Major Porter; the post-war reminiscences of Phelps's rock-solid first sergeant and Civil War successor, James Stewart; and the diary of sutler William A. Carter.

Nothing but Your Success: Johnston's Reassignment and Optimism

Precisely how Johnston came to be Harney's successor is unclear. The fact that he was the new colonel of an equally new regiment fighting Indians throughout Texas would seem to have made him an unlikely candidate for Utah. On the other hand, Johnston's 1855 selection to lead the elite Second Cavalry by Secretary of War Davis, General Scott, and President Pierce signaled great confidence in him. That Johnston had a very able executive officer in Colonel Lee probably made his reassignment from Texas feasible. In all likelihood, Johnston's selection to command the Utah Expedition was a function of not only his reputational standing but the inescapable fact that the War Department had run out of senior officers who were both available and suitable. That Harney had become unavailable and that the Fifth Infantry and Second Dragoons were led by their executive officers rather than by their colonels reflected the extent of this army-wide leadership shortfall.

Johnston attributed his assignment solely to General Scott, noting that he had no connection to Buchanan and had never met the president.[1]

LEE TO JOHNSTON, 1 AUGUST AND 25 OCTOBER 1857, SIBLEY, ED., "ROBERT E. LEE TO ALBERT SIDNEY JOHNSTON, 1857," 100–107.

Genl Twiggs recd a letter by mail last evg from New York, in which it is stated that you are intended to command the expedition to Utah, & Genl Harney to remain in Kansas.[2] Mr. Radziminski has written from Washington to Dr. McCormick to the same effect, & the N.Y. Herald of the 17th announces the same. I suppose therefore Utah is to be your destination, & I have thought you would like to know what is said on the subject. Although I consider it highly complimentary to you to be selected for this service, over others more convenient accessible, still I am sorry you are taken away from the Regt. & sent so far. You will have the consolation however of doing your duty, & we will probably follow.[3]

Tell Mrs. Johnston wives are a perfect drug [drag] out there, & if I was her I would not go. Besides Brigham's 50 female saints will look upon her as a poor imposed on sinner, & she will not be appreciated in that community. I fear too the season is too far advanced for her to venture. However, you will be able to see when you reach Washn & things may be better than they now appear.[4]

Wherever you go Colonel I wish you every happiness & success, & may all happiness attend you and yours

25 Oct. 1857

I have been intending to write you a long letter, in reply to your very welcome one,[5] on your return to Louisville from Washington, & have only waited till you could survey the difficulties of your present situation, before taking up your attention. . . .

Your friends here are all well, and you & Mrs. Johnston are much missed & inquired after. I hope you hear good accounts from her, & that you, my dear Colonel, are successfully prosecuting the business before you. I feel confident of your rising superior to the difficulties by which you are surrounded, & though I sympathize with you in the delicate position in which you are placed, & feel the paucity of the means with which you have been furnished,

---

[1] Johnston to N. J. Eaton, 11 October 1858, quoted in Johnston, *The Life of Albert Sidney Johnston*, 232.

[2] Brevet Maj. Gen. David E. Twiggs was commander of the Department of Texas with headquarters co-located with those of the Second Cavalry in San Antonio. It is clear that Johnston did not know the nature of his new assignment when he left Texas, just as Harney was uncertain of his when ordered to Kansas from Florida in April.

[3] In the spring of 1858 Lee and the Second Cavalry were briefly ordered north from Texas to reinforce Johnston from Kansas, a transfer that was soon rescinded.

[4] Mrs. Johnston remained home in Louisville, Kentucky.

[5] This Johnston–Lee letter has not been located.

> I anticipate nothing but your success, & an increase of your present high estimation in the army & country. . . .
>
> All the officers & their families here are well, except Major [Henry] Prince. I know all would send their kindest regards if they were aware I was writing. Please present mine to Major [Fitz John] Porter. I am glad you have him with you. He is an able aid[e] in the field, & valuable everywhere.

When Johnston reached Fort Kearny on 24 September, a week after departing Leavenworth, he paused to write to his old friend Capt. Amos Beebe Eaton. For Eaton, Johnston was full of optimism as well as caution about how best to obtain newspaper coverage for his campaign:

> The weather is fine, the sky for the last four days without a cloud, grass excellent as far as Laramie, beyond I learned it is not good, or rather that there is none as far as 150 miles west. This will not delay the march of the Dragoons as they will be provided with corn. There is no indication of an early winter and I now can have no doubt of a successful accomplishment of the march of all the troops destined for Utah. Do not have anything published I write, if you choose, there is no objection to your giving publicity in your own language to any information of interest contained in this & future letters.[6]

So Little Thus Far Accomplished: Captain Phelps's Frustrations on Hams Fork

Without question the most complete, vivid account of Colonel Alexander's march up Hams Fork toward Sublette's Cutoff and back appears in one of the unpublished segments of Capt. John W. Phelps's diary.

Phelps was a Vermonter and member of the West Point class of 1836. Once commissioned he served in the early Seminole wars in Florida, in the Mexican War, and in Texas fighting still other tribes. By the time of the Utah Expedition, Phelps's Battery was in Kansas Territory. His diaries are invaluable because their editorial comments and observations go well beyond the typical frontier journal entries focused on matters of wood, water, and grass. What one finds in Phelps's diaries is his prejudice against non-Americans, an interesting point of view since more than half of his artillerymen, including his valued first sergeant, were born outside of the United States.[7]

As commander of the Fourth U.S. Artillery's Light Battery B, Phelps was one of the Utah Expedition's principal unit commanders. Accordingly,

---

6 Johnston to Capt. Amos Beebe Eaton, 24 September 1857, Beinecke Library.

7 For a fictional account of life in Phelps's Battery during the Utah War, see Moss, *Soldiers 'n Saints.*

although only a captain by rank, he was included in the councils of war on 6 and 19 October by which Alexander decided to move on Salt Lake City via the northern route and then fatefully decided to retrace his steps. Through Phelps one experiences the wasted month of Indian summer and early snowfalls that set the stage for Albert Sidney Johnston's desperate November trek from Hams Fork, up Blacks Fork, to Fort Bridger in a series of blizzards. With these October segments, we now have more of Phelps's fascinating diary to join the excerpts published fifty years ago by the Hafens.[8]

The entries presented here start as Phelps's Battery, eight companies of the Tenth Infantry, ten companies of the Fifth Infantry, and Reno's Battery—all now gathered on Hams Fork near its juncture with Blacks Fork and the overland trail—first received word of Lot Smith's raid. [9]

Phelps Diary, 5 October–3 November 1857, Hamilton Gardner Transcription, Utah State Historical Society, from Original in New York Public Library.

Monday Octr. 5th

A day of excitement. The Mormons set fire to the grass in the valley some two or three miles above us and a considerable portion of the 10th Infy. as also of my own command were engaged all the morning in preventing its spread. Fortunately the wind has been gentle from the S.E. sweeping up the valley; but a great deal of grass has been consumed which would be indispensable if we are to remain here long.

The 5th Infantry and the [Reno] Ordnance train have arrived in the valley, and a report has been brought by ox drivers from Green River that two ox trains containing provisions were burnt at that point last night by an armed party of Mormons. There are 160 ox wagons with us—each of which carries from four to five thousand pounds. The train with our clothes is still behind.

An express arrived from Fort Leavenworth. The commanding officer of this expedition had not arrived at that post as late as the 10th of September. The Governor was to leave on the 15th of Sepr. Six companies of Dragoons had been ordered to Utah. . . .

Another Indian summer day—warm, whilst the night was very cold.

Tuesday Octr. 6

On a Council of War at the tent of Col. Alexander, the ranking officer present. The other officers were [Brevet] Col. [Carlos A.] Waite [5th Infy.], [Brevet] Lieut. Col. [E. R. S.] Canby, Major of the 10th, Capt. Marcy acting Major of the 5th, Capt. [Henry F.] Clark[e] Commissary Dept, [Brevet] Capt. [Jesse L.]

[8] The Hafens' book, *Mormon Resistance*, 89–138, used Phelps's diary through 30 September 1857.

[9] The editor has omitted Phelps's daily recording of cloud formations and wind conditions.

Reno of the Ordnance, the adjutant of the 10th—[1st] Lieut. [Henry E.] Maynadier and myself. There was also a guide Jim [Tim] Goodale present.

The question was whether to go back to Wind River Valley, to stop near here, say at Henry's Fork, or go on. The majority seemed to be in favor of going on—by the way of Bear River Valley.[10]

There was never a military command in such a position as ours—so far from resources, these and free intercourse with home about to be shut out by the snows of winter, our trains in the rear and the grazing in front being ~~burnt and~~ assailed with fire by the enemy, that enemy outnumbering us five to one; and our governor and the officer assigned to the command absent together with their instructions and an uncertainty as to when they will arrive.

The order to the troops however is clear—it is to establish a fort at or near Salt Lake City, and this should be attempted whatever may be the consequences. . . .

It was very cold this morning; but the day has been warm.

Mounted Mormons have shown themselves upon the hills near us to-day.

The 12 pdr Battery moved up the Fork above us this morning. It consists of 4 12 pd guns, 2 32 pdr Howitzers, 1 Battery wagon and 1 Forge.[11]

It is under the command of Capt. Reno of the Ordnance. He has some 12 or 15 ordnance men, 32 men (instructed artillerists) who were sent to Fort Leavenworth from [the recruit depot on Governor's Island] New York for my Battery (originally 40 but eight deserted) and one company of the 5th Infy. of one officer and 50 men. A few teamsters are also employed as drivers. There are with the Battery 47 wagons—viz—12 containing chiefly ordnance stores of some kind probably ammunition for small arms, 7 belonging to the Infantry company and 28 for forage and baggage. The Infantry company had been with the Battery from Fort Laramie here. From Fort Leavenworth to Fort Laramie there was a detachment of some 60 mounted Dragoon Recruits under [2d] Lieut. [John] Green. The Battery has half a supply of ammunition. The rest with half of my am[m]unition and other ordnance supplies are back in some ox train. The Battery when passing up to-day had eight horses, to each piece and four to each caisson—the two rear chests of the caissons being carried in the wagons. The Forge was drawn by mules.[12]

Wednesday Octr. 7

Col. Alexander issued orders assuming command of the troops present

---

[10] The Wind River Mountains due north of South Pass had several sheltered valleys along the Popo-Agie River's branches teeming with elk and warmed by hot springs. Magraw's Pacific Wagon Road crew had already gone into winter quarters there as frequently did the region's Shoshone and Crow bands.

[11] "Pound" referred to the weight of the projectile that the gun threw and was the standard way of describing an artillery piece. Here Phelps describes Reno's heavy (siege) battery; his own light battery was equipped with six-pounder field howitzers.

[12] Here Phelps may be displaying a little professional rivalry vis à vis Reno, who was the expedition's ordnance officer doing double-duty in a role for which he was not trained—artillery officer.

and directing a continuation of the advance day after to-morrow. But he has sent back four Infantry companies to Green River to see about the burning of the wagons and the forward movement will probably be delayed. It is much to be regretted, for our corn is getting scarce and the grazing bad. . . .

Thursday Octr. 8

A circular was issued from head quarters suspending the forward movement for the present.

Received twenty men of the 40 that were originally sent from the New York Harbor to Fort Leavenworth for my battery. The 12 remaining ones have been assigned to the 12 pdr Battery brought along by the ordnance Department. Those received are deficient not only in instruction but also in clothing. Some of them have no great coats, others no blankets, and all of them have but one pair of shoes or boots and most of them but one pair of pants. This clothing is all very much worn and is of the Infantry pattern.

Have been busy in reaming out shells and case shot, and preparing the battery for action. . . .

One of my men went out gunning [hunting] yesterday and has not been heard of since. He joined the company last June and is a German from Holstein where he had been a soldier.[13]

The 5th Infantry moved up the fork yesterday and they will take last grass between here and the burnt region. Grazing is consequently getting scarce. We ought to go on and take Fort Bridger garrison and then proceed down Bear River. . . .

Snow has seemed to fall at times in every direction, without reaching the earth however in any shape.

Friday Octr. 9th

Still in camp, overhauling the Battery wagons and limber chests, making a coal-pit, drilling recruits, etc.—it has occupied every minute of my time all day.[14]

It was very cold last night, water freezing solid in a basin. It was nearly clear this morning but has been gradually over clouding during the day. Cumuli were seen along the N.W. and smooth darkish cirrus along the S.E. From both snow seemed to descend, the former over a low range of mountains called Bear mountains, not far distant, and the latter over the Uintah Mountains. The Temperature has been mild and pleasant . . .

Saturday Octr. 10th

The four companies of Infantry that were sent back to Green River returned last evening, and orders are issued for resuming the march to-morrow morning.

---

[13] This was Pvt. Charles H. Wilcken, formerly of the Prussian army, in which he had been decorated with the Iron Cross. See Seifrit, "Charles Henry Wilcken," 311.

[14] The coal pit was probably adjunct to the functioning of the battery's important forge.

Received, as have ~~all~~ the other officers commanding corps a roll of late numbers of the Deseret News from Brigham Young. . . .

Mr. Smith, our guide, was sent back to Laramie as an express.

The earth this morning was covered with an inch of snow. It has gradually melted away until at sundown little if any is left. . . .

Several flocks of ducks were noticed during the morning, flying along the stream. Rabbits are numerous here.

A snow squall passed along the S.W. about mid afternoon.

Sunday Octr. 11th

The whole command commenced the movement up the Fork this morning—viz, two half filled regiments of Infantry and two batteries with their numerous wagons numbering altogether (ox and mule) about 400. We marched 9.12 miles.

The valley of the stream is about a half a mile in width. The stream is skirted with willows and was bordered with grass, tho' this has been nearly consumed by fire. We find enough however for our some 5000 animals. The banks of the valley are ~~two or three~~ at least a hundred feet in height, and on ascending them one sees a desolate country covered with shingles thro' which runs the deep valley of Ham's Fork. . . .

It was overcast this morning with clouds that moved to the south. During the march the wind beat in our faces from the W and N.W. occasionally bringing mingled sleet and rain—a cold raw day, causing the horses to shrink and tremble. . . .

Saw a human skull glaring at us ~~to-day~~ from the surface of the ground. We asked the guide if it was of an Indian. He said yes, because its forehead was low. We asked if the Indians did not bury their dead. Sometimes they do, he said, but at others they cover them over with bushes in the spot where they happen [to] die and so leave them.

One of my horses gave out and was abandoned, after sending back for him and trying to get him into camp.

Monday Octr. 12th

The command marched up the Fork 9.44 miles. The rear guard did not come up until 4 P.M.

Two men by the name of Hickman, brothers to Bill Hickman who is celebrated in this country as one of the "Destroying Angels" came into our camps yesterday with a letter from their Brother Bill to the sutler of the 10th Infantry.[15] One of them had a sword belt in his possession which had belonged to the man (Vilkins) [Wilcken] who went out gunning on the 7th inst. and had not been heard from since. These men say that Vilkins deserted; and that they saw him at Fort Bridger; that one of them exchanged with him a common belt

[15] These were Thomas Jefferson Hickman and Dr. George Washington Hickman.

for the sword belt, and that he was on his way to Salt Lake and California. They say moreover that Forts Bridger and Supply are burned—i.e. all the wood work about them. They disclaim being Mormons;[16] but one of the guards took them up and they will probably be detained for the present. Col. Alexander gave them an examination to-day. Our Indian agent, they say, has been carried off by the Utah Indians.[17]

A snow squall came up suddenly during the night and covered the earth with about an inch of snow. The air was filled with fog until half past ten A.M. when both fog and snow rapidly disappeared. This fog, where it settled upon the beard or poils [fringes] of the dress became frozen. Why should it freeze there and not in the air? . . .

9 P.M. It is said that the oxen of the wagons which were burnt at Green River were being driven up the fork following us to-day when the drivers were assailed by mounted Mormons and their oxen driven away from them.

The grass has been burned over thus far, tho' we find large patches that have escaped, and the grazing to-night is very good.

Tuesday Octr. 13th

Made a tedious 8.08 miles, up and down hill and thro' sage bushes. It is now sunset and the wagons of the 5th Infantry are not all in yet. I doubled teams twice—the worst marching that we have yet had,—it is thro' an unbroken country where perhaps a half dozen vehicles never before ventured. The hills close in upon the valley of the stream and compell us to go over them. There is such a place just ahead of us, which we have to pass over to-morrow morning—steep tho' not very high. We could pass through it better had not some beavers dammed up the stream and thus over flowed to some extent the narrow pass through which it runs.[18]

Small parties of men appear to be watching us along the heights above the valley.

It has been clear to-day, and comfortably warm, with a slight breeze from the west; at least as felt in the valley; up upon the hills it may be stronger.

Wednesday Octr. 14th

Marched 5.24 miles—the worst day's work that we have done yet, and [we] have still a bad one before us. One of our wagons upset at the outset this morning while crossing the stream and was entirely submerged in the water. Fortunately nothing was materially injured, tho' the delay thus occasioned was grievous. All the trains are up, however, earlier than they were yesterday.

---

[16] T. W. and G. W. Hickman were not members of the LDS church, although their brother Bill was.

[17] This refers to Indian Agent Garland Hurt's dramatic September escape from a Nauvoo Legion detachment approaching his Spanish Fork Indian farm. Hurt fled with the help of a small group of Ute braves loyal to him and reached Johnston's camp near South Pass on 23 October after a circuitous route through the mountains.

[18] Dams and flooded ditches were also part of the Legion's defenses being constructed in Echo Canyon.

We are encamped on the slopes of the hills, and numerous camp fires, ~~like~~ resembling the lights of a city, remind one of the immense outlay which this expedition has occasioned, and of the comparatively small results which are likely to flow from it. . . .

A led horse fell down a steep [bank] this morning into the stream and soon died.

Thursday Octr. 15th

Marched 6.45 miles by a better—less hilly route than we anticipated and encamped at an early hour (half past ten A M) near the old Oregon and California route which, coming from the South pass by what is called [Sublette's Cut-off] here crosses the valley of Ham's Fork. The numerous wagons all ~~coming~~ came up in good season. We have thus followed up the Fork into the range of Bear Mountains nearly fifty miles from the Green River route to Salt Lake City; our course being North of West. We are to leave the Fork here and pass over into the valley of Bear River. On our arrival at this point the grass was on fire at two different ~~points~~ places, but we find enough between those two ~~points~~ places for the time that we shall remain here, that is until day after to-morrow.

Abandoned two horses to-day. They fell down whilst on the march and could not be ~~lifted up to stand~~ set up again on their feet so as to stand. One of them had done nothing for nearly a month and had always had the same rations as the other horses. He was very poor—"got down" about a month ago and had never "picked up" since. And so too of the several other horses which have died or been left behind since our arrival in this valley. They have four pounds of corn a day besides grazing.

We have several guides—mountaineers—two French men and two American. Some of them have all their ~~whole~~ possessions along—Indian wives, ponies, cattle, lodges etc. Their lodges, bedding, cooking utensils etc. they carry on their ponies; the poles for the lodge being fastened to the animal by one of their ends and the other end trailing on the ground ~~by the~~ We saw a party of women with all the establishment, ponies, cattle and all, coming down a nearly perpendicular bank of the valley. It was a mode of travelling that the animals were evidently accustomed to, and the sight was truly patriarchal. Some of these scenes ought to be well portrayed upon canvass.[19]

Buffalo skulls are occasionally seen; and sage hens and rabbits are numerous.

It was very cold last night, and to-day it is quite warm. . . .

Friday October 16th

Remain in camp. Had an alarm—one section [of artillery] was harnessed, the horses of another led up, and the third made ready for action. It was occasioned by the report of an officer that another officer had seen 500 Mormons

[19] In 1859, after the conclusion of the Utah War, Albert Bierstadt and several other artists accompanied Frederick W. Lander's Pacific Wagon Road crew and painted magnificent scenes of the Wind River mountains and South Pass area.

and that one of the Regiments of Infantry was under arms, the bottom of all which is unknown, except that there was no occasion for it.

Capt. Marcy of the 5th went out with about a hundred men on a reconnossance to find a road towards Henry's Fork; and a party of ten wagons. Marcy (mounted) met a party of some 40 mounted Mormons. As they passed they first exchanged salutations, such as Good morning Sir! then when some little distance off, abusive epithets, and finally (when beyond rifle range), shots—by which one Mormon it is thought was wounded. One shot was sent by the Mormons and forty by our party.[20]

The Colonel commanding called for reports to-day concerning the condition of the animals of the command. Whilst they are all failing, the ox trains are said to be less fitted for resuming the march than any other. The jaunt from here to Bear River presents thirty miles of hilly road. In the meantime not a word is heard from the governor or officer assigned to the command of the expedition or of the ox trains containing many of our necessary supplies. The colonel, as he well might be, is considerably perplexed.

The nights are very cold—I was told by one of the surgeons of the command that the thermometer had ranged from 18 to 90 during 24 hours at one time, and from 18 to 75 at another. Yet the consumptives [tubercular cases] of the command appear to be thriving; one of these is an officer's lady.[21]

'Twas very cold last night. . . .

Saturday Octr. 17th

Still in camp. Was notified to meet with other commanders of corps and chiefs of staff at the Colonel's tent at 8 A.M. Capt. Marcy's party had brought in two prisoners during the night upon whose persons some important letters and papers had been found, and we were called together in order to consult upon the new phase which those papers seemed to give to our movement in this direction.

One of the persons apprehended was styled as major [Joseph] Taylor of the Mormon Army, and the other was his adjutant [Lt. William R. R. Stowell]. The paper of chief consequence was a letter of instructions to Major Taylor from Lieut. General Wells. He Major was to proceed down Bear River to its elbow and harass us in all possible ways by burning grass, alarming our camps, stampeding our animals, etc. The Major looked to me as if he might be an impostor, even in his pretensions to Mormonism. Both letters which I saw were of a military character, and both concluded with the expression—"Your brother in Christ."

---

[20] Marcy and his infantrymen were mounted on mules and were described by the better-mounted Nauvoo Legionnaires as "jackass cavalry." This encounter was with Lot Smith's party and is described in vivid detail in "Narrative of Lot Smith," Hafen and Hafen, eds., *Mormon Resistance*, 239–42. Smith recorded that no one in his party was wounded, although one man's hat was pierced by a bullet and two of his horses were shot.

[21] Another was Indian Supt. Jacob Forney.

This Major Taylor claims a birth place in Kentucky. He is a man of fine personal appearance and about 30 years of age. He estimates the Mormon army at 25000 men; had been told and believed that we were a mob coming upon them to destroy both women & children; was a poor, laboring innocent true spoken man who never inquired into matters of state; could not read or write; wanted our protection &c.

In short he is a favorable specimen of the American character in the ultimate extreme of its licence, shrewdness—crime and wickedness, for he has killed his man it is said—he is to all appearances a perfectly unshaped chaos of ~~intelligence~~ shrewdness and stolidity, and differs in no wise, morally, from the brute Bohemian or benighted Bulgarian the victim of long centuries of despotism who tills the land of the Danubian principalities, Turkey and Greece. The change that took place with Nebuchadnezzer in his transferrence from the palace to herd among the beasts of the field,[22] was no greater than it is with the American Character as exhibited on the one hand by the signer of the declaration of independence and on the other by this Major Taylor of the Mormon Army.[23]

He says however that he has a leaning toward us; that we are not so bad as he took us to be; that he has so expressed himself in presence of his Mormon friends, and that in consequence his command which consisted of 50 men has been taken away from him.[24]

By the officers called together our views as to the best course to be pursued was again discussed. One proposition was to return to the other side of the South Pass—to Wind River Valley; & Henry's Fork was again mentioned as a good wintering place. Another proposition was to burn up all our ox wagons and provisions over and above a forty days supply and march directly upon the City of Salt Lake by the way of Bear River. The majority seemed to be in favor of going on by the way of Bear River as we have commenced to do, taking every thing with us as far as we can, and stop only when compelled so to do. Such at all events was my own opinion expressed to the Colonel. As to what conclusion was arrived at I do not know since after giving my opinion I withdrew and have not heard much from the council since.

In the meantime nothing is heard from the Governor or our commanding officer or the troops and trains on the road following us. It is uncertain what route they will take whether by Fort Bridger or by the road which we are now on, and this ~~road~~ uncertainty renders our position the more embarrassing.

---

[22] Daniel 4:32–33.

[23] One of Captain Phelps's several prejudices was against those who were not native-born Americans. In the election of 1880 he ran for president as the candidate of the nativist American party and received a total of 707 votes. McClaughry, "John Wolcott Phelps," 263–90.

[24] Joseph Taylor's account of his capture on 16 October and interrogation appears in the same series as Lot Smith's narrative. See Junius F. Wells ["Vaux"], "The Echo Canyon War," 380–83. Taylor claimed that when he exaggerated the size of the Legion to Colonel Alexander at twenty to twenty-five thousand men, "I could have hung my hat on his eyes."

COL. EDMUND B. ALEXANDER, TENTH U.S. INFANTRY
He was the Utah Expedition's senior officer present until Colonel Johnston arrived at Hams Fork in early November. Preoccupied with inconsequentials such as the number of steps per minute at which the troops marched, Alexander drew the ridicule of his officers as timid, indecisive, and supercilious ("the old woman"). This was the type of leadership about which Ben McCulloch had warned Harney and Floyd in July. With the shock and embarrassment of Lot Smith's raid to the army's rear, Alexander reluctantly assumed the overall command that he had avoided and then led a disastrous trek and counter-march along Hams Fork in a failed attempt to reach Salt Lake by the looping northern (Bear River) route. *Courtesy of Massachusetts MOLLUS Collection (Image L6540), U.S. Army Military History Institute, Carlisle Barracks, Pennsylvania.*

Our expresses back, it ~~would seem~~ is suspected have been cut off; tho' Major Taylor says not.

One of the Hickmans mentioned as being prisoners some days since has been allowed to go to Salt Lake with permission to return if he chooses.

From here to Bear River Valley it is about 30 miles of very hilly tho' old well beaten road. Thence on down to the elbow or Soda Springs it is some sixty miles of good level road; thence onward to Fort Hall on the Oregon Route it is 66 miles with excellent grass and where hundreds of fat beeves could probably be got. From Soda springs down the River to the Mormon settlements it is sixty or seventy miles. Thus by a march of some 160 miles we might reach a point less than one hundred miles from the city, and where the people could not destroy the grass or other resources without injuring themselves as well as us;[25] and where the Oregon and California routes would be open to us, where we could comply with the orders which we have received and is to establish a post at or near Salt Lake City, and where in fine we might compell the Mormons to such a distinct avowal either of rebellion or submission as to enable the United-States to act with desision next season.

[25] Phelps had not yet grasped Mormon willingness to destroy their own resources, possessions, and infrastructure.

By retracing partly our route, occupying and garrisoning the points of Forts Bridger and Supply and sending our animals to graze on Henry's Fork, we could have South Pass and Bridgers Pass open to us if not clogged with snow, and we should hold one of the avenues to the city; but we should thus probably remain in an undecided attitude with respect to the Mormons and hence not comply with the intentions of the government.

In Bear River Valley the guides say our stock would perish. At Henry's Fork we might save ~~them~~ it; tho' the grass can be either burned or covered with snow in either locality.

We cannot expect supplies from the Atlantic states until next July or August, and we have not sufficient to last us till then.

Our oxen they say would all die if driven down Bear River Valley and we should not have them for beef; whereas, on Henry's Fork they might be saved for that purpose.

Such are some of the considerations that still present themselves and which receive a new aspect as each revolving day comes round. We have corn for only ten or fifteen days [of forage] and hence must go somewhere now for we can't stay here—at a point which is nearly the highest ~~point~~ level of travelled route between the Atlantic and Pacific. . . .

At this hour, half past 8 P.M. there is a driving snow storm from the North of East.

Three wild geese were seen flying towards the South.

This snow storm had commenced by sunset at the South Pass.

Sunday Octr. 18th

At 9 A.M. the snow storm having prevailed during the night was still continuing ~~having prevailed during the night~~ and had covered the earth to the depth of several inches. But at 10 it began to break away in the N.E. and the sun became visible. . . . Our poor horses have been pawing away the snow to find some grass—they suffer very much. One died last night from having fallen into a hole and strained himself the night before while ~~chilled~~ benum[b]ed with the cold.

Have at length heard from the rear—by Mr. [Ben] Ficklin. Two companies of the 10th Infantry under [Brevet] Col. [Charles F.] Smith were six days march from here, i.e. two days march on the other side of the South Pass waiting for the ox trains to come up. This was four days ago.

The Colonel commanding received letters from Brigham Young and Lieut. General Wells. They are both of ~~which are of~~ a hostile tenor. That of Brigham is six pages long.

One of the First Sergeants of the 10th Infantry died yesterday (of bilious cholic) and was buried this evening. The funeral procession reached the hillside where his grave had been dug; and the dirge like notes of the march had ceased and the ceremonies were being performed just as the last rays of the sun were gilding the tops of the eastern hills. The wintry ~~barrenness~~ coldness of the scene, the land being covered with snow; the good character of the deceased and the suddenness of his death all contributed to render the spectacle peculiarly desolate and gloomy.[26]

Col. Smith writes that he is out of corn; and it is said that with his two companies he is to escort 150 ox wagons.

Monday October 19th

It was finally decided to retrace our steps down the Fork and establish winter quarters at Fort Bridger and on Henry's Fork; and ~~accordingly~~ to this end the ox wagons were divided into three trains of 50 each and the troops assigned to them as escorts. The first division moved this morning and both the others will probably follow to-morrow.[27]

~~One section of my battery has been ordered to go with the rear division.~~

The 5th Infantry, it is said, have lost about a dozen mules and are in consequence breaking up some of their wagons giving the wheels to officers to make tent pins of.

It was very cold last night—the stream freezing over in the stiller places. But the snow has thawed away considerably to-day and the ice is all gone. . . .

Another express from the rear came in, but it is not known what it brings since it went on to overtake the commanding officer who is with the first division.

Tuesday October 20th

Marched back about twelve miles—I say about because the odometer is with the left section which is detached.

Received an order by which Col. Johnston assumes command. He is somewhere near the South Pass and will be up in the course of seven days. Our course in seeking the region of Henry's Fork as winter quarters appears to be approved by him.

Received another copy of the Deseret News from Brigham Young. It came thro' Col. Alexander.

Abandoned two horses which had become too much debilitated to stand.

It was still very cold last night, tho' not as cold as the night previous. . . . The snow has not melted to-day; ~~it lies in patches The breath has congealed~~

---

[26] Curtis R. Allen of Centerville, Utah, identifies this man as Sgt. John McDonnell, age 28, of Company E, Tenth U.S. Infantry; Allen to MacKinnon, e-mail message, 7 September 2006. A first sergeant was the senior enlisted man of each company.

[27] As a result of this decision, Private Scott of Phelps's Battery wrote in his diary, "Orders to return, the command divided into three divisions 10 miles back on the fork[:] 'The King of France marched up the hill. And then marched down again.'" Stowers and Ellis, eds., "Charles A. Scott's Diary of the Utah Expedition," 166, entry for 20 October 1857. Scott was quoting from the Mother Goose poem: "The king of France, the king of France, with 20,000 men, marched up the hill and then marched down again; and when they were up, they were up; and when they were down, they were down; and when they were only halfway up, they were neither up nor down." The lines have been used multiple times to express frustration with seemingly pointless government actions.

~~in the beard,~~ it lies in patches covering the ground by about one third. It has been sufficiently cold most of the time to congeal the breath in the beard.

Fortunately, we have found some grazing that the horses can eat. They are fond of brushing away the snow with their lips and taking the grass from under it. I could hear the animals throughout the night pawing at the stiff icy snow in search of food. I had for my horses about 4 lbs. of grass which I had cut before the storm and three pounds of corn, and a warm place among the bushes.

Wednesday Octr. 21st

Marched about 10 miles—our division of 50 ox wagons coming in at an early hour in the afternoon. The 1st division is only a mile or two ahead of us.

It is much easier to come over a road that has been broken by carriages than thro' sage bushes. On coming back it is frightful to see what my poor horses did in leading the way; and all to no purpose.

It was again very cold last night, the wind prevailing from the N of W; but the horses were well sheltered by the willows and had something to eat. Some of them were as warm as if in a stable.

The wind has been pretty fresh from the N.W. It is a cold wind; and it seemed to-day to come down from above since no hill s~~ee~~ furnished any protection from it. . . .

Thursday Octr. 22nd

Marched about seven miles and encamped on comparatively good grass, tho' it is but indifferent at best. We are over all the hills but one which were traversed during our up-river march. With the same outlay of horsework we might now have ~~been~~ arrived at this time in Bear River Valley and had a good road before us towards the Mormon settlements. The Mormons have grain for our horses but no money, and long before spring many of them would be glad I think to exchange one for the other.[28]

It was again quite cool last night, but without wind. It has been mild and warm to-day, the columns of smoke rising upright in the air with Indian summer tranquility. . . .

Friday Octr. 23rd

Remain in camp. Col. Johnston has ordered us back some forty miles or more to Fontenelle Creek, where it empties into Green River, and we are waiting to hear from him with regard to our previously formed plan of going to Henry's Fork to winter.

Some bands or companies of Mormons have been watching our movements from the banks of the valley. They caught up one of our wagon masters who was behind looking for stray animals; and after keeping him over night sent him in yesterday with a note from Capt. [William] Maxwell who

[28] More wishful thinking by Phelps.

said that he had tuk him and might have tuk twenty wagons; but he sent him in and requested that Major Taylor might be sent back in his place.

Had a fine dish of trout this evening, which were taken from the stream by one of the sergeants. . . .

Saturday Octr. 24th

Remain in camp writing letters for the next opportunity to the States. It is one month since we have heard from there.

A mild warm day. Last night as usual very cold. Yesterday morning and this the vapor stood up from the stream like thick long fir. Little or no wind at the surface. . . .

Sunday Octr. 26 [25]th

Still in camp. One of my horses is down flat and seems paralized, especially in his hind quarters. He seems otherwise to be in good health; has made many attempts to get up and has been lifted up by the men but all to no purpose, he falls back as if under an incubus. It is, perhaps, the alternation of cold nights and warm days, together with his reduced condition, that has occasioned a paralysis. A horse generally turns his hind quarters to the storm and it is in those quarters that he is most affected.

The earth was again covered with snow this morning, tho' to no great depth for by midday only the old sparse patches of the preceeding snow remained. . . .

Monday Octr. [26]

Remain in camp—until the grazing is consumed three times over.

But we have at length heard from Col. Johnston and in consequence shall move to-morrow to Black's Fork.

A part of the Infantry went out among the hills to-day and, concealing themselves, sent one of their number in advance. A party of Mormons saw this one and came down upon him, but when at the distance of about 250 yards the Infantry arose and fired upon them. They were well mounted and ran away rapidly. It is not known whether any of them were hit. A strange state of warfare this. . . .

Lost a horse last night—the one mentioned yesterday.

Tuesday Oct. 27

The Col. (Alexander) received an express last night and we are to meet Col. Johnston at Black's Fork—near where we encamped when coming out; and accordingly we are to move slowly, since the Col. was to come there from South Pass, a distance of nearly 100 miles while we have only about 30 to go, & while there is some grass here on this fork (notwithstanding the Mormon efforts to burn it all up) and little or none on Black's Fork.

We shall be out of corn in a ~~few~~ two or three days, and we should therefore endeavor to be amidst good grass—say on Henry's Fork, before it entirely fails. Else we may loose more animals than necessary. We marched only one hour this morning.

Received back the left [artillery] section from its service with the 3rd division of ox wagons, and sent the middle section in its place.

Found a stray horse in our camp—too poor to work—but brought him along.

It was perfectly clear this morning after a cold night. . . .

This cold, pure, dry air stimulates the appetite and conduces to the health. The men don't find 18 ozs. flour (tho' made doubly heavy with water) enough to satisfy their hunger, and are constantly running to the commissary to buy more. When mixed with water without leaven and baked in a Dutch oven it is about as heavy as lead; and yet, only one man has the fits.

Wednesday Octr. 28

Remain in camp.

The horses get pretty well filled up.

Encounter a current of little miseries. 1st a man had lost his knapsack, and to hear the story one could not tell whether stupidity or knavery was at the bottom of it.

2nd. One of the sentinels had broken a musket [illegible] during the night and was not honest enough to acknowledge it.

3rd ~~and last~~. A wagon tail was negligently left open during the night and a horse discovered ~~that~~ (much to his surprise and disgust no doubt) that both beans and rice were carried in bags as well as corn.

4th. The Doctor's Tent took fire before our eyes and burned up, injuring his bedding and every thing else more or less contained therein. It was one of the most awful conflagrations that I ever witnessed. All that a dozen of us could do was to stand appaled and gaze at the wholesale distruction. . . .

Thursday Octr. 29th

Marched 7.03 miles and encamped near the ground which we left on the 11th inst. . . .

Friday Octr. 30th

Remain in camp. Sent off the horses about two miles to graze. Lost a horse last night. It was the third that seemed to be afflicted with indigestion. They ate till the last; but their food seemed to do them no good. They became thinner and more languid every day, until they were no longer able to stand, and their hind quarters seemed paralyzed. They have had no salt for some time. The idea occurs of mixing glauber salts with their food.

This last horse that died was one of a lead span to a gun which was drawn by four horses most of the way from Fort Leavenworth. They are both dead. They were young horses and willing workers while one of the wheel horses of their team—a sorrel, with four white feet and a white nose, is now really fat. He has shirked all the way.

It is unpleasant to see these horses dying off after such a long companionship with them in which nothing but their hard work is remembered. Their last two sacks of corn is now being kept against a days hard work. For the first time they have had none to night.

The weather has been quite mild and pleasant to-day. . . .

Saturday Octr. 31st

Marched 8.40 miles and encamped nearly a mile below our first encampment on this Ham's Fork—it being exactly one month since our arrival here.

Mustered at 3 P.M.[29] The day has been quite warm . . .

The strange horse mentioned on the 27th inst. was down flat this morning; and as 20 men couldn't lift him he was left behind. . . .

Sunday Nov. 1st 1857

Remain in camp.

Another express came in from Brigham Young.

One of the officers of the command brought letters of introduction to some of the principal Mormons. He sent them on not long since with a note saying that he hoped soon to call in person—and to-day he received an answer from one of them about a dozen pages long.[30]

The night as usual was very cold; but the day has been more than usually warm. . . . The northern flanks of these [Uintah] mountains are, as they were when we first saw them, covered with snow. Their aspect of wintry repose is intense; and the clouds, in their slow march along their flanks, give them an air of peculiar grandeur and solemnity. The association of mountains with the clouds is exceedingly elevating and pleasant to the thoughts and feeling—Perhaps it reminds us that we of the earth—we too may become the associates of higher and more etherial beings.

Monday Nov. 2nd

Marched 8.72 miles and encamped on Black's Fork, not far from where we encamped on the 29th of Sepr. The 5th Infantry is just above us and the 10th Infantry just below. It was expected that Col. Johnston would meet us here to day; but he has not yet made his appearance. There is but poor grazing here for our some four thousand animals. It is not pleasant to see so many tents, such an outlay of wagons and animals on so long a march and with so little thus far accomplished. A company of Infantry fired yesterday one thousand yards at 30 or forty Mormons.

As usual it was very cold last night. But has been mild during the day. . . .

Abandoned another horse to-day—too weak to stand—fell down whilst

[29] Under army regulations, each unit stood muster and inspection on the last day of every other month beginning with February.

[30] The officer to whom Phelps refers was Capt. R. B. Marcy of the Fifth Infantry, who had New York friends in common with Apostle John Taylor from his days as editor of *The Mormon* in Manhattan. The long letter was written by Taylor as an exposition of the Mormon case and position and is Taylor to Marcy, 21 October 1857, House Ex. Doc. No. 71, Serial 956, 57–62.

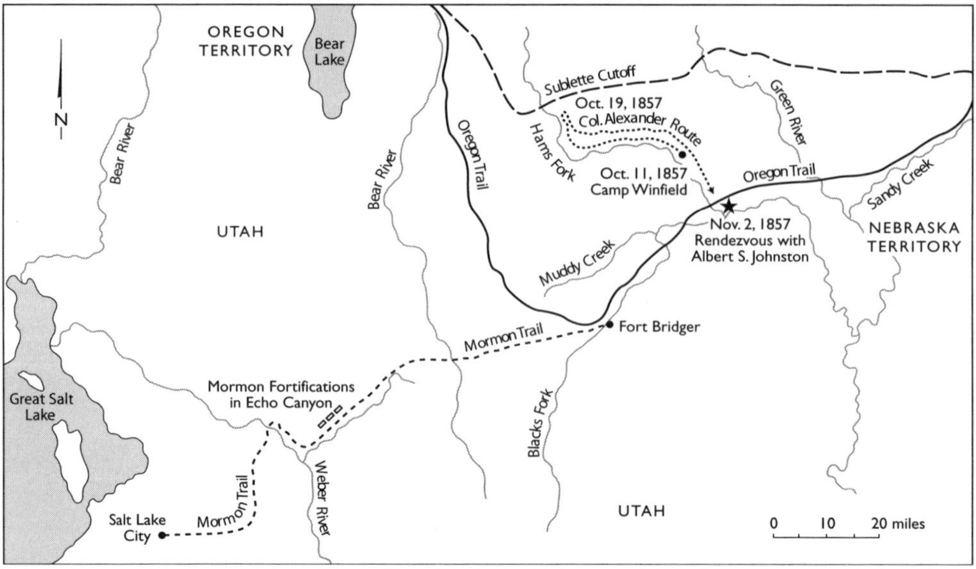

Routes Followed by the U.S. Army Expedition in 1857–58
This sweeping map shows the area between South Pass and Salt Lake City, including the routes taken by the army during its frustrating October march and counter-march along Hams Fork and the ordeal of its November slog up Blacks Fork to Fort Bridger. Adapted from Gowans and Campbell, *Fort Bridger: Island in the Wilderness. Map drawn by Bill Nelson.*

eating the frost killed grass which constitutes our grazing. One of the accompaniments of such debility is a loss of power in the muscles that move the eye-balls as well as the limbs.

I am writing this by the light of the moon. We are probably some 5000 feet above the level of the sea. The difference of level between this point and the highest point attained in the valley of Ham's Fork (distant from here 55 miles) is, I should say, between 2 and 3 thousand feet. The track that our carriages have made up the valley crosses the Fork nearly a dozen times, so that it would be hardly passable for carriages perhaps in the month of May or the early part of June, but later in the season it would be a good route, I think from Fort Kearny by the way of Bridgers Pass to either Oregon or California. It would be at least a hundred miles shorter than the way by Fort Laramie; would not offer steeper hills, and would furnish better grazing and water. It is decidedly the better route of the two for a Pacific railroad.

The white flanks of the Uintah Mountains could be plainly seen last night at this hour reflecting the light of the moon, tho' some sixty miles distant. . . .

Tuesday Nov. 3rd

Col. Johnston arrived upon the Fork to-day with two companies of the 10th Infy, two of Dragoons and a long train of upward of 340 wagons, containing supplies for the troops and sutlers stores. By this arrival we shall receive medical and ordnance stores both of which we could have ~~hardly done without had we advanced on Salt Lake~~ stood very much in need and especially if we had advanced on Salt lake as we set out to do three weeks ago.

With the train comes the Chief Justice (Eccles) [Eckels] and also Mr. Morrell, the post master for Salt Lake City. We get a few letters and papers. . . .

It has been a very cheerless day. . . .

One Magnificent Struggle from the Beginning: The Accounts of Porter, Johnston, Stewart, and Carter

When Maj. Fitz John Porter, a New Hampshireman, was detailed as Colonel Johnson's adjutant in late August, he had been serving in the same role with Brevet Maj. Gen. Persifor F. Smith, commander of the Department of the West. Both officers were West Pointers, although as a member of the class of 1845, Porter was nineteen years junior to Johnston. On the trail west of Fort Leavenworth, these officers became tentmates and close friends.

Porter's letter to his counterpart at General Scott's headquarters covers the period from the resumption of march on 6 November to soon after his arrival at Fort Bridger on 17 November. From this material, which found its way into the *Washington Union*, emerges not only a view of the hardships endured but a typical army officer's uncomplimentary view of Mormons. Here one also finds Porter's open admiration for the willingness of Colonel Johnston to share his troops' hardships.

Porter to McDowell, "Interesting Information from the Utah Expedition," 29 November 1857, *Washington Union*, 24 January 1858, 2/5–6.

I left you [with my last letter] on Black's Fork, 16 miles from Fort Bridger, on the 7th instant, after one day's march from the point of uniting the commands by Col. Johnston. You now find us in this camp, named in honor of our cherished chief [Scott], whose forethought and action has placed us in winter-quarters, under excellent shelter, without the blow of an axe. Our first day's march was over a dreary waste, made more desolate by the fall of snow two days previous, and the driving storm of snow and wind which met us in the middle of the march, miles from wood, water, grass, or shelter. To return was destruction; to advance was, apparently, to court it. The number of animals was insufficient to move either our mule or contractors' trains. Still we struggled on, losing strength hourly by the destruction of our animals; and on the evening of the 8th we prepared for the contest again. On the morning of the 9th a portion struck camp and advanced to the next place of shelter; there, while waiting the arrival of the rear, to have our animals struck down by cold, hunger, and thirst. The rear (5th infantry) could not make a march of five miles in a day to overtake us without leaving the supplies behind. Without sustenance for animals almost starved before we joined the main body, almost without fuel, that regiment, and the trains it escorted, passed the day travelling against one of the most severe storms of snow and wind I have experienced for many years, and camped in a dreary spot, open to the full blast of the storm, with the thermometer at 6° below zero at 6, A.M., where we were under shelter of bluffs. The orders [enclosed] will show our march. It was one magnificent struggle from the beginning to this place. One more day's march and our meat ration—beef, horse, and mule—would have been diminutively small for the winter. The last company of the 10th infantry, escorting the last of the supply-trains to Fort Bridger, reached this camp at 10, P.M., on the 22d; thus requiring six days to move our little army and its supplies less than six miles. In its limbs the giant's strength was expended; but the will which moved this force, and the spirits which have this will vitality, were brighter and stronger as the constitution became weaker; and if he had said on, on we would have gone, feeling that what he would direct would be right. The assurances you gave me of confidence in my commander have been more than realized, and he now has, I believe, the unbounded confidence of the army. You will see from his letters and orders how he grappled with the difficulties in his path, and I hope the spring will see him the conqueror. This little army is in fine health and in cheerful spirits. The men have borne their trials without a murmur—duty is severe upon officers and men; but not a word of complaint have I heard. We have all endured alike, and the fact that Colonel Johnston has on the march "footed it," as did the men; suffers the same exposure, and will not permit the officer to receive more than the soldier, has endeared him to all.[31]

Johnston himself sent a private account of this march to "Captain" N. J. Eaton, a close friend and West Point classmate who had been "dropped" by the army in 1839 as the result of a still-murky affair.[32]

---

[31] When the *Union* printed this letter, neither author nor recipient were identified. A parallel but rougher account of this march appears in Diary of Fitz John Porter, Manuscript Division, Library of Congress. In this journal, once at Camp Scott, Porter commented, "as I cannot be with my loved ones at home, I would rather be here than any other place except some 110 miles further on [in Salt Lake]."

[32] N. J. Eaton is not to be confused with Amos Beebe Eaton, another member of Johnston's class of 1826. N. J. Eaton left the army as a lieutenant, so the title used by Johnston was honorific, perhaps related to his connection to Mississippi River steamers.

Johnston to Eaton, 5 February 1858,
Johnston, *Life of Albert Sidney Johnston*, 213–14.

On our march from the South Pass we had fine roads and fine weather, and effected the march in eight days, uniting the troops and supplies on the 3d of November, with the exception of Cooke's command. Two days were occupied in distributing clothing and making arrangements to resume our march.

On the 6th of November it was resumed, and then commenced the storm and wintry cold, racking the bones of our men and starving our oxen, and mules, and horses, already half starved. They died on the road and at our camps by hundreds, and so diminished were their numbers that from camp to camp, only four or five miles, as many days were required to bring them all up, as it was necessary to give time to rest the animals, now incapable of protracted efforts, and to hunt for food. In this way fifteen days were consumed in making thirty-five miles to this place, the nearest and best place for shelter and fuel for the troops, and for shelter and grass for the animals. The struggle then amid snow and arctic cold (the thermometer 10° below zero) was for a place of safety. If any doubt existed before this storm of the propriety of risking the troops on the mountains before us before spring, or of the ability to accomplish the march, the destruction among our draught-animals the necessity of saving all the oxen left for food, even if capable of further exertion, now dispelled that doubt and solved the question.

Colonel Cooke's command arrived here with the rear of the main body on the 19th of November. The storm which he encountered on the Sweetwater, and on through the South Pass, destroyed more than half of his horses and a large number of his mules, although he had corn for them. In that high region, much higher than where we were, the cold must have been much more intense than experienced by us, and his animals, I presume, perished mainly from cold. I have the satisfaction to say that the privations of the march were endured by officers and men without complaint, or, perhaps, I might more justly say with cheerfulness. The troops are in fine health and condition. . . .

The Mormons have declared, as fully as words and actions can manifest intentions, that they will no longer submit to the Government, or to any government but their own. The people of the Union must now submit to a usurpation of their territory—to have a government erected in their midst, not loyal to, or rather not acknowledging any dependence upon, or allegiance to the Federal Government—and what is not less impolitic and entirely incompatible with our institutions, must allow them to ingraft their social organization upon ours and make it a part of our system, or they must act with the vigor and force to compel them to submit. This is due to the dignity and honor of the Government.

Two of Captain Phelps's enlisted artillerymen left vivid accounts of the nightmarish scene following the 6 November resumption of the march to

Fort Bridger. The diary of Pvt. Charles A. Scott has been published and is readily accessible.[33] But the Utah War reminiscences of Phelps's Scottish-born first sergeant, James ("Jock") Stewart, are not easily found, embedded as they are in obscure publications devoted primarily to Civil War experiences. It is not surprising that Stewart's recollections of the Utah War are in such material, for his valor at the battle of Gettysburg as a first lieutenant commanding Phelps's old Light Battery B was extraordinary and far overshadowed what he did in 1857–58. In this material one finds a view of the trek to Bridger "closer to the ground" than that of the expedition's commander, Albert Sidney Johnston, and his adjutant, Fitz John Porter.

"Capt. Stewart's Memoir of Early Service in the Battery," Augustus Buell, *The Cannoneer*, 389–98.

When we reached the river [Hams Fork in late September] we found about 3,000 Snake Indians in camp, and as they had seen us coming they did what they could to make a great impression on us. . . . They certainly did not make much of an impression upon us as samples of the "noble Red Men" that we had read so much of in [James Fenimore] Cooper's novels. It was in this camp that I abandoned my horse, "Tartar," with whom you afterward became so well acquainted [during the Civil War].[34] For over a month we were marched up one creek and down another waiting for Gen. Albert Sydney Johnston to arrive and assume command. But before he arrived, the Mormon Destroying Angels burnt three large wagon trains and all the grass along the creeks to prevent our stock from obtaining any grazing. The General arrived about the 1st [3d] of November, and the following day we took up the march toward Fort Bridger. We started on the march in a very heavy snow storm, some of the horses being taken out of the harness and turned loose nearly every mile. When we reached camp that afternoon the Captain ordered me to take four men and go back and do our best to bring to camp the horses that had given out on the march. After dinner we went back to where we had started from in the morning, but all we could do was to bring three of the number that had given out, we getting back to camp about midnight. Some of the men had pitched my tent during my absence, and when I entered it there was 10 inches of snow in it. Fortunately, I had a lot of saddle blankets, and, throwing them on the snow, turned in, in boots and spurs and all my clothing. The following morning when I woke up I found 12 horses frozen at the picket rope. The cooks were doing their best to get breakfast ready, but it was a hard

33 Stowers and Ellis, eds., "Charles A. Scott's Diary of the Utah Expedition, 1857–1861," 154–76.

34 Stewart retrieved Tartar from Washakie's Shoshones near Fort Bridger in the spring of 1858 and later rode him during the battle of Gettysburg. Schindler, "Tartar the War Horse."

thing to accomplish. However, after considerable time we had our breakfast, and as soon as the men had finished I had them fall in and sent every man to the creek to cut willow branches and give them to the horses to nibble at, as there was not a quart of grain in the whole command. The thermometer that morning stood 45 degrees below zero. The number of animals that died of cold and starvation that night was estimated at 600.

We remained in that camp two days and then started on the march, making about four or five miles. It certainly was a sight to see us make the attempt to start. Every driver had to lead his horses, and one-half of the Cannoneers would take hold of the leading piece and caisson and push them up on the horses, the poor animals simply staggering along like so many drunken men. I had bought a pony from the Indians, and had it not been for him it would have taken us several hours longer before we could have reached camp. I just tried him as an experiment, and, although he had never had a collar on his neck, he pulled like a good fellow. At last we reached Fort Bridger, having taken 13 days to march about 30 miles. During all this march the cold was excessive, thermometer ranging from 38 to 46 degrees below zero,[35] and nearly every man was frozen in feet or hands. We made our Winter camp a little below the fort.[36]

As Colonel Johnston, Major Porter, Captain Phelps, and 1st Sergeant Stewart began their desperate trek out of Hams Fork, Lt. Col. Philip St. George Cooke and the expedition's rear guard were in even greater peril east of South Pass. What Cooke, his dragoons, and accompanying civilians endured was captured in the diary of thirty-seven-year-old sutler William A. Carter, a veteran of both the Seminole Wars (with the Second Dragoons) twenty years earlier and an 1850 transcontinental journey to California's gold fields. Carter, destined to be one of Wyoming's leading merchants and judges, recorded not only the endurance of men and animals but Colonel Cooke's superb leadership.

"DIARY OF JUDGE WILLIAM A. CARTER—1857,"
TRANSCRIPTION BY DAVID L. BIGLER FROM ORIGINAL IN CARTER PAPERS,
WYOMING ARCHIVES AND HISTORICAL DEPT., CHEYENNE.

[November] 10th [Near Rocky Ridge] Last night was an awful night, the most disagreeable I think that I ever felt. The wind blew a storm all night sweeping the snow in our direction. The piteous cries of the famished mules was heart rending. They crowd around our camp fire, and seemed to beg for

[35] From the distance of thirty-three years, Stewart's recollection is faulty. Most other sources agree that the lowest temperature during this period was about –15°F.

[36] A similar but somewhat later version of this material is found in Stewart, "Battery B Fourth United States Artillery at Gettysburg."

food in the most supplicating cries but we had none to spare them. When we awoke this morning, the storm was still raging and the air dark with snow, mules were strewn about dead and some in the last agonies of death. It was a difficult matter to get them to stand long enough to feed them and put the harness on. One of the government trains left its mules mired in a slew with all the harness on. Some 50 loose horses and mules were left in camp it being impossiblel to drive them [illegible]. With great difficulty we succeeded in ascending the hill. The storm still raged furiously. We had 14 miles to make, but fortunately the wind blew in our backs most of the time all day. The wind swept with wild fury drifting the snow around us and up across our road. At every half mile a mule was turned loose unable to proceed any further. We reached camp on Sweet Water late in the evening and winding among the willow bushes and succeeded in finding a spot to shelter ourselves somewhat from the furious wind. We gave our mules a little corn and then shoveled away the deep snow and succeeded in kindling a fire. It was only by constant exertion in cutting willows that we could keep ourselves from freezing. The night was extremely cold and a great number of stock died.

11th. The morning, contrary to the anticipation of all was miled. We succeeded before night in reaching Dry Sandy 20 miles and encamped in the sage brush in a gully just above the Command.

12 The night was intensely cold but the sun is shining warmly. Poor Tiny our faithful mule is dying. The command will not be able to go much further. We left camp at one oclock [P.M.] not being able to collect our stock any sooner. We left 2 of our faithful animals lying in the rear of our wagons. They were unable to rise and seemed to select this spot as their last resting place to be near us.

It was with feelings of sadness that we left them but it was out of our power to render them assistance. Our road was beautiful today firm and level. We reached Little Sandy, 12 miles distant from Dry Sandy just as the sun was setting, but Col. Cook had gone onto Big Sandy and we were compelled to follow. He had turned off from the main road to the right and struck the stream high up about 6 miles from Little Sandy. We did not reach camp until after dark but although the night was cold soon succeeded in kindling a comfortable fire with sage brush and willows.

13th. The morning is pleasant. We have found some grass a few miles above camp and Col. Cook has given orders that we halt here today to refresh the Stock as there is only one feed of corn left. We are now distant from Green River about 28 miles and have nearly accomplished a march which will reflect credit upon our gallant Colonel.

Under all the circumstances no expedition has ever been conducted with more sound judgement more order and complete success than this. Under ordinary circumstances and under the conduct of an inexperienced officer, the Expe-

> dition would have proved a complete failure. A march across this direct country at the most pleasant time of the year is one of great [t]oil and ~~loss~~ sacrifice, but, at the most rigorous season it is almost a miracle without the loss of a single man and the sacrifice of a comparatively small amount of stock.[37] The storm and the intense cold the almost entire want of fuel ~~and~~ grass and water have offered no impediment to ~~impede~~ the progress of the march. The bugle sounded to the march and all was in motion. The brave Col at the head of his command faced the storm and ploughed through the snow drift, determined to accomplish the object ~~the object~~ of his duty. He suffered nothing to deter him from his purpose. The lives of his soldiers and the property of his Government were in his hands and he knew not what suffering a day's delay might bring upon him. The mountains had to be crossed for return was impossible. The forage for his animals was nearly exhausted and the little grass to be found was buried beneath the snow. He persevered and has been crowned with success. Great credit is due to Lieut Beufort [John Buford] the Regimental Quarter Master who never shrunk from his duty. I have often seen him when a wagon was overturned laboring in the snow to right it again and to permit no delay in the march. Not a murmur was heard from an officer or soldier all shared alike in the toils and privations consequent upon so severe a march. No person who has not made the trip across the plains has any correct notions in regard to it. The descriptions given of it by journalists are so meager that those who have read their descriptions and then traveled over the road acknowledge that they had not the most remote conception of the country.[38]

Small wonder that when Colonel Cooke and his command followed the rest of the Utah Expedition into the ruins of Fort Bridger on 19 November, he described what he saw on the road from Hams Fork as "hundreds of dead and frozen animals which for thirty miles nearly block the road; with abandoned and shattered property, they mark, perhaps, beyond example in history, the steps of an advancing army with the horrors of a disastrous retreat."[39]

[37] The Second Dragoons did sustain one fatality, the loss of a private to lockjaw.

[38] A published but less accurate version of this material appeared without attribution to the transcriber in "Diary of Judge William A. Carter," *Annals of Wyoming* II (April 1939): 75–110.

[39] Cooke to Asst. Adjt. Gen. F. J. Porter, 21 November 1857, House Ex. Doc. No. 71, Serial 956, 99.

Thomas L. Kane,

Mormon Friend and Self-Appointed Intermediary

Ignored by President Buchanan, attacked by Judge Drummond, and beset by medical and family problems, Kane withdrew from Mormon affairs in the spring of 1857. Re-energized and alarmed by the further, potentially bloody deterioration in Mormon-federal relations, he returned to the fray in early November for an inconclusive visit with the president. This was prelude to his Christmas return to the White House and year-end mission to Utah. This photo, a rare pre–Civil War image of Kane, shows him at age 37 in 1859. *Courtesy of Ronn Palm, Museum of Civil War Images, Gettysburg, Pennsylvania.*

Chapter 15

"My Thoughts upon Utah Matters" Origins of Kane's Mission

I was perhaps leaving undone that which I ought to have done.

—Thomas L. Kane on his November 1857 thoughts about Utah

Arrival on the Atlantic Coast of troubling rumors about Utah in late October and early November 1857 produced in Thomas L. Kane restlessness—and with it his return to the fray. The result was Kane's famous but mysterious peace mission to Utah, begun with his departure from Philadelphia on 4 January 1858. Kane returned nearly six months later in ruinous health but with substantial notoriety. It was a mission that made an enormous difference in the character of the Utah War's resolution and impacted the dynamics of federal-Mormon relations for decades. Together with the Mountain Meadows massacre, Brigham Young's proclamation of martial law, Maj. Lot Smith's raid, Capt. Randolph B. Marcy's epic march to New Mexico, and the dramatic Move South, Kane's intervention was one of the conflict's truly bold strokes.

There are at least three principal mysteries shrouding the origins of Kane's adventure: the reasons for his fateful withdrawal from Utah affairs during the crucial spring of 1857; his motives for re-engaging in early November; and the extent to which Kane was or was not Buchanan's emissary in early January. James Buchanan's reluctance to discuss the mission publicly, even after its conclusion, complicates an understanding of the president's motives, as well as Kane's. Although vastly different in temperament, both men had a long history of behavior that was secretive, manipulative, and even self-serving, as well as noble. As a result their decisions and actions involving Utah affairs were far from transparent. The written accounts they left were frustratingly terse in Buchanan's case but surprisingly lengthy in Kane's. Both men recorded their thoughts after the mission, doing so with intent to publish as each worked to protect, if not burnish, his own reputation.

The story of Kane's Utah mission is a Byzantine one that evokes Winston Churchill's later characterization of Russia as "a riddle wrapped in a mystery inside an enigma."[1] Here—in the aftermath of Lot Smith's raid—one sees Thomas L. Kane and James Buchanan maneuvering in their own ways.

Kane's frustrating attempt to help the Mormons during March, his disgust with Buchanan's fecklessness and apparent indiscretion, the public attack on him by W. W. Drummond, the nature of Kane's personal and family problems, and his consequent withdrawal to the mountains of northwestern Pennsylvania have been discussed in an earlier chapter. Precisely what stirred Kane to re-enter this troubled arena in early November—only a few days before shocking news of Lot Smith's raid arrived—is difficult to determine. Presumably one stimulus was the backwash from Elder Samuel W. Richards's unsuccessful attempt to meet with Kane on Brigham Young's behalf in mid-September.

He Had Been in the Country: S. W. Richards's Failed Attempt to Brief Kane

Rather than trust the security of the mails still functioning east of Independence, Brigham Young chose to brief Kane on his strategy through a personal emissary, Samuel W. Richards. Given the upheaval in responsibility for the mail route across the plains and Young's deep suspicion of non-Mormon postmasters, this decision made sense except for the fact that it failed to anticipate Kane's extended withdrawal from Philadelphia. When Richards called at Kane's unoccupied office, he made a fateful decision: to push on to New York, Boston, and Liverpool rather than spend a few more days hunting for Kane in what Richards called "the country." There could have been multiple reasons for Richards's decision: lack of energy or resourcefulness; inflexibility in deviating from his trans-Atlantic travel plans; preoccupation with the need to brief the British Mission on Young's plans; or a failure to appre-

[1] Winston S. Churchill, radio broadcast, 3 October 1939.

ciate the significance of Kane's unique role in the volatile world of Mormon-federal relations. The net effect of Richards's failure to meet with Kane in September was that again—as in the summer of 1856 and the spring of 1857—Kane was out of position to help Brigham Young with the Buchanan administration at a critical time.

Although Richards's travels to New York, Boston, and Liverpool were not secret, his specific assignment to visit Kane was confidential. Nonetheless Buchanan's political "organ" in Washington took notice of the urgency of Richards's travels. Four months later that newspaper, the *Washington Union*, guessed inaccurately that Young's emissary ("an express, direct from Utah, with extraordinary despatch, through Kansas to Boston") was part of a Mormon anti-slavery conspiracy with New England's Emigrant Aid Company.[2]

Richards's report to Brigham Young upon his unsuccessful return from Philadelphia was, with hindsight, remarkably prosaic, and—as with John M. Bernhisel's March withdrawal from Washington—there is no documentary sign that Young later took his agent to task for his decision:

> We called at Col. Kane's office in Philadelphia, found he had been in the country several weeks and would be out for some weeks to come. I was furnished his address and wrote to him, informing him of our arrival from Utah, and call at his office, to communicate with him upon the present state of affairs, and doings of Government, relative to Utah, tendered him assurances of your confidence and respect, and informed him how he could forward any communication he might be pleased to make to you upon any matters touching the interests of Utah. I shall no doubt have an opportunity of seeing him after my return from Europe; and should there be another opportunity of forwarding by Express this Fall Dr Clinton may make it convenient to have an Interview and send you the result.[3]

Notwithstanding Richards's wishful thinking, there is no evidence that Jeter Clinton, the Mormon branch president in Philadelphia, subsequently called on Kane. And so Kane's direct awareness of Utah affairs during much of the fall was presumably limited to Richards's letter of 16 September, a document so steeped in worries about communications security that it was as bland as his subsequent report to Brigham Young. If Young's intent in August had been to impart a sense of urgency to Kane through Richards, the likelihood is that he had succeeded only in shifting Kane's thoughts, but not necessarily actions, to Mormon affairs.

---

[2] "The Mormons in Kansas," *Washington* (D.C.) *Union*, 20 January 1858, 2/3.

[3] Richards to Young, 19 September 1857, LDS Archives.

Richards to Kane, 16 September 1857,
Kane Papers, Beinecke Library.

I beg you will excuse the liberty I take in addressing you.

Having just arrived from Utah I took the liberty of calling at your office in Philadelphia at the instance of Gov. B. Young to communicate to you such items as you might be pleased to learn relative to the State of things in Utah the intentions of the Authorities there &c. and also to learn of you any thing that you might have in your possession and be pleased to communicate, relating to the present movements of Government and their designs against us in that Territory.

I anticipated this interview with much pleasure from the short but very agreeable opportunity I had with you while on my way to England in the fall of 1851.

I left G.S.L. City on the 13th ult. [August] . . . reach[ed] this city on the 10th making the distance of near 2700 miles in 23 traveling days—more than 13 hundred of it performed with animals. . . .

Only one [of us] came to this city with me Elder Geo. G. Snyder who accompanies me to Liverpool for which place we expect to sail from Boston on Wednesday next, 23d

The crops in Utah were very abundant and every body almost was engaged gathering the harvest. The wheat harvest was nearly over when I left.

The movement of Government sending Troops to Utah came to our ears before my departure and their refusal of the Mail to be carried under Mr. Kimball's contract, all of which, together with the universal cry and voice of the Nation that the Mormons must quit the practice of their religious of the institutions, indicate to us that the present intention of Gov. towards us are extremely hostile and that in all probability they will make an effort to break us up in the mountains. From the knowledge you have of us, Dear Col., and the character of Prest. Young, you must well know that we could never submit to be interfered with in our religious views and practices, after what we have already passed through.

I consider therefore that the present state of things may result in a very serious consequences, both to us and the Government. The result however we do not fear, we most firmly believe it will tend greatly to our advantage, and that it will hasten the day when our oppressors shall cease to have power over us.

If you have any information in your possession which you would like to communicate to Gov. Young, you can do so with safety by addressing him, under cover, to William Felshaw, Florence, N.T. with a request to forward.[4] An Express will leave Florence about the first of Octr.

---

[4] The understanding was that "forward" meant placing any Kane–Young letter in an envelope addressed to a Salt Lake City recipient other than Brigham Young so as to minimize the likelihood of interception.

In the mean time if you would allow me to hear from you before my departure from Boston next Wednesday I should esteem it a very great favor.

Gov. Young was quite willing I should tell you of his full intentions relative to the Government and the course he should pursue, esteeming you as a warm friend, and worthy of that confidence. Of course I should not feel to commit to paper with the same freedom that I would speak.

I expect to return from England in the course of two or 3 months and in the spring to Utah. On my return to the states I may do myself the pleasure of calling upon you.

My Mission is to the Churches in the States and Europe.

Messrs Kimball, Wells, and others wished a very warm remembrance to you.

Praying God to increase your power and influence in the Earth, I am with much esteem,

P.S. Please address me care of C. F. Cleary, 9 Genesee St Boston.

During the interval between Richards's 13 August departure from Salt Lake City and Bernhisel's on 14 September, much had happened in Utah: implementation of Young's earliest war strategy; the Mountain Meadows massacre; Captain Van Vliet's visit; and the governor's proclamation of martial law. Accordingly, Young decided to take advantage of Bernhisel's return to Washington to write a letter to Kane, to be hand-carried by Bernhisel. Notwithstanding the security implicit in this arrangement, Young's 12 September letter was curiously unspecific and non-directive rather than candid and prescriptive. At times the letter was even a bit quirky, as with Young's comment, "Well, say you, I find you again in trouble." Filled also with rhetorical flourishes and prolix complaints, it gave no hint of either his imminent martial-law proclamation or the gunrunning mandate contained in the letters Young wrote on the same day to Jeter Clinton in Philadelphia, William I. Appleby in New York, and Orson Pratt in Liverpool. Perhaps most importantly, Young chose not to ask Kane to do anything specific, apparently leaving it to Kane's intuition to determine what he could and should do on the Mormons' behalf at that juncture.

Based on Bernhisel's travels, the letter reached the Atlantic Coast—Washington or New York—on about 27 October. In what would appear to be another case of inexplicable passivity, Bernhisel then simply dropped Young's letter in the U.S. mail to Kane rather than delivering it in person. Lost in the process was the opportunity to present Kane with his own valuable insights into what was happening in Utah and Washington.

When I Came Down upon the World Again: Prelude to Mission

Kane and his family returned to Philadelphia on 3 October. On 9 November, alarmed by some combination of Richards's and Young's letters, rumors of belligerence in Utah affairs, and the unsettling report that Captain Van Vliet delivered to Washington on 27 October, Kane traveled to the capital to meet with James Buchanan. He did so only days before the first substantial news of Lot Smith's raid reached Washington on 13 November.[5]

The president was a man well known to Kane's father, Judge John K. Kane, but apparently not a person whom Thomas had met. Whether the introduction was arranged by Judge Kane or by a political intermediary such as James C. Van Dyke is unknown. The meeting occurred four weeks before Congress reconvened, at which time Buchanan would need to speak publicly for the first time about Utah affairs.

Kane, Memorandum, July 1858, Kane Collection, American Philosophical Society.

When I came down upon the world again, which was in October, and learned the true state of affairs at that time, I was inexpressibly shocked. Besides the news which the public at large were possessed of, I had a letter from Utah post marked N. York from an individual with whom I had not corresponded for some time, and which probably came to my hands either through Doctor Bernheisel or Captain Van Vleet [*sic*] as I surmise, showing me beyond question that the Mormons were determined to resist our troops and were, the most staid and reliable men among them, in an exceedingly unhappy and distempered state of mind.[6]

An intimate friend of the President also, George Plitt Esq.[7] had a long conversation with me upon the subject of the Utah difficulties, and took pains to state to me that he did not believe that the President did not or was not

[5] The date of the Kane-Buchanan meeting can be determined from his wife's diary, although unfortunately she made no comments on what Thomas told her of the interactions during this session. Elizabeth W. Kane, "Journal," entry for 10 November 1857, Thomas L. and Elizabeth W. Kane Papers.

[6] This letter was presumably Young to Kane, 12 September 1857, carried east by Bernhisel.

[7] George Plitt of Philadelphia was a Democratic Party supporter of James Buchanan as early as the 1830s. The Plitts served as foster parents for Buchanan's orphaned niece, Harriet Lane, until Buchanan assumed the guardianship. When in 1857 Buchanan engineered Plitt's relinquishment of a patronage position and then failed to deliver another, it created a blow to the family finances that soured Mrs. Plitt on both politics and Buchanan while dampening George's ardor for the president. Klein, *President James Buchanan*, 252–53. Here was a collapse of a long-time Buchanan relationship similar to troubles that marked his relations with such close supporters as John W. Forney, Dr. Jonathan M. Foltz, and even James C. Van Dyke.

at any time prepared to attach full weight to any representations which I might be inclined to make to him.[8] I did not inquire whether this gentleman spoke to me at the instance of the President. I thought otherwise. But I remember his saying that he wished the President would send me [as] Commissioner to Utah, and that he urged me to go to Washington and see the President.

To be brief here, I went on to Washington[,] it was in November sometime in the 2d week of November[,] conversed with the President (A rough time I had of it at first too. He was so reluctant to admit that he had committed any error.), learned from him that the advance of the troops would be slow, that their orders and the instructions to Governor Cumming were of a character to prevent a precipitate advance; but I do not know why I thought myself fortunate in evading a proposal on his part to appoint me to proceed to Utah—I really thought that it was too late in the season for me to force my way among the Mormons, and I will admit was sufficiently recreant a citizen to congratulate myself upon not having the responsibility put upon me of refusing the President to make an effort at that time to save the administration and the country.

My thoughts turning after this upon Utah matters and examining fully into the subject the conviction gained upon me that I was perhaps leaving undone that which I ought to have done. Inquiring about among Mormons and others, I learned more than I had known of the different [travel] approaches to the Basin and learned that whatever might be the case with regard to myself, other men were able at that very date to penetrate to Salt Lake City. Let me remind you that domestic affliction came about this time to remind me that the sum of duty might not consist *in promoting the happiness* of my family &c.[9]

Policy of the Government Not Yet Definitely Fixed Upon

As Thomas L. Kane returned home from the White House, the *New York Herald*'s Washington correspondent also turned to Utah affairs and discerned ambiguity in the administration's Mormon policy.

---

[8] This convoluted description of Buchanan's lack of confidence in Kane may reflect more of Kane's view—forged in what he perceived as Buchanan's March 1857 rebuff—than Plitt's.

[9] Whatever the precise nature of the intimate, very private concerns afflicting the Kanes during November and perhaps December, Elizabeth described the period and the related gap in her journal-keeping as follows: "I cannot write about all the horrors we have passed through since I wrote last [12 November]. god has mercifully brought out of them one great blessing already, in uniting Tom and me in the bonds of a common faith." Even during the next April she referred to "the ghastly November days." Elizabeth W. Kane, "Journal," entries for 26 December 1857 and 4 April 1858, Thomas L. and Elizabeth W. Kane Papers.

"Interesting from Washington . . . Policy of the Administration on the Mormon Question," *New York Herald*, 11 November 1857, 4/6–5/1.

Washington, Nov. 10, 1857.

. . . The Mormon question will occupy a prominent position in the forthcoming [presidential] message. The policy of the government towards the fanatical people is not yet definitely fixed upon. All history proves that fanaticism cannot be overcome by force. This rather tends to strengthen the stubborn and embolden the timid. Peace policy alone will avail, unless the government has determined to put the whole people to death by the sword, which cannot be the case in this Christian age. What that peace policy will be is yet to be determined.

The troops now sent to Utah are to back up the authority of Gov. Cumming—not to make war upon the Mormons. Of this fact Maj. [Capt.] Van Vliet endeavored to satisfy them, when lately in Salt Lake City; and he did not altogether fail. Some of the leading men admitted that their apprehensions had been allayed, and that they were no longer opposed to the entrance of the troops; but Brigham Young had prophesied that they would not enter the valley this season, and that prophecy must be fulfilled, unless Young should have another revelation from Heaven, which will be the case if he finds that Col. Johnston is likely to take up his winter quarters in the Salt Lake Valley. Young has but one way to back out of his treasonable position, and that will be by another revelation; and I confidently predict that this will be made, if not this fall, then early in the spring, before the troops can operate against him.

If the snows have kept off, it is believed that Col. Johnston is at this time in Utah. He is provided with winter tents, and will not enter Salt Lake City for the present. Should his forces be attacked, he has two thousand men with which he will have to fight his battles and defend himself the best way he can. Among these are two complete batteries of light artillery; and the Mormons being wholly destitute of artillery, their crowds of excited populace would be but food for powder and balls. It is not contemplated by the government to send any other troops to Utah this season.

Major Van Vliet represents the passes through the mountains for sixty miles to be exceedingly narrow and difficult, and easily defended; but Salt Lake City is situated in the open valley just at the base of a table land three miles in extent, and from which a six pounder could destroy the whole town, which is built of sun dried brick.

The major was treated most kindly by the Mormon leader and his principal men. He dined with several of them, and was shown over their houses and introduced to many of their wives. The senior Mrs. Young was an elderly lady of agreeable and easy manner, and seemed to have a superintendence over the other fifteen wives. All of them appeared to be happy, each in the discharge of her respective duty. In the evening they all assembled in a handsomely furnished parlor, and were as noisy as a flock of blackbirds, full of life and merry conversation. It was said that he had a large number of wives located in colonies at his several saw mills in and around Salt Lake City.

Dr. Bernheisel [*sic*], the delegate to Congress, who has always been too modest in Washington to admit himself a married man, has three wives—one of them about twenty-eight years of age, and decidedly a good looking woman. The doctor is evidently a moderate as well as a modest man. Elder Taylor numbers thirty-seven wives.

It seems not to be generally known that plurality of wives is a new doctrine in the Mormon church.[10] Joe Smith preached against it, and only justified it in himself on the ground of special indulgence. The bible printed in 1852, in London, prohibits it in terms.

---

[10] The principal of plural marriage was hardly new, having been introduced secretly by Joseph Smith in 1843 and announced publicly in August 1852. The correspondent's account of Captain Van Vliet's social interactions in Salt Lake City and the number of Bernhisel and Taylor wives was highly inaccurate.

Chapter 16

"Much Easier to Plan than Execute"
Buchanan and Diplomats React to Lot Smith

The Mormons, in my opinion, are mad and angry with religious fanaticism. You mark if events do not show it. . . . It is now simply necessary to reduce the Territory to obedience, and punish its people for their treason and attendant barbarities, which I fear will be much easier to plan than execute.

—U.S. Army captain Rufus Ingalls to Lt. Col. Thomas Swords, 29 December 1857

Unofficial and fragmentary first news of Lot Smith's raid on the Utah Expedition's supply trains drifted eastward into the Kansas-Missouri frontier during the second week of November. On 11 November telegraphers flashed it to the nation's newspapers. The deceptive period of no news was over, replaced by the specter of imminent bloodshed if not federal defeat.

On 13 November first confirmation of the attack reached the cabinet through a letter from Utah chief justice Delana R. Eckels to Sec. of State Lewis Cass, written from an army bivouac on the Sweetwater River east of South Pass exactly a month earlier. A few days after this letter reached Washington, Albert Sidney Johnston's reports arrived via General Scott's headquarters at West Point. These reports appeared in newspapers almost immediately and were soon followed by Johnston's dispatch transmitting Brigham Young's 15 September proclamation of martial law. The result was a national shock wave—strangely eclipsing Atlantic Coast indignation over news of the Mountain Meadows massacre, arriving in late November.

President Buchanan should have been prepared for problems but was not. On 27 October Captain Van Vliet had arrived in Washington with an alarming assessment of Mormon resistance and a recommendation that Johnston's expedition should not enter Utah in 1857. Subsequently, on 10 November, the president had met with an agitated Thomas L. Kane. Neither visitor perceived anxiety or a sense of urgency in the White House any more than Bill Hickman had in Brigham Young's office on 24 June. But when Judge Eckels's and Colonel Johnston's reports arrived a few days after Kane returned home, newspapers reported an immediate flurry of cabinet meetings. Secretary Floyd swung into action by ordering General Scott to Washington for consultation.

Among Scott's earliest recommendations was one freighted with symbolism—to recognize Albert Sidney Johnston's leadership and bolster his morale by promoting him. Johnston became a brigadier general by brevet effective 18 November, although he was unaware of his promotion until the next March. This was to be the only brevet awarded by the government during the entire campaign.

Perhaps as a result of recommendations by Colonels Johnston and Alexander for a coordinated thrust from both the Pacific Coast and Kansas, or perhaps because of earlier unsolicited advice from Maj. George H. Thomas, the War Department focused immediately on California. Of special interest was the feasibility of inserting troops and supplies into southern Utah through the Gulf of California and the largely unexplored Colorado River. New intelligence-gathering instructions were sent to 1st Lt. Joseph C. Ives, the engineer-husband of Floyd's niece, who was then preparing to ascend the Colorado under unrelated earlier instructions to determine the river's head of navigation.

Unknown to the army, the small Ives Expedition had already caught Brigham Young's attention. Ives's imminent presence near Utah's southern flank and his consequent threat to any potential Mexican escape route stimulated Young's insatiable appetite for intelligence about the army. Here was a focus already fueled by Young's long-standing interest in exploiting the Colorado River for commercial purposes. The army's explorers were to be watched.

By 21 November Floyd had also sought the military advice of Scott's friend and immediate subordinate, Brevet Maj. Gen. Persifor F. Smith. General Smith happened to be in Washington in search of medical treatment, although his department headquarters were co-located with Harney's at Fort Leavenworth. By 24 November Smith had produced an extraordinary memo recommending reinforcement of Johnston from Kansas while opening a second multiple-pronged thrust against Utah from the Pacific Coast. The scale of Smith's recommendations was gargantuan. Planning for both initiatives began immediately. As word of Smith's views spread, public speculation arose as to whether Scott or some other senior officer would travel west to direct any Pacific-based move on Utah. At the end of November, General Harney again collected his thoughts on the Utah campaign and sent his views directly to President Buchanan, bypassing both Secretary Floyd and General Scott.

Writing at year-end from the Columbia River to his superior in San Francisco, Quartermaster Rufus Ingalls volunteered his own military views. Ingalls had news of the Lot Smith raid, and was aware of Lieutenant Ives's imminent ascent of the Colorado River. Additionally, he had heard rumors of a possible Mormon mass exodus to the Russian or British Pacific Coast possessions. On balance, Ingalls recommended reinforcing Johnston through the Columbia River–Fort Hall route, the general region that had attracted Brigham Young's visit during the previous spring.

Coincident with completion of General Smith's memo, the Interior Department's commissioner of Indian Affairs wrote to New Mexico's Indian superintendent in Santa Fe to counsel vigilance. Livid about reports of Mormon tampering with the northern Plains tribes as well as the language of Brigham Young's own reports, Commissioner James W. Denver worried about possible Mormon attempts to establish anti-government tribal alliances in the Southwest. His concerns ultimately brought into action the legendary Christopher (Kit) Carson, U.S. Indian agent for the Navajos at Taos, New Mexico Territory.

If the Buchanan administration was alarmed about developments in Utah, so too was Washington's diplomatic corps, especially the ambassadors of Great Britain, Russia, and perhaps Mexico. Rufus Ingalls was not the only one listening to rumors of Mormon flight to the Pacific.

The fat was in the fire. As December and the return of Congress approached, plans were in motion to press Utah from multiple directions with the full force of an embarrassed, anxious U.S. government. Key unknowns at the end of November were what President Buchanan would say to Congress about Utah, what action he would recommend to a country already gripped by a major economic downturn, and which defensive steps were being contemplated by the foreign ministries of the European powers with a stake in the Pacific Northwest.

Getting on Here Very Quietly & Pleasantly: A Deceptive Calm in Washington

September–October 1857, the period during which the Utah Expedition marched beyond the range of telegraphic and even postal communications, brought a deceptive quiet about Mormon affairs in Washington.[1] With this communications lag, Congress still in recess, and the return of Captain Van Vliet in the future, the nation focused not on Utah but on pending elections in Kansas and the recent stock market crash in Manhattan. The latter incident was an ominous development, confirming the onset of America's worst financial panic since 1837.[2] It triggered severe economic dislocations throughout the United States that, in turn, called into question the cost if not the wisdom of the War Department's western expeditionary commitments.

On 26 October, the day before Captain Van Vliet reached Washington, James Gordon Bennett's *New York Herald* was in an editorially relaxed mood:

> Exaggerated statements of Mormon power and Mormon hostility to the general government have been going the rounds of the press for some time, and the military expedition now on its way to the Great Salt Lake City is regarded as incurring almost as much peril as if it were moving to the relief of Lucknow.[3] We do not share in these apprehensions. All this talk and bluster about the hostile preparations that are being made in Utah is mere absurdity. Brigham Young may indulge in big talking before the Saints in the Bowery, and brother Kimball may make them laugh by telling them that his wives are strong and numerous enough to drive out Uncle Sam's troops; but there is no real intention on the part of the Mormons to offer any open resistance to the expedition. Brigham Young is a shrewd Yankee, and is altogether too sensible a man to entertain for a moment any such ridiculous idea. He knows very well that if he were to get up his Mormon followers to the point of armed rebellion against the government and people of the United States, he and they would be swept off the face of the earth. He has quite too good a time of it to desire any such summary proceeding. Instead of sending out his Danites to form ambuscades and to harass our troops, he will probably go to meet them him-

---

[1] See, for example, Secretary Floyd's announcement to his wife that "I am get[t]ing on here very quietly & pleasantly." Floyd to Sallie Buchanan Preston Floyd, 10 September 1857, Trigg-Floyd-Johnston Collection.

[2] In discussing the Panic of 1857, economists and historians have almost wholly avoided the impact of the enormously expensive Utah Expedition. See Huston, *The Panic of 1857*, 130–31 and 174–75; Calomiris and Schweikart, "The Panic of 1857," 807–35; and Rezneck, "The Influence of Depression upon American Opinion 1857–1859," 1–23.

[3] A reference to the siege and relief of Lucknow, India, during the 1857 sepoy mutiny.

self, accompany them into Salt Lake, and treat them to the best the place affords. The Saints may talk, but they will not fight. There need be no apprehension felt on that score. We will have no Mormon rebellion yet.[4]

Prior to the mid-November arrival of Judge Eckels's and Colonel Johnston's dispatches, the only first-hand news to reach Washington about Mormon affairs came from Capt. Stewart Van Vliet, who arrived in the capital on 27 October as Delegate Bernhisel reached New York. Van Vliet's several reports—written en route and upon arrival in Washington—have been published elsewhere.[5] Nonetheless it is useful to consider Delegate Bernhisel's description of this material in his 2 November letter to Brigham Young. Bernhisel provided Young with not only his understanding of what the captain reported to Buchanan but with four other pieces of information ranging in importance from the crucial to the titillating: the administration's largely dismissive reaction; prediction of an "intense excitement" to follow any armed collision; the debilitating impact of the ongoing financial panic; and an alert of reporter Albert G. Browne, Jr.'s, presence with the Utah Expedition.

BERNHISEL TO YOUNG, 2 NOVEMBER 1857, LDS ARCHIVES.

Captain Van Vliet is at Washington, and has had an interview with the President, and made his report. He informed his Excellency that Governor Young had stated that the United States Troops should not enter Salt Lake Valley, and that he should prevent them from doing so by force of arms, but neither the administration nor the public press believe that the troops will meet with any resistance. . . .

There has recently been a tremendous crash among the banks, brokers and mercantile establishments throughout the country. Every bank east of the Rocky mountains (I am not aware that there is a single exception,) has suspended specie [gold] payments, and the failures among the brokers and merchants throughout the length and breadth of the land are very numerous, and in many instances very heavy. . . .

Captain Van Vliet on all proper occasions stated that he had been very kindly received, and hospitably entertained at Salt Lake City. The officers whom we met on the Sweetwater were surprised to see him, for it had been reported that he was a prisoner and in chains.

---

[4] Editorial, "The Mormon Question—Will the Saints Show Fight?" *New York Herald*, 26 October 1857, 4/6

[5] House Ex. Doc. 71, Serial 956, 24–26; "Report of the Secretary of War," Senate Ex. Doc. 11, Serial 920, 35–38; Hafen and Hafen, eds., *Mormon Resistance*, 50–55.

The Mormon Problem Is Solved: Sour News from the Sweetwater

Judge Eckels's letter reached Secretary Cass on 13 November. He wrote from a camp on the Sweetwater River east of and eight days' travel from the destruction at Big Sandy and Green River. Although the full text of Eckels's letter cannot be found, substantial newspaper excerpts appeared within days thanks to the then-porous nature of the governmental departments.[6] The earliest and most extensive extract is printed below.[7]

Eckels to Cass, 13 October 1857, "The Mormon Outrage," *National Intelligencer*, 17 November 1857, 3/3.

An express has just arrived from Green river, and reports that on the night of October 5 a train of twenty-six wagons was captured by the Mormons, twenty-five miles from the Pacific Spring. At the same time two other trains were taken near Green river, in all seventy-eight wagons and loading. The Mormons said they had seven hundred men there and fifteen hundred more at Salt Lake City.

Col. Alexander is encamped on Ham's Fort [*sic*], thirty miles in advance of the front train, which is destroyed. He sent Captain Marcy with four hundred men back to Green river to enable the teamsters to collect their cattle.

The Mormons killed no one, for the reason that no resistance was made.

[Lt.] Col. [Charles F.] Smith will collect the trains on this side and escort them forward. One train is now before us and two behind. We are in good spirits, and that is a great help to all. The Mormons will likely attack us in a day or two, and may rue their impudence. We have forty-seven men in this command, but Col. Smith is a host within himself. We have determined, if attacked, to use the rifles in the lines. We shall most likely take the [northern looping] route on Bear river for Salt Lake City. The want of forage for our mules is the greatest hindrance, but we will go on if we have to walk and carry our provisions.

---

[6] A relatively recent search by the staff of the National Archives has failed to find Eckels's letter in the territorial records of the state department. Archivist Sally Kuisel to MacKinnon, e-mail messages, 9 and 29 April 2003. The editor believes it likely that Secretary Cass took Eckels's letter to a White House meeting and that through transmittal between cabinet secretaries it came to rest in the files of some other unknown department.

[7] Also of interest is another far more freewheeling letter written by Judge Eckels on the same day to the Cincinnati *Daily Enquirer*. Eckels wrote the second dispatch in his role as the newspaper's pseudonymous "Kenton." Between the two documents we have Eckels's full views as well as a fascinating glimpse into the private and public persona of Utah's new chief justice. Eckels ("Kenton") to Editor, 13 October 1857, *Daily Enquirer* (Cincinnati), 12 November 1857, 2/2. With minor differences, this letter was reprinted in *New York Times*, 16 November 1857, 1/1. For a discussion of Eckels's reportorial activities as "Kenton," see MacKinnon, "Epilogue," 34–35.

Several days later another Washington newspaper printed the same excerpt but added,

> The above dispatch, showing the first overt act of Mormon treason, was immediately laid before the President of the United States, who summoned the members of the Cabinet for consultation upon its contents. The intelligence was considered in Cabinet meeting in the afternoon, but no definite action determined on. The Secretary of War thinks it would be hopeless to attempt to send reinforcements or supplies so late in the season as this. Dispatches are anxiously looked for from Colonel Johns[t]on, who is in command of the army for Utah. The Government officers do not fully credit the report received from Judge Echols.[8]

The day after Judge Eckels's dispatch reached Washington, the *New York Herald* ran an editorial as alarmed as that of 26 October had been complacent. Like the judge, the *Herald* found a silver lining ("good news") in the midst of an embarrassment—a critical incident on which to rationalize draconian measures against the Mormons. As discussed below, this editorial struck a nerve with the British minister to Washington as well as with the *Herald*'s New York readers.

"Startling News from the Mormons—The War Commenced . . . ,"
New York Herald, Editorial, 14 November 1857, 4/3–4.

> A few days since it was reported from the West that the Mormons among the Rocky Mountains had captured the advanced provision trains of seventy-eight wagons belonging to the United States army corps *en route* for the Great Salt Lake. A special correspondent at Washington now informs us that the President has received official confirmation of this intelligence through a despatch from Judge Echols [*sic*], (appointed for Utah as the new Chief Justice of that Territory, and accompanying the army corps,) dated at the army camp on the Sweet Water, twenty-one miles east of the South Pass. . . .
>
> These acts of treason and rebellion appear to have been committed at several points, within two hundred miles of Great Salt Lake City; and as the army route over this interval lies through a confused mass of wild and desolate mountains, with frequent difficult passes and defiles highly favorable for guerilla [*sic*] warfare, we may reasonably infer that, having crossed the Rubicon, the Mormons will follow up their work in a stubborn defence of these mountain approaches to their capital. We should not, therefore, be surprised if the next information from this new seat of war were tidings of the destruction of an advanced detachment or two of the United States army by the infatuated followers of the Mormon prophet.

[8] *National Era* (Washington, D.C.), 17 November 1857, 187.

The inhospitable region into which the government troops were penetrating affords subsistence for neither man nor beast. The emigrant trail through this howling wilderness is perhaps as thickly strewn with the skeletons of wasted caravans as the desert route to Timbuctoo [Morocco]. The season is advanced. Ere this those Utah or Uintah mountains and their defiles are covered with the snows of a long winter; and if an army force of less than two thousand men, despoiled of their main supplies of subsistence, shall still be able to push through to the Salt Lake, it may be considered a very fortunate or a very wonderful achievement. More likely, from the loss of their provisions, the government troops will be compelled to fall back upon the plains, and wait the return of spring before resuming their expedition.

All our advices of the last three months from the Salt Lake have foreshadowed this plan of operations on the part of the Mormons, as commenced in the capture of these provision trains. It was certainly anything but a wise movement to send them so far in advance of the troops. The usual rule is to bring up the baggage and provisions in the rear of the army. To be sure, with all their threatenings and military preparations, it was not supposed that the Mormons would be so foolish as to invite the alternative of a forcible expulsion from the country, by an overt act of rebellion; but a good soldier guards against all possible contingencies, and is particularly careful of those supplies upon which the very existence of his troops depends.

We see now that Brigham Young is really in earnest, and that his programme is a desperate struggle to maintain his dictatorship and his polygamy. We have been led to believe, from his speeches and his movements, that he expects to be able to beat back the present army expedition of the government; that by the next spring he proposes to organize all Mormondom into a moveable camp, and with the approach of an army force which cannot be resisted, his plan will most probably be to evacuate Utah with the whole Mormon community, burning or destroying everything in their retreat which they cannot carry away. From his tour of exploration last spring, the Mormon prophet will thus, perhaps, move northward, across Oregon and Washington Territories into the British Possessions, to try the hospitality of Queen Victoria. It is certain, at all events, that Brigham Young is fully aware of the extreme folly of attempting to maintain by arms his occupation of Utah against the United States government. Accordingly, we think it a safe conclusion that his scheme is to beat back the present government expedition, and to evacuate Utah in an Israelitish exodus, or by a peaceable dispersion of the Saints in the Spring, to be recollected together again at some new Canaan, as their means and facilities may permit.

In this light we consider this intelligence of the capture of the government army trains as good news. It reduces this Mormon difficulty to a simple and easy solution. The chief and his whole gang of pestilent polygamists have chosen the alternative of rebellion. They must now prepare to submit to the strong hand, or to move their camp beyond the limits of the United States. We have no doubt they have made up their minds to repel this first government expedition, and to prepare for a complete evacuation against the approach of another. There is no longer any peace or security for them and their adulterous and incestuous habits in Utah. They are fully convinced of this; and the policy of the administration henceforth should be that active military policy which will most speedily operate to relieve the country of the nuisance of Mormonism without the effusion of blood. Give Brigham Young and his chief conspirators no promises of mercy; but leave every avenue open for their peaceable retreat to some other part of the world, and let them go. Should they pass over into the dominions of Victoria, let them go—for the most of them will thus be returning to their first allegiance.[9] This news from the Sweet Water is good news, as it indicates an early removal of the Mormons beyond our boundaries.

Waiting All Day to See the Secretary: The Colorado River as Invasion Route

Brigham Young's interest in the Colorado River and its multiple uses was nearly as long-standing as that of the U.S. Army, which began to chart the river's lower reaches at the close of the Mexican War.[10] With the advent of the Utah War, Maj. George H. Thomas of Albert Sidney Johnston's Second U.S. Cavalry volunteered his observations and recommendations about the Colorado River.[11] Thomas had recently changed post from Fort Yuma to Fort Mason, Texas, and undoubtedly he hoped that Adjutant General Cooper would share his letter with Secretary of War Floyd. Cooper indeed did so, and on 2 September 1857—after a long delay prompted by his disabling back pain—Floyd directed him to send a copy to Lieutenant Ives in California. Signifi-

[9] Most of Utah's European converts had emigrated from Great Britain, as had several of Brigham Young's most literate advisors: John Taylor (England), James Ferguson (Belfast), and George Q. Cannon (Isle of Man).

[10] For a description of Lt. George H. Derby's January 1851 survey of the lower Colorado below the newly established Fort Yuma, see Stewart, *John Phoenix, Esq.*, 65–72. Brigham Young's concerns about non-Mormon exploration of the river appear in First Presidency to Lyman and Rich, Journal History, entry for 23 October 1851, LDS Archives. An acceleration of Young's interest in exploring and exploiting the Colorado for commercial purposes during 1855 appears in Young to Hammond, 2 February 1855, and Brown to Young, 23 June 1855, both in LDS Archives, as well as in "Message of His Excellency Gov. B. Young," 11 December 1855, *Deseret News*, 9 December 1855, 4/1–3.

[11] During the Civil War, Thomas, dubbed "the Rock of Chickamauga," would become one of the Union Army's most accomplished major generals.

cantly, there is no sign that General Scott was part of this flow of communications. It is difficult to believe that Major Thomas's recommendations did not enter the discussion in Washington during the third week of November 1857 on how best to re-direct Ives's expedition.

THOMAS TO COOPER, 7 JULY 1857,
BEINECKE LIBRARY, YALE UNIVERSITY.

Whilst stationed at Fort Yuma I made repeated inquiries of the Indians living on the Colorado river above the post as to the navigability of that stream, and am of the opinion from what they have told me, and from what I could learn from other sources, that small steamers can ascend it very nearly to the point where the whites suppose the Rio Vergen [*sic*] empties into it.

If upon examination the Colorado proves to be navigable [up to the confluence with the Rio Virgin], it will be not only the most direct but the most convenient and safest route to convey supplies to the troops stationed in Utah Territory. Such being my belief I recommended its exploration to the Commanding Officer of the Dept of the Pacific in 1854. The Hamok-an Indians . . . say there is no stream of any size emptying into the Colorado from the west, but one which comes in from the east, about the size of the Gila, far above. This I understood, from their description of it, to be the Little Colorado. It is inhabited on its south bank by a tribe which they call Huallo-pay or pine woods people. The Huallo-pays are now at war with their neighbours on the north side of this small stream. These they call Havisoh-pays or *Blue* people, because their favorite color is blue. The Havisoh-pays are represented as being wealthy in horses, sheep & goats and have frequent intercourse with the whites.[12] Judging from this circumstance and from the similarity of sound I think the Navahoes and Havisoh-pays are the same people. When asked if they knew of the Pay-Utahs they informed me that they were the next tribe above them on the West bank of the river. If this [Indian] story be true they are well acquainted with the Colorado as far north as the Pay-Utah country, and from their account of the river I believe it will be found to be navigable to within one or two hundred miles of Salt Lake City.[13] Believing this information of some importance at this time I have taken the liberty of communicating it in this irregular manner.

From Hams Fork on 9 October Colonel Alexander had pleaded with the adjutant general for reinforcements and more supplies in the spring, adding, "I would further respectfully suggest that troops should be sent from California and Oregon. It is said that the road from California to Salt Lake is passable all winter, and it is certainly so much earlier in the spring than that

[12] Here Thomas presumably means Mormons.

[13] Thomas was almost as inaccurately optimistic as Brigham Young was in 1855.

from the States." On 18 October, writing from South Pass, Colonel Johnston recommended to army headquarters that spring reinforcement come from Kansas and—independent of Alexander—observed that, "A movement of troops from California, Oregon, and by this route [across the plains] would terminate a war with the Mormons speedily and more economically than if attempted by insufficient [unreinforced] means."[14] In forwarding Johnston's report to Secretary Floyd, General Scott vigorously supported Johnston's management of the beleaguered expedition's march west but had his adjutant add the following endorsement: "As to the expeditions from the Pacific, he [Scott] is confident the Colonel is not aware of the difficulties which would attend them,—and this part of the dispatch is not concurred in, as it is the opinion of the Genl-in-Chief that he can be reinforced earlier and far more effectually from this side."[15] Nonetheless, planning for a thrust from the Pacific Coast continued, although not necessarily with Scott's full awareness.

Floyd's penchant for bypassing Scott was especially noticeable in his dealings with Lieutenant Ives through the army's corps of topographical engineers. Key players there were its chief, Col. J. J. Abert, and his highly independent subordinate, Capt. Andrew A. Humphreys, chief of the corps's Bureau of Western Explorations and Surveys. Reflecting his anxiety over sending mail via the next Panama-bound mail packet, Humphreys hastily wrote two letters to Ives in rapid succession on 18 November, delivered to Ives at the Colorado by an Indian runner on 22 December. Because of their similarity in substance only one of the two letters—the first, more informal one—is included here. It conveys a sense of the anxiety that surrounded Floyd's department as well as the secretary's direct involvement in affairs that the absent General Scott no doubt would have considered his province.

Humphreys to Ives, 18 November 1857, Records of the Office of the Chief of [U.S. Army] Engineers, RG 77, National Archives.

I have been waiting all day to see the Secy [Floyd] and have only just succeeded and as it is half past two o'clock I have but a few minutes to write you. I will send an official letter tomorrow which may or may not be in time for the

[14] Alexander to Cooper, 9 October 1857 and Johnston to McDowell, 18 October 1857, House Ex. Doc. 71, Serial 956, 32 and 37–38.

[15] McDowell to Floyd, 10 December 1857, endorsement on Johnston to McDowell, 18 October 1857. When Johnston's dispatch was published at Congress's request as part of House Ex. Doc. 71, this endorsement was excluded and so remains unpublished. It may be found with the copy of Johnston's dispatch in folder "Correspondence Regarding Utah Expedition" (HR 35A-D12.3), House Committee on Military Affairs, RG 233, National Archives.

California Steamer.[16] The Mormons, we have just heard, are in open hostilities, with the troops in Utah. The Secretary desires you to proceed therefore up the Colorado with great caution—and it would probably be better not to leave your boat in Depot at the head of navigation but send it back to Ft. Yuma reporting the result as to the navigation of the river. If it should appear to you hazardous to proceed beyond the head of navigation, do not do so. It is suspected [?] that the Mormons may attempt to move Southward into Sonora.

War Dept. may wish to send a strong force to Great Salt Lake by the Colorado river & Virgin river—and the Secretary suggests that you might take your steamboat and a sufficient, strong escort with a howitzer in the boat & run up to the Virgin river and ascertain roughly [?] if the Colorado is practicable for light steamers and also the character of the Virgin river in its lower course, but in reference to the Virgin, merely *to ascertain if troops can march along it on the lower course.* It is supposed you might run up to the Virgin and back to Ft. Yuma in 10 days—If there is no great cañon where the Virgin empties into the Colorado, that is if it is not in the cañon Country, we may be pretty certain troops can march along it, and that is the object of inquiring.

You are the best judge whether this [trip? march?] up the river can be safely made or not. Of course the Secry does not wish it made if it cannot be done [?] safely. Write immediately so that the information will be in the Dept. at the earliest day practicable. Inform the Comdg officer at Ft. Yuma also of the result so that the Comdg officer of the troops in California may be acquainted with it.

Repeat both for the mail.

Interestingly, when Humphreys wrote his annual report for Floyd on 30 November—a document intended for publication—there was reference to neither the Utah War nor to his supplemental instructions to Ives of 18 November. The brief three-paragraph discussion of Ives's expedition included only the cryptic phrase, "The nature of this duty required peculiar preparations, which have been made."[17] It was an opaque message worthy of Brigham Young's own communications style.

Even after Ives's new instructions were aboard the New York–Panama steamer, Washington's topographical engineers and other staff officers continued to comb the capital for people knowledgeable about the Colorado River. Natural prey for such seekers was Capt. Samuel P. Heintzelman—on leave from his post in Arizona—as he wended his way through the governmental bureaus

[16] In his push to catch the Panama steamer, Humphreys succeeded in sending the formal second letter on 18 rather than 19 November.

[17] Humphreys, "Report from Bureau of Explorations and Surveys," *Annual Report of the Secretary of War,* Senate Ex. Doc. 11, Serial 920, 39.

in an attempt to pursue a patent application and to settle his army accounts. Heintzelman's Washington journal for the last week in November reveals the intensity of efforts to revise strategy for the Utah War. It was a topic that commanded the capital's attention as it had not done earlier in the fall.

Heintzelman, Journal Extracts, 13–30 November 1857, Heintzelman Papers.

** Mon., Nov. 16, 1857 . . . In the evening the [news]papers bring full confirmation of the burning of the trains by the Mormons. I had a talk with Van Vliet. He agrees with me that the Mormons will abandon the country. He thinks this winter & move to Mexico. I think in the spring, or so soon as they learn the Gov[ernment] is sending a sufficient force to subdue them.

** Sat., Nov. 21, 1857 . . . I met Capt. [Seth] Williams [Assistant Adjutant General] last evening & he told me that an expedition of 8,000 men is talked of, from the Pacific. I have thought for some time that would be a good plan. I would enter from the Colorado. Go up to near the mouth of the [Rio] Virgin.

. . . I met Capt. Humphreys at the hotel. He told me that they sent by the last steamer to Lieut. Ives to explore the Colorado re whether it is navigable as far as the Virgin in anticipation of an expedition from the Pacific side to Salt Lake. If they would call upon me I would tell them some things they don't appear to know. They have been closeted with Gen. Smith, but his information is second hand.

** Fri., Nov. 27, 1857 . . . I was in the Qr. Mtr. Genl's [office] & had a talk with him [Quartermaster General Thomas S. Jesup] about the Colorado. . . .

** Mon., Nov. 30, 1857 . . . I met Capt. Humphreys before I went [to see a lecture by Lola Montes on beautiful women]. He has been to [see] me several times to learn about the Colorado & the desert. I am tired [of] giving others information for which I get no credit.

Approach Them in Three Columns: General Smith's Advice

The extent to which General Scott was fully aware that Secretary Floyd had entered into intensive consultation with General Persifor F. Smith is unclear. The two senior officers were close friends, but Scott and General Smith were often out of contact as Smith roamed the country on leave in search of medical treatment for an unspecified illness that would take his life in May 1858. One can only imagine Floyd's and Buchanan's thoughts upon receiving General Smith's recommendation for a reinforced Utah Expedition the size of the entire U.S. Army.

Smith to Floyd, 24 November 1857, Persifor Fraser Smith Papers. In answer to your question asked me today as to my opinion of the force necessary to operate with success in Utah and of the manner in which that force can be best employed, I have the honor to submit the following observations.

1. The Mormons can assemble at Salt Lake City or at any other point where their establishments, stores and families may be collected six thousand men.
2. If they operate away from such point they must leave a strong guard which will, pro tanto, diminish the force in the field.
3. The approach to the valley of Salt Lake from the Eastward is through defiles easily to be defended with proper skill and means, by a small force against a large one.
4. To attack them to advantage these defiles must be turned, by other approaches on the East, of which the valley of Bear River is one, and by a movement from the Western settlements.
5. We should approach them in three columns, one from California and Oregon, one by Bear river valley and another by the defiles on the usual road.[18]
6. If we use two columns only, one being of necessity that of the Pacific Coast, the other must approach by the Bear River valley and its rear would be open to attacks from the defiles on the direct road.
7. Each of the three columns should be able to meet *all* the force the Mormons can bring into the field; for they may be unable to form a junction of any two before being attacked.
8. It is proper to estimate your enemy as your equal in value [competence] and to endeavor to surpass him in numbers, each column should therefore consist of about 5,000 men.[19]
9. I would propose to organize them into three divisions of two Brigades each with a proper amount of Cavalry and Artillery in each division.
10. The Division would then consist of Six Regiments of foot one of horse and two mounted batteries of mountain Howitzers.
11. As it is impossible to keep the ranks of the regiments full under any circumstances and after a march of a thousand miles casualties must increase; we may calculate the strength of each Division as follows.

Six Regiments of Infantry each with six hundred men	3600
One Regiment of Cavalry	600
Two mounted batteries each 120 men	240
Two Mountain Howitzer batteries each 100 men	200
Total	4640

[18] Surprisingly, Smith never provides a recommended route by which a California column should enter Utah, such as over the Sierra Nevada or by the southern road from either San Bernardino or the Colorado–Rio Virgin river access point.

[19] This recommendation for a force of fifteen thousand troops matched the size of the entire U.S. Army in 1857.

These with the ordnance men, Engine[e]rs soldiers &c would bring the Division up to 5000 men.

12. We have disposable in Oregon and California the 9th Infantry 10 Companies of Artillery and six companies of the 1st Dragoons.

In Kansas and neighboring territories we can supply the sixth Infantry—3rd Artillery—1st Cavalry and the companies for two batteries of mountain batteries.

13. We require 18 regts of foot, 3 of horse 6 mounted batteries, 6 mountain batteries and the Engineer and Ordnance soldiers.

	Foot	Horse	Artillery	Engineer C^{os}	Ordnance
Required	18 Regts.	3 Regts.	12 Batteries	1½ C^{os}	180 men
Available	4 "	1⅗ "	8 "	—	——
To be Provided	14 "	1⅖ "	4 "	1	100 men

14. I would suggest that 7 Regts of Infantry, one of Mounted Riflemen, and one of Cavalry be added to the Regular Army—that the batteries be manned from the Regiments of Artillery now in service but an additional Engineer C° and the necessary Ordnance can be raised; this would leave 7 Regiments of foot still to be raised—and for this purpose that seven regiments of volunteer infantry be called into service—Two in California and Oregon and five in the States East of the Rocky mountains.

15. In increasing the regular army, provide that on the termination of the present necessity there be retained from the whole Army the number of General, Field, Company, and staff officers, Regiments Companies and men that Congress may determine as proper to compose the Peace Establishment— To be selected by the President and organized on the principles heretofore suggested.

16. That a General officer be sent immediately to the Pacific to organize the Division there[20] and put it in motion as soon as the [1858] season will permit, that each Division should as nearly as possible consist of 2 old Reg^{ts}, 2 new ones and 2 of volunteers—the half of each old and new Reg^{t} to be mutually transferred, so that one half of each company may be experienced officers and men. The Mounted Rifles and Cavalry to be mixed in the same way with the new raised corps.

17. That the two other Divisions be [perfected?] in the same way as near as possible to St Louis and sent forward by Brigades before the grass is ready, having trains of forage and wheat and accompanying the Brigades until the forage is exhausted and the grass springs.

18. I would urge that all the Mounted Batteries be of 12 pdr guns and 32

[20] On 27 November the *New York Herald*'s Washington correspondent speculated that this officer might be Oregon's territorial delegate in Congress, Joseph Lane, a former brevet major general in the Mexican War. See reprinted dispatch, "The War in Utah," *Putnam* [County] *Republican Banner* (Greencastle, Ind.), 9 December 1857, 2/4.

pdr [siege] Howitzers with if necessary 8 horses each and that 2 18 pdrs be sent in the reserve, to overthrow such artificial defences as may be strongly erected; and that a large quantity of powder and sacks be furnished for opening [exploding] picket works and barricades.[21]

19. It would be very desirable that the appropriation be made for two years; for after the first year expires it will be past the season of operations before the reserves provided in the second year can reach the Army. There is little time enough now to prepare for moving in April and delay would be fatal.
20. If the Indians on the plains are troublesome or those west of the Rocky Mountains hostile, a larger force chiefly of volunteers must be provided.
21. I calculate on the troops not included in the expedition to protect the line of communication as far as the Rocky Mountains on this side and to the entry of the valley of the Salt Lake on the other. The Army of Utah must secure its own positions and communications beyond those points.
22. Such part of the force as comes from Oregon had better move out by the Columbia River and join that from California, North West of Salt Lake valley at a point to be agreed on.
23. All the mounted corps require better fire arms than they have. The pistol-carbines should be discarded at once.

I may observe that if we send a strong force to Utah from this side, the Indians on the plains will be quiet for it is only when they see our strength that they believe in it.

On the day that General Smith delivered this memorandum to Secretary Floyd, Nauvoo Legionnaire Philo Dibble, Jr., completed his own written contribution nearly two thousand miles to the west. A cavalry veteran of Lot Smith's famous raid a month earlier as well as a victim of an accidental gunshot wound to the head soon thereafter, Dibble spent 24 November 1857 in his courier's bivouac high among the cliffs overlooking the little-used Hastings Trail as it wound through Spring Valley between Fort Bridger and Echo Canyon. At this isolated, freezing, but beautiful perch, Private Dibble laboriously inscribed on the rocks a large rendering of his name and the date; in the process, he left to posterity one of the Utah War's most striking, enduring markers far better known today to trail enthusiasts than Gen. Persifor F. Smith's lost advice.[22]

As the consultation and planning process unfolded, the *New York Herald*'s

[21] The reference to "sacks" is to linen bags in which charges of gunpowder would be packaged.

[22] Eldredge, *Illustrated Emigrants' Guide*, 32–35.

Washington correspondent speculated wildly that "It is proposed to capture some two thousand saints now located in California, as well as Dr. Bernhisel, Brigham Young's delegate to Congress, and hold them as hostages until it is ascertained what the Prophet designs doing. General Cass seems to think this cannot be done under the Constitution, but the President thinks differently. A state of rebellion, he says, actually exists, and martial law must prevail."[23]

The Kind Feelings You Entertain for Me: Harney Weighs In

With General Smith dispensing Utah advice to the administration at Secretary Floyd's request and newspaper speculation beginning to grow, General Harney was unable to remain silent. At the end of November, a week before Buchanan was to send his first annual message to Congress, Harney sent unsolicited observations and recommendations to the president from Fort Leavenworth. Substantially more modest than the size of the force with which General Smith wanted to pacify Utah, Harney nonetheless invoked the desirability of a large force equivalent to between half and two-thirds of the entire army.

Harney to Buchanan, 29 November 1857, James Buchanan Papers, Historical Society of Pennsylvania.

Your very kind letter of the 22nd was duly received by me & I feel most grateful to you for the generosity with which you have been pleased to receive my humble efforts to serve you in this country. . . .

Under the circumstances of so large a force being here, and the almost certainty that some decided action must be taken early in the Spring against the Mormons, I think it would be proper for me to remain with my command during the winter, & not visit Washington, as I at first proposed—

We have no time to lose in preparing for Utah—I would suggest, it would be well for Congress to legislate at an early day upon such measures as you may recommend in your message, to enable the War Department to direct, this winter, the preparatory steps for the movements of the Expedition as soon as the grass will permit in the Spring—many important preparations can be made this winter, such as, the making and equipping the necessary number of Wagons, the purchase of animals, the preparation of Ordnance Stores, that they may be ready to be sent here by the first opportunity in the Spring &c.

[23] Reprinted dispatch, "The Mormon Rebellion," Cincinnati *Daily Enquirer*, 25 November 1857, 1/6.

A force of eight or ten thousand men may yet spare bloodshed, while a less force would but invite hostility.—it is of the first importance that such a force should arrive in Utah early in the season, & in an efficient condition—for this service, at least half of this force should be regulars.

Capt. Pleasonton has told me of the kind feelings you entertain for me, and that you are disposed to entrust the Command of this expedition to my judgment.—I can only now thank you for this evidence of your confidence, but I hope the result will show how earnest & sincere are my feelings of admiration, esteem & friendship for you, both personally & as the distinguished head of this great nation.

No Friend to the Mormons: Gratuitous Advice from Captain Ingalls

With detailed descriptions of General Smith's recommendations appearing in the press,[24] Captain Rufus Ingalls, quartermaster for the Department of the Pacific, did as first Maj. George H. Thomas and then General Harney had done independently. From Fort Vancouver, Washington Territory (opposite Portland), he gratuitously sent to his superior in San Francisco his own views on how best to prosecute and supply the Utah War.

There is logic to Ingalls's initiative, for he had spent the winter of 1854–55 in the Salt Lake Valley as the Steptoe Expedition's quartermaster, and had crossed the plains to Utah from Fort Leavenworth as well as traversed a new route from Salt Lake Valley to San Francisco Bay. What neither this record nor Ingalls's memorandum indicated, however, was that he was grinding a substantial anti-Mormon axe relating to his April 1855 indictment in Salt Lake City for attempting to abduct and impair the morals of a thirteen-year-old Mormon girl.[25]

Ingalls to Lt. Col. Thomas Swords, 29 December 1857, Yale Collection of Western Americana, Beinecke Library.

Events may render it necessary to dispatch troops in the early Spring to Utah from this Military Department, and I trust you will not hold me as being too forward or officious if I enclose you descriptive lists of some of

[24] See "From Washington," *Daily Enquirer* (Cincinnati), 12 December 1857, 1/6.

[25] MacKinnon, "Sex, Subalterns, and Steptoe." David L. Bigler makes a difficult case that Ingalls "might have acted out of honorable motives and resented the accusation of misconduct" in his attempt to depart Utah with young Rachael Nowell. Bigler points to Edward Potter's earlier well-intentioned effort to help two teenaged girls flee to California with the William Hollister emigrant train rather than marry the bishop of Fillmore, Utah. This argument in defense of Ingalls's conduct overlooks the character of his comrades' social interactions in Utah during the winter of 1854–55. Bigler to MacKinnon, e-mail message, 3 January 2007.

the immigrants routes from this Coast to the Great Salt Lake City as observed by us in 1855, and further give you some hints of other routes. . . .

The enclosed lists will be sufficiently explanatory.[26] From them you will observe that it will be difficult to find *any* road leading from *California* to the Great Salt Lake of less than 900 or 1000 miles in length. I am of opinion that quite *all the routes* that lead from *Central* California are impracticable from the Sierra Nevada across the Basin earlier than the middle of June for a column of troops. The Humbolt River Valley, I should say, would certainly be so, and trains cannot pass to the south of the Lake by Carson's river earlier than July, unless a route has been discovered since we were there. . . .

The route, via San Bernardino and the Mohave is by no means a short one. I do not believe it possesses rescources [*sic*] for animals *in any numbers.* It answers well enough for expresses &c. for it is open all the year though the best season to pass over it is in February and March. San Pedro is the terminus on the Coast. Were it practicable, it would answer well, for it touches the most southern Mormon settlements, where I think there are more better disposed people than nearer the chief city.[27]

Were the Colorado River already explored I think it would be found that it is navigable for small steamers to the Great Bend which is only some 25 miles from Los Vegas, a Mormon town just south of the southern rim of the Basin, and about 500 miles from Salt Lake City, over a good road. The facts, however, cannot be made known until Lt Ives has made explorations; but *in any event,* the route via the Gulf of California would be a long and expensive one, answering perhaps the wants of commerce, but no way at all for troops.[28]

[Brevet] Major [John S.] Hatheway and myself sent a train in 1849 from the Umpqua Valley, Oregon, to Fort Hall, under Lieut [George W.] Hawkins—the distances, character of country &c are not now with me but Gen[l] [Joel] Palmer, late Superintendent of Indian Affairs here, was the guide, and in a few days will furnish me notes of the route—It is not, probably, worth attention for any purposes now under consideration.[29]

---

[26] Not printed here for reasons of brevity.

[27] When Ingalls departed Utah in the spring of 1855, it was via the northern route. His brother officer, 1st Lt. Sylvester Mowry, led a detachment to California through Utah's southern settlements and would have disagreed vigorously with Ingalls about the disposition of the settlers based on the hostility he encountered. In December 1857 President Buchanan, Bernhisel, and Kane were all apprehensive about the reaction that Kane would receive from southern Utahns.

[28] At this time Ives was just beginning his ascent of the Colorado River.

[29] In addition to seeking his old field notes from Palmer, on 29 December Ingalls also sent an urgent note across the Columbia River to Robert ("Doc") Newell, one of the region's most experienced mountaineer-guide-interpreters. From Newell, Ingalls wanted advice as to the best route and season for funneling troops into the Salt Lake Valley from Oregon. Remarkably, within two days Newell responded from Champoeg, Oregon, with a long letter. Although he had dated his letter to Swords on 29 December, Ingalls held it back until hearing from Palmer and Newell, revised it, constructed an appendix of routes and distances, and mailed all of this material to San Francisco on 7 January 1858. Newell to Ingalls, 31 December 1857; photocopy in editor's possession.

The distance from Fort Leavenworth to the Great Salt Lake City by the nearest road is over 1200 miles—If the detour by Sublette's cutt off, and Soda Springs at the Great Bend of Bear River, is made, the distance must be over 1400 miles—Soda Springs, you will observe, is near (40 Miles) to Fort Hall, and the latter place is 196 miles from Salt Lake City. This leads me, Colonel, to suggest *the* line, that probably (and for aught I know, the one already decided upon at Head Quarters) is the *shortest, most open defensible,* and practicable earlier in spring than any other. That is the line of the Columbia River to Walla Walla—thence by Boise and the southern tributary of the Columbia—the Snake—to near Fort Hall—thence over the northern rim of the Basin (there very low) to Bear River into the settlements of Utah. Walla Walla is about 350 miles from Astoria, and *I think, not to exceed* 600 miles, by a wagon road practicable from March, or April, (dependant on the winter preceding) to Great Salt Lake City. The Hudson's Bay Company people have usually called it 600 miles from Walla Walla to Fort Hall; but they think the distance much over estimated. But I see no reason for going as far *north* and *east* as Fort Hall. I know of no obstacle in turning down on the Humbolt road where it crosses Raft, or Cache river, *though I am not personally acquainted with this country.* See descriptive list of my route.

With this point for a Deposit [Depot], and the Dalles, Walla Walla and (perhaps) Boise for Entrepots, the line would appear to be the most eligible in every point of view. By it Utah can be more *easily accessible,* and the troops there *more cheaply supplied* than from any other point.

All supplies can be put at Wal!a Walla *by water,* and from thence transported in ox and mule trains, probably *cheaper* than by the South Pass, and more rapidly.

In former years we had a *monthly mail* from this point to Great Salt Lake City the year round, and were it necessary communication might be had with that City from this river any month by expressmen who know the country.

For all offensive operations, I regard the entrance into the Valley of the Salt Lake by Bear river *on the north* as far the most easy and eligible in every respect. Should the Rebels attempt an escape to British or Russian America, which, by the way, I do not believe they think of, they might be cut off by a force from this quarter.[30] This force *should be a regular one,* if possible, though from the present prospect the regulars now in the Country will be required here to hold the Indians in check. If Volunteers are called upon I have no doubt a good description of men could be raised in California.

The Mormons, in my opinion, are mad and Crazy with religious fanaticism. You mark if events do not show it. Brigham Young *does not see the end* of his insensate conduct. He believes he is right and that he is going to *conquer* by aid of God, and he and his devotees will probably fight with unexampled fierceness and perseverance, unless something unforeseen shall arrest them.

[30] As discussed below, both destinations were under consideration in at least some passing fashion by Brigham Young during the war.

To Keep Them Quiet: Heading off Mormon Tribal Influence

As noted, throughout the Utah War Mormon leaders viewed Secretary of the Interior Thompson as a leader of the perceived war faction in James Buchanan's cabinet. Given that background it is interesting to examine what took place in the Interior Department's Office of Indian Affairs as well as in the War Department once news of Lot Smith's raid reached Washington.

Even before that event, the new commissioner of Indian Affairs, James W. Denver, had launched a written attack on Brigham Young on 11 November 1857 that ranged far beyond the purview of the Indian office. Denver did so with Thompson's support and in language as rough as any Brigham Young would experience from any other federal official, including President Buchanan. The vehicle for Denver's attack was a stern written rebuttal to Young's most recent letter of 12 September. Young's message, written without certainty as to what had happened the day before at Mountain Meadows, had complained at length about the Interior Department's expense-reimbursement and tribal-gifts policies, as well as about the episodic emigrant practice of shooting Indians on sight. Assessing the impact of the latter behavior on the tribes, Young commented: "I find it of the utmost difficulty to restrain them. The sound of war quickens the blood and nerves of an Indian. The report that troops were wending their way to this Territory has also had its influence upon them." Unknown to Denver, this was a far softened version of Young's emotional comments on the same subject written on the same day to Jeter Clinton and Apostle Orson Pratt and encompassed in his earlier unpublished discourse of 16 August.[31]

Barely able to control himself, Commissioner Denver sent Young what one newspaper described as "a sharp rebuke."[32] Whether he wrote solely from personal conviction or with an eye to public opinion is an interesting imponderable.[33] Irrespective of one's view of Denver's charges or his motives, it is clear that he wrote with an intensity comparable to that in some of Brigham Young's own letters and discourses.

[31] Young to Clinton and Young to Pratt, 12 September 1857, LDS Archives.

[32] *Daily Pioneer & Democrat* (St. Paul, Minnesota Territory), 27 November 1857, 2/4–5.

[33] Buchanan was about to appoint Denver as governor of Kansas. Once into that role, Denver sent the territorial legislature a message warning of what he perceived as a violent Danite-style society operating in Kansas on the Utah model. "Gov. Denver's Message," *Washington* (D.C.) *Union*, 17 January 1858, 3/1–2.

Denver to Young, 11 November 1857,
House Ex. Doc. 71, Serial 956, 186–87.

> [T]his department has information from reliable sources, that, so far from encouraging amicable relations between the Indians and the people of the United States outside of your own immediate community, you have studiously endeavored to impress on the minds of the Indians that there was a difference between your own sect, usually known as Mormons, and the government and other citizens of the United States—that the former were their friends and the latter their enemies.
>
> In addition to this, you have been denouncing this government and threatening an armed resistance to the authorities sent out by the President. Indeed, unless you and your coadjutors are most grossly misrepresented, and your language misquoted, the appearance of those authorities among you is all that is necessary to prompt you to an overt act of treason. It could never have been intended, when the appropriations were made by Congress, that the money should be used in arousing the savages to war against our own citizens, or to enable a subordinate officer to carry on treasonable practices against his government. . . .
>
> It is much to be regretted that such a state of affairs should exist, and it is always with great reluctance that we arrive at the conclusion that American citizens should at any time require the strong arm of power to compel obedience to the laws, or that a subordinate officer should so far forget his duty as to use his official position to injure one portion of his fellow-citizens, and to alienate another portion from loyalty to their government. But, when convinced of the existence of such facts, the chief executive has no alternative left but to crush out rebellion; and for this purpose all the powers of the government are placed under his control.

In large part the severity of Denver's comments must have been grounded in his awareness of earlier Mormon-Indian controversies in Missouri and Illinois as well as long-standing, corrosive complaints going back to 1851 about Mormon misconduct among the Plains tribes around Utah. In the fall of 1857 one of the chief complainants was Thomas S. Twiss, Denver's agent at the Upper Platte Agency. Twiss was no conventional bureaucrat. In 1826 he had graduated second in the West Point class that included Albert Sidney Johnston, but three years later Twiss resigned his commission. By 1855 Twiss had assumed the Indian agency for the Upper Platte, following which he married bigamously into a Sioux band. With the roll-up of the Y. X. Carrying Company, Twiss moved his headquarters from the vicinity of Fort Laramie to the recently evacuated Mormon mail and emigrant-aid station at Deer Creek, Nebraska Territory.

Fathoming Twiss's perspective is crucial to understanding Denver's November reaction to Brigham Young, but assessing Twiss's credibility is difficult because of swings in his behavior, his marital ties to the Sioux, and widely varying assessments of his character by both contemporaries and historians. Several of Twiss's letters critical of the Mormons were used by President Buchanan in early 1858 to justify the Utah War to Congress. One of them has long been considered by some historians to have been instrumental in bringing on the war, an erroneous judgment since Twiss wrote that letter in July 1857, well after the Utah Expedition had been launched.[34]

Denver to Thompson, 7 November 1857, House Ex. Doc. 71, Serial 956, 193.

I have the honor to state, for your information and consideration, that I have just received from Agent Twiss a communication, in my opinion, of much importance. He informs me that he had, at the date of his letter, the 15th of September, just returned from a visit to the western part of his agency, undertaken in consequence of a rumor that the Mormons had been tampering with the various Indian tribes of that region, and that he learned from the Arapahoes that they had been told by the Mormons that they were one people in customs, laws, and religion, and ought to be more closely united, as the President was sending troops to Utah for the purpose of dispossessing the Mormons of their lands, and when that was effected it would be an easy matter to dispossess the several Indian tribes; and he was further informed by the Arapahoes that they had also held "talks" with the Snake, Crow, Flathead, and Nez Percé tribes.

The agent advises that some one should be sent to all the tribes along the base of the Rocky mountains, to the north and northeast of Utah, for the purpose of counteracting the probable ill effect of these evil communications, and proposes to undertake the performance of the service himself this winter, and estimates that the outfit and necessary presents to secure the proposed object will not exceed five thousand dollars.

I agree with the agent as to the expediency of the measure, and would recommend that he be selected and instructed, at once, to act in the premises.

I send up herewith a copy of the agent's letter, and would respectfully advise that it be brought to the attention of the President.

As the policy of employing Indian volunteers may form the subject of a

[34] MacKinnon, "The Buchanan Spoils System and the Utah Expedition," 130.

future communication from me, I beg leave to direct your attention to the remark of Mr. Twiss, that "the Arapahoes are true to the government, and will cheerfully volunteer to accompany the troops to Utah, if their services are required."[35]

On 11 November, the day he rebuked Brigham Young, Denver wrote to Twiss's superior in St. Louis to authorize, in his name and Thompson's, Twiss's proposed mission to the western and northern tribes "to obviate the effects of any ill advice which they may receive from these misguided or badly disposed persons, by convincing them of the folly of doing otherwise than remaining upon friendly terms with the government, by persuading them of the interest which the government has in their welfare and happiness, and by exposing the entirely selfish and bad ends which they are invited to assist in accomplishing, but which can never be carried out."[36]

With news a few days later of the Lot Smith raid, Secretary Thompson and Commissioner Denver turned from the perceived Mormon threat among the northern Plains tribes to the unsettled state of affairs among the Indians to Utah's south. On the same day that General Smith submitted his long report to Secretary Floyd, Denver sent instructions to Santa Fe counseling vigilance.

Denver to Indian Superintendent J. L. Collins, 24 November 1857, House Ex. Doc. 71, Serial 956, 188–89.

You are, doubtless, aware of the condition of affairs in the Territory of Utah, and of the fact that the President has found it necessary, in consequence of the attitude which the Mormons, so called, have placed themselves in towards the government, to send a portion of the army to that country. The department has been advised that steps have been taken by persons of that sect to endeavor to alienate some of the tribes of the Upper Platte from their allegiance to the United States; and, presuming that it is not improbable that the same means may be used, or attempted, with the tribes of the Territory of New Mexico bordering upon Utah, or that they may be excited by the scenes which may occur between the troops and that misguided people, it is necessary that every precaution should be taken to keep them quiet. You are, therefore, instructed to use every endeavor in your power to effect this object. If it is necessary that you should visit them in person you are required to do so, and to use all

[35] It is not clear what became of this provocative Arapaho offer, but the use of Indian auxiliaries by either side (as at Mountain Meadows) was an incendiary issue that aggravated finger pointing in the Utah War. Although there is no proof that the Utah Expedition actually used Indian auxiliaries, the tone with which this Arapaho offer was discussed, the Bannock-Shoshone raid on Mormon Fort Limhi in February 1858, and Albert Sidney Johnston's unexecuted January and March plans to use Uintahs and hire Shoshones to operate and defend the Green River ferries raises serious questions about the appearance if not the defensibility of federal behavior in the field among the tribes.

[36] Denver to Haverty, 11 November 1857, House Ex. Doc. 71, Serial 956, 195–96.

funds in your hands applicable to such a purpose, if requisite, in making presents, or otherwise, for the purpose of conciliating them. Indeed, you are authorized to draw upon this office, if absolutely demanded, for a sum not exceeding ten or fifteen thousand dollars, which can be so applied. Yet, all pains should be taken to observe the strictest economy in its expenditures, taking care to satisfy yourself that strong reasons exist for every item laid out.

Should you fail in your efforts to keep the Indians in a state of peace and quiet, then your aim should be to array them against such other Indians as may be found on the side of the enemies of the government, and to spare no pains to prevent them from attacking the whites. The object of the government is to keep them quiet, if possible; but if that cannot be done, then to control them in such a manner as to direct their attacks only against those savages who may take up arms against our people.

It will be necessary for you to proceed with great caution and delicacy in this matter, so as not to excite the minds of the Indians. By keeping a vigilant watchfulness over their movements you will be able to inform yourself whether it may become necessary to take any steps in the premises, and for this purpose you should notify the agents of your superintendency to keep you well informed of the temper and intentions of the Indians in their agencies. They should have every facility afforded them to ascertain the feelings of the Indians, and to keep them on good terms with our citizens.

The [Taos] location of Agent [Kit] Carson will make his position, in the present emergency, a very important one, and he, particularly, should be cautioned to leave nothing undone to carry out the wishes of the government.[37]

They Will Turn to the North: Pacific Coast Jitters

Among the rumored destinations for a fugitive Mormon population were northern Mexico, coastal Central America, an island in the Dutch East Indies, the Sandwich (Hawaiian) Islands, Montana's Bitterroot Valley, and—most alarming to the European ambassadors—Russian America (Alaska) and Vancouver's Island. The latter possessions were relatively undefended; in both cases they were administered not as colonies but as commercial franchises operated exclusively by trading organizations—the Russian-American Company and the Hudson's Bay Company, respectively. By coincidence, the charters under which both companies operated were expiring, and so questions of renewal or termination were under consideration by their national governments.

Probably unknown to Great Britain and Russia as they assessed Mormon

[37] For the background of Indian affairs in New Mexico at this juncture and Kit Carson's role, see Heaston, "The Governor and the Indian Agent," 137–46; Moody, "Kit Carson, Agent to the Indians in New Mexico," 1–20.

intentions, President Buchanan and the U.S. minister to Mexico had since spring been actively contemplating the notion of an American military protectorate over northern Sonora and Chihuahua, a move for which the president eventually sought congressional sanction in December 1858. There is no evidence that in either 1857 or 1858 it was the Mormon problem that drove Buchanan to such a key military-political policy.[38] But the prospect of such a military protectorate unquestionably would have forced a shift in Brigham Young's thinking from any southern escape route to a northerly one.[39] So too would have Mormon apprehensions over the strategic implications of the U.S. Army's Ives Expedition and rumors of a military thrust into southern Utah from Texas or California. Such a northern alternative left open the option of staging from Fort Limhi for a subsequent overland migration into Montana and perhaps even across the British interior possessions to multiple destinations on the Pacific Coast.

Vancouver's Island was a twelve-thousand-square-mile, heavily wooded wilderness that was sparsely populated except by a few resident tribal bands, seasonal Indian visitors, and a tiny British settlement at what became Victoria. This wholly unexploited property was the largest island off North America's West Coast, almost ten times the area of New York's Long Island. The background of British anxieties over Mormon intentions and capabilities was older and more complex than the tsar's worries about the security of Russian America. Even before Joseph Smith, Jr.'s, 1844 assassination, there had been active planning, exploration, and therefore rumors of a Mormon move from the Midwest to the Far West—perhaps as far as gigantic Vancouver's Island. With the murder of Joseph and Hyrum Smith and the realization that Nauvoo was no longer a safe haven, these plans continued under Brigham Young's early leadership, generating speculation about the likely destination of what became the 1846 exodus from Illinois.[40]

---

[38] Buchanan's Mexican policy is described in Klein, *President James Buchanan*, 321–23, and Wilson, "James Buchanan's Proposed Intervention in Mexico," 687–701. Buchanan's proposed protectorate—prompted by chaos, lawlessness, and feckless government in northern Mexico—failed in the Senate during 1859. For newspaper speculation about a Mormon exodus to Sonora, see "Probability of the Mormons Occupying Sonora," *New York Times*, 25 November 1857, 2/5 in which the newspaper's Washington correspondent asserted that "Mr. Buchanan is anxious to acquire the Province of Sonora." See also "Brigham Young's Next Move," *New York Herald*, 22 November 1857, 4/4.

[39] For fears of an army thrust into the south beyond worries about the Ives Expedition, see Briggs, "Cultural Studies of the 1857 Southern Utah Militiamen."

[40] Esplin, "'A Place Prepared,'" 85–111. The best descriptions of these considerations are found in Munro, "Mormon Colonization Scheme for Vancouver Island," 278–85; and Bennett and Jewsbury, "The Lion and the Emperor," 37–62.

As Sir William Napier, Britain's minister to Washington, contemplated the implications of Lot Smith's raid and active press speculation about a Mormon move on Vancouver's Island, his principal action was to send the British foreign secretary, the Earl of Clarendon, a long memorandum setting forth the Utah situation as understood in Washington on 16 November 1857.[41] In this dispatch Napier urged that the Hudson's Bay Company be alerted to a possible Mormon threat to the security of the island. Napier was clearly motivated in part by the *New York Herald*'s alarming 14 November editorial, which had speculated on, if not encouraged, a possible Mormon northwest exodus across the company's territory to the Pacific Coast. After summarizing the movements of the Utah Expedition as then known, Napier concluded:

> It will not escape your Lordship's attention that it is reported that the Mormons intend thereafter to break up from Utah and force their way across Oregon and Washington Territories to Her Majesty's possessions. This rumour cannot be founded in an accurate knowledge of the designs of the Mormon Chiefs but it is accredited by their previous emigration from Nauvoo to the Salt Desert and the journey, however arduous, might perhaps be accomplished by scattered parties with a great sacrifice of Life and property. Her Majesty's Government may consequently prepare the authorities of the Hudson's Bay Company for an attempt of this kind in order that they may give directions to their agents adapted to such a contingency.[42]

At some point in 1858, probably during January, President Buchanan asked Delegate Bernhisel directly about the Mormons' northern interests. As Bernhisel later reported Buchanan's query, "[He] inquired where Gov. Young went last Spring. On being informed, asked why it had not been published. I answered that an account of his visit was published at the time. Spoke of the report of our being about to remove to the British possessions."[43] In the spring of 1858 British defensive actions on the Pacific would unfold, including creation of the new province of British Columbia. This successor organization to the Hudson's Bay Company's administration was intended as a bulwark against an unlikely but feared Mormon onslaught.

In the case of what is now called Alaska, the Russians—like the British—were acutely aware of their possession's military vulnerability and the admin-

---

[41] "The Mormon War in Utah—England Alarmed for Her Boundary Rights," (London) *Post*, 28 November 1857, reprinted in *New York Herald*, Editorial, 15 December 1857, 2/2.

[42] Napier to Clarendon, 16 November 1857, Foreign Office, Public Record Office, London; Copy in Manuscript Division, Library of Congress.

[43] Bernhisel, "Account of Conversations with President James Buchanan," LDS Archives.

istrative shortcomings of the Russian-American Company.[44] On 20 November 1857 Edward A. de Stoeckel, Russian minister to Washington, wrote a memo to Prince Aleksandr M. Gorchakov, Russian foreign minister, summarizing his very recent conversation with President Buchanan. Along with John M. Bernhisel's monthly reports to Brigham Young and Thomas L. Kane's papers, this dispatch provides one of the few records of Buchanan's first-hand comments on any aspect of the Utah War. It was a strange, almost quirky interview:

> Meanwhile, Brigham Young, by a seditious proclamation and by the destruction of a Federal wagon train, has defied the Government. It is claimed, however, that the Mormons, although animated with the most warlike resolution, foresee the eventuality of a new emigration and are resigned thereto in advance. It is added that in this case they will turn to the north to establish themselves on the territory of the Hudson's Bay [Co.] *or in our American possessions.*
>
> Recently the President [Buchanan] in conversation with me smilingly alluded to that eventuality. I asked him whether the Mormons would resort to us as conquerors or as peaceful colonists. "It is for you," he said to me, "to settle that question; as for us, we shall be very happy to be rid of them". This rumor circulated at San Francisco and our Vice Consul[45] who is also agent of the Russian American Company, asked me what there was to it.
>
> I do not need to add that this is a rumor which at present seems still premature, but which, if it should be realized, would place before us the alternative of providing an armed resistance or of giving up part of our territory.[46]

When Gorchakov received this dispatch in St. Petersburg, his concern matched Stoeckl's; he immediately submitted the memorandum to Tsar Alexander II. The tsar reacted by endorsing Stoeckl's dispatch with the comment: "This supports the idea of settling henceforth the question of our American possessions." By the end of December Gorchakov instructed Stoeckl to signal to the U.S. government that Russia was amenable to opening discussions about sale of its North American possessions. Ten years later—with a hiatus large-

[44] In the mid-1850s the Russian-American Company habitually portrayed itself as militarily beleaguered and, with only approximately two hundred troops, extremely vulnerable to attack by the roughly forty thousand Tlinglit tribesmen surrounding the company's posts. Even its headquarters at Sitka on Baranov Island were attacked in 1855. Bolkhovitinov, *Russian-American Relations*, 128 and 138.

[45] Petr Stepanovich Kostromitinov.

[46] Extract of Memorandum from E. A. de Stoeckl to Prince A. M. Gorchakov, 20 November/2 December 1857, Archive of the Foreign Policy of Russia, Moscow; Records of the U.S. Department of State, Washington. With Russia's conversion from the Julian to Gregorian calendar in 1918, many documents and historical narratives use dates corresponding to both calendars, which were twelve days apart. Stoeckl's dispatch and Tsar Alexander II's endorsement on it were written in French, the translation of which appears in Miller, *The Alaska Treaty*, 45.

ly attributable to the American Civil War—Alaska changed ownership for $7.2 million. The November 1857 Stoeckl-Buchanan conversation about the Utah War was neither the reason for this sale, nor even its catalyst, but it was a factor. Multiple other factors and motivations had also been at work—some for years previous—and after 1857 still other issues came to the fore.[47]

Whether Brigham Young was really interested in Russian America as a destination during the Utah War is difficult to assess, with only a few tantalizing clues. What is known is that both the British and Russian governments were concerned.[48] On 5 March 1858 Brigham Young wrote one of his long monthly letters of instruction to Delegate Bernhisel in Washington. In the middle of this letter—seemingly apropos of nothing—Young inserted a telegraphic sentence: "We have our eyes on the Russian possessions." On the same day he wrote in almost identical language to the president of the British Mission, Asa Calkin.[49] Thirty years ago the only American scholars to have focused on the Utah War–Alaskan issue concluded that such a Brigham Young interest was a myth, if not a ruse. In a 1977 article they quickly passed over Young's comment to Bernhisel as simply bewildering and missed completely the companion letter to Liverpool: "He had written nothing about Alaska before, and he apparently wrote nothing about it afterwards, and what he meant, or why he attached this isolated sentence to his letter to Bernhisel, only Brother Brigham could know."[50]

The editor believes otherwise. Brigham Young's own words—written to Bernhisel and Asa Calkin during Thomas L. Kane's first visit to Salt Lake

[47] Professor N. N. Bolkhovitinov, today's leading Russian authority on the sale of Alaska, argues that "Although the information received from Stoeckl about the Mormons was of a very unlikely nature, it aided the rebirth of the idea of the sale of Russian America." Bolkhovitinov, *Russian-American Relations*, 104. See also Bolkhovitinov to MacKinnon, message attachment to e-mail message from Professor Alexander Petrov to MacKinnon, 18 October 2000.

[48] David L. Bigler makes a strong case for Brigham Young's interest in and the importance of Fort Limhi to Mormon colonizing closer to the Missouri River's head of steam navigation at Fort Benton, Montana Territory. In doing so, Bigler keys to the unusual nature of Young's April–May 1857 trek into Oregon Territory together with his military reinforcement of Fort Limhi in October at a time when all other outlying Mormon colonies had been abandoned. Ardis E. Parshall argues that Young's 1851 prolonged personal exploration of Utah south of Parowan with a large entourage bears a striking resemblance to the northern journey six years later and calls into doubt both the uniqueness of the trek to Fort Limhi and the notion that Young planned to flee the territory during the Utah War. Parshall also argues that a total evacuation of Utah for a northern exodus was a far more daunting undertaking than the 1847 move to the Salt Lake Valley and therefore not a likely one. See Bigler, *Fort Limhi*, and "Mormon Missionaries, the Utah War, and the 1858 Bannock Raid on Fort Limhi," 30–53; Parshall to MacKinnon, e-mail message, 5 May 2006.

[49] Young to Bernhisel and Young to Calkin, 5 March 1858, LDS Archives.

[50] Sessions and Stathis, "The Mormon Invasion of Russian America," 35.

City and three days before news of the northern disaster at Fort Limhi reached the city—warrant serious thought, if not credence, rather than dismissal. That Thomas L. Kane arrived in Salt Lake City only a week before Young wrote these letters raises the question of whether he influenced Young's thinking. As discussed in Chapter 18, the fact that Kane traveled west with the intent to raise with Young the possibility of a Mormon exodus from the United States made the cryptic phrasing of his letters to Bernhisel and Calkin all the more intriguing. When one considers the wide range of strategic and tactical action options that Brigham Young examined during 1857–58, it is not unreasonable to view the Alaskan possibility as one that he also considered. Whether, as rumored, such consideration was as early as late 1857 and was of a strong, sustained nature is unclear and probably doubtful. But if in November 1857 Brigham Young was enthusiastic about bows as weaponry for the Nauvoo Legion, it is not unreasonable to consider the possibility of another non-traditional notion—that during 1857–58 President Young considered in some way and then rejected a substantial Mormon refuge in coastal Russian America—or elsewhere on the Pacific Coast.

Nervousness about Mormon intentions was confined to neither European diplomats nor to the tidal settlements of the Pacific Coast. The citizens of Los Angeles and inland San Bernardino—in an uproar since first reports of the Mountain Meadows massacre arrived in early October 1857—were as apprehensive as they were indignant. On the same day that Sir William Napier wrote to Lord Clarendon, seventy-one presumably non-Mormon residents of San Bernardino County sent a lively petition to Brevet Brig. Gen. Newman S. Clarke, commander of the U.S. Army's Department of the Pacific in San Francisco. After reciting accusations of Mormon disloyalty to the U.S. government, tampering with the allegiance of the Indians, gunrunning, and Danite threats of arson, the petitioners concluded, "We therefore petition, and demand protection of you; against our common enemies, the Mormons; and their *Allies*, the Indians. We would suggest to your Honor that two companies of Dragoons be stationed in this vicinity, to protect the citizens on the frontiers. And will ever pray for your success."[51]

[51] Petition of Citizens of San Bernardino, Calif. to Brevet Brig. Gen. N. S. Clarke, 16 November 1857, Records Department of Pacific (RG 393), National Archives.

Chapter 17

"Into Winter Quarters"
Sidney Johnston Takes Charge

The Adjutant General climbed up into a wagon-box and in a clear loud voice announced that the soldiers had gone into winter quarters, at Fort Bridger. Thus verifying my dream at this announcement. Pandemonium broke forth, cheer after cheer resounded through the rocky defiles of the mountains. Most truly it was a canyon to cheer in.

—Nauvoo Legion private Asa S. Hawley,
Echo Canyon, Late November 1857

With the arrival of the Utah Expedition's rear guard at Fort Bridger's charred ruins on 19 November 1857, its disparate elements—including the commander—were together for the first time.[1] Now the Legion's patrols had trouble determining whether Johnston was pausing to regroup or going into winter quarters. It was a life-or-death issue in view of Brigham Young's latest orders authorizing lethal force west of Bridger. There was good reason for the Mormons' uncertainty. Upon arrival Colonel Cooke and other officers had passionately urged Johnston to try to seize Salt Lake City with the dragoons and a pack train unencumbered by wagons. Notwithstanding Cooke's élan, Johnston went into winter quarters during the last week of November. His letters dropped use of the embarrassing notation "en route to Salt Lake City."

Satisfied that at last he was inside Utah, Alfred Cumming took the gubernatorial oath of office on 21 November. Simultaneously he issued a procla-

[1] The accompanying civilian appointees included Gov. Alfred Cumming, Sec. John Hartnett, Chief Justice Delana R. Eckels, U.S. Atty. John M. Hockaday, U.S. Marshal Peter K. Dotson, Supt. of Indian Affairs Jacob Forney, Indian Agent Garland Hurt, and the postmaster for Salt Lake City, Hiram F. Morrell. Associate judges Charles E. Sinclair and John Cradlebaugh did not arrive in Utah until the fall of 1858.

mation to announce his assumption of office and to command dispersal of rebellious groups. In Salt Lake City, Brigham Young pronounced Governor Cumming's installation irregular, declined to recognize him, and ignored the dispersal order. As discussed earlier, Young ordered that Cumming be kept out of the Salt Lake Valley if captured.

Johnston immediately took measures to quarter, defend, police, reinforce, and resupply the Utah Expedition. To avoid further embarrassment by the Nauvoo Legion, he instituted aggressive perimeter patrols and established picket posts to protect three adjacent camps: the ruins of Fort Bridger, the sprawling bivouac named Camp Scott, and a warren of eclectic civilian accommodations dubbed Eckelsville.

To police Camp Scott itself Johnston appointed Capt. Cuvier Grover of the Tenth Infantry as provost marshal. Grover, in turn, organized a system of passwords and a squad of formidable non-coms to enforce military discipline. Even with these measures, there were justifiable concerns that the Utah Expedition harbored an unknown number of Mormon spies. Brigham Young later boasted to Thomas L. Kane that his intelligence from Camp Scott–Eckelsville was such that he was aware even when one of the civilian appointees "visited the willows," as he phrased it. Correspondent A. G. Browne reported, "The system of espionage practiced toward this expedition by the Mormons has been complete and successful. Not a single detachment of troops, nor a train, nor hardly even a party of civilians traveling across the plains either on business or for pleasure, left the Missouri border during the Summer without being accompanied by a Mormon spy in some subordinate capacity, such as teamster or cook."[2]

Notwithstanding Jim Bridger's questionable ownership, Quartermaster John Dickerson leased Fort Bridger from him and turned its scorched stone walls into an improvised supply depot. Into this makeshift storage area went the contents of hundreds of wagons as well as the newly butchered carcasses of the expedition's weakest beef cattle and draught oxen—the ingredients of bad soup and worse garrison humor. To defend this vital installation Colonel Johnston stationed two infantry companies near the walls and protected them further with artillery emplacements (lunettes) and fortified ditches.

[2] Orton, "The Mormons in Johnston's Army," 24–27, discusses several cases in which the Utah Expedition had both enlisted and employed at Fort Laramie Mormon lads who had dropped out of the handcart companies during the previous fall. "Later from Utah," A. G. Browne, Jr., dispatch (Camp Scott), 3 January 1858, *New-York Daily Tribune*, 1 March 1858.

BREVET BRIG. GEN.
ALBERT SIDNEY JOHNSTON, U.S. ARMY
This is a rare portrait of Johnston wearing the brevet brigadier's star awarded for his leadership of the Utah Expedition's desperate November crawl from Hams Fork to Fort Bridger on Blacks Fork. This engraved etching was originally published in 1896 by New York artist Jacques Reich from his pen-and-ink sketch, probably after a contemporary photo. *From the editor's private collection.*

To avoid interdiction while improving communications from his rear, Johnston dispatched a small party eastward through Bridger's Pass rather than South Pass to determine the better winter route to Fort Laramie. From that post he began the months-long process of replacing the most urgently needed provisions, including salt. Johnston dealt with Mormon gunrunning by seizing Nicholas Groesbeck's cache at Platte Bridge. He reinforced his earlier embargo on all movement of people, goods, and mail beyond Fort Bridger. With that order the civilian freighters and merchants accompanying the Utah Expedition also settled into winter quarters with their substantial wagon train of goods, including a covert shipment of gunpowder intended for Salt Lake City's William H. Hooper.

To deal with the devastating loss of livestock, Johnston sent Capt. Randolph B. Marcy and a sixty-man detachment toward the army posts of New Mexico Territory to purchase mules, sheep, and salt on a grand scale. Over the subsequent six months, theirs was to be the most arduous winter march in American military history—shorter but even more daunting than the dragoons' twelve-hundred-mile bad-weather trek from Fort Leavenworth. Three

Panoramic View of the Army's Camp outside Fort Bridger's Scorched Walls
This recently discovered pencil sketch by Capt. Albert Tracy depicts the Utah Expedition's winter camp outside the ruins of Fort Bridger. Blacks Fork is in the foreground with units quartered in the new teepee-shaped Sibley tents shown in background. *Courtesy of the Yale Collection of Western Americana, Beinecke Library.*

days later Johnston dispatched Ben Ficklin and eleven other civilian volunteers in the opposite direction—to Oregon Territory to buy animals from the region's nomadic Flatheads and nervous mountaineers. Here was a remount effort with a continental sweep.

With an eye to reinforcements, Colonel Johnston had recommended to army headquarters in October a coordinated spring thrust from the Pacific side as well as Kansas. In early December Johnston followed up on this need by completing the recruitment and organization of a four-company battalion of volunteer infantrymen, a move accomplished by virtually impressing more than three hundred unemployed teamsters. This draft supplemented

the October high-pressure enlistment of Magraw's disgruntled Pacific Wagon Road crew. With this move Johnston partially replaced the desertions in Kansas while simultaneously bringing under military discipline a young, unruly group that Brigham Young viewed as a mob and that Chief Justice Eckels, with even better information, characterized as "St. Louis wharf rats."[3]

If Alfred Cumming began acting like a governor in late November, during December Judge Eckels went into the judicial business. In concert with U.S. Attorney John M. Hockaday, Eckels empanelled a grand jury of civilian camp followers. Based on Brigham Young's martial-law proclamation, the military orders captured with Legion major Joseph Taylor, and Maj. Lot Smith's destructive raid, the grand jury returned treason indictments against Young and more than a thousand other Mormons. It was a charge perhaps unique in American jurisprudence until the even more sweeping accusations of the Civil War.

[3] Eckels to Sen. Jesse Bright, 13 December 1857, photocopy in editor's possession.

Toward the end of December Indian Agent Garland Hurt and a few of his faithful Ute protectors rode south out of Camp Scott to visit the tribal bands wintering in the deep snows of the Uintah Mountains. Because Hurt's mission was murky, reports of it—along with notice of Ficklin's assignment—stimulated corrosive accusations in Salt Lake City. With some justification, these ran to one of the Utah War's most volatile issues—Indian "tampering." Mormons would have been even more alarmed had they known that even as Magraw was assuming a command in the volunteer battalion, he was also seeking an unauthorized role as a "special Indian agent."[4]

Once General Wells concluded that Johnston did not intend to move on Salt Lake City that winter, Brigham Young and he sent their troops home. They left in Echo Canyon fewer than one hundred men and several even smaller detachments to monitor the army's activities along Blacks Fork from atop Bridger's Butte and the ridges overlooking the valley of Yellow Creek.

Young then pursued some of his earlier ideas such as a "Standing Army" of one to two thousand men to complement the episodic availability of the territorial militia. He also began to develop plans for a spring offensive designed to intercept the returning Marcy expedition, propel Mormon raiders as far east as Fort Laramie, Nebraska Territory, and activate pre-positioned arsonists in cities across the country. Here again one sees Brigham Young thinking on a scale far broader than Utah and with a potential for violence unrecognized in the mythology of the Utah War as bloodless.

In this scene of continental hyperactivity, one subject notably failed to engage Brigham Young and D. H. Wells, as well as Albert Sidney Johnston, Alfred Cumming, and James Buchanan—the appalling tragedy at Mountain Meadows. By mid-November all five leaders had heard about the massacre from a variety of sources. Yet none possessed the curiosity, compassion, or sense of alarm even to mention—let alone pursue—one of the great crimes of nineteenth-century America. In the case of Young and Wells, they failed to probe a monumental atrocity committed by troops under their command while remaining indifferent to the well-being of its seventeen child-survivors. In Utah there was an unwillingness even to bury the victims properly, and so, uninterrupted, the wolves at Mountain Meadows finished their autumnal work.

---

[4] When the U.S. commissioner of Indian Affairs in Washington later became aware of Magraw's putative role he disavowed it ("Mr. McGraw has had no appointment from this Department"). Acting Commissioner Charles E. Mix to Rep. F. P. Blair, Jr., 6 Feb. 1858, transcription in Federal Writers' Project Typescripts, Utah Indian Affairs, Correspondence 1855–1859, U.S. Indian Affairs Dept., Utah State Historical Society. See also Magraw to Buchanan, 2 February 1858, James Buchanan Papers, Historical Society of Pennsylvania.

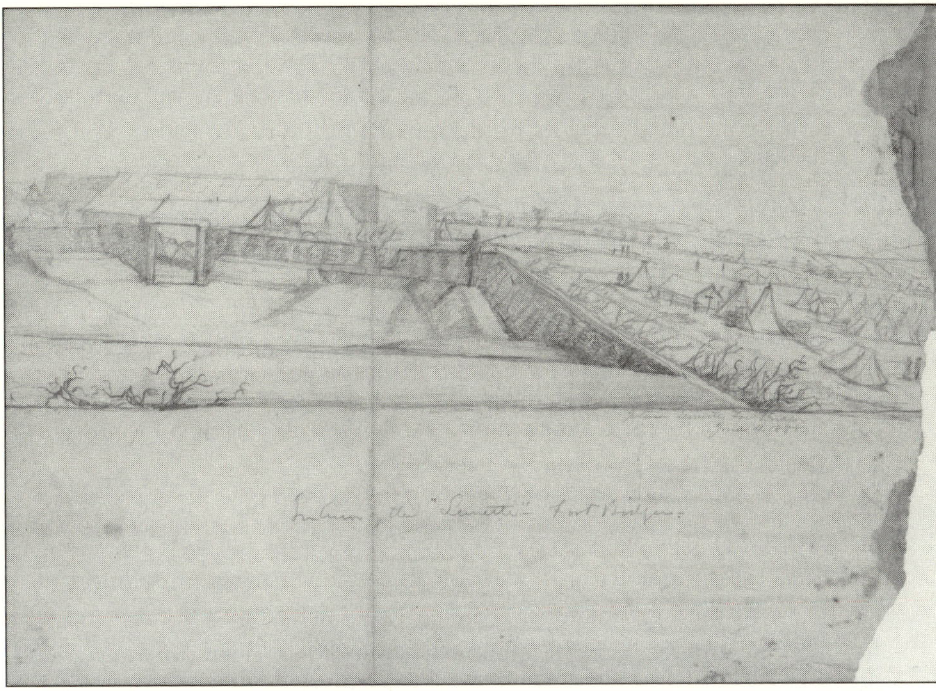

Fort Bridger's Interior after the November Fortification
This is the only extant contemporary view of Fort Bridger's interior, and shows artillery lunettes constructed by Johnston in late November to strengthen this trading post's defences against a Legion attack. This is a recently discovered sketch by Captain Tracy. *Courtesy of the Yale Collection of Western Americana, Beinecke Library.*

Men in Very Deep Thought: The Dilemma of Army Intentions

In mid-November General Wells's major worry was whether Colonel Johnston would move west of Fort Bridger. Unknown to the Nauvoo Legion and most historians, during the third week of November a debate, if not an argument, broke out atop the Utah Expedition's command at Fort Bridger on whether to go into winter quarters. Colonel Cooke argued vigorously for a march on Salt Lake City by the Second Dragoons alone, and when overruled nursed a grudge with Johnston and his adjutant that lasted for decades. In 1889 Cooke told Gen. William Tecumseh Sherman, "I was long an intimate friend [of Johnston], until a connextion with one F[itz]. J[ohn]. P[orter]. befell him. Then I first discovered his weakness in not marching on to Salt Lake City that fall [of 1857]."[5] A. G. Browne provided his readers with a muted description of the debate and its resolution, including the revealing confession that "Our present fear is that what we are debarred from undertaking will be accomplished from the side of California before we can move in the Spring. The 'Army of Utah' will then . . . see whatever glory was to be gained from the expedition inure to others."[6]

The letters to Brigham Young from his generals during the last half of November reflected their anxiety over Johnston's uncertain intentions as he approached and then seemed to pause at Fort Bridger. At stake was the possible escalation of the confrontation into a lethal one. It was the most uncertain two weeks of the Utah War.

In addition to reflecting these tensions, the letters shed light on the Legion's probable tactics if the army were to move on Salt Lake City. As discussed earlier, this correspondence also provides an extraordinary glimpse into the extent to which the Legion's most senior officers deferred to Young's judgment—seeking and receiving his counsel on even minor operational details. Displayed in the process were the Legion's intelligence-gathering capabilities, including detection of Captain Marcy's 27 November departure for New Mexico from Fort Bridger. Finally, the exchange of correspondence reveals the Legion's unique religious character—not only in terms of the letters' ecclesiastical phrasing but through an extraordinary expression of the pastoral relationship between Brigham Young and his most senior commander-counselor. During November 1857 General Wells was, among other things, a grieving father absent from home but comforted by his prophet as his infant daughter lay dead and a baby son struggled to shake off serious illness.

Perhaps the most revealing letter of the period was that written by General Wells to Brigham Young on 21 November from Echo Canyon, at which point Johnston had reached Bridger and decided to go into winter quarters, although Wells was not yet aware of either development.

WELLS TO YOUNG, 21 NOVEMBER 1857, LDS ARCHIVES.

In regard to the army they do not act a particle like they were going into Winter Quarters. . . . But I firmly believe that it has been their intention to leave

[5] Cooke to Sherman, 7 May 1889, Cooke Papers. See also Cooke to 1st Lt. William R. Hamilton, 8 March 1886, Brigham Young University Library.

[6] "Late from the Utah Expedition," Browne dispatch, 26 November 1857, *New-York Daily Tribune*, 18 January 1858.

> their heavy trains at Ft Bridger and come into the City with their light Artillery and their best mule teams and the principal part of the Army, leaving of course a strong guard made up however of their most fatigued and incapable men. . . . Night surprises may be made by attacking their Picket guards and driving them and fireing into their camps and their scouting parties may be ambushed and cut off, all of which we are calculating on doing to the best of our ability. They move very cautious, throwing out strong scouting parties and exploring every inch of the ground before they enter to occupy it. They keep a very close watch of their horses and mules. Our boys although about them nearly all the time, have not seen them outside of their camp grazing since they left the crossing at Ham's Fork, hence their slow progress grazing as they come. . . . We trust therefore if it comes to a crisis to give a good account of it, but withal our trust is in the Lord of Hosts . . . [the brethren] seem to feel well only a little chagrined at the slow movement of the enemy, but I feel that this is all right. I would rather lie in their path ten or twenty years, thereby blocking up their way than let them enter our peaceful city, or settlements with the train of Hell which follows after and is already in their midst.[7] I have constantly prayed that it might be turned aside and no collision take place this fall or winter, in hopes that something might transpire to avert it altogether as whenever it comes it will be soon enough. And reason would dictate to me that Col. Johnston and the office[r]s with him would not be so void of common sense as to undertake to force their way into the heart of an enemy's country at this season of the year where they could neither receive assistance, supplies, nor make good their retreat but judgeing from their movements and actions, we are compelled to believe they intend to try it. It would also seem as though they would also feel desirous of avoiding a collision, if it could be done without compromising themselves, rather than plunge a Territory into a civil war. How far these considerations go with them, I cannot say, but if they attempt the passage to the city this way, and none other is now left them where they can go with wagons, I shall take it as a sure indication that the Lord wants them used up and shall do what little I can towards accomplishing so desirable a result.[8]

In the midst of this high-level agonizing, Legion private Asa Hawley, home from the plains but on duty again in Echo Canyon, found a simpler means of divining the Utah Expedition's plans for the winter. He consulted his dreams:

> We were sleeping in a wagon-box [in Echo Canyon]. After retiring I lay awake, well, I do not know how long, meditating and thinking over the stirring events that were transpiring and what would be the final outcome. I thought of my little wife and my baby boy, my aged parents, and in fact, of all our people back in the valley, wondering if they had heard that the soldiers had passed

[7] Here again is Mormon concern about the behavior of the army's undisciplined civilian camp followers.

[8] "Used up" was one of the common euphemisms in Utah for killing.

Fort Bridger and if so, how great must be their anxiety. With those thoughts in mind I fell asleep, or at least it seemed so, and I imagined myself back near Fort Bridger, which part of the country was familiar to me. I was very anxious to see the soldiers. I finally beheld them this [west] side of Bridger. They were standing still. I could also see their officers, they seemed to me like men in very deep thought. In a quandary, not knowing which way to go or what to do. Most earnestly did I watch their every move. Finally there was a stir amongst them and they took up their line of march an to my surprise they started back toward Fort Bridger.[9]

Curiously Wrought Chimneys: Building Camp Scott

Virtually every soldier and camp follower who could write described how the wilderness of Blacks Fork and the charred remains of Jim Bridger's former trading post became the nation's largest military garrison. Even as Colonel Cooke wrote his report and fumed over Johnston's rustication of his dragoons to herding duty on Henrys Fork, the huge encampment near Bridger took shape. Camp Scott soon sprawled for miles along the icy, pristine, trout-filled waters of Blacks Fork. Among the crispest descriptions of this scene was Albert G. Browne's dispatch.

A. G. Browne, Jr., Dispatch, "Late from the Utah Expedition," 26 November 1857, *New-York Daily Tribune*, 18 January 1857.

Our Winter camp is in the narrow valley of Black's Fork, sheltered by high bluffs, which rise abruptly on each side of the bottom, at the distance of six or seven hundred yards from the channel of the stream. The banks of the Fork are lined with willow brush and cottonwood trees blasted in one or two places by attempts which were made by the Mormons before the evacuation of Fort Bridger to deprive us of fuel as well as of grass. The trees and brushes were fortunately too green to burn, and the fire swept through acres of wood, doing no other damage than to consume the dry leaves and scorch the bark. The water of the Fork is clear and pure, and ripples noisily over a stony bed, between two unbroken lines of ice. The headquarters are upon a little green knoll, around which the stream makes a gentle bend. The 5th infantry are camped on the left, toward Fort Bridger; the artillery batteries and the 10th infantry on the right. The dragoons will be distributed along Henry's Fork, on which the grass is unburnt. All the cattle and mules which survive will also be sent there to recruit.

[9] Narrative of Asa S. Hawley, 1912, LDS Archives.

> The work of killing cattle and jerking the beef, has been prosecuted busily during all the week; but the meat has suffered some deterioration in quality from the circumstance of having been beaten with oxwhips over a thousand miles of road since the beginning of the Summer. Indeed, to speak plainly, it is reduced to muscle and gristle. To increase the unsavory prospective, is added the fact that there has been no salt in camp for more than a fortnight. . . . I shook the final grains from my salt-cellar today, over a superb Mormon turnip taken from a cache unearthed at Fort Supply.
>
> The civil officers of the Territory have founded a Gentile city in a nook in the wood above the camp of the 10th Infantry, and by the talk about "twenty feet front," and "corner lots," a passer-by might almost imagine himself in boom-town Kansas. The Governor occupies a scollop in the eastern line of the wood, on which he has planted his tents and unloaded his wagons. Next comes the Chief Justice, who has excavated a quadrangle, fourteen feet square, and built a rough log hut over the hole. His establishment is more complete than that of the Indian Agent, which is progressing on a similar plan, but larger scale. The half-dozen Utes who are at work on it, handle the shovel and pick-ax with more dexterity than I had believed that Indians could acquire. The Marshal, and a son [David A. Burr] of the Surveyor-General, together with Mr. [Charles] Mogo, the Deputy Surveyor, are building a cabin which will surpass in size any other in the row except the projected court house.

An upbeat view of the camp comes to us through the "voice" of the Utah War's most familiar diarist—Capt. Albert Tracy, commander of the Tenth Infantry's Company H. Presented below is Tracy's letter to an unidentified friend, as run pseudonymously in his hometown newspaper.[10] The document is interesting for multiple reasons, as Tracy's earliest Utah War comments; a contrarian view of living conditions at Camp Scott; a reflection of the army's interest in Albert G. Browne's *Tribune* dispatches; and a glimpse into the antipathy between Colonel Alexander and his subordinates. Tracy's editor in Buffalo—who printed the letter over the signature "T."—prefaced its text with a comment that it was "spicily written." He noted, "We are reluctantly compelled to suppress some remarks concerning Col. Alexander, which, as the letter was not intended for publication, might involve a betrayal of the author's confidence on our part.[11] It is sufficient to say that the opinion prevails at Fort Bridger, as well as here, that had Col. Johnston held the command of the advance column, it would have wintered in Salt Lake City."

---

[10] None of Tracy's letters to family and friends have surfaced for the Utah War period except for two unexploited 1857 notes in the *Buffalo Commercial Advertiser*. His earliest surviving diary begins with the entry for 1 March 1858.

[11] In July 1858 Colonel Alexander would prefer charges of insubordination against Captain Tracy and force him to stand trial by court martial.

"T"[RACY] TO "N.," "A LETTER FROM THE UTAH ARMY," 10 DECEMBER 1857, *COMMERCIAL ADVERTISER* (BUFFALO, N.Y.), 3 FEBRUARY 1858, 2/1–2.

I should not wonder if you should see in the papers, before two months, letters calculated to produce the impression that this army is in a suffering condition. Let me tell you beforehand that such is not the truth, and that the prospect is very flattering that it will not be the case. . . . You will probably also see it stated that we are on short "grub." This can hardly be considered as a true presentment. The flour element of the ration has been reduced five ounces (leaving the daily allowance to each soul, as also to every person without a soul, and entitled to subsistence, thirteen ounces) but the beef component was at the same time raised (increased) eight ounces, the other items remaining as heretofore. This reminds me of a little matter it is as well to mention. We have had *no salt* for a month or more, so that, as regards that item of the ration, "heretofore" must be considered inapplicable. But most of us don't mind it much now. . . .

[T]he New York *Tribune* has a correspondent in camp. It being his business to pick up news, he doubtless gathers many items of which I may hear nothing in so large a camp as this.—Though no believer in the [anti-slavery] heresies of that paper, I am willing to believe that its correspondence may, sometimes, be reliable; in this case I hope to find it so. From some acquaintance with its correspondent here, I think he will only state facts, or what he believes to be facts. I understand the campaign on Ham's Fork was served up and sent forward by last mail, and that the controlling spirit in that lustreless performance has been handled without gloves.[12] I hope the simple facts have been related: they are quite sufficient, without varnish. I wish you would send me copies of the *Tribune* containing letters from Utah, and to increase my chances of getting them, perhaps it would be as well to send *two* copies of each number containing a letter, and in *separate* envelopes. . . .[13]

So far we have not had as cold weather this month as we had in November, and we are told by the mountaineers that we may not have a severe winter, if so, I shall get along very well as to animal comfort, for even now I can make my tent more comfortable than our parlor at Fort Ripley [Minnesota Territory] was the winter you were there, and when I shall have completed some improvements I have in view, I expect I shall get on admirably. Today is so warm that my fire has nearly gone out without inconvenience to me. My general health continues good.

---

[12] Probably a reference to A. G. Browne's scathing dispatch for the period 13–29 November, which the *Tribune* ran on 18 January 1858 with headlines including "Mismanagement of the Campaign" and "A Court of Investigation Desired."

[13] Tracy was as apprehensive of Mormon mail interceptions as Brigham Young was cynical about the intrusions of U.S. postmasters.

Capt. Albert Tracy, Tenth U.S. Infantry
This is the only extant image of Tracy, the Utah Expedition's best-known diarist-artist. Tracy was a persistent critic of Colonel Alexander, who finally court-martialed him for disrespect in 1858. His newly discovered letters from 1857 shed light on the war before the March 1858 start of his published journal. This photo depicts Tracy as a Union Army infantry major. *Courtesy of the Maine National Guard.*

Remain in the Vicinity of My Fort: Magraw among the Shoshones

One of Albert Sidney Johnston's defensive strategies for the fall and winter involved dealing with Indians. Whether this effort went beyond the matter of neutralizing the tribes to take on an offensive character is an intriguing but largely unexamined question. It is an especially important issue in view of accusations of Mormon attempts to subvert tribal allegiances; Indian Agent Garland Hurt's shadowy December mission from Fort Bridger to the Uintahs; the subsequent association of Ben Ficklin—Magraw's former employee—with the February Bannock-Shoshone attack on Fort Limhi; and Johnston's March 1858 decision to hire Chief Washakie's Shoshones to operate and defend the important Green River ferries. Into this thicket of tribal intrigue plunged W. M. F. Magraw during October in the self-assumed role of "special Indian agent." When they heard of it, Secretary of the Interior Thompson and Indian Affairs commissioner Charles E. Mix disavowed such a role for Magraw. Whether Superintendent Forney, if not Colonel Johnston, encouraged and perhaps enabled Magraw's pretensions is a matter awaiting examination.

The most extensive description yet discovered of what Magraw was doing among the tribes during the fall of 1857 appears in his year-end letter to President Buchanan.

MAGRAW TO BUCHANAN, 2 JANUARY 1858,
JAMES BUCHANAN PAPERS, HISTORICAL SOCIETY OF PENNSYLVANIA.

> I received from the Commissioner of Indian Affairs five hundred dollars for the purchase of goods to be given as presents to the Indians through whose country I might pass. Having learnt that the Mormons were tampering with the Indians, and especially with the Snakes [Shoshones], I sent for Wash-Kee the Chief of that Tribe, and his band, and distributed amongst them the whole of the goods intended for presents.[14] These were the first he had ever received direct from the Government, but he said he had occasionally got ~~some occasionaly~~ some few articles from Brigham Young, who always represented them as presents from the Mormons. I advised him not to return to the Mormons but to remain in the vicinity of my fort this winter. . . . [T]he Snakes are now at the boiling spring, to which point they had followed the Buffalo.[15]
>
> I learnt much from Wash-Kee of the attempts made by the Mormons to join an alliance with him and his people. In accomplishing this treason they were always thwarted, as Wash-Kee is one of the most remarkable Indians I have ever seen, and decidedly one of the most intelligent of his race. I hope the Government will carry out the promise I made to them to the effect that some arrangement would be entered into by which his people would receive regular annuities. Before leaving Washington Gov. Denver requested me to ascertain from Wash-Kee, whether or not he would not wish to visit Washington, and see his "Great Father"; he agreed to do so, if I would take him along with me when I went in, in company with a few of his people, the principle men. If such an arrangement should be desirable there will be sufficient time to acquaint me with it. There is much in my letter that you may think properly belongs to different Departments, but my position being rather a novel one I have concluded to advise you direct.[16]

[14] Among Magraw's presents were "a rifle, a Colt's revolver, and a saddle gaudily trimmed with blue and red morocco, and embellished with silver studs." A. G. Browne, Jr., dispatch, 18 October 1857, "Important from the Mormon War . . . Indians Neutral," *New-York Daily Tribune*, 11 December 1857.

[15] Magraw probably meant Fort Thompson (near today's Lander, Wyo.), the winter bivouac for the remnants of his Pacific Wagon Road crew, rather than Fort Bridger.

[16] Although Magraw was willing to pander to Secretary Thompson by naming his fort after him, he had no hesitation in bypassing him to deal directly with Buchanan. It was behavior worthy of Harney's circumvention of General Scott to communicate with Buchanan and Floyd.

Lt. Col. Barnard Elliott Bee, Battalion of U.S. Volunteers
A captain and company commander in the Tenth, Bee's December election as commander of the four-company "volunteer" infantry battalion forcibly recruited at Fort Bridger was engineered by Johnston, a comrade-in-arms during the Texas Revolution with Bee's father, the new republic's secretary of war. After an embarrassing clash with Johnston, Governor Cumming appointed Bee a lieutenant colonel on his staff. During their nine months of service, Bee's battalion of Pacific Wagon Road men and unemployed teamsters underwent essential training and discipline while effectively increasing Johnston's troop strength by about 25 percent. Because of Bee's frontier service and early death in 1861, images of him are rare. This portrait, painted in 1898 by Johan Stolle, depicts Bee as a Confederate brigadier. *Brigadier General Barnard Elliott Bee, C. S., Johan Stolle (American, active 1870–1907) oil on canvas, Gibbes Museum of Art/Carolina Art Association, XX 1923, Charleston, South Carolina.*

Or Be Starved on the Road: Volunteering under Duress

The most famous unit in Utah military history is, of course, the Mexican War's Mormon Battalion. The least known is another independent volunteer infantry battalion—the one organized ten years later at Camp Scott. The great irony of these two organizations is that circumstances pitted the latter against veterans of the former.

Lt. Col. Barnard E. Bee, commander of the Utah War's Battalion of U.S. Volunteers, later became famous as a Confederate brigadier. But his volunteer battalion and its troops are historical phantoms. They lack a unit history, and even a simple listing of those who served was not published until 2006.[17] Lost with the volunteer battalion's identity is a colorful story worth resurrecting and preserving. Impressed into uniform in a wilderness, the unit's

[17] Nielson, *Roll Call at Old Camp Floyd, Utah Territory*, 201–16.

very origins belied the volunteer character of its name and service. Its commander was a South Carolina West Pointer who later died heroically in the Civil War's battle of First Bull Run only hours after coining Gen. Thomas J. Jackson's enduring nickname, "Stonewall." Present at the creation of Bee's Utah War battalion and commander of its first company was the notorious W. M. F. Magraw, who was supported by his former employee, William Porter Finlay, now the battalion's senior enlistee as its sergeant-major. Finlay was described by Britain's First Lord of the Admiralty as "a young man of great military promise, having fought well at the Cape [of Good Hope], indeed only too fond of fighting which has been his infirmity."[18]

This is not the place for a unit history, but a glimpse of the Battalion of U.S. Volunteers is warranted. After all, the unit's recruitment increased Johnston's troop strength at Camp Scott by nearly 25 percent. A few documents follow describing the battalion's organization as well as the insider account left by Capt. W. M. F. Magraw of Company A and more of the colorful newspaper dispatches sent to the *Saint Louis Leader* by Sergeant-Major Finlay as the pseudonymous "W. P. F." The battalion's story starts in late October 1857 as Magraw—nervous about the self-induced collapse of his Pacific Wagon Road assignment as well as the menacing attentions of Bill Hickman and Lot Smith—sought a safe haven.[19] It was a critical juncture in terms of both time and place as Albert Sidney Johnston sought to reinforce and re-equip his own troubled expedition. For Magraw, the stars of federal largesse once more came into fortuitous alignment—this time over the valley of the Sweetwater River near South Pass.

Magraw to Buchanan, 2 January 1858, James Buchanan Papers, Historical Society of Pennsylvania.

From a request made by you to me before I left Washington last Spring, that I should write to you occasionally, as Mr Hockaday purposes leaving for the States in a day or two. I take the opportunity of sending to you some few particular events which have taken place on the Wagon Road Expedition; and

---

[18] First Lord of the Admiralty Sir James Graham to Duke of Newcastle, 6 December 1853, Public Record Office, Victoria, Melbourne, Australia.

[19] Ever since assaulting Mormon James Gemmell in Independence during the early summer, Magraw had been nervous about possible Mormon retaliation. As far east as Fort Laramie and as early as 5 September, Magraw's assistant chief engineer noted critically, "A few evenings since the camp was astonished by his [Magraw's] entertaining (liquoring) one of [Brigham] Young's principal men [Porter Rockwell?] and relating the circumstances of Gamble [Gemmell], trying to excuse himself. Now he appears to be particularly anxious to allow the army to get between him and Salt Lake City." Henry K. Nichols, Jr., to A. H. Campbell, 5 September 1857, Records of the Pacific Wagon Road Office, National Archives.

also what I have seen in my new position with the Army of Utah, which may be interesting to you. . . .

Directly East of the South Pass, I met Captain Van Vliet on his return from Salt Lake, and was by him informed of the hostile intentions of the Mormons, and advised by him to proceed no further in that direction. Having been for some time previously fully satisfied from actual observation that the Mormons were watching my movements, and dogging my trains, requiring on my part the utmost vigilance to protect the animals and other property from being carried off by a surprise, I felt it incumbent upon me to take up some secure position. . . .

[Upon hearing of hostilities] I at once tendered him [Col. Johnston] the entire amount of transportation in my charge, and offered him the services of myself and my men as Volunteers. This offer was readily accepted. . . . I brought back to [Johnston's] head Quarters command thirteen wagons and one hundred and ten mules, escorted by a company of forty one men, who have volunteered, and elected me their Captain, joining the Head Quarters on the eight[h] day. The volunteers were mustered into the service of the United States for six months from the 24th day of October, (being the first volunteers in this army) & I turned the property over to the Quarter Master receiving his receipt for the same. . . . On our arrival at this Camp [Scott] . . . I with my Company renewed our enlistment for three months longer, on the understanding with Col. Johnston that we should be mustered out of the service at an earlier period if our services could be dispensed with.

I have been somewhat minute in giving you a statement of my movements, as I feel it incumbent upon me to do so. For the responsibility which I have taken upon myself I am accountable to you, and your Administration, and I trust that my course may be sustained. What I have done I considered was for the best, being thrown entirely upon my own judgment, and actuated solely by a sence of duty to my Country. . . . After hostilities broke out, the employees themselves expressed their wishes to be permitted to assist in quel[l]ing the rebellion of the miserable traitor Brigham Young, and his marauding followers, and bringing to the justice they so richly merit their insolent offenders against the laws of our Country. . . .

If it would not be considered improper in me, I would humbly request if there should be any promotion that these two Gentlemen [Captains Marcy and Bee] should not be overlooked, for in my opinion their services richly merit the confidence of the Government. They are both in the prime of life, healthy, strong, and energetic.[20]

[20] Upon Marcy's return to Camp Scott from New Mexico, Johnston assigned him honorific duty as the Department of Utah's inspector general and favorably endorsed his application for a six-month paid leave of absence. On 29 May 1858 Gen. Scott recommended to Secretary Floyd that he award Marcy a majority by brevet, but inconceivably no apparent action was taken. On 22 August 1859 Marcy was promoted to major in the paymaster department. Hollon, *Beyond the Cross Timbers*, 225n7; Heitman, *Historical Register* 1:689. Bee also received a leave in 1858.

There is another Gentleman whom I cannot pass by unnoticed in my communication to you. It is young Wm Porter Finlay. . . . At Laramie I requiring some additional assistance in my Engineer Department, I was recommended to procure M^{r}. Finlay's services, which I accordingly did.[21] When I made known the request of Co^{l}. Johnston to which [I referred] in the previous part of this letter, young Finlay promptly responded, and joined my company as a private in which capacity he remained until the formation of the Battalion, when he was immediately selected by Col. Bee for the important duty of Sergeant-Major, this being the only position which could be given him. . . .[22]

M^{r}. Hockaday will give you all the news here, so I will trouble you no further, but will conclude by wishing you a hap[p]y new year, and a prosperous Administration

[P.S.] I do not intend this as an official communication unless you see proper to make it so.

Unknown to Captain Magraw, a quite different account of life with the volunteers was flowing from within his own unit to the readers of the *Saint Louis Leader*. From that newspaper's exchanges with sister publications, the entire country became aware of "W. P. F."'s irreverent views of his inept but politically connected benefactor.

William Porter Finlay, "The Army for Utah,"
30 November 1857, *Saint Louis Leader*, 14 January 1858, 4/3–4.

Real life is more romantic than fiction, but the way in which I became a volunteer is nothing out of the way. The wagon road expedition, in fact, became a busted institution, Magraw, the Superintendent, having succeeded in first quarrelling with all his engineer department, with his disbursing agent, and with his medical man, ended by declaring to our great surprise in the winter quarter on Wind river, that he had no supplies for us for the winter, that he could obtain no provisions on credit from any of the trading posts within 150 miles, and had no money, and that he must send nearly all back to the States, at the same time just mentioning that he could not furnish us sufficient transportation or food to take us there, and stating his private opinion that we

[21] Magraw sloughs over the fact that near Fort Laramie, his wagon road party began to disintegrate, with some clerical and professional employees quitting in disgust over his mismanagement and drunken, overbearing behavior. MacKinnon, "The Buchanan Spoils System and the Utah Expedition," 139–40. The hiring of Finlay was noted with some ridicule by Magraw employees who considered him "English." In his later dispatches to the *Saint Louis Leader*, Finlay took pains to portray himself as Irish.

[22] A sergeant-major's duties in an American regiment or independent battalion were often more administrative than as the chief enforcer of unit discipline. In Finlay's case his education and writing skills ran to his advantage as Bee sought to organize a battalion de novo. Since Finlay had accompanied the Tenth between Forts Leavenworth and Laramie, he would have been known to Bee as well as to the two officers whom he took from that regiment to form the volunteer battalion's cadre, Lieutenants James Deshler and James H. Hill.

> would all, or nearly all, be starved on the road. . . . Before we had recovered from our surprise at the unexpected and rather alarming statement of the Superintendent, he commenced a flourishing speech, full of high-sounding words and unfinished sentences, appealing to our patriotism, valor, and other noble qualities which it is presumed we all possessed, calling upon us to volunteer to the army in Utah, and hinting what a capital selection we would make in choosing him, W. M. F. Magraw, as captain. Now, I will venture to say there were few men, if any, in all the expedition who would not at once have come forward cheerfully and willingly to render their services, no matter what might be the inclemency of the season or the nature of the country in which operations were to be carried on. Hesitation or any unmanly reluctance to participate in the hardships to which all expected the troops composing the army for Utah would be this winter exposed, there was none, but to be in this fashion forced to volunteer or run the greatest risk of perishing from cold and hunger on the road to the States, was most revolting to the feelings of all. It was neither more nor less than pressing into the service, and the hardest sort of pressing at that; Hobson's choice, either go for a soldier or go and be d—d. With considerable hesitation, at last the men of the expedition said they would go, and of course Magraw was chosen Captain, as, being Superintendent, how else was transportation or food on the road for the troops to be procured. J[ames]. Knowles, of Independence, and C. H. Hamilton, of Weston [Missouri], were elected, in a sort of way, Lieutenants, and then the Superintendent issued a sufficiency of whisky to celebrate his election and to make such a scene of drunken rioting in the camp as it has seldom been my fortune to witness. The principal performers in this latter part of the proceedings were Irish laborers, and consequently no really serious injuries were given or received, but those conversant with the manners and customs of the natives of the Emerald Isle, can fancy the delightful scenes which were enacted by these gallant defenders of their adopted country, on the evening of their first day's service.

With the army's arrival at Fort Bridger and the decision in short order to go into winter quarters, Colonel Johnston immediately set out to recruit additional volunteer companies. By early December three more companies were raised with the persuasive help of Russell, Majors and Waddell's Charlie Morehead. Another motivator for enlistment was Johnston's edict that teamsters not volunteering would be barred from heading for Salt Lake City. If they chose to return east it would be afoot with only a few days of government rations—a virtual death sentence.

As with the formation of Magraw's unit (later designated Company A), the former teamsters in what became Companies B, C, and D elected their officers. There are signs that the elections in these three companies were sub-

CAPT. GEORGE WASHINGTON CHERRY, BATTALION OF U.S. VOLUNTEERS
Cherry, an unemployed teamster, was elected to command Company C because of his performance during Indian raids on the plains and his prior volunteer military experience in Oregon and in Central America with filibusterer William Walker. Photographed in the uniform of a private, his Oregon rank during 1855–56, this image of Cherry may have been taken by David A. Burr at Camp Scott in late 1857 before he could acquire the shoulder straps of his new rank as a captain. *Courtesy of the late LaVonne Cherry Ketchum, Biggs, California.*

stantially more open than that held among Magraw's men, with commissions going clearly to those who were either seasoned wagonmasters or men with prior military experience. For example, Samuel Foster, the new captain of Company D, was a long-service wagonmaster and one of the men from whom Judge Eckels sought an affidavit on 4 November at Hams Fork about the Lot Smith and related raids. George Washington Cherry, a teamster, became captain of Company C probably because of his earlier service with an Oregon volunteer unit during an Indian war and his subsequent filibustering experience in Central America with William Walker, the notorious "Grey-Eyed Man of Destiny." In Company B, teamster James F. Bennett was elected captain because of his grit in leading resistance to a Cheyenne attack at Ash Hollow during the summer march. Recognizing that he was only nineteen, Bennett insisted on exchanging ranks with an older man, Daniel McLaughlin, whom he then served as Company B's first lieutenant.

Albert G. Browne was on the scene as Bee's battalion took shape and recorded an informed outsider's view of the process still different than the widely varying accounts of Captain Magraw and Sergeant-Major Finlay.

A. G. Browne, Jr., "Later form the Utah Expedition,"
13 December 1857, *New-York Daily Tribune,* 2 February 1858.

Four companies of volunteers have been organized and equipped up to this date, and it is possible that one or two more may be added to the number.[23] With the assent of the Commander-in-Chief, they have been consolidated into a separate battalion, and have elected Capt. Barnard E. Bee, of Company D, 10th Infantry, to be their commander. He has accepted the position, with the temporary rank of Lieutenant-Colonel. His staff consists of Lieut. James H. Hill, Adjutant, and James Deshler, Quartermaster, both also of the 10th. . . .[24]

This battalion, when properly drilled, is likely to do good service. Most of the men are thoroughly acclimated, and all of them are burly, hardy fellows, who came from the States as ox-drivers. It is rather an abuse of language, however, to call their enlistment voluntary. I was walking with an officer down the bottom toward Fort Bridger, a day or two ago, when we met half-a-dozen men loaded with blankets, bake-ovens, frying-pans, tin dippers, and rifles, traveling in the opposite direction. Supposing them to have arrived in camp, we hailed them, and asked who they were, and where they were going. "Oh," said one of them, "my name is 'Zekel Thompson. I came out a drivin' a bull team for Russell & Waddell, and now that they've turned us out, we can't get anything to eat, and so we're a goin' up to volunteer. I s'pose there's no choice 'cept between volunteerin' and starvin'."[25]

A. G. Browne, Jr., Dispatch,
"Christmas and New Year's in the Camp,"
2 January 1858, *New-York Daily Tribune,* 1 March 1858.

The Army was mustered day before yesterday [31 December] . . . the battalion of volunteers by Brevet Lieut.-Col. Chapman, of the 5th Infantry. The volunteers presented a creditable appearance, considering the few weeks during which they have been subjected to drill. I subjoin a list of the officers of their battalion, as I have already forwarded to you a list of the officers on duty with the regular army:

Lieut.-Col. Barnard E. Bee (Capt. 10th Inf.), Commanding.
Second Lieut. James H. Hill (10th Inf.), Adjutant.
Second Lieut. James Deshler (10th Inf.), Quartermaster.
Capt. W. M. F. Magraw, Company A.
Capt. Daniel McLaughlin, Company B.
Capt. George W. Cherry, Company C.

[23] The size of the battalion stayed at four companies.

[24] Aside from his other qualifications, Hill was Bee's brother-in-law.

[25] Thompson does not appear on the volunteer battalion's published muster rolls for 30 June 1858, but may have been among the troops discharged earlier. Nielson, *Roll Call at Old Camp Floyd,* 201–16.

Capt. Samuel Foster, Company D.
First Lieut. James Knowles, Company A.
First Lieut. James [F.] Bennett, Company B.
First Lieut. Henry K. Hartley, Company C.
First Lieut. George W. Fuller, Company D.
Second Lieut. W. P. Cowne, Company A.[26]
Second Lieut. Joseph R. Chauncey, Company B.
Second Lieut. Benj. F. Thomas, Company C.
Second Lieut. W. O. Clarkson, Company D. . . .

A petition in the following language has been signed by the entire volunteer battalion, and will be presented in Congress at an early day:

"To the Honorable the Senate and House of Representatives of the United States, in Congress assembled:

We, the undersigned, members of the volunteer companies serving with the Army of Utah, respectfully request from you an early consideration of the circumstances in which we are placed.

Trusting entirely to the magnanimity of the Government, we have entered the service of the United States at a time when we thought we were in duty bound to do so, without any appropriation having been made for our pecuniary reward. We are situated in peculiarly embarrassing circumstances, many of us being without funds, and all the sutlers, with a single exception, refusing us credit. Consequently, we are deprived of many comforts, and, indeed, of some of the necessaries of life. Such being the case, we respectfully hope that you will give this, our memorial, your earliest consideration."

Very little comment, certainly is needed on such a petition. No well-informed gentleman can question the wisdom of Col. Johnston in assuming authority to enlist and organize the battalion. It has afforded employment and subsistence to men whom the inclemency of the season and their distance from home would otherwise have rendered pensioners on military charity throughout the Winter; and its organization has contributed to the quiet, order, and discipline of the camp. It has shown discretion in selecting so excellent an officer as Col. Bee for its commander, and before the Summer, through his efforts and those of his staff, it will be in condition to render valuable service in the field. I can imagine no reason why Congress shall not immediately indorse its enlistment and organization, provide for its pay, and place its officers on the same footing in respect to emoluments and commissions as those of the volunteer regiments employed in the Mexican war.

---

[26] Cowne was elected to replace 2nd Lt. Charles H. Hamilton, who resigned soon after commissioning under Magraw to take his chances on returning to Missouri rather than spend the winter at Camp Scott. "Latest from Utah. Statement of Lieut. C. H. Hamilton," *Western Journal of Commerce* (Kansas City, Mo.), 6 February 1858.

It Will Be Much to My Credit: Marcy to New Mexico

Aside from the epic foul-weather march of the Second Dragoons, the Utah Expedition's most noteworthy display of grit was Capt. Randolph B. Marcy's perilous winter trek to New Mexico and back. Thanks to his own reports published in 1858, his 1866 book, and the work of a competent twentieth-century biographer, the broad outline of the Marcy Expedition's experiences and its commander's role are relatively well known.[27] But the names of the others who went to New Mexico with Captain Marcy on the most arduous winter march in American military history are largely unknown. Many of Marcy's anonymous veterans would go on to experience notoriety, including Pvt. William Gentles, the inappropriately named infantryman who mortally bayoneted Lakota chief Crazy Horse in 1877; Corp. Ralph Pike, whose 1859 assassination as a sergeant in Salt Lake City prompted Utah's longest-running (thirty-one-year) criminal case; Jenny Goodale, the Indian wife of a guide who not only accompanied Marcy but sacrificed her pet pony to feed the starving detachment along the Continental Divide; and Hispanic packer Mariano Medina, later the founder of Loveland, Colorado.[28]

The following material serves to introduce their story. Notwithstanding Marcy's vast experience with army exploration expeditions in the West during the prior twenty years—the reason for his selection—this material indicates that he and his troops seriously underestimated the hazards awaiting them. For example, on 20 November Marcy wrote to his daughter Nellie from Fort Bridger:

> We have a long winter before us and shall no doubt find it exceedingly dull, but if I remain here I shall read a great deal. I think however that I shall be sent with a command to New Mexico in a few days for the purpose of bringing out supplies early in the spring. If I go I shall have three officers and (100) men and I think it will be much to my credit.[29] Moreover I shall be much more comfortable there than here. I have not yet received the order but have been told that I should probably be sent.[30]

[27] Marcy, *Thirty Years of Army Life on the Border*, 224–63; Hollon, *Beyond the Cross Timbers*, 215–30.

[28] MacKinnon, "Epilogue to the Utah War," 214, 235.

[29] Marcy was overly optimistic. He was to be the only officer, and Johnston detailed to him only sixty-two other people, including forty enlisted men and twenty-two civilian employees. Recognition and the possibility of promotion were clearly on Marcy's mind; the phrase "much to my credit" also appeared in another family letter once he reached New Mexico.

[30] Marcy to Mary Ellen (Nellie) Marcy, 20 November 1857, George B. McClellan Papers.

A week later A. G. Browne provided a description of what type of soldier volunteered to accompany Marcy to New Mexico and for what reason:

> Capt. Marcy of the Fifth Infantry will start tomorrow for New-Mexico with a picked company of 35 men, 23 of whom have been furnished from the 10th Infantry, and the remainder from the 5th.[31] His object is to procure supplies of salt, and make arrangements for forwarding mules to the army in the early Spring. The trail which he will eventually strike leads to Taos. Notwithstanding the dangers to which such an expedition is exposed at this season of the year, the prospect of inactivity throughout the Winter has caused a general desire among officers and men to be attached to it. Each company of the infantry regiments was called upon to furnish a list of five men [with twenty companies, a total of 100], from which its quota was to be selected, and in one instance, that of Company A, 10th Infantry, commanded by [1st] Lieut. [Henry B.] Kelly, every private applied for a place upon the list.[32]

On 24 November Captain Marcy received his eagerly awaited orders for New Mexico.[33] On the same day—in Washington—Commissioner Denver wrote to New Mexico's superintendent of Indian Affairs to warn him of potential Mormon machinations among the territory's tribes and to suggest the services of Kit Carson. High above Utah's Spring Valley, Legion courier Philo Dibble, Jr., carved his name and the date into a cliff face while awaiting the next message linking the Mormon posts at Bridger's Butte and Echo Canyon. Dibble's was the intelligence network that would immediately detect and report to Brigham Young Marcy's departure for New Mexico.

With Rifles, Pistols, Swords, and Other Warlike Weapons: Log Cabin Indictments

On 30 December 1857 a federal grand jury composed of civilians at Eckelsville returned an indictment of treason and other offenses against Brigham Young

[31] Browne described only the number of privates selected, which was thirty-six (rather than thirty-five). He overlooks the additional presence of two sergeants and two corporals, selected equally from the Fifth and Tenth, for a total of forty enlisted men—fifteen from the former regiment and twenty-five from the latter. This imbalance may have reflected the smaller size of the Fifth (due to desertions) or a perceived qualitative difference in the troops running to the Tenth's advantage.

[32] "Late from the Utah Expedition," A. G. Browne, Jr., Dispatch (Camp Scott), 26 November 1857, *New-York Daily Tribune*, 18 January 1858.

[33] Marcy's orders provide the only known listing by name, regiment, and company of the non-commissioned officers, privates, and guides detailed to accompany him as well as the number (but not names) of packers, herders, mulemasters, and workmen who also were part of the expedition. The limitations of space preclude listing these names here. See Special Orders No. 50, Head Quarters, Army of Utah (Camp Scott), 24 November 1857, Records, U.S. House Committee on Military Affairs, National Archives.

and as many as one thousand other people, only nineteen of whom could be identified by name. A prime mover in these proceedings was not only Judge Eckels but Utah's U.S. attorney, John M. Hockaday.

Normally grand-jury proceedings are secret. As a result the very fact of this indictment, let alone the names of the accused and rationale for their indictments are largely missing from the Utah War's historiography. Several indictees had been involved in high-profile incidents such as the proclamation of martial law, the Lot Smith raid, and the capture of Maj. Joseph Taylor. Unquestionably they were included because of their roles in these affairs. But beyond these relatively few individuals, it appears that the grand jury swept in the entire First Presidency, several Legion generals, an occasional apostle, several of Brigham Young's most notorious agents, and the editor of the *Deseret News*. Inclusion of several other names is truly puzzling, as in the case of Brigham Young's brother, Phineas, and their nephew William Young.[34]

Because Albert G. Browne, Jr., was the clerk of Judge Eckels's court, he had broad access to legal records. This proximity, combined with Browne's journalistic employment, meant that New York's *Tribune* fortuitously carried accounts of the December grand-jury proceedings unavailable elsewhere, including the names of the jurors.[35]

In considering the composition and perspective of the grand jury, one needs to be mindful that judicial proceedings and jury selection had long been one of the prime issues in dispute between Utah's Mormon leadership and non-Mormon federal appointees. Usually this involved conflicts over the role of county probate courts and the frequently all-Mormon composition of their juries. The character of the federal grand jury empanelled in a log cabin at Eckelsville raises similar questions from the opposite perspective in view of the backgrounds of the sixteen jurors involved and their likely impact on objectivity.

With respect to backgrounds, jury foreman John D. ("Jack") Radford was a partner in the mercantile firm of Radford & Cabot, which operated out of the Kansas-Missouri frontier and served as sutler for the Fifth U.S. Infantry.

---

[34] Phineas and William Young may have come to the grand jury's attention not because of their involvement in an act of treason, war, or rebellion but because of their role in a quite different incident on Hams Fork in mid-September. There both Youngs, Porter Rockwell, and Lewis Robison attempted unsuccessfully to force Mormon apostates James Wadsworth and his wife to return to Salt Lake City. Browne, the clerk of Eckels's court, was well aware of this conflict and reported it to his New York readers. A. G. Browne, Jr., Dispatch, 15 November 1857, "Late from the Utah Expedition," *New-York Daily Tribune*, 18 January 1858.

[35] See "Later from the Utah Expedition . . . Opening of the Territorial Court," A. G. Browne, Jr., Dispatch, 13 December 1857, *New-York Daily Tribune*, 2 February 1858.

CIVILIANS' WINTER QUARTERS AT "ECKELSVILLE"
This David A. Burr photo shows the makeshift quarters near Fort Bridger for Utah's new federal appointees and civilian camp followers. The little community was under constant Mormon surveillance and was named for a prominent resident, Chief Justice Delana R. Eckels of Greencastle, Indiana. From the David H. and David A. Burr Collection. *Courtesy of the Division of Rare and Manuscript Collections, Carl A. Krock Library, Cornell University, Ithaca, New York.*

His firm and that of Joseph C. ("Doc") Irwin (Weston, Missouri) were greatly inconvenienced and threatened financially by the halt of their trains at Fort Bridger by Colonel Johnston. In Irwin's case, he was still doggedly seeking compensation from the government as late as 1887, as was Jim Bridger's family.[36] Anyone familiar with the backgrounds of jurors Jacob Forney, Hiram F. Morrell, Jim Bridger, and Charles Mogo would recognize that they had experienced significant conflicts with leaders of the Mormon hierarchy about

[36] "Old Mormon War Claims, Hearing on Behalf of Freighters During the Johnston Campaign," *Salt Lake Tribune*, 23 July 1887, 4/3.

whom testimony was being presented by U.S. Attorney Hockaday. That officer, in turn, had multiple bones to pick with Brigham Young over the 1856 fate of his mail business with Magraw and the Salt Lake City tannery operated with his brother Ike Hockaday.[37]

Perhaps the extreme case of likely antagonism was that of Mogo, who had fled Utah—leaving his pregnant wife, Margaret, behind—on 29 July 1857 after receiving repeated threats and a severe beating. On 1 November 1857 Mrs. Mogo, a Mormon apostate, had crossed into the Utah Expedition's snowy lines bearing the dead body of her newborn son after an arduous carriage ride from Salt Lake City. She was a captive under escort by a mounted Legion detachment and was, in effect, exchanged for a prisoner-brother of Bill Hickman.[38]

Although little or nothing is known about the background of the rest of the grand jurors, it is unlikely that any of the sixteen were Mormons. If at Camp Scott there were those who believed that turnabout was fair play, it was a volatile, dangerous behavior in the world of grand juries and capital offenses.

A. G. Browne, Jr., Dispatch, "Indictment of Mormon Leaders for High Treason," 30 December 1857, *New-York Daily Tribune*, 1 March 1858.

The Grand Jury of the District Court of the United States for this county returned into Court today the following indictment for treason, against certain Mormons who have been prominently identified with the acts of violence perpetrated thus far in the rebellion. It is to be regretted that the evidence presented to the jury did not justify the addition to the list of the name of John M. Bernhisel, the Mormon Delegate to Congress. The position in which he is placed by the revolt of his constituency, is such that great curiosity exists in camp to learn how he has demeaned himself at Washington. . . .[39]

---

[37] The likely bias of the grand jurors was discussed in 1930 by B. H. Roberts, one of the few historians to express an awareness of the 30 December 1857 indictments. Roberts, *A Comprehensive History of the Church* 4:317–18.

[38] Affidavit of Margaret H. Mogo, 16 November 1857, A. G. Browne, Jr., Dispatch (Camp Scott), 22 November 1857, "Late from the Utah Expedition . . . Affidavits Concerning Mormon Outrages," *New-York Daily Tribune*, 18 January 1858. Six weeks after his grand jury returned its indictment, Charles Mogo compiled a summary of his complaints against Brigham Young and the Mormons. See Mogo (Camp Scott) to Thomas A. Hendricks, Commissioner, U.S. Gen. Land Office, 15 February 1858, photocopy of typescript transcription in editor's possession.

[39] It is conceivable that by departing Salt Lake City at dawn on 14 September (with Captain Van Vliet) Bernhisel unwittingly escaped inclusion in the indictment by a day because of the jury's later fixation with 15 September as the crucial date in the alleged treason conspiracy.

Indictment[40]
1st Count

United States of America.
Territory of Utah.
Green River County ss.

District Court of the United States.
December Term. Eighteen Hundred and Fifty-Seven.

The Grand Jurors of the United States of America empannelled, charged, and sworn to inquire for the said United States within and for the said Territory and the body of the District and County aforesaid, upon their oath present:

That Brigham Young, Heber C. Kimball, Daniel H. Wells, John Taylor, George D. Grant, Lot Smith, Porter Rockwell, William A. Hickman, Albert Carrington, Joseph Taylor, William Stowell, Lewis Robinson [*sic*], Joshua Terry, John Harvey, Daniel Jones, Phineas Young, William Young, Robert Burton, James Ferguson, Ephraim Hanks,[41] late of the County aforesaid, yeomen, with a great multitude of persons (whose names to the Grand Jurors aforesaid are at present unknown) to the number of one thousand persons and more, being inhabitants of the said Territory and resident therein, and under the protection of the Constitution and Laws of the said United States, and owing allegiance and fidelity to the said United States, not weighing the duty of their said allegiance, but wickedly devising and intending the peace and tranquillity of the said United States to disturb and to stir, move, and excite insurrection, rebellion, and war against the said United States, on the fifteenth day of September in the Year Eighteen Hundred and Fifty Seven,[42] within the Territory, District, and County aforesaid, and within the jurisdiction of this Court, unlawfully, falsely, maliciously and traitorously did compass, imagine, and intend to raise and levy war, insurrection, and rebellion against the said United States;

---

[40] Third District Court Case Files, Utah State Archives, Salt Lake City; dispatch of Albert G. Browne, Jr., 30 December 1857, *New-York Daily Tribune*, 1 March 1858. Although Browne included much if not all of the indictment in his dispatch, the text of the following indictment is taken from the court case files in Utah as more official. It has been excerpted here to eliminate redundancies and unhelpful legal jargon. The text of Brigham Young's 15 September 1857 martial-law proclamation and General Wells's 4 October 1857 instructions to Maj. Joseph Taylor were exhibits internal to the indictment not included here because they are published in full in earlier chapters.

[41] All of these names will be familiar to readers of the preceding chapters, with the possible exception of Joshua Terry (a prominent raider with the Nauvoo Legion), John Harvey (a lieutenant in the Nauvoo Legion formerly assigned to Fort Supply and one of the men identified by Mrs. Mogo as having been in her escort from Salt Lake City), and William Young (a nephew of Brigham Young resident in Pleasant Grove).

[42] The only apparent significance of this date is its linkage to the timing of Brigham Young's martial-law proclamation, with which most of the indicted were uninvolved. If that is why this date was selected, it adds credibility to the likelihood that an earlier proclamation of martial law was *not* circulated.

and in order to fulfil and bring to effect the said traitorous compassings, maginations, and intentions of them, . . . [did] array and dispose themselves in a warlike and hostile manner against the said United States. . . . Contrary to the duty of their said allegiance and fidelity, against the form of the Act of the Congress of the said United States in such case made and provided, and against the Constitution peace and dignity of the said United States.

2nd Count.

. . . That [the accused] . . . intending the peace and tranquillity of the said United States to disturb, and to prevent the execution of the laws thereof within the said Territory, . . . to fulfil and bring to effect the said traitorous intention . . . did falsely and traitorously assemble and combine against the said United States, . . . did array and dispose themselves in a warlike and hostile manner against the said United States, . . . [and] did levy war against the said United States. . . .

3rd Count.

. . . That . . . Brigham Young . . . did issue a . . . proclamation . . . [and] William Stowell . . . did have in his possession . . . [a] treasonable communication from the said Daniel H. Wells to the said Joseph Taylor . . . levying war against the said United States, and . . . [the accused did] issue wicked, malicious, and traitorous speeches, writings and proclamations, . . . set fire to and burn commissary stores belonging to the said United States, . . . disarm divers citizens of the said United States having charge and custody of the commissary stores aforesaid, . . . steal, take, and drive away oxen, horses, and mules, belonging to the said United States, . . . and . . . oppose the march of the army of the said United States by the erection of military fortifications on a public highway, [thereby] levying war against the said United States. . . .

4th Count.

. . . That . . . an open, public, and traitorous rebellion and war against the United States of America, was and yet is prosecuted and carried on within the Territory of Utah aforesaid by . . . traitors against the said United States . . . [who] with force and arms . . . adhere to and give aid and comfort to the said enemies of the said United States, by traitorous speeches, writings, and proclamations, . . . by assembling and gathering together, armed and arrayed in a warlike manner, . . . by furnishing intelligence, provisions, and munitions of war, . . . by setting fire to and burning commissary stores belonging to the said United States, . . . by disarming divers citizens of the said United States having charge and custody of the commissary stores aforesaid, . . . by stealing, taking, and driving away oxen, horses, and mules belonging to the said United States, . . . and . . . by opposing the march of the army of the said United States by the erection of military fortifications on a public highway, adhere to and give aid and comfort to the enemies of the said United States so as aforesaid rebelling and levying war against the said United States . . .

John M. Hockaday Pros Atty

A True Bill.

J. D. Radford
Foreman

Tut, Tut, None of That Mr. Ferguson: The Captivity of Charlie Becker

If Brigham Young was well informed about activities at Camp Scott, Albert Sidney Johnston occasionally picked up information as to Mormon activities and intent. For the most part Johnston's sources were an occasional eastbound traveler who had passed through Salt Lake City or wily Native Americans seeking to benefit from both sides of the conflict. At the end of December Johnston reaped an intelligence windfall of sorts with the return from Salt Lake City of three Utah Expedition captives. The narratives of one of these former prisoners—Charles W. (Charlie) Becker, a discharged civilian teamster—appears below. This new Utah War "voice" is presented because it sheds light on benevolent Mormon treatment of a low-level, economically unrewarding, non-threatening prisoner in sharp contrast to the violent Yates captivity.

When Charlie Becker wrote a narrative of his Utah War experiences as a teamster, he was a respected pioneer rancher in his late eighties living on the arid high plains of eastern Oregon's Malheur County. Working from notes and memory while adding a dash of hyperbole, Becker generated in the early 1920s one of the more interesting and unexploited of the Utah Expedition's captivity narratives.

"The History of the Expedition against the Mormons in the Year of 1857," Narrative by Charles W. Becker, LDS Archives.

At this time [probably in late October 1857] an incident happened which took me to Salt Lake City ahead of our expedition, rather against my will. It was my turn to be on the afternoon guard, on the outside limits of the herd, about two miles from the main camp. We were waiting our turn to be moved to winter quarters at Fort Bridger. Along toward evening I noticed a party, consisting of at least a dozen men, dismounted, hiding behind some sand rock cliffs. They seemed to be watching our camp, but thinking it some of our own scouts I paid no more attention to them. . . . They told me they were a Mormon raiding party, and that they intended to drive off a bunch of our cattle, that I must go with them, that there might be no alarm spread. . . . Darkness was coming on, with no help yet in sight. I had no bedding, and the night promised to be extremely cold. I concluded to surrender on as favorable terms as I could get. The Captain of the enemy party, whom I learned later was Captain Warren Snow, of Sante Pete, stepped out and pledged himself to protect me, a pledge which was faithfully kept, and then some.[43] He promised that I would be turned over to the headquarters of the Mormon Legion, as they call their Army. It was under command of General Wells, father of ex-governor Wells, whose acquaintance I made thru my lamented friend Fred Kiesel, as I soon found out was located on Bear River.[44]

As I stepped out they all came up and shook hands with me, as though I had been a long lost brother just found. Seeing that I was barefooted inside of my shoes a young Mormon reached back under his buckskin coat and handed me a pair of heavy home-knitted new woolen socks. I refused at first, but he insisted, saying that I would have a long night's ride, and that my feet would freeze without socks. I thanked him and put them on, thinking that there was surely one good Mormon. . . . Of course they relieved me of my rifle and revolver, telling me that I should be paid for them before they sent me back.

We rode until about midnight before we reached their camp, which consisted of a covered wagon, drawn by four mules. It was a bitter cold night. We were given something to eat by the two Mormons who were in charge of the wagon. Then they put me in the covered wagon and we started out again. Had it not been for those warm, woolen socks, and a live sheep the Mormons carried along in their wagon, which I drew down over me, I would have suffered severely. . . . We traveled that afternoon, and toward evening got into headquarters camp, in the sheltered valley on Bear River of the Nauvoo legion, under the command of General in Chief H. Wells. General Wells got up and shook hands with me, spoke to me in a most kindly way, assuring me that I was perfectly safe. His own cook was then ordered to prepare me something to eat.

After supper, while sitting around a big log fire, they asked many questions concerning Johnson's Army. I would not answer all their questions. James Ferguson, adjutant General of Wells' Staff, a hot headed, impulsive Irishman, spoke up very abruptly and said "Answer our questions more directly, or we'll find a way of forcing you to do so". General Wells quickly answered, "Tut, tut, none of that Mr. Ferguson". Then General Wells told me to answer the questions I thought best, and that no harm should come to me.

[43] Warren Stone Snow of Manti, Sanpete County, was a Nauvoo Legion major at the time of the Utah War; he later became bishop of Ephraim, Utah.

[44] Heber Manning Wells served as Utah's first state governor beginning in 1896. If Becker first met Fred J. Kiesel during the Utah War, the latter was then about eighteen years old. Kiesel, from Ogden, served on the constitutional committee just prior to Utah statehood, and became a state senator. He died in 1919.

In the course of a few days General Wells got information through his own scouts that Johnson's Army had settled down in their winter quarters, and would make no more attempts to reach Salt Lake City. . . .

A number of teams came in from Salt Lake City, loaded with supplies for Wells' [new] camp [in Echo Canyon]. A man named Charles Decker was with one of these parties. He took a friendly interest in me, and told me if I would promise him not to attempt an escape, that he would try to get permission from General Wells to take me home to his family. There I could do the chores and make myself useful around his place while he was away from home. I readily promised, escape being impossible anyway, and Wells gave permission. I was to be delivered later at headquarters in Salt Lake City. He told me confidentially, later, that I would be better and safer living with his family, about six miles from Salt Lake City.[45]

On arrival at Mr. Decker's farm I found a very nice little place, well equipped with comfortable buildings, I learned that Mr. Decker was a son-in-law of Brigham Young, having married his oldest daughter, Lena, a most beautiful and highly intelligent woman. They had three beautiful children, who were as good as they were beautiful. I found there another younger woman, also a wife of Mr. Decker.[46] Polygamy was in common practice at that time. These two women seemed to be getting along splendidly, like an older and a younger sister.[47] They both treated me with consideration while I remained with them, and I tried to make myself as useful to them as I could. There was also a young lady at the place, doing the housework, a most estimable young woman, who came from England as a Mormon convert. She told me many things about the inner and private life of the Mormons. She had been married to a young Mormon, but when he brought his second wife in through the front door she went out the back door. . . .

I had been living with this most lovable Mormon family about six weeks when one evening Mr. Decker came home from Salt Lake City and said that he had some bad news for us, that he had received orders from Wells to bring me in, that I was to be sent with some other prisoners back to Fort Bridger.

While staying at the place I met Brigham Young several times, as he came to visit Lena. We all ate dinner together as a family, and he asking many questions concerning Johnson's Army. I formed rather a favorable opinion of him. I was sorry to leave those good people, and they assured me that they were sorry to have me go.

---

[45] Decker may have been mindful of the October and November fate of Richard Yates and the Aiken party without a Mormon protector.

[46] Charles Franklin Decker reportedly crossed the plains at least fifty times in the capacity of mail carrier and express rider, as well as in assisting emigrant companies. His first wife was Vilate Young, Brigham Young's second eldest daughter; the couple had four children at the time Becker was captured. Decker had married his second wife, Margaret Jane Maxfield, earlier in 1857.

[47] Hence the Mormon term "sister wives" to describe the relationship between multiple women married to the same husband. Some such relationships were as Becker describes, while others were less congenial.

When we reached Salt Lake, I was guarded in a wooden building on Main Street, called Steptoe's Barracks, with two other prisoners who were being sent back.[48] We were furnished with an old cook stove and plenty of provisions, such as vegetables, beef and flour, the best to be had in those days. They put a guard over us with an old musket, a good natured Dan[e]. One night while the Mormons were having a great gathering, we were rather lonesome and sought to have a little amusement of our own. We started a game of blind man's buff. We got our guard to deposit his gun behind the door and play with us, and we managed to keep the good Danish man blindfolded most of the time, while he fell over benches and stools we put into his way. This made a great racket, which could be heard on Main Street below, and soon we heard someone rushing up the stairs. It was Bill Hickman, Provost-Marshal of Salt Lake City. He found our guard standing in the middle of the room, blindfolded, and at once ordered him under arrest and took him away.[49] Then he brought a monstrous big Swede, a very surly fellow, who wouldn't make up with us. . . .

The morning we started [back] General Wells came over and talked to us in a very friendly manner and gave me a package of papers to deliver to Col. Sidney Johnson. . . . On our arrival at the Fort I proceeded at once to Col. Johnson's tent and delivered my package of papers. He treated me very kindly and ordered the Commissary sargeant to give me what clothing I needed. also medicine for my frosted feet, and anything else I was in need of, all which orders the good sargeant he generously fulfilled. Of course Col. Johnson asked me many questions regarding how the Mormons treated us while they kept us prisoners and what preparations they had made to oppose his army. Of course, all of which I gladly answered to the best of my ability. The Colonel asked me many questions regarding my experiences, the treatment we received, and the arrangements they had made to oppose his Army. He also expressed his satisfaction that we had been so kindly treated.[50]

---

[48] "Steptoe's Barracks" is an unfamiliar Salt Lake City landmark, but it probably was a building rented during the winter of 1854–55 to quarter the U.S. troops of Brevet Lt. Col. E. J. Steptoe before they moved on to California.

[49] This incident may be related to the fact that on Christmas Day Legion adjutant general Stout "Attended a Court martial as Judge Advocate where John Redman & Isaac Rowley were tried for mal-conduct as guards over the U.S. prisoners. The charges were sustained and they & the officer of the guard repremanded." Entry for 25 December 1857, Brooks, ed., *On the Mormon Frontier* 2:649.

[50] Typescript versions of some or all of Becker's multi-part narrative, prepared for publication but never printed, are in several repositories: Oregon Historical Society (Portland), the library of Utah State University (Logan), and in Salt Lake City, at Utah State Historical Society and LDS Church Archives. The material reproduced here was prepared from the copy at LDS Archives. An unknown editor indicated that Becker prepared this material to be read at meetings of the Malheur County Pioneer Reunions before his death in 1925 at age 90. Charlie Becker claimed to have been a Pony Express rider during 1860–61, an experience that has not been verified.

Chapter 18

"To Avert a War of Extermination" Converging Destinies of Kane, Buchanan, and Young

He is full of courage, and if his judgment is correct, he may be able to avert a war of extermination against a poor deluded race.

—James C. Van Dyke's description of Thomas L. Kane to President Buchanan, 9 December 1857

With the arrival of December 1857 James Buchanan faced the return of Congress, absent from Washington since early March. On 8 December a messenger hand-carried Buchanan's constitutionally required annual message to Congress—what today is called a State of the Union address. Incredibly, this document contained Buchanan's first public explanation of his reasons for intervening in Utah six months earlier.[1]

With Congress already in an investigatory mode, the Utah portion of the message was a mixture of two thrusts: justifications, echoing the accusations of Judges Kinney and Drummond as well as those of other federal appointees; and indignation, spawned by the recent shock of Lot Smith's raid and Brigham

[1] By today's standards this silence is easily interpreted as weak presidential communications skills. But historian David Herbert Donald argues that in the nineteenth century there was "the traditional view that the President, once elected, had no direct dealings with the public. His job was to administer the government and to report his actions and wishes to the Congress. Presidents rarely left the capital city, except for brief vacations; they almost never made public addresses; and they maintained, in theory, a sublime indifference to public opinion and political pressures." Nonetheless, when there was an issue of great importance to Buchanan, he found a way to take his case to the public. An example, in contrast to his long silence over Utah, is his nationally published 15 August 1857 letter to leading citizens of New Haven, Connecticut, rebutting their criticism of the administration's Kansas policy. Donald, *Lincoln*, 440.

Young's proclamation of martial law. The message was vintage Buchanan: lawyerly and careful in its construction of a "case" against Brigham Young, yet ambiguous on such key issues as whether Utah was indeed in a state of rebellion. The message was wholly silent on news of the Mountain Meadows massacre, already the catalyst for a public uproar in California, but not the focus of significant indignation on the Atlantic Coast. Secretary Floyd's own annual report left no doubt that he believed Utah to be in rebellion. Neither Buchanan nor Floyd signaled future actions remotely resembling negotiations or conciliation efforts.

Brigham Young's annual message, read by James Ferguson to Utah's legislative assembly in Salt Lake City on 15 December, stood in stark contrast to these federal documents in terms of tone, focus, and perspective. The subjects that Young chose to ignore were even more startling than those that he addressed.

Also returning to Washington in December was Thomas L. Kane, the Latter-day Saints' oldest and most influential non-Mormon friend. This time Buchanan's political protégé James C. Van Dyke accompanied Kane. There, in a White House session immediately after Christmas, the three men held discussions that led to Kane's year-end decision to go to Utah. As discussed in a succeeding volume, Kane's would be a high-stakes mission with enormous impact on resolution of the Mormon-federal conflict. In sharp contrast to this scene of holiday political machinations at a bachelor-president's lonely White House is the account of Brigham Young's pastoral remarks to the large, complex family gathered about him on Christmas Day 1857.

Following the holiday, President Young turned to the unsettling intelligence reports arriving in his office from Mormon travelers in an aroused southern California. Concurrently Kane resigned his only source of livelihood, a clerkship in his father's Philadelphia's federal district court. During this post-Christmas period Kane also attempted to reconcile his skeptical wife, parents, and siblings to his abrupt, highly disruptive departure for an uncertain mission with questionable outcome and an unknown timetable. For Kane it was a quasi-messianic mission, a highly personal attempt at conflict resolution while proving, if not establishing, his own worth. Messrs. Buchanan and Van Dyke spent the closing days of 1857 crafting four letters for Kane to take west—three from Buchanan to Kane and one from Van Dyke introducing Kane to Utah's U.S. attorney, John M. Hockaday. To Kane's disappointment

Buchanan and Van Dyke designed these letters to be helpful but without committing the administration to any responsibility or substantive support for his mission. Fundamentally, they were merely expressions of good wishes.

Unknown to Kane as he left Philadelphia on his long journey on 4 January 1858, he also carried in his small trunk a fifth letter: a highly pessimistic admonition from his father, Judge John K. Kane. Here was a message in stark contrast to the type of patriarchal blessing that Mormon men typically received before embarking on such a mission, or for that matter the one Brigham Young had received on Christmas Day from his brother. This was to be the last word Thomas L. Kane would ever have from his revered father, James Buchanan's Democratic Party intimate.

His Power Has Been, Therefore, Absolute: Explaining Utah

The thrust of Buchanan's message to Congress was hardly the Mormon problem. It was a subject in an address largely unexamined by Utah War historians to which he allocated only five lawyerly paragraphs, or 4 percent of the total address.

Buchanan, "First Annual Message to Congress," 8 December 1857, Moore, Ed., *The Works of James Buchanan*, 10:129–63.

Whilst Governor Young has been both governor and superintendent of Indian affairs throughout this period [since 1850], he has been at the same time the head of the church called the Latter-Day Saints, and professes to govern its members and dispose of their property by direct inspiration and authority from the Almighty. His power has been, therefore, absolute over both church and State.

The people of Utah, almost exclusively, belong to this church, and believing with a fanatical spirit that he is governor of the Territory by divine appointment, they obey his commands as if these were direct revelations from Heaven. If, therefore, he chooses that his government shall come into collision with the government of the United States, the members of the Mormon church will yield implicit obedience to his will. Unfortunately, existing facts leave but little doubt that such is his determination. Without entering upon a minute history of occurrences, it is sufficient to say that all the officers of the United States, judicial and executive, with the single exception of two Indian agents, have found it necessary for their own personal safety to withdraw from the Territory, and there no longer remains any government in Utah but the des-

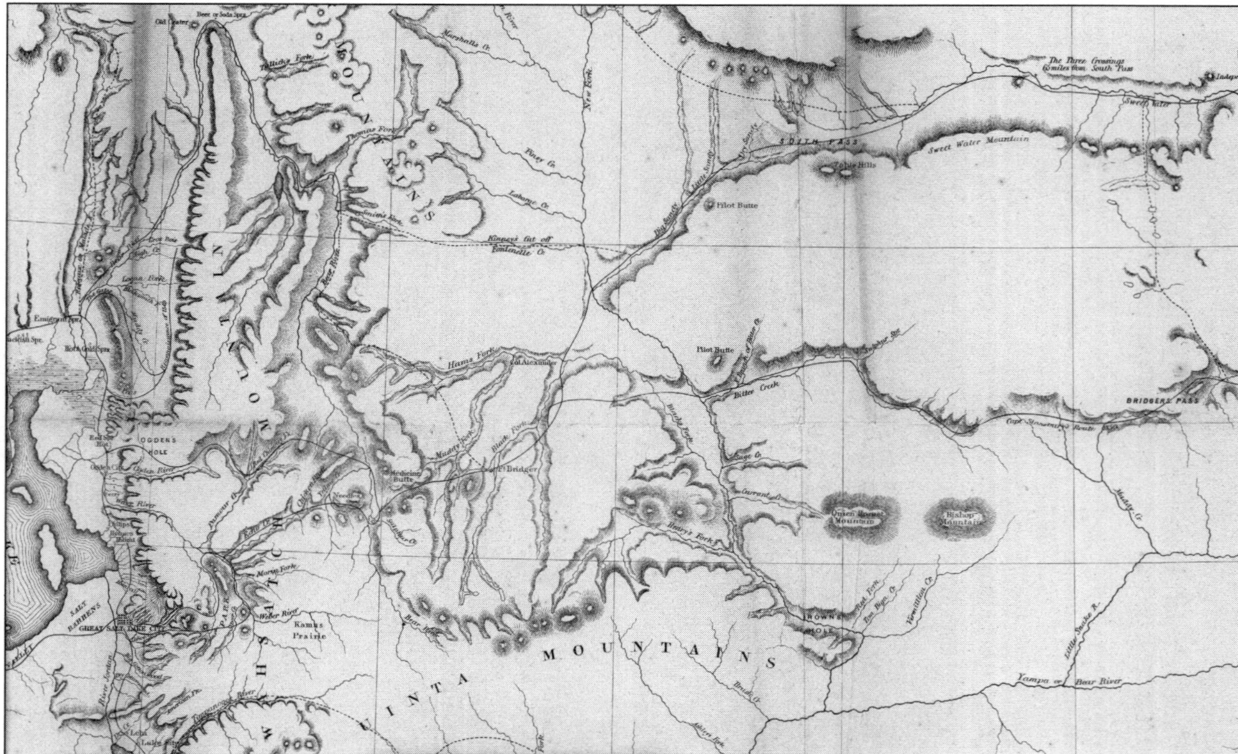

"Sketch of the Country Between
South Pass & The Great Salt Lake," 1857 (portion)

Based on the October reports of Alexander and Johnston, this map marks Alexander's "Camp Winfield" at the juncture of Hams and Blacks Fork. No indication is made of plans to go into winter quarters at Fort Bridger, thus reflecting an incomplete understanding in Washington of the Utah Expedition's situation when Buchanan and Floyd finalized their annual reports in December 1857. From "Report of the Secretary of War, 1857," U.S. Senate Exec. Doc. 11, 35th Cong., 1st Sess., Serial 920. *Courtesy of Noel Carmack, Merrill-Cazier Library, Utah State University.*

potism of Brigham Young.[2] This being the condition of affairs in the Territory, I could not mistake the path of duty. As Chief Executive Magistrate, I was bound to restore the supremacy of the Constitution and laws within its limits. In order to effect this purpose, I appointed a new governor and other federal officers for Utah, and sent with them a military force for their protection, and to aid as a *posse comitatus,* in case of need, in the execution of the laws.

With the religious opinions of the Mormons, as long as they remained mere opinions, however deplorable in themselves and revolting to the moral and religious sentiments of all Christendom, I had no right to interfere. . . . My instructions to Governor Cumming have therefore been framed in strict accordance with these principles. At their date a hope was indulged that no necessity might exist for employing the military in restoring and maintaining the authority of the law; but this hope has now vanished. Governor Young has, by proclamation, declared his determination to maintain his power by force, and has already committed acts of hostility against the United States. Unless he should retrace his steps the Territory of Utah will be in a state of open rebellion. . . .[3]

There is reason to believe that Governor Young has long contemplated this result.[4] . . . He has, therefore, for several years, in order to maintain his independence, been industriously employed in collecting and fabricating arms and munitions of war, and in disciplining the Mormons for military service.[5] As superintendent of Indian affairs he has had an opportunity of tampering with the Indian tribes, and exciting their hostile feelings against the United States. This, according to our information, he has accomplished in regard to some of these tribes, while others have remained true to their allegiance, and have communicated his intrigues to our Indian agents.[6] He has laid in a store of provisions for three years, which, in case of necessity, as he informed Major Van Vliet, he will conceal, "and then take to the mountains, and bid defiance to all the powers of the government."[7]

A great part of all this may be idle boasting; but yet no wise government

[2] The Indian agents were Dr. Garland Hurt and George Armstrong, a Mormon.

[3] The all-important matter of whether a rebellion against federal authority did or did not exist in Utah Territory is muddied in this address. Here the president uses substantively different—and conflicting—phrasing in successive paragraphs, an ambiguity at odds with the direct assertions in Secretary Floyd's accompanying report as well as the army's internal communications and Governor Cumming's 21 November proclamation. In his 1866 book the president described Utah as being in "actual rebellion"; Buchanan, *Mr. Buchanan's Administration on the Eve of the Rebellion,* 35.

[4] Buchanan's repeated use of the title governor at this late date presents another ambiguity. Buchanan's own treasury department considered Brigham Young's governorship to have ended 21 November 1857—the date of Governor Cumming's formal assumption of office—and terminated his salary accordingly. General Harney had abandoned use of "governor" for Young in July.

[5] See Chapter 10 for discussion of the extensive Mormon quest for arms and munitions.

[6] This section reflects the inputs of Secretary Thompson, Commissioner Denver, and Indian Agent Twiss.

[7] Stewart Van Vliet was then a captain and was not promoted to major until 3 August 1861. Heitman, *Historical Register,* 1:984.

> will lightly estimate the efforts which may be inspired by such frenzied fanaticism as exists among the Mormons of Utah. This is the first rebellion which has existed in our Territories; and humanity itself requires that we should put it down in such a manner that it shall be the last.[8] To trifle with it would be to encourage it and to render it formidable. We ought to go there with such an imposing force as to convince these deluded people that resistance would be vain, and thus spare the effusion of blood. We can in this manner best convince them that we are their friends, not their enemies. In order to accomplish this object, it will be necessary, according to the estimate of the War Department, to raise four additional regiments; and this I earnestly recommend to Congress.[9] At the present moment of depression in the revenues of the country I am sorry to be obliged to recommend such a measure;[10] but I feel confident of the support of Congress, cost what it may, in suppressing the insurrection and in restoring and maintaining the sovereignty of the Constitution and laws over the Territory of Utah.

Accompanying Buchanan's message were the annual reports of Secretary of War Floyd and Secretary of State Cass—the cabinet officers with jurisdiction over the army and territorial affairs—as well as the comparable report of General Scott, the army's general in chief. Consistent with the extent to which Cass and Scott had been subordinated to Buchanan and Floyd, respectively, neither officer mentioned Utah or Mormons in his report, a remarkable omission, especially for General Scott. Secretary Floyd's report differed from Buchanan's. It provided more operationally oriented comments; it explicitly linked Kansas and Utah; and it ranged into the political as well as social arena. Floyd, as did Brigham Young in his letters of 12 September, described Utah's greatest threat as its strategic position astride America's transcontinental emigration routes:

Floyd, Annual Report, 5 December 1857, Senate Ex. Doc. 11, 6–9.

> From the first hour they fixed themselves in that remote and almost inaccessible region of our Territory, from which they are now sending defiance to the sovereign power, their whole plan has been to prepare for a successful secession from the authority of the United States and a permanent establishment of their own. . . .
>
> But, unfortunately for these views [of governmental forbearance], their set-

[8] This sentence is Buchanan's most famous utterance about the Utah War—the federal counterpart, in the conflict's folklore, to Lot Smith's "for His sake" assertion two months earlier.

[9] Buchanan's choice of words—leaving ambiguous whether "additional" regiments meant regulars or volunteers—touched off a hopeful flurry of military organizing in virtually every state of the union. At that time the regular U.S. Army consisted of twenty regiments. Floyd's annual report recommended five additional regiments, including one for Indian warfare in Texas.

[10] A reference to the Financial Panic of 1857; see Chapter 16.

> tlements lie in the great pathway which leads from our Atlantic States to the new and flourishing communities growing up upon our Pacific seaboard. They stand a lion in the path;[11] not only themselves defying the military and civil authorities of the government, but encouraging, if not exciting, the nomad savages who roam over the vast unoccupied regions of the continent to the pillage and massacre of peaceful and helpless emigrant families traversing the solitudes of the wilderness. The rapid settlement of our Pacific possessions; the rights in those regions of emigrants unable to afford the heavy expenses of transit by water and the isthmus; the facility and safety of military, commercial, political, and social intercommunication between our eastern and western populations and States, all depend upon the prompt, absolute, and thorough removal of a hostile power besetting this path midway of its route, at a point where succor and provisions should always be found, rather than obstruction, privation, and outrage. However anxiously the government might desire to avoid a collision with this or any other community of people under its jurisdiction, yet it is not possible for it to postpone the duty of reducing to subordination a rebellious fraternity besetting one of the most important avenues of communication traversing its domain, and not only themselves defying its authority, but stimulating the irresponsible savages hovering along the highway to acts of violence and indiscriminately upon all ages, sexes, and conditions of wayfarers.

Such were the only explanations offered by the Buchanan administration publicly during 1857 as its reasons for intervening militarily in Utah Territory. In early 1858, subsequent to transmittal of his annual message, the president provided raw reports and correspondence relating to Utah affairs as requested by Congress, but did so on a highly incomplete basis. No additional narrative account of logic, rationale, or decision making was forthcoming.[12]

He Is Full of Courage: Van Dyke and Kane's December White House Meeting

The day after President Buchanan forwarded his message to Congress, his closest Philadelphia political advisor, James C. Van Dyke, moved to refocus Buchanan on resolution of the Mormon problem through Thomas L. Kane.

[11] Interestingly, this was the phrase used in 1850 by General Scott, then acting secretary of war, to describe the U.S. Army's role in blocking an anticipated "invasion" of the embryonic New Mexico Territory by Texas state troops in a border dispute.

[12] After the active phase of the Utah War, brief comments on this subject appeared in Buchanan, "Second Annual Message of the President," 6 December 1858, Moore, ed., *The Works of James Buchanan*, 10:242–43. In his post-presidential defense of his administration, Buchanan dealt with Utah matters in summary fashion but only through excerpts from his first and second annual messages; Buchanan, *Mr. Buchanan's Administration*, 233–39.

Van Dyke's efforts came just as Congress began to shift aggressively into an investigatory, partisan posture vis à vis the administration's Utah policy.

As discussed earlier, Van Dyke was largely invisible as a presidential advisor, but his influence was substantial if not supreme behind the scenes.[13] It was Van Dyke who had urged the president to see John M. Hockaday on the state of affairs in Utah during the previous April, and it was he who would broker Kane's urgent trip to Washington at Christmas time. As a person close to both Hockaday and Kane as well as to Buchanan, Van Dyke was one of the few senior Utah War protagonists who heard several sides of the story, if not the Mormon perspective, directly.

It was against this background that Van Dyke wrote to President Buchanan on 9 December 1857 to describe Kane's current thinking about Mormon affairs. He proposed a White House meeting to explore Kane's desire to serve as an independent intermediary.[14]

Van Dyke to Buchanan, 9 December 1857,
James Buchanan Papers, Historical Society of Pennsylvania.

It has been my intention to visit Washington before this, but I have found it impossible, and it is now uncertain when I shall be able to get down. If there I had intended to mention to you the wishes of Col. Thos L. Kane in relation to the condition of Mormon affairs. . . . Col. Kane from his long association with that people, has much influence with the Mormons, and especially with their chief. He thinks he can do much to accomplish an amicable peace between them and the United States. He is willing to make an expedition to Salt Lake this winter, even at his own expense, if hostilities have not advanced to such a point as would render useless any efforts on his part. He has conversed with me much, on this subject, and my conclusion from all he has said has been, that it would not be an unprofitable thing if you would have a consultation with him, and hear his views. He does not wish to annoy you, unless you desire to see him. Would you have any objection in expressing in a private note to me a desire to see him, which note I might show him, but not to be used, or in writing to him.[15] He is full of courage, and if his judgment is correct, he may

---

[13] In arguing Van Dyke's influence while obscure, I am mindful of Alex Beam's comment that "[i]t is risky for a writer to assert the importance of someone unknown to history, because the contrary case already exists." Beam, *New York Times Book Review*, 16 June 2002, 14.

[14] Historian Richard D. Poll has speculated without documentary support that Kane rather than Van Dyke might have been the real author of this letter based on its tone. Poll, "Thomas L. Kane and the Utah War," 112–35.

[15] This convoluted communications procedure reflected the working methodologies of the Buchanan administration as well as a likely desire to limit their political liabilities from the escalating Mormon controversy. It is unknown whether Buchanan responded to Van Dyke's request for such a note.

be able to avert a war of extermination against a poor deluded race. He expected me to speak to you when I came to Washington, but he does not know that I have written, nor will I tell him I have done so, unless my suggestion, that you express a willingness to see him, meets your views.

Van Dyke's letter to Buchanan did not produce results until Christmas. In the meantime, Kane had taken the initiative to consult Delegate Bernhisel. According to Kane, they met in Pennsylvania before Congress convened on 7 December:

> The month of December was on us when I wrote far and wide letters to a timid Bernheisel [*sic*] who received one of them at a place in Perry County where he was lying perdu.[16] He came down to see me in the sick room which I then occupied and confessed to me the worst which I had reason to fear with respect to the designs of the Mormons. News had been received at Washington of a character calculated to excite grave apprehensions with respect to the safety of our troops. He confirmed the worst of it. ~~He~~ I asked ~~me~~ him on the score of my old friendship for his people to collect for me all the authentic information which he could lay hands on. He did so and imparted it to me most freely.[17]

Slightly later, on the same day that Van Dyke wrote to President Buchanan to stimulate a visit from Kane, Bernhisel wrote to Kane to solicit arguments that the delegate might use in defending Utah. Either because he feared mail monitoring or because he intended to hand the text of Kane's arguments to President Buchanan, Bernhisel made an unusual request—Kane should provide this material in someone else's handwriting. Significantly, Bernhisel refers here to Kane's personal "anxieties and troubles," allusions consistent with Kane's own account of their earlier having met in his "sick room."[18]

A week after making this request of Kane, Bernhisel reported to Brigham Young on the Washington scene. Reflecting his own as well as President Young's concern over the privacy of sensitive messages passing through the U.S. mails, Bernhisel confined his main message to a single, cryptic, disconnected sentence buried in the middle of the letter: "Colonel K[ane] is still our friend."[19]

---

[16] Kane's English-French phrase "lying perdu" could be interpreted to mean "lying low." This reference to what Kane viewed as Bernhisel's timidity presumably runs to his puzzling avoidance of Buchanan in late March and November–December 1857 when it was clear that the president was unhappy with Utah.

[17] Kane, "Concerning the Mormons and Pres. Buchanan."

[18] Bernhisel to Kane, 9 December 1857, Kane Papers, Stanford University Libraries.

[19] Bernhisel to Young, 17 December 1857, LDS Archives.

Poisoned Fangs So Deeply Buried: Young's Annual Message

Although in the eyes of the U.S. government Brigham Young was no longer in office, he nonetheless sent a gubernatorial address of the annual type to Utah's legislative assembly on 15 December. It was a message quite different than President Buchanan's. Essentially it mixed the mundane with a prolix recitation of Utah's colonial treatment. In the process Young omitted all reference to such highly relevant events as the appointment of his successor, mobilization of the Nauvoo Legion, the Mountain Meadows massacre, and his proclamation of martial law. The presence of the Utah Expedition, then in winter quarters within the territorial borders, was treated as a mere rumor. Young dismissed the policies of the Buchanan administration as "treasonous"—interesting phrasing in view of the fact that he was then the target of a federal grand jury contemplating treason indictments near Fort Bridger. Young's was a truly extraordinary address that contained his most extensive published comments on the process by which the Utah War started.[20]

Governor's Message to the Utah Legislative Assembly, 15 December 1857, *Deseret News*, 23 December 1857, 3/1–4, 4/1–4, 5/1–3.

It is a matter of deep regret that officers of a Government, . . . have become so sunken in degradation. . . . Reckless office-holders and office-seekers have their poisoned fangs so deeply buried in the vitals of the body politic and are so thoroughly organized and drilled in the defence and attack of the spoils . . . that it is a discouraging task to attempt arresting the turbid current of official corruption. . . .

The members and officers of the last Legislative Assembly, familiar with the evils visited upon the innocent by the miserably bad conduct of certain officials heretofore sent here by Government . . . respectfully memorialized the President and Senate to appoint officers for Utah in accordance with an accompanying list containing the names of persons who were her first choice for the offices placed opposite those names, but if that selection did not meet with approval, they were solicited to make the appointments from a list containing other and a larger number of names of residents who were also the choice of the people, and if that selection was also rejected, to appoint from any part of the Union, with the simple request, in such event, that the

[20] See also Browne, dispatch of 4 January 1858, "The Mormon Legislature—Brigham Young's Message," *New-York Daily Tribune*, 1 March 1858.

appointees be good men.[21] In this matter of appointment of officers, what more rights could the most tyrannical in a Republican Government ask a Territory to waive? Yet up to this date no official information concerning the action, if any, taken upon that memorial has ever reached us.

Time glided by, and travelers and newspapers began to confirm the rumor that the present Executive and a part of his Cabinet had yielded to the rabid clamor raised against Utah by lying editors, corrupt demagogues, heartless office hunters and the ignorant rabble, incited by numbers of the hireling clergy, and were about to send an army to Utah with the sole and avowed purpose, as published in almost every newspaper, of compelling American citizens, peacefully, loyally and lawfully occupying American soil, to forego the dearest Constitutional rights, to abandon their religion, to wallow in the mire and worship at the shrine of modern civilization and Christianity, or be expelled from the country, or exterminated. . . .

[I]t must needs be that President Buchanan, if he has ordered an army to Utah as reported, for he has not officially notified me of such a movement by his order, has at length succumbed, either of choice or through being overcome, to the cruel and nefarious counsels of those enemies, and is endeavoring to carry out a usurpation of power which of right belongs only to the people, by appointing civil officers known to be justly objectionable to freemen and sending a so-called army under mere color of law to force those officers upon us at the point of the bayonet, and to form a nucleus for the collection and protection of every gambler, cut throat, whoremaster and scoundrel who may chose to follow in their train. . . . [W]hat were the legitimate inferences to be drawn from the rumors that the President had sent a batch of officials with an army to operate as their posse? That he had willfully made the official appointments for Utah from a class other than good men, and placed himself, where tyrants often are, in the position of levying war against the very Nation whose choice had made him its chief executive officer. . . .

No one has denied or wishes to deny the right of the Government to send its troops when, where and as it pleases, so it is but done clearly within the authorities and limitations of the Constitution, and for the safety and welfare of the people; but when it sends them clearly without the pale of those authorities and limitations, unconstitutionally to oppress the people, as is the case in the so-called army sent to Utah, it commits a treason against itself which commands the resistance of all good men, or freedom will depart our Nation. . . . That the President and the counselors, aiders and abettors of the present treasonable crusade against the peace and rights of a Territory of the United States, may reconsider their course and retrace their steps is earnestly to be desired.

[21] This paragraph is another reflection of Brigham Young's belief—originated by Bernhisel—that the legislative assembly's 6 January 1857 memorial and petition—suppressed upon receipt by Buchanan—were catalysts for Buchanan's decision to intervene in Utah.

To Exterminate or Drive Us from the Mountains: Pacific Coast Fury

As Apostle Ezra Taft Benson returned to Utah from the British Mission during the fall, he encountered a wide range of anti-Mormon attitudes and plans during his travels through New York, Panama, and California. He reported what he observed to Brigham Young privately from San Pedro, California, on 5 December, noting that "The hornets seem to be raging & all hell is ready to boil over. . . . I am informed by a Gentleman on board the Boat that the Government intends to have Ten thousand troops on the march for Utah the Southern Rout[e] within 3 months time & another ~~will~~ company will approach the Territory on the North."[22] Seven weeks later Benson spoke to thousands of attendees at Sunday services in Salt Lake City. In his tabernacle discourse Apostle Benson described what he had seen and heard as preparations for a war of extermination filled with anticipated scenes of execution:

> They have all sworn, old Harney included, that they will not give sleep to their eyes nor slumber to their eyelids until they have destroyed the "Mormons." They design in their hearts to blot "Mormonism" out of existence. . . . The halters are already made which they design shall hang the Governor, the members of the Legislative Assembly, and every faithful Elder in the Church; for they feel determined to swing you up between the heavens and the earth. We understand their plays and their schemes, for we have been in their midst.[23]

On a more personal level, Mormon missionary William M. Wall of Provo provided a report even more alarming than Apostle Benson's. Wall had left his home in Provo on 13 May 1856 and returned with a group of Australian converts in December 1857 by way of an action-packed loop that included Carson Valley, San Francisco, Tahiti, Australia, San Pedro, and San Bernardino. Wall arrived in southern California just ahead of Benson in the immediate aftermath of Mountain Meadows. The furor he encountered there was a preview of what Howard Egan and Thomas L. Kane would later face. On 11 December 1857, after crossing the southern desert and journeying to Salt Lake City, Wall reported directly to Brigham Young and received his blessing. The next day he appeared in George A. Smith's Historian's Office to dictate a long, vivid account of his adventures, only a small portion of which

[22] Benson to Young, 5 December 1857, LDS Archives; a very brief description of this letter appeared in *Deseret News*, 6 January 1858, 349/1. This multi-pronged thrust was fundamentally Gen. P. F. Smith's advice to Secretary Floyd of a few weeks earlier.

[23] Tabernacle Discourse, Ezra T. Benson, 24 January 1858, *Journal of Discourses*, 6:177–84.

appears here. Although he was not a member of President Young's inner circle, Wall's narrative—virtually unknown to historians—provides a glimpse of one of Mormonism's cooler, more resourceful frontiersmen.

Wall, Statement, 12 December 1857, Salt Lake City, History of Brigham Young, LDS Archives.

I arrived at the [Los] Angelos at [on 12 October 1857] . . . I soon discovered that there was great excitement in the town against the Mormons, on account of a company being massacred by the Indians, which they laid to the Mormons. Mr. Chatman, Quartus S. Sparks, Dr. Andrews and many other apostates, whose faces I knew, but could not call by name, gathered around me and threatened to hang me; they seemed to be very much excited.[24] I hear Dr. Andrews say, that he would sooner see Gov. Young's heart's blood run, than to see cold spring water when he was dry. They threatened most furiously to hang me, and gathered round me, about 25 of them; they finally drew off from me a little, and I called for my room and went to bed early in the evening. About 10 o'clock at night there came a company and knocked at the door and asked if William M. Wall was in there. I told them he was. They said they had some business with him and wished him to open the door. I told them it was after my business hours and I would wait on them in the morning. They then said there was no use in any of my damned pass-running, they had got to hang me and were going to do it. . . . I told the mob that I should not unlock the door, but they could kick it down if they wished, as it was very shaky, but there was one thing certain the man that came in first I should kill. . . . [In the morning] . . . [I] became satisfied that they would kill me, and bore them a faithful testimony of the truth of the Gospel, of Joseph being Prophet, and also of the Prophet Brigham. . . . I told them there was one little particular I wished to impress upon their minds, and that was that some of them had got to die in the operation . . . they stepped back a little and I got into my carriage and rode towards San Bernardino. . . .

I was threatened considerably while in San Bernardino, by Jerome Benson and others.[25] . . . I had at that time a splendid double barrelled shot gun, three revolvers, a good bowie knife, and a legging knife all in sight; they looked very savage at me, but said nothing. . . .

We travelled slowly, and on the 10th or 11th [of November] fell in with [U.S.

[24] The multiple feuds, legal actions, and even assaults in which Charles Chapman, Quartus S. Sparks, Woodville M. Andrews, and their supporters participated are described throughout Lyman, *San Bernardino*. Chapman had signed the 16 November 1857 petition of San Bernardino non-Mormons to General Clarke detailing Mormon disloyalty.

[25] Benson, a Mormon apostate, had become embroiled in a vicious land dispute with the Mormon leadership at San Bernardino in early 1857. His heavily fortified ranch—dubbed "Fort Benson"—became headquarters for the local anti-Mormon faction. Lyman, *San Bernardino*, 339–40. Several Bensons signed the 16 November petition to General Clarke.

Navy lieutenant Edward F.] Beale's train near the foot of the Mohave . . . I had a conversation with the wagon master. . . . He then said the United States had got into a difficulty with the Mormons and he feared it would be a serious difficulty before it was ended. I said I presumed it would be a small matter for the United States to settle the difficulty. He said he thought it would not be so damned easy as there was from 20, to 30,000 fighting men, and the hell of it was they were all united, and commanded by the smartest man in the United States. . . . He also said the Mexican War was no comparison to this difficulty. . . . I then told him [I was a Mormon and] I had two wives of my own that God had give me; they had been faithful and true to me and I should defend them while I had strength in my body to do so—I did not deny them in any nation or country. He then patted me on the shoulder and said he gloried in my grit, that he did not blame me at all for my feelings. . . .

I arrived in this City last evening and made the report of my mission to President B. Young—he spent two hours asking me questions, and blessed me and said I was welcome home.

Silent Night: Christmas with Brigham Young and the Utah Expedition

A Christmas Day gathering at Brigham Young's "residence" was attended by some unknown portion of his large family of nearly one hundred siblings, wives, and children. We are fortunate to have a wonderful record of what took place.[26] The family meeting began with the dispensation of a patriarchal blessing for Brigham Young by his older brother, John. In the Mormon world such blessings were not unusual as a Latter-day Saint undertook some difficult, perilous church assignment. With a restive U.S. Army expedition camped only 113 miles to the east and California ablaze with anti-Mormonism, Young's family was mindful of the burdens that beset even a prophet, seer, and revelator. John Young's blessing recounted his brother's God-given responsibilities, talents, and future rewards. Some of the latter were otherworldly, but some clearly related to the more mundane, immediate challenges of the ongoing Utah War:

> . . . no power shall overcome you; you never shall fall by the hand of an enemy, for that is not the mind of the Spirit, but the mind of the Lord is that you

[26] The meeting was recorded by one of Young's stenographic clerks, John V. Long, and his wife Sophia. For a contrasting, almost Scrooge-like observance of Christmas in Salt Lake by the city's overworked postmaster and probate court judge, see entry for 25 December 1857, Thomas, comp. "Elias Smith's Journal," Utah State Historical Society.

shall escape . . . you shall not only have power over the United States but over the nations of the earth, and you shall do a mighty work. . . . Notwithstanding your enemies may hunt you like a Roe [buck] upon the mountains yet you shall escape as a bird from the hands of the Fowler and not a hair of your head shall fall, but you shall be sustained in all times and places.[27]

Then Brigham Young shared his thoughts.

YOUNG FAMILY MEETING, MINUTES, 25 DECEMBER 1857, GENERAL CHURCH MINUTES, LDS ARCHIVES.

Now give me your attention and I will take a text; this will please Sister Fanny for she is fond of text preaching.[28] . . .

We have come here to the mountains, and the Lord has done this, and he had it in his mind when this Church was built to plant it in these mountains at a certain time. He knew this and he took his own means and time to bring it about.

Ten years ago last July when we were down upon that Temple Block, and I think by sister Whitney's house I stated that if we were let alone for ten years we would not ask any odds of our enemies, and I think that it was ten years precisely that we were let alone at that time.[29]

Well the United States has been a free government since they declared their independence 80 years ago. From the day that the signers of the declaration put their names to the paper till this last summer, there never has an army or troops of men that have met with a perfect bluff, a perfect snagg as has these troops now upon our borders, and never were they made to use up and overdo themselves, and hop up and bite their own noses off till this army that have come to Utah, and all that is necessary is for me to point my finger[30] and tell them to stay there, and they will wilt and dry up, and be known no more.

This Church and kingdom will still increase. There is not a City there is not a Government . . . [that is not] watching the result of certain movements, and when they find that the United States has taken up a crusade like fighting the air against shadows or against the fog, they will watch for them [to] dwindle into their own shadows, and be lost therein, and the fire will blaze, and the news will go that there [is] a people in the mountains called mormons, and that they are in the fastnesses of the rocky mountains, and the

---

[27] Patriarchal blessing of Brigham Young, 25 December 1857, by John Young, Patriarchal Blessings, Vol. 27, 326, LDS Archives.

[28] Brigham Young's older sister, Fanny Young Murray.

[29] Helen Mar Kimball Whitney, who was daughter of Heber C. Kimball, widow of Joseph Smith and wife of Horace Whitney.

[30] The pointing or crooking of Brigham Young's finger was a gesture loaded with symbolic imagery and violence, even at a family Christmas gathering. See Chapter 3. William M. Wall had even heard a reference to this feared Brigham Young gesture in the midst of a Los Angeles lynch mob the previous October.

> United States can do nothing with them, and the time will soon be that their name and sound, and the pride of the people will be "I am from Utah," and I am a Latter day saint, and this will strike terror to the christian and to the heathen world, and that time is close at hand. . . .
>
> I feel like kicking every body out of doors that will not honor it [the Mormon priesthood]; and . . . I feel that I could sling mountains from me when the power of the priesthood rests upon me. Let me know the mind and will of God and I am stronger than a thousand millions of Gentiles. [W. W.] Phelps called me the "Lion of the Lord," and I feel like a thousand lions. Only get the Spirit of God upon you, have it like a fire within you; that is the way it is with me, whether I speak or not. The power of the priesthood is here.

As Brigham Young and his family observed Christmas, a quite different celebration unfolded at Camp Scott. Although Capt. John W. Phelps proclaimed it to be "one of the mildest, pleasantest days that we have had for a long time," the temperature dipped as low as 3 degrees Fahrenheit: "Christmas. One of the officers' ladies had egg nog and a set-out which would have graced any point on the [Atlantic] seaboard. The eggs were from hens that were brought along in coops."[31] Amidst these festivities Russell, Majors and Waddell's agents Charles R. Morehead and James Rupe feverishly prepared for a twelve-hundred-mile trek from Camp Scott to Fort Leavenworth—alone and with only three mules between them. It was to be a winter ordeal of almost unimaginable hardship and fortitude. Their self-imposed task was delivery of the army-receipted bills of lading by which their firm might claim payment from the War Department and stave off financial ruin. Provisioned by Albert Sidney Johnston with a ham, Johnston's own box of prairie matches, and a supply of hard bread, Morehead and Rupe set out on a journey that would bring not only the first substantive year-end news of the Utah Expedition but would provide—as Morehead later claimed—the inspiration for an all-weather pony express service.[32]

Christmas at the White House: Kane, Van Dyke, and Buchanan

There are two accounts of how Thomas L. Kane and James C. Van Dyke came to meet with James Buchanan at the White House at Christmas time 1857, a session presumably prompted by Van Dyke's 9 December letter to the presi-

[31] Entry for 25 December 1857, Phelps diary transcription, Hamilton Gardner Collection.

[32] "Personal Recollections of Charles R. Morehead," *Doniphan's Expedition*, 610–11.

dent. The first of the differing narratives—written by Kane in July 1858 for his family and perhaps publication—omitted all reference to a role by Van Dyke but was filled with self-serving posturing and convoluted phrasing.

THOMAS L. KANE, "CONCERNING THE MORMONS AND PRES. BUCHANAN," JULY 1858, KANE PAPERS, AMERICAN PHILOSOPHICAL SOCIETY.

[After evaluating Dr. Bernhisel's Utah information] I proceeded to Washington where I had a decisive interview with the President.

I went on in the night of December 25th, a day to which none of you strove with more difficulty to impart a festive [Christmas] character than myself who knew the purpose in my heart. The President received me in a manner for which, thinking it over, I didn't intend to forget that I ought to be grateful. He had heard of the intention of the Mormons to assail our little army at a very early day. He knew they must succumb. He had, I have since understood, been opposed to pushing the army beyond Laramie.[33] He knew that disaster to the army would be before the country a disgrace to his administration. I don't think that he believed there was a chance of escape open for any of them, but the constant burden of his remarks was to urge an old friend's grandson[34] to give up all thought of an enterprise which he assured him must be vain, rash and foolhardy and which promised no other possible result than the sacrifice of his own life which would be adding to the weight of the public indignation against the unfortunate Mormons.

One of the difficulties which I experienced was to convince Mr. Buchanan that I was determined to go, whether with his approbation or not, and that the only question at last for him to resolve was, whether in case I should succeed in reaching Salt Lake city, I should not be provided by him with my proper means of influence. He then again displayed a degree of consideration, for which I ought to remember I must thank him. I had to convince his reason why I must refuse an appointment from him, by showing him how important it was that I could be warranted in assuring the Mormons that I was not a Government agent or removed from the impractical position of a private citizen. In a letter which he wrote for me he stated this at my request. But he afterwards urged me and I remember how much it seemed to be upon his mind at the close of our last interview to receive compensation for my services or at least for my expenses from the public treasury. I was obliged I remember to remind him how important it might be for my personal safety to be without credentials; But it was not enough for me to say because I failed to show him why I must refuse a price for risking my life in the service of my coun-

[33] It is astonishing that Kane or the president would assert that Buchanan had opposed movement of the army beyond Fort Laramie in 1857. Generals Scott and Harney had, of course, offered such advice to Floyd and Buchanan, respectively, without success during that spring.

[34] The grandson was Kane, whose grandfather would presumably have been the merchant Elisha Kane (1770–1834).

try. Finally, I remember this with pleasure, "Well, you can be compensated for your *expenses*", laying emphasis upon the word, from the secret service fund. Though the expression of his face was most affectionate, when he said this, I probably showed the twinge which I felt at the word[s] secret service fund in my own less expressive countenance. For he grasped my hand, and asking me with much fervor to excuse him said, "I promise you, I promise you, to say no more of this—at least until you return."[35] —To be sure after this he still persisted in urging me to believe that if I went I would not return.

I say what you do not like to have me say, but many a time after when I was hard driven, I was helped to carry myself through by remembering not merely the particular confidence to which it was a compliment that he admitted me whom he had never known except as his [political] opponent in our State, but numerous express kind and friendly words, rallying my pride of family, and convincing me that at least I would not be forgotten by him, if my life was thrown away.

While Kane was meeting with Buchanan, his wife recorded in her journal:

I cannot write about all the horrors we have passed through since ~~we~~ I wrote last [12 November 1857]. God has mercifully brought out of them one great blessing already, in uniting Tom and me in the bonds of a common [Christian] faith. Tom thinks he may be of service to Him by bringing about a peace between Utah & the U.S. and went ~~on~~ to Washington last night to see the President about it. May God give him wisdom to do right, and may His peace be with him. And oh, may He guide Papa.[36]

The second participant narrative dealing with Kane's December White House visit was quite different than the first. It was dictated in March 1859 by Van Dyke at Kane's request from what Van Dyke characterized as his "vivid recollection." This memorandum described their visits with the president and

[35] The matter of compensation and expense reimbursement for Kane's Utah mission by either the U.S. government or the LDS church is complex and unclear. This was a matter not only of principle, as Kane saw it, but one of significant practical consequences for his wife and chilren whom he was leaving without lodgings or income in his absence. Discussion of the subject appears in decades of the Kane family papers at Brigham Young University and calls for careful analysis. The staff of the National Archives has searched the records for Buchanan's office as well as those for the departments of treasury and state and have been unable to locate indications of what Kane described as a presidential "secret fund." Archivist Wayne T. DeCesar (National Archives) to MacKinnon, e-mail message, 9 September 2004. Nonetheless, in November 1857 Governor Cumming recommended to Secretary of State Cass that Utah's U.S. Marshal Dotson be compensated from a "fund for secret service" rather than the traditional fee-for-service arrangement for such officers. Cumming to Cass, 28 November 1857, State Department Territorial Papers. Utah Series, Vol. 1 (30 April 1853–24 December 1859), microfilm copy, Utah State Historical Society.

[36] Entry for 26 December 1857, Elizabeth W. Kane Journal, Thomas L. and Elizabeth W. Kane Papers.

Van Dyke's related session with Bernhisel. This narrative, like Kane's, was developed by a man who was an attorney with an eye to posterity; both men probably wrote with some sort of public use in mind. For example, Kane had asked Van Dyke in 1859 for his recollections only six days after shaking off another illness to address the New-York Historical Society on the subject of Governor Cumming's role in the Utah War's outcome. Kane did so as a major step in his successful campaign to prevent a vulnerable Cumming's removal by Buchanan. Because of its length, only excerpts from this important Van Dyke memorandum appear below.[37]

Van Dyke, Memorandum for Kane, 28 March 1859,
Kane Collection, Pennsylvania State Archives.

During the week preceding the first of January 1858 I accompanied you to the City of Washington for the purpose of assisting as far as I could in arranging some of the necessary preliminaries of your intended expedition to Utah with a view of effecting a peace with that people. I think we arrived in Washington on the morning of Saturday, December 26, 1857.[38] I called upon the President and informed him that you were in Washington for the purpose of having another interview with him in relation to your intended trip. The President asked me if you were still determined upon going; and said he considered the undertaking a very hazardous one, fraught with dangers and difficulties on all sides; that he did not believe it was possible for you to reach Salt Lake at that season of the year; and that even if you should he could not help doubting whether any good would result from your visit. I told him that your mind was fully made up, that you intended to go with the sanction and approbation of the Administration if they saw fit so far to aid you; but if such prestige and aid was withheld, you would go without it; that go you would. I said also to the President that I was satisfied you had some influence with that people, and that you believed the American Army was in great peril and thought you could, in a great measure, avert the coming danger.

My impression is that in this conversation I said to the President that I had reason to believe that Mr. Bernheisel [*sic*] thought well of your intentions and did not doubt your power to do something if you could get into the country. I recollect distinctly that in reply to a remark made by me of which the above is the substance, the President said "And have you seen Mr. Bernhisel?—He does not come to see me." I replied that I had not, but that I thought,

[37] This valuable twenty-nine-page holograph memo was part of a broader set of materials transcribed by Elizabeth W. Kane, probably in 1902, for Richard Whitehead Young, a talented, attorney-grandson of Brigham Young who frequently wrote about Utah's territorial period, including the Utah War.

[38] The 26th of December did fall on a Saturday in 1857.

I could see him before I left the city. It was in consequence of this conversation that I requested you to procure for me an interview with Mr. Bernhisel. This you did at your own room on Saturday afternoon.

In the course of the conversation with Mr. B[ernhisel], I remarked that you had determined upon, what was considered my [by] many of your friends, a hazardous undertaking. He said, Yes, he thought so, but that you seemed fully bent upon your purpose; that while he would desire to persuade you not to go, he was nevertheless constrained, under the circumstances, to give you all the aid in his power. I asked him why he considered the experiment a dangerous one. He said that it was very doubtful whether you could arrive at Salt Lake in safety; that his own people had at that time arrived at such a point of hostility to the United States that they would sacrifice you if they discovered your design in visiting them. He said that such was the feeling, especially among the outer [southern] settlements through which you would of necessity pass, that he feared very much whether you would ever be able to reach the city; that if you should be able to do so, however, you would be safe enough, for he considered the kind feelings of Gov. Young and the better class of the people towards you *personally*, were such that you would be perfectly safe—though he seemed somewhat in doubt whether the time for your intended friendly offices had not transpired.[39] . . .

He said the Mormons were fully prepared for resistance; that his belief was they would resist to the last; and that although they might not try their strength in any regular action, they would nevertheless be able to cut off our supplies, and by various annoyances to our army keep up a protracted war and greatly embarrass this Government. He also said that the troops at Fort Bridger were in danger, but I could not learn from him in what respect, although I tried to do so. . . .

He certainly did complain about the removal of Gov. Young as Commissioner of Indian Affairs without any notice to him; and said that the consequence was that depredations had been committed by the Indians for which their people thought the government at Washington was responsible;[40] and that this had tended much to increase the bad state of feelings against the U.S. and any person who should be sent there to compel a submission. It is, however, due to Mr. Bernhisel to say that while stating these thoughts, as well as in his whole conversation with me, he appeared greatly to deprecate the existence of hostilities, and manifested a lively interest in anything which might have a tendency to avert the consequence of their continuance. It was in this

---

[39] Perhaps Bernhisel as well as President Buchanan feared for Kane's safety in this region of Utah because of reports of the Mountain Meadows massacre that had reached Washington in November.

[40] This reference to Indian depredations may have been an attempt by either Bernhisel—or subsequently Van Dyke—to deflect accountability for the September 1857 Mountain Meadows massacre from the responsible parties. Young had been a superintendent, not commissioner, of Indian Affairs.

connection that he spoke of you and of the unlimited confidence many of the Mormon leaders and people had in your word as a gentleman; and said that there was no person here nor there who could exercise such a wholesome influence as yourself. He said he had no doubt they would rely upon any statement you might make; and that anything said by you as to the sentiments and views of the President in relation to the designs of our government would have a power[ful] weight with the Mormons.

He expressed great regret that you had not thought of going out at an earlier date; and said he had no doubt that had you gone there during the latter part of the summer and given them assurances of the prosecution of offenders and of the pardon from the President of such persons as they might desire, his belief was that you could have exerted a powerful influence in persuading his people to return to their allegiance to the U.S. He seemed, however, to doubt whether anything could then be accomplished, inasmuch as all their preparations had been made to attack our army, and that many of the people had become so anxious for an opportunity for revenge that he feared even your influence would be of no avail; but that if any one could produce a better state of feelings in that country it would be yourself, provided you could arrive there in safety—That so great was the danger in this respect that he could not think you would be justified in making the effort.

His remarks upon your influence with the Mormons were so pointed an[d] decided that I felt some curiosity to know how it was that you had ingratiated yourself into the affections of this strange people. I remarked to him, "How is it that Col. Kane has such influence with your people?" I said jocosely, "He is no Mormon, and does not, I believe, approve of those peculiarities in their religion which appear to be the principal obstacle to a cordial affiliation between you and the rest of the U.S." He said, "Oh no! He is no Mormon, and of late years has treated us very coldly; we think on account of our religion which we all very much regret; but our friendship for and confidence in him is of a different nature."[41] . . .

I have in the foregoing remarks given you the substance of the conversation referred to. . . . But so much died [did] this conversation satisfy me that you were right, notwithstanding the wishes of all your friends (including the President) that you should not at that season of the year persist in your determination to visit Utah, that I repeated to the President all that had occurred between Mr. Bernhisel and myself. I may also add that it seemed to make a favorable impression upon him.

---

[41] That Kane was not a member of the LDS church is best explained in Whittaker, "New Sources on Old Friends," 90–94. As Elizabeth Kane's journal makes clear, the more relevant question was that of whether Thomas was even a Christian. As indicated below, Buchanan wrote an unsigned editorial for the *Washington Union* denying Kane was a Mormon.

Lord, Please Put into the President's Mouth Right Words: Year-End Maneuverings

Thomas L. Kane returned to his home from Washington on the evening of 29 December 1857 determined to go to Utah if he could clear two hurdles: obtaining an appropriate understanding and related set of credentials from Buchanan; and negotiating the approval of his family. Maneuvering in both arenas was a complex group that included Van Dyke, Delegate Bernhisel, multiple members of the extended Kane family, and, of course, President Buchanan. Back in Philadelphia, Van Dyke immediately informed the president:

> Col. Kane has returned from Washington perfectly charmed with his interview with you, and satisfied that it is your determination to speed him all you can in his intended expedition to Utah. There is one subject about which he has talked to me. It is in regard to the form of the letter to be used by him amongst the Mormons. The statement that Col. "Kane[']s personal word would have great weight with you in your exercise of executive clemency" was intended by him to be doubly serviceable—enabling him not only to reward the deserving but also to menace the refractory who should fear to forfeit his good will. Powers to declare a general amnesty would not perhaps be as desirable to him. This is his idea and I repeat it to you for consideration. He is determined to sail, and has taken his passage in the steamer of the 5th from N.Y.[42]

Meanwhile, Elizabeth Kane recorded her further thoughts on her husband's trip to the White House and its immediate aftermath.

Elizabeth W. Kane Journal, December 1857, Thomas L. and Elizabeth W. Kane Papers.

28th December [1857] Sunday [Monday] Night. I feel sure that God will guide and support dear Papa and provide for him in a way my short sighted humanity sees not. I trust Him. And, Father, I feel willing now, should it prove Thy will, to yield my dear husband to Thy hands if Thou needest him to bring peace to those lost sheep of Israel. Lord, if I give Him to Thee cheerfully wilt Thou deign to accept it as my Thank[s] offering for Thy infinite goodness in making him a Christian. Lord Thou knowest that it is a sacrifice for us to part when we are in trouble, and Thou wilt in mercy strengthen and help us. Lord wilt Thou show us what Tom ought to do about his business, his *daily* [family and professional] duties? We do not quite see how to reconcile his neglecting them with his performing this. Lord, please put into the President's mouth right words. May they make the right course for Tom to pursue plain. Give us strength to follow it when we see it, and oh, let the peace which Thou only canst give, shine in our hearts.

---

[42] Van Dyke to Buchanan, 29 December 1857, James Buchanan Papers, Historical Society of Pennsylvania.

Help me to be a faithful wife to him, a faithful mother to our children, and to do my duties at home rightly, whether my dear companion is with me, or away.

For Christ's sake, amen!

Tuesday [Wednesday] 30th Dec. Tom returned last night. He gives up his clerkship day after tomorrow, and on the 5th of January sails, God's will be done! Then [Saint] Paul answered, "What mean ye to weep and to break mine heart? for I am ready not to be bound only, but to die at Jerusalem for the name of the Lord Jesus. And when he would not be persuaded, we ceased saying. The will of the Lord be done."[43]

I am going to give him my little Bible, and also have been copying some of our favorite pieces of poetry But it makes me sorrowful so I shall leave it for the present.

As Elizabeth Kane was recording her thoughts about her husband's visit to the White House, his father, Judge John K. Kane, wrote to his old Pennsylvania political friend, the president. The judge thanked Buchanan both for seeing Tom and providing him with cautionary advice of the sort already dispensed by the judge. By today's standards his was an extraordinary letter for a sitting federal judge to send to a president. It contained not only Kane's personal feelings about the Mormons and his son's imminent mission to Utah, but candid comments about the political dilemma posed by Senator Douglas's concept of popular sovereignty. Most extraordinary, though, was the judge's belief, after talking with his son, that he had broached to Buchanan his intent to pursue the possibility of a Mormon exodus from the United States and that the president was not adverse to supporting such a departure. Here was a view attributed to Buchanan consistent with his comment a few weeks earlier to the Russian ambassador that "we shall be very happy to be rid of them." It was also an intent of Thomas L. Kane that renders more explainable Brigham Young's assertion to Bernhisel and Asa Calkin about a week after meeting with Kane, that "We have our eyes on the Russian possessions."[44]

Judge John K. Kane to Buchanan, 31 December 1857, Private Collection of Mrs. Anne Richards Horton, San Marino, California.

I have heard from my son how fully and in what a friendly spirit you sustained the views I had expressed to him before he visited you. I thank you very cordially.

I have been aware for a ~~very~~ long time of the influence he might exert over

[43] Acts 21:13–14.

[44] Young to Bernhisel and Young to Calkin, 5 March 1858, LDS Archives. See Chapter 16.

that strange people, and have thought of the possibility of his intervention for good in the controversy that is now so imminent. But it is only since his return from Washington that I have in any wise yielded my assent to the sacrifice which he meditates.

Yet, foregoing my feeling as a father, I believe that he is right, and that by an act of self-devotion wh[ich] I am afraid to contemplate, he may achieve a great good to his country and to his fellow men. For I do believe, that in the the [*sic*] providence of God it has been reserved for your Administration to undergo the severest trials for this Union, to which it has ever been subjected; and I hold that there are principles interlocked with one branch at least of the Mormon question, which however offensive morally in their application to the particular case, it would be unwise to denounce.[45] I do not know better office to be rendered at this time by a mere citizen than the peaceful amotion of Mormonism beyond our borders.[46] It has passed by force of circumstances beyond the sphere of direct executive intervention, but I am glad to learn that, so far as consists with a prudent reserve, you have not been unwilling to aid my son in the effort.

I will not deny myself the pleasure of saying, before I close this letter, how heartily I go with you in each and every particular of your doctrine and action in the Kansas case. It was an effort of self restraint, such as I have rarely submitted to, that kept me from perilling my sense of judicial propriety when invited to preside at the late meeting.[47] I do not find my own views in any of the speeches, though they are implied perhaps in Mr. Rush's summary. But I need not expand them to one who has considered the whole subject from the highest point of view.

I might indeed confess, if we had not already followed Mr Douglas so far, that the doctrine of squatter sovereignty is more palatable to me as an abstraction than as a dogma of practical politics. To devolve absolutely the organic legislation of a state on the first ten or twenty or thirty thousand emigrants or outcasts as it may happen from all nations and tribes under the sun, who may intrude or plant themselves as neighbors on the public lands, seems to me of dangerous policy. I would rather trust the wisdom of a convention, or even of Congress, to pass on the questions of Religious Equality, Corporate Endowments, State Liabilities, the Currency, the Judicial tenure, and the like, than any unfledged gathering such as I have read of in and about Salt Lake.

---

[45] This is a convoluted reference to the relationship between polygamy and popular sovereignty.

[46] As indicated in an earlier chapter, at the time there was substantial press speculation that Brigham Young was contemplating a Mormon mass exodus to northern Mexico or to the Pacific Coast possessions of Great Britain or Russia. Judge Kane's use of the now archaic "amotion" introduces a flavor of eviction, removal, ouster, and deprivation of property that goes beyond the notion of voluntary emigration.

[47] Judge Kane is probably referring to a recent mass political meeting held in Philadelphia in support of admitting Kansas to statehood under a constitution adopted at Lecompton, perhaps Buchanan's highest-risk and most controversial political embroilment at the time.

> But all this, except as it goes to apologise for the action at Lecompton, it would not be well to say now.[48]

Also at year-end John M. Bernhisel wrote to Brigham Young a letter to be hand-carried west by Kane. This message discussed Kane's deep anxiety over not yet having received Buchanan's promised letters. Reflected here is Kane's fear that either these letters would not be forthcoming or that they might lack the ambassadorial leverage that Kane felt he needed in dealing with both friends and adversaries in the West. There can be multiple interpretations of the several Kane directives to Bernhisel that the delegate reported in this letter to Young. One is that Kane had been trying to inveigle Bernhisel into a late-December meeting with the president in hopes that the delegate would induce Buchanan to describe verbally his backing of Kane in terms far more supportive and directive than the president was apt to commit to Kane in writing. Under this interpretation, if Bernhisel recorded such a conversation with Buchanan in a report to Young, Bernhisel would, in effect, be providing Kane with a second-hand (indirect) presidential authorization that could be useful in Utah. Unfortunately for Kane, Bernhisel did not see Buchanan until 5 January 1858, the day Kane left New York for California via Panama. The delegate's year-end letter to Brigham Young—delivered to him in Salt Lake City by Kane seven weeks later—contained little of help to Kane.[49]

Buck All Over: Plausible Deniability and Buchanan's Letters

By Thursday, 31 December—with passage booked for 5 January on the S.S. *Moses Malone* out of New York—Thomas L. Kane grew anxious in Philadelphia at not having received letters from President Buchanan. On the last day of 1857 Kane wrote a polite but persistent reminder to the president of the timing involved.[50] The president, in turn, wrote three letters to Kane on the

[48] The editor is deeply grateful to Mrs. Horton, a descendant of Brigham Young's late second counselor Dr. Willard Richards, for access to this letter, a copy of which Judge Kane sent or gave to his son before he left for Utah. The original is not in any of the known collections of Buchanan's papers.

[49] Bernhisel to Young, 31 December 1857, LDS Archives. Young described Kane's delivery of this message to him in a letter to Bernhisel of 5 March 1858, ibid.

[50] Thomas L. Kane to Buchanan, 31 December 1857, James Buchanan Papers, Historical Society of Pennsylvania.

same day which crossed his in the mail.[51] They arrived just in time before Kane's departure.

In Buchanan's transmittal note—signed "Ever your friend"—for his other two letters he characterized them as messages "as strong as I can write them after taking a review of the whole ground & I hope they may prove satisfactory." Buchanan added the thought, "If you had not expressed an inflexable [*sic*] determination, I would again advise a reconsideration of your purpose. If you go, may Heaven protect you! The purity of your motives & the energy of your character are beyond all question." Accompanying this transmittal was a generic letter of introduction from Buchanan that Kane might use with any U.S. officers encountered during his journey:

> As you have been impelled by your own sense of duty to visit Utah & having informed me that nothing can divert you from this purpose, it affords me pleasure to commend you to the favorable regard of all officers of the United States whom you may meet in the course of your travels. Possessed as you are of my confidence & being well informed as to passing events, you may have it in your power to impart to them useful information from this side of the Continent. I do not doubt that they will, in the exercise of whatever descretion [*sic*] their instructions may permit, render you all the aids & facilities in their power in expediting you on your journey undertaken of your own accord, to accomplish the pacific & philanthropic objects you have in view. Heartily wishing you success.

The second letter transmitted by Buchanan on 31 December was for a different purpose and reads like a memorandum written to build a legal defense:

> You furnish the strongest evidence of your desire to serve the Mormons by abandoning the comforts of friends, family & home & voluntarily encountering the perils and dangers of a journey to Utah at the present inclement season of the year, at your own expense and without official position. Your only reward must be a consciousness that you are doing your duty. Nothing but pure philanthropy & a strong desire to serve the Mormon people could have dictated a course so much at war with your private interests.
>
> You express a strong conviction in which, however, I do not participate, that a large portion of the Mormons labor under a mistake as to the intentions of the Federal Government towards them. If this be so, my late [annu-

[51] Buchanan to Kane, 31 December 1857, Thomas L. and Elizabeth W. Kane Papers. These letters may also be found in James Buchanan Papers, Historical Society of Pennsylvania, and—with the exception of the transmittal letter—in Moore, ed., *The Works of James Buchanan*, 10:167–69, and Hafen and Hafen, eds., *Mormon Resistance*, 266–68.

> al] message will disabuse their minds. My views therein expressed, as I have already informed you, have undergone no change. These sentiments were expressed in sincerity & truth, & I trust that your representations of them may meet with the success you anticipate. I hope that the people of Utah may be convinced ere it is too late that there exist no duties of higher obligation than those which they owe to their country. They cannot doubt your friendship and the services which you have rendered to them in times past will conciliate their regard.
>
> At the same time I deem it my duty to say, that whilst reposing entire confidence in the purity of patriotism of your motives and entertaining a warm personal regard for yourself, I would not at the present moment in view of the hostile attitude they have assumed against the United States send any agent to visit them on behalf of the Government. If the case were otherwise, however, I know no person to whom I should more cheerfully confide such a mission than yourself.[52] With every sentiment of personal regard.

Aside from these confidential messages, James Buchanan made no known private or public comment on Kane's mission and the understandings surrounding it other than through a single, muted sentence buried in his December 1858 second annual message to Congress: "I cannot, in this connection, refrain from mentioning the valuable services of Colonel Thomas L. Kane, who, from motives of pure benevolence, and without any official character or pecuniary compensation, visited Utah during the last inclement winter for the purpose of contributing to the pacification of the Territory."[53]

In a last minute attempt to be helpful, James C. Van Dyke supplemented Buchanan's multiple letters with one of his own. It was a letter of introduction for Kane written on the stationery of the Philadelphia U.S. attorney's office by Van Dyke to Utah's U.S. attorney, John M. Hockaday. In this document Van Dyke described Kane as "the friend of our party, and the personal and political friend of the President. He may have matters of importance about which to consult you." Van Dyke went on to comment, "He is a gentleman of high honor in whose statements you can rely with the utmost confidence. I am sure you will extend to him every facility in your power, towards the accomplishment of the patriotic designs for which he visits the great valley. Any kindness, of a personal character, and every aid which pro-

[52] This description of Kane as a non-agent/agent is classic Buchanan phrasing second only to his handling of the matter of Utah's status as a rebellious or almost-rebellious territory.

[53] "Second Annual Message of the President," 6 December 1858, Moore, ed., *The Works of James Buchanan,* 10:245. This sentence later reappeared in Buchanan, *Mr. Buchanan's Administration,* 238.

fessionally you shall extend to him will be highly esteemed by your friends here, and especially by [me]."[54]

Given this cordial but largely unsubstantial documentary support from the president and his closest counselor, it is fascinating to read Kane's perhaps fanciful July 1858 description of the understanding he then believed he had reached with Buchanan during their late December meeting:

> My powers you have understood rightly from Mr. Buchanan were the same as those of Messrs. Powell and McCullough sent out in April [1858] as [Peace] Commissioners.[55]
>
> I know this from Mr. Buchanan reading over to me their instructions last week. The only difference between us was that they were the bearers of a proclamation of general pardon, while I had a discretionary power as pardons were to be granted upon my recommendation. I still however remember a human expression of the President[']s which I wrote down at the time and afterwards repeated with good effect—"I should be glad to pardon *the whole* of them."[56]

Whether Kane was correct in asserting that Buchanan had verbally empowered him to recommend pardons in individual cases is crucial to an understanding of the December Kane-Buchanan discussions and the psychological as well as political underpinnings for Kane's mission. Judge Kane's 4 January letter to Thomas (see below) implies his belief that his son had received some sort of informal understanding from the president; Van Dyke's and Bernhisel's letters of 29 and 31 December to Buchanan and Young, respectively, indicate that Kane was aggressively seeking such support. No record has been found of any Utah pardons recommended by or attributable to Thomas L. Kane.

One of the most intriguing sources on what power and authority Buchanan

---

[54] Van Dyke to Hockaday, 3 January 1858, Private Collection. Kane carried this letter west with the expectation that he would meet Hockaday at Camp Scott. Because Hockaday left Camp Scott in early January 1858 and did not return until late May, they did not meet. Van Dyke's unused letter of introduction remained in Kane's papers until auctioned in 2003. Text provided to MacKinnon by Ms. Sallie Connelly, 27 September 2003.

[55] Unknown to Kane in December 1857, Lazarus W. Powell—former governor of Kentucky and that commonwealth's U.S. senator-elect—and Ben McCulloch—former Texas Ranger, U.S. marshal for the eastern district of Texas, and Buchanan's first choice as Brigham Young's successor—would be appointed presidential commissioners in April 1858. Their mission was to tender a blanket presidential pardon for Utah's population if Brigham Young would accept it without negotiation, as he did.

[56] Thomas L. Kane, "Concerning the Mormons and President Buchanan," July 1858. Kane drafted this account while recovering from a post-Utah bout of feverish ill health and at a time when he was alternately savaged and lionized in the press over his poorly understood mission, an ambiguity to which Kane as well as Buchanan contributed during the last half of 1858.

did or did not bestow on Kane in late December 1857 is an editorial on this subject published in the *Washington Union.* Whether this unsigned piece was written by Buchanan—as was sometimes his practice—or merely reflected his views cannot be determined.[57] What is clear, though, is that the *Union*'s editorial would not have appeared without Buchanan's sanction, especially since it ran in July 1858 subsequent to Kane's return from Utah and at a time when the hostile *New York Times* had pointedly written:

> This proceeding [Kane's mission] does not seem to us quite in keeping with the ordinary openness and integrity of American diplomacy. It has not been customary thus to amuse the public with pretentious designs, which secret agents were commissioned to thwart. The public is entitled to know whether Dr. KANE was or was not a public agent—clothed with authority to speak and act for the President—and what were the instructions under which he acted. Will the Washington *Union* be good enough to enlighten us on this point?[58]

In response, the *Union* ran a long editorial, the opening paragraphs of which savaged the *Times* as "a common demoralizer and disorganizer, scrupling not to make itself an apologist of Mormonism, a conduit for the erotic effusions of the free-lovers, and a ready sewer for the discharge upon the public of all the abominations and heresies of the day." Having set this tone, the *Union* went on to discuss the Buchanan-Kane understandings:

> Dr. Kane, [was] a mere private citizen without power or authority of any sort. . . . He was a personal acquaintance of the President and possessed his esteem, and hence, we believe, took with him letters of introduction to officers of the army from Mr. Buchanan as from an [private] individual. But he went neither as agent of the President nor as officer of the government; neither as secret agent nor as public officer; but simply on an individual, self-imposed mission, as a private citizen, philanthropist, well-wisher of the Mormons, or what you will. He took no message from the President, other than the President had publicly announced [in his annual message], in regard to the Mormons. . . . But no pretension of the kind is too preposterous and stupid for the Times.[59]

---

[57] For example, on 20 or 21 May 1858 Thomas L. Kane's brother Pat visited Buchanan to complain of the *Union*'s lack of support for Kane's Utah mission. Elizabeth Kane recorded that at that session Buchanan "with his own hand wrote a notice to the Union, saying that Tom was no Mormon, but a worthy brother of Elisha's, a noble enterprise—etc, etc." An unsigned editorial in these words appeared in the *Union*'s 21 May issue. Elizabeth W. Kane Journal, entry for 21 May 1858, Thomas L. and Elizabeth W. Kane Papers; "Col. Thomas L. Kane," *Washington* (D.C.) *Union*, 21 May 1858, 2/3.

[58] "The Mormons—Light Needed," *New York Times*, 5 July 1858, 4/3.

[59] "Rebellion Complains of Bad Faith," *Washington* (D.C.) *Union*, 8 July 1858, 2/1–2.

Whatever their understandings were of Buchanan's intent, both Thomas L. Kane and Judge Kane responded immediately to the president's letters. The judge wrote: "My son has allowed me to see your letters to him which arrived this morning. I hardly find words to express to you the gratitude with which I recognize your kindness. If, as indeed I fear, he shall at last sacrifice himself in the cause of that which he conscientiously regards as duty, I shall always remember your gallant solicitude in his behalf and the provident spirit in which you have sought to guard him." His son informed the president: "I am in the last preparations for my departure and have only a moment to thank you for your letters. I may not see into the future; but I cannot think that I shall fail to reach my destination—and in time to effect some good—I will not be a disappointed man unless I fail to prove myself."[60]

Notwithstanding the effusive thanks which Kane and his father promptly sent to the White House, the son must have been disappointed in the letters as he packed for the West. Given the criticism of his Utah policy then developing in Congress, what Buchanan had written for Kane in his cautious, lawyerly, and secretive fashion was a model of what in today's presidential politics and intelligence work would be called "plausible deniability." The letters were a means of distancing Buchanan from Kane if his secret mission should become known, controversial, or a failure while providing signs that on at least a personal basis he had wished Kane well—thin gruel and cold comfort. From the distance of Philadelphia, George Plitt and John W. Forney—jaundiced former friends of the president—and Pat Kane (Thomas's brother) immediately recognized the letters as such. Elizabeth Kane recorded their reactions and commented: "[they] think Mr. B. has behaved badly. His exceedingly non-committal letters are, they say, 'Buck all over, so that if Mr. K. succeeds, he may approve him, if he fails disavow him.'"[61]

In 1950, unaware of Buchanan's unpublished transmittal letter to Thomas L. Kane of 31 December 1857 or Kane's own subsequent memoranda of these year-end machinations, historian Dale L. Morgan tried to discourage a colleague's hunt for documentary evidence of presidential duplicity. At the same time Morgan raised the matter of plausible deniability. "There are practically no Buchanan letters through 1857–58, and of course it is unrealistic to

---

[60] John K. Kane and Thomas L. Kane to Buchanan, 2 and 3 January 1858, respectively; both in James Buchanan Papers, Historical Society of Pennsylvania.

[61] The assessments by Messrs. Plitt, Forney, and Pat Kane were recorded in Elizabeth W. Kane, "Journal," entry for 16 April 1858, Thomas L. and Elizabeth W. Kane Papers.

hope that anything would be found to controvert his pubilshed statements when he wholly disavowed Kane in any other terms than a disinterested person. Had Buchanan had a secret understanding with Kane and been willing to have it known, I think he would have brought it into the light of day when the letters to Kane I here send you were published. That way, he could have claimed credit for some master-minding; [if it surfaced] later he would have put himself on record as being simply a liar."[62]

God Bless and Speed Him with All My Heart: Cross-Currents among the Kanes

Although outwardly supportive of her husband's mission, Elizabeth Kane confided to her journal: "I tried to help him as far as I could, before he went, and to keep his heart, and kept a cheerful look on my face as he looked the last look as his vessel bore him off . . . I often say, that were it not for the grief it would cause Tom, and the good I may be able to do the children, I would just as lieve die as live." Her brother-in-law John, Tom's younger brother, wrote to her from France at a time when he was uncertain about whether Tom would decide to go to Utah. He expressed admiration for Elizabeth but implied disapproval of the mission among his siblings: "I wrote merely to say God bless you. That I feel with you in your trial and to thank you for the noble manner in which you have behaved. I knew how you acted when I read that Tom had gone even before I read [sister] Bessie Kane's note telling me about it. You will see by the family letter what are my thoughts with regard to Tom's action."[63]

If Thomas L. Kane's wife and siblings had qualms about his mission, his father was bluntly opposed to it and pessimistic about its chances for success. Notwithstanding Elizabeth Kane's perception that her husband "considered himself insulted by Floyd, [by] the War Secretary's bearing towards him," Floyd later commented sympathetically that the son "acted under a deep conviction of duty, against the advice of his excellent father, Judge Kane, since deceased, and other members of his family."[64] A letter written to Thomas

[62] Morgan to McQuown, 27 February 1950, McQuown Collection. By this letter Morgan transmitted a transcription of Buchanan's two published year-end letters to Kane but not the amplifying unpublished cover note.

[63] Elizabeth W. Kane, "Journal," entry for 16 January 1858. John Kane, Jr.'s, letter of 4 January 1858 is pasted in Elizabeth's journal at 10 February 1858.

[64] Elizabeth W. Kane, "The Story of the Mother of the Regiment," unpublished ms., Thomas L. and Elizabeth W. Kane Papers; Floyd to Lazarus W. Powell and Ben McCulloch, 12 April 1858, "Report of the Secretary of War," U.S. Cong., 35th Cong., 2d sess., House Ex. Doc. 2, Serial 942, 162.

by his father—hidden in his trunk by Elizabeth and presumably opened at sea while steaming for Panama—contained cross-currents of parental disapproval, apprehension, and love. It was a letter substantially more apprehensive and downbeat than that written by Judge Kane to Buchanan as recently as 31 December upon Thomas's return from Washington. To some unknown extent Judge Kane's later comments must have been grounded in the loss of his eldest son, Elisha, far from home and less than a year earlier. It was the last letter that Kane received from the judge, who would die during the last week of February—virtually on the eve of Thomas's exhausted, secretive, but dramatic arrival in Salt Lake City. There—in Utah—Tom Kane was to begin the work and seek the destiny which at year-end beckoned so strongly through his new-found but non-Mormon Christianity.

Judge John K. Kane to Thomas L. Kane,
4 January 1858, Thomas L. and Elizabeth W. Kane Papers.

I have been so strenuous an opponent of your whole project, and have said so many things against it which may come back unpleasantly to your memory that I think it right to say to you once and for all, at the moment of our parting, that you carry with you all the blessing that a father's prayers can involk [*sic*].

Yet I do not think you are to succeed; and I want you to be prepared for the worst. The Mormons can hardly have misconceived the honest and kindly aims and purposes of the President, and I do not believe you will be able to impress them with the feeling of our American people. You know, and I know, how anxious Mr. Buchanan is to prove himself their friend; and you know—or if you do not, I do—that if the Mormons once assail our troops, the sentiment of the country will never be satisfied while a Mormon community survives on this continent.[65]

Yet such is the judicial blindness that seems to cover your friends in Utah—gallant and far-sighted as I know many of them to be—and such, too, are the initial embarrassments in which evil counsel and precipitate action have involved the question, that I have very faint hopes connected with your mission. Mr. Buchanan's letters to you are certainly strong and clear enough if they could be met in a corresponding spirit. You wrong him and me too, if you suppose that my opposition to your scheme has made their phraseology less definite than his oral pledges to yourself. Coming from a statesman of his heralded integrity and habitual caution, they have surprised me by their strength. Were I the President, I could not have committed myself, even to you, as fully as he has done.[66] Naturally these letters engage him for all that you can honestly ask.

[65] Apparently Judge Kane did not view the Lot Smith raid as having constituted such a flash point.

[66] These are the words of a judge-father who once had Thomas jailed for contempt of court over a real but minor infraction.

Still, I repeat it; you are going, I apprehend, to fail, and I close this letter by a farewell assurance to you that the Home Welcome in all its cordiality, awaits you, whether you fail or succeed.

God bless you, dear Tom,

[P.S.] I have concluded to let your wife throw my letter into your trunk; it may make a home-reminiscence for you when you find it.[67]

Perhaps the most fascinating of the documents surrounding Thomas L. Kane's year-end departure for Utah was that written from Paris by his younger brother, John K. Kane, Jr. Unlike John's earlier letter to Elizabeth, this one was written to the entire family and with full knowledge that his brother was indeed going to Utah. Written by a young student far from home who had already lost two of his brothers and might lose a third, John Kane, Jr.'s, letter provides perhaps the definitive familial assessment of what drove Thomas L. Kane. Tom had told President Buchanan that in going to Utah "I will not be a disappointed man unless I fail to prove myself." After he returned from Utah, Kane told Delegate Bernhisel that "he would have the world know that he m[a]de his journey at his own expense, in the interest of the whole United States, and of humanity as well as the friends he loves in Utah."[68] For the family, young John Kane put it differently—in terms of Thomas's psyche.

John K. Kane, Jr., to Family, 21 January 1858,
John K. Kane Collection, American Philosophical Society.

I am glad the family did not make him unhappy by useless remonstrances for whatever be the result those sort of things give no pleas[ur]e in the retrospect. I am moreover not so sure of an unsuccessful termination to the affair. I have great confidence in Tom's long head and unbounded energy and however impossible a thing may seem I regard the fact of Tom's having undertaken it as more than half a success. Then too when I reflect that Tom is never so well as when exposed to what would kill most men of his build, and that hard life in open air (no matter how hard) always agrees with him better than the most tranquil of sedentary existence. . . . Tom is weak and sickly it is true but I travelled with him the summer before last and I was astonished during our hard journey over the mountains, when our horse broke down and we had to foot it over the rugged pine barrens under a boiling August sun to find that what was exhausting me acted like a tonic to Tom who eat [*sic*] with an appetite slept soundly gained color in his cheeks and actually began to grow fat on what would have killed me in a month's time. At home Tom's big soul was preying on his body. The loss of dear Elish. And the crushing blow which

[67] Judge Kane died of pneumonia at age 62 on 21 February 1858 as his son passed through Utah's southern settlements three days before his arrival at Salt Lake.

[68] Bernhisel to Young, 11 December 1858, LDS Archives.

this financial crisis gave to his hopes of organizing a new expedition [to the Arctic] were killing him by inches. He is too great a man to occupy himself with trifles. Look at him whenever by any accident a McKean & Elk Co. Coal Company or Sunbury & Erie Railroad or some other such thing capable of supplying some dozens of respectable Mr. Fraileys and Cressons with mental nourishment for a lifetime come in his way.[69] Why he turned to like a hungry giant having captured a red bird seized it tore it to atoms and devoured it at a single bolt. His life full of occupation and usefulness in other peoples eyes was objectless in his own and he was unhappy. No man can have health who is not at least contented. The venist lout of a Tom Leiper [Kane] becomes dyspeptic and villious while for a man like Tom it is death. Now he has got an object large enough and noble enough to draw his thoughts away from the poor self on which they were fading and I cant help hoping that his physical man will improve in consequence. However be the result of what it may the object is grand and noble and does him and the family honor and I for one say God bless and speed him with all my heart.[70]

[69] These were major commercial projects in western Pennsylvania's McKean and Elk counties with which Thomas L. Kane became involved, perhaps with Frailey and Cresson. Kane was a director of the Sunbury & Erie Railroad and "one of the men who made certain that this promising venture would pass through McKean County and [the town of] Kane, a move criticized by railroad historians as the reason why this railroad proved to be less successful than it might have been." Treese, *Railroads of Pennsylvania*, 127.

[70] Transcription courtesy of Dr. Matthew J. Grow.

Bibliography

This bibliography has separate sections for secondary sources (books and articles and book chapters), published primary sources, unpublished primary sources, and newspapers.

Secondary Sources: Books

Adams, George Rollie. *General William S. Harney: Prince of Dragoons.* Lincoln: University of Nebraska Press, 2001.

Arrington, Leonard J. *Brigham Young: American Moses.* New York: Alfred A. Knopf, 1985.

Auchampaugh, Philip G. *Robert Tyler, Southern Rights Champion 1847–1866: A Documentary Study Chiefly of Antebellum Politics.* Duluth, Minn: Himan Stein, 1934.

Bagley, Will. *Blood of the Prophets: Brigham Young and the Massacre at Mountain Meadows.* Norman: University of Oklahoma Press, 2002.

———, ed. *"A Bright, Rising Star": A Brief Life of James Ferguson, Sergeant Major, Mormon Battalion; Adjutant General, Nauvoo Legion.* Collector's Edition Keepsake for volume 4 of the *Kingdom in the West* series, *Army of Israel.* Spokane, Wash: The Arthur H. Clark Co., 2000.

Baker, Jean H. *James Buchanan.* New York: Times Books/Henry Holt, 2004.

Bayard, Samuel J. *Life of George Dashiell Bayard, Late Captain, U.S.A., and Brigadier-General of Volunteers, Killed in the Battle of Fredericksburg, Dec. 1862.* New York: G.P. Putnam, 1874.

Beck, Paul N. *The First Sioux War: The Grattan Fight and Blue Water Creek, 1854–1856.* Lanham, Md: University Press of America, 2004.

Belohlavek, John M. *Broken Glass: Caleb Cushing & the Shattering of the Union.* Kent, Ohio: The Kent State University Press, 2005.

Bigler, David L. *Forgotten Kingdom: The Mormon Theocracy in the American West, 1847–1896.* Spokane, Wash: The Arthur H. Clark Co., 1998.

———. *Fort Limhi: The Mormon Adventure in Oregon Territory, 1855–1858.* Spokane, Wash: The Arthur H. Clark Co., 2003.

Bolkhovitinov, N. N., and Richard A. Pierce, trans. *Russian-American Relations and the Sale of Alaska, 1834–1867.* Kingston, Ont. and Fairbanks, Alaska: Limestone Press, 1996.

Boller, Paul F., Jr. *Presidential Anecdotes.* New York: Oxford University Press, 1996.

Bringhurst, Newell G. *Brigham Young and the Expanding American Frontier.* Boston, Mass: Little, Brown, 1986.

Brooks, Juanita. *The Mountain Meadows Massacre.* Norman: University of Oklahoma Press, 1962.

Chalfant, William Y. *Cheyennes and Horse Soldiers: The 1857 Expedition and the Battle of Solomon's Fork.* Norman: University of Oklahoma Press, 1989.

Clausen, Henry C. and Bruce Lee. *Pearl Harbor: Final Judgment.* New York: Crown Publishers, 1992.

Cross, Croy F. *Justin Smith Morrill, Father of the Land-Grant Colleges.* East Lansing: Michigan State University Press, 1999.

Curtis, George Ticknor. *Life of James Buchanan, Fifteenth President of the United States.* 2 vols. New York: Harper & Bros., 1883.

Denning, Greg. *Mr. Bligh's Bad Language: Passion, Power and Theater on H. M. Armed Vessel Bounty.* Cambridge, U.K: Cambridge University Press, 1992.

Donald, David Herbert. *Charles Sumner and the Coming of the Civil War.* New York: Alfred A. Knopf, 1961.

———. *Lincoln.* New York: Simon & Schuster, 1995.

Eldredge, John. *Illustrated Emigrants' Guide to the Historic Sites along the Hastings/Mormon Trail, Fort Bridger to the Salt Lake Valley.* Salt Lake City: TrailBuff.com Press, 2006.

Emerson, Ken. *Doo-dah! Stephen Foster and the Rise of American Popular Culture.* New York: Simon & Schuster, 1997.

Farley, Steven E. *The Mormon Mountain Meadows Massacre: From the Diary of John I. Ginn.* Bloomington, Ind: 1st Books Library, 2003.

Fehrenbacher, Don E. *The Dred Scott Case: Its Significance in American Law & Politics.* New York: Oxford University Press, 1978.

Fielding, Robert Kent. *The Unsolicited Chronicler: An Account of the Gunnison Massacre, its Causes and Consequences, Utah Territory, 1847–1859: A Narrative History.* Brookline, Mass: Paradigm Publications, 1993.

Firmage, Edwin Brown, and Richard Collin Mangrum. *Zion in the Courts: A Legal History of the Church of Jesus Christ of Latter-day Saints, 1830–1900.* Urbana and Chicago: University of Illinois Press, 1988.

Foltz, Charles S. *Surgeon of the Seas, The Adventurous Life of Surgeon General Jonathan M. Foltz in the Days of Wooden Ships.* Indianapolis, Ind: Bobbs-Merrill Co., 1931.

Furniss, Norman F. *The Mormon Conflict, 1850–1859.* New Haven, Conn: Yale University Press, 1960.

Garavaglia, Louis A., and Charles G. Worman. *Firearms of the American West 1803–1865.* Albuquerque: University of New Mexico Press, 1984.

Gates, Barbara T. *Victorian Suicide: Mad Crimes and Sad Histories.* Princeton: Princeton University Press, 1998.

Gates, Zethyl. *Mariano Medina: Colorado Mountain Man.* Boulder, Colo: Johnson Publishing, 1981.

Gordon, Leo V., and Richard Vetterli. *Powerderkeg.* Novato, Calif: Lyford Books, 1991.

Goetzmann, William H. *Army Exploration in the American West, 1803–1863.* New Haven, Conn: Yale University Press, 1959.

Hafen, LeRoy R., and Francis Marion Young. *Fort Laramie and the Pageant of the West, 1834–1890.*

Glendale, Calif: The Arthur H. Clark Co., 1938; reprinted, Lincoln: University of Nebraska Press, 1984.

Hardy, B. Carmon, *Solemn Covenant: The Mormon Polygamous Passage*. Urbana and Chicago: University of Illinois Press, 1992.

Hedren, Paul L. *Fort Laramie in 1876: Chronicle of a Frontier Post at War*. Lincoln: University of Nebraska Press, 1988.

Hilton, Hope A. *"Wild Bill" Hickman and the Mormon Frontier.* S.L.C: Signature Books, 1988.

Hollon, W. Eugene. *Beyond the Cross Timbers: The Travels of Randolph B. Marcy, 1812–1887*. Norman: University of Oklahoma Press, 1955.

Holzer, Harold. *The Lincoln-Douglas Debates*. New York: HarperCollins Publishers, 1993.

Huseman, Ben W. *Wild River, Timeless Canyons: Baldwin Mollhausen's Watercolors of the Colorado.* Fort Worth, Tex., and Tucson, Ariz: Amon Carter Museum and University of Arizona Press, 1995.

Huston, James L. *The Panic of 1857 and the Coming of the Civil War.* Baton Rouge: Louisiana State University Press, 1987.

Ipson, Kathryn H. *Ever Faithful, The Life of Joseph Leland Heywood*. n.p., 1999.

Isaacson, Walter. *Benjamin Franklin: An American Life*. New York: Simon & Schuster, 2003.

Jackson, W. Turrentine. *Wagon Roads West: A Study of Federal Road Surveys and Construction in the Trans-Mississippi West, 1846–1869*. Berkeley and Los Angeles: University of California Press, 1952.

Jenson, Andrew. *LDS Biographical Encyclopedia*. 4 vols. S.L.C: Andrew Jenson History Co., 1901.

Johannsen, Robert W. *Stephen A. Douglas*. New York: Oxford University, 1973.

Johnson, Melvin C. *Polygamy on the Pedernales: Lyman Wight's Mormon Villages in Antebellum Texas, 1845–1858*. Logan: Utah State University Press, 2006.

Johnston, William Preston. *The Life of Albert Sidney Johnston, Embracing His Services in the Armies of the United States, the Republic of Texas, and the Confederate States*. New York: D. Appleton and Company, 1878.

Klein, Philip S. *President James Buchanan: A Biography*. University Park: Pennsylvania State University Press, 1962.

Knowlton, Ezra Clark. *The Utah Knowltons: History and Genealogy of Three Generations of Sidney Algernon Knowlton and His Descendants*. S.L.C: Knowlton Family Organization, 1971.

Leland, Joy, ed. *Frederick West Lander: A Biographical Sketch* (1822–1862). Reno, Nev: Desert Research Institute, 1993.

Lyman, Edward Leo. *San Bernardino: The Rise and Fall of a California Community*. S.L.C: Signature Books, 1996.

Madsen, Brigham D., ed. *Exploring the Great Salt Lake, The Stansbury Expedition of 1849–50*. S.L.C: Tanner Trust Fund, University of Utah Library and University of Utah Press, 1989.

Mahon, John K. *History of the Second Seminole War, 1835–1842*. Gainesville: University of Florida Press, 1967.

McConnell, William F. *Remember Reno: A Biography of Major General Jesse Lee Reno*. Shippensburg, Penn: White Mane Publishing Co., 1996.

McCullough, David. *Mornings on Horseback*. New York: Simon and Schuster, 1981.

McGavin, E. Cecil. *U.S. Soldiers Invade Utah*. Boston, Mass: Meador Publishing Co., 1937.

Miller, David Hunter. *The Alaska Treaty.* Kingston, Ont: Limestone Press, 1981.

Moorman, Donald R., with Gene A. Sessions. *Camp Floyd and the Mormons: The Utah War.* S.L.C: University of Utah Press, 1992; reprinted 2005.

Morris, Edmund. *Theodore Rex.* New York: Modern Library, 2002.

Moss, Robert H. *Soldiers 'n Saints, An Historical Novel.* Springville, Ut: Cedar Fort, Inc., 1996.

Mullis, Tony R. *Peacekeeping on the Plains: Army Operations in Bleeding Kansas.* Columbia: University of Missouri Press, 2004.

Nadeau, Remi. *Fort Laramie and the Sioux.* Lincoln: University of Nebraska Press, 1982.

Paige, Glenn D. *The Korean Decision: June 24–30, 1950.* New York: The Free Press, 1968.

Paul, R. Eli. *Blue Water Creek and the First Sioux War, 1854–1856.* Norman: University of Oklahoma Press, 2004.

Peskin, Allan. *Winfield Scott and the Profession of Arms.* Kent, Ohio: Kent State University Press, 2003.

Pinnegar, Charles. *Brand of Infamy: A Biography of John Buchanan Floyd.* Westport, Conn: Greenwood Press, 2002.

Quinn, D. Michael. *The Mormon Hierarchy: Extensions of Power.* S.L.C: Signature Books, 1997.

Rankin, Robert S. *When Civil Law Fails: Martial Law and Its Legal Basis in the United States.* Durham, N.C: Duke University Press, 1939.

Richards, Kent D. *Isaac I. Stevens: Young Man in a Hurry.* Pullman: Washington State University Press, 1979.

Roberts, Brigham H. *A Comprehensive History of the Church of Jesus Christ of Latter-day Saints, Century I.* 6 vols. S.L.C: Deseret News Press, 1930.

Roland, Charles P. *Albert Sidney Johnston: Soldier of Three Republics.* Lexington: University Press of Kentucky, 1964; reprinted 2001.

Schindler, Harold. *Orrin Porter Rockwell: Man of God, Son of Thunder.* S.L.C: University of Utah Press, 1983.

Searight, Thomas B. *The Old Pike: A History of the National Road.* Uniontown, Pa: n.p., 1894.

Settle, Raymond W., and Mary Lund Settle. *Empire on Wheels.* Stanford, Calif: Stanford University Press, 1949.

———. *War Drums and Wagon Wheels: The Story of Russell, Majors and Waddell.* Lincoln: University of Nebraska Press, 1966.

Sharpe, Mike. *Thou Shalt Not Kill Unless Otherwise Instructed (Poems and Stories).* Armonk, N.Y: M.E. Sharpe, Inc., 2005.

Simpson, John Eddins. *Howell Cobb: The Politics of Ambition.* Chicago, Ill: Adams Press, 1973.

Singer, Jane. *The Confederate Dirty War: Arson, Bombings, Assassination and Plots for Chemical and Germ Attacks on the Union.* Jefferson, N.C: McFarland & Co., 2005.

Smith, Elbert B. *The Presidency of James Buchanan.* Lawrence: University Press of Kansas, 1975.

Smythe, Donald. *Pershing: General of the Armies.* Bloomington: Indiana University Press, 1986.

Sohn, Anton Paul. *A Saw, Pocket Instruments, and Two Ounces of Whiskey: Frontier Military Medicine in the Great Basin.* Spokane, Wash: The Arthur H. Clark Co., 1998.

Stampp, Kenneth M. *America in 1857: A Nation on the Brink.* New York: Oxford University Press, 1990.

Stewart, George R. *John Phoenix, Esq., the Veritable Squibob.* New York: Henry Holt & Co., 1937.

Thompson, Jerry. *Henry Hopkins Sibley: Confederate General of the West.* Natchitoches, La: Northwestern State University Press, 1987.

Treese, Loretta. *Railroads of Pennsylvania: Fragments of the Past in the Keystone Landscape.* Mechanicsburg, Pa: Stackpole Books, 2003.

Tullidge, Edward W. *History of Salt Lake City.* S.L.C: Star Printing Co., 1886.

Van Noord, Roger. *King of Beaver Island: The Life and Assassination of James Jesse Strang.* Urbana and Chicago: University of Illinois Press, 1988.

Van Wagenen, Michael Scott. *The Texas Republic and the Mormon Kingdom of God.* College Station: Texas A&M University Press, 2002.

Varley, James F. *Brigham and the Brigadier: General Patrick Connor and His California Volunteers in Utah and Along the Overland Trail.* Tucson, Ariz: Westernlore Press, 1989.

Walker, Ronald W. *Wayward Saints: The Godbeites and Brigham Young.* Urbana and Chicago: University of Illinois Press, 1998.

Wallner, Peter A. *Franklin Pierce: New Hampshire's Favorite Son.* Concord, N.H: Plaidswede, 2004.

West, Elliott. *The Contested Plains: Indians, Goldseekers, and the Rush to Colorado.* Lawrence: University Press of Kansas, 1998.

Whall, Les. *The Salt Lake City Post Office, 1849–1869.* S.L.C: The Author, 1982.

Wilson, Mark R. *The Business of Civil War: Military Mobilization and the State, 1861–1865.* Baltimore: Johns Hopkins University Press, 2006.

Woldman, Albert A. *Lincoln and the Russians, The Story of Russian-American Diplomatic Relations During the Civil War.* Cleveland, Ohio: World Publishing Co., 1952.

Woodward, Arthur. *Feud on the Colorado.* Los Angeles: WesternLore Press, 1955.

Young, Otis E. *The West of Philip St. George Cooke, 1809–1895.* Glendale, Calif: The Arthur H. Clark Co., 1955.

Secondary Sources: Articles and Book Chapters

Abbott, Keene. "The Sound of Running Water," *The Outlook* 9 (28 October 1911).

Agnew, James B. "General Barnard E. Bee," *Civil War Times Illustrated* 14 (December 1975).

Aird, Polly. "'You Nasty Apostates, Clear Out': Reasons for Disaffection in the Late 1850s," *Journal of Mormon Hist.* 30 (Fall 2004).

"Albert Gallatin Browne," *Report of the Harvard Class of 1853, 1849–1913, Issued on the Sixtieth Anniversary for the Use of the Class and Its Friends.* Cambridge, Mass: Harvard University Press, 1913.

Alexander, John K. "Working a 'Gold Mine': Scholars of Early America and Their Manuscript Collections at The Historical Society of Pennsylvania," *Pennsylvania Magazine of Hist. and Biography* 124 (January/April 2000).

Alexander, Thomas G. "Wilford Woodruff and the Mormon Reformation of 1855–57," *Dialogue: A Journal of Mormon Thought* 25 (Summer 1992).

Alter, J. Cecil and Robert J. Dwyer, eds. "Journal of Captain Albert Tracy, 1858–1860," *Utah Hist. Qtly.* 13 (1945).

Auchampaugh, Philip G. "James Buchanan, the Court and the Dred Scott Case," *Tennessee Hist. Magazine* 9 (January 1926).

———. "John B. Floyd and James Buchanan," *Tyler's Qtly. Hist. and Genealogical Magazine* 4 (April 1923).

Baker, Anni P. "Daughters of Mars: Army Officers' Wives and Military Culture on the American Frontier," *The Historian: A Journal of Hist.* 67 (Spring 2005).

Balla, Wesley, Peter Wallner, and Jane and Craig Venzke. "Revealing Relationships: The Family and Friends of Franklin Pierce," *Hist. New Hampshire* 59 (Spring 2005).

Ballantine, Henry Winthrop. "Unconstitutional Claims of Military Authority" *Yale Law Journal* 24 (1915).

Belohlavek, John M. "The Politics of Scandal: A Reassessment of John B. Floyd as Secretary of War," *West Virginia Hist.* 31 (April 1970).

Bennett, Richard, and Arran Jewsbury. "The Lion and the Emperor: The Mormons, the Hudson's Bay Company, and Vancouver Island, 1846–1858," *BC Studies* 128 (Winter 2000/2001).

Bigler, David L. "Mormon Missionaries, the Utah War, and the 1858 Bannock Raid on Fort Limhi," *Montana: The Magazine of Western Hist.* 53 (Autumn 2003).

———. "Garland Hurt, the American Friend of the Utahs," *Utah Hist. Qtly.* 62 (Spring 1994).

———. "Sources of Conflict: Mormons and Their Neighbors, 1830–90," unpublished lecture delivered to the Salt Lake [City] Theological Seminary, 25 July 2003.

———. "The Aiken Party Executions and the Utah War, 1857–1858." *Western Hist. Qtly.* 38 (Winter 2007).

Blodgett, Peter J. "Using Our Faculties: Collecting the Papers of Western Historians at the Huntington Library," *Western Hist. Qtly.* 34 (Winter 2003).

Bohl, Susan. "A War on Civilians: Order Number 11 and the Evacuation of Western Missouri," *Prologue: The Journal of the National Archives* 36 (Spring 2004).

Briggs, Robert H. "Cultural Studies of the 1857 Southern Utah Militiamen." Unpublished paper, Mormon History Association annual conference, May 2006, Casper, Wyo.

Brock, R. A. "General John Rogers Cooke," *Southern Hist. Society Papers* 18 (1890–91).

Bush, Lester E., Jr. "Brigham Young in Life and Death: A Medical Overview," *Journal of Mormon Hist.* 5 (1978).

Calomiris, Charles W., and Larry Schweikart, "The Panic of 1857: Origins, Transmission, and Containment," *The Journal of Economic Hist.* 51 (December 1991).

Cannon, M. Hamlin. "Winfield Scott and the Utah Expedition," *Military Affairs: Journal of the American Military Institute* 5 (Fall 1941).

Chapin, David. "'Science Weeps, Humanity Weeps, the World Weeps': America Mourns Elisha Kent Kane," *The Pennsylvania Magazine of Hist. and Biography* 123 (October 1999).

Cohen, Samuel. "Martial Law in Washington Territory," *Pacific Northwest Qtly.* 27 (July 1936).

"Constitutional Law. Federal Constitutional Limitation on Military Powers of State Governor," *Virginia Law Review* 22 (May 1936): 825–26.

Corwin, Edward S. "Martial Law, Yesterday and Today," *Political Science Qtly.* 47 (1932).

Cubbison, Douglas R. "'Look Out for Hell Some Place Soon': The 2nd Colorado Cavalry in Missouri February–September, 1864," *Military Hist. of the West* 32 (Spring 2002).

Culmer, Frederick A. "'General' John Wilson, Signer of the Deseret Petition," *California Hist. Soc. Qtly.* 26 (1947).

Cutrer, Thomas W. "'A Lion in Her Path': Texas, New Mexico, and the United States Army, 1850," *Military Hist. of the West* 34 (2004).

Davidson, Lee, "America's Forgotten War, LDS Raiders Kept Army at Bay in 1857-58," *Deseret Morning News*, 9 July 2006.

Esplin, Ronald K. "'A Place Prepared': Joseph, Brigham and the Quest for Promised Refuge in the West," *Journal of Mormon Hist.* 9 (1982).

Eyal, Yonatan. "With His Eyes Open: Stephen A. Douglas and the Kansas-Nebraska Disaster of 1854," *Journal of Illinois State Hist. Soc.* 91 (Winter 1998).

Gibson, Harry W. "Frontier Arms of the Mormons," *Utah Hist. Qtly.* 42 (Winter 1974).

Godfrey, Audrey M. "Housewives, Hussies, and Heroines: The Women with Johnston's Army," *Utah Hist. Qtly.* 54 (Spring 1986).

Godfrey, Kenneth W. "William Bowker Preston: Pioneer, Colonizer, Civic Leader, Church Official, Husband, and Father," *Mormon Hist. Studies* 5 (Spring 2004).

———. "Did the Bishop Murder the Morrisite Mrs. Bowman? The Arrest and Trial of Robert T. Burton." Unpublished paper, Mormon History Association annual conference, May 1999, Ogden, Ut.

Golder, Frank. "The Purchase of Alaska," *American Hist. Review* 25 (1920).

Gray, John S. "Fact Versus Fiction in the Kansas Boyhood of Buffalo Bill," *Kansas Hist: A Journal of the Central Plains* 8 (Spring 1985).

Groesbeck, Nicholas Harmon. "Narrative" in "They Came in 1856: John Banks Company," *Treasures of Pioneer History*. 6 vols. S.L.C: Daughters of Utah Pioneers, 1952–57.

Hamilton, William R. "History of the Mormon Rebellion of 1856–57," *The United Services, a Monthly Review of Military and Naval Affairs* (1890–91).

Harmon, George D. "President James Buchanan's Betrayal of Governor Robert J. Walker of Kansas," *Pennsylvania Magazine of Hist. and Biography* 53 (1929).

Hatfield, Mark O. (with Senate Historical Office). "Strained Relations with Buchanan," "John C. Breckinridge (1857–1861)," *Vice Presidents of the United States, 1789–1993*. Washington: U.S. Government Printing Office, 1997.

Heaston, Michael D. "The Governor and the Indian Agent: 1855–1857," *New Mexico Hist. Review* 45 (April 1970).

Hendrickson, Rya C. "Clinton's Military Strikes in 1998: Diversionary Uses of Force?" *Armed Forces and Society* 28 (2002).

Hershey, H. J. "Power and Authority of Governor and Militia in Domestic Disturbances," *Harvard Law Review* 34 (1921).

Hinton, Wayne. "John D.T. McAllister: The Southern Utah Years, 1876–1910," *Journal of Mormon Hist.* 29 (2003).

Holland, James W. "Memoir of Roberts Bartholow," *Transactions of the College of Physicians of Philadelphia* 26 (1904).

Hubbard, George U. "Abraham Lincoln as Seen by the Mormons," *Utah Hist. Qtly.* 31 (Spring 1963).

Isley, William H. "The Sharps Rifle Episode in Kansas History," *The American Hist. Review* 12 (April 1907).

Johannsen, Robert W. "National Issues and Local Politics in Washington Territory, 1857–1861," *Pacific Northwest Qtly.* 42 (January 1951).

Johnson, Kenneth R., ed. "A Southern Student Describes the Inauguration of President James Buchanan," *Alabama Hist. Qtly.* 31 (Fall/Winter 1969).

Johnson, Norman K. "Taking a Page from the Canny Comanche, Henry Sibley Devised a New Tent for the Western Frontier," *Wild West* (October 1991).

Jorgenson, Lynne Watkins. "John Hyde, Jr., Mormon Renegade," *Journal of Mormon Hist.* 17 (1991).

Klein, Philip S. "The Inauguration of President James Buchanan," *Journal of the Lancaster Co. Hist. Soc.*, 61 (October 1957).

Lieber, G. Norman. "What Is the Justification of Martial Law?" *North American Review* 163 (1896).

Lokken, Roy N. "The Martial Law Controversy in Washington Territory, 1856," *Pacific Northwest Qtly.* 43 (April 1952).

Lyman, Edward Leo. "Larger than Texas: Proposals to Combine California and Mormon Deseret as One State," *California Hist.* 80 (Spring 2001).

MacKinnon, William P., and Richard D. Poll. "Causes of the Utah War Reconsidered," *Journal of Mormon Hist.* 20 (Fall 1994).

——— and Richard N. Ellis. "Edwin Vose Sumner," Howard R. Lamar, ed., *New Encyclopedia of the American West.* New Haven, Conn: Yale University Press, 1998.

———. "Epilogue to the Utah War: Impact and Legacy," *Journal of Mormon Hist.* 29 (Fall 2003).

———. "'Like Splitting a Man Up His Backbone': The Territorial Dismemberment of Utah, 1850–1896," *Utah Hist. Qtly.* 71 (Spring 2003).

———. "'Lonely Bones': Leadership and Utah War Violence," *Journal of Mormon Hist.* 33 (Spring 2007).

———. "Loose in the Stacks: A Half-Century with the Utah War and Its Legacy," *Dialogue: A Journal of Mormon Thought* 40 (Spring 2007).

———. "125 Years of Conspiracy Theories: Origins of the Utah Expedition of 1857–58," *Utah Hist. Qtly.* 52 (Summer 1984).

———. "Stranger in a Strange Land: My Forty-Five Years with the Utah War and What I Have Learned," *Yale University Library Gazette* 80 (October 2005).

———. "Review Essay [Floyd]," *New Mexico Hist. Review* 78 (Fall 2003).

———. "Review Essay [Harney]," *New Mexico Hist. Review* 76 (October 2001).

———. "Sex, Subalterns, and Steptoe: Army Behavior, Mormon Rage, and Utah War Anxieties," *Utah Hist. Qtly.*, forthcoming 2008.

———. "The Buchanan Spoils System and the Utah Expedition: Careers of W. M. F. Magraw and John M. Hockaday," *Utah Hist. Qtly.* 31 (Spring 1963).

———. "The Gap in the Buchanan Revival: The Utah Expedition of 1857–58," *Utah Hist. Qtly.* 45, no. 1 (Winter 1977).

———. "'Unquestionably Authentic and Correct in Every Detail': Probing John I. Ginn and His Remarkable Utah War Story," *Utah Hist. Qtly.* 72 (Fall 2004).

Madsen, Brigham D., ed. "John Gunnison's Letters to His Mormon Friend, Albert Carrington," *Utah Hist. Qtly.* 59 (Summer 1991).

Mazour, Anatole. "The Prelude to Russia's Departure from America," *Pacific Hist. Review* 10 (1941).

McClaughry, John. "John Wolcott Phelps: The Civil War General Who Became a Forgotten Presidential Candidate in 1880," *Vermont Hist.* 38 (Autumn 1970).

Merrill, Irving R., and Merle Wells. "Tim Goodale Comes Home," *Overland Journal: The Official Journal of Oregon-California Trails Association* 17 (Summer 1999).

———. "Goodale's Cutoff from Boise Valley to Powder River," *Overland Journal: The Official Journal of Oregon-California Trails Association* 4 (Spring 1996).

Miller, David H. "Brigham Young, Edward J. Steptoe, and the 1854–55 Gubernatorial Controversy." Unpublished paper, Utah State Historical Society annual meeting, September 1978, Salt Lake City.

Miller, Rod. "Bill Cody Gets Buffaloed," in James A. Crutchfield, ed. *The Way West: True Stories of the American Frontier.* New York: Forge Books, 2005.

Moody, Marshall D. "Kit Carson, Agent to the Indians in New Mexico 1853–1861," *New Mexico Hist. Review* 28 (January 1953).

Morgan, Wanda. "The Pony Express Rider and the President," *Signal Mountain* 1 (Fall 1998).

Mullis, Tony R. "The Dispersal of the Topeka Legislature, A Look at Command and Control (C2) During Bleeding Kansas," *Kansas Hist: A Journal of the Central Plains* 27 (Spring–Summer 2004).

Munro, J. B. "Mormon Colonization Scheme for Vancouver Island," *Washington Hist. Qtly.* 25 (1934).

Musick, Michael P. "War in an Age of Wonders: Civil War Arms and Equipment," *Prologue: The Journal of the National Archives* 27 (Winter 1995).

Nickles, David Paul. "Telegraph Diplomats: The United States' Relations with France in 1848 and 1870," *Technology and Culture* 40 (January 1999).

Orton, Chad M. "The Mormons in Johnston's Army," *Pioneer* (Winter 1998).

Parshall, Ardis E. "'Pursue, Retake & Punish': The 1857 Santa Clara Ambush," *Utah Hist. Qtly.* 73 (Winter 2005).

Peterson, Charles S. "A Portrait of Lot Smith Frontiersman," *Western Hist. Qtly.* 1 (October 1970).

Peterson, Paul. "The Mormon Reformation of 1856–1857: The Rhetoric and the Reality," *Journal of Mormon Hist.* 15 (1989).

Pinney, Marie. "Charles Becker, Pony Express Rider and Oregon Pioneer," *Oregon Hist. Qtly.* 67 (September 1966).

Poll, Richard D, and Ralph W. Hansen. "'Buchanan's Blunder': The Utah War, 1857–1858," *Military Affairs* 25 (Fall 1961).

——— and William P. MacKinnon. "Causes of the Utah War Reconsidered," *Journal of Mormon Hist.* 20 (Fall 1994).

———. "The Mormon Question Enters National Politics, 1850–1856," *Utah Hist. Qtly.* 25 (April 1957).

———. "Thomas L. Kane and the Utah War," *Utah Hist. Qtly.* 61 (Spring 1993).

Ponce, Pearl T. "Pledges and Principles: Buchanan, Walker, and Kansas in 1857," *Kansas Hist: A Journal of the Central Plains* 27 (Spring–Summer 2004).

Quinn, D. Michael "LDS 'Headquarters Culture' and the Rest of Mormonism, Past and Present," *Dialogue, A Journal of Mormon Thought* 34 (2001).

Rezneck, Samuel. "The Influence of Depression upon American Opinion, 1857–1859," *Journal of Economic Hist.* 2 (May 1942).

Richmond, Robert. "Some Western Editors View the Mormon War, 1857–1858," *Trail Guide* 8 (March 1963).

Robitscher, Jonas, "Buchanan." Typescript 1976, chapter for unpublished monograph on presidential health; photocopy in editor's possession.

Rutherford, Phillip R. "The Arabia Incident," *Kansas Hist: A Journal of the Central Plains* 1 (Spring 1978).

Ryan, Garry David. "Camp Walbach, Nebraska Territory, 1858–1859: The Military Post at Cheyenne Pass," *Annals of Wyoming* 35 (April 1963).

Schindler, Harold. "Firearms in the West: Guns, Handy in Early Utah, May Have Kept Arguments from Getting to Trigger Point, Settlers in Utah Produced Copycat Colts," *Salt Lake Tribune,* 20 February 1994.

———. "Tartar the War Horse," *Salt Lake Tribune,* 4 September 1994.

Scroggins, Mark. "Georgia, New York, and Muskets on the Eve of the Civil War," *Georgia Hist. Qtly.* 89 (Fall 2005).

Seifrit, William C. "Charles Henry Wilcken, An Undervalued Saint," *Utah Hist. Qtly.* 55 (1987).

SenGupta, Gunja. "Bleeding Kansas," *Kansas Hist: A Journal of the Central Plains* 24 (Winter 2001–2002).

Shengold, David. "From the Other Shore: Aleksandr Herzen on James Buchanan," *Slavic Review* 51 (Winter 1992).

Sheridan, Richard C. "Brigadier-General James Deshler, Professional Soldier," *Alabama Hist. Qtly.* 26 (Summer 1964).

Sessions, Gene A., and Stephen W. Stathis. "The Mormon Invasion of Russian America: Dynamics of a Potent Myth," *Utah Hist. Qtly.* 45 (Winter 1977).

Smith, Marion O. "In Quest of a Supply of Salt Peter and Gunpowder in Early Civil War Tennessee," *Tennessee Hist. Qtly.* 56 (Summer 1997).

Solberg, Winton U. "No Rest for the Weary," *Christian Hist.* 19 (May 2000).

Stephen, Sir Leslie, and Sidney Lee, eds., *Dictionary of National Biography*. 63 vols. New York: Macmillan, 1885–1900.

Thompson, Jerry. "When Albert Sidney Johnston Came Home to Texas: Reconstruction Politics and the Reburial of a Hero," *Southwestern Hist. Qtly.* 103 (April 2000).

Walker, Ronald W. "Raining Pitchforks: Brigham Young as Preacher," *Sunstone* 8 (May–June 1983).

Watt, Ronald G. "The Beginnings of 'The Journal of Discourses': A Confrontation Between George D. Watt and Willard Richards," *Utah Hist. Qtly.* 75 (Spring 2007).

———. "Sailing 'The Old Ship Zion': The Life of George D. Watt," *Brigham Young University Studies* 18 (Fall 1977).

Watts, Dale E. "How Bloody Was Bleeding Kansas? Political Killings in Kansas Territory, 1854–1861," *Kansas Hist: A Journal of the Central Plains* 18 (Summer 1995).

———. "Plows and Bibles, Rifles and Revolvers: Guns in Kansas Territory," *Kansas Hist: A Journal of the Central Plains* 21 (Spring 1998).

Weida, Jason Collins. "A Republic of Emergencies: Martial Law in American Jurisprudence," *Connecticut Law Review* (Summer 2004).

Wells, Junius F. [Vaux], "The Echo Canon War," *Contributor* 3 (1881–82).

Whittaker, David J. "New Sources on Old Friends: The Thomas L. Kane and Elizabeth W. Kane Collection," *Journal of Mormon Hist.* 27 (Spring 2000).

Williams, David A. "President Buchanan Receives a Proposal for an Anti-Mormon Crusade, 1857," *Brigham Young University Studies* 14 (Autumn 1973).

Wilson, H. L. "James Buchanan's Proposed Intervention in Mexico," *American Hist. Review* 5 (1899).

Wilson, Mark R. "The Politics of Procurement: Military Origins of Bureaucratic Autonomy," *The Journal of Policy Hist.* 18 (2006).

Published Primary Sources

Adams, F. G. *Transactions of the Kansas State Historical Society, 1889–1896.* 5 vols. Topeka: Kansas State Printing Co., 1896.

Americanization Dept., ed. *America, Great Crises In Our History Told by Its Makers. A Library of Original Sources.* 25 vols. Chicago: Veterans of Foreign Wars, 1925.

[Anonymous.] *Mormoniad.* Boston, Mass: A. Williams and Co., 1858.

Basler, Roy P. *The Collected Works of Abraham Lincoln.* 9 vols. New Brunswick, N.J: Rutgers University Press, 1953–55.

Bigler, David L., ed. *A Winter with the Mormons: The 1852 Letters of Jotham Goodell.* S.L.C: University of Utah Tanner Trust Fund, 2001.

———, and Will Bagley, eds., *Army of Israel: Mormon Battalion Narratives.* Spokane, Wash: The Arthur H. Clark Co., 2000.

Brooks, Juanita, ed. *On the Mormon Frontier: The Diary of Hosea Stout, 1844–1861.* 2 vols. S.L.C: University of Utah Press and Utah State Historical Society, 1964.

Brown, J. Robert. *Journal of a Trip across the Plains of the U.S., from Missouri to California, in the Year 1856 Giving a Correct View of the Country, Anecdotes, Indian Stories, Mountaineers' Tales, Etc.* Columbus, Ohio: The author, 1860.

Brown, Lorenzo. *The Journal of Lorenzo Brown, 1823–1900.* [S.L.C.?: By the family, ca. 1985].

[Browne, Albert G., Jr.]. "The Utah Expedition; Its Causes and Consequences," *The Atlantic Monthly. A Magazine of Literature, Art, and Politics* 3 (March–May 1859).

Buchanan, James. *Mr. Buchanan's Administration on the Eve of the Rebellion.* New York: D. Appleton and Co., 1866.

Buell, Augustus. *"The Cannoneer": Recollections of Service in the Army of the Potomac.* Washington, D.C: National Tribune, 1890.

Carter, William A. "Diary of Judge William A. Carter," *Annals of Wyoming* 11 (April 1939).

Chittenden, Hiram Martin, and Alfred Talbot Richardson, eds. *Life, Letters and Travels of Father Pierre-Jean DeSmet, S.J., 1801–1873.* 2 vols. New York: Arno Press and the New York Times, 1960.

Civil War Papers Read before the Commandery of the State of Massachusetts Military Order of the Loyal Legion of the United States. 3 vols. Boston; reprinted Wilmington, N.C: Broadfoot Publishing Co., 1993.

Clark, William. "A Trip Across the Plains in 1857," *Iowa Journal of Hist. and Politics* (1922).

Cooley, Everett L., ed. *Diary of Brigham Young 1857.* S.L.C: Tanner Trust Fund and University of Utah Library, 1980.

"Correspondence Between the Late Secretary of War and General Wool." *House Exec. Doc. 88* (35-1), 1858, Serial 956.

"Covode Investigation." *House Report 648* (36-1), 1860, Serial 1071.

Crosby, Jesse W. "Journal of Pvt. Jesse W. Crosby," *Annals of Wyoming* (July 1939).

Dunbar, Seymour, and Paul C. Phillips, eds. *The Journals and Letters of Major John Owen, Pioneer of 1850–1871, Embracing His Purchase of St. Mary's Mission; the Building of Fort Owen; His Travels; His Relation with the Indians; His Work for the Government; and His Activities as a Western Empire Builder for Twenty Years.* 2 vols. New York: Edward Eberstadt, 1927.

Gardner, Hamilton, ed. "March of 2d Dragoons, Report of Lieutenant Colonel Philip St. George Cooke on the March of the 2d Dragoons from Fort Leavenworth to Fort Bridger in 1857," *Annals of Wyoming* 27 (April 1955).

Gunnison, John W. *The Mormons or Latter-day Saints, In the Valley of the Great Salt Lake.* Brookline, Mass: Paradigm Publications, reprinted 1993.

Hafen, LeRoy R., and Ann W. Hafen, eds. *Mormon Resistance: A Documentary Account of the Utah Expedition, 1857–1858.* Lincoln: University of Nebraska Press, reprinted 2005 from *The Utah Expedition, 1857–1858: A Documentary Account of the United States Military Movement under Colonel Albert Sidney Johnston, and the Resistance by Brigham Young and the Mormon Nauvoo Legion.* Glendale, Calif: The Arthur H. Clark Co., 1958; reprinted 1982.

Hammond, Otis G., ed. *The Utah Expedition 1857–1858: Letters of Capt. Jesse A. Gove, 10th Inf., U.S.A., of Concord, N.H., to Mrs. Gove, and Special Correspondence of the New York Herald.* Concord: New Hampshire Historical Society, 1928.

Heitman, Francis B. *Historical Register and Dictionary of the United States Army 1789–1903.* 2 vols. Washington, D.C., 1903.

Hickman, William A., with J. H. Beadle. *Brigham's Destroying Angel: Being the Life, Confession, and Startling Disclosures of the Notorious Bill Hickman, the Danite Chief of Utah.* S.L.C: Shepard Publishing Co., 1904.

Homer, Michael W., ed. *On the Way to Somewhere Else: European Sojourners in the Mormon West, 1834–1930.* Spokane, Wash: The Arthur H. Clark Co., 2006.

"Hooper & Williams, Livingston, Kincaid & Co., Gilbert & Gerrish, and Others," *House Report 521* (36-1), 1860, Serial 1070.

Hulbert, Archer Butler, ed. *Letters of an Overland Mail Agent in Utah.* Worcester, Mass: American Antiquarian Society, 1929.

Humphreys, Capt. A. A. "Report from Bureau of Explorations and Surveys," *Annual Report of the Secretary of War, 1857.*

Hyde, John. *Mormonism: Its Leaders and Designs.* New York: W. P. Fetridge, 1857.

Jones, Daniel W. *Forty Years Among the Indians: A True Yet Thrilling Narrative of the Author's Experiences Among the Natives.* S.L.C: Bookcraft, 1960.

Journal of Discourses, 26 vols. London: Latter-day Saints Book Depot, 1854–1886.

Kenney, Scott G., ed. *Wilford Woodruff's Journal, 1833–1898.* 9 vols. Midvale, Ut: Signature Books, 1983–1985.

Lowe, Percival G. *Five Years a Dragoon ('49 to '54) and Other Adventures of the Great Plains.* Kansas City: Franklin Hudson Pub. Co., 1906.

Majors, Alexander and Prentiss Ingraham, ed. *Seventy Years on the Frontier: Alexander Majors' Memoirs of a Lifetime on the Border.* Columbus, Ohio: Long's College Book Co., 1950.

Marcy, Randolph B. *Thirty Years of Army Life on the Border.* New York: Harper & Brothers, 1866.

Martin, George W., ed. *Collections of the Kansas State Hist. Soc.* 12 (1911–12).

Martineau, James H. "A Scouting Party," *Contributor,* August 1890.

Moore, John Bassett, ed. *The Works of James Buchanan, Comprising his Speeches, State Papers, and Private Correspondence.* 12 vols. New York: Antiquarian Press Ltd., 1960.

Morehead, Charles R. "Morehead's Narrative" (Appendix C) in William E. Connelley, *War with Mexico, 1846–1847: Doniphan's Expedition and the Conquest of New Mexico and California.* Topeka, Kans: Crane & Co., 1907.

Morrison, James L., Jr., ed. *The Memoirs of Henry Heth.* Westport, Conn: Greenwood Press, 1974.

Myers, Robert Monson, ed. *The Children of Pride, A True Story of Georgia and the Civil War.* New Haven, Conn: Yale University Press, 1972.

Nielson, Roger B. *Roll Call at Old Camp Floyd, Utah Territory: Soldiers of Johnston's Army at the Upper Camp 8 July to 8 September 1858.* Springville, Ut: n.p., 2006.

Owens, Kenneth N. *Gold Rush Saints: California Mormons and the Great Rush for Riches.* Spokane, Wash: The Arthur H. Clark Co., 2004.

Remy, Jules. *A Journey to Great-Salt-Lake City.* 2 vols. London: W. Jeffs, 1861.

"Report of the Secretary of War, 1857." *Senate Exec. Doc. 11* (35-1), Serial 920.

Scott, Winfield. *Memoirs of Lieut.-General Scott, L.L.D., Written by Himself.* 2 vols. New York: Sheldon & Co., 1864.

Sibley, Marilyn McAdams, ed. "Robert E. Lee to Albert Sidney Johnston, 1857," *The Journal of Southern Hist.* 29 (February 1963).

"Statistical Report on the Sickness and Mortality in the Army of the United States, Compiled [by Richard H. Coolidge, M.D.] from the Records of the Surgeon General's Office; Embracing a Period of Five Years, From January, 1855, to January, 1860." *Senate Exec. Doc.* 52 (36-1), 1860, Serial 1035.

Stewart, James. "Battery B Fourth United States Artillery at Gettysburg," *Sketches of War Hist.* 4 (1893).

Stowers, Robert E., and John M. Ellis, eds. "Charles A. Scott's Diary of the Utah Expedition, 1857–1861," *Utah Hist. Qtly.* 28 (April 1960).

Terry, James Parshall [Unohoo]. "Johnston's Army Incidents," *Juvenile Instructor* 28 (May 1893).

Townsend, George Alfred. *The Mormon Trials at Salt Lake City.* New York: American News Company, 1871.

Turnley, Parmenas Taylor. *Reminiscences of Parmenas Taylor Turnley, from the Cradle to Three-Score and Ten, by Himself, from Diaries Kept from Early Boyhood.* Chicago, Ill: Donohue & Henneberry, 1893.

U.S. Opinions of the Attorney General. 8 U.S. Op. Atty. Gen. 365 (3 February 1857).

"Utah Expedition." House Exec. Doc. 71 (35-1), 1858, Serial 956.

Ware, Eugene F. *The Indian War of 1864.* New York: St. Martin's Press, 1960.

White, David A., comp. *News of the Plains and Rockies 1830–1865*. 8 vols. Spokane, Wash: The Arthur H. Clark Co., 1996–2001.

Wills, John A. "The Twin Relics of Barbarism," *Publications of the Historical Society of Southern California*, multiple vols. (Los Angeles: Evening Express Co., 1890, reprinted Dawson's Book Shop, 1965).

Young, Brigham. *Proclamation of Martial Law*, 15 September 1857. Brigham Young Collection, LDS Archives.

Young, John R. *Memoirs of John R. Young, Utah Pioneer 1847, Written by Himself.* S.L.C: Deseret News, 1920.

Unpublished Primary Sources

Arrington, Leonard J. Papers. Utah State University, Logan.

Bagley, John. Record Book, Written 1894. Unpublished typescript. Private collection of Mr. Will Bagley.

Becker, Charles W. Narrative. LDS Archives.

Black, Jeremiah S. Papers. Library of Congress.

Buchanan, James. Papers. Historical Society of Pennsylvania, Philadelphia.

Buchanan, James. Papers. Waidner-Spahr Library, Dickinson College, Carlisle, Pa.

Buchanan, James, to Naperville, Ill., Committee, 14 March 1857. Naperville (Ill.) Historical Society; copy in Utah State Historical Society.

Burr, David A. and David H. Papers. Special Collections, Krock Library, Cornell University, Ithaca, N.Y.

Cannon, M. Hamlin. Papers. Tutt Library, Colorado College, Colorado Springs, Colo.

Carrington, Albert. Collection. Marriott Library, University of Utah, Salt Lake City.

Carrington, Albert. Diary. Daughters of Utah Pioneers, Salt Lake City.

Carter, William A. Papers. Auerbach Collection, Firestone Library, Princeton University.

Cass, Lewis. Papers. William L. Clements Library, The University of Michigan, Ann Arbor.

Child, Warren Gould. Autobiography and journal. LDS Archives.

Cobb, Howell. Papers. Hargrett Library, University of Georgia, Athens.

Colt, Samuel. Papers. Connecticut State Library, Hartford, Conn.

Colt, Samuel, to Daniel H. Wells, 16 February 1852. Utah State Archives, Salt Lake City.

Confederate Records (RG 109). National Archives.

Cooke, Philip St. George. Papers. Library of Virginia, Richmond, Va.

Cumming Family Papers. Augusta Richmond County Historical Society and Special Collections, Reese Library, Augusta [Georgia] State University.

Cushing, Caleb. Papers. John Hay Library, Brown University, Providence, R.I. and Manuscript Division, Library of Congress.

Davis, W. W. H. Papers. Yale Collection of Western Americana, Beinecke Library, Yale University.

Douglas, Stephen A. Papers. Special Collections Research Center, University of Chicago Library.

Drake, Samuel Adams. Recollections of the Old Army in Kansas. Yale Collection of Western Americana, Beinecke Library, Yale University.

Drummond, William W., to Caleb Cushing, 1 October 1855. Yale Collection of Western Americana, Beinecke Library, Yale University.

Federal Writers' Project Typescripts. Utah Indian Affairs, Correspondence 1855–1859, U.S. Indian Affairs Dept. Utah State Historical Society, Salt Lake City.

Ferguson, James, to Jane R. Ferguson. Letters of 31 October and 17 November 1857. Private Collection of Mr. Tom Schleve.

Floyd, John B. Papers. Swem Library, College of William and Mary, Williamsburg, Va.

Gardner, Hamilton. Collection. Utah State Historical Society, Salt Lake City.

General Church Minutes. LDS Archives.

Ginn, John I., "Mormon and Indian Wars: The Mountain Meadows Massacre, and Other Tragedies and Transactions Incident to the Mormon Rebellion of 1857. Together with the Personal Recollection of a Civilian Who Witnessed Many of the Thrilling Scences [*sic*] Described." Typescript. Yale Collection of Western Americana, Beinecke Library, Yale University.

Hamelin, Joseph P., Jr. Journal. Yale Collection of Western Americana, Beinecke Library, Yale University.

Hawley, Asa S. Autobiography. LDS Archives.

Headquarters of the Army. Letters Sent (RG 108). National Archives.

Headquarters, Troops Serving in Kansas. Letters Sent (RG 393). National Archives.

Heintzelman, Samuel P. Papers. Manuscript Division, Library of Congress.

Historian's Office, Journal. LDS Archives.

Historian's Office. Letterpress copybooks. LDS Archives.

History of Brigham Young. LDS Archives.

Hooper, William H. Collection. Yale Collection of Western Americana, Beinecke Library, Yale University.

Hollon, W. Eugene. Papers, UM 35, University of Toledo Archives, Ward M. Canaday Center, University of Toledo, Ohio.

Journal History of the Church of Jesus Christ of Latter-day Saints. LDS Archives.

Kane, John K., to James Buchanan. Letter of 31 December 1857. Private Collection of Mrs. Anne Richards Horton, San Marino, Calif.

Kane, Thomas L. Collection. American Philosophical Society, Philadelphia.

Kane, Thomas L. Papers. Yale Collection of Western Americana, Beinecke Library, Yale University.

Kane, Thomas L. Collection. Pennsylvania State Archives, Harrisburg, Pa.

Kane, Thomas L. Papers. Stanford University Libraries, Palo Alto, Calif.

Kane, Thomas L. and Elizabeth W. Papers. L. Tom Perry Special Collections, Harold B. Lee Library, Brigham Young University, Provo, Ut.

King, Hannah Tapfield. Journals. LDS Archives.

Lyman, Amasa. Collection. LDS Archives.

Marcy, William L. Papers. Library of Congress.

Margetts, Elizabeth Batemen and Phillip. Letters. Private Collection.

Martineau, James H. William R. Palmer Collection, Sherratt Library, Southern Utah University, Cedar City, Ut.

McClellan, George B. Papers. Manuscript Division. Library of Congress.

McQuown, Madeline R. Collection. Special Collections, Marriott Library, University of Utah, S.L.C.

Moorman, Donald R. Collection. Weber State University, Ogden, Ut.

Morris, Robert M. Journal. Yale Collection of Western Americana, Beinecke Library, Yale University.

Nauvoo Legion (Utah). Adjutant General's Record 1851–1870. LDS Archives.

Nauvoo Legion Papers. Yale Collection of Western Americana, Beinecke Library, Yale University.

Oriental and India Office Collections. The British Library, London.

Patriarchal blessing of Brigham Young, 25 December 1857. Patriarchal Blessings, 27:326. LDS Archives.

Pierce, Franklin, to Cabinet, 4 March 1857. J. Pierpont Morgan Library, New York.

Poll, Richard D. Papers. Marriott Library, University of Utah, S.L.C.

Preston, William B. Papers. Special Collections & Archives, Merrill-Cazier Library, Utah State University, Logan.

Pulsipher, John. "A Short Sketch of the History of John Pulsipher, Written by Himself." LDS Church History Library.

Quinn, D. Michael. Papers. Beinecke Library, Yale University.

Roylance, Ward Jay. Collection. LDS Archives.

Rumfield, Hiram S. Papers. Yale Collection of Western Americana, Beinecke Library, Yale University.

Schroeder, Theodore. Collection. LDS Archives.

Scott, Winfield. Papers. William L. Clements Library, The University of Michigan, Ann Arbor.

Smith, George A. Papers. LDS Archives.

Smith, Persifor Fraser. Papers. Historical Society of Pennsylvania, Philadelphia.

Stevens, Isaac Ingalls. Papers. Yale Collection of Western Americana, Beinecke Library, Yale University.

Trigg-Floyd-Johnston Collection. Wylie Library, University of Virginia's College at Wise, Va.

Taylor Family Papers. Marriott Library, University of Utah, S.L.C.

Terry, James Parshall. Autobiography. L. Tom Perry Special Collections, Harold B. Lee Library, Brigham Young University, Provo, Ut.

Thomas, Sarah C., comp. "Elias Smith's Journal." Typescript 1984. Utah State Historical Society, S.L.C.

Toucey, Isaac. Papers. Connecticut State Library, Hartford, Conn.

U.S. Army. Adjutant General's Office. Letters Received (RG 94). National Archives.

U.S. Army. Dept. of the Pacific. Records (RG 393). National Archives.

———. Records of Office of the Chief of Engineers (RG 77). National Archives.

———. Quartermaster General. Letters Sent (RG 92). National Archives.

U.S. Attorney General. Correspondence from the President, Letters Received (RG 60). National Archives.

U.S. Dept. of the Interior. Records of the Pacific Wagon Road Office. National Archives.

U.S. Dept. of State. Miscellaneous Letters. National Archives.

———. Territorial Papers, Records of Territories 1764–1873 (RG 59). National Archives

U.S. Records. House Committee on Military Affairs. National Archives.

U.S. Records of the War Department (RG 98). National Archives.

U.S. Secretary of War, Letters Sent (RG 107). National Archives.

Utah Territory. Legislative Assembly. "Memorial and Resolutions to the President of the United States, Concerning Certain Officers of the Territory of Utah, 6 January 1857," Utah State Archives, S.L.C.

Watt, George D. Papers. LDS Archives.

Wills, Daniel H., to William H. Dame. Letters of 1 and 13 August 1857. William R. Palmer Collection, Sherratt Library, Southern Utah University, Cedar City, Ut.

Young, Brigham. Collection. LDS Archives.

Young, Brigham. Financial Records. Special Collections & Archives, Merrill-Cazier Library, Utah State University, Logan.

Young, Brigham to Howard Egan, 6 January 1858. Yale Collection of Western Americana, Beinecke Library, Yale University.

Young, Brigham. "Message of Gov. Brigham Young to Utah Legislative Assembly, 11 December 1855." Utah State Archives, S.L.C.

Newspapers

Alta California (San Francisco, Calif.)

Brooklyn Daily Eagle (Brooklyn, N.Y.)

Church News (*Deseret News*) (Salt Lake City)

Commercial (Cincinnati)

Commercial Advertiser (Buffalo, N.Y.)

Congressional Globe (Washington, D.C.)

Daily Enquirer (Cincinnati)

Daily Pioneer & Democrat (St. Paul, Minn.)

Daily Republican (Binghamton, N.Y.)

Daily Union (Sacramento, Calif.)

Deseret News (Salt Lake City)

Farmer's Cabinet (Amherst, N.H.)

Millennial Star (Liverpool, U.K.)

Missouri Republican (St. Louis)

Mormon (New York, N.Y.)

National Era (Washington, D.C.)

National Intelligencer (Washington, D.C.)

New York Herald
New York Daily Times
New-York Daily Tribune
New York Times Book Review
New York World
News of the World (London)
Northern Whig (Belfast, Ireland)
Post (London)
Press (Lexington, Mo.)
Putnam Republican Banner (Greencastle, Ind.)
Republican (Lawrence, K.T.)
Saint Louis Leader
Salt Lake Tribune (Salt Lake City)
Sun (Baltimore)
Sun (Pittsfield, Mass.)
Valley Tan (Salt Lake City)
Washington Union (Washington, D.C.)
Weekly Tribune (Liberty, Mo.)
Western Journal of Commerce (Kansas City, Mo.)

Index

The Editor

William P. MacKinnon's interest in Utah, the Mormons, and the most significant territorial-federal conflict in American history reaches back to his undergraduate years at Yale University in the late 1950s. His senior essay on the Utah Expedition, written for Yale's History Honors Program at the encouragement of Professor Howard R. Lamar and Curator Archibald Hanna, won the Yale Library's Walter McClintock prize. He is an alumnus of the Mount Hermon (Massachusetts) School and in 1960 earned a B.A. degree magna cum laude from Yale University, where he was elected to Phi Beta Kappa. He has been Chairman of the Yale Library Associates and is an Associate Fellow of Yale's Davenport College. In 1962 MacKinnon received an M.B.A. degree from the Harvard Graduate School of Business Administration.

As an independent historian, MacKinnon has written articles, essays, and book reviews on Utah's territorial period as well as on the U.S. Army's western campaigns that have appeared in more than thirty scholarly journals and encyclopedias. Since 1988 MacKinnon has been Founder and President of MacKinnon Associates, a strategy consulting firm providing counsel on organizational and management issues to Boards, CEOs, and other senior officers. Prior to that he was a financial and human resources executive with General Motors Corporation in New York and Detroit for twenty-five years, becoming a vice president in 1982. As a community volunteer, he has been Chairman of Children's Hospital of Michigan.

MacKinnon served during 1962–68 in squadrons of the New York Air National Guard following active duty with the U.S. Air Force. He currently resides with his wife Patricia in Santa Barbara, California.

Kingdom in the West Series

The role of the Church of Jesus Christ of Latter-day Saints in the settlement of the American West has been a subject of controversy and fascination for 160 years. Kingdom in the West: *The Mormons and the American Frontier,* a series from The Arthur H. Clark Company, explores the story of the Mormon people and their part in the wider history of the American West. Using primary source documents, most of them never before published, the projected set of twenty volumes examines the Mormons' religious vision and political ambitions, revealing how they saw themselves and how they appeared to others.

The series' first volume, *The Pioneer Camp of the Saints,* brought the Latter-day Saint people to the Great Basin via the Mormon Trail journals of Thomas Bullock. In *Forgotten Kingdom: The Mormon Theocracy in the American West, 1847–1896,* David L. Bigler provided a narrative overview of the Latter-day Saint movement in the American West. *Scoundrel's Tale: The Samuel Brannan Papers* told the audacious story of the most colorful Mormon in California's history. *Army of Israel: Mormon Battalion Narratives* used source documents to tell the story of one of the West's most amazing adventures. In Volume 5, *Defending Zion: George Q. Cannon and the California Mormon Newspaper Wars of 1856–1857,* Roger Robin Ekins collected writings from the *Western Standard* and the opposition press, painting a vivid picture of the debate over Mormonism that led to the Utah War. In *Fort Limhi,* David Bigler returned to tell the story of the Mormon adventure in Oregon Territory from 1855 to 1858 and its surprising impact on the resolution of the Utah War. With Ken Owens's *Gold Rush Saints,* the series returned to look at California Mormons during the great rush for riches. Michael Homer's *On the Way to Somewhere Else* gathered a rich array of accounts by European sojourners to the Great Basin. Carmon Hardy's *Doing the Works of Abraham,* the ninth volume in the series, outlined the theory and practice of Mormon polygamy and its central role in the faith's political struggles of the late nineteenth century. The current volume by Bill MacKinnon, *At Sword's Point, Part 1: A Documentary History of the Utah War to 1858,* is the first of a two-volume set on that significant event. Subsequent volumes will focus on the Mountain Meadows massacre, Mormon-Indian relations, dissenters in the Mormon West, and the trail to southern California from Salt Lake.

Series subscriptions are welcomed. Manuscript proposals of a documentary nature may also be submitted. Address inquiries to the publisher:

The Arthur H. Clark Company
2800 Venture Drive
Norman, Okla. 73069-8216
(405) 325-5609